The Economics of Ecosystems and Biodiversity in National and International Policy Making

The Economics of Ecosystems and Biodiversity in National and International Policy Making

Edited by Patrick ten Brink

An Output of TEEB:
The Economics of Ecosystems and Biodiversity

from Routledge

First published in 2011 by Earthscan

First issued in paperback 2018

Earthscan Ltd, Dunstan House, 14a St Cross Street, London EC1N 8XA, UK
Earthscan LLC, 1616 P Street, NW, Washington, DC 20036, USA
Earthscan publishes in association with the International Institute for Environment and Development

For more information on Earthscan publications, see www.earthscan.co.uk
or write to earthinfo@earthscan.co.uk

ISBN 978-1-84971-250-7 (hpk)
ISBN 978-1-84971-250-7 (pbk)

Typeset by Domex e-Data Pvt. Ltd
Cover design by Susanne Harris

The recommended full citation for this volume is as follows:
TEEB (2011), The Economics of Ecosystems and Biodiversity in National and International Policy Making. Edited by Patrick ten Brink. Earthscan, London and Washington

An example of the recommended citation for a single chapter from this volume is as follows:
ten Brink, P., Eijs, A., Lehmann, M., Mazza, L., Ruhweza, A., and Shine, C., (2011). Transforming our approach to natural capital: the way forward. In The Economics of Ecosystems and Biodiversity in National and International Policy Making, pp451–479. Edited by Patrick ten Brink. Earthscan, London and Washington

Disclaimer
The designations employed and the presentation of the material in this publication do not imply the expression of any opinion whatsoever on the part of the United Nations Environment Programme concerning the legal status of any country, territory, city or area or of its authorities, or concerning delimitation of its frontiers or boundaries. Moreover, the views expressed do not necessarily represent the decision or the stated policy of the United Nations Environment Programme, nor does citing of trade names or commercial processes constitute endorsement.

A catalogue record for this book is available from the British Library

Library of Congress Cataloging-in-Publication Data

The economics of ecosystems and biodiversity in national and international policy making / edited by Patrick ten Brink.
    p. cm.
"An Output of TEEB: The Economics of Ecosystems and Biodiversity."
Includes bibliographical references and index.
ISBN 978-1-84971-250-7 (hardback)

1. Environmental policy. 2. Environmental policy–United States. 3. Environmental economics.
4. Environmental protection–Social aspects. I. Brink, Patrick ten. II. International Institute for Environment and Development.

GE170.E3755 2011
333.95'16–dc22

2010039482

To Catherine, daughters Chloé and little Éléa,
and to all the other new generations.
May they enjoy and benefit from nature as we do.

Contents

List of Figures, Tables and Boxes   *xi*
List of Contributors   *xix*
Acknowledgements   *xxiii*
Foreword   *xxv*
Preface   *xxvii*
List of Acronyms and Abbreviations   *xxix*

Introduction   **1**

Part I — The Need for Action

1   The Global Biodiversity Crisis and Related Policy Challenge   **7**
     What is biodiversity and why does it matter?   10
     The biodiversity crisis: Scale and causes   13
     Economic dimensions of the biodiversity crisis   26
     Human dimensions of the biodiversity crisis   34

2   Framework and Guiding Principles for the Policy Response   **47**
     Why is biodiversity neglected in decision making?   50
     Using economic information to improve policy coherence   52
     Guiding principles for policy change   59
     The TEEB toolkit for policy change   71

Part II — Measuring What We Manage: Information Tools for Decision Makers

3   Strengthening Indicators and Accounting Systems for Natural Capital   **79**
     What measurement problems do we face?   83
     Improving measurement of biodiversity and ecosystem services   84
     'Greening' our macroeconomic and societal indicators   102
     Integrating ecosystems into national income accounting   107
     Building a fuller picture: The need for 'GDP of the poor'   113
     Annex 1 Country-based calculations of GDP of the poor   124

4   Recognizing the Value of Biodiversity: New Approaches to Policy Assessment **129**
     Understanding the value of ecosystem services   132
     Expanding monetary valuation of ecosystem services   141
     Integrating economic thinking into policy assessment   151

Next steps: The need to build assessment capacity 164
Annex 1 Overview of methodologies used in assessing value of
ecosystem services 168
Annex 2 Stages of a policy assessment, proposed actions and ways to
address biodiversity 173

Part III — Available Solutions: Instruments for Better Stewardship of Natural Capital

5 Rewarding Benefits through Payments and Markets 177
Payments for ecosystem services (PES) 181
International PES: REDD+ and beyond 199
Redirecting tax and payment mechanisms for environmental benefit 212
Sharing benefits derived from genetic resources 221
Developing markets for green goods and services 231
Expanding markets through green public procurement (GPP) 242

6 Reforming Subsidies 259
Subsidies and their implications 263
Why do some subsidies miss their mark? 265
Specific impacts of subsidies across key sectors 270
Making reform happen 283
Targeting subsidy reform at today's priorities 290

7 Addressing the Losses through Regulation and Pricing 299
Basic principles for halting ongoing losses 303
Regulating to avoid damage: Environmental standards 305
Compensating for losses: Offsets and biodiversity banks 310
Setting more accurate prices: Market-based instruments 317
Monitoring, enforcement and criminal prosecution 330
Making it happen – Policy mixes to get results 336

8 Recognizing the Value of Protected Areas 345
Protecting areas for biodiversity and people 348
Weighing the benefits and costs of protected areas 355
Improving effectiveness through economic evaluation 368
Securing sustainable financing for protected areas 373
Strengthening policy and institutional support 385
Creating a workable future for protected areas 388
Annex 1 Key elements for successful implementation and relevant
policy provisions 399

9 Investing in Ecological Infrastructure 401
Is natural capital a worthwhile investment? 404

Providing benefits beyond the environmental sector 416
Investing in ecosystems for climate change adaptation 425
Proactive strategies for making investment happen 430
Annex 1 Direct costs and potential benefits of restoration:
Selected examples by ecosystem 442

Part IV — The Road Ahead

10 Transforming Our Approach to Natural Capital: The Way Forward **451**
Future vision: Working with the value of nature 456
A framework for sustainable action 462
Delivering change 472

Index *481*

List of Figures, Tables and Boxes

Figures

1.1	The pathway from ecosystem structure and processes to human well-being	12
1.2	Map of forest areas	13
1.3	Map of coral reefs	17
1.4	State of exploitation of selected stock or species groups for which assessment information is available, by major marine fishing areas, 2004	18
1.5	Main direct drivers of change in biodiversity and ecosystems	23
1.6	Natural capital: Its contribution to the economy and livelihoods	26
1.7	Distribution of benefits over different geographic scales	29
1.8	Land-use choices and trade-offs of ecosystem service provision	32
1.9	The mangrove and the shrimp farm; a comparison of values	33
1.10	Value of selected provisioning and regulating ecosystem services under different land-use scenarios in the Leuser National Park, Indonesia	34
1.11	Substitution potential for ecosystem services	37
2.1	TEEB policy options overview	71
3.1	The policy cycle	85
3.2	Drivers, pressures, status, impact and responses (DPSIR)	86
3.3	Deforestation in Haiti and the Dominican Republic	116
4.1	Understanding ecosystem changes	133
4.2	The benefits pyramid	135
4.3	Mapping links between supply of ecosystem services and beneficiaries	138
4.4	Application of a total economic value framework to ecosystem services	139
4.5	Ecosystem services values from forests	145
4.6	Drivers of forest decline	155
5.1	Increasing rewards for ecosystem services provision through PES	183
5.2	PES and the polluter pays principle	184
5.3	PES stakeholders and their interactions	186
5.4	Public water quality contracts for PES – A schematic	192
5.5	Strategies for marketing biodiversity joint service provision	196
5.6	Opportunities for regional PES: Example of the Amazonian 'water pump'	200
5.7	National carbon and biodiversity map for Panama	205
5.8a	Comparative maps of biodiversity hotspots and major wilderness areas and the UN's Human Development Index (HDI): Global Biodiversity 'priority areas' map	210
5.8b	Comparative maps of biodiversity hotspots and major wilderness areas and the UN's Human Development Index (HDI): Human Development Index (HDI) map	211

5.9	Three mechanisms for maintaining or restoring the tropical forest eco-utility	212
5.10	Ecological fiscal transfers in Brazil	218
5.11	Protected areas overlaid over municipal borders in Saxony, Germany	219
5.12	Percentage change in general lump-sum transfers	220
5.13	Forest area certified by major certification schemes (2000–2009)	233
5.14	FSC-certified forest per region, as of 1 January 2008	239
7.1	Appropriateness of compensation in relation to the importance of impacted biodiversity and availability of reliable compensation options	312
7.2	Cost recovery in water pricing: Towards an economic perspective	324
7.3	Environmental taxes as a percentage of total tax receipts in 2006	327
7.4	Patrols and buffalo populations	335
8.1	Schematic for analysing the value of protected areas over time	349
8.2	Food security and protected areas	357
8.3	Total benefits of conservation compared to benefits from conversion	363
8.4	Schematic distribution of benefits and costs of conserving PAs in developing countries as a percentage of the value of total benefits	365
8.5	Map of Chile showing PAs and threats to ecosystem	370
8.6	Financing gaps by region for existing protected areas	375
9.1	Conceptual framework for restoration, rehabilitation and reallocation at the landscape level	407
9.2	Summary of cost ranges of restoration efforts	410
9.3	Images of the Aral Sea: (a) 1989; (b) 2003; and (c) 2009	415
10.1	Eroding natural capital base and tools for an alternative development path	474

Tables

1.1	Examples of potential ecosystem service values from tropical forests	28
2.1	Global conventions addressing biodiversity issues	53
2.2	Where are economic insights useful to the policy process?	56
2.3	How biodiversity policies affect development policy and poverty alleviation	60
2.4	Catastrophic events creating 'windows of opportunity' for policy change	65
2.5	Examples of initiatives to facilitate good governance practices	70
3.1	Thresholds and responses: Examples from the fisheries sector	86
3.2	Updated indicators for assessing progress towards the 2010 biodiversity target	88
3.3	Hypothetical examples of key attributes and generic limits that define acceptable condition in two habitat types	91
3.4	Examples of ecosystem service indicators	95
3.5	Differences in forest dependence, vulnerability to climate change impacts and factors affecting the vulnerability of different forest user groups for the State of Para, Brazil	115
3.6	GDP of the poor and share of GDP	117
3.A1	Equity-adjusted income of the poor	127

4.1   Evaluation of multiple functions of forests   148
4.2   Adapting standard questions to cover biodiversity and ecosystem services   154
4.3   Different alternatives for flood protection in the CBA (Phase One:
       Different measures; Phase Two: Optimization)   158
4.4   Distributing total economic value from forestry between stakeholders   159
4.A1   Valuation methods in more detail   170
4.A2   Stages of a policy assessment, proposed actions and ways to
       address biodiversity   173
5.1   Possible scope of creditable activities in a REDD+ mechanism   201
5.2   Market sectors dependent on genetic resources   222
5.3   Global supply of roundwood from certified resources (2007–2009)   234
6.1   Aggregate subsidy estimates for selected economic sectors   265
7.1   Examples of sectoral regulations that can benefit ecosystem services   306
7.2   Examples of different uses of MBIs to protect biodiversity and ecosystems   321
8.1   Internationally recognized system of PA categories   351
8.2   Examples of protected area benefits and costs accruing at different scales   361
8.3   Existing funding mechanisms for protected areas, including lessons learned
       concerning their effectiveness   377
8.A1   Key elements for successful implementation and relevant policy provisions   398
9.1   Feasibility and time scales of restoring or rehabilitating different
       types of ecosystems: Examples from Europe   409
9.2   Alien species in Europe generating some of the highest costs   418
9.3   Effects of land conversion in the Waza floodplain and costs and
       benefits of restoration   422

Boxes

1.1   Key definitions: Biodiversity, ecosystems and ecosystem services   11
1.2   Global assessments and the use of scenarios to make future projections   20
1.3   Key ecological risks, tipping points and measures to alleviate
       pressures resulting in biodiversity loss   21
1.4   Fact box: How human demand can affect biodiversity   25
1.5   Natural capital: Its relationship to productivity   27
1.6   Value for money from natural capital   30
1.7   To convert or not to convert – deciding between mangroves
       and a shrimp farm   32
1.8   Forests, rural communities and mutual benefit   35
1.9   The links between biodiversity, marine ecosystem services and livelihoods   38
2.1   Examples of policies that have provided biodiversity conservation benefits   50
2.2   Trade and environment   54
2.3   Multiple values of wetlands: Example of the Daly River catchment (Australia)   55
2.4   Using valuation as part of a decision support system   58
2.5   Economic valuation of damages to enforce liability rules   58
2.6   Actors and stakeholders at different scales of marine policy   61
2.7   Rewarding environmental leaders: Examples of national practice   62

2.8	Upholding traditional knowledge through People's Biodiversity Registers (India)	63
2.9	Obstacles to success: Example of a carbon sink project, Colombia	64
2.10	How do 'property rights' apply to biodiversity and ecosystem services?	66
2.11	Policy challenges related to uncertain property rights in the Amazon	67
2.12	Impact of minority rights on conservation in China's Wolong Nature Reserve	68
2.13	Applying 'ecological footprint analysis' to the world's regions	68
3.1	Examples of ESS indicators across environmental policy areas	97
3.2	Examples of ESS indicators across sector policies	98
3.3	Using the 'ecological footprint' indicator in policy: Some examples	99
3.4	Using 'final ecosystem services' (FES) indicators in national accounting	100
3.5	Four types of capital	104
3.6	The Stiglitz–Sen–Fitoussi Commission's critique of GDP	106
3.7	Marginal costs of timber production in China	106
3.8	Environmental degradation and vulnerability: Haiti and the Dominican Republic	116
3.A1	Country GDP of the poor calculations: India	124
3.A2	Country GDP of the poor calculations: Brazil	125
3.A3	Country GDP of the poor calculations: Indonesia	126
4.1	Coastal capital: The value of coastal ecosystems in Belize	133
4.2	Spatial and temporal boundaries in ecosystem-rated cost–benefit calculations	136
4.3	Considering the spatial distribution of cost and benefits to allow for appropriate compensation levels	136
4.4	The inherent value residing in the preserving options for the future: River restoration in Denmark	140
4.5	Valuing ecosystem services to inform land-use choices: Opuntia scrubland in Peru	142
4.6	Use of benefits transfer of values for non-timber forest products	144
4.7	Collected evidence on the values of ecosystem services	145
4.8	Values of water provision in New Zealand	146
4.9	Three cases of using valuation to assess levels of compensation in legal claims	146
4.10	Using valuation to justify payment of local tax revenues for forests in Japan	148
4.11	Entry fees for parks	149
4.12	Valuing ecosystem services at the country and regional level in the Mediterranean	149
4.13	The main policy assessment processes: EIA and SEA	151
4.14	Valuation study to determine a watershed tax rate in Japan	152
4.15	Has SEA helped? Lessons learned in the European Union	152
4.16	Making a case for biodiversity in mainstream policy assessment	153
4.17	Example of analysis of drivers of biodiversity loss	155
4.18	Implementing an integrated landscape approach in India	156

4.19   The choice of the discount rate   157
4.20   An integrated valuation approach for the Scheldt (Belgium–Netherlands)   157
4.21   Identifying the three different levels of stakeholders   160
4.22   International backing for public participation in environmental
       decision making: The Aarhus Convention (1998)   161
4.23   Valuing keystone species: The case of the Asian elephant, India   161
4.24   Applying ecosystem-level SEA in the Sperrgebiet Land Use Plan, Namibia   162
4.25   Capacity building for integrated assessment by UNEP   164
5.1   Definition of PES   182
5.2   An evolving nationwide scheme: The Pagos por Servicios
       Ambientales (PSA), Costa Rica   187
5.3   Mexico's Programme for the Payment of Hydrologic Environmental
       Services of Forests (PSAH)   188
5.4   PES incentives to conserve agricultural ecosystem services in Japan   190
5.5   Private sector contracts for PES: The example of Vittel
       mineral water, France   191
5.6   Public water quality contracts for PES: The example of
       farmers in Germany   192
5.7   Recent large-scale PES to alleviate poverty and reduce
       deforestation in Ecuador   193
5.8   Phased performance payments under PES schemes on
       Mafia Island, Tanzania   198
5.9   The evolution of REDD+ under the UNFCCC   201
5.10   The costs and benefits of reducing GHG emissions from deforestation   202
5.11   Example of a multiple-benefits REDD project in Madagascar   207
5.12   Examples of international funding initiatives to address deforestation   208
5.13   Think PINC: The 'Proactive Investment in Natural Capital' proposal   212
5.14   Stimulating international biodiversity demand through a
       Green Development Initiative   213
5.15   Tax incentives for conservation easements and ecological gifts in
       North America   215
5.16   'Green Funds Scheme' in The Netherlands (Regeling groenprojecten)   216
5.17   Using low interest rates to provide incentives for urban greening in Japan   216
5.18   Ecological fiscal transfers in Brazil   218
5.19   Modelling intergovernmental fiscal transfers for conservation in Germany   219
5.20   Goose Management Scheme, Scotland   220
5.21   Rewarding conservation of golden eagles by the Sami in Finland   221
5.22   Examples of benefit sharing and payments under bioprospecting contracts   225
5.23   Learning from practitioners: Benefit-sharing perspectives from enterprising
       communities   229
5.24   Forest certification schemes   233
5.25   Volume and value of fisheries certified by the Marine Stewardship
       Council (MSC)   234
5.26   Using rice labelling to support habitat restoration and economic
       benefits in Japan   235

5.27   Biodiversity benefits from nature-based tourism in the Philippines   236
5.28   Biomimicry: Examples of economic gain linked to learning from nature   237
5.29   Social stock exchange for companies providing services of public benefit   241
5.30   MSC risk-based support framework for smaller fisheries   241
5.31   Strengthening regulations for GPP implementation in China   242
5.32   Tightening criteria for centralized procurement: Timber purchasing
       in the UK   243
5.33   Energy and water savings through green procurement in Denmark   244
5.34   Cost savings identified through WLC in Germany   245
5.35   Joint procurement through the EcoProcurement Service,
       Vorarlberg, Austria   245
5.36   Phased implementation of green food procurement in
       East Ayrshire, Scotland   246
5.37   Compatibility of GPP with free trade rules and disciplines   246
6.1   Subsidies: Different definitions for different contexts   264
6.2   Estimated distributional impact of energy subsidies in four
       developing countries   266
6.3   The EU Common Agricultural Policy (CAP) and its impacts on biodiversity   271
6.4   Reforming production subsidies: The EU CAP and the Agenda 2000 reforms   272
6.5   The environmental impact of subsidies to the small-scale sector in Senegal   274
6.6   Sunken billions   274
6.7   Fisheries subsidies: The good, the bad, and the ugly   276
6.8   Removing fishery subsidies in Norway   277
6.9   Reforming water subsidies in the Czech Republic   279
6.10   Targeting water pricing against social objectives   280
6.11   Fuel subsidy reform in Ghana   281
6.12   Removing fuel subsidies in Indonesia   282
6.13   The CBD's headline target for incentives, including subsidy reform   284
6.14   Developing a roadmap for subsidy reform: A checklist for policy makers   285
6.15   Enhancing transparency of farm subsidies in the European Union   288
6.16   Removal of agricultural and fisheries subsidies in New Zealand   289
6.17   Minimum criteria for subsidy programme design   292
7.1   Fundamental principles for incorporating costs of biodiversity loss   304
7.2   Scope and flexibility of environmental regulation   305
7.3   Agro-ecological zoning to consolidate ecosystem service provision in Brazil   306
7.4   Regulatory success stories: Tackling air pollution and promoting sustainable
       forestry   308
7.5   Feeding catchment assessment data into the regulatory process,
       South Africa   309
7.6   Biodiversity compensation mechanisms   310
7.7   Offsetting deforestation in Flanders, Belgium   312
7.8   BBOP Principles on Biodiversity Offsets   315
7.9   Biodiversity compensation and offsets in Australia and the US   316
7.10   Use of volume-based waste fees to reduce waste generation in Korea   318
7.11   Experience with tradable fishery quotas in New Zealand   319

7.12	Scope of environmental liability rules	319
7.13	Experience of water use rights in reducing water consumption in China	323
7.14	Full cost recovery as a tool to reduce over-exploitation: Water pricing examples	324
7.15	Tradable development rights to control urban sprawl and preserve open space: The case of Montgomery County (Maryland, US)	325
7.16	Creating synergies: Using MBI revenues to finance biodiversity policies	326
7.17	Using economic valuation to determine mandatory compensation rates in India	329
7.18	Analysing willingness to pay (WTP) to adjust fee structures in the Antilles	330
7.19	What are environmental crimes?	331
7.20	Wider impacts of pollution and dumping	332
7.21	The economics behind environmental crimes	333
7.22	Investigating bat crime in the UK	334
7.23	Enforcement at Serengeti National Park	335
7.24	Environmental/ecological tax reform	337
8.1	Definitions of protected areas	350
8.2	Main direct pressures posing risks to protected areas	353
8.3	Protected areas support for local livelihoods	355
8.4	Maintaining food security: Crop wild relatives and protected areas	357
8.5	Using economic arguments to support conservation in Indonesia	369
8.6	Valuation for decision support: Regional conservation planning in Chile	370
8.7	Compensation through insurance against elephant damage in Sri Lanka	371
8.8	Financial sustainability of protected areas (PAs) in Latin America and the Caribbean	374
8.9	Using tourism revenue to support the protection of dolphins at Samadi Reef	381
8.10	Options for financing a new network of protected areas in Sierra Leone	382
8.11	Inequalities in benefit distribution in China's Wolong Nature Reserve	383
8.12	The importance of monitoring in forest protected areas, Panama	384
8.13	The CBD Programme of Work on Protected Areas (PoWPA)	385
8.14	Micronesia Challenge commitment to protected area implementation	387
9.1	Key definitions and the expanding focus of restoration	406
9.2	Cost-effectiveness of protection and restoration over engineered solutions: Example of a US watershed	411
9.3	A natural capital 'mega-project': Example of the Aral Sea restoration	414
9.4	The economic case for government-led rapid response to invasive species	418
9.5	Valuation of livelihood benefits arising from ecosystem rehabilitation in South Africa	417
9.6	Socio-economic benefits from grassland restoration projects, South Africa	420
9.7	Multiple benefits from wetland restoration in the Everglades, Florida	421
9.8	Reducing poverty by investing in floodplain restoration in Cameroon	421
9.9	Restoration failures: An example from coastal protection in the Philippines	423
9.10	Dams, irrigation and the spread of schistosomiasis in Senegal	424
9.11	The restoration of wetlands and lakes in the Yangtze River Basin	426
9.12	Climate change adaptation in Bolivia	428

9.13   Restoration and conservation strategy of mires and peatlands
in Germany   429
9.14   Ecosystem gains from sustainable agricultural practices   429
9.15   Launch of the Sloping Land Conversion Programme after flooding
in China   431
9.16   Investing in the environment during the financial crisis: The case
of South Korea   432
10.1   Visions for the future: Variations on a theme   460
10.2   The CBD Strategic Plan for the period 2011–2020   465
10.3   Four steps to put natural capital at the heart of national policy making   469

List of Contributors

Coordinating lead authors (CLA)

Patrick ten Brink, Institute for European Environmental Policy (IEEP), Belgium
Bernd Hansjürgens, Helmholtz Centre for Environmental Research (UFZ), Germany
Marianne Kettunen, IEEP, Finland
Markus Lehmann, Secretariat of the Convention on Biological Diversity (SCBD), Canada
Carsten Neßhöver, UFZ, Germany
Christoph Schröter-Schlaack, UFZ, Germany
Stephen White, European Commission: DG Environment EC, Belgium

Lead authors (LA)

James Aronson, Centre National de la Recherche Scientifique (CNRS), France
Samuela Bassi, IEEP, UK
Augustin Berghofer, UFZ, Germany
Joshua Bishop, International Union for Conservation of Nature (IUCN), Global
James Blignaut, University of Pretoria, South Africa
Aaron Bruner, Conservation International (CI), USA
Nicholas Conner, International Union for Conservation of Nature/World Commission on
    Protected Areas (IUCN/WCPA), Australia
Nigel Dudley, Equilibrium Research, UK
Sonja Gantioler, IEEP, Belgium
Sarat Babu Gidda, SCBD, Canada
Haripriya Gundimeda, Indian Institute of Technology, Bombay (IITB) India
Celia A. Harvey, CI, USA
Katia Karousakis, Organisation for Economic Co-operation and Development (OECD)
Marianne Kettunen, IEEP, Finland
Markus Lehmann, SCBD, Canada
Anil Markandya, University of Bath, UK
Andrew J. McConville, IEEP, UK
Kalemani Jo Mulongoy, SCBD, Canada
Paulo A. L. D. Nunes, Fondazione Eni Enrico Mattei (FEEM), Italy
Luis Pabon, The Nature Conservancy (TNC), USA
Irene Ring, UFZ, Germany
Alice Ruhweza, Katoomba Group, Uganda
Clare Shine, IEEP, France
Benjamin Simmons, UNEP, Switzerland
Pavan Sukhdev, UNEP, UK
Patrick ten Brink, IEEP, Belgium
Graham Tucker, IEEP, UK
Alexandra Vakrou, EC, Belgium
Stefan van der Esch, Ministry of Housing, Spatial Planning and the Environment (VROM),
    The Netherlands

Madhu Verma, Indian Institute of Forest Management (IIFM), India
Jean-Louis Weber, European Environment Agency (EEA), Denmark
Sheila Wertz-Kanounnikoff, Center for International Forestry Research (CIFOR), Indonesia
Stephen White, EC, Belgium
Heidi Wittmer, UFZ, Germany

Contributing authors (CA)

Jonathan Armstrong, IEEP, Belgium
Samuela Bassi, IEEP, UK
Meriem Bouamrane, UNESCO, France
James Boyd, Resources for the Future, UK
Ingo Bräuer, Ecologic, Germany
Stuart Chape, UNEP/WCMC, UK
David Cooper, SCBD, Canada
Arthur Eijs, Ministry of Infrastructure and the Environment (IenM),
    The Netherlands
Florian Eppink, UFZ, Germany
Naoya Furuta, IUCN, Japan
Leen Gorissen, VITO, The Netherlands
Pablo Gutman, World Wildlife Fund (WWF), North America
Bernd Hansjürgens, UFZ, Germany
Sarah Hodgkinson, IEEP, UK
Alexander Kenny, SCBD, Canada
Marianne Kettunen, IEEP, Finland
Sophie Kuppler, UNEP, Switzerland
Markus Lehmann, SCBD, Canada
Inge Liekens, VITO, Belgium
Leonardo Mazza, IEEP, Belgium
Katherine McCoy, IEEP, UK
Patrick Meire, University of Antwerp, Belgium
Anja von Moltke, UNEP, Switzerland
Paul Morling, Royal Society for the Protection of Birds (RSPB), UK
Karachepone Ninan, Institute for Social and Economic Change, India
Valerie Normand, SCBD, International
Ece Ozdemiroglu, Eftec, UK
Carlos Muñoz Piña, Instituto Nacional de Ecologia, Mexico
Matt Rayment, GHK, UK
Alice Ruhweza, Katoomba Group, Uganda
Christoph Schröter-Schlaack, UFZ, Germany
Burkhard Schweppe-Kraft, The Federal Environment Ministry (BMU), Germany
Andrew Seidl, IUCN, Global
Clare Shine, IEEP, France
Sue Stolton, Equilibrium Research, UK
Pavan Sukhdev, UNEP, Global
Ben ten Brink, Netherlands Environmental Assessment Agency (PBL)
Patrick ten Brink, IEEP, Belgium
Rob Tinch, Eftec, Belgium

Mandar Trivedi, International Canopy Programme, UK
Alexandra Vakrou, EC, Belgium
Kaavya Varma, Green India States Trust (GIST), India
Francis Vorhies, Earthmind, Switzerland
Stephen White, EC, Belgium
Jeffrey Wielgus, World Resources Institute (WRI), USA
Sirini Withana, IEEP, UK
Heidi Wittmer, UFZ, Germany

Other contributors and reviewers

These are noted at the end of each chapter

Acknowledgements

This volume of TEEB is a tribute to the commitment, inspiration and effort of its ten 'Chapter Teams' of authors (see above), its Core Team members, other contributors and reviewers from many disciplines and all continents (see chapters). Without the strategic input, personal commitment and genuine interest of all the above, this book would not have seen the light of day.

Special thanks are due to the Core Team of motivated and skilled professionals who guided and in many cases wrote great parts of this book. They include Alexandra Vakrou (European Commission), Alice Ruhweza (Katoomba Group, Uganda, and now UNDP), Benjamin Simmons (UNEP), Bernd Hansjürgens (UFZ), Christoph Schröter-Schlaack (UFZ), Heidi Wittmer (UFZ), Helen Mountford (OECD), James Vause (Defra, UK), Jean-Louis Weber (EEA), Katia Karousakis (OECD), Madhu Verma (IIFM, India), Marianne Kettunen (IEEP), Mark Schauer (UNEP), Markus Lehmann (SCBD), Meriem Bouamrane (UNESCO), Stefan van der Esch (VROM, The Netherlands, and now PBL), Stephen White (European Commission), Sylvia Kaplan (BMU-Germany) and Clare Shine (IEEP), who was also invaluable in the language edit of the whole book.

We are most grateful to TEEB Study Leader, Pavan Sukhdev, for his inspiration and vision, to Georgina Langdale (UNEP) for communications, to Mark Schauer and Benjamin Simmons (UNEP) for administration and financial management at the UNEP Office in Bonn and to the UFZ team (Heidi Wittmer, Carsten Neßhöver, Augustin Berghöfer and Christoph Schröter-Schlaack) for scientific coordination and support.

Thanks also to our TEEB colleagues who coordinated TEEB's other volumes, Pushpam Kumar (University of Liverpool), Heidi Wittmer (UFZ), Haripriya Gundimeda (IITM) and Joshua Bishop (IUCN), for their collaboration and regular inputs.

We are also indebted to members of the TEEB Advisory Board – Joan Martinez-Alier, Giles Atkinson, Edward Barbier, Ahmed Djoghlaf, Jochen Flasbarth, Yolanda Kakabadse, Karl-Göran Mäler, Julia Marton-Lefèvre, Peter May, Jacqueline McGlade, Ladislav Miko, Herman Mulder, Walter Reid, Achim Steiner and Nicholas Stern – for their advice, support and guidance.

I'd also personally like to thank colleagues at IEEP for their encouragement, patience and unwavering support. While many are noted as authors and contributors, I'd particularly like to thank Clare Shine, Barbara Akwagyiram, Jonathan Armstrong, Sonja Gantioler, Leonardo Mazza, Graham Tucker and Marianne Kettunen. I am also grateful to David Baldock and IEEP's Board of Trustees for their support and encouragement.

For the original inspiration and commitment to initiate TEEB, I'd like to thank Stavros Dimas, Sigmar Gabriel, Ladislav Miko and Jochen Flasbarth; Patrick Murphy for helping launch it operationally; and Janez Potočnik for ongoing support and encouragement.

And, finally, of course, thanks are due to the funders who are supporting the TEEB initiative – the European Commission and the German, UK, Dutch, Swedish, Norwegian, Belgian, Swiss and Japanese governments. They not only offered crucial funding but also expertise and direct engagement in the work itself. Heartfelt thanks also to the many organizations who offered important in-kind contributions, including the EEA, OECD, UNEP and the Secretariat of the CBD.

Patrick ten Brink (IEEP)
Coordinator, TEEB for National and International Policy Makers

Foreword

All countries have an interest and a responsibility in understanding the importance of their country's natural assets – its land and forests, its coast and marine areas, its inland waters and wetlands, its biodiversity – the species, the ecosystems in which they live and their genes. This is the natural capital that provides a country, its economy and its people with a flow of goods and services that are fundamentally important for prosperity, livelihoods and well-being. The values we receive from our natural capital are immense, and failure to adequately take these values into account in our decisions exposes us to the risk of losing yet more of it.

A forward-looking country/government will recognize the need to understand what these flows of value are and how to work with nature to maintain these ecosystem services that come from the stock of natural capital – the productivity of fisheries, forests and soils, the quality of water supply, carbon storage and natural hazard mitigation, as well as the cultural, spiritual and tourism values of natural assets. We need to understand the dynamic relationship between people, the economy and natural systems better and take account of these insights in decisions – at the policy level, and indeed also at the business and citizen level.

I have therefore followed TEEB with interest and am committing my country, Brazil, to undertake a 'TEEB Brazil' assessment, focusing on those issues of particular relevance to us, namely the forests and savannas, the marine and coastal areas, the use of agricultural lands, the importance of water ... Other countries naturally will focus on issues pertinent to their specific natural assets, their relations with their neighbours and of course their position within the global context.

There is no time to lose in understanding and responding to the values of nature, and transforming our approach to natural capital. Working with nature offers the potential to achieve many of our objectives cost-effectively, offers significant savings, and promises many policy synergies, notably with climate change, water security, poverty eradication and in general improving the well-being of citizens. It also provides an opportunity for innovation and for a transition to a sustainable green economy, mindful of nature's resource and ecosystem limits, and respecting the rights and dreams of each of our nation's children and grandchildren.

We will build on the knowledge and insights of practice across the globe presented in this TEEB in Policy Making book. And we look forward to sharing our own insights from our national assessment with the wider community – at the CBD COP11 in India and at the UN Conference on Sustainable Development (Rio+20) in Brazil in 2012.

Izabella Teixeira
Minister of the Environment, Brazil

Preface

Pavan Sukhdev
Study Leader, TEEB

It is a rare privilege to write a preface to a book which not only is timely and policy relevant, but one which in its preliminary form (as a TEEB Report, 'TEEB for National and International Policy-Makers', 2009) has already gained so much traction with policy makers. As I write, the World Bank together with UNEP and others have announced plans at CBD COP-10, Nagoya, for a multi-year project to incorporate Natural Capital into national accounts – one of the main recommendations of this book (*The Economics of Ecosystems and Biodiversity in National and International Policy Making*, referred to in short form as 'TEEB in National Policy'). The governments of Brazil and India have announced their decisions to undertake 'country TEEB' studies inspired by TEEB, to help integrate the value of ecosystem services into their respective policy making frameworks. Such traction for any policy oriented publication is indeed commendable, but it also places on the TEEB community a significant onus of public responsibility: to be available to support these implementation initiatives as they progress towards their laudable goals.

The problems of biodiversity loss and ecosystem degradation had been described and sized in economic and human welfare terms by our 'Interim Report' in May 2008. Shortly thereafter, the core team of TEEB had to decide expeditiously how to sequence its 'end-user' focused work on economically justifiable policy solutions to these problems. Significant interest from end-users, including TEEB's donor nations, led to a decision that 'TEEB for National and International Policy-Makers' would have to be first off the block. This represented a considerable challenge of urgency for its authors and reviewers – as well as a challenge of coordination, since the underlying science and economics were simultaneously being compiled by our foundational report 'TEEB – Ecological and Economic Foundations'. It is to the credit of all these authors, reviewers and coordinators that this report and its book form were delivered on time and to high standards of quality.

While the TEEB suite aims to address all major groups of decision makers – policy makers, administrators, businesses, communities and individuals – the fundamental importance of policy reform and action in recognizing and integrating the value of ecosystem services cannot be over-emphasized. It is a prerequisite for changing both business drivers and consumer behaviours in order to reduce the loss of biodiversity and degradation of ecosystems. It is a foundation for improving the measurement and management of public wealth, such as most of our ecological infrastructure. And perhaps most important of all, it is essential for evolving viable and sustainable strategies to eradicate persistent poverty.

Addressing challenges for policy makers

'TEEB in National Policy' was first unveiled as a TEEB Report in Brussels, in November 2009. This book updates and reinforces the key messages of its earlier report version, and adds new findings and material that have become available since the report version was written. 'TEEB in National Policy' addresses the key challenges to national and international policy makers. What are the key areas of policy within this broad domain that can and should be changed? And what are the economic justifications for these changes – measured holistically, taking account of the 'public wealth' component of natural capital and the impacts of policy changes thereon? The latter question is not one of secondary importance, as it goes to the heart of many policy failures that we observe today. We tend to allow decision making frameworks to persist in which explicit or implicit trade-off choices are made without recognizing losses of public wealth – especially if it is natural capital, and not man-made capital. This is not likely to be a strategy for human progress.

For example, land-use change decisions from natural ecosystems to agriculture or habitation cannot be considered economic if decided (implicitly or explicitly) on the basis that 'there is no price, hence no value' for the ecosystem services lost due to that land-use change. And yet that is exactly what we find happens in most cases of forest clearance, mangrove removal, wetland reclamation, etc. Significant cost externalization to society takes place while enhancing some private profits, and often public wealth destruction can exceed private wealth creation. This decision making pattern is questionable as a source of sustainable prosperity for society as a whole.

Solving deep-rooted and extensive problems such as the ongoing loss of biodiversity and ecosystems will need significant changes in policy at both national and local levels, as well as changes in business behaviour and citizen awareness. Some of these changes will need institutions to take on fundamental reforms. For example, reflecting natural and human capital formation and destruction in the accounts of society could provide strong support for policy and budgetary responses to invest in 'public wealth' such as natural capital (see Chapter 3, a recommendation that feeds into the World Bank lead project for Ecosystem Valuation and Wealth Accounting). Expanding the reach of market-based mechanisms by enabling payments for ecosystem services (PES) could provide economic incentives for conservation (Chapter 5 of this book expands on this idea). Taxing what we take (resource extraction) and not what we make (profits from goods and services) could encourage natural resource-efficient production and consumption; and so on. These are all big changes, each of which would address the root causes of biodiversity loss and ecosystem degradation.

Recognizing, demonstrating and capturing value

Although it includes market-based mechanisms as solutions, it should be emphasized that TEEB is anything but a cost–benefit-based design for planetary stewardship. A common thread running through the recommended suite of solutions is multi-layered recognition and valuation of nature's benefits to society. Economic valuation can be very helpful in communicating the value of nature to diverse groups of decision makers precisely because it uses *economics*, the language of our prevailing economic–political paradigm.

TEEB suggests a tiered approach in analysing problems and suitable policy responses. We find that at times it suffices just to *recognize value* – be it intrinsic, spiritual or social – to create a policy response favouring conservation or sustainable use (e.g. sacred groves; legal Protected Areas or community-based Conservation Areas). No economic valuation is made as such in these instances, but, rather, valuation at a societal level (see Chapter 4, TEEB Foundations, 2010).

At other times we may need to *demonstrate economic value* in order for policy makers to respond – such as a wetland conserved near Kampala (see TEEBCase on www.TEEBweb. org) for its sewage treatment function instead of reclaiming it for agriculture. We caution that it is not a 'risk-free' exercise to demonstrate value by deriving and propagating shadow prices. There is always the risk that misguided policy makers or exploitative interests may want to use these prices for the wrong ends. Therefore, our proposition is that the act of valuing the flows and stocks of Nature is ethically valid so long as the purpose of that exercise is, first and foremost, to demonstrate value in order to change behaviour, and to prevent damaging trade-offs based on implicit valuations that are involved in causing the loss of biodiversity and degradation of ecosystems.

Finally, TEEB has also focused considerably on changes that *capture economic value* by rewarding and supporting good conservation through a variety of means – payments for environmental services, environmentally harmful subsidy (EHS) reforms, eco-certification, biodiversity or ecosystem services offsets, direct investment in natural capital, etc. (see examples in this book, Chapters 4–9). In most instances, the valuation of services rewarded is an important input for an effective policy solution which is backed by sound economics. However, we do not suggest that putting values must lead to *tradability* of the assets or flows being valued. That is a separate societal choice which potentially affects survival of species as well as of poor forest-dependent and ocean-dependent people, and such choices cannot be made lightly or on other than an ethical plane, involving as they do both intra-generational and inter-generational equity. Placing blind faith in the ability of markets to optimize social welfare, or privatizing the ecological commons and letting markets discover prices for them, is not what TEEB recommends. Rather, as this book bears out, TEEB documents a responsible and multi-layered approach towards recognizing, demonstrating and capturing the value of ecosystem services in order to reform policies, change business incentives, and inform and influence societies, communities and individuals as decision-makers and agents of change.

'Mainstreaming' TEEB

To summarize, modern society's predominant focus on market-delivered components of well-being, and its almost total dependence on market prices to indicate value, means that we generally do not measure or manage economic value that is exchanged other than through markets, such as the public goods and services that comprise a large part of nature's flows to humanity. Society generally also ignores third-party effects of private exchanges (so-called 'externalities') unless they are actually declared illegal.

TEEB has assembled much evidence that the economic invisibility of nature's flows into the economy is a significant contributor to the degradation of ecosystems and the loss of biodiversity. This in turn leads to serious human and economic costs, which are being felt now, have been felt for much of the last half-century and will be felt at an accelerating pace if we continue to do 'business as usual'.

There are serious risks to societies and economies, as well as significant opportunities, in recognizing and responding to biodiversity losses and ecosystem degradation. Assessment and evaluation of these risks and opportunities must therefore be undertaken as a priority. Evaluations of any kind are a powerful 'feedback mechanism' for a society that has distanced itself from the biosphere upon which its very health and survival depends. Economic valuations, in particular, communicate the value of ecosystems and biodiversity, and their largely unpriced flows of public goods and services in the language of the world's dominant economic and political model. Mainstreaming this thinking, and bringing it to the attention of policy makers, administrators, businesses and citizens, is in essence the central goal of TEEB, and of this book.

List of Acronyms and Abbreviations

AAU	assigned amount units
ABS	access and benefit sharing
ADNI	adjusted disposable national income
AHTEG	Ad hoc Technical Expert Group
A/R	afforestation and reforestation
BAT	best available techniques
BCRLIP	Biodiversity Conservation and Rural Livelihood Improvement Project
BioCF	World Bank BioCarbon Fund
BMU	The Federal Environment Ministry, Germany
CAP	Common Agricultural Policy
CBA	cost–benefit analysis
CBD	Convention on Biological Diversity
CCBA	Climate, Community and Biodiversity Alliance
CCS	carbon capture and storage
CDM	Clean Development Mechanism
CERCLA	Comprehensive, Environmental Response, Compensation and Liability Act (US)
CI	Conservation International
CIFOR	The Center for International Forestry Research
CITES	Convention on International Trade in Endangered Species of Wild Flora and Fauna
CLA	coordinating lead authors
CMS	Convention on the Conservation of Migratory Species of Wild Animals
COP	Conference of the Parties
COWI	Consultancy Within Engineering, Environmental Science and Economics
CPET	Central Point of Expertise for Timber
CU	conservation units
CVM	contingent valuation methods
CWR	crop wild relatives
DPSIR	drivers, pressures, status, impact and responses
EC	European Communities
EEA	European Environment Agency
EEZ	exclusive economic zones
EFR	ecological fiscal reform
EHS	environmentally harmful subsidies
EIA	environmental impact assessment
ESA	European Space Agency
ESMAP	Energy Sector Management Assistance Programme
ESS	ecosystem services
ETR	environmental tax reform
FAO	Food and Agriculture Organization of the United Nations
FCPF	Forest Carbon Partnership Facility
FEEM	Fondazione Eni Enrico Mattei
FiRST	Financial Resource Support for Tef

FSC	Forest Stewardship Council
GAISP	Green Accounting for Indian States Project
GATT	General Agreement on Tariffs and Trade
GDI	Green Development Initiative
GDM	Green Development Mechanism
GDP	gross domestic product
GEF	Global Environment Facility
GFCF	gross fixed capital formation
GHG	greenhouse gas
GIS	geographic information system
GIST	Green India States Trust
GMES	Global Monitoring for Environment and Security
GPP	green public procurement
GTZ	Gesellschaft für Technische Zusammenarbeit
HANPP	human appropriation of net primary production
HDI	Human Development Index
HNV	high nature value
IAASTD	International Assessment of Agricultural Knowledge, Science and Technology for Development
IAS	Invasive alien species
ICBG	International Cooperative Biodiversity Groups
IDRC	The International Development Research Centre
IEA	International Energy Agency
IEEP	Institute for European Environmental Policy
IenM	Ministry of Infrastructure and the Environment, The Netherlands
IFOAM	International Federation of Organic Agriculture Movements
IFRC	International Federation of Red Cross and Red Crescent Societies
IISD	International Institute for Sustainable Development
IITB	Indian Institute of Technology, Bombay
INRA	French National Institute for Agricultural Research
IPBES	Intergovernmental Science-Policy Platform on Biodiversity and Ecosystem Services
IPCC	Intergovernmental Panel on Climate Change
ITTO	International Tropical Timber Organization
IUCN	International Union for Conservation of Nature
IUFRO	International Union of Forest Research Organizations
IUU	illegal, unreported and unregulated
IVM	Institute for Environmental Studies, Amsterdam
JPY	Japanese Yen
KWS	Kenya Wildlife Service
LA	lead authors
LCA	life cycle assessment
LULUCF	Land Use, Land-Use Change and Forestry
LWEC	Living With Environmental Change
MA	Millennium Ecosystem Assessment
MAFF	Forestry Agency, Ministry of Agriculture, Forestry and Fisheries of Japan
MBI	market-based instrument
MDG	Millennium Development Goal

MEA	multilateral environmental agreement
MEFT	Ministère de l'Environnement des Forêts et du Tourisme
MNP	Netherlands Environmental Assessment Agency
MPA	marine protected area
MSY	maximum sustainable yield
NBSAP	National Biodiversity Strategy and Action Plan
NEPAD	New Partnership for Africa's Development
NMVOC	non-methane volatile organic compound
NOAA	National Oceanic and Atmospheric Administration (US)
NPV	net present value
NRCS	Natural Resources Conservation Service
NTFP	non-timber forest product
ODA	official development assistance
OECD	Organisation for Economic Co-operation and Development
OPEC	Organization of the Petroleum Exporting Countries
PA	protected area
PBL	Planbureau voor de Leefomgeving
PBR	People's Biodiversity Register
PEFC	Programme for the Endorsement of Forest Certification Schemes
PES	payments for ecosystem services
PINC	Proactive Investment in Natural Capital
PoWPA	Programme of Work on Protected Areas
PPP	polluter pays principle
PSA	Pagos por Servicios Ambientales
PSE	Producer Support Estimate
PSIA	poverty and social impact assessment
PWC	Price Waterhouse Coopers
R&D	research and development
REACH	Registration, Evaluation, Authorisation and Restriction of Chemicals
REDD	Reducing Emissions from Deforestation and Forest Degradation
RNC	renewable and cultivated natural capital
RSPB	Royal Society for the Protection of Birds
RTA	reduced tidal area
SAC	Scottish Agricultural College
SBSTTA	Subsidiary Body on Scientific, Technical and Technological Advice
SEA	strategic environmental assessment
SEEA	System of Environmental and Economic Accounting
SER	Society for Ecological Restoration
SERI	Sustainable Europe Research Initiative
SFM	sustainable forest management
SMART	specific, measurable, achievable, realistic and time-specific
SNA	System of National Accounts
TAC	total allowable catch
TBGRI	Tropical Botanical Garden and Research Institute
TDR	tradable development rights
TEV	total economic value
TFP	total factor productivity
TNC	The Nature Conservancy

TSV	total system value
UFZ	Helmholtz Centre for Environmental Research
UNCCD	UN Convention to Combat Desertification
UNCTAD	UN Conference on Trade and Development
UNDP	United Nations Development Programme
UNECE	United Nations Economic Commission for Europe
UNEP	United Nations Environment Programme
UNEP-WCMC	United Nations Environment Programme World Conservation Monitoring Centre
UNCSD	United Nations Conference on Sustainable Development
UNFCCC	United Nations Framework Convention on Climate Change
UNSD	United Nations Statistics Division
UNWWAP	United Nations World Water Assessment Programme
USAID	United States Agency for International Development
VBWF	volume-based waste fee
VROM	Ministerie van Volkshiisvesting, Ruimetelijke Ordening en Milieubeheer (Dutch Ministry of Housing, Spatial Planning and the Environment)
WCPA	World Commission on Protected Areas
WfW	Working for Water
WLC	whole life costing
WRI	World Resources Institute
WSSD	World Summit on Sustainable Development
WTO	World Trade Organization
WTP	willingness to pay
WWF	World Wide Fund for Nature

Introduction

Patrick ten Brink

'Biodiversity' is an umbrella term covering all life on the planet, from genes and species up to habitats and ecosystems on land and in water. Biodiversity provides a range of ecosystem services that fuel our global economy and underpin human and societal well-being. However, its many values mostly go unrecognized in the markets and in decision making by politicians, administrators, businesses and individuals. Because nature is almost invisible in the choices we make at every level, we are steadily drawing down our natural capital. We do so without understanding what it really costs to replace services provided free by nature – or whether man-made alternatives are even feasible.

Damage to global biodiversity is acute and accelerating. While the overarching driver is linked to pressures from steadily rising consumption and production, we make the problem worse by excluding nature's value from our decisions – and miss opportunities for solutions.

The Economics of Ecosystems and Biodiversity in National and International Policy Making provides a toolkit and a way forward. New momentum is under way to develop more balanced and accountable approaches based on nature's values and fairer distribution of its benefits. This book presents an evidence base of experience and best practices from around the world.

Structure of the book

Part I outlines the need for action and sets the scene for the book's substantive chapters.

Chapter 1 presents the economic and social rationale for urgent action. It highlights the causes of current biodiversity loss, the seriousness of this trend and the scale of human dependence on ecosystem services and biodiversity, particularly for the poor. After explaining the critical importance of ecosystem services for economic prosperity, it shows how valuation can support informed and cost-effective policy trade-offs and investments.

Chapter 2 presents a framework and guiding principles for the policy response. It outlines obstacles to policy change linked to the lack of economic information on ecosystem services and biodiversity. Guiding principles for policy change are presented, followed by a summary of the range of instruments available to decision makers, cross-referenced to relevant chapters of this book.

Part II focuses on measurement and assessment which is essential to provide the evidence base for decision makers.

Chapter 3 looks at strengthening indicators and accounting systems for natural capital. It analyses existing indicators used for biodiversity and ecosystem services in economic decision making and shows how we can use them better. It then assesses national accounting frameworks and natural capital accounts and proposes steps to incorporate information on the stock of natural capital into relevant measurement systems. Lastly, it argues for progress towards a new measure – 'GDP of the poor' – to ensure proper recognition of the critical importance of natural capital for the world's poorest, consistent with the Millennium Development Goals (MDGs).

Chapter 4 discusses tools and best practices to integrate ecosystem and biodiversity values into policy assessment. It presents practical examples adapted to different regions and contexts, showing how countries have carried out valuation of ecosystem services derived from biodiversity and how these have influenced policy design, instrument choice and investment decisions. Specific consideration is given to the need for a holistic approach that covers benefits and losses at both private and societal levels and also at local, national and global levels, and addresses implications for future generations.

Part III focuses on policy responses adapted to the improved evidence base and ways to combine different instruments to ensure better and more inclusive stewardship of natural capital.

Chapter 5 analyses tools to reward those who maintain the flow of ecosystem services. These include payments for ecosystem services (PES) ranging from schemes for local water supply to the global REDD+ scheme under the UN Framework Convention on Climate Change. It shows how taxes, compensation regimes and contractual frameworks for fairer sharing of benefits derived from genetic resources can all provide positive incentives for conservation. The chapter ends with a detailed consideration of more familiar tools to stimulate and target market supply and demand for 'greener' goods and services, including eco-labelling, certification schemes and green public procurement.

Chapter 6 addresses the need for comprehensive reform of subsidy policies to reduce harm to biodiversity and ecosystem services, and make public expenditure more effective, particularly at this period of economic crisis. It provides data on current subsidy levels and areas of inefficiency, proposes priorities for reform and gives practical guidance on tackling specific obstacles, building on a review of tools and programmes already implemented in a range of countries.

Chapter 7 presents ways to increase accountability for the cost of damage to biodiversity and ecosystem services in order to curb further losses. It shows how economic information can be used to inform and target environmental regulations and standards, and ensure a proportionate approach. It examines compensation schemes designed to ensure no net loss or a net gain of biodiversity and ecosystem services, followed by the scope and limitations of market-based instruments for delivering additional conservation gains and stimulating innovation. The critical need for better enforcement and international cooperation in the area of environmental crime is underlined.

Chapter 8 focuses on protected areas – designated sites that are the 'crown jewels' of biodiversity. Without ignoring their fundamental role in safeguarding biodiversity's intrinsic values, the chapter concentrates on the values to the economy, society and individuals provided by ecosystems within protected areas. It demonstrates that these anthropocentric values very often make a complementary and convincing case for designation and appropriate site management and investment to meet conservation objectives and secure continued provision of a range of ecosystem services.

Chapter 9 takes a broader approach to natural assets and explores the economics of restoration. It considers ways to augment renewable natural capital by investing in the maintenance, restoration and rehabilitation of damaged or degraded ecosystems. Such investments can promote many different policy goals, including secure delivery of clean drinking water, natural disaster prevention or mitigation and climate change adaptation.

Part IV concludes with a vision for biodiversity in a green economy and proposes a practical framework for sustainable action. It starts by tackling key questions. What role can – and should – policy makers play? How? At what level? Who else should be involved? How can we differentiate roles and responsibilities? The chapter then sets out concrete steps for institutions and their partners, and identifies priorities for implementation, including target actions for the next five years and key tools to achieve lasting results.

In summary, this book shows how and why existing prices, markets and policies fail to reflect the true value of ecosystem services and biodiversity, and the true cost of ongoing damage. It argues for urgent action and demonstrates the huge range of opportunities we already have to respond to the value of nature. Decision makers are given a roadmap to guide reform of policy frameworks at all levels, based on lessons learned and innovative solutions from around the world.

Part I

The Need for Action

Chapter 1

The Global Biodiversity Crisis and Related Policy Challenge

Coordinating lead author
Patrick ten Brink

Lead authors
Marianne Kettunen, Alexandra Vakrou, Heidi Wittmer

Contributing authors
Jonathan Armstrong, Leonardo Mazza, Clare Shine, Matt Rayment,
Alice Ruhweza, Ben ten Brink

See end of chapter for acknowledgements for reviews and other contributions

Contents

Key messages   9

Summary   10

1 What is biodiversity and why does it matter?   10

2 The biodiversity crisis: Scale and causes   13
   2.1   How much of our natural capital is being lost?   13
   2.2   Global projections of future loss   19
   2.3   What is driving these losses?   23

3 Economic dimensions of the biodiversity crisis   26
   3.1   How do ecosystem services underpin the economy?   26
   3.2   Understanding the value of ecosystem services   27
   3.3   Using valuation to assess trade-offs, costs and benefits   31

4 Human dimensions of the biodiversity crisis   34
   4.1   Ecosystem services: A lifeline for the poor, a necessity for everyone 34
   4.2   Substitution potential: Limits and implications   36
   4.3   Engaging communities to define policy solutions   38

Notes   39

Acknowledgements   39

References   40

Key messages

Ecosystems and their biodiversity underpin the global economy and human well-being, and need to be valued and protected. The world's 'natural capital' is not a luxury for the rich but a necessity for all. The figures speak for themselves: over a billion people in developing countries rely on fish as a major source of food, around 1.1 billion people are dependent on forests for their livelihoods and over half of all commercial medicines derive from natural substances, mostly sourced in rainforests.

Damage to global ecosystem services and biodiversity is acute and accelerating. In the last century we have lost 35 per cent of mangroves, 40 per cent of forests and 50 per cent of wetlands. 60 per cent of ecosystem services have been degraded in 50 years. Species are being lost 100 to 1000 times faster than in geological times and this will get worse with climate change. 80 per cent of the world's fisheries are fully or over-exploited. Critical thresholds are being passed and coral reefs risk collapse if CO_2 emissions are not urgently reduced.

Ecosystem damage carries costs for business and society: the number of sectors benefiting from natural capital represents a far larger share of the economy than many policy makers appreciate. It is not just the agricultural, forestry and fisheries sectors, but also water, food and drink, pharmaceuticals, health, recreation and tourism. Failure to halt biodiversity loss on land will also lead to major losses from lost provisioning services (e.g. food, fuel, water), regulating services (e.g. lost carbon storage; air, water and waste purification; natural hazards management) and cultural services (e.g. recreation and tourism). At sea, for provision services alone, unsustainable fishing reduces potential fisheries output by an estimated $50 billion/year.

Growing demand from an expanding and wealthier global population is a key cause of biodiversity loss. At a deeper level, economic signals from policy and market prices fail to reflect the true value of biodiversity. Incentives are not in place to encourage sustainable practices or to distribute costs and benefits efficiently and fairly. The imbalance between private gain and public loss runs through most of today's policy failures.

Understanding value is critical to inform trade-offs in decision making on land conversion and ecosystem management. When the true value of ecosystem services are included, traditional trade-offs may be revealed as unacceptable. The cost of acting to sustain biodiversity and ecosystem services can be significantly lower than the cost of inaction.

Policies that seek to integrate environmental, economic and social concerns need to recognize the limited substitution potential of ecosystem services and the sheer scale of the human impacts caused by loss or degradation of natural capital. Finding alternative sources – e.g. for water, fuelwood and food – or creating artificial substitutes – e.g. water purification – can strain poorer communities, increase costs and raise prices of the most basic commodities, putting them beyond the reach of some groups. In some cases (e.g. species extinction) there are no substitutes.

Maintaining and investing in natural capital not only makes economic sense but is also critical for meeting social objectives and fundamental to meeting the Millennium Development Goals. This book will describe the potential for win–win–win opportunities (biodiversity, economic and social) in responding to the biodiversity crisis.

Summary

In our every deliberation, we must consider the impact of our decisions on the next seven generations. (From *The Great Law of the Iroquois Confederacy*)

Chapter 1 provides an overview of key issues and priorities related to the global biodiversity crisis. Section 1 introduces policy makers to basic terms, concepts and the reasons for urgent concern at the highest levels. Section 2 highlights the seriousness of current biodiversity loss, backed by concrete examples, and analyses the causes of ongoing and future projected losses. Section 3 explains the critical importance of ecosystem services for economic prosperity and shows how valuation can support informed and cost-effective policy trade-offs and investments. Section 4 emphasizes the scale of human dependence on ecosystem services and biodiversity, particularly for the poor with limited access to alternatives, and the need to engage communities in developing and implementing policy solutions.

1 What is biodiversity and why does it matter?

'Biodiversity' is an umbrella term that covers all life on the planet, from the genetic level up to species to habitats and ecosystems on land and in water. It underpins our global economy as well as human well-being. Biodiversity offers essential benefits to people and contributes to society as a whole by providing knowledge, protection, medicine and community identity. Ecosystems in their turn provide a range of vital services, including regulation of nutrient and carbon cycles (see Box 1.1 for key terms).

Despite its benefits for society, damage to global biodiversity is acute and accelerating. Before we even consider future predictions (see Section 2), alarming statistics already highlight the scale of past losses. Species are going extinct 100 to 1000 times faster than in geological times (Pimm et al, 1995). During the last century, the planet lost 50 per cent of its wetlands, 40 per cent of its forests and 35 per cent of its mangroves. Around 60 per cent of global ecosystem services have been degraded in just 50 years (MA, 2005a).

These losses harm the economy (see Section 3) and human well-being (see Section 4). Unfortunately, we usually appreciate what we have lost too late and/or where there are no available substitutes. The poorest people and developing countries are hit hardest but richer nations are not immune. For example, the loss of bees has sparked worldwide concern because it directly affects natural pollination capacity. We know that over half of the world's fish stocks are already fully exploited and another quarter over-exploited or depleted (FAO, 2009a). This decline affects us all but especially the one billion or more people in developing countries who rely on fish for their main source of protein.

The relationship between biodiversity, ecosystems and their ability to deliver vital services is complex and variable. Ecosystems are components of biodiversity, and species are essential components within those ecosystems. The loss of any components of biodiversity will trigger a change in services provided by the ecosystem concerned. Depending on the circumstances, such changes can (initially) be subtle or make ecosystems less stable and more vulnerable to collapse. If an entire ecosystem is lost, this will have a significant structural impact with direct human, social and economic costs.

Box 1.1 Key definitions: Biodiversity, ecosystems and ecosystem services

Biological diversity means 'the variability among living organisms from all sources, including terrestrial, marine and other aquatic ecosystems and the ecological complexes of which they are part; this includes diversity within species, between species and of ecosystems' (UN, 1993). The term covers every form of life on Earth (plants, animals, fungi and micro-organisms), the diversity of communities that they form and the habitats in which they live. It encompasses three levels: ecosystem diversity (i.e. variety of ecosystems); species diversity (i.e. variety of different species); and genetic diversity (i.e. variety of genes within species).

Ecosystem means 'a dynamic complex of plant, animal and micro-organism communities and their non-living environment interacting as a functional unit' (UN, 1993). Every ecosystem is characterized by complex relationships between living (biotic) and non-living (abiotic) components (resources), sunlight, air, water, minerals and nutrients: the quantity (e.g. biomass, productivity), quality and diversity of species (e.g. richness, rarity) all play an important role. The functioning of an ecosystem often hinges on certain species or groups of species that perform key functions e.g. pollination, grazing, predation, nitrogen fixing.

Ecosystem services refer to the flow of benefits[1] that people obtain from ecosystems (MA, 2005a). These include:

- *provisioning services* (e.g. food, fibre, fuel, water);
- *regulating services* (benefits from ecosystem processes that regulate e.g. climate, floods, disease, waste and water quality);
- *cultural services* (e.g. recreation, tourism, and aesthetic, spiritual and ethical values);
- *supporting services* necessary for the production of all other ecosystem services (e.g. soil formation, photosynthesis, nutrient cycling).

'Habitat services' is also a separate classification to highlight the importance of ecosystems to provide habitats for migratory species (e.g. as nurseries) and as gene pool 'protectors' (maintain gene pool diversity and vitality) (see TEEB Foundations, 2010).

Ecosystem services flow from the 'natural capital stocks', like interest or dividends from the stock (also sometimes termed 'natural assets'). 'Natural capital' is an 'economic metaphor for the limited stocks of physical and biological resources found on earth' (MA, 2005a). See Section 3 and Chapter 3 for additional definitions and insights on 'natural capital', and TEEB Foundations (2010).

Many factors influence ecosystem resilience and the likely extent and rate of changes to ecosystem services. Examples include species abundance, level of biomass, quality and structure of natural habitats, and level of genetic diversity. Some services are directly linked to species' detailed composition and diversity (e.g. pollination, many cultural services). Others, like flood regulation, depend on the role of physical structures and processes at the ecosystem scale (for more detailed scientific discussion, see TEEB Foundations, 2010) (see Figure 1.1).

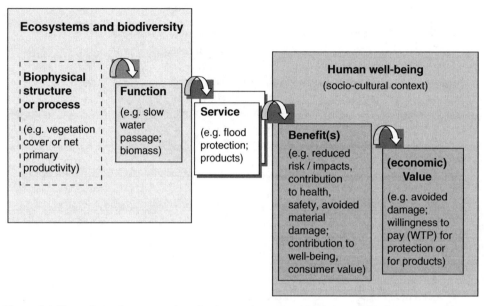

Figure 1.1 *The pathway from ecosystem structure and processes to human well-being*

Source: Adapted from Haines-Young and Potschin (2009) and Maltby (2009)

Many economic sectors depend on biodiversity and ecosystem services to a varying extent, including agriculture, fisheries, forestry, development, health, energy, transport and industry. Several need 'natural capital' for their flow of inputs, research, new products and business innovation (see Section 3.1 and Figure 1.6 below). Examples include the pharmaceutical industry and ecotourism, which requires a high-quality environment: in 2000, estimates by the World Tourism Organization showed global ecotourism spending growing by 20 per cent a year, about five times the average rate of growth in the tourism industry as a whole (TIES, 2006). Biomimicry (learning from nature) is expanding in areas as diverse as architecture, engineering and product development (see Chapter 5). With appropriate investment, it offers major potential for new markets.

Policy makers have a powerful incentive to maintain this natural capital – to avoid significant financial costs. Nature frequently offers the same services as man-made technological solutions for far less money (see Section 3). Particularly in this period of cutbacks to public and private budgets, avoiding unnecessary costs is fundamental to good governance and effective administration.

Failing to take steps to halt global biodiversity loss carries increasing costs in terms of damage to human health and property, erosion of ecosystem services and reduced economic opportunities. The consequences are socially inequitable and economically inefficient. Despite this, our balance sheets and national accounting systems give almost no visibility to biodiversity-related costs and benefits – or to the way they are distributed (see Chapter 3).

2 The biodiversity crisis: Scale and causes

Our natural environment is critical to intelligent economic growth and it is very easy to take for granted what nature provides for free. (Chris Carter, Minister of Conservation, New Zealand, 2006)

2.1 How much of our natural capital is being lost?

This section provides key facts about the planet's natural capital (see Section 3 and Chapter 3), the scale, importance and current rates of loss. Information and examples are grouped by ecosystem types for ease of reference. The socio-economic implications of species and genetic diversity loss are discussed in Sections 3 and 4.

Forests

Forests in different forms cover an area of around 4 billion hectares[2] (30.3 per cent of total global land area) (see Figure 1.2) and contain 80 to 90 per cent of the world's remaining terrestrial biodiversity (Costanza et al, 1997, see also FAO, 2000). They provide many valuable goods and services, including timber, food, fodder, medicines, climate regulation, provision of fresh water, soil protection, carbon sequestration, cultural heritage values and tourism opportunities (Shvidenko et al, 2005). It has been estimated that around 1.1 billion people depend on forests for their livelihoods (Vedeld et al, 2004; UN Millennium Project, 2005) and that 1.6 billion people around the world depend to some degree on forests for their livelihoods (World Bank, 2004).

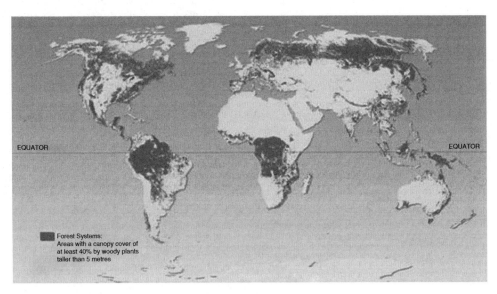

Figure 1.2 *Map of forest areas*

Source: MA (2005b)

FAO's most recent *Global Forest Resources Assessments* (FAO, 2010) reports the following findings:

- About 13 million hectares were converted to other uses or lost through natural causes each year in the last decade, with the highest net losses of forest reported for South America and Africa, with 4 and 3.4 million hectares respectively.
- The net loss of forest area was reduced to 5.2 million hectares per year between 2000 and 2010, down from 8.3 million hectares annually in the 1990s. The net annual loss of forests in 2000 to 2010 is equivalent to an area about the size of Costa Rica or Slovakia.
- The slowing down of the net annual loss of forest area is due both to a reduction of deforestation rates in Brazil and Indonesia, which had the highest loss of forests in the 1990s, and ambitious tree planting programmes in countries such as China, India, the US and Vietnam. During 2005 to 2010, the area of planted forest increased by about 5 million hectares per year. Three-quarters of all planted forests consist of native species while one-quarter comprises introduced species.

Standing forests are an important net carbon sink. Old-growth tropical forests are estimated to absorb up to 4.8Gt CO_2 per year, equivalent to around 0.67t CO_2 per capita (IPCC, 2007; Eliasch, 2008; Lewis and White, 2009). Globally, carbon stocks in forest biomass decreased by an estimated 0.5Gt a year in 2000 to 2010, mainly due to a reduction in total forest area (FAO, 2010). This is assumed to amount to approximately 15 per cent of annual human-induced CO_2 emissions. Conversely, deforestation releases CO_2 into the atmosphere and, at current rates, may account for 18 to 25 per cent of global CO_2 emissions (Stern, 2006; UNEP 2009).

Natural and semi-natural grasslands

Grasslands (land used for grazing) cover an estimated 52.5 million km². This is about 40.5 per cent of terrestrial land cover and can be broken down into wooded savanna and savanna (13.8 per cent), open and closed shrub (12.7 per cent), non-woody grassland (8.3 per cent) and tundra (5.7 per cent) (FAO, 2005b).

The biggest change to ecosystem structure has been the transformation of nearly a quarter (24 per cent) of the Earth's terrestrial surface to cultivated systems (MA, 2005b). Since 1945, 680 million hectares out of 3.4 billion hectares of rangelands have been affected: 3.2 million hectares are currently degraded every year (FAO, 2005b). Over 50 per cent of flooded grasslands/savannas and tropical and subtropical grasslands/savannas have been destroyed, together with nearly 30 per cent of montane grasslands and shrublands (WWF, 2006). Conversion of grassland to cultivated areas has led to problems of access to water for livestock and wildlife, loss of lean season grazing, obstruction of migration routes, and loss and fragmentation of wildlife habitat.

Soil degradation has damaged the productive capacity of both natural rangelands and cultivated lands (FAO, 2005b). This is a global problem with serious implications for food security but it also has significant local impacts. In Africa, 40 per cent of farmland suffers from nutrient depletion rates greater than 60kg/ha/year, with the highest rates in Guinea, Congo, Angola, Rwanda, Burundi and Uganda (Henao and Baanante, 2006).

Agricultural land

The Earth's land surface area totals 13.5 billion hectares, of which about 8.3 billion hectares are currently grassland or forest and 1.6 billion hectares cropland (Fischer, 2008):

- An additional 2 billion hectares are considered potentially suitable for rain-fed crop production. However, this figure should be used prudently as it also includes forests and wetlands which are extremely important as carbon sinks and for the provision of ecological services (FAO, 2008).
- Additional demand for agricultural production is linked to the conversion of available land to cultivate biofuel crops. The existing and predicted increase in biofuel production, together with recent food shortages due to adverse climatic conditions, have already had a very sharp impact on the price of agricultural commodities and this trend is expected to continue. Prices of agricultural commodities such as coarse grains and vegetable oil are projected to rise 12 to 15 per cent above the levels that would normally have prevailed in 2017, even if biofuel production levels were kept at their 2007 levels (OECD–FAO, 2008).
- FAO estimates that 1.02 billion people were undernourished in 2009, the vast majority in the Asia–Pacific region and sub-Saharan Africa (907 million). The core problem here is not about agricultural production and yields but that the poor cannot pay these higher food prices – a situation aggravated by the current economic crisis (FAO, 2009c).
- Enough food could be produced on land already under cultivation to feed the projected global population of 9 billion by 2050 (UNESA, 2009) if adequate investment were made in sustainable management, including agricultural intensification and innovation, and if further land conversion (i.e. forestry loss) was avoided.

Significant local risks are generated by loss of agricultural production or productivity. This can result from erosion and soil degradation caused by agricultural practices and/ or climate change. Soil quality and production capacity may also decline where over-abstraction reduces groundwater aquifer levels until they either fall below a critical threshold, allowing saltwater intrusion, or become too low for agricultural access, compromising yields, activities and livelihoods.

Freshwater systems

These are aquatic systems which contain water of almost no salt content and include lakes and ponds, rivers and streams, reservoirs, groundwater and wetlands. At global level:

- they provide most drinking water resources, water resources for agriculture, industry and sanitation and food such as fish and shellfish;
- they also provide recreational opportunities and a means of transportation;
- they cover 0.8 per cent of the Earth's surface and contain 0.009 per cent of its total water (Daily, 1997; Huges, 1999);
- they house 40 per cent of all known fish species (Master et al, 1998).

All continents unsustainably exploit freshwater resources. Between 5 and 25 per cent of global freshwater use exceeds long-term accessible supply (Vörösmarty et al, 2005). Water withdrawals from rivers and lakes for irrigation, urban uses and industrial applications doubled between 1960 and 2000. The construction of dams and other structures along rivers has moderately or strongly affected flows in 60 per cent of the world's large river systems, fragmenting aquatic ecosystems (MA, 2005a). Water abstraction for human uses has reduced the flow of several major rivers, including the Nile, Yellow and Colorado Rivers (Postel, 2000).

Forest loss, watershed degradation, wetland drainage and infrastructure that accelerates water run-off all reduce the potential for this 'natural infrastructure' to store, purify and provide water. Associated risks occur at both local and regional level. The possible future loss of the 'Amazon water pump' is an example of potentially dramatic international impact (see Chapter 5).

Terrestrial and coastal wetlands

Wetlands include swamps, marshes, mangrove swamps, forests and wet prairies, and cover 6 per cent of the Earth's land surface. They help maintain the water cycle by capturing and holding rainfall and snowmelt, retaining sediments and purifying water and provide a natural wastewater treatment system for some cities. Wetlands are important biodiversity areas and provide breeding grounds for fish, grazing lands and the source of staple food plants. They also act as carbon sinks, provide protection from floods and storms and help control soil erosion. Since 1900, the world has lost around 50 per cent of wetlands (UNWWAP, 2003).

Coastal wetland loss in some places is running at 20 per cent a year (Agardy et al, 2005). Taking mangroves as an example, 20 per cent (3.6 million hectares) of total coverage has been lost since 1980 (FAO, 2007) but this figure rises to 80 per cent in some countries due to conversion for aquaculture, over-exploitation and storm damage (MA, 2005a).

Another 2 per cent of the planet's land surface is covered by valuable coastal ecosystems such as estuaries, dunes, seagrass beds and lagoons. Coastal ecosystems are highly productive and have been estimated to account for up to 40 per cent of the total value of global ecosystem services. They yield 90 per cent of global fisheries and produce about 25 per cent of global biological productivity. (Valiela et al, 2001; UN, 2002).

Many natural ecosystems act as important buffers for natural hazards: wetlands for flood control, mangroves against sea surges and tsunamis, forests against landslides and mudslides, and mixed forests for reduced fire risk. This means that hazard risks rise along with mangrove conversion, deforestation and wetland drainage. During typhoon Wukong in Vietnam in 2000, for example, areas planted with mangroves were relatively unharmed while neighbouring provinces suffered significant losses of life and property (Brown et al, 2006).

Tropical coral reefs

Reefs cover just 1.2 per cent of the world's continental shelves but are the most diverse marine ecosystems (SCBD, 2010). They are often likened to oases within marine nutrient 'deserts' as they have a crucial role in shaping tropical marine systems which are highly productive despite very low nutrient conditions (Odum and Odum, 1955; see also Figure 1.3):

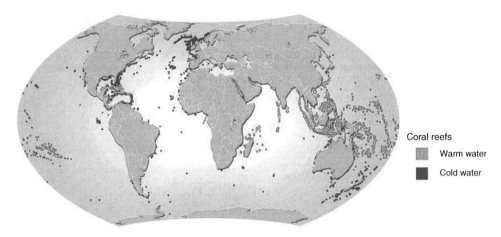

Coral reefs
Warm water
Cold water

Figure 1.3 *Map of coral reefs*

Source: Nellemann et al (2008)

- Reefs harbour an estimated 1 to 3 million species, including over a quarter of all marine fish species (Allsopp et al, 2009).
- They often have even higher levels of biodiversity than tropical forests.
- 20 per cent of reefs have been destroyed (MA, 2005a; Wilkinson, 2008).
- 30 per cent have been seriously damaged through destructive fishing practices, pollution, disease, coral bleaching, invasive alien species and tourism (UNEP-WCMC, 2006; Wilkinson, 2008).
- 58 per cent of the world's reefs are potentially threatened by human activities at the global scale (Bryant et al, 1998).

The risks of climate change for coral reef biodiversity and ecosystems now look greater than initial forecasts. Predicted temperature rise is expected to make major (further) loss of warm water coral reefs inevitable. New scientific evidence points to the fact that coral reef recovery is seriously hampered by CO_2 concentrations above 350ppm (Veron, 2009).

Marine systems

Oceans account for 90 per cent of the habitable volume for life on Earth and contain 90 per cent of global biomass (Rogers, 2009). Recent statistics demonstrate their importance as a provider of food and other goods but also the level of pressure on marine resources:

- In 2006, global capture fisheries represented 92 million tonnes of fish, of which nearly 90 per cent were harvested from the sea (FAO, 2009a).
- Since industrial fishing began, the total mass of commercially exploited marine species has been reduced by 90 per cent in much of the world (MA, 2005a).

- Current yields are lower than maximum potential due to excess fishing pressure in the past, with no possibilities in the short or medium term for further expansion and with an increased risk of further decline (World Bank, 2008).
- 52 per cent of marine fisheries are fully exploited (at or near maximum sustainable yields), 17 per cent over-exploited, 7 per cent depleted and 1 per cent recovering. 18 per cent are moderately exploited with only 2 per cent 'under-exploited' (FAO, 2009a) (see Figure 1.4).

Lowered biomass and habitat fragmentation resulting from fisheries impacts have led to local extinctions, especially among large, long-lived, slow-growing species with narrow geographical ranges (Pauly et al, 2005).

Improved governance could greatly increase economic benefits from existing fisheries. The difference between the potential and actual net economic benefits from marine fisheries is in the order of US$50 billion/year in an industry with an annual landed catch value of US$86 billion (World Bank, 2008). The cumulative loss to the global economy over the last three decades is estimated to be in the order of US$2 trillion (FAO, 2009a). There is also enormous waste: by-catch (unused catch) amounts to 38 million tonnes/year or 40 per cent of total catch (Davies et al, 2009).

Under current policies, there is an increased risk of fish stocks undergoing a series of collapses. This would impact on target stocks, entire marine ecosystems, food security, protein input and economies. In the near future, global fleets still have potential for substitution but local fleets will not always be able to find alternative sources of fish (see Section 4.2). Even at the global level, fishery substitution potential will also decrease with time.

Species and genetic diversity

Historically, natural loss of biodiversity occurred at far slower rates and was countered by the origination of new species (MA, 2005a). Current extinction rates are estimated to be 100 to 1000 times faster than those in geological times.

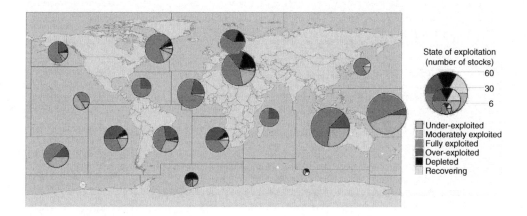

Figure 1.4 *State of exploitation of selected stock or species groups for which assessment information is available, by major marine fishing areas, 2004*

Source: FAO, 2005a

Recent tracking of losses by trend (the Living Planet Index) and rarity (IUCN Red List) offer similarly bleak pictures of the situation. Several terrestrial, marine and freshwater species are in steady decline (WWF, 2008) and the number of globally threatened species has been steadily increasing for the past ten years. Latest estimates in the Red List (IUCN, 2008; 2009a) indicate that:

- Nearly a quarter (21 per cent) of the world's assessed known mammal species and a third (30 per cent) of known amphibian species are known to be threatened or extinct.
- Over a third (17,291 species) out of the assessed 47,677 species are threatened with extinction.
- 12 per cent of the world's bird species are under threat.
- The highest levels of threat are found in islands: 39 to 64 per cent of mammals are threatened in Mauritius, Reunion and the Seychelles and 80 to 90 per cent of amphibian species are endangered or extinct in the Caribbean (Hilton-Taylor et al, 2009).

Species extinction and population loss in different ecosystems has reduced global genetic diversity. This reduces the fitness and adaptive potential of both species and ecosystems, thus limiting the prospects for recovery after possible disturbance. More specifically, agricultural intensification – coupled with selective breeding and the harmonizing effects of globalization – has significantly reduced the genetic diversity of cultivated plants and domesticated animals in agricultural systems. A third of the 6500 breeds of domesticated animals are estimated to be threatened or already extinct due to their very small population sizes (MA, 2005a; FAO, 2009b).

2.2 Global projections of future loss

Under current policies, the losses outlined above are expected to continue, leading to an increasingly acute global biodiversity crisis. Recent global environmental assessments provide specific projections on the scale of likely changes in biodiversity, based on potential scenarios and policies (see Box 1.2).

The assessments are unanimous in that pressures causing biodiversity loss will continue to increase under all considered policy scenarios, resulting in rates of biodiversity loss projected to accelerate and exceed that of the last century. Predictions for the period 2000 to 2050 include:

- **Terrestrial biodiversity:** Under business-as-usual scenarios, a further 11 per cent of biodiversity would be lost, with higher rates of loss in Africa and Latin America (OECD, 2008). Even under global sustainability policies, 7.5 per cent would be lost, with higher rates of 10.5 per cent and 9 per cent in Africa and Latin America/ Caribbean respectively (UNEP, 2007).
- **Forest cover** would continue to decrease under all scenarios. Even under the sustainability scenarios rate of loss in forest cover would not decrease significantly, which in large part can be ascribed to increased land demand for biofuel cultivation (UNEP, 2007; SCBD, 2010).
- **Agriculture:** Poor agricultural practices associated with unfavourable socio-economic conditions could create a vicious circle in which poor smallholder

---

Box 1.2 Global assessments and the use of scenarios to make future projections

In 2005, the Millennium Ecosystem Assessment (MA, 2005a) assessed the consequences of ecosystem change for human well-being and established the scientific basis for actions to enhance their conservation and sustainable use. It was followed by the Global Environment Outlook 4 (GEO-4; see UNEP, 2007), the OECD Environmental Outlook (OECD, 2008), the International Assessment of Agricultural Science and Technology (IAASTD, 2008) and, most recently, the Global Biodiversity Outlook 3 (GBO-3; see SCBD, 2010).

Scenarios used in the assessments

Assessments typically use a set of different scenarios outlining likely global situations (the best known is the IPCC's Special Report on Emissions Scenarios). The MA and the GEO-4 have developed broadly comparable sets, based on four categories:

1. **conventional markets**: continued focus on liberalized markets, leading to rapid economic and technological growth with a reactive approach to environmental protection;
2. **global sustainable development**: a global response to sustainability issues, average economic and technological growth and proactive approach to environmental protection;
3. **competition between regions**: countries shun global cooperation in favour of protectionist policies, leading to slower economic and technological growth and a reactive approach to environmental protection;
4. **regional sustainable development**: sustainable development is prioritized at a regional level without cooperation at a global scale, leading to average economic and technological growth.

Key findings from these models are noted in the text. The projections for biodiversity are likely to be underestimates as the models do not consider invasive species impacts or ecological tipping points. The marine models are also hampered by lack of information and are likely to underestimate fishing effort, particularly artisanal.

---

farmers are forced to use marginal lands, increasing deforestation and overall degradation. The assessments are unanimous that increased productivity is key to protecting terrestrial biodiversity as it reduces the need to convert remaining natural areas to cultivation. If this does not occur, biodiversity loss would be even higher than projected. IAASTD (2008) suggests that more recent scenarios reflect an emerging agreement that by 2050 land demand for agriculture could increase by approximately 10 per cent, even assuming high investment in agricultural productivity leading to substantial increases in yield. GBO-3 suggests that, although efforts to alleviate poverty might increase demand for food and energy and have negative effects on biodiversity, habitat destruction could also locally be reduced through virtuous cycles of sustainable intensification of agriculture and poverty alleviation. Next to substantial increases in protected areas, more sustainable meat production is seen as having the greatest positive impacts on biodiversity.

- **Energy demand:** Globally, this is projected to almost double between 2000 and 2030 under business-as-usual scenarios (IAASTD, 2008). For biofuels, the International Energy Agency (IEA) in its *World Energy Outlook 2006* presented various scenarios for growth to 2030. Its reference scenario projects that around 2.5 per cent of arable land would be needed to satisfy growing demand. Under its alternative policy scenario, which assumes a faster deployment of biofuels, meeting the demand for biofuels would even require a land conversion of 3.8 per cent by 2030.
- **Trade liberalization** may stimulate more efficient use of resources (OECD, 2008) but could potentially also contribute to an increase in agricultural production in Africa and South America where the land and labour costs are lower. This would have an unintended net negative impact on biodiversity due to impacts on grasslands and tropical forests.
- **Fisheries:** One study predicts a global fish stock collapse by 2048 without major additional policy response, noting that 29 per cent of edible fish stocks have already declined by 90 per cent (Worm, 2006). Assessments looking into fisheries (UNEP, 2007) suggest improvements if ecosystem-based conservation policies are deployed (e.g. total catch limits, designated fishing seasons and zones, regulated fishing methods, elimination of capacity subsidies) although this would obviously depend on regional policies and their enforcement.

Box 1.3 Key ecological risks, tipping points and measures to alleviate pressures resulting in biodiversity loss

The GBO-3 underlined the range of ecological risks and losses expected in the future under current trends (economic growth, population, consumption, innovation). Key results suggest that under a business-as-usual scenario:

- Tropical forests would continue to be cleared for crops and pastureland and potentially for biofuel production.
- Climate change, invasive alien species, pollution, water extraction and dam construction would put further pressure on freshwater biodiversity and the services it underpins.
- Overfishing would continue to damage marine ecosystems and cause the collapse of fish populations, leading to the failure of fisheries.

It also noted the risk of critical ecological tipping points (see Chapter 3) being passed. For example:

- The Amazon Forest could undergo a widespread dieback, due to the interaction of deforestation, fire and climate change, changing from rainforest to savanna or seasonal forest over wide areas. The Forest could move into a self-perpetuating cycle in which fires become more frequent, drought more intense and dieback accelerates.
- The Sahel in Africa, under pressure from climate change and over-use of limited land resources, shifts to alternative degraded states, further driving desertification.

- Island ecosystems are afflicted by a cascading set of extinctions and ecosystem instabilities, due to the impact of invasive alien species. As invaded communities become increasingly altered and impoverished, vulnerability to new invasions may increase.
- Freshwater eutrophication is caused by the build-up of phosphates and nitrates from agricultural fertilizers, sewage effluent and urban stormwater run-off. Freshwater bodies become algae dominated (eutrophic state). As algae decay, oxygen levels in the water are depleted and there is widespread die-off of other aquatic life, including fish.
- The combined impacts of ocean acidification and warmer sea temperatures make tropical coral reef systems vulnerable to collapse. Together with the bleaching impact of warmer water, and a range of other human-induced stresses, reefs increasingly become algae dominated with catastrophic loss of biodiversity.

Within TEEB a quantitative assessment was carried out by the PBL-Netherlands Environmental Assessment Agency, supported by the Dutch government, building on the model underlying the GBO-3 projections. This produced the following key results:

- Diet: changing to healthier diets could offer major potential benefits for biodiversity. Reducing to a 65g/day/capita of meat would save approximately 10 million km^2 of natural areas by 2050, which would reduce the net loss of natural area to about zero. Moving to a full vegetarian diet would save around 18 million km^2, which would reverse the loss of natural area into 8 million km^2 gain compared to the year 2000. In terms of mean species abundance (MSA), the projected loss by 2050 would be reduced by 35 per cent and 55 per cent respectively.
- Protected areas: expanding protected areas by 20 per cent or 50 per cent would lead to savings of 2 million km^2 or 9 million km^2 respectively. In terms of MSA the projected loss would be reduced by 10 per cent and 50 per cent respectively.
- Mitigating climate change: a policy response without bioenergy would have no impact on the projected loss of natural area. However, with bioenergy it would result in a significant additional loss of 5 million km^2. In terms of MSA the projected loss would be reduced by 10 per cent and increased by 10 per cent respectively.
- Increasing agricultural yields also has major potential for reducing the negative impacts noted in the business-as-usual scenario – potentially saving around 6 million km^2 of natural areas. In terms of MSA the projected loss would be reduced by 30 per cent.

For an ambitious yet feasible combination of options (i.e. expanding protected areas by 20 per cent and switching to a lower meat diet), the global net loss of natural area would be close to zero, and the loss in terms of MSA would be halved.

To halt biodiversity loss completely would clearly require additional measures, such as integration across sectors, synergies with other policy objectives, measures to change the economic signals for biodiversity preservation, greening of the markets, regulation and enforcement, and investment in natural capital, including restoration (see Chapters 5 to 9 of this book).

The biophysical results produced in the above-mentioned study (PBL, 2010) have also been used as a basis for estimating the *monetary* benefits of the option scenarios; these benefit estimates are being juxtaposed with cost estimates (where available). This analysis is part of a wider body of quantitative assessment work for TEEB. As this volume goes to press, the work on costs and benefits – by the Scottish Agricultural College (SAC) and IVM et al – was still ongoing and will be discussed in context in subsequent books in the Earthscan TEEB series.

Sources: SCBD (2010); PBL (2010)

2.3 What is driving these losses?

The global assessments identify a range of direct causes and key underlying drivers for biodiversity and ecosystem losses.

Direct causes for biodiversity loss

These can be grouped into five main categories. The extent to which they contribute to ecosystem degradation and biodiversity loss will vary between ecosystems and regions (see Figure 1.5 below).

Habitat loss results from land-use change, mainly through conversion for agriculture and urban, industrial and infrastructure development, and is affecting over 2000

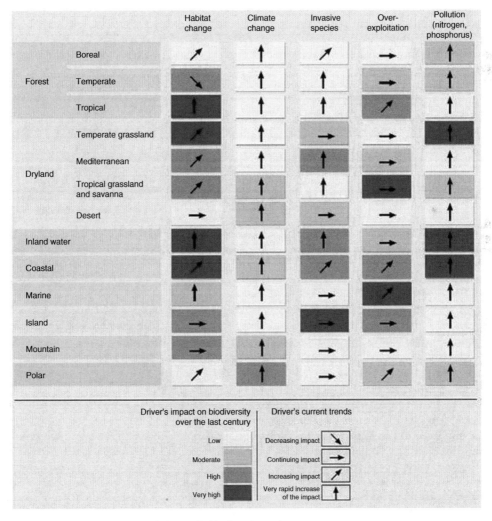

Figure 1.5 *Main direct drivers of change in biodiversity and ecosystems*

Source: MA (2005b, p16)

mammal species (IUCN, 2009b). **Over-exploitation** of resources, such as fish, energy, minerals and soil, reflects increased prosperity as well as poverty (see Box 1.3). Use of species for their (perceived) medicinal properties affects over 900 mammal species, mainly in Asia (IUCN, 2009b). **Pollution** from multiple sources contributes to cumulative impacts on natural capital and results from a wide range of mainstream economic sector activities.

Climate change impacts on biodiversity and ecosystems are now considered likely to be greater than initial forecasts. Although scientists indicate that ecosystems will be able to adapt to a certain extent to rising temperatures and sea levels and to changes in evapotranspiration, the combination of human-induced pressures and climate change will increase the risk of losing numerous systems. Coral reefs are a well-documented example (see TEEB *Climate Issues Update*, 2009).

Invasive alien species (IAS) have wide-ranging impacts on the food web, habitat structure and ecosystem functions. Recent data confirm that numbers of IAS are increasing in all environments and among all taxonomic groups: in Europe, for example, they increased by 76 per cent over the period 1970 to 2007 (Butchart et al, 2010).[3] This upward trend is difficult to halt, let alone reverse (MA, 2005a). A key economic study, based on six countries, estimated that globally the potential costs of damage and control could reach almost 5 per cent of global gross domestic product (GDP) (US$1.4 trillion/year) (Pimentel et al, 2001; 2005). At the EU level, the impacts of IAS have already cost EU stakeholders around €12 billion per year over the past 20 years and it has been estimated that a failure effectively to address threats by IAS might lead to even greater costs in the future (Kettunen et al, 2009; Shine et al, 2010). Environmental degradation already creates favourable conditions for some introduced species to establish and spread. Climate change may in turn modify the whole process of an invasion, increase ecosystem vulnerability and alter species' distributions (Capdevila-Argüelles and Zilletti, 2008).

Underlying drivers

The assessments identify growing demand for goods and services from an increasingly wealthy and expanding population as the main underlying cause of biodiversity loss and ecosystem conversion or degradation.

This type of consumption, which often goes well beyond the fulfilment of basic needs, is based on choice. In contrast, those living below the poverty line are more likely to depend for their livelihood and even survival on local resources or land. Short-term needs will inevitably take precedence over long-term considerations, particularly where there is no clear and immediate incentive to preserve undervalued ecosystems.

Over-consumption of specific goods and services is partly driven by economic signals from policy and market prices which rarely reflect the true value of biodiversity and the social costs and benefits of ecosystem services. Most ecosystem services are unpriced or underpriced (see Chapters 5 and 7), such as:

- **Water:** Groundwater extraction is rarely subject to full cost charging (see Chapter 6).

Box 1.4 Fact box: How human demand can affect biodiversity

- Global meat, fish and dairy consumption causes around 30 per cent of biodiversity loss.
- 80 per cent of agricultural area is currently devoted to meat and dairy production.
- On average, a world citizen consumes 39kg of meat per year. In the US, this figure is 121kg, in EU-15 91kg, in China 54kg and in Africa 14kg.
- 10 per cent of the world's population consumes 25 per cent of animal protein (fish, meat and dairy).
- World consumption of animal protein has doubled since 1970.
- In sub-Saharan Africa, 71 per cent of world heritage sites are affected by over-extraction of resources (illegal hunting or fishing, fuelwood collection, etc.) and 38 per cent by encroachment for agriculture.

Source: PBL, 2009

- **Fish in the high seas:** Access to this common resource is not subject to exploitation charges (see Chapter 7).
- **Forests:** These are often in fact 'commons'. Payment systems that do exist are generally too low to reinvest in future forests (see Chapter 7).
- **Regulating services provided by ecosystems:** Land managers rarely receive income for carbon storage, water regulation and other services (see Chapter 5) and have little incentive to manage ecosystems to maintain them rather than producing marketable commodities.

Many ecosystem services are difficult or impossible to price or trade in conventional markets. There is nevertheless a clear rationale for public intervention to protect services with the following characteristics:

- **Public goods:** Services like air quality maintenance and climate regulation are *non-excludable* (i.e. people cannot be excluded from consuming them) and *non-rival* (one person consuming them does not prevent another from doing so).
- **Services with strong externality effects:** For a range of regulating services (e.g. water supply, pollination, erosion control), the actions of some landowners and managers generate benefits to neighbouring landowners and communities but these tend to be difficult to capture in market transactions.
- **Services for which markets are hard to design:** For example, fisheries are not pure public goods but are rarely priced because organizing and policing markets in fishing rights is complex.

More often than not, negative impacts generated by the primary production, transport, mining and energy sectors are not monetized. Until recently, compensation for damage has only rarely – and then only partially – been payable (see Chapter 7). There is an imbalance between rewards derived from providing private marketable goods/services for current consumption and those from providing services that benefit the wider population, including future generations.

Responding to these drivers will be critical to address the biodiversity challenge. Current losses reflect multiple failures of public policy and, too often, the lack of high-level political backing for conservation of natural assets. We can turn the situation around by better appreciating the value of ecosystems and biodiversity, and integrating such values into all areas of policy making (see Chapters 2 and 4).

3 Economic dimensions of the biodiversity crisis

We need to understand the value of today's natural capital to assess what will be lost if biodiversity and ecosystem loss is not halted, as well as the potential added value of investing in nature.

3.1 How do ecosystem services underpin the economy?

Economic prosperity depends on the flow of services from at least four types of capital: man-made capital (buildings, machines and infrastructure), human capital (skills and creativity), social capital (cooperation, trust and rule of law) and natural capital.[4] Natural capital is an input to intermediate consumption by many sectors of the economy and also a direct input for final 'consumption'. Public and private sectors and households can play a role both as consumers of and investors in natural (and social) capital (see Figure 1.6).

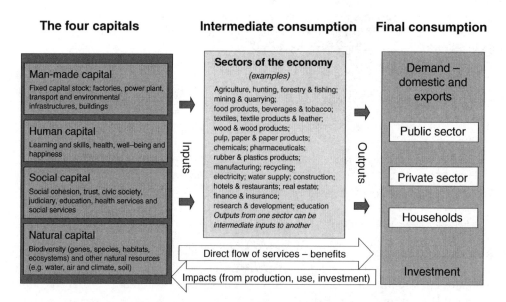

Figure 1.6 *Natural capital: Its contribution to the economy and livelihoods*

Source: own representation, Patrick ten Brink

GDP builds on natural capital. This can be done sustainably by working within the limits of ecosystems. However, GDP more often relies on unsustainable extractive uses and either draws down natural capital (e.g. deforestation, overfishing) or creates man-made capital at the expense of natural capital (e.g. building over natural habitats).

The number of sectors benefiting from natural capital represents a far larger share of the economy than many policy makers appreciate. This dependence is obvious for some sectors (primary production, water supply, nature-based tourism) but less so for others that derive huge economic benefits from biodiversity (e.g. cosmetics, chemicals, plastics, food, drink and ornamental fish). Data for 2006 (see Chapter 5 and TEEB in Business, 2011) shows how products derived from genetic resources contributed to the economy, including:

- a significant share of the pharmaceutical sector's turnover (total industry turnover US$640 billion) is derived from genetic resources (IMS, 2007);
- enzymes, micro-organisms and other products used in biotechnology (total sector value US$70 billion) (Ernst and Young, 2007);
- all agricultural seeds (US$30 billion) (SCBD, 2008; see also TEEB in Business, 2011).

Box 1.5 puts this into economic context.

Box 1.5 Natural capital: Its relationship to productivity

Environmental economists have long maintained that the importance of natural capital as a production factor is often overlooked. Traditionally, an economy's growth rate is split into (i) weighted growth rates of the various factors of production; and (ii) total factor productivity (TFP) covering growth not accounted for by productive inputs (e.g. technological progress). However, many TFP estimates do not adequately account for draw-down of the stock of natural capital (Repetto et al, 1989; Dasgupta and Mäler, 2000; Ayres and Warr, 2006). Failing to internalize the cost of environmental externalities (i.e. damage) is equivalent to using an unpaid factor of production.

TFP estimates may be biased upwards once the environment is not classified as a factor of production. This makes it possible to attribute part of the economy's productivity growth to natural capital and, conversely, to reveal that continued loss of natural capital has a negative impact on productivity and will compromise the potential for future growth (Vouvaki and Xeapapadeas, 2008).

3.2 Understanding the value of ecosystem services

Appreciating the value of natural assets is critical to change the way we make policy and investment decisions. Any given area provides multiple services and offers a unique set of benefits. Focusing on a single service from an area risks ignoring the wide range of other services. This can lead to potentially important losses in terms of costs and of opportunities forgone.

Valuing the full range of services

The first step is to understand the whole set of services: what they are, what helps create them, their link to on-site activities, who benefits and where. The second is to express changes in these ecosystem services in quantitative and in monetary terms (see Chapter 4). The actual values per hectare will vary depending on the nature of the land, its use and the proximity and wealth of groups using the service.

Table 1.1 shows that tropical forests can have significant value for regulating services even though their economic importance is often perceived only in terms of products (timber and non-timber). Case studies show that it is not atypical for about two-thirds of forest value to derive from regulating services and only one-third from provisioning food, raw material and genetic material for pharmaceuticals (for a

Table 1.1 Examples of potential ecosystem service values from tropical forests

Service	Value
Food, fibre and fuel	Provisioning services for Cameroon's forests (per hectare average discounted net present values) were estimated at US$560 for timber, US$61 for fuelwood and US$41–US$70 for non-timber forest products (NTFPs) (Lescuyer, 2007, based on a review of previous studies). Tribal communities living in the Rajiv Gandhi National Park derived 4691 rupees (US$109) per household per year from NTFPs (Ninan et al, 2007).
Climate regulation	Value of climate regulation by tropical forests in Cameroon at US$842–US$2265 per ha (Lescuyer, 2007, based on a review of previous studies). Value of carbon stored in above-ground biomass in Guyana's forests, estimated at between $6500 and $7000 per ha at $20 per tonne, but could rise to over $20,000 per ha at potential values of $60–80 per tonne in near future (Office of the President Republic of Guyana, 2008).
Water regulation	Value of flood protection by tropical forests in Cameroon estimated at US$24 per ha/year (Yaron, 2001).
Groundwater recharge	Contribution to groundwater recharge of a 40,000ha tropical forest watershed in Ko'olau, Hawaii, estimated at (net present value (NPV) using shadow prices) US$1.42–2.63 billion (Kaiser and Roumasset, 2002).
Pollination	Average value of pollination services provided by forests in Sulawesi, Indonesia, estimated at €46 per hectare. Due to ongoing forest conversion, continued decline of pollination services is expected to directly reduce coffee yields by up to 18 per cent and net revenue/ha by up to 14 per cent within 20 years (Priess et al, 2007).
Existence values	A contingent valuation study in the UK and Italy evaluated non-users' willingness to pay (WTP) for a proposed programme of protected areas to conserve Brazilian Amazonia at $US43 per household per year (Horton et al, 2003). The value of natural forest in the Herbert River District, North Queensland, was estimated through choice modelling at AUS$18 per ha/year (approximately US$11) (Mallawaarachchi et al, 2001).
Opportunity cost	The value of land use lost by NOT deforesting, on average, is approximately $1000 per ha (present value over 30 years, Grieg-Gran, 2008), varying with geographical and economic details. The values of ecosystem services lost by deforestation (see above) will very often exceed this. In particular the climate regulation values are likely to be higher. Office of the President Republic of Guyana (2008) suggests that the cost of carbon abatement via side-payments to avoid deforestation would be only $2–11 per tonne of carbon dioxide.

detailed discussion of methodologies and examples, see TEEB Foundations 2010, Appendix 3).

As noted, values are site and time specific. The value of coral reefs for tourism, for example, can range from low to extremely high in cases where the sector is a key source of income and economic development. At the top end of the range, their value can be up to US$1 million per ha/year, e.g. in Hawaii which is accessible to high-income markets (Ruitenbeek and Cartier, 1999; Cesar et al, 2002; TEEB Foundations, 2010, Appendix 3). Even when these extreme values are put aside, the economic potential of coral reefs for tourism is considerable and highlights the economic risks associated with losing these natural assets.

Identifying benefits at different scales

Benefits can arise at different geographic scales, depending on the ecosystem service (see Figure 1.7 for an illustrative split of services across geographic scales). These again vary on a case-by-case basis and over time. Services with global benefits (outer shading of the figure) include carbon storage and genetic resources for developing new medicines, while others are mainly national or local (e.g. pollination, water purification – represented by the inner shaded area). Many services can deliver benefits at several levels, e.g. ecotourism, recreation.

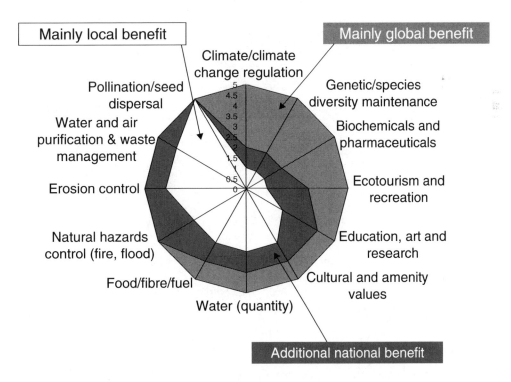

Figure 1.7 *Distribution of benefits over different geographic scales*

Source: own representation, Patrick ten Brink

Saving costs by working with natural capital

Avoiding unnecessary or excessive costs is in the interests of all policy makers and economic sectors. Many services can be more efficiently provided by maintaining or restoring 'ecological infrastructure' than by artificial structures or processes, including fire protection from native vegetation, natural soil fertility and genetic diversity as insurance for future food security (for other examples, see Box 1.6).

Box 1.6 Value for money from natural capital

Natural solutions for water regulation, filtration and treatment

Forests and wetlands filter and clean much more cheaply than water treatment plants:

- Catskill Mountains, US: US$2 billion natural capital solution (restoration and maintenance of watershed) versus a US$7 billion technological solution (pre-treatment plant).
- New Zealand: The Central Otago conservation area (Te Papanui Catchment) saved the city of Dunedin NZ$93 million (approximately US$65 million) in water supply costs (BPL, 2006).
- Venezuela: The national protected area system prevents erosion, flooding and water supply fluctuation that would reduce farm earnings by around US$4 million/ year (based on data provided in Gutman, 2002, updated by the authors to account for inflation and increase in land under irrigated agriculture).
- A third of the world's hundred largest cities draw a substantial proportion of their drinking water from forest-protected areas (Dudley and Stolton, 2003).

Forest investments to reduce flooding

In China, following severe Yangtse River flooding in 1999, the government committed to invest over US$40 billion in the Sloping Land Conversion Programme by offering farmers along the river cash incentives to cede their land for forest conversion to decrease erosion and mitigate flood impacts (Bennett and Xu, 2007; Tallis et al, 2008; see Chapter 9).

Fish stock regeneration through protection of fish nurseries in mangroves

In Cambodia, the Ream National Park provides fish breeding grounds and other subsistence goods from mangroves worth an estimated US$600,000 per year and an additional US$300,000 in services such as storm protection and erosion control (Emerton et al, 2002; see also Chapter 8).

Carbon capture and storage

Finding cost-effective means to mitigate climate change is essential, given the scale of the challenge. Proposed man-made solutions include allocating substantial funds to artificial carbon capture and storage (CCS) e.g. by pumping CO_2 into the ground. Natural ecosystems (forests, agricultural land, wetlands) already store vast quantities of carbon above ground and in water or soil and absorb additional amounts every year: deforestation or degradation can lead to very significant emissions (FAO, 2010; see Chapter 5). For example in Mecklenburg-Vorpommern in Germany an area of 30,000 hectares was restored, saving up to 300,000 tonnes CO_2 equivalent of emissions. This amounts to an avoidance cost of between €8 and €12 per tonne CO_2. If alternative land-use options are used (e.g. extensive grazing, reed production or alder forest) costs decrease to between €0 and €4 per tonne CO_2 (Federal Environment Agency, 2007; MLUV MV, 2009; Schaefer, 2009).

3.3 Using valuation to assess trade-offs, costs and benefits

Distributional impacts – who wins and who loses? – are a fundamental element of decision making. For ecosystem services, this question has not only a geographic dimension (see Figure 1.7 above) but also a time dimension. Converting natural systems can create short-term wealth and employment but evidence shows that keeping natural ecosystem services would provide wealth and jobs indefinitely, albeit often at lower levels. How we compare impacts now and in the future is critical (on use of the discount rate, see Chapter 4 and also TEEB Foundations, 2010, Chapter 6).

Costs and benefits of land conversion

Any land-use choice involves trade-offs. Decisions to convert land imply that the benefits are considered to outweigh the costs. However, such decisions are often systematically biased as they do not account for the value of all ecosystem services affected by the particular decision.

The choice of land use will affect the services produced and, as a result, determine who benefits or loses and by how much. Land conversion decisions thus have important distributional impacts. Valuation helps to clarify the trade-offs not only between services but also between respective groups of beneficiaries. Decision making (e.g. on spatial planning applications) should address these implications through the evidence base.

Figure 1.8 gives a simplified example of trade-offs involved in a decision to leave land in a natural state, convert it to extensive agriculture or convert it to intensive agriculture (excluding pollution issues). It shows that concentrating on food provision entails greater loss of other services. In some cases, this may be essential and the benefits will outweigh the losses of other services. In others, however, the main benefits from increased food provision may go to a different private interest than the former beneficiaries of the other services.

Existing policy frameworks usually give explicit consideration to some trade-offs e.g. between road/house construction and designation of natural areas for protection. However, this decision-making process rarely factors in all benefits and costs, e.g. loss of carbon stored in the soil when converting forests to biofuels production, impact on species migration caused by dam building.

Once ecosystem services values are understood and included, what seemed an 'acceptable' trade-off may prove to have net costs (see example in Box 1.7). Conversely, including too little information in decision making can inadvertently lead to 'lose–lose' decisions.

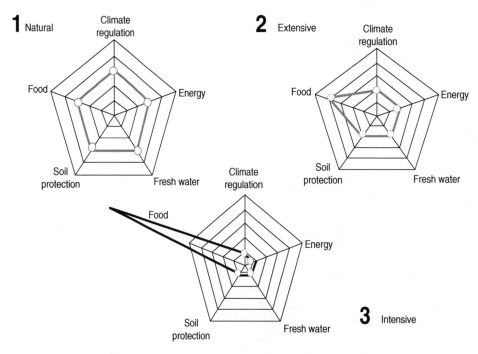

Figure 1.8 *Land-use choices and trade-offs of ecosystem service provision*

Source: B. ten Brink (2008)

Box 1.7 To convert or not to convert – deciding between mangroves and a shrimp farm

A case study in Southern Thailand estimated benefits from commercial shrimp farming at around US$9632/ha (Hanley and Barbier, 2009). Returns to private investors were particularly high because the shrimp farms received subsidies and the investors did not have to pay for restoring the original ecosystem (open-access mangroves) or for property depreciation at the end of the farms' operating life. For those making the private gain, the conversion decision was clearly an easy one.

However, the conclusion changed once the full picture of costs and benefits to society were considered. By adjusting to account for the shrimp farm subsidies and the pollution generated, the farms' economic return was reduced to US$1220/ha and turned negative once rehabilitation costs (around US$9318/ha) were also included (Hanley and Barbier, 2009). Conversely, the benefits of retaining the mangroves (mostly to local communities) were estimated at around US$584/ha for collected wood and NTFPs, US$987/ha for fish nurseries and US$10,821/ha for coastal protection against storms (Barbier, 2007). The total value of the mangroves was therefore around US$12,392/ha.

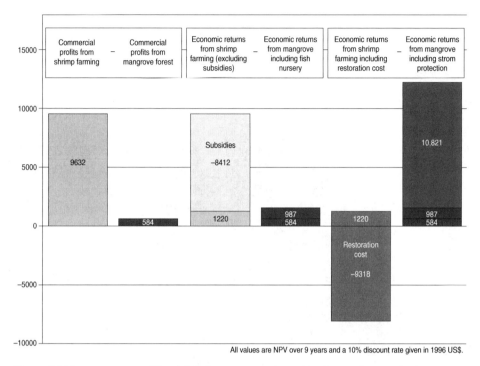

Figure 1.9 *The mangrove and the shrimp farm; a comparison of land-use values per hectare*

Note: All values are NPV over nine years, with a productive life of five years of the shrimp farm, and a 10 per cent discount rate. They are 1996 US$.

Source: Adapted from Hanley and Barbier (2009)

Putting private gain above public loss is a very common factor in decisions leading to loss of ecosystem services and biodiversity. A private investor who receives public subsidies without having to pay for pollution or resource impacts of the activity has no incentive to avoid such damage (see Chapter 6). The result is a potentially major public loss – at community, national or global level – for a smaller private gain.

Cases like this point up the need for active public policy. They can only be avoided through a fuller approach to valuation and cost–benefit analysis and an appropriate policy response (e.g. subsidy reform, payment of meaningful compensation, refusal of a permit).

Costs and benefits of pro-conservation policies

The issue of trade-offs is equally important for pro-conservation policies (see Chapter 8). Choosing to protect a site has implications for those already benefiting from the site and for those hoping to use the site in another way:

- Existing and potential beneficiaries include direct users (e.g. those harvesting timber) and indirect users (e.g. those who gain from clean water and air).

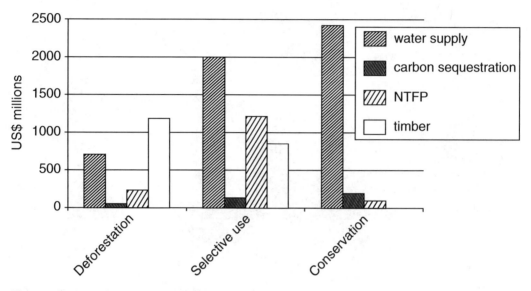

Figure 1.10 *Value of selected provisioning and regulating ecosystem services under different land-use scenarios in the Leuser National Park, Indonesia*

Source: Van Beukering et al (2003)

- A site not designated for conservation will provide a range of benefits (e.g. extractive benefits of timber for a private user) and other services depending on the nature of the land, the links to population groups and the nature of the extractive activity.
- Designation of land for conservation is usually designed to reduce extractive use and pollution, and to increase provision of other ecosystem services. This may lead to a net benefit but it will often be necessary to pay compensation to former users, address incentives for lost opportunity costs and pay for site management.
- There is a clear case for pro-conservation policies when such benefits (measured in terms of the ecosystem services provided to wider society) outweigh the costs (including financial costs and opportunity costs).
- However, the costs of implementing conservation are generally met locally whereas the benefits occur at multiple levels. Policy makers need to consider who should pay for conservation and what mechanisms are needed (see Chapters 5 and 8).

The use of economic analysis to inform policy trade-offs can be illustrated with an example from Indonesia. In the Leuser National Park, controlled and uncontrolled logging and unsustainable harvesting of NTFPs is degrading key ecosystem services, leading to a decline in overall benefits from the forest ecosystem; associated revenues are mainly captured by elites with fewer benefits for local people. Conservation and selective use of the forest ecosystem would support maintenance of a broad range of services with greater benefits for the local population. The value of 11 ecosystem services was therefore compared for the period 2000 to 2030 under different land-use scenarios (van Beukering et al, 2003). Their total economic value (TEV) (see Chapter 4) was estimated at US$9.5 billion under the conservation scenario and US$9.1 billion under the selective-use scenario compared to an estimated income of US$7 billion under the deforestation scenario. Figure 1.10 presents the TEV for four of these ecosystem services under the different scenarios, using a discount rate of 4 per cent.

4 Human dimensions of the biodiversity crisis

4.1 Ecosystem services: A lifeline for the poor, a necessity for everyone

It is not just wealth that is in danger but also 'well-being' – both individual well-being and health (human capital), and social well-being and stability (social capital). Nature and healthy natural systems are vital to us all at different levels. Engaging local communities is central to tackling current threats to biodiversity and ecosystem services.

The poor often depend most directly on ecosystems for basic goods and services and are therefore the first to suffer the impacts of biodiversity loss or degradation. Natural resources are a basic source of their income generation (see the discussion on 'GDP of the poor' in Chapter 3). Moreover, healthcare needs for the world's poor are mostly met by traditional medicines and treatments extracted from natural sources: loss of this biodiversity hits them doubly hard as the cost of industrial medicines is often prohibitive. The TEEB Interim Report (2008) underlined that there are critically important links between ecosystem services (loss) and the feasibility of achieving the Millennium Development Goals (MDGs) (UN, 2000).

Beyond material dependency, biodiversity often plays an important role in religious beliefs, traditional knowledge and social institutions. Many communities are enmeshed with the ecosystems within which they live and this connection forms the basis of their identity and culture (see Box 1.8).

Box 1.8 Forests, rural communities and mutual benefit

Over 90 per cent of the world's poorest people depend on forests for their livelihoods, with some populations having no other source of resources (e.g. indigenous forest peoples).

The average annual value of NTFPs is variously estimated at between US$1/ha and US$100/ha (SCBD, 2001). However, in certain countries, NTFPs represent a much higher share of household income, e.g. 40 to 60 per cent in Chivi, Zimbabwe (Lynam et al, 1994); 47 per cent in Mantandia, Madagascar (Kramer et al, 1995); and 49 per cent in Madhya Pradesh, Orissa and Gujarat, India (Bahuguna, 2000). Forest loss can seriously impact on income/well-being for population groups that often have no easy substitute available.

At the same time, communities can and do play an important role in maintaining healthy forests and there are strong arguments for making them part of the solution to deforestation and degradation. Communities own 22 per cent of all developing country forests. Community tenure is expected to double again by 2020 to more than 700 million hectares (Molnar, 2003).

Some countries already reward communities for their management efforts, including:

- **Ecuador:** The municipal government pays communities US$11 to US$16 per ha/year to maintain natural forest cover and ensure clean water supplies in the Pisque watershed.
- **Uganda:** ECOTRUST pays villagers US$45.60 per ha/year (US$8 per tonne of carbon sequestered) for reforestation with native trees.

Source: Borges (2007)

Vulnerability to climate shocks is unequally distributed. Hurricane Katrina provided a potent reminder of human frailty in the face of climate change, even in the richest countries. Across the developed world, public concern over exposure to extreme climate risks is mounting with every flood, storm and heat wave. Yet climate disasters are heavily concentrated in poor countries.

Some 262 million people were affected by climate disasters annually from 2000 to 2004, over 98 per cent of them in the developing world. In richer countries forming part of the Organisation for Economic Co-operation and Development (OECD), 1 in 1500 people was affected by climate disaster over this period. The comparable figure for developing countries was 1 in 19 (UNDP, 2007).

4.2 Substitution potential: Limits and implications

Typically, if we lose or damage something, we ask ourselves where to find a replacement. When a natural resource is depleted, we look for ways to acquire a substitute, e.g. another fishing ground, another forest for fuel or another aquifer for water. This substitution of ecosystem services can sometimes happen by natural means: the services lost from the original ecosystem may be (partly) substituted by exploiting another, similar ecosystem in some other location. In other cases, substitution can be by artificial means, through use of technical solutions e.g. desalinated water or bottled water.

However, there are limits to substitution potential and this has very important human implications. For some services and groups of society, there are:

- no alternatives;
- only degraded alternatives; or
- much more costly – even unaffordable – alternatives.

Resource depletion has direct social impacts in such cases. Fuelwood provides a stark example. The more time has to be spent on collecting fuel or earning money to pay for it, the less is available for cooking, heating and other needs. In some countries the poor traditionally depend heavily on wood and charcoal as an energy source and women and children may spend 100 to 300 work days a year gathering wood: in Mali, already in the late 1980s, some collection trips required walking 15km one way and in urban areas, an average of 20 to 40 per cent of cash income had to be set aside to buy wood or charcoal (FAO, 1987). With most alternative fuels becoming increasingly expensive and deforestation resulting in fuelwood becoming a scarce resource, covering energy needs is becoming more and more costly for the world's poorest, undermining the prospect of achieving the Millennium Development Goals (UNDP, 2005).

Figure 1.11 shows the social and cost implications of seeking substitutes. The values are again case-specific and illustrative: real costs would obviously depend on location.

Limits on substitution potential also depend on time scale and geography. Global fishing fleets can move from one fishery to the next, which gives them substitution potential for the short and probably also medium term. In the long term, however, they will also hit a threshold without proper fisheries management/governance. For local fishermen, fish stock collapse can rapidly deprive them of any substitute. This means that the level of global incentives compared to local incentives can be fundamentally different.

The situation is similar for fish protein. Rich urban populations will hardly be affected by a loss of a fishery in one part of the world as there will still be fish in the supermarket, whereas local populations dependent on artisanal fishing may have no immediate substitute for the loss of fish protein in their diet. This will either have health implications or knock-on effects in terms of them searching for protein elsewhere. It may also affect livelihoods as they may have fewer opportunities in the short term to find substitute employment (see Box 1.9).

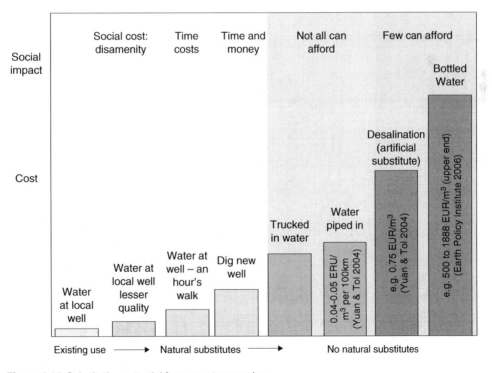

Figure 1.11 *Substitution potential for ecosystem services*

Source: P. ten Brink et al (2009)

Box 1.9 The links between biodiversity, marine ecosystem services and livelihoods

There are several well-documented cases where changes to biodiversity have led to the degradation or collapse of ecosystem services with consequent impacts on livelihoods. Some examples are given below for the marine environment:

- In the late 1980s, the invasion of the Black Sea by a comb jellyfish and the subsequent collapse of the fishing industry led to the loss of 150,000 jobs. Environmental degradation also led to a reported loss of US$300 million in tourist industry revenue (Lubchenco, 1997).
- The Canadian cod fishery in Newfoundland, Canada provided 80 to 100 per cent of income in some communities, employing 20 per cent of the population. Its collapse led to more than 40,000 people losing their jobs, including 10,000 fishermen (Vilhjálmsson et al, 2010).
- 1300 fishermen lost their jobs due to the degradation of the former Lake Karla in Greece, the consequent impact on commercial fisheries and the lack of alternatives (Zalidis and Gerakis, 1999).
- Following the 1998 coral reef bleaching event in the Indian Ocean, predicted total economic damages over the next 20 years could reach US$8 billion, including US$1.4 billion in lost food production and from fisheries, US$3.5 billion in lost tourism revenue and US$2.2 billion in lost coastal protection. Economic losses from coral bleaching in the Philippines are estimated at between US$6 million and US$27 million, depending on the coral reef's recovery (Pratchett et al, 2008).

Substitution is of course more complex than simply finding other sources of the ecosystem service. Ecosystems are often interdependent and individual components cannot be extracted and replaced without impacting on other associated ecosystems.

4.3 Engaging communities to define policy solutions

Engaging communities to be part of the process and part of the solution is invaluable. Local knowledge of ecosystems, biodiversity and plant properties can reveal many opportunities (medicines, pharmaceuticals, other uses of biomimicry). Without local input, implementation may be inefficient, ineffective or inequitable (see Chapter 5 regarding payments for ecosystem services (PES), Chapter 8 regarding protected areas (PAs)).

Existing incentives can make converting forests or hunting for bush meat or rare species attractive to local people. Adjusting incentives to take opportunity costs into account can foster support and participation at community level, and avoid solutions that look good on paper but fail in practice.

This book provides many concrete examples of success stories building on local engagement. For the most part, it is local people who are now paid to maintain or restore watersheds, forests and wetlands through payments for ecosystem services (PES) or carbon storage programmes supported through REDD+ (Reducing Emissions from Deforestation and Forest Degradation). Their traditions and expertise can make bioprospecting more cost-effective: due sharing of the benefits can facilitate future cooperation (see Chapter 5).

Communities also play fundamental roles in the management of protected areas (see Chapter 8), and also in the management of common resources (e.g. fisheries) or community resources (e.g. lands under community property rights regime (e.g. forests); see also Chapters 2 and 5).

Other innovative approaches now link natural capital and the creation of social capital. In many southern African countries, for example, community-based natural resource management is considered a good strategy not only to develop multi-resource livelihood activities, but also to stimulate local self-reliance and poverty alleviation. In Tanzania local communities often preserve and cultivate endemic species on their village lands not only for household needs but also to support crop diversity (Wily, 2000; Benjaminsen et al, 2002).

This type of programme typically focuses attention on restructuring the rights of access to and use of communal and/or state lands. To be successful, the role of farmers in conserving biodiversity on their farmlands needs to be recognized, particularly the fact that rural communities through different uses have created a diversified landscape.

A country or region where the natural capital is acutely run down will find it particularly difficult to meet the Millennium Development Goals. A concerted effort to restore natural capital by establishing or reinforcing institutional arrangements, building upon existing social capital, should therefore be an essential part of any strategy to address social challenges and improve community health and livelihoods.

Notes

1 It can be useful to distinguish between ecological phenomena/ecosystem *functions*, their direct and indirect contributions to human welfare (*services*) and the actual *benefits* that they generate. For wider discussion on the classification and insights on the relationships between biodiversity/ecosystems, the functions, the service flows and the benefits see Chapters 1 and 2 of TEEB Foundations (2010).
2 Using the agreed global definition of forests as areas of a minimum threshold of 5m for the height of trees, at least 10 per cent crown cover (related to area shaded on the ground) and minimum forest areas of 0.5ha (FAO, 2006). The UNFCCC uses a slightly different definition, with a range of height of 2 to 5m, minimum patch of 0.01–1ha and crown cover of 10 to 30 per cent.
3 For information on IAS and current trends in Europe, see the DAISIE database www.europe-aliens.org/.
4 Immaterial capital (e.g. patents, licences, brands) also plays a core role in modern economic development.

Acknowledgements

The authors would like to thank David Baldock, IEEP, UK; Leon Braat, Wageningen University, The Netherlands; Kaley Hart, IEEP, UK; Pushpam Kumar, University of Liverpool, UK; Indrani Lutchman, IEEP, UK; A. J. MacConville, IEEP, UK; Carsten Neßhöver, UFZ, Germany; Rosimeiry Portela, Conservation International, US; Robert Tinch, Eftec, UK; Graham Tucker, IEEP, UK; Sander van der Ploeg, Wageningen University, The Netherlands; Emma Watkins, IEEP, UK; and Stephen White, European Commission, DG Environment, Belgium.

References

Agardy, T., et al (2005) *Ecosystems and Human Well Being: Current State and Trends* (Volume 1), Island Press, Washington, DC

Allsopp, M., Page, R., Johnston, P. and Santillo, D. (2009) *State of the World's Oceans*, Springer. www.springerlink.com/content/978-1-4020-9115-5, accessed 26 October 2009

Ayres, R. and Warr, B. (2006) 'Accounting for growth: The role of physical work', *Structural Change and Economic Dynamics*, vol 16, no 2, pp211–220

Balmford, A., Rodrigues, A. S. L., Walpole, M., ten Brink, P., Kettunen, M., Braat, L. and de Groot, R. (2008) *The Economics of Biodiversity and Ecosystems: Scoping the Science*, European Commission (Contract: ENV/070307/2007/486089/ETU/B2), Cambridge, http://ec.europa.eu/environment/nature/biodiversity/economics/pdf/scoping_science_report.pdf, accessed 16 October 2009

Bahuguna, V. (2000) 'Forests in the economy of the rural poor: An estimation of the dependency level', *Ambio*, vol 29 , no 3, pp126–129

Barbier, E. B. (2007) 'Valuing ecosystem services as productive inputs', *Economic Policy*, vol 22, no 49, pp177–229

Benjaminsen, T., Cousins, B. and Thompson, L. (eds) (2002) *Contested resources: Challenges to the Governance of Natural Resources in Southern Africa*, Programme for Land and Agrarian Studies, University of the Western Cape, Cape Town

Bennett, M. T. and Xu, J. (2008) 'China's sloping land conversion program: Institutional innovation or business as usual?' *Ecological Economics*, vol 65, no 4, pp699–711, www.cifor.cgiar.org/pes/publications/pdf_files/China_paper.pdf, accessed 27 July 2010

Borges, B. (2007) *Payments for Ecosystem Services: Strengthening Rural Livelihoods and Environmental Conservation*, Presentation at the 12th Poverty Environment Partnership 19–21 November 2007, Washington, DC, http://archive.povertyenvironment.net/?q=filestore2/download/1504/Borges-Payments forEcosystem Services.pdf, accessed 17 September 2009

BPL (Butcher Partners Limited) (2006) *Evaluation Study of the Economic Benefits of Water in Te Papanui Conservation Park* (Prepared for the New Zealand Department of Conservation of New Zealand), www.doc.govt.nz/upload/documents/conservation/threats-and-impacts/benefits-of-conservation/economic-benefits-te-papanui.pdf, accessed 28 July 2010

Brown, O., Crawford, A. and Hammill, A. (2006) *Natural Disasters and Resource Rights: Building Resilience, Rebuilding Lives*, International Institute for Sustainable Development, Manitoba, Canada

Bryant, D., Burke, L., McManus, J. and Spalding, M. (1998) *Reefs at Risk*, World Resources Institute, Washington, DC, http://pdf.wri.org/reefs.pdf, accessed 26 October 2009

Butchart, S., Walpole, M., Collen, B., van Strien, A., Scharlemann, J., Almond, R., Baillie, J., Bomhard, B., Brown, C., Bruno, J., Carpenter, K., Carr, G., Chanson, J., Chenery, A., Csirke, J., Davidson, N., Dentener, F., Foster, M., Galli, A., Galloway, J., Genovesi, P., Gregory, R., Hockings, M., Kapos, V., Lamarque, J.-F., Leverington, F., Loh, J., McGeoch, M., McRae, L., Minasyan, A., Hernández Morcillo, M., Oldfield, T., Pauly, D., Quader, S., Revenga, C., Sauer, J., Skolnik, B., Spear, D., Stanwell-Smith, D., Stuart, S., Symes, A., Tierney, M., Tyrrell, T., Vié, J.-C. and Watson, R. (2010) 'Global biodiversity: Indicators of recent declines', *Science*, vol 328, no 5982, pp1164–1168

Capdevila-Argüelles, L. and Zilletti, B. (2008) *A Perspective on Climate Change and Invasive Alien Species*, Convention on the Conservation of European Wildlife and Natural Habitats, T-PVS/Inf (2008) 5 rev., Strasbourg

Carter, C. (2006) 'Te Papanui delivering $136m to New Zealand', the website of the New Zealand Government: Press Releases, www.beehive.govt.nz/node/26025, accessed 16 October 2009

Cesar, H. S. J., van Beukering, P. J. H., Pintz, W. and Dierking, J. (2002) *Economic Valuation of the Coral Reefs of Hawai'i*, Hawai'i Coral Reef Initiative, University of Hawai'i, Honolulu

Costanza, R., d'Arget, R., de Groot, R., Farber, S., Grasso, M., Hannon, B., Limburg, K., Naeem, S., O'Neill, R., Paruelo, J., Raskin, R., Sutton, P. and van den Belt, M. (1997) 'The value of the world's ecosystem services and natural capital', *Nature*, 387, pp253–260

Daily, G. C. (ed) (1997) *Nature's Services*, Island Press, Washington, DC

Dasgupta, P. and Mäler, K.-G. (2000) 'Net national product, wealth and social well-being', *Environment and Development Economics*, vol 5, pp69–93

Davies, R. W. D., Cripps, S. J., Nickson, A. and Porter, G. (2009) 'Defining and estimating global marine fisheries by catch 2009', *Marine Policy*, vol 33, no 4, pp661–672

Dudley, N. and Stolton, S. (2003) *Running Pure: The Importance of Forest Protected Areas to Drinking Water*, World Bank/WWF Alliance for Forest Conservation and Sustainable Use, WWF, Gland, Switzerland, http://assets.panda.org/downloads/runningpurereport.pdf, accessed 26 October 2009

Earth Policy Institute (2006) *Bottled Water: Pouring Resources Down the Drain*, www.earth-policy.org/Updates/2006/Update51.htm, accessed 22 September 2010

Eliasch, J. (2008) 'Climate change: Financing global forests', *The Eliasch Review*, Earthscan, London, www.official-documents.gov.uk/document/other/9780108507632/9780108507632.pdf, accessed 27 October 2010

Emerton, L., Seilava, R. and Pearith, H. (2002) 'Bokor, Kirirom, Kep and Ream National Parks, Cambodia: Case studies of economic and development linkages, field study report', in *Review of Protected Areas and their Role in the Socio-Economic Development of the Four Countries of the Lower Mekong Region*, International Centre for Environmental Management, Brisbane and IUCN Regional Environmental Economics Programme, Karachi, http://cmsdata.iucn.org/downloads/casestudy03ream.pdf, accessed 19 October 2009

Ernst and Young (2007) *Beyond Borders: The Global Perspective*, http://webapp01.ey.com.pl/EYP/WEB/eycom_download.nsf/resources/BB2006_Global.pdf/$FILE/BB2006GlobalPerspective.pdf, accessed 9 July 2010

FAO (Food and Agriculture Organization of the United Nations) (1987) 'Socio-economic aspects of using wood fuels', in *Technical and Economic Aspects of Using Wood Fuels in Rural Industries*, FAO, Rome, www.fao.org/docrep/006/ab780e/AB780E00.htm#TOC, accessed 27 July 2010

FAO (2000) *Global Forest Resource Assessment*, FAO, Rome

FAO (2005a) *Review of the State of World Marine Fishery Resources*, FAO, Rome, ftp://ftp.fao.org/docrep/fao/007/y5852e/y5852e00.pdf, accessed 19 October 2009

FAO (2005b) *Grasslands of the World*, FAO, Rome, ftp://ftp.fao.org/docrep/fao/meeting/007/w0750e.pdf, accessed 12 August 2009

FAO (2006) *Global Forest Resource Assessment 2005*, FAO, Rome, ftp://ftp.fao.org/docrep/fao/008/A0400E/A0400E00.pdf, accessed 12 August 2009

FAO (2007) *The World's Mangroves 1980–2005*, FAO Forestry Paper, Rome, ftp://ftp.fao.org/docrep/fao/010/a1427e/a1427e00.pdf, accessed 12 August 2009

FAO (2008) *The State of Food and Agriculture. Biofuels: Prospects, Risks and Opportunities*, FAO, Rome

FAO (2009a) *State of World Fisheries and Aquaculture 2008*, FAO, Rome, ftp://ftp.fao.org/docrep/fao/011/i0250e/i0250e.pdf, accessed 16 October 2009

FAO (2009b) *2010 Biodiversity Indicators Partnership: Headline Indicator 'Trends in Genetic Diversity'*, www.twentyten.net/Indicators/HL_Trendsingeneticdiversity/Geneticdiversityofdomesticatedanimals/tabid/74/Default.aspx, accessed 12 August 2009

FAO (2009c) *The State of Food Insecurity in the World: Economic Crises – Impacts and Lessons Learned*, Rome, ftp://ftp.fao.org/docrep/fao/012/i0876e/i0876e.pdf, accessed 27 July 2010

FAO (2010) *Global Forest Resources Assessment*, Rome, www.fao.org/forestry/fra/fra2010/en/, accessed 26 July 2010

Federal Environment Agency (2007) *Economic Valuation of Environmental Damage: Methodological Convention for Estimates of Environmental Externalities*, Federal Environment Agency, Dessau, Germany, www.umweltdaten.de/publikationen/fpdf-l/3482.pdf

Fischer, G. (2008) 'Implications for land use change', paper presented at the Expert Meeting on Global Perspectives on Fuel and Food Security, 18–20 February 2008, FAO, Rome

Forest Trends (2010) www.forest-trends.org/program.php?id=58

Gutman, P. (2002) 'Putting a price tag on conservation: Cost benefit analysis of Venezuela's National Parks', *Journal of Latin American Studies*, vol 34, no 1, pp43–70

Grieg-Gran, M. (2008) 'The cost of avoiding deforestation: Update of the report prepared for the Stern Review of the Economics of Climate Change', London, available at http://www.iied.org/pubs/pdfs/G02489.pdf, last accessed 4 November 2010

Haines-Young, R. and Potschin, M. (2009) 'The links between biodiversity, ecosystem services and human well-being', in D. Raffaelli and C. Frid (eds) *Ecosystem Ecology: A New Synthesis*, BES Ecological Reviews Series, Cambridge University Press, Cambridge

Hanley, N. and Barbier, E. B. (2009) 'Valuing ecosystem services', in *Pricing Nature: Cost-Benefit Analysis and Environmental Policy*, Edward Elgar, London

Henao, J. and Baanante, C. (2006) 'Agricultural production and soil nutrient mining in Africa: Implications for resource conservation and policy development', International Center for Soil Fertility and Agricultural Development summary report, http://ictsd.org/i/agriculture/3495/, accessed 27 July 2010

Hilton-Taylor, C., Pollock, C. M., Chanson, J. S., Butchart, S. H. M., Oldfield, T. E. E. and Katariya, V. (2009) *State of the World's Species*, http://data.iucn.org/dbtw-wpd/html/RL-2009-001/section5.html, accessed 27 October 2010

Horton, B., Colarullo, G., Bateman, I. and Peres, C. (2003) 'Evaluating non-user willingness to pay for a large-scale conservation programme in Amazonia', *Environmental Conservation*, vol 30, no 2, pp139–146, www.uea.ac.uk/~e436/Horton_Peres_et_al_Willingness_to_pay_Amazonia.pdf, accessed 28 July 2010

Huges, R. (1999) 'Aquatic ecosystem', in D. E. Alexander and R. W. Fairbridge (eds) *Encyclopaedia of Environmental Sciences*, Kluwer Acadmic Publishers, The Netherlands

IAASTD (International Assessment of Agricultural Science and Technology) (2008) *Agriculture at a Crossroads*, www.agassessment.org/reports/IAASTD/EN/Agriculture%20at%20a%20Crossroads_Global%20Report%20(English).pdf, accessed 19 October 2009

IEA (International Energy Agency) (2006) *World Energy Outlook 2006*, Paris, www.iea.org/textbase/nppdf/free/2006/weo2006.pdf, accessed 19 October 2009

IMS (2007) *Intelligence 360: Global Pharmaceutical Perspectives 2006*, IMS Health, Tokyo, Japan

IPCC (Intergovernmental Panel on Climate Change) (2007) 'AR4 Synthesis Report', *Summary for Policy Makers*, IPCC Fourth Assessment Report, Cambridge University Press, New York, www.ipcc.ch/#, accessed 22 September 2009

IUCN (International Union for Conservation of Nature) (2008) 'Summary statistics of species listed on the 2008 IUCN Red List', www.iucn.org/about/work/programmes/species/red_list/2008_red_list_summary_statistics/, accessed 27 July 2010

IUCN (2009a) 'Extinction crisis continues apace', Press Release, 3 November 2009, www.iucn.org/?4143/Extinction-crisis-continues-apace, accessed 27 July 2010

IUCN (2009b) 'The IUCN Red List of Threatened Species – Mammals – Analysis of Data', www.iucnredlist.org/initiatives/mammals/analysis, accessed 27 July 2010

Kaiser, B. and Roumasset, J. (2002) Valuing indirect ecosystem services: The case of tropical watersheds', *Environment and Development Economics*, vol 4, no 7, pp701–714

Kettunen, M., Genovesi, P., Gollasch, S., Pagad, S., Starfinger, U., ten Brink, P. and Shine, C. (2009) 'Technical support to EU strategy on invasive species (IAS) – Assessment of the impacts of IAS in Europe and the EU', final draft report for the European Commission, Institute for European Environmental Policy (IEEP), Brussels, Belgium, available at http://ec.europa.eu/environment/nature/invasivealien/docs/Kettunen2009_IAS_Task%201.pdf, accessed 19 November 2010

Kramer, R., Sharma, N. and Munasinghe, M. (1995) *Valuing Tropical Forests: Methodology and Case Study of Madagascar*, Environment Paper No 13, World Bank, Washington, DC

Lescuyer, G. (2007) 'Valuation techniques applied to tropical forest environmental services: Rationale, methods and outcomes', Paper presented at the West and Central Africa Tropical Forest Investment Forum: Issues and Opportunities for Investment in Natural Tropical Forests, sponsored by ITTO, 28–30 August 2007, Accra, Ghana

Lewis, S. L. and White, L. (2009) 'Increasing carbon storage in intact African tropical forests', *Nature*, vol 457, pp1003–1006

Lubchenco, J. (1997) 'The Black Sea – common ground', Religion, Science and the Environment Symposia, www.rsesymposia.org/more.php?catid=114&pcatid=49, accessed 9 July 2010

Lynam, T. J. P., Campbell, B. M. and Vermeulen, S. J. (1994) *Contingent Valuation of Multi-purpose Tree Resources in the Smallholder Farming Sector, Zimbabwe*, Working Paper Series 1994/8, Studies in Environmental Economics and Development, Department of Economics, Gothenburg University, Sweden

MA (Millennium Ecosystem Assessment) (2005a) *Ecosystems and Human Well-Being: Biodiversity Synthesis*, World Resources Institute, Washington, DC, www.millenniumassessment.org/documents/document.354.aspx.pdf, accessed 26 October 2009

MA (2005b) *General Synthesis Report*, World Resources Institute, Washington, DC, www.millenniumassessment.org/documents/document.356.aspx.pdf, accessed 27 July 2010

MA (2005c) *Inland Water Systems*, www.millenniumassessment.org/documents/document.289.aspx.pdf, accessed 27 July 2010

Mallawaarachchi, T., Blamey, R. K., Morrison, M. D., Johnson, A. K. L. and Bennet, J. W. (2001) 'Community values for environmental protection in a cane farming catchment in Northern Australia: A choice modelling study', *Journal of Environmental Management*, vol 62, no 3, pp301–316

Maltby, E. (ed) (2009) *Functional Assessment of Wetlands: Towards Evaluation of Ecosystem Services*, Woodhead, Abington, Cambridge

Master, L. L, Flack, S. R. and Stein, B. A (1998) 'Rivers of life: Critical watersheds for protecting freshwater biodiversity', A NatureServe Report, www.natureserve.org/library/riversoflife.pdf, accessed 16 October 2009

McKinsey and Co. (2008) *Pathways to a Low Carbon Economy for Brazil*, www.mckinsey.com/clientservice/ccsi/pdf/pathways_low_carbon_economy_brazil.pdf, accessed 16 October 2009

Ministerium für Landwirtschaft, Umwelt und Verbraucherschutz Mecklenburg-Vorpommern (2009) *Konzept zum Schutz und zur Nutzung der Moore: Fortschreibung des Konzeptes zur Bestandsicherung und zur Entwicklung der Moore, Schwerin*, Germany, http://service.mvnet.de/_php/download.php?datei_id=11159

Molnar, A. (2003) 'Forest certification and communities: Looking forward to the next decade', Forest Trends, Washington, DC, available at www.forest-trends.org/documents/files/doc_126.pdf, accessed 19 November 2010

Nellemann, C., Hain, S. and Alder, J. (eds) (2008) *In Dead Water: Merging of Climate Change with Pollution, Over-Harvest, and Infestations in the World's Fishing Grounds*, United Nations Environment Programme (UNEP), GRID-Arendal, Norway, www.unep.org/pdf/InDeadWater_LR.pdf, accessed 27 July 2010

New Zealand Department of Conservation (2006) *The Value of Conservation: What Does Conservation Contribute to the Economy?* www.doc.govt.nz/upload/documents/conservation/value-of-conservation.pdf, accessed 22 September 2010

Ninan, K. N., Jyothis, S., Babu, P. and Ramakrishnappa, V. (2007) 'Nagarhole – The Context of Tribal Villages Located Within and Near a National Park', in K. N. Ninan (ed) *The Economics of Biodiversity Conservation: Valuation in Tropical Forest Ecosystems*, Earthscan, London

Odum, H. T. and Odum, E. P. (1955) 'Trophic structure and productivity of a windward coral reef at Eniwetok atoll, Marshal Islands', *Ecol. Monogr*, vol 25, pp291–320

OECD (Organisation for Economic Co-operation and Development) (2008) *OECD Environmental Outlook to 2030*, Paris, www.oecd.org/document/20/0,3343,en_2649_34305_39676628_1_1_1_37465,00.html, accessed 26 October 2009

OECD–FAO (Organisation for Economic Co-operation and Development and Food and Agriculture Organization of the United Nations) (2008) *OECD–FAO Agricultural Outlook 2008–2017*, Paris, www.oecd.org/dataoecd/54/15/40715381.pdf, accessed 19 October 2009

Office of the President Republic of Guyana (2008) *Creating incentives to avoid deforestation*, http://gina.gov.gy/booklet%20on%20avoided%20deforestationf.pdf, accessed 4 November 2010

Pabon, L. (2009) *Valuing Nature: Assessing Protected Area Benefits*, The Nature Conservancy, www.nature.org/initiatives/protectedareas/files/valuing_nature_assessing_protected_area_benefits.pdf, accessed 26 October 2009

Pauly, D., Alder, J., Bakun, A., Heileman, S., Kock, K., Mace, P., Perrin, W., Stergiou, K., Sumaila, U. R., Vierros, M., Freire, K., Sadovy, Y., Christensen, V., Kaschner, K. and Palomares, M. (2005) 'Marine fisheries systems', in *Millennium Ecosystem Assessment. Ecosystems and Human Well-Being: Current States and Trends*, Island Press, Washington, DC, pp745–794

PBL (Planbureau voor de Leefomgeving) (2009) *Milieubalans 2009*, www.rivm.nl/bibliotheek/rapporten/500081015.pdf, accessed 23 October 2009

PBL, Netherlands Environmental Assessment Agency (NEAA) (2010) *Rethinking Global Biodiversity Strategies: Exploring Structural Changes in Production and Consumption to Reduce Biodiversity Loss*, The Hague/Bilthoven, available at www.pbl.nl/en, accessed 28 October 2010

Pimentel, D., McNair, S., Janecka, J., Wightman, J., Simmonds, C., O'Connell, C., Wong, E., Russel, L., Zern, J., Aquino, T. and Tsomondo, T. (2001) 'Economic and environmental threats of alien plant, animal, and microbe invasions', *Agriculture, Ecosystems and Environment*, vol 84, pp1–20

Pimentel, D., Zuniga, R. and Morrison, D. (2005) 'Update on the environmental and economic costs associated with alien invasive species in the United States', *Ecological Economics*, vol 52, pp273–288

Pimm, S. L., Russell, G. J., Gittleman, J. L. and Brooks, T. M. (1995) 'The future of biodiversity', *Science*, vol 269, pp347–350

Postel, S. L. (2000) 'Entering an era of water scarcity: The challenges ahead', *Ecological Applications*, vol 10, no 4, pp941–948, www.cee.mtu.edu/~nurban/classes/ce5508/2008/Readings/SandraPostel00.pdf, accessed 27 July 2010

Pratchett, M. S., et al (2008) 'Effects of climate induced coral bleaching on coral reef fishes – ecological and economic consequences', *Oceanography and Marine Biology: An Annual Review*, vol 46, pp251–296

Priess, J. A., Mimler, M., Klein, A.-M., Schwarze, S., Tscharntke, T. and Steffan-Dewenter, I. (2007) 'Linking deforestation scenarios to pollination services and economic returns in coffee agroforestry systems', *Ecological Applications*, vol 17, no 2, pp407–417

Repetto, R., Magrath, W., Wells, M., Beer, C. and Rossini, F. (1989) *Wasting Assets: Natural Resources in National Income Accounts*, World Resources Institute, Washington, DC

Rogers, A. D. (2009) 'International Commission for Land Use Change and Ecosystems: The oceans', Zoological Society of London, presentation given at Rome G8+5 Legislators Forum, Italian Chamber of Deputies, 12–13 June 2009

Ruitenbeek, H. J. and Cartier, C. M., with contributions from Bunce, L., Gustavson, K., Putterman, D., Spash C. L., van der Werff ten Bosch, J. D., Westmascott, S. and Huber, R. (1999) 'Issues in applied coral reef biodiversity valuation: Results for Montego Bay, Jamaica', *World Bank Research Committee Project RPO#682-22 Final Report*, World Bank, Washington, DC

SCBD (Secretariat of the Convention on Biological Diversity) (2001) *The Value of Forest Ecosystems* (CBD Technical Series No 4), Montreal, available at www.cbd.int/doc/publications/cbd-ts-04.pdf, accessed 16 October 2009

SCBD (2008) *Access and Benefit-Sharing in Practice: Trends in Partnerships Across Sectors* (CBD Technical Series No 38), Montreal, www.cbd.int/doc/publications/cbd-ts-38-en.pdf, accessed 29 June 2010

SCBD (2009) *Biodiversity, Development and Poverty Alleviation – Recognizing the Role of Biodiversity for Human Well-Being*, Montreal, Canada

SCBD (2010) *Global Biodiversity Outlook 3*, Secretariat of the Convention on Biological Diversity, Montreal

Schäfer, A. (2009) 'Moore und Euros – die vergessenen Millionen', *Archiv für Forstwesen und Landschaftsökologie*, vol 43, no 4, pp156–159

Shine, C., Kettunen, M., Genovesi, P., Essl, F., Gollasch, S., Rabitsch, W., Scalera, R., Starfinger, U. and ten Brink, P. (2010) 'Assessment to support continued development of the EU Strategy to combat invasive alien species', final report for the European Commission, Institute for European Environmental Policy (IEEP), Brussels, Belgium, available at http://ec.europa.eu/environment/nature/invasivealien/docs/IEEP%20report_EU%20IAS%20Strategy%20components%20%20costs.pdf, accessed 19 November 2010

Shvidenko, A., et al (2005) 'Forest and Woodland Systems', in R. Hassan, R. Scholes and N. Ash (eds) *Ecosystems and Human Well-Being: Current State and Trends*, Island Press, Washington, DC

Stern, N. (2006) *Review on the Economics of Climate Change*, Cambridge University Press, available at www.webcitation.org/5nCeyEYJr, accessed 26 July 2010

Tallis, H., Kareiva, P., Marvier, M. and Chang, A. (2008) 'An ecosystem services framework to support both practical conservation and economic development', *PNAS*, vol 105, no 28, pp9457–9464

TEEB (The Economics of Ecosystems and Biodiversity) (2008) *TEEB Interim Report*, www.teebweb.org/LinkClick.aspx?fileticket=5y_qRGJPOao%3d&tabid=1018&language=en-US, accessed 16 October 2009

TEEB (2009) *Climate Issues Update*, www.teebweb.org/LinkClick.aspx?fileticket=L6XLPaoaZv8%3D&tabid, accessed 21 October 2009

TEEB Foundations (2010) *The Economics of Ecosystems and Biodiversity: Ecological and Economic Foundations* (ed P. Kumar), Earthscan, London

TEEB in Business (2011) *The Economics of Ecosystems and Biodiversity in Business and Enterprise* (ed J. Bishop), Earthscan, London

ten Brink, B. (2008) Presentation at the workshop: 'The Economics of the Global Loss of Biological Diversity', 5–6 March 2008, Brussels

ten Brink, P., Rayment, M., Bräuer, I., Braat, L., Bassi, S., Chiabai, A., Markandya, A., Nunes, P., ten Brink, B., van Oorschot, M., Gerdes, H., Stupak, N., Foo, V., Armstrong, J., Kettunen, M. and Gantioler, S. (2009) *Further Developing Assumptions on Monetary Valuation of Biodiversity Cost of Policy Inaction (COPI)*, European Commission project – final report, Institute for European Environmental Policy (IEEP), London and Brussels

TIES (The International Ecotourism Society) (2006) *Ecotourism Statistical Fact Sheet*, Washington, DC, www.ecotourism.org/atf/cf/%7B82a87c8d-0b56-4149-8b0a-c4aaced1cd38%7D/TIES%20 GLOBAL%20ECOTOURISM%20FACT%20SHEET.PDF, accessed 22 September 2010

UN (United Nations) (1993) *Convention on Biological Diversity*, United Nations Treaty Series, vol 1760, I-30619, www.cbd.int/doc/legal/cbd-un-en.pdf, accessed 26 July 2010

UN (United Nations General Assembly) (2000) *United Nations Millennium Declaration*, www.un.org/ millennium/, accessed 16 October 2009

UN (United Nations) (2002) *Ensuring the Sustainable Development of Oceans and Coasts*, Co-Chairs' Report from The Global Conference on Oceans and Coasts at Rio+10, www.un.org/jsummit/html/ documents/backgrounddocs/unescoreport.pdf, accessed 27 July 2010

UNDP (United Nations Development Programme) (2005) *Energy Services for the Millenium Development Goals*, www.unmillenniumproject.org/documents/MP_Energy_Low_Res.pdf, accessed 27 July 2010

UNDP (2007) *Human Development Report 2007/2008*, New York, http://hdr.undp.org/en/media/ HDR_20072008_EN_Complete.pdf, accessed 27 July 2010

UNEP (United Nations Environment Programme) (2007) *Global Environment Outlook 4: Environment for Development*, United Nations Environment Programme (UNEP), Nairobi, Kenya, www.unep.org/ geo/geo4/report/GEO-4_Report_Full_en.pdf, accessed 27 July 2010

UNEP (2009) *The Role of Ecosystem Management in Climate Change Adaptation and Disaster Risk Reduction*, Copenhagen Discussion Series, Paper 2, June 2009, www.unep.org/climatechange/LinkClick. aspx?fileticket=rPyahT90aL4%3D&tabid=129&language=en-US, accessed 26 July 2010

UNEP-WCMC (United Nations Environment Programme World Conservation Monitoring Centre) (2006) *In the Front Line: Shoreline Protection and Other Ecosystem Services from Mangroves and Coral Reefs*, UNEP-WCMC, Cambridge, UK, www.unep.org/pdf/infrontline_06.pdf, accessed 27 July 2010

UNESA (2009) *World Population Prospects: The 2008 Revision*, Population Division, United Nations Department of Economic and Social Affairs, Washington, DC, http://esa.un.org/unpd/wpp2008/peps_ documents.htm, accessed 10 July 2010

UN Millennium Project (2005) *Investing in Development: A Practical Plan to Achieve the Millennium Development Goals, Overview*, United Nations, New York

UNWWAP (United Nations World Water Assessment Programme) (2003) *Water for People, Water for Life*, http://webworld.unesco.org/water/wwap/facts_figures/protecting_ecosystems.shtml, accessed 16 October 2009

Valiela, I., Bowen, J. L. and York, J. K. (2001) 'Mangrove forests: One of the world's threatened major tropical environments', *BioScience*, vol 5, no 10, pp807–815

van Beukering, P. J. H., Cesar, H. J. S. and Janssen, M. A. (2003) 'Economic valuation of the Leuser National Park on Sumatra, Indonesia', *Ecological Economics*, vol 44, pp43–62, www.public.asu. edu/~majansse/pubs/ee2003.pdf, accessed 27 July 2010

Vedeld, P., Angelsen, A., Sjaasrad, E. and Berg, G. (2004) *Counting on the Environment: Forest Income and the Rural Poor*, Environmental Economics Series No 98, World Bank, Washington DC

Veron, J. E. N. (2009) *The Coral Reef Crisis: Scientific Justification for Critical CO_2 Threshold Levels of <350ppm, Output of the Technical Working Group Meeting*, Royal Society, http://static.zsl.org/files/1c-the-coral-reef-crisis-the-critical-importance-of-350-ppm-co2-967.pdf, accessed 23 September 2010

Vilhjálmsson, H., et al (2010) 'Fisheries and aquaculture in the Newfoundland and Labrador Seas, Northeastern Canada', in *The Encyclopaedia of Earth*, Section 13.4 of the *Arctic Climate Impact Assessment*, www.eoearth.org/article/Fisheries_and_aquaculture_in_the_Newfoundland_and_Labrador_ Seas,_Northeastern_Canada, accessed 27 July 2010

Vörösmarty, C. J., Lévêque, C., Revenga, C., Bos, R., Caudill, C., Chilton, J., Douglas, E. M., Meybeck, M., Prager, D., Balvanera, P., Barker, S., Maas, M., Nilsson, C., Oki, T. and Reidy, C. A. (2005) 'Fresh Water', in *Millennium Ecosystem Assessment: Current State and Trends Assessment*, Island Press, Washington DC, pp165–207

Vouvaki, D. and Xeapapadeas, A. (2008) 'Total factor productivity growth when factors of production generate environmental externalities', Working paper, http://mpra.ub.uni-muenchen.de/10237/1/VX_ TFP_Externalities_28_August_2008.pdf, accessed 27 July 2010

Wilkinson, C. (ed) (2008) *Status of Coral Reefs of the World: 2008*, Global Coral Reef Monitoring Network and Reef and Rainforest Research Center, Townsville, Australia

Wily, L. A. (2000) *Making Woodland Management More Democratic: Cases from Eastern and Southern Africa*, IIED Dryland Issues Paper 99, www.iied.org/pubs/pdfs/9029IIED.pdf, accessed 20 October 2009

World Bank (2004) *Sustaining Forests: A Development Strategy*, World Bank, Washington DC

World Bank (2008) *The Sunken Billions: The Economic Justification for Fisheries Reform*, The International Bank for Reconstruction and Development/The World Bank, Washington, DC

Worm, B. (2006) 'Impacts of biodiversity loss on ocean ecosystem services', *Science*, vol 314, pp787–790

WWF (World Wide Fund for Nature) (2006) *Living Planet Report 2006*, Gland, Switzerland, http://assets.panda.org/downloads/living_planet_report.pdf, accessed 26 July 2010

WWF (2008) *Living Planet Report 2008*, Gland, Switzerland, http://assets.panda.org/downloads/living_planet_report_2008.pdf, accessed 16 October 2009

Yaron, G. (2001) 'Forest, plantation crops or small-scale agriculture? An economic analysis of alternative land use options in the Mount Cameroun Area', *Journal of Environmental Planning and Management*, vol 44, no 1, pp85–108

Yuan, Z. and Tol, R. S. J. (2004) 'Evaluating the costs of desalination and water transport', *Water Resources Research*, vol 41, no 3

Zalidis, G. C. and Gerakis, A. (1999) 'Evaluating sustainability of watershed resources management through wetland functional analysis', *Environmental Management*, vol 24, pp193–207

Chapter 2

Framework and Guiding Principles for the Policy Response

Coordinating lead author
Bernd Hansjürgens

Contributing authors
Marianne Kettunen, Christoph Schröter-Schlaack,
Stephen White, Heidi Wittmer

Editing and language check
Clare Shine

See end of chapter for acknowledgements for reviews and other contributions

Contents

Key messages   49

Summary   50

1   Why is biodiversity neglected in decision making?   50

2   Using economic information to improve policy coherence   52
    2.1   Mainstreaming biodiversity and ecosystem services   52
    2.2   How can economics help?   55
    2.3   When can economic values help?   56

3   Guiding principles for policy change   59
    3.1   Address the right actors and balance diverse interests   61
    3.2   Pay attention to the cultural and institutional context   62
    3.3   Take property rights, fairness and equity into account   63
    3.4   Base policies on good governance   69

4   The TEEB toolkit for policy change   71

Acknowledgements   72

References   73

Key messages

Reducing biodiversity loss and ecosystem degradation helps to secure benefits from our natural capital – now and in the future. Neglecting biodiversity in decision making is economically inefficient and socially inequitable. When economic values inform policy, we improve the quality and durability of the choices we make across all sectors and levels.

Changing the tide: Using economic information to improve public policies

Economic analysis needs to make visible and explicit the full value of biodiversity and ecosystem services to society. This can expand understanding and integration of these issues at all political levels and also demonstrate the risks and costs of inaction.

Economic information should be fed into each stage of the policy making and review process to:

- identify opportunities to build on successful practices developed elsewhere;

- evaluate and improve existing biodiversity policies so that they reach their full potential;

- prioritize and guide the design of new policies;

- provide a solid basis for integrating biodiversity concerns into all relevant sectoral and cross-sectoral plans, policies and programmes;

- help reform policies and consumption patterns in areas and sectors shown to cause damage to biodiversity and ecosystem services.

Internationally agreed mechanisms to ensure policy coordination and coherence between different sectors and levels of government – such as National Biodiversity Strategy and Action Plans under the Convention on Biological Diversity – need to be applied more rigorously and effectively.

Guiding principles for policy change

Key factors to maximize social acceptance and meet policy objectives efficiently and fairly include:

- addressing the right actors and balancing diverse interests between and within different groups, sectors and areas, supported by robust coordination mechanisms;

- paying attention to the specific cultural and institutional context to ensure that proposed policy solutions are appropriate, timely and harness local knowledge;

- taking property rights, fairness and equity into account and considering distributional impacts of costs and benefits, including on future generations, throughout the policy development process;

- basing all policies on good governance: access to economic information leads to increasing transparency and supports good governance practices, while good governance opens the field for economic information.

Summary

Chapter 2 calls for stronger public policy to tackle the global biodiversity crisis. Section 1 outlines obstacles to policy change linked to the lack of economic information on ecosystem services and biodiversity. Section 2 shows, through concrete examples, how and when economic values can be incorporated into decision making. Section 3 sets out guiding principles for policy change, paying particular attention to equitable distribution of costs and benefits. Section 4 summarizes the range of instruments available to decision makers, with cross-references to relevant chapters of this book.

1 Why is biodiversity neglected in decision making?

> Poverty and environmental problems are both children of the same mother, and that mother is ignorance. (Ali Hassan Mwinyi, Tanzanian President, 1998, quoted in Chau, 2008)

Biodiversity policy is not a new field. In recent decades, nearly all countries have adopted targets and rules to conserve species and habitats and to protect nature against pollution and other damaging activities. Policies and measures that have positively affected biodiversity and ecosystem services can take many forms (see Box 2.1).

Despite this progress, the scale of the global biodiversity crisis (see Chapter 1) shows that current policies are simply not enough to tackle the problem efficiently.

Box 2.1 Examples of policies that have provided biodiversity conservation benefits

- expanding terrestrial and marine protected area systems in developed and developing countries and investing in and managing them to meet conservation objectives and preserve critical habitats (e.g. through the Natura 2000 network of the EU Habitats and Birds Directives and designations as RAMSAR sites or UNESCO biosphere reserves);
- developing integrated water resource management (e.g. EU Water Framework Directive);
- legal recognition of liability for environmental damage (e.g. for oil spills);
- incentives to reward biodiversity management (e.g. payments for ecosystem services);
- market-based instruments (e.g. inter-state green tax transfers, wetland mitigation banks, taxes and charges on products, pollution and use of natural resources, appropriate subsidies);
- certification of products (e.g. timber, fish, organic food, eco-labelled products) and services (e.g. sustainable tourism);
- regulations to stop or limit the release of pollutants into rivers and groundwater systems, improve air quality and reduce the emissions of greenhouse gases (GHGs) into the atmosphere;
- bans on the production or use of dangerous substances (e.g. ozone depleting substances, some pesticides) or of products that can harm the environment (e.g. plastic bags);
- stricter technical norms (e.g. making double-hulled oil tankers mandatory) and practices (e.g. banning dynamite fishing or bottom trawling);
- investment programmes for environmental infrastructure (e.g. waste collection and treatment), innovation and low-impact technologies (e.g. some types of renewable energy) and restoration of natural habitats and services (e.g. floodplains, mangroves);
- sustainable management practices (e.g. for agriculture, fisheries, forestry).

Some of the reasons are only too familiar to policy makers, such as lack of financial resources, lack of capacity, information and/or expertise, overlapping mandates and weak enforcement. But there are also more fundamental economic obstacles which need to be understood to make meaningful progress.

A key aspect is that biodiversity is the ultimate cross-cutting issue. Many policy areas have significant implications for biodiversity, including sector policies (e.g. agriculture, forestry, fisheries), cross-sectoral policies (tourism, transportation, trade, land-use policy, regional planning, etc.) and general economic and development policies. In practice, policy making which impacts on biodiversity and ecosystem services is often fragmented and does not adequately reflect their important role for the economy and society.

A root cause of this neglect is that biodiversity and ecosystems can be characterized as a public good:

- **Their benefits take many forms and are widespread.** This makes it difficult to 'capture' value and ensure that beneficiaries pay for it. For example, a forest provides local benefits to local people (timber, food and other products); the forest ecosystem regulates water flows and provides regional climate stability; and forests are globally important because they sustain biodiversity and act as long-term carbon sinks.
- **Existing markets and market prices only capture some ecosystem services,** mainly 'provisioning services' for e.g. food or fibre (Millennium Ecosystem Assessment, 2005). More commonly, individuals and businesses can use what biodiversity provides without having to pay for it, while those who provide the service rarely get due recognition or payment.
- **The costs of conservation and restoration have to be paid immediately, often at local level, yet many benefits occur in the future.** For example, creating a protected area to save endangered species can cause short-term losses to user groups, which may mean little or no weight is given to the possible long-term benefits (e.g. discovery of medicinal traits in conserved species).

Other relevant factors include:

- **Uncertainty about potential future benefits is matched by ignorance about the risks of inaction.** We know too little about why each species is important, what its role in the food web is, what could happen if it goes extinct and the 'tipping points' of different ecosystems. For policy makers, spending money on policies with clear returns is generally preferable to those with less assured outcomes.
- **Deterioration of biodiversity and ecosystem services often occurs gradually: marginal impacts of individual and local actions can add up to severe damage at the global scale.** For example, small-scale assessment of individual development projects (e.g. forest clearance for agriculture or housing) can indicate a positive cost–benefit ratio but their cumulative impacts in terms of deforestation and habitat fragmentation can be far higher.

These factors all contribute to a systematic bias in the way we make policies and decisions. First, when trade-offs have to be made between conservation and other policy objectives (e.g. increasing agricultural productivity, expanding transport or energy infrastructure), the apparent lack of compelling economic arguments means that decisions very often go against biodiversity and ecosystem services. Second, and even more important, neglecting their economic value means that public decision making tends to be presented in terms of mutually exclusive objectives rather than as a quest for integrated and coherent policy solutions.

Sometimes, trade-offs certainly do exist and will survive robust scrutiny. In other cases, claiming that such trade-offs exist and hard decisions must be taken may be too hasty. Providing economic information on the role of biodiversity and ecosystems will help to distinguish the former from the latter.

2 Using economic information to improve policy coherence

> We should not limit our attention to protected areas. If we do we will be left with a patchwork quilt: pockets of nature in a desert of destruction. (José Manuel Durão Barroso, President of the European Commission, 2009)

There is a compelling rationale for governments to lead efforts to safeguard biodiversity and ecosystem services. Public environmental policy needs to be based on moral values (concern for human well-being), intrinsic values (not letting species go extinct) and good stewardship, while taking economic considerations into account. These overarching values need to guide and shape new policy responses to reduce current losses and invest in healthy functioning ecosystems for the future.

Private actors (businesses and consumers) have a growing role to play in choices that affect our natural capital. However, a strong policy framework is needed to ensure that decisions are efficient (society gets the most it can from its scarce biodiversity) and equitable (the benefits of biodiversity are distributed fairly). Appropriate regulation provides both the baseline from which markets for certain ecosystem services can evolve as well as the mechanisms to monitor their effectiveness.

2.1 Mainstreaming biodiversity and ecosystem services

The issue is not just to design a better biodiversity policy alongside other policy areas. The economic survival of various production sectors, and of the people who depend on those sectors for their livelihoods, is intricately connected to ecosystem services and the biodiversity that underpins them. For this reason, biodiversity concerns need to be mainstreamed into sectoral and cross-sectoral plans, programmes and policies as well as poverty reduction plans and national sustainable development plans.

Mechanisms to ensure policy coordination and coherence between different sectors and levels of government are therefore essential, both within and between countries. Spatial planning is an important part of this equation. Most environmental decision making takes place close to the ground, especially permitting, inspection, planning decisions and enforcement. Local administrations and actors therefore need to be aware, involved and adequately resourced (see TEEB in Local Policy, 2011).

Policy makers can build on the globally agreed targets and implementation frameworks developed under international treaties relevant to aspects of biodiversity (see examples in Table 2.1). In 2010, Parties to the overarching Convention on Biological Diversity (CBD) adopted a global Strategic Plan for CBD implementation to 2020: this puts strong emphasis on economic analysis and valuation and the application of economic tools (see Box 2.1).

Table 2.1 Global conventions addressing biodiversity issues

Name of Convention	Adoption	Parties as of 2010	Aim	Further information
Convention on Biological Diversity (CBD)	1992	193 parties (168 signatories)	Conservation of biodiversity; sustainable use of its components; and fair and equitable sharing of the benefits arising out of the utilization of genetic resources.	www.cbd.int
World Heritage Convention	1972	187	Promote cooperation among nations to protect heritage of outstanding value.	http://whc. unesco.org/en/ convention
Convention on International Trade in Endangered Species of Wild Fauna and Flora (CITES)	1973	175	Ensure that international trade in specimens of wild animals and plants does not threaten their survival.	www.cites.org
Convention on Wetlands (Ramsar Convention)	1971	160	Conservation and wise use of wetlands through local, regional and national actions and international cooperation.	www.ramsar.org
International Treaty on Plant Genetic Resources for Food and Agriculture	2001	125	Recognize the contribution of farmers to crop diversity; establish a global system to provide farmers, plant breeders and scientists with access to plant genetic materials; and ensure benefit sharing from the use of genetic materials within the originating countries.	www. planttreaty.org
Convention on the Conservation of Migratory Species of Wild Animals (CMS)	1979	114	Conservation of terrestrial, marine and avian migratory species throughout their range.	www.cms.int
International Convention on Whaling	1946	88	Provide for proper conservation of whale stocks.	www.iwcoffice. org

The CBD also requires Parties to develop National Biodiversity Strategy and Action Plans (NBSAPs). This process has evolved into the main national mechanism to achieve coordinated and coherent biodiversity policy implementation across sectors and levels of government. CBD Parties have now initiated an ambitious process of revising and updating their NBSAPs, which need to be strengthened and made more effective.

Adopting the ecosystem services approach may involve amending international conventions or standards in other policy sectors. For example, current WTO rules prohibit the introduction of certain environmental measures as they would violate free trade principles (see Box 2.2). In Finland, payments to compensate fishers for lost catch caused by recovering seal populations were found to conflict with EU state aid regulations and were thus phased out after only two years (Similä et al, 2006).

Box 2.2 Trade and environment

The links between trade and environment are multiple, complex, and important. Trade liberalization is – of itself – neither necessarily good nor bad for the environment. Its effects on the environment in fact depend on the extent to which environment and trade goals can be made complementary and mutually supportive. (UNEP and IISD, 2005)

Governments have obligations not only under the WTO, but also various multilateral environmental agreements (MEAs) such as the CBD and the UNFCCC. Debate often arises over a perceived risk of conflict between these different international conventions and rules. Although there have been no WTO legal disputes to date regarding a conflict between specific MEA provisions and the WTO, governments may have to balance WTO-related obligations not to discriminate in traded goods with MEA-related obligations to limit or ban the import of goods produced under environmentally harmful conditions or that contribute to environmental degradation.

Another potential issue exists for goods and products that have been produced according to criteria that safeguard ecosystems and mitigate environmental pressures. The external costs of their production (i.e. costs that society has to bear) are lower than those of competing goods not produced under such conditions. It has been argued that to ensure a level playing field, goods produced under environmentally friendly criteria should be rewarded for the lower costs transferred to society as a whole. This could have implications for international trade, depending on how governments decide to reflect these cost differences (e.g. through standards, labelling schemes or use of taxes).

Trade-offs may exist between the long and short term; between economic development and environmental and living conditions; and between natural capital and GDP. These are especially relevant for developing countries. Restricting trade in products by obliging certain production standards, or by favouring certain products over others, limits the flexibility (also in time) that developing country governments have to set their own priorities, while compliance can pose a significant challenge to small and medium-sized businesses in these countries. On the other hand, short-term development by 'mining' natural resources could mean long-term impoverishment.

While the effects of trade liberalization on economic development have been thoroughly investigated, this is much less true for its impacts on ecosystems and the environment (Verburg et al, 2009). Some studies have found that liberalizing trade in agricultural products could lead to large biodiversity losses especially in Latin America and Africa yet would decrease losses in Europe and North America due to transfers in agricultural production (ten Brink B. et al, 2007).

Sources: Sampson (2005); UNEP and IISD (2005); Verburg et al (2009); ten Brink B. et al (2007)

2.2 How can economics help?

Focusing on the services provided by biodiversity and ecosystems is critical to overcome their traditional neglect. The Millennium Ecosystem Assessment (see Chapter 1) paved the way for indicators to measure the status of ecosystem services (see Chapter 3). TEEB goes one step further by using data on the value of such services to support more informed decision making.

The transition from acknowledging services to valuing them is a huge step towards raising awareness. We can now demonstrate that biodiversity and ecosystem services have value – not only in the narrow sense of goods and services in the marketplace but also because they are essential for our lives, survival and well-being. This is the case even if markets do not exist or if these values are not expressed in monetary terms: values can also be based on qualitative or semi-quantitative assessments. What we actually measure in monetized form is very often only a share of the total value of biodiversity and ecosystem services. 'True' values are usually much higher (see Chapter 4).

Valuation can help policy makers by shedding light on the contribution made by different ecosystem services, whether directly or indirectly (see Box 2.3).

Using economic values during the choice and design of policy instruments can help to:

- overcome the above-mentioned bias in decision making by demonstrating equivalence of values (between for example manufactured capital and natural capital, present and future benefits/costs, different resource types), even where these are not monetized or represented by market prices;
- demonstrate that even if biodiversity benefits are multifaceted and diffuse, they can be subsumed or aggregated within certain broader values (e.g. for forests);
- create new markets where none previously existed (e.g. the recently created markets for GHG emissions are powerful examples of what can be achieved where market-based approaches are developed for environmental goods within a strong policy framework); and

---

Box 2.3 Multiple values of wetlands: Example of the Daly River catchment (Australia)

A 2008 study to assess the value of one catchment in the Northern Territory covering over 350,000 hectares put its current use value at about Aus$390/ha (US$330/ha) (almost Aus$139 million (US$120 million) for the whole catchment). Estimated values per ha/year for different catchment benefits included:

- carrier function for crop growing, pastoralism and crocodile hunting: Aus$31/ha (US$26/ha);
- habitat function as a contribution to nature conservation: Aus$1/ha (US$0.85/ha);
- regulation function (water use, carbon sequestration): Aus$298/ha (US$251/ha);
- information/cultural function (tourism, recreational fishing): Aus$57/ha (US$48/ha).

Note: All values transformed by using 2008 average exchange rates
Source: de Groot et al (2008)

- make future benefits visible, rather than simply relying on today's costs (e.g. by identifying option values of plants from tropical forests that are relevant for pharmaceutical products or showing the potential of low-impact tourism) (see also Chapter 4).

2.3 When can economic values help?

There are many steps in the policy-making process where information on biodiversity and ecosystem service values can be systematically used. Economic data is an important vehicle to raise public awareness and to inform the process of agenda setting or policy formulation. It can form the basis for new policies – and also provide starting points for policy change (see Table 2.2).

Box 2.4 provides examples of how economic information can be applied at the decision-making stage.

Box 2.5 illustrates the use of economic valuation at a later stage, after damage has occurred, to guide legal remedies and the award of compensation.

Table 2.2 Where are economic insights useful to the policy process?

Stage	Major Steps	Type and role of economic information
Problem identification and agenda setting (Goal: To get safeguarding biodiversity and ecosystem services onto the political agenda)	• Make the case for biodiversity conservation by providing evidence of losses and ecological and economic impacts. • Illustrate the link between biodiversity and other environmental, economic or social pressures (e.g. climate change, financial crises, poverty reduction) to help policy coherence. • Involve other sectors in framing biodiversity concerns and link these to their concerns to foster engagement and ownership. • Carry out an analysis of the state of biodiversity and ecosystem services in advance to be prepared to take advantage of new windows of opportunity.	• Economic figures on the value of biodiversity losses. • Calculate the carbon value of forests. • Provide numbers on the option values of tropical forests with regard to pharmaceutical products. • Assess economic losses due to ineffective and/or environmentally harmful subsidies.
Policy formulation and decision making (Goal: frame alternative policy options and decide which alternative should be adopted)	• Analyse the root causes of the loss of biodiversity and ecosystem services. • Agree on objectives for potential policy solutions. • Set up rules for resolving biodiversity conflicts between stakeholders. • Formulate alternative policy solutions. • Agree on the criteria for comparing alternative policy solutions. • Select indicators for each criterion.	• Costs and benefits of policy alternatives (e.g. comparing technical water treatment facilities with constructed wetlands). • Developing indicators that measure the values associated with biodiversity loss and ecosystem service degradation (quantitative and monetary).

Table 2.2 Where are economic insights useful to the policy process? *(Cont'd)*

Stage	Major Steps	Type and role of economic information
	• Assess, compare and communicate to decision makers the impacts of each solution against the agreed indicators. • Decide on the most acceptable solution and define additional measures as needed to maximize synergies and minimize trade-offs.	
Implementation (Goal: Carry out the adopted policy including necessary planning to deliver expected policy outcomes and monitoring)	• Secure formal authorization and upfront resource allocation for implementation. • Conduct operational planning. • Ensure and manage stakeholder participation. • Strengthen administrative capacity by ensuring that monitoring systems are in place to measure pressures or impacts on biodiversity and ecosystem services and providing adequate funding (e.g. for managing protected areas or for monitoring activities).	• Evaluation of the costs of alternative monitoring schemes. • Identification of relevant stakeholders (beneficiaries and cost-carriers) and their respective interests. • Justify compensation payments for losers.
Evaluation (Goal: Determine whether a policy has been implemented successfully or not, based on the results of monitoring)	• Establish and make information available on the scope and criteria for evaluation, adapted to the purpose of evaluation and information requirements. • Involve statistical offices and determine from the outset which data/information systems to use. • Collect information through monitoring, conduct evaluation and involve stakeholders. • Draw conclusions, propose policy improvements and share lessons learned.	• For example by local authorities' monitoring stations, statisticians' analysis or companies' monitoring demonstrate that biodiversity loss and ecosystem degradation cause economic losses. • Ex-post valuation of benefits and costs.
Inspections, enforcement and response to non-compliance (Goal: Check whether policies are being implemented and, if not, address this by suitable means)	• Provide adequate inspection capacity and inspection procedures. • Depending on national circumstances, request technical measures/changes, administer fines or initiate court proceedings for non-compliance response and penalties.	• Cost-effectiveness of inspection. • Implement the polluter pays principle. • Application of economic instruments – fines/penalties, compensation payments or remediation in kind.

Source: Adapted from UNEP (2000) in Howlett and Ramesh (2003)

Box 2.4 Using valuation as part of a decision support system

Indonesia

The Segah watershed (Berau District) contains some of the largest tracts of undisturbed lowland forest (150,000 hectares) in East Kalimantan which provide the last substantial orangutan habitat. A 2002 valuation study concluded that water from the Segah River and the nearby Kelay River had an estimated value of more than US$5.5 million/year (e.g. regulation of water flow rates and sediment loads to protect infrastructure and irrigation systems). In response to these findings, the Segah Watershed Management Committee was established to protect the watershed.

Uganda

The Greater City of Kampala benefits from services provided by the Nakivubo Swamp (catchment area >40km^2) which cleans water polluted by industrial, urban and untreated sewage waste. A valuation study looked at the cost of replacing wetland wastewater processing services with artificial technologies (i.e. upgraded sewage treatment plant, construction of latrines to process sewage from nearby slums). It concluded that the infrastructure required to achieve a similar level of wastewater treatment to that naturally provided by the wetland would cost up to US$2 million/year compared to the costs of managing the natural wetland to optimize its waste treatment potential and maintain its ecological integrity (about US$235,000). On the basis of this economic argument, plans to drain and reclaim the wetland were reversed and Nakivubo was legally designated as part of the city's greenbelt zone.

Sources: Emerton and Bos (2004); TNC (2007); UNDP-UNEP Poverty-Environment Facility (2008)

Box 2.5 Economic valuation of damages to enforce liability rules

The shipwreck of the *Exxon Valdez* tanker in 1989 triggered the application of contingent valuation methods (CVM) in studies conducted pursuant to the US Comprehensive, Environmental Response, Compensation and Liability Act (CERCLA) to assess the level of liability for damage caused to natural resources. A panel headed by Nobel laureates K. Arrow and R. Solow was appointed to advise the US National Oceanic and Atmospheric Administration (NOAA) on the suitability of CVM for use in natural resource damage assessments. In its report the panel concluded that CVM studies, including passive use values, can produce estimates reliable enough to be the starting point of a judicial process to assess such damages. To enable CVM to be used appropriately, the panel drew up a list of guidelines for contingent valuation studies. While some of these guidelines have attracted criticism, the majority have been accepted widely.

Source: Navrud and Pruckner (1997)

Economics can highlight that there are policies that already work well, deliver more benefits than costs, and are effective and efficient. For example, the REDD scheme (Reducing Emissions from Deforestation and Forest Degradation), introduced as a key climate policy instrument in 2007, has already stimulated broader interest in payments for ecosystem services (PES) (see Chapter 5). Several countries and organizations have gathered case studies on REDD design and implementation that can be useful for other countries and applications (Parker et al, 2009). Other examples of approaches that could be used more widely for biodiversity objectives include green public procurement (see Chapter 5), instruments based on the polluter pays principle and targeted incentive-based instruments, such as taxes, tradable quotas or liability rules, to improve the cost-effectiveness of policy measures (see Chapter 7).

Economic analysis can help existing instruments work better. Using assessment tools (see Chapter 4) to measure and compare the efficiency and cost-effectiveness of existing policies can ensure that instruments can reach their full potential. Assessment provides ongoing opportunities to review and improve policy design, adjust targets and thresholds and make the positive effects of protection visible (e.g. for protected areas). The process increases transparency and can contribute to acceptance of restrictive policies by stakeholders.

Economic assessment can make explicit the unintended damage caused by measures taken in other policy areas, such as environmentally harmful subsidies. Policy instruments that do not take nature into account often have a net negative impact by enabling activities that damage biodiversity and ecosystem services. Examples include subsidies for housing that encourage land conversion and urban sprawl in natural areas, and subsidies for fisheries and agriculture that encourage activities of a kind or at a level of intensity that exceed ecological sustainability thresholds (see Chapter 6).

Economic information enables policy makers to simultaneously address poverty issues and social goals where the analysis covers the distribution of costs and benefits between different groups in society. Such analysis can highlight the importance biodiversity and ecosystem services have for poorer segments of the population in many countries. Biodiversity policies designed to address these issues can contribute to alleviating poverty (see Table 2.3).

3 Guiding principles for policy change

Success will require two major shifts in how we think – as policy makers, as campaigners, as consumers, as producers, as a society. The first is to think not in political or economic cycles; not just in terms of years or even decade long programmes and initiatives. But to think in terms of epochs and eras [...] the second is to think anew about how we judge success as a society. For 60 years we have measured our progress by economic gains and social justice. Now we know that the progress and even the survival of the only world we have depends on decisive action to protect that world. (Gordon Brown, former British Prime Minister, 2009)

Table 2.3 How biodiversity policies affect development policy and poverty alleviation

Project	Country	Conservation achievements	Development/ poverty alleviation	Further information
Quito's Water Fund	Ecuador	• 3.5 million trees planted • Nine park guards hired • Hydrology monitoring programme started	• Alternative income (jobs) • Education • Clean water • Conflict resolution training • Technical capacity building	UNEP (2004)
China's Sloping Land Programme	China	• 14.6 million hectwes reforested by 2010	• Alternative income • Targeted support for ethnic minority groups • Flood control	Bennett and Xu (2005)
Il'Ngwesi Ecolodge	Kenya	• Wildlife populations increased • Poaching controlled	• Alternative income • Education (school funded) • Security (reduced poaching)	Il Ngwesi (2009)
Namibia's Conservancy Programme	Namibia	• Wildlife populations increased • Overgrazing controlled • Landscape connectivity improved	• Alternative income • Property rights • Cultural equality • Gender equality	Namibian Association of Community Based Natural Resource Management (CBNRM) Support Organisations (NACSO) (2010)
Cape Peninsula Biodiversity Conservation Project	South Africa	• Invasive plants eradicated • Antelope species reintroduced • Raptor populations increased • Protected areas established	• Improved infrastructure • Alternative income	FFEM (2007)

Source: Adapted from Tallis et al (2008)

As well as taking economic values into account, policy makers need to consider the following factors when designing an effective process:

• many different actors are concerned, with highly diverse interests;
• each country's cultural and institutional context is different;
• ethical considerations and distributional issues are critical to fair and durable solutions; and
• good governance must underpin successful policy implementation.

3.1 Address the right actors and balance diverse interests

Decisions affecting biodiversity and ecosystem services are made and influenced by many different actors and affect groups in different ways. Governments and public authorities are responsible for setting policy but a whole series of other groups (industry and business, consumers, landowners, NGOs, lobbyists, indigenous peoples, etc.) also make decisions that affect the natural environment (see Box 2.6). The challenge is to identify all relevant actors, mobilize 'leaders' and ensure that they have the necessary information and encouragement to make the difference.

Box 2.6 Actors and stakeholders at different scales of marine policy

Key players at sea range from those who use its resources to those who pollute its waters. Relevant policy areas cover not only shipping and dumping of waste at sea but also border/customs operations, land-based industry and agriculture (e.g. run-off from nitrates or chemicals). Very often, these same actors have a direct interest in conserving water quality (e.g. local communities, fishermen, public authorities). While some groups may be able to adapt to policy change and mitigate their negative impacts (e.g. by adjusting shipping routes), others like small-scale fishers may have greater difficulty in reducing their impact or dependence on marine resources and services.

Source: Berghöfer et al (2008)

Involving stakeholders is essential and has many advantages. People affected by damage to biodiversity and ecosystem services often have access to information or expertise that is not available to the general public. These groups also stand to win or lose most from policy changes and can play a central role in setting policy targets and implementing concrete solutions. One option is to reward local 'champions' who contribute to successful take-up of new challenges (see Box 2.7).

Even within single sectors, there will be a broad range of different stakeholders and interests. Production patterns can vary from environmentally sensitive to high impact. Within agriculture, for example, eco-farming is associated with sustainable land-use practices and reduced soil depletion or erosion whereas industrialized farming involves monocultures and intensive use of fertilizers and pesticides.

Additional challenges arise where policy making involves several governmental levels, e.g. global negotiation rounds or supranational organizations, national policy makers, regional administrations and local interest groups. At the multilateral level, many agreements and mechanisms are in place to formalize cooperation across boundaries. To improve water resource management, for example, more than 80 special commissions linking three or more neighbouring countries have been established in 62 international river basins (Dombrowsky, 2008).

**Box 2.7 Rewarding environmental leaders:
Examples of national practice**

In 2004, the Chinese Environmental Award was established to reward outstanding efforts to safeguard natural resources and capital (State Environmental Protection Administration of China, 2005). It has so far been granted to five groups and individuals. The 2006 award for Best Ecological Performance on Environmental Protection went to the Forest Police Station of Xi Shuang Ban Na, Yunnan Province, a biodiversity hotspot (www.cepf.org.cn/en/Leading).

Similar programmes include:

- the KEHATI award in Indonesia (www.kehati.or.id/);
- the Premio de Reportaje sobre Biodiversidad in South America (www. premioreportaje.org); or
- the Equator Prize for outstanding efforts to reduce poverty and biodiversity conservation (www.equatorinitiative.org).

3.2 Pay attention to the cultural and institutional context

Policy makers need to consider local culture and institutions when deciding which policies are likely to be appropriate or acceptable. The success of policy reforms may also be influenced by timing.

A country's cultural context (e.g. religious norms or morality, level of civil society engagement) and institutional context (e.g. laws, regulations, traditions) usually provide useful entry points for biodiversity conservation.

The importance of traditional knowledge related to biodiversity is increasingly recognized by scientists, businesses and policy makers. In some countries, scaling up traditional use patterns and local management practices to the regional or national level may be more easily accepted than top-down approaches. The first step towards this goal involves the systematic collection of relevant local knowledge (see example in Box 2.8).

Policy options may be easier to implement and enforce when they fit easily into existing regulations and do not need substantial legislative changes or reallocation of decision-making powers. Establishing a protected area or restricting use of a certain resource can be easier if this is consistent with religious norms. Market-based tools to manage ecosystem services may be more easily accepted in countries that already use markets for pollution control or nature protection (e.g. the US) than in regions relying mainly on traditional regulatory norms (e.g. many European countries).

On the other hand, one country's move is often another country's opportunity to follow. Political 'champions' who propel a new problem up the policy agenda and offer innovative solutions (e.g. PES in Costa Rica, REDD in Guyana) can catalyse progress at a regional or global level. Sharing information about success stories is an important and practical way to learn from experience elsewhere and to develop solutions appropriate to national needs and priorities.

As in any policy area, new instruments and measures can face difficulties not only when being negotiated but also in day-to-day implementation and enforcement. Good design, good communication and good will are all important to boost compliance with

---

Box 2.8 Upholding traditional knowledge through People's Biodiversity Registers (India)

People's Biodiversity Registers (PBRs) were initiated in India in 1995 to record rapidly eroding folk knowledge of medicinal uses of plants. Their focus has since been broadened to cover wild varieties of cultivated crops to support on-farm conservation and promotion of farmer's rights. PBRs record information on species, their habitats, the price of biological produce and regulations governing harvests.

The most ambitious PBR to date covers 52 sites in seven states. This huge database is designed to:

- facilitate community regulation of access to biodiversity resources leading to sustainable harvests;
- promote knowledge-based sustainable management of agriculture and the sustainable use of livestock, fish and forests to improve public health and the quality of life of community members;
- generate funds by charging collection fees for access to biodiversity resources;
- stimulate conservation of valuable natural resources; and
- achieve fair sharing in the benefits of commercial application of local knowledge.

Sources: India's Third National Report on Implementation of the CBD (2005); Gadgil et al (2006); Verma (2009)

---

environmental policy instruments because these need backing from affected stakeholders to be fully effective. For example, payment schemes to reward biodiversity-friendly agricultural practices will only work well if people fully understand the scheme and do not face other obstacles when participating (see example in Box 2.9).

'Windows of opportunity' can help decision makers secure policy change. These can open in response to increased awareness of environmental problems (e.g. concern over ozone led to the Montreal Protocol; concern over climate change, to the REDD mechanism, which has great potential for broader application to biodiversity conservation; see Chapter 5). Crises can also provide opportunities for reform, for instance to phase out expensive agricultural or fisheries subsidies harmful to biodiversity (see Chapter 6). Policy windows can also open as part of a response to catastrophe (see Table 2.4).

3.3 Take property rights, fairness and equity into account

> It took Britain half the resources of the planet to achieve its prosperity; how many planets will a country like India require? (Mahatma Gandhi, quoted in Goodland, 1992)

New strategies and tools for protecting biodiversity and sustaining ecosystem services often involve changes in existing rights to manage, access or use resources ('property rights'). The distributional implications of policy change, particularly for vulnerable groups and indigenous people, need to be identified up front and fully addressed in consultations throughout the policy development process.

Box 2.9 Obstacles to success: Example of a carbon sink project, Colombia

Objectives

The PROCUENCA project in the Chinchiná River Basin was launched in 2001 to use sustainable forestry to improve water provision in an area suffering from deforestation due to agricultural and grazing expansion. Financial support to landowners was originally provided through a national reforestation programme to establish plantations for timber production: soon afterwards this was designated as a forest carbon project in collaboration with the FAO.

Lessons learned

Although participants managed their plantations independently, the project created constraints on land use without having properly informed local land users on the possible risks and benefits involved in reforestation and forest carbon projects. Funds for reforestation were reported to be unequally distributed: most were directly channelled to the project, which meant that smaller landholders received only a small share insufficient to sustain their livelihood and to cover opportunity costs.

Income from the timber is not expected until after 20 years, a period that is too long for most landowners to go without revenues. Uncertainty related to process, prices and approvals meant that local farmers could not tell if income generated through carbon credits would cover the loans taken out to join the project.

Capacity building and take-up through community-based participation is reported to be limited. Few farmers attended special training, some local leaders denied the existence of the forest carbon programme and 78 per cent of farmers surveyed mentioned logging and sales as perceived economic benefits. Moreover, the project may have stimulated the replacement of natural forests by plantations with a negative biodiversity impact (GFC, 2008).

Project adjustment

Despite these shortcomings the project was developed further in collaboration with Conservation International to ensure its additionality in terms of carbon storage and biodiversity conservation (CI, 2010). These efforts contributed to the successful approval of the project for the Clean Development Mechanism (CDM) under the UN Framework Convention on Climate Change (UNFCCC, 2010). Once the reduction in GHG emissions has been verified, landowners will be able to sell carbon credits on the international carbon market from 2011.

Most people would agree that other species have a right to co-exist with us on Earth and that it is important to maintain biodiversity in a state able to provide benefits to humans.

The above statement raises ethical issues and practical questions of responsibility for policy makers. Should a landowner have to stop using part of his land to help a

Table 2.4 Catastrophic events creating 'windows of opportunity' for policy change

Event (natural catastrophe; hazard or accident)	Policy Results
1976 industrial accident in chemical plant near Seveso, Italy: released highly toxic TCDD (dioxin) contaminating four communities.	Introduction of EU Seveso Directive (1982/1996/2003) requiring the establishment of emergency plans, regular security checks and inspections to reduce industrial accidents related to dangerous substances (EC, 2009a)
1999 oil spill of *Erika* tanker: 10 million litres of oil caused the death of up to 100,000 birds near the French Atlantic coast.	Within the EU, the 'Erika I package' (legislation for double-hulled ships and Liability Directive). (Europa, 2007). In the US in 2005, 79 per cent of tanker calls (US-flag and foreign-flag) at US ports were by double-hull tankers. (United States Government Accountability Office, 2007)
2000 pollution of Danube River: caused by a cyanide spill from tailings of a metals recovery plant near Baia Mare/Romania	EU Mining Waste Directive 2006, requiring a waste plan containing expected waste quantities, qualities and measures of disposal, to be verified by inspectors (EC, 2009b).
2004 tsunami in South-east Asia: caused the death of more than 200,000 civilians	A range of international projects and investments in mangrove restoration to strengthen natural coastal barriers to increase security against waves (e.g. EU Asia Pro-Eco II B Post Tsunami Project, Mangrove Action Project; EC, 2009c)
2005 Hurricane Katrina in the US: caused nearly 2000 casualties and had an estimated cost of more than US$80 billion (costliest tropical cyclone in history) (Knabb et al, 2006).	Arguably triggered greater support for a commitment to addressing climate change and for wetland restoration in general (see also Chapter 9). Rising awareness and mainstreaming, e.g. mass media, documentary *An Inconvenient Truth*.
2010 Deepwater Horizon oil spill in the Gulf of Mexico: preliminary estimates indicate a discharge of approximately 40,000 barrels per day (*New York Times*, 2010).	Post-accident: Administration established system for real-time updating of information on coastal water quality (EPA, 2010). June 2010: The oil company responsible (BP) created a US$20 billion escrow compensation fund; ceiling increased in July when BP set aside a pre-tax charge of US$32.2 billion to cover liabilities (BP, 2010). 21 July 2010: A US$1 billion oil spill response and containment system for deepwater Gulf of Mexico jointly established by four other oil companies (McNulty and Kirchgaessner, 2010).

threatened species? Plant trees to protect freshwater resources? Be compensated for losses or reduced gains as a result of new biodiversity policies? Should people have to leave land to which they do not hold formally registered rights, even if they have lived there for generations? When a pharmaceutical company discovers an important drug derived from a plant species in a tropical rainforest, who should reap the benefits? The company? The country of origin? The forest people?

At least three arguments support consideration of property rights and distributional impacts as an integral part of policy development:

- Reasons of equity: fairness in addressing changes of rights between individuals, groups, communities and even generations is an important policy goal in most countries.
- Taking distributional issues into account makes it much more feasible to achieve other goals when addressing biodiversity loss, particularly those related to poverty alleviation and the Millennium Development Goals (see Table 2.2 above).
- There are almost always winners and losers from policy change. In most cases, loser groups will oppose the new measures. If distributional aspects are fully considered when designing policies, the chances of successful implementation can be improved.

Rights to use or benefit from natural resources can take many forms, including informal rules such as traditional norms or tenure rights (see Box 2.10). In some countries, the

---

Box 2.10 How do 'property rights' apply to biodiversity and ecosystem services?

'Property rights' is a generic term covering a bundle of different rights over a resource (P). Not all of these are necessarily held by the same person, as explained below:

- **The Right to Use:** Party A has a right to use resource P.
- **The Right to Manage:** Party A has a right to manage resource P and may decide how and by whom P shall be used.
- **The Right to the Income:** Party A has a right to the income from resource P, in other words they may use and enjoy the fruits, rents, profits, etc. derived from P.
- **The Right of Exclusion:** Others may use resource P if and only if party A consents (if party A consents, it is prima facie not wrong for others to use resource P; if party A does not consent, it is prima facie wrong for others to use resource P).
- **The Right to Transfer:** Party A may temporarily or permanently transfer user rights to specific other persons by consent.
- **The Right to Compensation:** If party B damages or uses resource P without party A's consent, then A typically has a right to receive compensation from B.

Two other rules are also relevant to the concept of property rights:

- **Punishment Rule:** If party B interferes with party A's use of resource P or uses P without A's consent, then B may be punished in an appropriate way.
- **Liability Rule:** If use of resource P causes damage to the person or property of party B, then party A (as P's owner) may be held responsible and face a claim for damages.

Source: Birner (1999)

law underpins rights to recreational services e.g. the right to walk through private woodlands or to access beaches and sea or lake shores.

What complicates matters for the policy maker is that different rights are often held by different people or groups in society. A forest might be owned by the state, local people might have a right to use some of its products, rights for water coming from this area might be held by third parties and international companies might hold concessions for deforestation. This legal and historic complexity needs to be considered when adjusting or introducing policies for ecosystem services and biodiversity (see Box 2.11).

Moreover, as the Nobel laureate Elinor Ostrom has shown through her extensive empirical work, successful management of natural resources may not always be achieved by solely assigning complete private property rights (Ostrom, 1990; 2005). Economic theory distinguishes between four broad types of management regimes: state property regimes, private property regimes, common property regimes and open access regimes (Bromley, 1998). The best option in a given situation will depend on the resource in question and the evolution of the institutional set-up in society.

The ability to enforce property rights, whether by governments or by those owning the rights (e.g. local communities), will depend on institutional capacities. These include inspection powers and capacity in the former case and access to a functioning judiciary in both cases. Transparency and access to information are critical (see Section 3.4 below).

Box 2.11 Policy challenges related to uncertain property rights in the Amazon

Only 14 per cent of private land in the Amazon is backed by a secure title deed (Barreto et al, 2008). Uncertainty over landownership leads to violence between different groups, makes it hard for public authorities to prevent illegal deforestation and encourages short-term management (i.e. destruction of the forest through cutting timber and cattle grazing). In practice, deforestation has often been used as a way of establishing property rights.

In 2009, Brazil announced its intention to transfer around 670,000km^2 (roughly the size of France) into private ownership 'to guarantee that people have ownership of land, to see if we can end the violence in this country' (President Lula, BBC News, 2009). Under the proposal:

- the smallest areas (<100 hectares) would be handed over for free;
- medium-sized plots would be sold for a symbolic value; and
- larger estates (>1500 hectares) would be auctioned at market prices.

However, this fundamental change in property rights is contentious among Brazilians. Some NGOs have argued that this proposal amounts to an amnesty for land-grabbers and that the 'bill will be a major signal indicating to the people who enjoy impunity that it is worth committing a crime in the Amazon' (BBC News, 2009).

Sources: Barreto et al (2008); BBC News (2009)

Box 2.12 Impact of minority rights on conservation in China's Wolong Nature Reserve

This Reserve was established in 1975 as a flagship project to conserve endangered giant pandas. Research carried out-25 years later (Liu et al, 2001) showed increased fragmentation and a decrease in the Reserve's forested area, leading to a significant loss of panda habitat. The rate of habitat loss was actually 1.15 times higher within the Reserve than in the surrounding area.

The reasons for this unexpected result are mainly socio-economic. The local population belongs to an ethnic minority which is not covered by China's one child rule. The population inside the Reserve almost doubled from 1975 to 1995. Most inhabitants make their living by farming, fuelwood collection, timber harvesting, road construction and maintenance – all leading to continuous destruction of forested areas. Outside the Reserve, the one child rule applied and people gradually switched to other types of energy, reducing the demand for wood.

Source: Liu et al (2001)

The specific social context of each country will also influence the design and likely success of policy initiatives (see Box 2.12).

Distributional impacts occur at different levels: between nations, regions, sectors, groups in society and generations (see regional example in Box 2.13). An important function of TEEB is to present a range of practical tools to identify and address such impacts.

Specific distributional issues arise where benefits of ecosystem conservation go beyond local level. For example, restricting land use upstream is often necessary to maintain freshwater provision at adequate levels and quality for downstream users.

Box 2.13 Applying 'ecological footprint analysis' to the world's regions

Ecological footprint analysis compares human demands on nature with the biosphere's ability to regenerate resources and maintain ecosystem services. It does this by assessing the biologically productive land and marine area required to produce the resources consumed and to absorb the corresponding waste, using available technology.

Analysis carried out at the global level shows that since the mid-1980s, global human demand for natural capital has exceeded the planet's capacities to regenerate. Between 1961 and 2005 the per capita footprint of the Asia–Pacific, Latin American and Caribbean regions remained stable, while North America and Europe nearly doubled their per capita uptake of natural resources during that period (WWF, 2008).

Where distributional impacts are perceived as unfair, compensation may be necessary to ensure full implementation of selected policies. Some countries have introduced schemes for downstream water users to compensate upstream landowners (e.g. Mexico; see Chapter 5).

Decision making today affects tomorrow's societies. The species we commit to extinction are clearly not available to future generations. If ecosystems can no longer provide important regulating services, they will have to provide for them in a different manner. This has enormous implications. Based on a 4 per cent discount rate, our grandchildren 50 years from now have a right to only one-seventh of what we use today (see TEEB Interim Report (2008), Chapter 4 and TEEB Foundations (2010), Chapter 6).

3.4 Base policies on good governance

Good governance is perhaps the single most important factor in eradicating poverty and promoting development. (Former UN Secretary-General Kofi Annan, 1998)

Good governance means that decisions are taken and implemented in an effective, transparent and accountable manner by all relevant institutions, with respect for the rule of law and human rights.

Good governance is needed to avoid bias or misuse of economic values in decision making. Bias can take different forms (e.g. considering the interests of the elite over those of other social groups; excluding or concealing the amount and distribution of policy costs and benefits; failing to take account of local and indigenous property rights). This is often unintentional given the sheer complexity of biodiversity and the number of affected interests. However, there may also be other reasons related to the way information is used. Well-informed interest groups may be better placed to voice their concerns in decision-making processes (e.g. allocation of sectoral subsidies).

Economic information can provide strong support to good governance. Systematic and balanced information on costs and benefits makes it clear how different groups in society are affected by policy options and helps resist pressure of vested interests. This can be further supported by a broad approach of stakeholder participation.

Tools to consider the costs and benefits of projects and policies affecting social and environmental interests are already in place in many countries (e.g. environmental impact assessments, cost–benefit analysis and strategic environmental assessments). Feeding quality data on the value of biodiversity and ecosystem services into assessment frameworks can help decision makers at relevant levels reach more informed decisions and improve policy design (see Chapter 4, and also TEEB in Local Policy, 2011).

Many regional processes and initiatives support international collaboration to improve governance and public decision making. Some of the most important agreements are listed in Table 2.5 below.

Table 2.5 Examples of initiatives to facilitate good governance practices

Countries	Strategy	Date	Description	Source
Organization of American States (OAS), 34 countries from the American continent	Inter-American – Convention against Corruption	1996	Promotes, facilitates and regulates cooperation between the Parties to ensure the effectiveness of its measures. Incorporates actions to prevent, detect, punish and eradicate corruption in the performance of public functions and acts of corruption specifically related to such performance.	OAS (2009)
Central Asia, Europe	Aarhus Convention	1998	Convention on access to information, public participation in decision making and access to justice in environmental matters	UNECE (2010)
OECD Member States, Argentina, Brazil, Bulgaria, Chile, Estonia, Israel, Slovenia, South Africa	Convention on Combating Bribery of Foreign Public Officials in International Business Transactions	1999	Incorporates legally binding standards to criminalize bribery of foreign public officials in international business transactions and provides for a series of related measures to make this effective.	OECD (2009a)
Australia	Good Governance Guiding Principles	2000	Set of criteria that must be aimed for in development assistance.	AUSAID (2000)
Europe	European Governance: A White Paper	2001	Concept of governance based on the rules, processes and behaviour that affect the way in which powers are exercised at European level. Emphasizes openness, participation, accountability, effectiveness and coherence.	EC (2001)
Africa	New Partnership for Africa's Development (NEPAD)	2001	Initiative to place Africa on a path of sustainable development encompassing good governance and prosperity with a consolidation of peace, security and informed policy choices.	NEPAD (2009)
Arab Countries	The Good Governance for Development Initiative	2005	Promotes broad reforms to enhance the investment climate, modernize governance structures and operations, and strengthen regional and international partnerships to facilitate investment in participating countries.	OECD (2009b)

4 The TEEB toolkit for policy change

This book aims to help policy makers consider the wider framework for policy change and innovation when addressing biodiversity issues. It provides concrete examples showing how economic information and values can help overcome current difficulties with many biodiversity policies and accelerate policy reform.

As noted in this chapter, policy makers have a range of options when taking action:

- build on good practices that have been proven to work elsewhere;
- ensure that existing instruments reach their full potential;
- reform policies and instruments to avoid unintended side-effects;
- develop and implement new policies.

Figure 2.1 provides an overview of available policy instruments analysed in the rest of this book. For ease of reference, it divides them into three broad groups:

1. instruments providing information for biodiversity policies;
2. instruments setting incentives for behavioural change; and
3. instruments directly regulating the use of natural resources.

Providing information

Providing information helps us to measure what we manage. Chapter 3 focuses on new approaches to indicators and national accounting systems to integrate the values of natural capital. Chapter 4 shows how valuation and policy assessment frameworks can be used more effectively to safeguard ecosystem services. These information tools feed into the design of all the policy instruments discussed in later chapters (dotted lines in Figure 2.1).

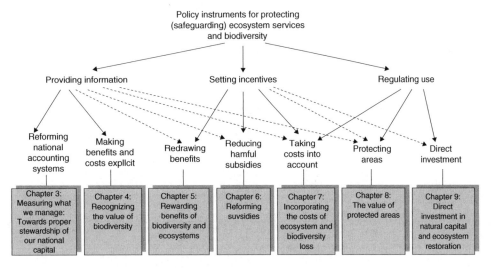

Figure 2.1 *TEEB policy options overview*

Source: Bernd Hansjürgens, own representation

Setting incentives

Instruments that influence resource-use decisions by setting incentives are increasingly used in biodiversity policy and open up new opportunities for policy makers. However, incentives set in other policy fields can also negatively impact biodiversity. Careful analysis of potentially conflicting provisions can be greatly improved by using economic valuation. Chapter 5 presents incentive-based instruments to reward biodiversity benefits and examines markets and procurement policies for green goods and services. Chapter 6 discusses ways to reform existing harmful subsidies that damage biodiversity and ecosystem services. Chapter 7 considers the scope for use of pricing mechanisms as part of a broad policy mix.

Regulating use

Regulating use involves three different sets of instruments: those that make the user or polluter pay; protected areas; and direct public investment. Chapter 7 analyses use of regulatory instruments in different contexts, including related issues of liability, compensation and enforcement. Chapter 8 shows how cost–benefit analysis and improved governance can strengthen the design and effectiveness of protected area instruments to safeguard biodiversity hotspots. Chapter 9 assesses options for direct public investment either in ecological infrastructure or by restoring degraded ecosystems.

Each approach has specific advantages and disadvantages depending on the characteristics of the ecosystem at hand and the concrete design and implementation issues. Some measures may be feasible for ecosystem management while others are not.

An appropriate mix is needed, which takes into account actors, institutions, the policy cycle, distributional implications and instrument design. Chapter 10 draws these strands together and presents a vision and practical framework for transforming our approach to natural capital.

Acknowledgements

The authors would like to thank Peter Bridgewater, Joint Nature Conservation Committee – JNCC, UK; Deanna Donavan, JNCC, UK; Stefan van Esch, Ministry of Housing, Spatial Planning and the Environment, Financial and Economic Affairs, The Netherlands; Jan Joost Kessler, Agency for International Development – AID, The Netherlands; Hugh Laxton, UK Nature Landscape Office, Belgium; Markus Lehmann, Secretariat of the Convention on Biological Diversity – SCBD, Canada; Eimear Nic Lughadha, Royal Botanical Gardens Kew, UK; Karachepone Ninan, Institute for Social and Economic Change, India; Alfred Oteng-Yeboah, Council for Scientific and Industrial Research – CSIR, Ghana; Benjamin Simmons, UNEP, Global; Monique Simmonds, Royal Botanical Gardens Kew, UK; Paul Smith, Royal Botanical Gardens Kew, UK; Patrick ten Brink, IEEP, Belgium; Graham Tucker, IEEP, UK; Alexandra Vakrou, European Commission – DG Environment, Belgium; James Vause, UK Government Department for Environment, Food and Rural Affairs – Defra, UK; Sirini Withana, IEEP, UK; and Carlos Eduardo Young, Federal University of Rio de Janeiro, Brazil.

References

Annan, K. (1998) 'Partnerships for global community: Annual report on the work of the organization', United Nations, New York, www.un.org/ecosocdev/geninfo/afrec/sgreport/index.html, accessed 10 October 2010

AUSAID (The Australian Government's Overseas Aid Program) (2000) 'Good governance: Guiding principles for implementation', www.ausaid.gov.au/publications/pdf/good_governance.pdf, accessed 10 October 2009

Barreto, P., Pinto, A., Brito, B. and Hayashi, S. (2008) *Quem é o Dono da Amazônia? Uma Análise do Recadastramento de Imóveis Rurais*, Instituto do Homem e Meio Ambiente da Amazônia, Belém, PA, www.imazon.org.br/novo2008/arquivosdb/QuemDonoAmazonia.pdf, accessed 23 July 2010

Barrett, S. (2003) *Environment and Statecraft: The Strategy of Environmental Treaty-Making*, Oxford University Press, New York

Barrosso, J. M. D. (2009) 'Biodiversity: Giving proper value to a priceless asset', speech at Biodiversity Protection – Beyond 2010, Athens, 27 April 2009, http://europa.eu/rapid/pressReleasesAction.do?reference=SPEECH/09/197&format=HTML, accessed 10 October 2010

BBC News (British Broadcasting Corporation) (2009) Amazon Bill Controversy in Brazil, http://news.bbc.co.uk/2/hi/science/nature/8113952.stm, accessed 23 July 2009

Bennett, M. T. and Xu, J. (2005) *China's Sloping Land Conversion Program: Institutional Innovation or Business as Usual?* www.cifor.cgiar.org/pes/publications/pdf_files/China_paper.pdf, accessed 10 October 2009

Berghöfer, A., Wittmer, H. and Rauschmayer, F. (2008) 'Stakeholder participation in ecosystem-based approaches to fisheries management: A synthesis from European research projects', *Marine Policy*, vol 32, pp243–253

Birner, R. (1999) *The Role of Livestock in Agricultural Development: Theoretical Approaches and Their Application in the Case of Sri Lanka*, Avebury, Aldershot

BP (British Petroleum) (2010) 'BP sets out Gulf of Mexico costs, further asset sales and strong operating performance', www.bp.com/extendedgenericarticle.do?categoryId=2012968&contentId=7063921, accessed 22 September 2010

Bromley, D. W. (1998) 'Property regimes in environmental economics', in H. Folmer and T. Tietenberg (eds) *The International Yearbook of Environmental and Resource Economics 1997/1998: A Survey of Current Issues*, Edward Elgar, Cheltenham

Brown, G. (2009) Speech on the 'Roadmap to Copenhagen manifesto on the challenge of climate change and development', London, http://webarchive.nationalarchives.gov.uk/+/number10.gov.uk/news/speeches-and-transcripts/2009/06/roadmap-to-copenhagen-speech-19813, accessed 22 November 2010

Chau, P. (2008) 'Population', University of California San Diego, Environmental Studies, http://ieng6.ucsd.edu/~pcchau/ENVR30/reader/txtbk/ch01.pdf, accessed 22 September 2010

CI (Conservation International) (2010) 'Credit for forests', www.conservation.org/FMG/Articles/Pages/credit_for_forests_colombia.aspx, accessed 13 July 2010

de Groot, D., Finlayson, M., Verschuuren, B., Ypma, O. and Zylstra, M. (2008) *Integrated Assessment of Wetland Services and Values as a Tool to Analyse Policy Trade-Offs and Management Options: A Case Study in the Daly and Mary River Catchments, Northern Australia*, Supervising Scientist Report 198, Supervising Scientist, Darwin NT

Dombrowsky, I. (2008) 'Integration in the management of international waters: Economic perspectives on a global policy discourse', *Global Governance* 14, pp455–477

EC (European Commission) (2001) *European Governance: A White Paper*, http://eur-lex.europa.eu/LexUriServ/site/en/com/2001/com2001_0428en01.pdf, accessed 23 July 2009

EC (European Commission) (2009a) 'European civil protection. Chemical accidents (Seveso II): Prevention, preparedness and response', EC Environment, http://ec.europa.eu/environment/seveso/index.htm, accessed 10 October 2009

EC (European Commission) (2009b) 'Mining waste', EC Environment, http://ec.europa.eu/environment/waste/mining/index.htm, accessed 10 October 2009

EC (European Commission) (2009c) *Indian Ocean Tsunami: The European Response*, http://ec.europa.eu/world/tsunami/rehab_reconstruc.htm, accessed 10 October 2009

Emerton, L. and Bos, E. (2004) *Value: Counting Ecosystems as an Economic Part of Water Infrastructure*, IUCN, Gland, Switzerland and Cambridge, http://data.iucn.org/dbtw-wpd/edocs/2004-046.pdf, accessed 10 October 2009

EPA (2010) 'EPA response to BP spill in the Gulf of Mexico, coastal water sampling', www.epa.gov/BPSpill/water.html, accessed 22 September 2010

Europa: Summaries of EU legislation (2007) 'Maritime safety: Accelerated phasing-in of double-hull oil tankers', http://europa.eu/legislation_summaries/transport/waterborne_transport/l24231_en.htm, accessed 22 September 2010

FFEM (Fonds Français pour l'Environnement Mondial) (2007) *Cape Peninsula Biodiversity Conservation Project*, www.ffem.fr/jahia/webdav/site/ffem/users/admiffem/public/Plaquettes_projet/Biodiversity_peninsuleCap_eng.pdf, accessed 10 October 2009

Gadgil, M., et al (2006) *Ecology is for the People: A Methodology Manual for People's Biodiversity Register*, http://ces.iisc.ernet.in/PBR/PBR%20Final%20document.pdf, accessed 23 July 2009

GFC (Global Forest Coalition) (2008) *Life as Commerce: The Impact of Market-Based Conservation on Indigenous Peoples*, www.globalbioenergy.org/uploads/media/0810_GFC_-_The_impact_of_market-based_conservation_on_indigenous_peoples.pdf, accessed 10 October 2009

Goodland, R. (1992) 'The case that the world has reached limits: More precisely that current throughput growth in the global economy cannot be sustained', *Population & Environment*, vol 13, no 3, pp167–182

Howlett, M. and Ramesh, M. (2003) *Studying Public Policy: Policy Cycles and Policy Subsystems*, Oxford University Press, Oxford

Il Ngwesi Group Ranch – People of Wildlife (2009) *Integrating Community Development and Sustainable Environmental Management*, www.ilngwesi.com, accessed 10 October 2009

India's Third National Report on Implementation of the CBD (2005) www.cbd.int/doc/world/in/in-nr-03-en.doc, accessed 23 July 2009

Knabb, R. D., Rhome, J. R. and Brown, D. P. (2006) 'Tropical cyclone report Hurricane Katrina', US National Hurricane Center, www.nhc.noaa.gov/pdf/TCR-AL122005_Katrina.pdf, accessed 10 October 2010

Liu, J., Linderman, M., Ouyang, Z., An, L., Yang J. and Zhang, H. (2001) 'Ecological degradation in protected areas: The case of the Wolong Nature Reserve for giant pandas', *Science*, vol 292, pp98–101

McNulty, S. and Kirchgaessner, S. (2010) 'Tracking the oil spill in the Gulf', *Financial Times:* 21 July 2010, London, www.ft.com/cms/s/0/73c055f0-94f6-11df-af3b-00144feab49a.html, accessed 22 September 2010

Millennium Ecosystem Assessment (2005) *Ecosystems and Human Well-Being: Current State and Trends*, www.maweb.org/documents/document.356.aspx.pdf, accessed 23 July 2009

Namibian Association of Community Based Natural Resource Management (CBNRM) Support Organisations (NACSO) (2010) 'What is NACSO?', www.nacso.org.na/index.php, accessed 10 October 2010

Navrud, S. and Pruckner, G. J. (1997) 'Environmental valuation: To use or not to use? A comparative study of the USA and Europe', *Environmental and Resource Economics*, vol 10, no 1, pp1–25

NEPAD (New Partnership for Africa's Development) (2009), www.nepad.org/system/files/framework_0.pdf, accessed 10 October 2010

New York Times (2010) 'Tracking the oil spill in the Gulf', www.nytimes.com/interactive/2010/05/01/us/20100501-oil-spill-tracker.html, accessed 22 September 2010

OAS (Organization of American States) (2009) *The Inter-American Convention Against Corruption*, www.oas.org/juridico/english/corr_bg.htm, accessed 10 October 2009

OECD (Organisation for Economic Co-operation and Development) (2009a) *OECD Convention on Combating Bribery of Foreign Public Officials in International Business Transactions*, www.oecd.org/document/21/0,2340,en_2649_34859_2017813_1_1_1_1,00.html, accessed 10 October 2009

OECD (2009b) *Initiative on Governance and Investment for Development*, www.oecd.org/pages/0,3417,en_34645207_34645466_1_1_1_1_1,00.html, accessed 10 October 2009

Ostrom, E. (1990) *Governing the Commons: The Evolution of Institutions for Collective Action*, Cambridge University Press, Cambridge

Ostrom, E. (2005) *Understanding Institutional Diversity*, Princeton University Press, Princeton

Parker, C., Mitchell, A., Trivedi, M. and Mardas, N. (2009) *The Little REDD+ Book*, Global Canopy Programme, Oxford

Sampson, G. P. (2005) *The World Trade Organization and Sustainable Development*, United Nations University, Tokyo

Similä, J., Thum, R., Varjopuro, R. and Ring, I. (2006) 'Protected species in conflict with fisheries: The interplay between European and National Regulation', *Journal for European Environmental & Planning Law*, vol 3, no 5, pp432–445

State Environmental Protection Administration of China (2005) *China's Third National Report on Implementation of the CBD*, www.cbd.int/doc/world/cn/cn-nr-03-en.pdf, accessed 23 July 2009

Tallis, H., Kareiva, P., Marvier, M. and Chang, A. (2008) 'An ecosystem services framework to support both practical conservation and economic development,' *PNAS*, vol 105, no 28, pp9457–9464

TEEB (2008) *The Economics of Ecosystems and Biodiversity: An Interim Report*, European Commission, Brussels, www.teebweb.org, accessed 13 July 2010

TEEB Foundations (2010) *The Economics of Ecosystems and Biodiversity: Ecological and Economic Foundations* (ed P. Kumar), Earthscan, London

TEEB in Local Policy (2011) *The Economics of Ecosystems and Biodiversity in Local and Regional Policy and Management* (ed H. Wittmer and H. Gundimeda), Earthscan, London

ten Brink, B., Alkemade, R., Bakkenes, M., Clement, J., Eickhout, B., Fish, L., de Heer, M., Kram, T., Manders, T., van Meijl, H., Miles, L., Nellemann, C., Lysenko, I., van Oorschot, M., Smout, F., Tabeau, A., van Vuuren, D. and Westhoek, H. (2007) *Cross-roads of Life on Earth: Exploring Means to Meet the 2010 Biodiversity Target*, CBD, Montreal

TNC (The Nature Conservancy) (2007) *Watershed Valuation as a Tool for Biodiversity Protection*, www. nature.org/initiatives/freshwater/files/watershed_report_02_02_07_final.pdf, accessed 23 July 2009

UNDP–UNEP Poverty-Environment Facility (2008) *Making the Economic Case: A Primer For Mainstreaming Environment in National Development Planning*, www.unpei.org/PDF/Making-the-economic-case-primer.pdf, accessed 23 July 2009

UNECE (2010) 'Introducing the Aarhus Convention: Access to information, public participation in decision making and access to justice in environmental matters', www.unece.org/env/pp/, accessed 22 September 2010

UNEP (United Nations Environment Programme) (2004) *FONAG: Quito's Water Fund – A Municipal Commitment to Protect the Watersheds*, www.unep.org/gc/gcss-viii/USA-IWRM-2.pdf, accessed 10 October 2009

UNEP (2009) 'Integrated policymaking for sustainable development', unpublished manuscript

UNEP (United Nations Environment Programme) and IISD (International Institute for Sustainable Development) (2005) *Environment and Trade: A Handbook*, UNEP, Geneva

UNFCCC (United Nations Framework Convention on Climate Change) (2010) 'PROCUENCA Project design document' (PDD), www.netinform.net/KE/files/pdf/Procuenca_PDD_version03_abril%2013.pdf, accessed 13 July 2010

United States Government Accountability Office (2007) 'Maritime security: Federal efforts needed to address challenges in preventing and responding to terrorist attacks on energy commodity tankers', available at www.gao.gov/new.items/d08141.pdf, accessed 13 July 2010

Verburg, R., Stehfest, E., Woltjer, G. and Eickhout, B. (2009) 'The effect of agricultural trade liberalization on land-use related greenhouse gas emissions', *Global Environmental Change*, vol 19, no 4, pp434–446

Verma, M. (2009) 'Role of traditional knowledge systems and efforts thereof for conservation of biodiversity in India – A few examples', Personal communication

Woodward, R. T. (2003) 'Lessons about effluent trading from a single trade', *Review of Agricultural Economics*, vol 25, no 1, pp235–245

WWF (World Wide Fund for Nature) (2008) *Living Planet Report 2008*, http://assets.panda.org/downloads/living_planet_report_2008.pdf, accessed 23 July 2009

Part II

Measuring What We Manage: Information Tools for Decision Makers

Chapter 3
Strengthening Indicators and Accounting Systems for Natural Capital

Coordinating lead author
Patrick ten Brink

Lead authors
Sonja Gantioler, Haripriya Gundimeda, Pavan Sukhdev,
Graham Tucker, Jean-Louis Weber

Editing and language check
Clare Shine

See end of chapter for acknowledgements for reviews and other contributions

Contents

Key messages 81

Summary 83

1 What measurement problems do we face? 83

2 Improving measurement of biodiversity and ecosystem services 84
   2.1 What role do indicators play? 84
   2.2 What should biodiversity indicators measure? 87
   2.3 Towards a biodiversity monitoring framework 90
   2.4 Measuring ecosystem services 93

3 'Greening' our macroeconomic and societal indicators 102
   3.1 Traditional approaches to measuring wealth and well-being 102
   3.2 Tools for more sustainable measurement 103

4 Integrating ecosystems into national income accounting 107
   4.1 The rationale for ecosystem accounting 107
   4.2 Limitations of conventional accounting systems 108
   4.3 Practical steps towards ecosystem accounting 109
   4.4 Using available information to meet policy makers' demands 112

5 Building a fuller picture: The need for 'GDP of the poor' 113
   5.1 A tale of two tragedies: The measurement gap around the rural poor 113
   5.2 Poverty and biodiversity: From vicious to virtuous circle 114
   5.3 Practical steps towards measuring the GDP of the poor 117

Notes 118

Acknowledgements 119

References 120

Annex 1 Country-based calculations of GDP of the poor 124

Key messages

Ecosystems and biodiversity are our stock of 'natural capital' – they lead to a flow of benefits that support societal and individual well-being and economic prosperity. We do not measure this capital well enough to ensure its proper management and stewardship. Without effective monitoring we cannot understand the range or scale of the impacts of biodiversity loss or choose the best response. Without suitable indicators or accounting, we lack a solid evidence base for informed policy decisions. The following improvements are urgently needed:

Improving the measurement and monitoring of biodiversity and ecosystem services

Headline indicators are needed to set and monitor specific, measurable, achievable, realistic and time-specific (SMART) targets. These should address the status of phylogenetic diversity (genetic diversity between species), species extinction risk, the quantity and ecological condition of ecosystems/biotopes and flows in related benefits. The status indicators should be part of an interlinked framework of driver, pressure, status, impact and response indicators.

More field data are required, especially from biodiversity-rich countries. Some monitoring can be carried out by remote sensing but more ground surveys are also required.

Data are also vital for economic evaluation and designing policy instruments, particularly to define baselines and set targets and conditions to ensure verifiability and additionality. Evaluation of performance and added value are essential to generate confidence in policy instruments such as payments for ecosystem services.

More effort is needed to develop indicators of ecosystem services. This will require further research to improve understanding of – and develop better indicators on – the link between biodiversity and ecosystem condition and the provision of ecosystem services. However, this should not delay the selection and use in the short term of headline indicators for biodiversity and ecosystem service targets, which can be subsequently refined.

Better macroeconomic and societal indicators

Macro-indicators need to take natural capital into account. The ecological footprint is a valuable concept for policy objectives and communication. The European Union's 'Beyond GDP' process is piloting an environmental index for use alongside gross domestic product (GDP) and launching macro-indicators to communicate key issues on sustainable development. The Stiglitz–Sen–Fitousi Commission on the Measurement of Economic Performance and Social Progress also supports well-being measurement within macroeconomic policy.

Adjusted Income and Consumption aggregates should be used to reflect under-investment in ecosystem maintenance, over-consumption of natural resource and ecosystem services and, where possible, positive investment in natural capital. They should be introduced as soon as feasible in the form of international standards in the core set of headline macroeconomic aggregates, alongside conventional GDP, national income and final consumption. To be effective and efficient in budgetary and public debates, these need to be computed and published at the same date as conventional indicators, i.e. in relation to fiscal year deadlines.

More comprehensive national income accounting

National accounts need to take the wider issues of natural capital into account, including well-being and sustainability dimensions. The 2003 UN System of Environmental and Economic Accounting (SEEA) manual upgrade needs to be completed rapidly to include physical accounts for ecosystem stocks, degradation and services as well as valuation rules. Natural capital accounts should be developed to take the full set of ecosystem services (private or common-pool economic resources as well as public goods) into account and be published regularly.

Towards GDP of the poor

The rural poor are the most vulnerable to loss of biodiversity and ecosystem services. Appropriate policies require an understanding of this link and ways to measure the importance of such services to their incomes and livelihoods. Measuring the GDP of the poor can clarify current dependence and highlight exposure to poverty and the threats to development and achieving the MDGs due to losses of natural capital.

Summary

Chapter 3 addresses the need to measure ecosystems and biodiversity for proper stewardship of our natural capital. Section 1 introduces the key issues, underlining the predominance of GDP and economic measurement in political decisions, and argues that this needs to be complemented by other measures. Section 2 looks at useful types of measurement in the policy cycle and then in more depth at the role of biodiversity indicators and tools for measuring ecosystem services. Section 3 shows how such indicators can feed into mainstream economic aggregates: it focuses on macro and societal indicators and indices to 'measure the true wealth of nations', comparing traditional tools with equivalent indicators that take nature into account. Section 4 presents indicators and aggregate measures as an integral component of accounting systems: it explains the current System of National Accounts and discusses ways to improve systematic measurement of nature within a national framework. Section 5 considers how to better measure the social dimension by looking at 'GDP of the poor'.

1 What measurement problems do we face?

> No one would look just at a firm's revenues to assess how well it was doing. Far more relevant is the balance sheet, which shows assets and liability. That is also true for a country. (Joseph Stiglitz, 2005)[1]

Newspapers, political speeches and policy decisions have traditionally focused on GDP growth, job losses/unemployment, trade issues and financial markets. Reporting on these issues is helped by the existence of accepted, timely and aggregated data. Despite their importance, it is increasingly recognized that such issues are only part of the picture. We also need to take account of our 'ecological footprint' – to measure how human demands on natural capital stocks affect the flows of ecosystem services which contribute to human well-being at all levels.

We measure economic transactions and assets through the System of National Accounts (SNA), which provides much-used aggregated indicators such as GDP (United Nations, 1968; United Nations et al, 2003). The SNA has evolved over time and is well respected for its core purposes. However, natural capital is almost totally excluded from the SNA and its depreciation is not reflected in the macroeconomic aggregates used by policy makers or discussed in the press. This means that loss or damage to fish stocks, forests, water and air quality, species and habitats has little or no visibility in national accounting systems.

This lack of measurement and reporting undermines efforts to secure the future availability of resources. Awareness of the status of and threats to ecosystem services is relatively poor, which hampers informed public discussion on what to do, where and by whom. If we don't know what we have, how can policy ensure its effective management?

Changes in natural capital stock are important to understand because they affect the flow of goods and services from nature. Taking fisheries as an example, the catch that can be landed in a year is not just a function of effort and fleet capacity but also depends on the size of available stocks and the status of each level of the food chain. This information is increasingly understood for fish as a resource but only partly taken into account in quotas, subsidies, monitoring and enforcement. The same applies to crop genetic diversity which is critical to long-term food security.

The current emphasis on 'evidence-based policy making' is hard to meet if even basic information on natural capital stock and its changes is missing (see Section 2). TEEB aims to help policy makers by providing information and tools to measure the value of what we manage.

2 Improving measurement of biodiversity and ecosystem services

2.1 What role do indicators play?

> Indicators arise from values (we measure what we care about) and they create values (we care about what we measure). (Dana Meadows, 1998)

'Indicators'[2] produce a manageable amount of meaningful information by summarizing, focusing and condensing it (Godfrey and Todd, 2001). Good indicators should be policy relevant, scientifically sound, easily understood, practical, affordable and sensitive to relevant changes (CBD 2003; see also TEEB Foundations (2010) Chapter 3).

Considering the huge complexity of biodiversity, its benefits for human well-being and the complicated linkages between the two, it is not easy to develop a commonly agreed set of indicators. Nevertheless, this task is vital because indicators can play a decisive role in:

- helping decision makers and the public to understand status/condition and trends related to biodiversity and the ecosystem services it provides;
- assessing whether international and national policies on land use and management provide the correct response to the biodiversity decline;
- clarifying the consequences of (in)action by measuring progress and the efficiency of measures taken (e.g. does a specific instrument actually help fish stocks to recover or slow rates of deforestation?); and
- benchmarking and monitoring performance in relation to defined targets and timelines and communicating results and lessons learned.

Biodiversity and ecosystem service indicators can be useful across different sectors and at different stages of the policy cycle. They can be applied to:

- problem recognition (e.g. endangered habitats and loss of ecosystem services);
- identification of solutions (e.g. management activities for favourable conservation status);
- assessing and identifying linkages between policy options (e.g. investment in protected areas, green infrastructure);

- the implementation process (e.g. subsidy reform, payment for ecosystem services); and
- ongoing monitoring and evaluation (e.g. status and trends).

Figure 3.1 shows how indicators can be fed into the iterative policy cycle, using the European Union's Natura 2000 Network as an example.

To make full use of their potential, indicators should be part of an analysis framework that addresses functional relationships between nature and human well-being, such as the widely used DPSIR (drivers, pressures, status, impact and responses) approach (see Figure 3.2). The DPSIR framework makes it possible to characterize and measure driving forces (e.g. population growth, consumption and production patterns), pressures on biodiversity state and ecosystem functions (e.g. intensive agriculture, climate change), their impact on the delivery of ecosystem services and on human well-being and, finally, the policy response.

We specifically need indicators to measure 'tipping points' or 'critical thresholds', in other words the point at which a species, habitat or ecosystem is lost or damaged so badly that provision of an ecosystem service is compromised. Used in this way, indicators can function as an early warning system to alert policy makers and managers to the need for targeted action. Table 3.1 demonstrates how such indicators can be applied to the fisheries sector to highlight linkages between catch levels, stock resilience and possible responses. In some cases it will be very difficult to assess where

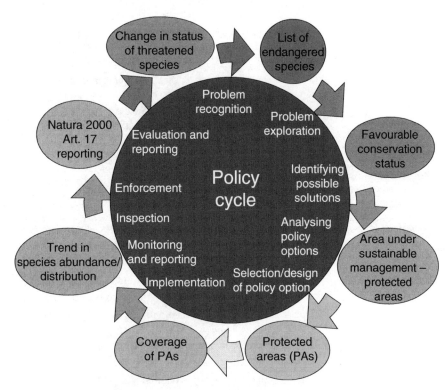

Figure 3.1 *The policy cycle*

Source: Patrick ten Brink and Sonja Gantioler, own representation

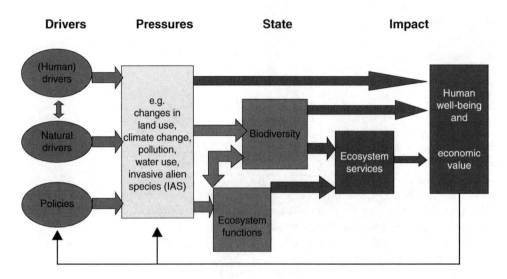

Figure 3.2 *Drivers, pressures, status, impact and responses (DPSIR)*

Source: Adapted by Chapter 3 authors from Braat and ten Brink (2008)

Table 3.1 Thresholds and responses: Examples from the fisheries sector

Thresholds	Examples
Natural critical thresholds	• Minimum population levels for stock viability (linked to fishing capacity and effort)
	• Minimum oxygen levels in water (linked to eutrophication)
	• Minimum habitat area for species survival (linked to fragmentation of rivers)
Scientifically established critical thresholds	• Scientific assessment of the above examples, and:
	• Maximum sustainable yield (MSY)
	• Maximum fleet capacity

Response	Examples
Political responses	• Commitment to sustainable use of marine ecosystems
	• Commitment to achieving good ecological status of ecosystems
	• Commitment to significantly reducing the rate of biodiversity loss
Regulatory responses	• Catch quotas, catch sizes, e.g. total allowable catch (TAC)
	• Designation of marine protected areas and no-take zones
	• Requirement for wastewater treatment, emission limit values and specific management practices
Stakeholder responses	• Support for increased protection of terrestrial/marine environment
	• Expressions of willingness to pay (WTP) for solution
	• Management practices consistent with sustainable take levels

Source: Adapted from ten Brink et al (2008)

critical thresholds are exactly; here indicators to present 'critical trends' can play a useful role (ten Brink et al, 2008).

Indicators are likely to be most effective if the data they generate are clearly presented. Maps can provide a powerful instrument to identify problems, communicate spatial information to different audiences and target policy measures, e.g. by helping to identify:

- those who create benefits associated with biodiversity and should be eligible to receive payments for ecosystem services (PES);
- those who benefit from these ecosystem services and should therefore contribute to payments to secure the future provision of such services (see Chapter 5 on PES).

However, indicators are not a panacea, whatever their field of application. They have to be used bearing in mind their limitations and risks. These include the risk of misinterpretation due to condensing of information, low data quality and limitations in clearly capturing causality. In summary:

> Determining that change has occurred does not [always] tell the story of why it has occurred. Indicators constitute only one part of the logical and substantive analysis needed ... The key to good indicators is credibility ... It is more helpful to have approximate answers to a few important questions than to have exact answers to many unimportant questions. (UNDP, 2002)

2.2 What should biodiversity indicators measure?

Current scope of measurement

We urgently need to better understand what is happening to biodiversity in order to conserve and manage ecosystem services effectively, as there is good evidence that biodiversity losses can have substantial impacts on such services. For example, the loss of functional groups of species can negatively affect overall ecosystem resilience (see Folke et al, 2004; TEEB Foundations, 2010, Chapter 2), biodiversity restoration can greatly enhance ecosystem productivity (Worm et al, 2008) and high-biodiversity regions can provide valuable ecosystem services (Turner et al, 2007).

The full range of biodiversity therefore needs to be conserved and monitored in broad terms. Concentrating on selected components that we currently consider to be of particular value is risky. Ecological processes are too complex and interlinked, and present too many unknowns for us to do this without risking grave damage to ecosystem services and wider aspects of biodiversity. 'To keep every cog and wheel', wrote Aldo Leopold, 'is the first precaution of intelligent tinkering' (Leopold, 1953).

A 'big picture' approach, going beyond the most characteristic species, is vital to keeping future options open. This is increasingly recognized. In 2002, CBD Parties made a landmark commitment to achieve a significant reduction in the current rate of biodiversity loss by 2010 at the global, regional and national levels. This target was endorsed by the World Summit on Sustainable Development (WSSD) and the United Nations General Assembly and incorporated within the Millennium Development

Goals as a contribution to poverty alleviation. Similar targets were adopted in other regions, with the EU adopting the more ambitious target of halting the decline of biodiversity in the EU by 2010 and restoring habitats and natural systems.

Setting these specific targets was a bold and important step but it is now clear that the CBD and EU targets have not been met (EC, 2008a; Butchart et al, 2010). These failures may be partly because the targets did not explicitly define the measures of biodiversity by which they could be monitored, which undermined their usefulness in terms of accountability (Mace and Baillie, 2007). More broadly, biodiversity monitoring is insufficient in most parts of the world and for most taxa groups to reliably measure progress towards targets (or key pressures or effectiveness of responses).

To address these constraints, CBD Parties agreed in 2004 on a provisional list of global headline indicators to assess global progress towards the 2010 target (Decision VII/30) and to communicate trends in biodiversity related to the CBD's three objectives. Parties subsequently distinguished between indicators considered ready for immediate testing and use, and those requiring more work (see Table 3.2). A similar and linked process of indicator development was also undertaken in the EU (EEA, 2007).

Table 3.2 Updated indicators for assessing progress towards the 2010 biodiversity target

Focal area	Indicator
Status and trends of the components of biological diversity	• **Trends in extent of selected biomes, ecosystems, and habitats** • **Trends in abundance and distribution of selected species** • **Coverage of protected areas** • **Change in status of threatened species** • **Trends in genetic diversity of domesticated animals, cultivated plants and fish species of major socio-economic importance**
Sustainable use	• **Area of forest, agricultural and aquaculture ecosystems under sustainable management** • *(Proportion of products derived from sustainable sources)* • *(Ecological footprint and related concepts)*
Threats to biodiversity	• **Nitrogen deposition** • **Trends in invasive alien species**
Ecosystem integrity and ecosystem goods and services	• **Marine Trophic Index** • **Water quality of freshwater ecosystems** • *(Trophic integrity of other ecosystems)* • **Connectivity/fragmentation of ecosystems** • *(Incidence of human-induced ecosystem failure)* • *(Health and well-being of communities who depend directly on local ecosystem goods and services)* • *(Biodiversity for food and medicine)*
Status of traditional knowledge, innovations and practices	• **Status and trends of linguistic diversity and numbers of speakers of indigenous languages** • *(Other indicators of status of indigenous and traditional knowledge)*
Status of access and benefit sharing	• *(Indicator of access and benefit sharing)*
Status of resource transfers	• **Official development assistance provided in support of the CBD** • *(Indicator of technology transfer)*

Note: Indicators considered ready for immediate testing and use are in **bold**. Indicators requiring more work are in *italic* in parentheses.

Source: CBD (2009)

Improving existing approaches

For reasons of necessity and practicality, the CBD indicators tend to rely on existing datasets rather than identifying future needs and devising appropriate monitoring programmes. This approach of adopting, adapting and supplementing existing data inevitably leads to compromises (Balmford et al, 2005; Dobson, 2005; Mace and Baillie, 2007). Data constraints mean that most indicators identified in the CBD process relate to pressures rather than the actual status of biodiversity.

More comprehensive and representative measures and monitoring are needed for biodiversity as a whole, alongside the development of specific ecosystem service (ESS) indicators (see Section 2.4 and TEEB Foundations, 2010, Chapter 3). It is particularly important that monitoring covers the three principal components of biodiversity (genes, species and ecosystems) in terms of their quantity, diversity and ecological condition.

Deficiencies in current monitoring were noted in 2009 in an International Expert Workshop on the 2010 Biodiversity Indicators and Post-2010 Indicator Development.[3] This concluded that 'the current indicator set is incomplete in a number of areas; e.g. wild genetic resources, ecosystem quality, ecosystem services, sustainable use, human well-being, access and benefit sharing and indigenous local knowledge, and both threats and responses more broadly' (UNEP-WCMC, 2009). Similar conclusions were reached in a review of the EU biodiversity indicator set (Mace and Baillie, 2007).

From a TEEB perspective, the gaps relating to genetic diversity, ecosystem quality (i.e. ecological condition) and ecosystem services are of particular concern (see also TEEB Foundations, 2010, Chapter 3). Proposals to address the first two gaps are given below: ESS indicators are considered in Section 2.4.

Monitoring genetic diversity in wild species would be especially valuable with respect to its linkage to ecosystem services (e.g. potential provision of new drugs). As genetic material is the raw material upon which natural selection and selective breeding acts, it is fundamental to enabling adaptation to environmental change (e.g. climate change) and longer-term evolution. At present, however, information on genetic diversity within species is largely confined to cultivated crops and domesticated animals and would be extremely difficult, time-consuming and costly to gather and monitor more widely.

For these reasons, its direct measurement and inclusion as a headline biodiversity indicator is currently impractical. However, a useful proxy indicator would be phylogenetic diversity (genetic diversity between species). This means the taxonomic difference between species, which can be measured as an index of the length of evolutionary pathways that connect a given set of taxa.

The main gap in the CBD indicator set that must and can be filled concerns the ecological condition of ecosystems (biotopes and habitats). Although existing indicators address some attributes of some habitats (e.g. marine habitats through the Marine Trophic Index), no habitats are adequately monitored with respect to all the key attributes that define their condition. This is a significant weakness for monitoring overall biodiversity status: many ecosystems can be degraded with little visible impact on the most frequently monitored species (e.g. birds, which are often less sensitive to habitat degradation than other species groups).

Monitoring ecosystem condition is particularly important with regard to ESS provision as it is often the most direct indicator of likely benefits. For example, some ecosystem services, such as climate regulation or water purification, tend to be related more to ecosystem processes and biomass (i.e. quantity) than to biodiversity itself. Others relate more to diversity, e.g. bioprospecting and genetic diversity (see Chapter 5).

Establishing a standardized global system for ecosystem condition indicators would be a major challenge and probably prohibitively time-consuming and not cost-effective. A possible solution would be to create a simple assessment framework that supports the establishment of national biodiversity indicators compatible with a global reporting template. This assessment framework could be established by expert working groups who would first identify a minimum set of attributes to define acceptable condition for each type of ecosystem. Generic standards could then be set for each attribute against which to judge ecosystem condition.

Under this approach, a subset of common indicators could be developed at global level, complemented by more and varied indicators at national, regional and local levels. Specific standards could be varied between countries/regions within agreed limits appropriate to local conditions, but would be published to enable scrutiny of how each country interprets the acceptable condition standards. Table 3.3 uses hypothetical examples to illustrate the concepts used to monitor protected area condition in the UK, based on generic standards within a common standards framework.[4]

Although a very large set of indicators would be used to measure the quality (condition) of all ecosystems, the results could be combined into one simple index of overall ecosystem condition if necessary, e.g. 'x per cent of ecosystems in acceptable condition'.

2.3 Towards a biodiversity monitoring framework

Integrating current approaches

Balmford et al (2005) noted that a global biodiversity monitoring system should not focus on a few aspects of biodiversity but cover a wide range of natural attributes, including habitat extent and condition. Similarly, the 2009 International Expert Workshop on Biodiversity Indicators (see Section 2.2) recommended that 'some additional measures on threats to biodiversity, status of diversity, ecosystem extent and condition, ecosystem services and policy responses should be developed in order to provide a more complete and flexible set of indicators to monitor progress towards a post-2010 target and to clearly link actions and biodiversity outcomes to benefits for people' (UNEP-WCMC, 2009).

On the basis of these observations and the discussions in Section 2.2, we suggest that the status of biodiversity could be measured according to an expanded CBD indicator set and the above framework, and then summarized into the following five headline indicators:

1   genetic diversity: taxonomic difference between species – phylogenetic trends (indicators to be developed);
2   population trends (e.g. based on a modified version of the Living Planet Index (Loh et al, 2005; Hails et al, 2008; Collen et al, 2009);

Table 3.3 Hypothetical examples of key attributes and generic limits that define acceptable condition in two habitat types

Attribute types	Temperate forest		Blanket mire	
	Attribute (and ecosystem service relevance)	Acceptable limits	Attribute (and ecosystem service relevance)	Acceptable limits
Size	Area of habitat patch (minimum area for key species and interior habitat)	>10ha	Area of habitat patch (maintenance of hydrology)	>100ha
Physical properties			Peat depth (maintenance of carbon)	>10cm
			Water level (vegetation requirements and peat protection)	<10cm below soil surface and <20cm above soil surface
Vegetation structure	Height/age classes (regeneration of habitat and underpins diverse community)	>20% mature trees, 2% to 5% seedlings		
Species composition	Native species (supports key species of biodiversity)	>90%	Sphagnum mosses (carbon sequestration depend on these species)	>20% cover
			Dwarf shrubs	<10%
Biomass	Tree density (timber production)	10–100 trees per ha	Not measurable in practice	
Productivity			Forage (for livestock and wild species)	>90% potential net primary production
Specific features	Dead wood (habitat for key species)	>10 cubic foot per ha		

3 species extinction risk trends (based on IUCN Red List criteria and the Red List index; see IUCN, 2001; Butchart et al, 2005; 2007; 2010; Baillie et al, 2008);
4 ecosystem extent (following CBD practice, with agreement on classes and definitions);
5 the condition of ecosystems according to key attributes (CBD indicators to be extended).

These five headline indicators could form the basis of SMART (specific, measurable, achievable, realistic and time-specific) targets for biodiversity status. Like their constituent indicators (e.g. for each habitat type), they are scalable and could therefore be used for targets and monitoring from local to global scales, subject to agreement on standards. Monitoring data could also be differentiated according to sample locations (e.g. to report on the condition and effectiveness of protected areas) or applied to corporate land holdings to assess their impacts on biodiversity and ecosystems.

As noted in Section 2.1, the value of indicators increases considerably if integrated within a DPSIR framework. Including indicators of drivers and pressures can warn of impending impacts and monitoring responses can help to assess the effectiveness of conservation measures: together, these facilitate the adoption of adaptive management practices (Salafsky et al, 2001). A framework that combines state indicators with indicators of related pressures and drivers would thus provide a comprehensive measurement and monitoring system to support effective management of biodiversity and many key ecosystem services at a global level. Specific ESS indicators would also be required for certain circumstances and locations (see Section 2.4 below).

Filling monitoring gaps

We already have enough species monitoring data to provide headline indicators of trends (species population, threat status) although representation of some taxa groups and regions needs to be much improved. We could also improve assessment of ecosystem coverage through better use of remote sensing data. Existing datasets could be used more effectively by developing software to create long time series and near-real-time data on land use, land cover and landscape fragmentation in collaboration with e.g. Global Monitoring for Environment and Security (GMES) and NASA.

The main gap in available data concerns ecosystem condition. This requires major investment in monitoring. Some monitoring can be done using existing and new remote sensing data (e.g. habitat fragmentation, vegetation cover, landscape diversity) but more on-the-ground sample surveys of key attributes are needed in managed ecosystems and more field data from countries with high levels of biodiversity (as is now the case in richer western countries).

With appropriate training and capacity building, such surveys could be carried out by local communities and other stakeholders, using simple but robust and consistent participatory methods (Danielsen et al, 2005; Tucker et al, 2005). This type of monitoring approach would also engage local people in biodiversity issues and provide employment benefits. It is essential that indicator development support local and national needs as much as the top-down needs of international institutions.

Biodiversity monitoring is currently inadequate mainly because funding is insufficient. Although creating a comprehensive biodiversity monitoring framework would require significant resources, this would almost certainly be a small fraction of the value of the ecosystem services currently lost through ineffective monitoring and management. Increasing funding for biodiversity monitoring would be highly cost-effective.

Funding improved monitoring

Responsibility for and funding of monitoring and measurement is not currently shared with those who use and benefit from biodiversity or with those who damage it. A significant proportion of monitoring costs are met by NGOs and their volunteers, or from public sources. A strong case can be made for using approaches based on the polluter pays principle to improve monitoring of biodiversity pressures and state.

Shifting more responsibility for monitoring to the private sector and/or introducing cost recovery for inspectorates' monitoring activities, could reduce the cost burden on public authorities. There is also potential for collaboration on monitoring between business and NGOs (see TEEB in Business, 2011).

Private sector impacts on biodiversity generally need to be better monitored and reported. Indicators for this purpose have in fact been developed but tend to be too general and inconsistently used to be of great value. We need to agree on approaches and standards that provide more meaningful and robust indicators of biodiversity impacts and are linked to SMART business targets (e.g. no net loss of biodiversity). Top-down generic indicators need to be completed by bottom-up approaches where local stakeholders report on impacts of relevance to them.

In May 2010, the CBD's Subsidiary Body on Scientific, Technical and Technological Advice (SBSTTA) considered monitoring of biodiversity targets in the context of the CBD's proposed post-2010 mission, strategic goals and targets. A discussion note[5] prior to this meeting (SBSTTA-14) noted many of the above-mentioned recommendations for setting and monitoring biodiversity targets. These included the need to develop SMART targets within a DPSIR or equivalent framework; to use targets focused on biodiversity outcomes (e.g. ecosystem extent and condition), enabling measures and ecosystem services; and to increase the biodiversity monitoring capacity of many countries. However, the recommendations adopted by the SBSTTA[6] were less ambitious and although generally supportive of progress, deferred further considerations to an Ad Hoc Technical Expert Group (AHTEG).

Furthermore, the proposed CBD strategic goals and targets discussed at SBSTTA-14 mainly focus on pressures and responses,[7] which means that the proposed indicators have a similar focus and contain few measures on biodiversity status. They do include further indicators on genetic components (e.g. genetic diversity of domesticated animals, cultivated crops and fish of major socio-economic importance) and ecosystem services but there seems to be no proposal for developing a more comprehensive framework for monitoring ecosystem condition. This gap therefore remains a priority issue that needs to be further addressed.

2.4 Measuring ecosystem services

Policy makers need information from ecosystem service measurement to support integrated decision making that responds to environmental, social and economic needs. If wisely used and well researched, ESS indicators can reveal the impacts of biodiversity and ecosystem loss/degradation on livelihoods and the economy. Moving from measurement of biophysical capacities to measurement of benefit flows and economic values of ecosystem services can provide an effective tool that takes the full value of natural capital into account.

State of play on ecosystem service indicators

Ecosystem service indicators make it possible to describe the flow of benefits provided by biodiversity. We can use them to better measure and communicate the impacts that change an ecosystem's capacity to provide services for human well-being and development. Within a DPSIR framework (see Figure 3.2 above), they can complement other indicators by focusing on the social impact of natural capital loss.

Compared to 'traditional' biodiversity indicators, ecosystem service indicators are a relatively new tool. The publication of the Millennium Ecosystem Assessment (MA, 2005) brought attention to ecosystem services in the political arena. This shift led to increased development and use of related indicators, often derived from other sectors (e.g. timber production and the forestry sector) and centred on provisioning services. The MA's final report in 2005 noted that 'there are at this time no widely accepted indicators to measure trends in supporting, regulating or cultural ecosystem services, much less indicators that measure the effect of changes in these services on human well-being' (MA, 2005).

This statement remains largely valid. The main reason is the complexity of functional relationships between ecosystem components and how they affect the provision of services, as well as the multidimensional character of these services. It is therefore essential to continue efforts to develop reliable indicators for key regulating, supporting and cultural services. Current technical difficulties largely reflect the relatively recent focus on these services. They are not a reason to stop exploring and promoting the application of existing indicators, which are already useful for policy discussions, and instrument choice and design.

Valuing what ecosystem service indicators measure

Table 3.4 provides a non-exhaustive first set of ecosystem service indicators, based on the MA framework, which are already in use or being developed. It includes a range of quantitative and some qualitative indicators.

For some services and some audiences, economic valuation is essential as quantitative and qualitative information is not considered sufficient. However, the absence of monetary values for regulating services (often non-marketed services) can create a bias towards provisioning services (usually captured by market prices) when considering potential trade-offs. Ways to monetize ecosystem service indicators are explored in Chapter 4.

Each type of information is important. Although qualitative indicators do not quantify and monetize benefits arising from ecosystem services, they are an important tool to underpin quantitative and monetary information and help to close gaps where no such information exists. It is possible to develop widely recognized qualitative indicators if based on sound judgement, experience and knowledge. This is particularly true for supporting services which, in the MA framework, include all natural processes that maintain other ecosystem services (e.g. nutrient cycling, soil formation). These have not been listed in Table 3.4 since there are still significant gaps in knowledge regarding the applicability of related indicators.

Applying ecosystem service indicators at the policy level

Some of the few existing and agreed indicators for regulating services have been developed in the environment sector (e.g. climate change and carbon sequestration/ storage rates, natural flood protection, see Box 3.1). Extending their application will more effectively link biodiversity with other environmental policy areas and instruments (e.g. REDD-plus, flood risk management) to improve synergies and communication, and facilitate potential trade-offs between stakeholders (e.g. companies, institutions, civil society, etc.).

Table 3.4 Examples of ecosystem service indicators

Ecosystem service	Ecosystem service indicator
Provisioning services	
Food Sustainably produced/harvested crops, fruit, wild berries, fungi, nuts, livestock, semi-domestic animals, game, fish and other aquatic resources	• Crop production from sustainable [organic] sources in tonnes and/or hectares • Livestock from sustainable [organic] sources in tonnes and/or hectares • Fish production from sustainable [organic] sources in tonnes live weight (e.g. proportion of fish stocks caught within safe biological limits) • Number of wild species used as food • Wild animal/plant production from sustainable sources in tonnes
Water quantity	• Total freshwater resources in million m^3
Raw materials Sustainably produced/harvested wool, skins, leather, plant fibre (cotton, straw, etc.), timber, cork, etc.; and sustainably produced/harvested firewood, biomass, etc.	• Forest growing stock, increment and fallings • Industrial roundwood in million m^3 from natural and/or sustainable managed forests • Pulp and paper production in million tonnes from natural and/or sustainable managed forests • Cotton production from sustainable [organic] resources in tonnes and/or hectares • Forest biomass for bioenergy in million tonnes of oil equivalent (Mtoe) from different resources (e.g. wood, residues) from natural and/or sustainable managed forests
Natural medicines: biochemicals and pharmaceuticals Sustainably produced/harvested medical natural products (flowers, roots, leaves, seeds, sap, animal products, etc.); ingredients/components of biochemical or pharmaceutical products	• Number of species from which natural medicines have been derived • Number of drugs using natural compounds
Ornamental resources Sustainably produced/harvested ornamental wild plants, wood for handcraft, seashells, etc.	• Number of species used for handcraft work • Amount of ornamental plant species used for gardening from sustainable sources
Genetic/species diversity maintenance Protection of local and endemic breeds and varieties, maintenance of game species gene pool, etc.	• Number of crop varieties for production • Livestock breed variety • Number of fish varieties for production
Regulating services	
Air quality regulation	• Atmospheric cleansing capacity in tonnes of pollutants removed per hectare
Climate/climate change regulation Carbon sequestration, maintaining and controlling temperature and precipitation	• Total amount of carbon sequestered/stored = sequestration/storage capacity per hectare × total area (Gt CO_2)
Moderation of extreme events Avalanche control, storm damage control, fire regulation (i.e. preventing fires and regulating fire intensity)	• Trends in number of damaging natural disasters • Probability of incident

Table 3.4 Examples of ecosystem service indicators (*Cont'd*)

Ecosystem service	Ecosystem service indicator
Water regulation Regulating surface water run-off, aquifer recharge, etc.	• Infiltration capacity/rate of an ecosystem (e.g. amount of water/surface area) – volume through unit area/per time • Soil water storage capacity in mm/m • Floodplain water storage capacity in mm/m
Water purification and waste management Decomposition/capture of nutrients and contaminants, prevention of eutrophication of water bodies, etc.	• Removal of nutrients by wetlands (tonnes or percentage) • Water quality in aquatic ecosystems (sediment, turbidity, phosphorus, nutrients, etc.)
Erosion control Maintenance of nutrients and soil cover and preventing negative effects of erosion (e.g. impoverishing of soil, increased sedimentation of water bodies)	• Soil erosion rate by land-use type
Pollination Maintenance of natural pollinators and seed dispersal agents (e.g. birds and mammals)	• Abundance and species richness of wild pollinators • Range of wild pollinators (e.g. in km, regular/aggregated/random, per species)
Biological control Maintenance of natural enemies of plant and animal pests, regulating the populations of plant and animal disease vectors, etc.	• Abundance and species richness of biological control agents (e.g. predators, insects, etc.) • Range of biological control agents (e.g. in km, regular/aggregated/random, per species)
Disease regulation of human health Regulation of vectors for pathogens	• Changes in disease burden as a result of changing ecosystems
Cultural and social services	
Landscape and amenity values Amenity of the ecosystem, cultural diversity and identity, spiritual values, cultural heritage values, etc.	• Changes in the number of residents • Changes in the number of visitors to a site to enjoy its amenity services • Number of products the branding of which relates to cultural identity
Ecotourism and recreation Hiking, camping, nature walks, jogging, skiing, canoeing, rafting, recreational fishing, animal watching, etc.	• Number of visitors to protected sites per year • Amount of nature tourism
Cultural values and inspirational services, e.g. education, art and research	• Total number of visits to sites, specifically related to education or cultural reasons • Total number of educational excursions at a site • Number of TV programmes, studies, books, etc. featuring sites and the surrounding area

Sources: Built on, among others, MA (2005); Balmford et al (2008); Kettunen et al (2009); TEEB Foundations (2010)

Ecosystem service indicators can also support more efficient integration of biodiversity considerations into other sector policies (e.g. agriculture, fisheries, forestry, energy, land-use planning). They can link biodiversity, economic and social indicators and measure how different sectors could be affected by impacts on capacity

Box 3.1 Examples of ESS indicators across environmental policy areas

Climate change: Carbon sequestration/storage rates

Total amount of carbon sequestered/stored in Gt CO_2 equivalent = sequestration capacity/storage per hectare × total area of ecosystem

Tropical forests have an annual global sequestration rate of around 1.3Gt of carbon (about 15 per cent of total carbon emissions resulting from human activities). It is estimated that tropical/subtropical forests together store nearly 550Gt of carbon, the largest amount across all biomes, which could be increased through reforestation and halting forest degradation (Lewis et al, 2009; Trumper et al, 2009). The potential of such carbon storage/sequestration measures to support often low-cost mitigation of climate change (Stern, 2006; IPCC, 2007; Eliasch, 2008) has led to significant political momentum and policy tools building on this indicator. These include EU support for a Global Forest Carbon Mechanism to achieve the objective of halting global forest cover loss by 2030 (see EC, 2008b) and international support under the UNFCCC for the REDD-plus mechanism (Reducing Emissions from Deforestation and Forest Degradation in developing countries) (see Chapter 5).

Urban air quality: Atmospheric cleansing capacity

Tonnes of particulates removed per hectare of ecosystem

Urban trees in the Philadelphia region of the US were found to have removed over 1000 tons of air pollutants from the atmosphere in 1994 (study by Nowak et al in Powe and Willis (2002) and references within), and in the Chicago region trees were found to remove around 5500 tonnes of air pollutants per year (McPherson et al, 1997). In the UK as a whole, trees can be seen to absorb large quantities of pollutants; between 0.4 and 0.6 million tonnes of PM_{10} (particulate matter) and 0.7 and 1.2 million tonnes of SO_2 are absorbed every year (Powe and Willis, 2002).

Urban planning can leverage this capacity of green infrastructure to achieve air quality standards. Values can be attached through the avoided morbidity and mortality impacts that result from its contribution to reduced air pollution levels (see TEEB in Local Policy, 2011).

Clean drinking water: Contribution of natural forests to water quality

Amount/percentage of nutrients removed; levels of sediment, turbidity, phosphorus, etc.

In Germany, an organic drink manufacturer (Bionade Corporation) initiated a project with the NGO Trinkwasserwald e.V. to create 130 hectares of 'drinking water forests' linked to their capacity to filter and clean water. Each hectare of conifer monoculture converted into deciduous broad-leaved forest is estimated to generate 800,000 litre/year for a one-off conversion cost of €6800/hectare, under 20-year contracts between the NGO and forest owners (Greiber et al, 2009; see also Chapter 5).

to provide ecosystem services, thus contributing to more 'joined-up thinking' and policy integration (see Box 3.2).

These examples show how sector policies have or could put ecosystem services to the top of their agenda. It is crucial to be aware of the risks of trade-offs between different ecosystem services but also to take opportunities to create synergies, e.g. reforestation to directly maintain benefits or investment in green infrastructure to avoid forest degradation.

Although existing policies do not mandate 'no net loss' of ecosystem services at regional or national level, or indeed corporate level (with some project exceptions), such targets could conceivably be adopted in the future (see Chapter 7 for examples

---

Box 3.2 Examples of ESS indicators across sector policies

Agriculture: Criteria linked to abundance, species richness and range of wild pollinators

The indicator can be used to identify what proportion of production depends on wild pollinators:

- The diversity and activity of wild pollinators (e.g. insects, mammals) can vary according to the distance between natural forest and cultivated land. For coffee, Ricketts et al (2004) show that sites near the forest were visited by a greater diversity of bee species, more frequently and had more pollen deposited than sites further away. Above 1km from the forest, wild pollination services became insufficient and about 20 per cent less coffee was produced.
- The global economic value of pollination services provided by insects (mainly bees) was calculated at (153 billion in 2005 for the world's main food crops (Gallai et al, 2009). This figure is equivalent to 9.5 per cent of the total value of world agricultural food production (Gallai et al, 2009). In the US, wild pollinators are estimated to account for about US$3 billion of annual fruit and vegetable production (Losey and Vaughan, 2006).
- This type of indicator makes it possible to link agri-environment payments to the capacity of farmland to provide pollination services and measure the effectiveness of management action (see Chapter 6 on reforming subsidies to agriculture to support extensive farming).

Health: Atmospheric cleansing capacity related to illness/mortality rate

Tonnes of particulates removed per hectare of forest

The UK study on air cleansing capacity (see Box 3.1) estimated the impact of higher air quality in terms of net health effects at 65 to 89 cases of avoided early mortality and 45 to 62 fewer hospital admissions per year. The estimated net reduction in costs ranged between £0.2 million and £11.2 million. Hewitt (2002) also found that doubling the number of trees in the West Midlands would reduce excess deaths due to particles in the air by up to 140 per year (Powe and Willis (2002) and references within). One measure to meet urban air quality and health standards (e.g. set by the World Health Organization) could include protected area investments to secure provision of tree cover (see Chapter 8).

of their current use at project level and also TEEB in Business (2011) for the indicators for business integration). Clearly defined policy goals will be essential to ensure the effectiveness of new indicators as an integration tool. A widely recognized and robust set of indicators on ecosystem quality and capacity to provide services will be necessary to measure progress towards targets and the efficiency of approaches taken, and to improve instrument design and credibility (quantify baselines, set conditions and performance indicators for additionality, assessment and verifiability) (see Chapter 5 on the importance of robust indicators for PES schemes).

A small executive set of headline indicators would arguably be sufficient for high-level target setting and communication by policy makers, politicians, the press and business, supported by wider sets for measurement and monitoring. Initiatives such as *Streamlining European 2010 Biodiversity Indicators* (EEA, 2009) and the CBD global headline indicators (see Table 3.2 above) already include a limited number of indicators for ecosystem capacity to provide services and goods (e.g. water quality of freshwater ecosystems) and for sustainable use of provisioning services (e.g. ecological footprint, see Box 3.3). These provide a better and more consistent basis to support decision makers than was the case only five years ago.

Such indicators could also be included in corporate reporting standards (e.g. Global Reporting Initiative) to communicate the impacts of lost services on company performance (e.g. forestry/paper industry, water quality/beverage industry) and the impacts of companies on ecosystem service provision (e.g. metals and mining) (see further TEEB in Business, 2011).

Even if headline indicators may be enough for high-level purposes, there is also value in having detailed ESS indicators for certain policy instruments. These include policy

---

Box 3.3 Using the 'ecological footprint' indicator in policy: Some examples

Ecological footprint analysis compares human demand on nature with the biosphere's ability to generate resources and provide services (see Chapter 2). It measures how much biologically productive land and water an individual, city, country, region or planet requires to produce the resources it consumes and to absorb the waste it generates.

SEBI 2010 includes the ecological footprint in its set of 26 indicators. The latest SEBI 2010 review suggests that natural resource use and waste generation in Europe is running at more than double the continent's natural capacity. This ecological deficit means that Europe cannot sustainably meet its consumption demands from within its own borders. EU-27 has a footprint of 4.7 global hectares per person, twice the size of its biocapacity.

The European Commission is actively considering how and where to integrate footprint measurement, notably as regards its impact outside EU territory. An analysis of the potential to use the footprint and related assessment tools in the EU Thematic Strategy on the Sustainable Use of Natural Resources has been carried out.

South Australia uses the ecological footprint as a regional target and aims to reduce its footprint by 30 per cent by 2050.

Sources: South Australia's Strategic Plan (2007); Ecologic et al (2008); EC (2009); Schutyser and Condé (2009); SEBI (2010)

assessments, environmental impact assessments (EIAs) and national accounting as well as procedures to analyse companies' economic dependency and impacts on ecosystem services through materiality or life cycle assessments (LCAs; see TEEB Foundations (2010) for more on LCA). Used in such assessments, indicators help us to answer questions on the economic, social and environmental consequences of different policy or planning options affecting biodiversity (see Chapter 4). They can also be integrated into Systems of National Accounts (SNA) through the development of satellite accounts (see Box 3.4 and, for details of national accounting, Sections 3 and 4 below).

Box 3.4 Using 'final ecosystem services' (FES) indicators in national accounting

Switzerland commissioned a feasibility study on the use of the FES approach, developed by Boyd and Banzhaf (2007), for its national income accounting. FES are defined as components of nature that are directly enjoyable, consumable or usable to yield human well-being. The schematic account matrix distinguishes between FES indicators attributable to four main benefit categories: health, safety, natural diversity and economic benefits. The study analyses in more detail the application of accounting indicators in the category 'health' and for the benefit of 'undisturbed sleep' (see example below) through natural sound absorption by and in nature.

Schematic account matrix for final ecosystem services (FES)

Product group	Benefit		Ecosystem services			Relevant interim products/ processes/ functions
Benefit category	Type of benefit	Description	Description	Unit		
Differentiation between:	Active benefit value	Benefit 1	Ecosystem Service 1	#person/year		
Health	Passive benefit value		Ecosystem Service 2	#person/year		
Safety						
Natural diversity	Existence value			#person/year		
Economic benefits		Benefit 2				
Example: Health	Passive benefit value	Undisturbed sleep	Nocturnal noise level below limit values (near residence)	#person/year without exceedance of limit values in dB(A) between 10.00pm and 6.00am		Natural sound absorbers

Source: Ott and Staub (2009)

Challenges and next steps

The readiness of ESS indicators for use depends on data availability, the capacity to summarize characteristics at multiple spatial and temporal scales and the communication of the results to non-technical policy makers (Layke, 2009).

There are more, and better, indicators available for provisioning services as these are incorporated into marketed commodities (e.g. wood for timber and fuel). The flow of benefits from regulating and cultural services is not as visible or easily measurable: many non-market services are therefore enjoyed for free. Proxy indicators can help us estimate associated benefits by referring to the capacity of an ecosystem to provide them, but these are only a short-term solution. We need to improve regulating and cultural service indicators in order to integrate the value of ESS more fully in our decision making (Layke, 2009).

ESS indicators need to take account of the sustainability of provisioning and other services over time to ensure that the long-term benefit flow of services is measured. Over-exploitation of benefits from provisioning services (e.g. fish stocks), cultural services (e.g. tourism) and regulating services (e.g. reforestation for carbon capture) could lead to their depletion and reduced social trade-offs. Relevant indicators should therefore take sustainable productivity into account, which calls for a clear definition of what 'sustainability' actually means with regard to those services.

It is crucial to develop a baseline to determine where critical thresholds (e.g. safe biological limits, critical loads) and alternative pathways under different policy scenarios may lie. However, setting such thresholds is hampered by ignorance, uncertainties and risks associated with ecological systems. Safe minimum standards may be a way to overcome these challenges (see TEEB Foundations, 2010, Chapter 5).

Not all ESS indicators can be measured in quantitative terms or converted to monetary values: there is a risk that policy makers focus more on those for which quantifiable information is available. As stated in TEEB Foundations (2010) Chapter 3, 'reliance on existing measures will in all likelihood capture the value of only a few species and ecosystems relevant to food and fibre production, and will miss out the role of biodiversity and ecosystems in supporting the full range of benefits, as well as their resilience into the future'. To avoid creating a policy bias by focusing on a subset of indicators high on the political or corporate agenda, efforts to find complementary non-quantified indicators should be increased.

In parallel, ESS valuations that focus on a single service need to be systematically cross-checked with broader measurements to assess ecosystem capacity to maintain delivery of the full range of services. This capacity depends on ecosystem robustness, integrity and resilience, not on asset value. Economic benefits from ESS exploitation need to be compared to the additional costs required to maintain ecosystem capital in the broadest sense (i.e. to mitigate overall degradation), rather than a narrow measurement of loss of benefits resulting from natural resource depletion.

To better identify ESS beneficiaries and those who guarantee ESS provision to society, research should focus on the link between biodiversity and ecosystem condition and ESS provision. This is particularly acute for indicators on regulating and cultural services: as noted, data are often insufficient and indicators inadequate to characterize the diversity and complexity of the benefits they provide (Layke, 2009).

TEEB Foundations (2010) Chapter 3 discusses in more detail the lessons learned from initial application of existing indicators and highlights opportunities and constraints arising from their use.

Improving measurement can be a long process but it is of fundamental importance to arrive at good solutions. In the long term, measurement is often a good investment and can be a cost-effective part of the answer – spotting risks early and addressing them efficiently can help avoid much higher damage costs later on. ESS indicators are not an isolated part of measurement but can effectively complement macroeconomic and social indicators to further describe interactions between nature and society. Ways to move to more sustainable measurement of the wealth of nations and well-being of societies are discussed in Sections 3.1 and 3.2 respectively.

3 'Greening' our macroeconomic and societal indicators

On GDP and well-being:

The welfare of a nation can scarcely be inferred from a measurement of national income ... Distinctions must be kept in mind between quantity and quality of growth, between its costs and return, and between the short and the long-term. Goals for more growth should specify more growth of what and for what. (Simon Kuznets, principle architect of the GDP concept 1934)

On GDP and social equity:

Progress measured by a single measuring rod, the GNP, has contributed significantly to exacerbate the inequalities of income distribution. (Robert McNamara, President of the World Bank 1973)

On GDP and natural capital:

A country could exhaust its mineral resources, cut down its forests, erode its soils, pollute its aquifers, and hunt its wildlife to extinction, but measured income would not be affected as these assets disappeared. (Robert Repetto et al, 1989)

On GDP and decision making:

Choices between promoting GDP and protecting the environment may be false choices, once environmental degradation is appropriately included in our measurement of economic performance. (Stiglitz–Sen–Fitousi Report on the Measurement of Economic Performance and Social Progress, Stiglitz et al, 2009)

3.1 Traditional approaches to measuring wealth and well-being

'Traditional' indicators to measure countries' economic performance include GDP, national income, final consumption, gross fixed capital formation (GFCF), net savings, international trade balance, international balance of payments, inflation, national debt and savings rates. On the social side, commonly used indicators relate to unemployment, literacy, life expectancy and income inequality. A useful combined indicator that straddles more than one domain is the Human Development Index (HDI).

These conventional aggregates are an integral part of national accounting systems (see Section 4) but they only tell part of the story as they do not systematically cover the loss of biodiversity. Biodiversity and ESS indicators are already a step in the right direction towards complementing them and, as Section 2 showed, they are increasing in number. Many argue that there are now too many separate tools to attract anything like as much public, press and political attention as the consolidated traditional economic indicators. CO_2 indicators may prove an exception but, while helpful, do not directly address ecosystems and biodiversity.

We can illustrate the slow process of change through the example of trade deficits, e.g. where imports exceed exports. These feature in the press every week yet there is little mention of green trade deficits, i.e. biodiversity impacts related to imports and exports of goods and services. Ecological footprint analysis (see Box 3.3 above) can help to fill this gap by identifying creditor and debtor nations from a biodiversity perspective. 'Water footprints' can also offer useful information to consumers (e.g. when bananas are imported, so are the water and the nutrients from the soil).

The most developed countries, in particular, are significant environmental debtor nations whereas most developing countries are creditor nations. This debt/credit is not reflected in traditional measurement and decision making or market signals, although some countries have recognized that continued footprint growth cannot go on for ever and are using the footprint as a policy target to reduce their environmental impacts or increase resource efficiency.

3.2 Tools for more sustainable measurement

For many economic terms used in everyday policy making, there are already corresponding concepts in use that do refer to nature.

Economic capital, natural capital

The concept of capital derives from economics: capital stocks (assets) provide a flow of goods and services which contribute to human well-being. The concept is traditionally equated with manufactured goods but this man-made capital is only part of the picture. We can also talk of 'human capital', 'social capital' and 'natural capital' – the stock of natural resources from which ecosystem services flow (see Box 3.5). While some prefer not to liken nature to natural capital, the term can help communicate the importance of nature in the economic context (see also Chapter 1, Figure 1.6).

Infrastructure and green infrastructure

Traditional infrastructure spending focused on roads, rail, schools, etc., but there is now increasing appreciation of the importance of investing in 'green infrastructure': protected area networks (Chapter 8), watersheds that provide water purification and provisioning services (Chapters 5 and 9), restoration of watercourse to provide habitat (see Box 4.2 for an example) and increase spatial connectivity between different nature areas, city gardens that provide amenities (see TEEB in Local Policy, 2011) and, in some countries, green roof programmes to help biodiversity and adaptation to climate change.

Box 3.5 Four types of capital[8]

Manufactured capital

Man-made capital includes produced assets that are used to produce other goods and services, such as machines, tools, buildings and infrastructure. This category can also include financial capital.

Natural capital

In addition to natural resources like timber, water, and energy and mineral reserves, this includes natural assets that are not easy to value monetarily (e.g. species diversity, endangered species, ecosystems that perform ecological services like air and water filtration) and can be considered as the components of nature linked directly or indirectly with human welfare. Forests, agricultural land and soil, grasslands, wetlands, rivers and coral reefs are examples of natural capital.

Human capital

This generally refers to the health, well-being and productive potential of individual people and includes mental and physical health, education, motivation and work skills. These elements not only contribute to a happy, healthy society but also improve the opportunities for economic development through a productive workforce.

Social capital

Like human capital, this is related to human well-being but on a societal rather than individual level. It consists of the social networks that support an efficient, cohesive society and facilitate social and intellectual interactions among its members. Social capital refers to those stocks of social trust, norms and networks that people can draw upon to solve common problems and create social cohesion, e.g. neighbourhood associations, civic organizations and cooperatives. The political and legal structures that promote political stability, democracy, government efficiency and social justice (all of which are good for productivity as well as being desirable in themselves) are also part of social capital.

Source: GHK et al (2005) building on Ekins (1992)

Man-made capital depreciates, natural capital 'appreciates'

Artificial infrastructure, like flood protection barriers and water treatment plants, degrades and requires maintenance with associated costs. Natural infrastructure can often do its own maintenance, e.g. mangroves for coastal flood protection. Proactive investment in natural capital formation is an implicit theme running through programmes for afforestation, investment in watersheds, forest management, restoration and investment in protected areas (see Chapters 5, 8 and 9).

Gross fixed capital formation (GFCF) and natural capital formation

Most governments regularly monitor the GFCF level (i.e. investment in infrastructure) but rarely the level of natural capital formation. Elements that are included give a very incomplete picture of natural capital. For example, when a forest is felled to convert to agricultural use, current SNA guidelines suggest recording a positive GFCF in an agriculture land asset up to the amount of the felling works.[9]

National net savings, 'genuine' savings

Countries measure how much money is saved on average as the result of all positive and negative economic transactions. Under the current SNA, economic revenue from rent on natural capital is considered as part of net savings even though part of these receipts should be reinvested to maintain sustainable income flow from natural capital (just as companies do with regard to depreciation of other types of capital).

The World Bank's 'adjusted net or genuine savings' indicators measure a 'truer' level of saving in a country by looking not just at economic growth but also taking into account the depreciation of produced capital, investments in human capital (as measured by education expenditures), depletion of minerals, energy, forests and damage from local and global air pollutants (World Bank, 2006). However, these indicators should also include the degradation of ecosystem capital which relates to maintenance of all ecological functions (instead of being limited to depletion which only concerns maintenance of income from forest exploitation).

GDP vs. national income that takes nature into account

GDP (the sum of sectors' value added) measures economic transactions during an accounting period but not a country's welfare, well-being or wealth. Because these transactions are the basis for taxation and closely correlated to employment, GDP has been overplayed in macroeconomic decisions and is sometimes misinterpreted as a welfare indicator by journalists and many economists. These limitations and flaws in GDP use have been addressed by the international Commission on the Measurement of Economic Performance and Social Progress (see Box 3.6 and Section 5).

Correcting the prices for consumption, imports and exports

Some people talk of 'greening GDP' when they actually mean 'greening the economy' (reducing impacts on nature). One way to do this is to change market signals to introduce pricing that takes nature into account (e.g. full cost recovery charges, resource costing, subsidy reform, application of the polluter pays principle through taxes, liability and regulation). The greening of markets and supply chains (e.g. via green public procurement) can also be a key step forward (see Chapters 5 to 7).

National accounts currently record household final consumption as well as imports and exports at purchasers' prices. These prices cover production/distribution costs (intermediate consumption, labour, taxes and financial costs), profit and compensation for fixed capital depreciation from wear and tear. However, national accounts do not record an element for depreciation of ecosystem capital, which means that purchasers' prices are underestimated where commodities are obtained by damaging ecosystems (see Box 3.7).

Box 3.6 The Stiglitz–Sen–Fitoussi Commission's critique of GDP

The Commission has stressed the need to pay more attention to other existing aggregates, e.g. national income and households' consumption, which might have more direct implications for people's well-being than economic production. It first considered the properties of the national income aggregate (derived from GDP), which aims to measure how much money we can dispose of freely for our own expenditures. Under the current system:

- where part of GDP is regularly sent abroad – e.g. to pay revenue to a foreign shareholder or to families of immigrant workers – GDP is adjusted for these revenue transfers with the rest of the world to produce the so-called 'gross national income';
- a second adjustment is made to account for the normal degradation of productive capital and the need to repair or replace it, to produce a net national income (national income).

The Commission examined which elements of this income are not disposable (e.g. income tax for the households sector) and which other imputations should be considered, e.g. non-market services supplied by the government sector. It proposed the compilation of a net disposable national income, mostly targeted at improving households' well-being.

If we take a step further to take account of the consumption of natural capital, we can propose the calculation of an adjusted net disposable national income. Being linked to production processes, this imputation will mostly draw upon business accounts.

Source: Building on Stiglitz et al (2009)

Box 3.7 Marginal costs of timber production in China

From 1949 to 1981 China logged some 75 million hectares, 92 per cent of which were natural rather than plantation forests. Total forest ecosystem services lost through deforestation in China between 1950 and 1998 were estimated at up to US$12 billion/year, including climate regulation, timber and fuel supply, agriculture productivity, water regulation, nutrient cycling, soil conservation and flood prevention. About 64 per cent of this loss was linked to supplying timber to the construction and materials sector.

The value of services lost due to timber production may be expressed in terms of the market price of timber (see TEEB in Business, 2011). This suggests that the 'true' marginal cost of timber production may have been almost three times greater than the prevailing market price. Following dramatic floods linked to deforestation in 1998, the Chinese government introduced a logging ban which led to increased imports of timber from other countries, suggesting that the environmental costs of timber consumption have been shifted at least in part to non-Chinese forests.

Source: TEEB in Business (2011) building on CIFOR (2005)

When policy makers set formal targets to maintain biodiversity and ecosystem capacity in a good state, the implicit value of ecosystem degradation potentially attached to each commodity unit needs to be considered as a concealed negative transfer to future generations and/or from suppliers to consumers. Measuring and valuing these concealed transfers is important to assess the reality of each country's economic performance. It sheds light on the sustainability of consumption patterns and on distributional effects resulting from distorted international trade.

Consumers keen to make responsible choices can be helped through the systematic implementation of product traceability (coming on stream for fair trade and organic products, see Chapter 5) and the provision of the full price (including information on the adverse environmental impacts which accrued for the production of a good, e.g. CO_2 labelling for products) alongside the market price. This can help protect sustainably managed industries against arguably unfair competition from competitors who do not pay for ecosystem degradation and thus receive an implicit subsidy (see Chapters 6 on subsidies and 7 on full cost recovery and polluter pays principle). This type of measurement approach would also help in policy design and lead to future GDP statistics being less out of step with nature.

4 Integrating ecosystems into national income accounting

4.1 The rationale for ecosystem accounting

Ecosystems are badly – and even equivocally – recorded in national accounts. They usually feature only as an economic resource able to generate monetary benefit for their owners (i.e. in proportion to private gain). Ecosystem services supporting production are treated as externalities, with free amenities and regulating services absent from the picture.

The TEEB project has always acknowledged accounting as an essential component because the protection of public goods and maintenance of ecosystem services goes to the heart of sustainable development and how it can accommodate economic growth. Proper accounting is necessary to support informed decisions. The indicators discussed in Sections 2 and 3 above need to feed directly into such accounting systems.

At present, accounts only cover the actual value of ecosystem services if they are incorporated into product prices or when the services are (at risk of being) lost and the cost of alternatives becomes apparent. When their market price is zero, services are in fact invisible and can be appropriated for production or degraded without record. These free services therefore need to be measured, valued and added to existing measures such as GDP to provide more inclusive aggregates to guide decisions by policy makers, businesses and consumers.

The need for change is widely acknowledged, not just in TEEB but also in processes like 'Beyond GDP'[10], the OECD's 'Global Project on Measuring the Progress of Societies'[11] and the Stiglitz–Sen–Fitoussi Commission (see Box 3.6 above). Economic commentators also recognize its importance, given the visibly unsustainable externalities from over-consumption of ecosystem services. Population growth and chaotic economic development in general also highlight the need to account for the real value of what we produce and consume.

Today's unparalleled multiple systemic crises – economic/financial, climate/energy and ecosystems/biodiversity – have jointly spawned crises of governance and trust.

Citizens, business and government are increasingly concerned about accumulating debts, the exposure of concealed debts and the ability of huge untested rescue packages to work. Social stability could be jeopardized. These crises share common features related to shortcomings in society's accounting mechanisms: over-destruction of financial, human and natural capital, over-consumption fuelled by debt, and the shifting of risks from the strongest to the weakest (the ever-increasing North–South debt) or to future generations. Underlying factors include:

- lack of transparency in consumer transactions of financial, food, fibre and energy products;
- misleading market price signals did not cover all costs and risks;
- neglect of public goods such as the built and natural infrastructure, security, cooperation, equity, nature, clean air and water.

Early warning signals could have been recognized before these crises: financial transactions accounting for more than 90 per cent of the world's total transactions; two-digit profit rates raised as an accounting standard for companies; pension liabilities putting pressure on public budgets/debts (which will increase markedly along with our ageing populations); the average very low progress towards the Millennium Development Goals (MDGs); increases in malnutrition in many countries; melting of ice caps and glaciers; and a rate of ecosystem degradation and species extinction unprecedented in the planet's history.

These crises highlight the need for governance to maintain all types of capital, meet the needs of today's and future generations and enhance citizen participation. Fair, transparent and robust accounts are an important support for any such governance model:

- robustness relates to the completeness of recording and the elimination of double counting: such properties are essential when calculating the true results of economic activity (profit of companies, taxable revenue of households or the nation's product, income and savings);
- fairness relates to distributional equity considerations between rich and poor within countries, between regions and between present and future generations;
- transparency concerns full disclosure of the use of different types of capital, the positive and negative impacts (externalities) of such uses and how their costs/benefits vary between today's needs and those of future generations.

4.2 Limitations of conventional accounting systems

The United Nations SNA is the globally recognized accounting framework that brings coherence to hundreds of mainly economic statistics available in many countries. Variables such as GDP, production, investment and consumption are produced annually, quarterly and sometimes even monthly from the SNA framework.

Historically the impetus for such accounts has come from the need to mobilize resources in times of crisis. From the first sets of accounts developed in the 17th and 18th centuries in England[12] and France[13] and the material balance of the USSR economy of 1925[14] to the first official national income statistics produced for the USA[15] in 1934, the UK[16] in 1941 and several European countries after 1945, the common purpose was either to mobilize resources to fight wars and/or to pay for peacetime reconstruction. After the Second World War, the Marshall Plan for post-war construction in Europe spawned the development of a first *Standardized System of National Accounts* published in 1952 (OECD, 1959).[17] The following year, the UN published a revised version for global use known as the 1953 SNA (United Nations, 1953).

This backdrop strongly influenced the SNA's almost exclusive focus on the economic factors of production and consumption. Its creators were well aware of these limitations. In his Nobel memorial lecture in 1984, the 'father' of the SNA, Richard Stone, stated that accounts for society ought to rest on three pillars: economic, socio-demographic and environmental. He highlighted that issues such as pollution, land use and non-renewable resources offered plenty of scope for accounting and that GDP should be complemented by other variables when considering overall societal welfare.

Since then, there has been only limited progress on including natural capital in SNA revisions. The 2008 revision still does not record subsoil assets depletion in the same way as fixed capital consumption (United Nations et al, 2008).

These intrinsic limitations led to the introduction of 'satellite' accounts in the 1993 SNA revision. One of these was developed as the System of Environmental and Economic Accounting (SEEA) (United Nations et al, 2003) but failed because it did not recognize the need for asset accounts in physical units or acknowledge the concept of ecosystem.

A few countries have developed satellite accounts for environmental protection expenditures, natural assets (subsoil, water, forest), pollution (emissions accounts) or other material flow accounts (see also TEEB Climate Issues Update, 2009). Because these accounts were generally underused, the London Group on Environmental Accounting – a group of national and environmental accountants from various OECD and developing countries – was created to revise the SEEA to better balance monetary and physical accounts.

The 2003 SEEA now offers best accounting practices for physical units for natural assets, such as land ecosystems and water systems. With respect to valuation issues, however, it still artificially divides ecosystems into resource components (timber, fish stocks, water in reservoirs, etc.) where depletion is calculated according to conventional economic rules and where valuation for 'environmental degradation' remains uncertain.

Addressing these shortcomings is a key challenge for the SEEA 2012/2013 revision, which will devote a specific volume to ecosystem accounts and valuation issues.

4.3 Practical steps towards ecosystem accounting

Against this background, elements for ecosystem accounting have been developed and are being tested by the European Environment Agency (EEA) with many partners. Several analyses and methodological approaches have been developed and presented in papers (Weber, 2007, 2008). Land accounting has been established on the basis of land-cover change detection for Europe (EEA, 2006) and can be applied to the global level, using similar methodologies developed with the European Space Agency (ESA), FAO, United Nations Environment Programme (UNEP), International Cooperative Biodiversity Groups (ICBG) and other relevant bodies.

Under TEEB auspices, the EEA has been working on ecosystem accounting for Mediterranean wetlands (EEA, 2010). This methodological case study provides insights on the potential contribution of environmental accounting to the economics of ecosystems and biodiversity, and has developed eight practical elements for guidance, which are detailed below.

1 The three geographical scales for ecosystem accounts

Ecosystem accounts can be implemented across the three geographical scales most relevant to prevailing governance models and societal welfare considerations.

The global/continental scale sets out general objectives through international conventions, and requires simplified accounts that monitor main trends and distortions for all countries. The national/regional scale involves the enforcement of environmental policies and regulations through environmental agencies, economic ministries, statistical offices and courts. The local scale supports action by local government and business, at site level and through management, projects and case studies: this is where assessing and valuing ESS is essential and feasible because informed actors can express their real preferences.

2 Assigning priorities for policy making

From a policy and data viewpoint, ecosystem accounting should be prioritized from a top-down perspective, not bottom-up.

Each of the above scales can be assigned a mission, data access and a time frame. The accounting strategy should consider the three interconnected scales and their feasibility when considering how to integrate the environment in economic decision making.[18]

3 Simplified global-scale accounts

Simplified global-scale accounts can be produced at short notice, on the basis of global monitoring programmes and international statistics, and annually updated to assess losses (gains) in total ecological potential of physical units and the cost of ecosystem restoration to maintain their functions and capacity to continue service delivery. This maintenance cost equates to ecosystem capital consumption which can be used in two ways:

i.   calculation of the value of domestic and imported products at their full cost in addition to their purchase price;
ii. subtraction from the GNP (together with fixed capital consumption) to calculate the new headline aggregate of adjusted disposable national income (ADNI).

4 Integration of national economic-environmental accounts with ecosystem accounts

To integrate national economic-environmental accounts with ecosystem accounts, the first task is to compute ecosystem capital consumption and use this to derive ADNI on the basis of national statistics and monitoring systems. The second is to integrate such ecosystem accounts with the national accounting matrixes and the monetary and physical indicators used for policy making. The process for implementing these national accounts is the revision of the UN SEEA by 2012/2013.

5 Local-scale ecosystem accounts

Local-scale ecosystem accounts would be very helpful for planning departments and environmental protection agencies to fully internalize environmental considerations when considering e.g. the costs/benefits of development proposals. Private actors and businesses are also interested, as shown by their response to carbon accounting and recent interest in biodiversity considerations. Guidelines could be developed based on these general principles but adapted to the needs of the various communities of users.

6 Socio-ecological systems

Socio-ecological systems are the appropriate analytical units for such accounting as they reflect higher levels of interaction between ecosystems and people. UNEP and EEA are developing an international standard ecosystem services classification for use in accounting. Priority accounts should cover stocks and flows of land cover, water, biomass/carbon and species/biodiversity in order to calculate the ecological potential[19] of many terrestrial socio-ecosystems. The type of formula (simplified/sophisticated) will depend on operational targets, scales and data availability.

7 Asset valuation

Asset valuation is very feasible and very useful in the context of cost–benefit assessment of project impacts. It helps policy makers achieve trade-offs between possible benefits from new development compared to present benefits from natural resources and non-market ecosystem services and to see if benefits compensate losses. Used in regular national accounting, this method contains several risks (e.g. ignoring or undervaluing non-use values of a public-good nature). For renewable assets, stock valuation is not necessary: what matters most is that the ecosystems are renewing so that their multiple functions can be maintained over time, whatever the current preference for a specific service. The degradation of ecological potential can be observed and measured in physical units, making it possible to calculate a restoration cost by reference either to the average cost of maintenance works or to the benefits/losses involved in reducing extraction or harvesting to a level compatible with system resilience.

8 Ecosystem capital maintenance

Ecosystem capital maintenance is the other approach to valuation and considers their present and future capacity to deliver services. Two elements need to be considered: actual expenditures for environmental protection and resource management, and additional costs potentially needed to mitigate degradation. When actual expenditures are insufficient to maintain the ecosystem, allowance may be made for additional necessary costs (as done by business and national accounts for 'cost of capital maintenance' or 'fixed capital consumption'). Ecosystem capital consumption should be calculated in the same way as fixed capital consumption and added to that figure to adjust the calculation of company profit or national income. As with fixed capital, this adjustment measures what needs to be reinvested to maintain the asset's equivalent productive/reproductive capacity. This amount should be set aside at the end of one accounting period and made available for restoration during the following one: it may lead to a lower dividend payment and/or lower taxes on profits (see above; EEA, 2010).

4.4 Using available information to meet policy makers' demands

The data issue requires a strategic response. On the bright side, we have made tremendous progress in the last 30 years through observation satellites, ground positioning systems, on-site real-time monitoring, databases, geographical information systems and the internet. Organizations have developed capacities and networks that now make it possible to move towards ecosystem accounting.

On the less positive side, the lack of guidelines for ecosystem accounting is particularly acute at local government/agency and business levels. Data are regularly collected (e.g. by protected area authorities) but compiling them into an integrated framework is a huge effort. Guidelines should consider the needs of local actors for information on physical state, costs and benefits in relation to their mandate.

Another difficulty concerns restrictions on data access by some public organizations. This is being addressed by new data policies of the major space agencies, open access policies of environmental agencies and initiatives to facilitate access to scientific knowledge: statistical offices have improved access to their databases and developed local statistics. However, more progress is needed, e.g. to merge statistical and geographic information system (GIS) data and develop grid databases.

Data collection will only develop if it meets the needs of policy makers, companies and the public. New products result from iterations between the supply and demand sides. The supply side identifies a need and technical capacities to meet it (sketches, models, prototypes, etc.). The demand side expresses needs and preferences, and validates the product by using it. Although environmental accounting methodologies have been proficiently designed over three decades and tested in various contexts, they have not yet met demand-side requirements.

Initiatives launched before the current crises (see Section 4.1) note that physical indicators are part of the response to better reflect the social and environmental interactions of economic development: all request new monetary indicators. The current crises amplify this need and make it essential for the supply side to develop new products on the basis of existing data. These products will be simple to start with but they will give users preliminary elements to better assess trade-offs and decisions based on past accounts and derived outlooks.

Some new products are already coming on stream and can provide a useful contribution to the post-2010 baseline discussion (see Section 2 above). They include:

- an interim 'basket of four' indicators (ecological footprint, human appropriation of net primary production (HANPP), landscape ecological potential and environmentally weighted material consumption developed by the 2007 Beyond GDP conference);[20]
- a 'cube' of six indicators that looks at elements of ecological potential to support accounting (total ecological potential, a multi-criteria weighted product of landscape ecological potential, ecosystem dependency, HANPP, biodiversity rarefaction, catchments exergy loss and healthy populations), proposed by the EEA.

Finally, at the CBD COP10 in Nagoya, Japan, the World Bank launched a new global partnership to 'green' national accounts, which promises to offer a useful step forward and new evidence base on integrating natural capital and their values into national accounts:

The natural wealth of nations should be a capital asset valued in combination with its financial capital, manufactured capital, and human capital. National accounts need to reflect the vital carbon storage services that forests provide and the coastal protection values that come from coral reefs and mangroves.

Through this new partnership, we plan to pilot ways to integrate ecosystem valuation into national accounts and then scale up what works to countries around the world. (Zoellick, 2010)

5 Building a fuller picture: The need for 'GDP of the poor'

The tools described above are necessary adjustments but insufficient if a significant set of beneficiaries are poor farming, pastoral or forest-dwelling communities. Here, we need a more encompassing measure of societal well-being that better reflects the position of society's poorest – those most at risk from the consequences of mis-measurement and loss of ecosystem services, particularly in transitional economies. The right income aggregate to measure and adjust is the 'GDP of the poor'.

5.1 A tale of two tragedies: The measurement gap around the rural poor

Traditional measures of national income, like GDP which measures the flow of goods and services, can be misleading as indicators of societal progress in mixed economies because they do not adequately represent natural resource flows. This misrepresents the state of weaker sections of society, especially in rural areas.

To move beyond paradigms focused on income, Human Development Indices (HDIs) have been developed to provide a broader-based measure of development. However, HDI also fails to take account of the contribution of natural resources to livelihoods. The World Bank has published total wealth estimates (Dixon et al, 1997) which seek to account for the contribution of natural capital, but this is a stock concept. There is also a need for a flow variable which adequately captures the value of natural resource flows, even though these are mainly in the nature of public goods.

Developing 'green accounts', with adjustments to GDP to account for natural capital depletion, is a step in this direction but does not show the social dimension. Similarly, the genuine savings indicator (Pearce and Atkinson, 1993) does not indicate the real cost of natural resource degradation at the micro level, even though this is where real and often acute costs are felt by the poorest and most vulnerable sections of society (see 5.3 below).

Particularly for developing countries, where many poor people are dependent on natural resources for employment and subsistence, the result is often a tale of two tragedies:

1. The exclusion of ecosystem service flows from society's accounting systems results in a lack of policy attention and public investment in ecosystem and biodiversity conservation. This risks triggering the well-documented 'tragedy of the commons' – in other words, an unsustainable future for generations to come.
2. The second, intra-generational, tragedy concerns the 'tyranny of the average' – in other words the implicit assumption that an increase in any measure of average

progress (e.g. GDP growth) reflects progress in the distribution of well-being within society at large.

Adopting a 'beneficiary focus' helps us to better recognize the human significance of observed losses of ecosystems and biodiversity. In this section, we propose an adapted measure – the 'GDP of the poor' – that can show the dependence of poor people on natural resources and the links between ecosystems and poverty (Section 5.2). This takes the form of a three-dimensional metric which integrates economic, environmental and social aspects, thereby indicating the vulnerability of these population groups if valuable natural resources are lost (Section 5.3). Once adjusted for equity, the real cost of biodiversity loss is different – so this indicator could reflect its impact on the 'real income' and well-being of the poor.

5.2 Poverty and biodiversity: From vicious to virtuous circle

The links between poverty and biodiversity can be examined from the perspective of livelihoods, distribution, vulnerability and causality.

In livelihood terms, abundant biodiversity and healthy ecosystems are important for food, energy and water security, health, social relations, freedom of choice and action. They provide the basic material for quality of life and guard against vulnerability (MA, 2005). Treating these socially valuable flows as externalities and omitting them from national accounts means that GDP is understated as a measure of total income. It mis-states the GDP of the poor who are the key beneficiaries of services like direct harvesting of food, fuelwood and non-timber forest products (NTFPs) and indirect flows of fresh water and nutrients to fields and forests. The main economic impact of ignoring these natural inputs is on the income security and well-being of the poor.

An analysis of vulnerability leads to similar conclusions. Natural resources are obviously used by society at large but the vulnerability of different user groups to changes in biodiversity varies according to their income diversity, geographical location and cultural background. Table 3.5 illustrates this by reference to end-users of forests in Brazil, showing their respective vulnerability to climate change and natural hazards. The highest vulnerability is found among local communities in and near forests, due to their lack of mobility and access to substitute resources.

Poverty–environment linkages are multidimensional and context-specific, reflecting geographic location, scale and the economic, social and cultural characteristics of individuals, households and social groups (Duraiappah, 1998). 'Poverty can be due to a range of lack of the various assets (and income flows derived from them): (a) natural resource assets; (b) human resource assets; (c) on-farm physical and financial assets; (d) off-farm physical and financial assets. A household might be well endowed in one asset but poor in another, and the type of poverty can influence the environment-poverty links' (Reardon and Vosti, 1995).

Poverty can be exogenous (external to the group) and endogenous (internal to the community) (Duraiappah, 1998). The root cause of environmental degradation is not only poverty but several other factors. Exogenous poverty – factors like greed, institutional and policy failures – leads to environmental degradation which in turn leads to endogenous poverty (e.g. due to degradation of natural assets). Services commonly affected by such degradation include reduced water availability, water quality, forest biomass, soil fertility and topsoil as well as inclement microclimates.

The two types of poverty thus reinforce each other. Poverty, where it leads to degradation of natural capital to support needs, reduces the services generated by ecosystems: with lack of investment resources, this leads to more poverty and thus creates a vicious circle.

An example of these linkages (see Box 3.8) is from Haiti, the poorest country in the western hemisphere with 65 per cent of its people surviving on less than US$1 a day. Deforestation was shown to have led to much higher vulnerability and loss of life (compared to the neighbouring Dominican Republic) as a result of a cyclone which affected both countries.

Table 3.5 Differences in forest dependence, vulnerability to climate change impacts and factors affecting the vulnerability of different forest user groups for the State of Para, Brazil

User group	Main goods and services	Level of vulnerability	Factors affecting sensitivity	Adaptive capacity
Federation	Biological diversity; timber and non-timber products; emission reductions; hydroelectric energy	Low for some goods and services; high for others	Deforestation and uncontrolled logging increases sensitivity	Mobility of resources; accessibility to technology, human and financial resources; diversity of land uses; biological diversity
State government (e.g. Para)	Biological diversity; timber and non-timber products; emission reductions	Medium to high	Deforestation and uncontrolled logging increases sensitivity	Limited mobility; limited access to technology and resources; limited diversity of land uses
Logging companies	Timber	High	Demand for timber; unauthorized forest conversion; forest degradation	Limited mobility and access to resources; sustainable forest management (SFM) and diversification of species harvested may increase adaptive capacity and reduce sensitivity
Forest communities in Para	Timber and non-timber forest products; drinking water; soil restoration	High to very high	High dependence on forest products and services in an area of high potential exposure	Diversity of uses; maintenance of biodiversity; very limited mobility and access to resources
Communities outside forests in Para	Some timber and non-timber forest products; energy from wood	High to very high	Market demand for agricultural products; poor soil management	Very limited mobility and access to resources; limited diversity

Source: Louman et al (2009)

Box 3.8 Environmental degradation and vulnerability: Haiti and the Dominican Republic

The relationship between environmental degradation and impacts on vulnerable populations is evidenced by the differing impact of Hurricane Jeanne in Haiti and the Dominican Republic (DR).

Haiti was originally fully forested but from 1950 to 1990 the amount of arable land was almost halved due to soil erosion. Deforestation reduced evaporation back into the atmosphere and total rainfall in many locations has declined by as much as 40 per cent, reducing stream flow and irrigation capacity. By 2004 only 3.8 per cent of Haiti was under forest cover, compared to 28.4 per cent of DR.

In Haiti, floods and Hurricane Jeanne killed approximately 5400 people due to destruction of mangroves and the loss of soil-stabilizing vegetation, causing landslides that led to most casualties. In DR, which is much greener and still has 69,600 hectares of mangroves, Jeanne claimed less than 20 lives (Peduzzi, 2005).

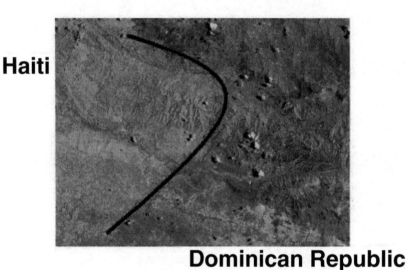

Figure 3.3 *Deforestation in Haiti and the Dominican Republic*

Source: NASA/Goddard Flight Center Scientific Visualization Studio

This stark difference reflects the impacts that deforestation and resource degradation have on the resilience of poor people in the face of environmental hazards. It also highlights the higher risks experienced by vulnerable populations that do not have enough disposable income, insurance or assets to recover from disasters. With an average monthly income of US$30.50, Haitians are deeply affected by the worsening state of the environment. This has translated into political turmoil, over-exploitation of resources that perpetuates the poverty–ecosystem degradation trap, health concerns and a flow of environmental refugees that has implications for stability and natural resources in neighbouring countries.

Source: Peduzzi (2005)

Natural resource degradation can thus aggravate loss of natural resources because of the poverty trap. It is essential to break this vicious circle through a proactive strategy of investment in natural capital to increase the generation of ecosystem services.

5.3 Practical steps towards measuring the GDP of the poor

Tackling poverty and biodiversity loss calls for efficient and sustainable utilization of natural resources. Development paradigms should take into account the nexus between growth, poverty and environment.

We should emphasize that degradation of ecosystems and loss of biodiversity has different impacts at the macro and micro level. At the micro level, it leads to the erosion of the resource base and environmental services. Viewed from an 'equity' perspective, the poverty of their beneficiaries makes these ecosystem service losses even more acute as a proportion of their incomes and livelihoods.

The first step for economies where rural- and forest-dweller poverty is a significant social problem is to use a sectoral GDP measure focused on and adapted to their livelihoods. At a micro level, including ecosystems and biodiversity as a source of economic value increases the estimate of their effective income and well-being provided that all services are systematically captured. Initially, adding the income from ecosystem services to the formal income registered in the economy will appear to reduce the relative inequality between the rural poor and other groups, as urban populations (rich and poor) are less dependent on free flows from nature. However, once natural capital losses are factored in, the picture of inequality changes as these affect the rural poor much more: it becomes clear that where natural capital is being lost, the rural poor are even less well-off.

Moving towards this kind of measurement is useful for policy making. Three case studies were conducted for India, Brazil and Indonesia to test this emerging methodology for country analysis purposes. The results are synthesized in Table 3.6 below and presented in the Annex.

Table 3.6 GDP of the poor and share of GDP

Natural resource-dependent sectors and ESS (2005)	Brazil	Indonesia	India
Original share of GDP (%): Agriculture, forestry, fisheries	6.1%	11.4%	16.5%
Adjusted share of GDP (%) + non-market + ESS	17.4%	14.5%	19.6%
Original per person unadjusted 'GDP of the poor' (US$/person)	51	37	139
Adjusted GDP of the poor per person (US$/person)	453	147	260
Additional GDP of the poor from ESS and non-market goods (US$/person)	402	110	121
Share of ESS and non-market goods of total income of the poor (%)	89.9%	74.6%	46.6%

Note: See Annex 1 for data, sources and calculations

Source: Authors' own calculations

The findings illustrate by how much income would change if all services were systematically quantified. The methodology considered the sectors in national accounts that are directly dependent on availability of natural capital i.e. agriculture and animal husbandry, forestry and fishing. If these sectors are properly accounted for, the significant capital losses observed have huge impacts on their respective productivity and risks. These collectively indicate the GDP of the (rural) poor registered in the economy, but to get the full measure, non-market products and services in these sectors also need to be added.

For India, the main natural resource-dependent sectors – agriculture, forestry and fisheries – contribute around 16.5 per cent to GDP. When the value of ecosystem services provided by forests and the value of products not recorded in GDP statistics are added, this increases the adjusted contribution of agriculture, forestry and fishing to GDP from 16.5 per cent to 19.6 per cent. For the rural poor, the average per person value from these combined sectors was US$138.80. When non-market goods are included as well as the value of ecosystem services, per person effective income goes up to US$260. This is a much larger increase than for the average across the economy as a whole.

A similar pattern, with even more significant increases, is also observed in the Brazilian and Indonesian case studies.

These estimates are useful not only to test the indicator but to illustrate the importance of the information that can be obtained. Though only a few of the ecosystem services could be added and generally conservative estimates have been used, the results underline the potential for its further development.

The analysis also emphasizes that even with the partial evidence available, the issue of the rural poor's dependency on income from non-market products and services is critical to factor into policy making. Their dependency and increasing loss of livelihood from the erosion of natural capital underlines the need for a strategy for investing in the natural capital stocks that support the GDP of the poor.

Notes

1   See *Foreign Affairs*, November/December 2005, www.foreignaffairs.com/
2   'Measures' are actual measurements of a state, quantity or process derived from observations or monitoring. 'Indicators' serve to indicate or give a suggestion of something of interest and are derived from measures. An 'index' is comprised of a number of measures in order to increase their sensitivity, reliability or ease of communication (see TEEB Foundations (2010) Chapter 3 for further definitions used in TEEB).
3   International workshop in Reading, UK, jointly organized by the CBD secretariat and UNEP-WCMC: www.cbd.int/doc/?meeting=EMIND-02.
4   www.jncc.gov.uk/page-2199.
5   www.cbd.int/doc/meetings/sbstta/sbstta-14/official/sbstta-14-10-en.doc.
6   www.cbd.int/doc/meetings/sbstta/sbstta-14/in-session/sbstta-14-recommendations-en.doc.
7   www.cbd.int/doc/meetings/wgri/wgri-03/official/wgri-03-03-en.doc.
8   In addition, immaterial capital (e.g. patents, licences, brands) plays a core role in modern economic development.
9   See 2008 SNA, 10.44, http://unstats.un.org/unsd/nationalaccount/SNA2008.pdf.
10 In November 2007, the European Commission, European Parliament, Club of Rome, OECD and WWF hosted the high-level conference 'Beyond GDP' with the objectives of clarifying which indices are most appropriate to measure progress, and how these can best be integrated into the decision-making process and taken up by public debate. A direct outcome of the conference was the

publication in 2009 of the Communication 'GDP and beyond: Measuring progress in a changing world' by the European Commission, which includes an EU roadmap (www.beyond-gdp.eu/index.html).

11 The project exists to foster the development of sets of key economic, social and environmental indicators to provide a comprehensive picture of how the well-being of a society is evolving. It also seeks to encourage the use of indicator sets to inform and promote evidence-based decision making, within and across the public, private and citizen sectors. www.oecd.org/pages/0,3417,en_40033426_40033828_1_1_1_1_1,00.html.

12 Known as *Verbium Sapienta* (1665). Produced by William Petty for resource mobilization during the second Anglo-Dutch war (1664–1667).

13 Known as *La dime royale* (1707). Published by Sebastien le Prestre de Vauban, and based on his experience of mobilizing resources for the construction of military forts on French borders.

14 Published by Wassily Leontief, Nobel Prize winner 1973, as *The Balance of the Economy of the USSR: A Methodological Analysis of the Work of the Central Statistical Administration* (1925).

15 Published by Simon Kuznets, winner of The Sveriges Riksbank Prize in Economics in Memory of Alfred Nobel, 1971.

16 Published by Richard Stone, winner of The Sveriges Riksbank Prize in Economics in Memory of Alfred Nobel, 1984.

17 Published by OEEC (precursor to OECD).

18 The difficulties of accounting for ecosystems, starting from cases studies and the valuation of ecosystem services, were considered in a recent article (Mäler et al, 2009). The authors state in the conclusion that 'when we deal with ecosystem services, we the analysts and we the accountants must figure out the accounting prices from knowledge of the working of every ecosystem. It is therefore – at least for now – impossible to design a standardised model for building a wealth based accounting system for ecosystems. We have to develop such an accounting system by following a step by step path, going from one ecosystem to another.'

19 The ecological potential is measured from multi-criteria diagnosis (rating) based on these accounts, possibly completed on indicators related to populations' health and to external exchanges.

20 See www.beyond-gdp.eu/

Acknowledgements

The authors would like to thank Camilla Adelle, IEEP, UK; Mubariq Ahmad, WWF, Indonesia; Barbara Akwagyiram, IEEP, UK; Jonathan Armstrong, IEEP, UK; Giles Atkinson, London School of Economics, UK; Jonathan Baillie, Institute of Zoology, UK; Lina Barrera, Conservation International; Thomas Brooks, Nature Serve; Stuart Buchart, Birdlife International, UK; Tamsin Cooper, IEEP, UK; Deanna Donovan, Joint Nature Conservation Committee (JNCC), UK; Annelisa Grigg, International Balance Ltd, UK; Mikkel Kallesoe, World Business Council for Sustainable Development (WBCSD); Ninan Karachepone, Institute for Social and Economic Change, India; Jan Joost Kessler, AIDEnvironment, The Netherlands; Eimear Nic Lughadha Royal Botanic Gardens, UK; Indrani Lutchman, IEEP, UK; Jock Martin, EEA, Denmark; Leonardo Mazza, IEEP, Belgium; Alastair Morrison, Department for Conservation, New Zealand; Aude Neuville, European Commission – DG Environment, Belgium; Andy Stott, JNCC, UK; Rosimeiry Portela, Conservation International, Brazil; Irene Ring, Helmholtz Centre for Environmental Research (UFZ); Monique Simmonds, Royal Botanique Gardens, UK; Stuart Simon, Conservation International; Paul Smith, Royal Botanic Gardens, UK; Nina Springer, ExxonMobile; James Spurgeon, Jacobs Consultants, UK; Dhar Uppeandra, National Academy of Sciences India (NASI), India; Madhu Verma, Indian Institute of Forest Management, India; Matt Walpole, UNEP World Conservation Monitoring Centre, UK; Mathis Wackernagel, International Print Network, North America and Switzerland; Stephen White, European Commission – DG Environment, Belgium; Oliver Zwirner, European Commission – DG Environment, Belgium; and other members of the TEEB for Policy Makers Core Group.

References

Baillie, J. E. M., Collen, B., Amin, R., Resit Akcakaya, H. R., Butchart, S. H. M., Brummitt, N., Meagher, T. R., Ram, M., Hilton-Taylor, C. and Mace, G. M. (2008) 'Toward monitoring global biodiversity', *Conservation Letters*, vol 1, pp18–26

Balmford, A. P., Crane, A., Dobson, R., Green, E. and Mace, G. M. (2005) 'The 2010 challenge: Data availability, information needs and extraterrestrial insights', *Philosophical Transactions of the Royal Society of London B*, vol 360, pp221–228

Balmford, A., Rodrigues, A. S. L., Walpole, M., ten Brink, P., Kettunen, M., Braat, L. and de Groot, R. (2008) *The Economics of Biodiversity and Ecosystems: Scoping the Science*, European Commission (contract: ENV/070307/2007/486089/ETU/B2) Cambridge, www.ec.europa.eu/environment/nature/biodiversity/economics/teeb_en.htm, accessed 22 September 2010

Boyd, J. and Banzhaf, S. (2007) 'What are ecosystem services? The need for standardized environmental accounting units', *Ecological Economics*, vol 63, pp616–626

Braat, L. and ten Brink, P. (eds) with Bakkes, J., Bolt, K., Braeuer, I., ten Brink, B., Chiabai, A., Ding, H., Gerdes, H., Jeuken, M., Kettunen, M., Kirchholtes, U., Klok, C., Markandya, A., Nunes, P., van Oorschot, M., Peralta-Bezerra, N., Rayment, M., Travisi, C. and Walpole, M. (2008) *The Cost of Policy Inaction (COPI): The Case of Not Meeting the 2010 Biodiversity Target*, European Commission, Brussels

Butchart, S. H. M., Stattersfield, A. J., Baillie, J. E. M., Bennun, L. A., Stuart, S. N., Akçakaya, H. R., Hilton-Taylor, C. and Mace, G. M. (2005) 'Using Red List indices to measure progress towards the 2010 target and beyond', *Philosophical Transactions of the Royal Society B*, vol 360, pp255–268

Butchart, S. H. M., Akçakaya, H. R., Chanson, J., Baillie, J. E. M., Collen, B., Quader, S., Turner, W. R., Amin, R., Stuart, S. N. and Hilton-Taylor, C. (2007) 'Improvements to the Red List Index', *Public Library of Science (PLoS) ONE*, vol 2, no 1

Butchart, S. H. M., Walpole, M., Collen, B., van Strien, A., Scharlemann, J. P. W., Almond, R. E. A., Baillie, J. E. M., Bomhard, B., Brown, C., Bruno, J., Carpenter, K. E., Carr, G. M., Chanson, J., Chenery, A. M., Csirke, J., Davidson, N. C., Dentener, F., Foster, M., Galli, A., Galloway, J. N., Genovesi, P., Gregory, R. D., Hockings, M., Kapos, V., Lamarque, J.-F., Leverington, F., Loh, J., McGeoch, M. A., McRae, L., Minasyan, A., Morcillo, M. H., Oldfield, T. E. E., Pauly, D., Quader, S., Revenga, C., Sauer, J. R., Skolnik, B., Spear, D., Stanwell-Smith, D., Stuart, S. N., Symes, A., Tierney, M., Tyrrell, T. D., Vie, J.-C. and Watson, R. (2010) 'Global biodiversity: Indicators of recent declines', *Science*, vol 328, no 5982, pp1164–1168

CBD (Convention on Biological Diversity) (2003) *Monitoring and Indicators: Designing National-Level Monitoring Programmes and Indicators*, CBD, Montreal, www.cbd.int/doc/meetings/sbstta/sbstta-09/official/sbstta-09-10-en.pdf, accessed 22 September 2010

CBD (2006) 'Decision VIII/15: Framework for monitoring implementation of the achievement of the 2010 target and integration of targets into the thematic programmes of work', in 'Decisions adopted by the conference of the parties to the convention on biological diversity at its eight meetings', 20–31 March 2006, www.cbd.int/decision/cop/?id=11029, accessed 22 September 2010

CBD (2009) '2010 biodiversity target: Indicators', www.cbd.int/2010-target/framework/indicators.shtml, accessed on 30 October 2009

CIFOR (The Center for International Forestry Research) (2005) *CIFOR Annual Report 2004: Forest for People and the Environment*, CIFOR, Bogor, Indonesia, www.cifor.cgiar.org/Knowledge/Publications/Detail?pid=1820, accessed 23 June 2010

Collen, B., Loh, J., Whitmee, S., McRae, L., Amin, R. and Baillie, J. (2009) 'Monitoring change in vertebrate abundance: The Living Planet Index', *Conservation Biology* 23, pp317–327

Danielsen, F., Burgess, N. D. and Balmford, A. (2005) 'Monitoring matters: Examining the potential of locally-based approaches', *Biodiversity and Conservation* 14, pp2507–2542

Dixon, J., Hamilton, K. and Kunte, A. (1997) 'Measuring the wealth of nations', in *Expanding the Measure of Wealth: Indicators of Environmentally Sustainable Development*, Environmentally Sustainable Development Studies and Monographs Series 17, Washington, DC, pp19–39

Dobson, A. (2005) 'Monitoring global rates of biodiversity change: Challenges that arise in meeting the Convention on Biological Diversity (CBD) 2010 goals', *Philosophical Transactions of the Royal Society of London B*, vol 360, pp229–241

Duraiappah, A. K. (1998) 'Poverty and environmental degradation: A review and analysis of the nexus', *World Development*, vol 26, no 12, pp2169–2179

EC (European Commission) (2008a) 'A mid-term assessment of implementing the EC Biodiversity Action Plan', (COM (2008) 864 final), Commission of the European Communities, Brussels

EC (2008b) 'Addressing the challenges of deforestation and forest degradation to tackle climate change and biodiversity loss', (COM (2008) 645/3), Communication from the European Commission to the European Parliament, the Council, the European Economic and Social Committee and the Committee of the Regions, Brussels

EC (2009) 'GDP and beyond: Measuring progress in a changing world', (COM (2009) 433) Communication from the Commission to the European Parliament, the Council, the European Economic and Social Committee and the Committee of the Regions, Brussels

Ecologic, SERI and Best Foot Forward (2008) *Potential of the Ecological Footprint for monitoring environmental impacts from natural resource use*, Report to the European Commission, DG Environment, www.ec.europa.eu/environment/natres/pdf/footprint_summary.pdf, accessed 22 September 2010

EEA (European Environment Agency) (2006) *Land Accounts for Europe 1990–2000*, EEA Report No 11/2006, prepared by R. Haines-Young and J.-L. Weber, EEA, Copenhagen, Denmark, www.reports.eea.europa.eu/eea_report_2006_11/en, accessed 29 October 2009

EEA (2007) *Halting the Loss of Biodiversity by 2010: Proposal for a First Set of Indicators to Monitor Progress in Europe*, EEA, Copenhagen, Denmark

EEA (2009) *Streamlining European 2010 Biodiversity Indicators*, EEA Report, March, available at http://biodiversity-chm.eea.europa.eu/information/indicator/F1090245995, accessed 28 October 2010

EEA (2010) *Ecosystem Accounting and the Cost of Biodiversity Losses – The Case of Coastal Mediterranean Wetlands*, EEA Technical Report No 3/2010, www.eea.europa.eu/publications/ecosystem-accounting-and-the-cost, accessed 28 July 2010

Ekins, P. (1992) 'A four-capital model of wealth creation', in P. Ekins and M. Max-Neef (eds) *Real-Life Economics: Understanding Wealth Creation*, Routledge, London and New York, pp147–155

Eliasch, J. (2008) *Climate Change: Financing Global Forests. The Eliasch Review*, www.official-documents.gov.uk/document/other/9780108507632/9780108507632.pdf, accessed 22 July 2010

Folke, C., Carpenter, S., Walker, B., Scheffer, M., Elmqvist, T., Gunderson, L. and Holling, C. S. (2004) 'Regime shifts, resilience, and biodiversity in ecosystem management', *Annual Review of Ecology, Evolution and Systematics*, vol 35, pp557–581

Gallai, N., Salles, J.-M., Settele, J. and Vaissiere, B. (2009) 'Economic valuation of the vulnerability of world agriculture confronted with pollinator decline', *Ecological Economics*, vol 68, pp810–821

GHK, IEEP, PSI, et al (2005) 'SRDTOOLS Methods and tools for evaluating the impact of cohesion policies on sustainable regional development (SRD)', Contract No 502485 Sixth Framework Programme Priority 8.3.1 Task 11 Regio Underpinning European Integration, Sustainable Development, Competitiveness and Trade Policies

Global Footprint Network (2009) 'Footprint for nations', www.footprintnetwork.org/en/index.php/GFN/page/footprint_for_nations/, accessed 29 October 2009

Godfrey, L. and Todd, C. (2001) 'Defining thresholds for freshwater sustainability indicators within the context of South African water resource management', Second WARFA/Waternet Symposium: Integrated Water Resource Management: Theory, Practice, Cases, Cape Town, South Africa

Greiber, T., van Ham, C., Jansse, G. and Gaworska, M. (2009) 'Final study on the economic value of groundwater and biodiversity in European forests' (070307/2007/486510), IUCN ROfE, IUCN ELC and CEPF, Brussels

Hails, C., Humphrey, S., Loh, J. and Goldfinger, S (eds) (2008) *Living Planet Report 2008*, WWF, Gland, Switzerland

Hammond, A., Kramer, W., Tran, J., Katz, R. and Walker, C. (2007) *The Next 4 Billion: Market Size and Business Strategy at the Base of the Pyramid*, World Resources Institute

Hassan, R. (2005) 'The System of Environmental and Economic Accounting', presentation given at FRANESA Workshop, 12–16 June 2005, Maputo, Mozambique

Hewitt, N. (2002) *Trees and Sustainable Urban Air Quality*, Lancaster University, www.es.lancs.ac.uk/people/cnh/

IPCC (Intergovernmental Panel on Climate Change) (2007) *Climate Change 2007: The Physical Science Basis* (Contribution of Working Group I to the Fourth Assessment Report of the IPCC), Cambridge University Press, Cambridge

IUCN (International Union for Conservation of Nature) (2001) *IUCN Red List Categories and Criteria: Version 3.1*, IUCN Species Survival Commission, Gland, Switzerland and Cambridge

Kettunen, M., Bassi, S., Gantioler, S. and ten Brink, P. (2009) *Assessing Socio-economic Benefits of Natura 2000: A Methodological Toolkit for Practitioners*, Output of the project Financing Natura 2000: Cost estimate and benefits of Natura 2000 (Contract No: 070307/2007/484403/MAR/B2), Institute for European Environmental Policy (IEEP), Brussels

Kuznets, S. (1934) 'National income, 1929–1932', 73rd US Congress, 2d session, Senate document no 124, p7, http://library.bea.gov/cdm4/document.php?CISOROOT=/SOD&CISOPTR=888, accessed 28 October 2010

Layke, C. (2009) *Measuring Nature's Benefits: A Status Report and Action Agenda for Improving Ecosystem Services Indicators*, Mainstreaming Ecosystem Services – Policy Series No 2, External review draft, World Resources Institute (WRI)

Leopold, A. (1953) *Round River*, Oxford University Press, Oxford

Lewis, S. L., Lopez-Gonzalez, G., Sonké, B., Affum-Baffoe, K., Baker, T. R., Ojo, L. O., Phillips, O. L., Reitsma, J. M., White, L., Comiskey, J. A., Marie-Noel, D., Ewango, C. E. N., Feldpausch, T. R., Hamilton, A. C., Gloor, M., Hart, T., Hladik, A., Lloyd, J., Lovett, J. C., Makana, J. R., Malhi, Y., Mbago, F. M., Ndangalasi, H. J., Peacock, J., Peh, K. S. H., Sheil, D., Sunderland, T., Swaine, M. D., Taplin, J., Taylor, D., Thomas, S. C., Votere, R. and Woll, H. (2009) 'Increasing carbon storage in intact African tropical forests', *Nature*, vol 457, pp1003–1006

Loh, J., Green, R. E., Ricketts, T., Lamoreux, J., Jenkins, M., Kapos, V. and Randers, J. (2005) 'The Living Planet Index: Using species population time series to track trends in biodiversity', *Philosophical Transactions of the Royal Society of London B*, vol 360, no 1454, pp289–295

Losey, J. E. and Vaughan, M. (2006) 'The economic value of ecological services provided by insects', *BioScience*, vol 56, pp311–323

Louman, B., et al (2009) 'Forest ecosystem services: A cornerstone for human well-being', in R. Seppälä (ed) *Adaptation of Forest and People to Climate Change: A Global Assessment Report*, IUFRO (International Union of Forest Research Organizations) World No 22, pp15–27

MA (Millennium Ecosystem Assessment) (2005) *Ecosystems and Human Well-being: Biodiversity Synthesis*, Millennium Ecosystem Assessment, World Resources Institute, Washington, DC

Mace, G. M. and Baillie, J. E. M. (2007) 'The 2010 biodiversity indicators: Challenges for science and policy', *Conservation Biology*, vol 21, pp1406–1413

Mäler, K. G., Aniyar, S. and Jansson, Å. (2009) 'Accounting for ecosystems', *Environmental & Resource Economics, European Association of Environmental and Resource Economists*, vol 42, no 1, pp39–51, www.springerlink.com/content/a7q1u4053v74120u/fulltext.pdf, accessed 30 October 2009

McNamara (1973) *The Nairobi Speech, Address to the Board of Governors by Robert S. McNamara, President, World Bank Group*. Nairobi, Kenya, September 24, 1973, http://siteresources.worldbank.org/EXTARCHIVES/Resources/Robert_McNamara_Address_Nairobi_1973.pdf, accessed 24 October 2010

McPherson, E. G., Nowak, D., Heisler, G., Grimmond, S., Souch, C., Grant, R. and Rowntree, R. (1997) 'Quantifying urban forest structure, function and value: The Chicago Urban Forest Climate Project', *Urban Ecosystems*, vol 1, no 1, pp49–61

Meadows, D. (1998) *Indicators and Information Systems for Sustainable Development – A Report to the Balaton Group*, The Sustainability Institute, Hartland, VT, www.sustainer.org/pubs/Indicators&Information.pdf

Mubariq, A. (2009) Mimeo based on experts' discussion in reference to various segmented forest valuation studies known in the circle of Forestry Department, Bogor Agriculture University

OECD (1959) *A Standardized System of National Accounts, 1958 Edition*, www.oecd.org/dataoecd/56/41/31075094.pdf, accessed 24 October 2010

Ott, W. and Staub, C. (2009) 'Wohlfahrtsbezogene Umweltindikatoren – Eine Machbarkeitsstudie zur statistischen Grundlage der Ressourcenpolitik', final draft report, Bundesamt fuer Umwelt, Bern

Pearce, D. W. and Atkinson, G. (1993) 'Capital theory and the measurement of sustainable development: An indicator of weak sustainability', *Ecological Economics*, vol 8, pp103–108

Peduzzi, P. (2005) 'Tropical cyclones: Paying a high price for environmental destruction', *Environment and Poverty Times*, vol 3, no 3, www.grida.no/publications/et/ep3/page/2587.aspx, accessed 28 July 2010

Pimm, S. L., Russell, G. J., Gittleman, J. L. and Brooks, T. M. (1995) 'The future of biodiversity', *Science*, vol 269, pp347–350

Powe, N. A. and Willis, K. G. (2002) 'Social and environmental benefits of forestry. Phase 2: Mortality and morbidity benefits of air pollution absorption by woodland landscape benefits', Report to the Forestry Commission, UK, www.forestry.gov.uk/pdf/airpollf.pdf/$FILE/airpollf.pdf

Reardon, T. and Vosti, S. (1995) 'Links between rural poverty and the environment in developing countries: Asset categories and investment poverty', *World Development*, vol 23, no 9, pp1495–1506

Repetto, R., Magrath, W., Wells, M., Beer, C. and Rossini, F. (1989) *Wasting Assets: Natural Resources in the National Income Accounts*, World Resources Institute, Washington, DC

Ricketts, T. H., Daily, G. C., Ehrlich, P. R. and Michener, C. D. (2004) 'Economic value of tropical forest to coffee production', *PNAS*, vol 101, pp12579–12582

Salafsky, N., Margoluis, R. and Redford, K. H. (2001) *Adaptive Management: A Tool for Conservation Practitioners*, Biodiversity Support Program, Washington, DC

Schutyser, F. and Condé, S. (2009) *Progress towards the European 2010 Target*, EEA Report No 4/2009, www.eea.europa.eu/publications/progress-towards-the-european-2010-biodiversity-target, accessed 30 October 2009

SEBI (2010) *Assessing biodiversity in Europe – the 2010 Report*, EEA Report No 5/2010, www.eea.europa.eu/publications/assessing-biodiversity-in-europe-84

South Australia's Strategic Plan (2007) 'Objective 3 – Attaining Sustainability', http://catalogue.nla.gov.au/Record/3944984, accessed 30 October 2009

Stern, N. (2006) *The Stern Review on the Economics of Climate Change*, Cambridge University Press, Cambridge

Stiglitz, J., Sen, A. and Fitoussi, J.-P. (2009) *The Measurement of Economic Performance and Social Progress Revisited – Reflections and Overview*, www.stiglitz-sen-fitoussi.fr/documents/overview-eng.pdf accessed 24 October 2010

TEEB (2009) *The Economics of Ecosystems and Biodiversity: Climate Issues Update*, www.teebweb.org, accessed 22 September 2010

TEEB Foundations (2010) *The Economics of Ecosystems and Biodiversity: Ecological and Economic Foundations* (ed P. Kumar), Earthscan, London

TEEB in Local Policy (2011) *The Economics of Ecosystems and Biodiversity in Local and Regional Policy and Management* (ed H. Wittmer and H. Gundimeda), Earthscan, London

TEEB in Business (2011) *The Economics of Ecosystems and Biodiversity in Business and Enterprise* (ed J. Bishop), Earthscan, London

ten Brink, P., Miller, C., Kettunen, M., Ramsak, K., Farmer, A., Hjerp, P. and Anderson, J. (2008) 'Critical thresholds, evaluation and regional development', *European Environment*, vol 18, pp81–95

Torras, M. (2000) 'The total economic value of Amazonian deforestation, 1978–1993', *Ecological Economics*, vol 33, pp283–297

Trumper, K., Bertzky, M., Dickson, B., van der Heijden, G., Jenkins, M. and Manning, P. (2009) *The Natural Fix? The Role of Ecosystems in Climate Mitigation*, A UNEP rapid response assessment, United Nations Environment Programme, UNEP-WCMC, Cambridge

Tucker, G. M., Bubb, P., de Heer, M., Miles, L., Lawrence, A., van Rijsoort, J., Bajracharya, S. B., Nepal, R. C., Sherchan, R. C. and Chapagain, N. (2005) *Guidelines for Biodiversity Assessment and Monitoring for Protected Areas*, King Mahendra Trust for Nature Conservation and UNEP-WCMC, Kathmandu, Nepal and Cambridge

Turner, W. R., Brandon, K., Brooks, T. M., Costanza, R., da Fonseca, G. A. B. and Portela, R. (2007) 'Global conservation of biodiversity and ecosystem services', *BioScience*, vol 57, pp868–873, www.uvm.edu/giee/publications/Turner%20et%20al.%20BioSci.%202007.pdf, accessed 22 September 2010

UNDP (United Nations Development Programme) (2002) *RBM in UNDP: Selecting Indicators*, Signposts in Development, UNDP, www.undp.org/cpr/iasc/content/docs/MandE/UNDP_RBM_Selecting_indicators.pdf, accessed 30 October 2009

UNEP-WCMC (2009) International Expert Workshop on the 2010 Biodiversity Indicators and Post-2010 Indicator Development, UNEP-WCMC, Reading, www.cbd.int/doc/meetings/ind/emind-02/official/emind-02-0709-10-workshop-report-en.pdf, accessed 22 September 2010

United Nations (1953) *A System of National Accounts and Supporting Tables*, United Nations, Department of Economic Affairs. Statistical Office, New York, 1953, http://unstats.un.org/unsd/nationalaccount/1953SNA.pdf, accessed 24 October 2010

United Nations (1968) *A System of National Accounts*, Studies in Methods, Series F, No 2, Rev. 3, New York

United Nations, European Commission, International Monetary Fund, Organisation for Economic Co-operation and Development, World Bank (2003) *Integrated Environmental and Economic Accounting (SEEA 2003)*, http://unstats.un.org/unsd/envAccounting/seea2003.pdf, accessed 22 September 2010

United Nations, European Commission, International Monetary Fund, Organisation for Economic Co-operation and Development, World Bank (2008) *System of National Accounts, (2008 SNA)*, http://unstats.un.org/unsd/nationalaccount/SNA2008.pdf, accessed 22 September 2010

van Beukering, P. J. H., Cesar, H. J. S. and Janssen, M. A. (2003) 'Economic valuation of the Leuser National Park on Sumatra, Indonesia', *Ecological Economics*, vol 44, pp43–62

Weber, J.-L. (2007) 'Implementation of land and ecosystem accounts at the European Environment Agency', *Ecological Economics*, vol 61, no 4, pp695–707

Weber, J.-L. (2008) 'Land and ecosystem accounts in the SEEA revision', Position paper for the UN London Group meeting, Brussels, 29 September to 3 October 2008

World Bank (2006) *Where Is the Wealth of Nations? Measuring Capital for the 21st Century*, The World Bank, Washington, DC

Worm, B., Barbier, E. B., Beaumont, N., Duffy, J. E., Folke, C., Halpern, B. S., Jackson, J. B. C., Lotze, H. K., Micheli, F., Palumbi, S. R., Sala, E., Selkoe, K. A., Stachowicz, J. J. and Watson, R. (2008) 'Impacts of biodiversity loss on ocean ecosystem services', *Science*, vol 314, pp787–790

Zoellick, R. B. (2010) World Bank Press Release no 2011/155/SDN, 28 October, http://web.worldbank.org/WBSITE/EXTERNAL/NEWS/0,,contentMDK:22746592~pagePK:64257043~piPK:437376~theSitePK:4607,00.html

Annex 1 Country-based calculations of GDP of the poor

Box 3.A1 Country GDP of the poor calculations: India

Agriculture and allied activities contribute around 16.5 per cent to the GDP, with per person income of US$2220 (adjusted for purchasing power parity). A large proportion of timber, fuelwood and NTFPs are not recorded in the official GDP, so these were added as adjustments. To these tangible benefits we have also added the contribution of ecotourism and biodiversity values and ecological services provided by forest ecosystems, based on estimates from the Green Accounting for Indian States Project (GAISP). The adjusted contribution of agriculture, forestry and fishing to GDP has increased from 16.5 per cent to 19.6 per cent.

More specifically:

* Not all of the contribution of agriculture, forestry and fishing can be attributed to poor people.
* We assumed that fuelwood and NTFPs are totally consumed by the poor.
* For ecotourism, we assumed that with international tourists, there is a leakage of around 40 per cent out of India and only the remaining 60 per cent is captured by the host country. Of this 60 per cent, part of the income accrues to the government, tour operators, hotels and restaurants (we assumed 50 per cent) and only the remainder goes to the local people. For domestic tourists, we also assumed that officially recorded revenue is captured by the formal sector and only the rest accrues to local people.
* For bioprospecting, from a strict 'equity' perspective, it can be argued that the entire revenue should be captured by locals. However, we assume that locals get a royalty of only 25 per cent and that the rest goes to the bioprospector or to the relevant government and agency. This is a very rough approximation: in practice, local people may often get considerably less than this (see also the section on access and benefit sharing in Chapter 5).
* The other ecological services considered are carbon sequestration, flood control, nutrient recycling and water recharge for which the locals directly benefit (except for carbon).

Based on this, the per person GDP accruing to the poor (whom we define as population holding less than one hectare of agricultural land, people dependent on forests and the small fishing community) is US$260/year. If this income is deducted from GDP, the per person income available for the rest of the community is US$435/year. However, if ecosystems are degraded, the cost may not be equal to the benefits forgone for the following reasons:

- The costs can be higher because if local people try to get the same benefits elsewhere, it costs them much more (marginal utility of income generated is always lower than marginal disutility from spending the money).
- The marginal utility of a dollar obtained by a poor person is always higher than that of a rich person.
- The poor do not have any buffer from degradation of ecosystem services in the form of institutions and financial resources, unlike the rich.

For these reasons, a loss of a dollar would hurt poor people more than a dollar to the rich. We therefore need to use equity weighting. We have used the ratio of mean per person expenditure on food of households at the top of the pyramid to that of the households at the bottom of the pyramid as the equity weight. This data has been taken from a survey by the World Resources Institute and calculations by the authors (Hammond et al, 2007).

Box 3.A2 Country GDP of the poor calculations: Brazil

In Brazil, agriculture and allied activities contribute only around 6.1 per cent to the GDP, with per person income of US$8151 (adjusted for purchasing power parity). After accounting for unrecorded goods and unaccounted services from forests in the national accounts, based on a study by Torras (2000) adjusted for inflation, the adjusted contribution of agriculture, forestry and fishing to GDP was calculated (section authors) to increase to 17.4 per cent. This is not surprising given that forests cover 87 per cent of Brazil's land area (of which primary forests cover 50 per cent of the land area). Brazil has an active market for environmental services, the benefits of which are shared by several stakeholders.

We assumed that climate regulation services provided by forests are captured by global populations and the rest of the ecological services will accrue to Brazilians. Of this we assumed that only 10 per cent of the benefits (except ecological services) and 2 per cent of ecological services (assumed in proportion to the area held by the poor) accrue to the rural poor (Brazil has only 14 per cent rural population). Based on this, the per person GDP accruing to the poor (whom we define as population holding less than four hectares of agricultural land, people dependent on forests and the small fishing community) is US$453/year and that available for the rest of the community is US$1416/year. After adjusting for the equity weighting (ratio of mean per person expenditure on food of households occupying the top of the pyramid to that of the bottom of the pyramid), the inequality-adjusted cost per person for the poor community is US$642.

Box 3.A3 Country GDP of the poor calculations: Indonesia

Agriculture and allied activities contribute around 11.4 per cent to the GDP, with per person income of US$2931 (adjusted for purchasing power parity). After accounting for unaccounted timber, fuelwood and NTFPs, ecotourism, biodiversity values and ecological values that are not recorded in the GDP, the adjusted contribution of agriculture, forestry and fishing to GDP has increased to 14.5 per cent. These values were taken initially from a study by van Beukering et al (2003). However, based on expert opinion in Indonesia (Mubariq, 2009), these values seem to be a little higher for the country as a whole: we have therefore revised the estimates upwards to reflect the reality.

As valuation is context and area specific, it is better to consider a range of values across the country rather than transferring one estimate for the entire region. The following conservative range of estimates seem to be an appropriate lower band, based on various studies conducted in Indonesia:

- unrecorded timber and fuelwood used directly by forest-dependent poor communities: US$40–US$60 per hectare/year;
- NTFPs: US$22–US$30 per hectare/year;
- ecotourism and biodiversity: US$12–US$20 per hectare/year;
- ecological services: US$40–US$60 per hectare/year.

The same study was used to calculate the proportion of benefits shared by poor people. The different groups of stakeholders identified as benefiting from forest ecosystems include:

- local communities (households, small-scale farmers and entrepreneurs);
- local government (the body responsible for maintaining infrastructure and collecting local taxes);
- the elite logging and plantation industry (owners of concessions);
- national government (law enforcement); and
- the international community (representing global concerns for poverty, climate change and biodiversity loss).

If the forests are harvested selectively, the share of benefits received by the local community is estimated to be 53 per cent, by local governments 10 per cent, by elite industries 14 per cent, by national governments 5 per cent and by the international community 18 per cent. In this study, we have assumed that poor people get 53 per cent of the total benefits. Based on this, the per person GDP accruing to the poor (whom we define as population holding less than four hectares of agricultural land, people dependent on forests and the small fishing community) is US$147/year and that available for the rest of the community is US$425/year.

As the loss of one dollar of benefits derived from ESS to the rich is not the same as one dollar to the poor, we should use equity-adjusted income (equity weights were derived by dividing the mean per person expenditure on food of households in the top of the pyramid to that of the bottom of the pyramid). Based on this, the inequality-adjusted cost per person for the poor community is US$327.

Source: Mubariq (2009)

Table 3.A1 Equity-adjusted income of the poor (adjusted for purchasing power parity, 2005)

		Brazil	Indonesia	India
Gross domestic product (US$ millions)	(1)	1,517,040	670,840	2,427,390
Contribution of agriculture, forestry, livestock and fishing (US$ millions)	(2)	92,397	76,715	401,523
Of which contribution by the poor (per hectare value multiplied with area of small holdings less than 1 ha) (US$ millions)	(3)	993	3708	48,867
Percentage contribution of agriculture, forestry and fishing to GDP	(4)	6.1%	11.4%	16.5%
Total population (millions)	(5)	186	229	1094
Of which poor (millions)	(6)	19.6	99	352
Per person agricultural GDP of the poor	(7 = 3/6)	**50.7**	**37.4**	**138.8**
Per person GDP for the rest of the population (less GDP of the poor and rest of the population)	(8 = (1 − 3)/ (6 − 7)	9104.6	5138.9	3208.0
Adjustments for unrecorded timber and fuelwood from forestry GDP (US$ millions)	(9)	5870	6660	16,477
Adjustments for contribution of NTFPs to the economy (US$ millions)	(10)	57,158	5230	11,691
Adjustments for ecotourism and biodiversity values (US$ millions)	(11)	28,866	1823	17,285
Adjustments for other ecological services (US$ millions)	(12)	79,193	6800	28,282.6
Adjusted contribution of agriculture, forestry and fishing to GDP	(13 = 9 + 10 + 11 + 12 + 2)	263,484	97,227	475,258
Adjusted contribution of agriculture, forestry and fishing to the poor	(14)	8870	14,579	91,580
Per person adjusted agricultural GDP for the dependent population	(15 = 14/6)	**452.6**	**147**	**260.1**
Per person adjusted GDP for the entire population	(16 = 13/5)	1416	425	435
Equity adjusted cost per person for agriculture dependent community	(17 = equity weight*15)	*641.9*	*327*	*307.0*
Contribution of ecological services to classical GDP (in US$ millions)	(18 = 13 − 2)	171,807	20,512	73,735
Additional contribution to GDP	(19 = 18/1)	11%	3.1%	3.1%
Total Share of GDP	(20 = 19 + 4)	**17.1%**	**14.5%**	**19.6%**
Contribution to the poor (in US$ millions)	(21 = 14 − 3)	7877	10,872	42,713

Note to Table 3.A1:

1. Figures from the World Bank: http://data.worldbank.org/. For the rest see country notes below:

2. Brazil: Brazil has a population of 20 million dependent on forests including 350,000 indigenous people. The figures include population with less than one hectare agricultural land and fishing population. The equity weights are based on the ratio of consumption expenditures on food of the top expenditure group to the bottom expenditure groups based on survey by the World Resources Institute.

3. Indonesia: Indonesia has 80 to 95 million people who are directly dependent on forests (based on a publication on forest-dependent population by FAO). The figures also include population with less than one hectare agricultural land and fishing population. Of the 40 million households who are dependent on agriculture, 14 per cent have less than 1 ha of land holdings in Indonesia. The equity weights are based on the ratio of consumption expenditures on food of the household occupying the top of the pyramid to those in the bottom of the pyramid based on a survey by the World Resources Institute.

4. India: The values for forests are based on the Green Accounting for Indian States Project (GAISP) floor values adjusted for the year 2005. For timber and fuelwood, only open forests are considered. For the rest, very dense and dense forests are considered. For the forest-dependent population, assumptions are based on the estimates of the World Bank's 2004 publication *Counting on the Environment: Forest Income and the Rural Poor,* suggesting that about 200 million people in India directly depend on forests. In this figure are included the population with less than one hectare agricultural land and the fishing population. The equity weights are based on the ratio of consumption expenditures on food of the agricultural households with more than four hectares agricultural land to the households having less than one hectare land.

5. The services to agriculture, fishery and livestock can be captured through the productivity approach method, i.e. any decrease or deterioration in services is already reflected in the value added in agriculture, livestock and fishing sectors. So these values were not calculated separately.

Chapter 4

Recognizing the Value of Biodiversity: New Approaches to Policy Assessment

Coordinating lead author
Stephen White

Lead authors
Patrick ten Brink, Benjamin Simmons

Contributing authors
Naoya Furuta, Inge Liekens, Karachepone Ninan, Patrick Meire,
Clare Shine, Robert Tinch, Jeffrey Wielgus

Editing and language check
Clare Shine

See end of chapter for acknowledgements for reviews and other contributions

Contents

Key messages   131

Summary   132

1   Understanding the value of ecosystem services   132
    1.1   The nature of value and valuing nature   132
    1.2   Three ways to analyse value: Qualitative, quantitative and monetary 133
    1.3   Applying total economic value frameworks to ecosystems   138

2   Expanding monetary valuation of ecosystem services   141
    2.1   How do common valuation methods work?   141
    2.2   Scope for extending benefits transfer methods   143
    2.3   Examples of valuation in practice   145
    2.4   Limits to monetary valuation   150

3   Integrating economic thinking into policy assessment   151
    3.1   What can policy assessments contribute?   151
    3.2   How can we make better use of available information?   153
    3.3   Best practices for more effective assessment frameworks   154

4   Next steps: The need to build assessment capacity   164

Notes   165

Acknowledgements   166

References   166

Annex 1 Overview of methodologies used in assessing value of ecosystem services   168

Annex 2 Stages of a policy assessment, proposed actions
         and ways to address biodiversity (UNEP, 2009b)   173

Key messages

The main cause of the biodiversity crisis is unsustainable growth in consumption and production, exacerbated by a tendency to undervalue biodiversity and the ecosystem services it supports.

Current decision making is biased towards short-term economic benefits because the long-term value of ecosystem services is poorly understood. Recognizing the value of ecosystem services can lead to better, more cost-efficient decisions and avoid inappropriate trade-offs. It is also an important step towards refocusing economic and financial incentives to achieve sustainability goals. Tools and techniques already exist for this purpose and are being constantly improved.

Understanding the value of ecosystem services

Decision makers need to understand that ecosystem services are generated by natural capital in which services are (at risk of) being lost, and they need to understand the economic costs of losing them, who faces these costs, where and when. Valuation can help develop the necessary evidence base and should address spatial relationships between sources and beneficiaries of impacts and services. Countries can cooperate to develop and integrate robust valuation procedures within their broader decision support systems.

Valuation procedures should, at a minimum, be based on a qualitative understanding of environmental and social impacts of changes to natural capital and associated ecosystem services. However, building capacity to quantify and monetize such impacts is an essential further step to make trade-offs explicit and increase transparency.

Expanding monetary valuation of ecosystem services

Quantitative and monetary valuation methodologies should strengthen their focus on long-term impacts (positive and negative) of resource-use decisions and compare them using a discount rate appropriate for ecosystem services.

Existing expertise should be maximized by building on past practice, undertaking more primary analysis and promoting benefits transfer of existing studies in accordance with available guidance.

Integrating economic thinking into policy assessment

Valuation is a tool to guide decisions, not a precondition for acting to protect biodiversity. Decision makers across all levels and sectors need to commit to systematic and timely analysis of proposed projects, programmes and policies through impact assessments, strategic environmental assessments and environmental impact assessments. The aim should be to have a fuller evidence base available at the right time to take the whole picture into account.

The precautionary principle should be applied in decision making affecting biodiversity and ecosystem services where impacts cannot be predicted with confidence and/or where there is uncertainty about the effectiveness of mitigation measures.

Each country needs to develop and institutionalize a culture of analysis, consistent with recognized best practices. This can be done by developing capacity and having an accepted, functional and supported policy assessment system in place.

Summary

Chapter 4 focuses on methods for valuing biodiversity and ecosystem services (ESS) and ways to feed better information more effectively into national and international policy formation. Section 1 provides an overview of different ways to analyse value and how these can be linked. Section 2 outlines methodologies for monetary valuation and demonstrates their practical application, before identifying certain limitations that need to be addressed (with additional details in the Annexes). Section 3 shows how structured assessment frameworks can support more informed and balanced policy making and sets out eight best practices to improve current approaches. Section 4 considers next steps and the critical need to build valuation and assessment capacity.

1 Understanding the value of ecosystem services

Earlier chapters of this book have shown how current losses of biodiversity and associated ecosystem services, driven by unsustainable patterns of production and consumption, have significant economic costs for local, national and international communities. This raises an important question: if biodiversity loss is so detrimental, then why do we allow it?

Part of the answer lies in our failure to understand and incorporate the long-term value of ecosystem services when we make policy decisions based on assessments of trade-offs. A much more robust approach is needed to correct the current bias in decision making towards short-term narrowly focused economic benefits.

1.1 The nature of value and valuing nature

What do we mean by the 'value' of ecosystem services? When people think of value, they usually consider an item's usefulness and importance. However, this value is rarely the price we actually pay for ecosystem services as these are often free to the 'user' or cost much less than their value to society as a whole. Moreover, many ecosystem services tend to be outside traditional markets and so do not have a market price.

In a few cases, such as provision of timber or seafood, some output from an ecosystem does have a market price. This reflects the fact that those outputs are bought and sold on an open market where the price reflects what people are willing to pay for them. Even in this situation, the price charged does not necessarily reflect their true value as it will only be partial. There are likely to be impacts on the wider ecosystem beyond those considered in the market transaction.

The absence of markets for most ecosystem services arises for a number of reasons, including the lack of clear property rights attached to such services (see Chapter 2). In many cases, ecosystem services have a 'public good' characteristic which would not be priced accurately by markets even if property rights were defined (e.g. genetic diversity of crops that has insurance value for future food security).

Difficulties in obtaining monetary estimates of ecosystem services mean that decisions tend to be based on incomplete cost–benefit assessments and, as noted, are biased towards short-term economic benefits. Because we underestimate the economic and social importance of such services, we have few incentives to safeguard them and society as a whole loses out (see Box 4.1).

Box 4.1 Coastal capital: The value of coastal ecosystems in Belize

A recent assessment evaluated the average annual contribution of reef- and mangrove-associated tourism, fisheries and shoreline protection services to the national economy of Belize. Coral reef- and mangrove-associated tourism contributed an estimated US$150 million to US$196 million to Belize's economy in 2007 (equivalent to 12 to 15 per cent of GDP). Annual economic benefits from reef- and mangrove-dependent fisheries is estimated at between US$14 million to US$16 million. Reefs and mangroves also protect coastal properties from erosion and wave-induced damage, equivalent to an estimated US$231 million to US$347 million in avoided costs per year.

The findings of this study, carried out by the World Resources Institute (WRI), received much publicity in Belize and successfully conveyed the value of coastal ecosystems. Belizean NGOs have used these results, together with scientific evidence of the continuing decline in reef fish and reef health, to advocate for tougher fishing regulations. In parallel, local groups are using the results to pressure the government to change existing mangrove legislation, by pointing to the high economic value of mangroves as a reason to increase penalties for illegal clearing.

The availability of credible economic valuation also helped Belize's Fisheries and Environment Departments to calculate damages for compensation after a container ship grounded on the barrier reef in January 2009.

Sources: Cooper et al (2008); Humes (2010); Supreme Court of Belize (2010)

1.2 Three ways to analyse value: Qualitative, quantitative and monetary

To put an economic value on changes to ecosystem services, we first need to understand what those changes are. Figure 4.1 illustrates the series of steps that have to be considered. Valuation usually comes at the end of the process and has to build on scientific information collected in the earlier stages.

Analysis of ecosystem services can be done at three levels – qualitative, quantitative and monetary:

- Qualitative analysis generally focuses on non-numerical information (e.g. health benefits from clean air; social benefits from recreation; security and well-being).
- Quantitative analysis focuses on numerical data (e.g. the number of people benefiting from wood from forests, of avoided health impacts, of visitors to a

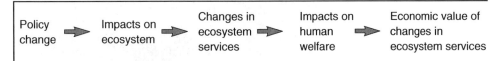

Figure 4.1 *Understanding ecosystem changes*

Source: Stephen White, own representation

natural site or beauty spot; quantity of quality water provision, carbon sequestered) (see also ecosystem service indicators in Chapter 3).
- Monetary analysis focuses on translating this data into a particular currency (e.g. the avoided costs of water purification or flood damage; the level of revenue or payments generated from tourism or from medicines and pharmaceuticals derived from natural products).

All three types of analysis are useful, but they provide different levels of information to a decision maker. We can illustrate this through the example of a scheme to increase agricultural production by converting grazing land to intensive cropping. If the financial benefits of intensification outweigh the financial cost of land clearance, this may seem appealing at first sight. However, this would only be a partial analysis as it only considers costs and benefits of the market transactions associated with the change of land use. To determine whether the policy would be beneficial at a societal level, we also need to consider non-market impacts, including impacts on untraded ecosystem services and biodiversity. For example, land conversion could release significant emissions of greenhouse gases (GHGs) and also reduce the land's capacity to absorb flood waters.
What would the different means of analysis deliver in this type of case?

- Qualitative analysis would simply describe the potential scale of these impacts (e.g. increased flood risk): the decision maker would have to make a judgement as to their importance relative to any financial costs and benefits.
- Quantitative analysis would directly measure the change in ecosystem services resulting from the change in land use (e.g. frequency/volume of estimated increase in flood risk/carbon dioxide emissions). The decision maker would then have a scientific measure of impacts to weigh up against financial costs and benefits.
- Monetary analysis would attach monetary values to the change in the flow of ecosystem services to put an estimated cost figure on whether a policy is likely to have a net benefit to society as a whole. It usually builds on quantitative analysis.

Which type of analysis to adopt will largely depend on the type of benefit being measured, the time and resources available and the significance of the decision. Qualitative analyses are usually easier and less expensive to conduct than quantitative analyses. Likewise, quantitative analyses usually require fewer resources than monetary analyses.
Figure 4.2 illustrates the different levels of resources required for each type of analysis. As one goes up the pyramid, there are fewer ecosystem services that can be assessed without increasing time and resources, due to the scarcity of policy-relevant data on costs and the need to assess the specific circumstances of every case. This insight is relevant because it may not always be practical to quantify changes in ecosystem services. In many cases, a qualitative assessment may be preferable: more resource-intensive analysis will inevitably be focused on the issues of most concern and potential value.
This highlights that valuation is only one input into the decision-making process but one that can be central. A pragmatic approach to valuation can be summed up as follows: 'always identify impacts qualitatively, then quantify what you can, then monetize (where possible).' The monetary value is only part of the total value of

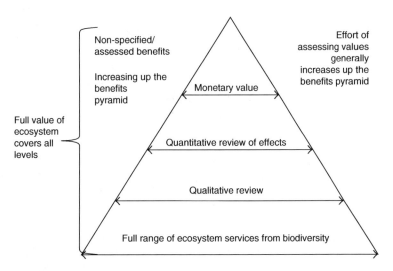

Figure 4.2 *The benefits pyramid*

Source: Patrick ten Brink, own representation

biodiversity – its 'total system value' (TSV) (O'Gorman and Bann, 2008). This combines the monetary, quantitative and qualitative insights, and also includes the values from the ecosystem that are not yet known or not captured by the assessment (e.g. as was the case in the past for carbon storage value). Biodiversity has value even if these are not assessed or not known about, though this value may be 'invisible' to some decision making. It is important not only to invest in assessing value where we are aware of services or associated benefits, but also to invest in understanding ecological processes and functions, to broaden our appreciation of these services and benefits. Box 4.2 shows the need to take into account the specific spatial and temporal boundaries in ecosystem service-related cost–benefit calculations.

In any type of analysis, it is also important to understand the spatial relationship linking the source supplying the ecosystem service to the various beneficiaries. This information is useful to identify:

- the impacts to be taken into account during the valuation;
- which stakeholders are likely to be winners or losers from any decision or cumulative trend;
- who should be involved or taken into account when designing ecosystem management approaches and choosing instruments to reward benefits (see Chapter 5), or avoid impacts (see Chapter 7).

Box 4.3 illustrates the extent to which collecting information on the spatial distribution of costs and benefits may, in some cases, be critical to the design of effective instruments to provide compensation to ensure the provision of ecosystem services where costs and benefits are not distributed evenly.

Box 4.2 Spatial and temporal boundaries in ecosystem-rated cost–benefit calculations

The North Wind's Weir (Washington State, US) salmon habitat restoration project aims to restore 0.8 hectares of critical habitat in the freshwater–saltwater transition zone by excavating and replanting native vegetation. This type of transition zone habitat is extremely scarce (it can only be located where fresh water meets tidal salt water, between 5.5 and 7 miles from the river mouth) and vital to maintaining viable salmon populations.

Cost–benefit calculations for this project (Batker et al, 2005) estimated the value of the site-specific ecosystem service improvements at $13,388–47,343 per year, totalling a present value of $384,000–$1.36 million. As the site is in a high development value area, land acquisition costs ($1.9 million) plus estimated restoration costs ($1.79 million) amounted to $3.69 million, significantly greater than the benefit.

However, this figure did not take account of the off-site impacts, and in particular the fact that transition habitat is critical for salmon conservation in the whole watershed. Taking its rarity into account, the authors estimated that it would be worth paying up to $19 million per acre for the restoration.

This case has a happy outcome because the restoration project went ahead, with contaminated soil removed in 2008/2009, construction work in 2009, and planting throughout 2010. It highlights the importance of ensuring that the boundaries – both spatial and temporal – of any cost–benefit calculations allow the full effects of any decision to be taken into account. Here, this required critical natural capital to be evaluated in the assessment by considering the interdependence of this project and many other actions leading to salmon conservation in the watershed: i.e. the project was treated as one piece in a bigger picture.

Source: Batker et al (2005)

Box 4.3 Considering the spatial distribution of cost and benefits to allow for appropriate compensation levels

Costs and benefits of individual projects are rarely distributed evenly. There will be winners and losers. This is true both over time (concepts of discounting and sustainability constraints seek to strike a balance across generations) and spatially (various approaches to equitable decision making may be applied, including payments for ecosystem services and other forms of compensation).

Several cost–benefit studies highlight the spatial distribution of impacts by conducting analysis at different levels.

Guyana: At the international level, the assessment of Guyanan deforestation (Office of the President, Republic of Guyana, 2008) contrasts the direct economic costs to local populations of forgoing forest development with the substantial global climate mitigation and biodiversity benefits of conservation. The report makes a powerful case that investing in Guyanan forest conservation would be a cost-effective method of carbon mitigation from a global perspective, while emphasizing that without side-payments, the economically optimal approach for Guyana would be to develop its forests. Even though the cost–benefit analysis (CBA) does not cover all possible impacts, it nevertheless leads to robust and important policy conclusions.

India: Studies of Rajiv Gandhi National Park and Dandeli Wildlife Sanctuary (Ninan et al, 2007a, 2007b) and a study of Finnish old-growth conservation (Kniivillä et al, 2002) focus on how benefit–cost ratios can vary for different populations at different radii around a study area. For the Rajiv Gandhi study, tribal communities living in the Park derive significant net present value (NPV) of 30,378 rupees (1999) ($705[a]) per household (at 12 per cent discount rate) from non-timber forest products, but the NPV falls to –3212 rupees (1999) (–$75) per household when the study scope is expanded to include coffee-growing communities outside the Park who suffer wildlife damage. On the other hand, expanding the scale further to cover the regional, national or global populations who benefit from the Park's tourism or biodiversity conservation aspects would reveal a positive NPV. The policy conclusion is that it may be necessary and/or desirable to compensate coffee growers for wildlife damage, both for equity reasons and to ensure successful conservation of wildlife in the park and surrounding areas.

Finland: The Finnish case reports regional NPVs of €186 million ($175 million[b]) at 3 per cent discounting, or €106 million ($100 million) at 5 per cent, from conservation of old-growth forests. Local NPVs are much lower and probably negative (from –€26.6 million to +€4.4 million (–$25.1 million to +$4.2 million) at 3 per cent, and –€21.5 million to +€1.3 million (–$20.3 million to +$1.2 million) at 5 per cent, depending on assumptions regarding where benefits from state-owned timber sales accrue). Again the point is simple, but with powerful policy implications: the recreation and non-use benefits of conservation are spread widely, whereas the lost economic opportunities are locally concentrated, implying that some compensation may be appropriate.

Mongolia: A further example is provided by the management and maintenance of the Khan Khentii Strictly Protected Area and Gorkhi-Terelj National Park in the Upper Tuul ecosystem in Mongolia. This area is the main source of water supplies for Ulaanbaatar. At present, there is an estimated Tug 24.6 billion ($21 million[c]) per year of tourism value, Tug 3.3 billion ($2.8 million) from herding, Tug 138 million ($0.11 million) timber, Tug 170 million firewood ($0.15 million) and Tug 77 million ($0.07 million) non-timber forest products. The total estimated value is around Tug 28.3 billion ($24 million), though only Tug 4 billion ($3.4 million) accrues to local populations.

However, this does not take account of the impacts on downstream water supply which have a present value of Tug 959–1095 billion ($822–939 million) depending on the scenario. The NPV of a 'conservation' scenario exceeds the alternatives of 'gradual degradation' by Tug 76 billion ($65 million) and 'no protection' by Tug 125 billion ($107 million). The investment of Tug 1 in the conservation of the Upper Tuul ecosystem has the potential to generate an additional Tug 15 in water-, land- and resource-use benefits over the next 25 years. The opportunity costs for local populations are Tug 5 billion ($4.2 million) for gradual deterioration and Tug 8 billion ($6.9 million) for conservation, compared with the no-protection scenario.

Even though nationally (and globally) it is very clearly optimal to conserve the Upper Tuul ecosystem, it is not in the immediate financial interest of local people. Again, this calculation shows clear policy conclusions highlighted in the report: 'It is neither realistic nor equitable to expect people in the upper watershed to subsidize the provision of water benefits for the inhabitants of Ulaanbaatar. A key challenge emerges: to generate funds to ensure adequate public investment in ecosystem conservation and protected area management and to set in place sufficient financial incentives to persuade land and resource users in the Upper Tuul to limit their land and resource uses to sustainable levels.'

Notes: a Converted at 43.06, the official exchange rate for 1999, http://data.worldbank.org/indicator/PA.NUS.FCRF
b Converted at 1.06, http://data.worldbank.org/indicator/PA.NUS.FCRF
c Converted at Tug 1,166 to $1, http://data.worldbank.org/indicator/PA.NUS.FCRF

Sources: Kniivillä et al (2002); Ninan et al (2007a, 2007b); Office of the President, Republic of Guyana (2008); Emerton et al (2009)

The diagram in Figure 4.3 uses the example of a partly forested watershed to show how an ecosystem provides different ecosystem services to different populations in the vicinity. Some benefit downstream from services provided; others in the area do not benefit; and a third group not only benefits from the ecosystem services but also influences them through activities that degrade or enhance the natural capital. It is critical to look at sufficient scale to understand the key interconnections between ecosystems and social and economic systems.

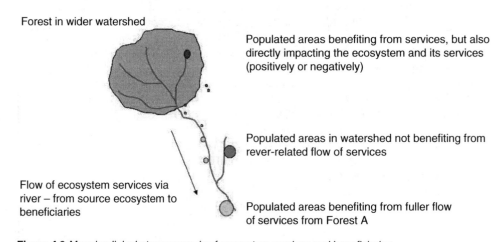

Forest in wider watershed

Populated areas benefiting from services, but also directly impacting the ecosystem and its services (positively or negatively)

Populated areas in watershed not benefiting from rever-related flow of services

Flow of ecosystem services via river – from source ecosystem to beneficiaries

Populated areas benefiting from fuller flow of services from Forest A

Figure 4.3 *Mapping links between supply of ecosystem services and beneficiaries*
Source: Adapted from Balmford et al (2008)

1.3 Applying total economic value frameworks to ecosystems

Despite the importance of qualitative analysis, the main challenge for policy makers is to promote more robust frameworks and capacity for quantitative and monetary analysis to reveal the economic value of ecosystem services. Valuation is a critical step towards correcting the current distortion in policy trade-offs and ensuring that ecosystem services are given the right weight in decisions.

Total economic value (TEV) provides a well-structured conceptual framework to consider all of the values supplied by an ecosystem to people, society and the economy.[1] It is based on two broad categories of value:

'Use values'

'Use values' include direct and indirect use of ecosystems and options for future use:

- *Direct use value* arises from the direct use of an ecosystem good or service and can include consumptive use (e.g. timber production) and non-consumptive use (e.g. wildlife viewing).
- *Indirect use value* refers to benefits derived from effects on other goods and services which people value (e.g. regulating services for water are valued because they protect people and property against flooding; pollination is important for food production).
- *Option use values* represent the value of having the option to use (directly and/or indirectly) the ecosystem good or service in the future.

'Non-use values'

'Non-use values' exist to the extent that people derive pleasure from simply knowing that nature and its elements (e.g. a rare species) exist (existence value) or because they wish to bequest it to future generations (bequest value) or to ensure that it is there for others in the present generation (altruist value). The bequest and altruist values are together termed 'philanthropic' values (see TEEB Foundations, 2010).

Figure 4.4 shows how the key elements of TEV can be applied to different types of ecosystem services.

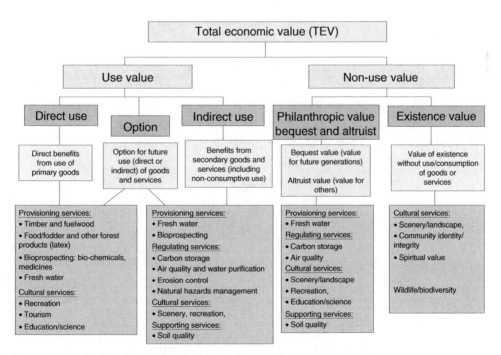

Figure 4.4 *Application of a total economic value framework to ecosystem services*

Source: Adapted from Kettunen et al (2009)

In addition, there is the 'insurance value' that depends on and is related to the ecosystem's resilience – its ability to resist pressures (e.g. pollution, climate change), stay in its stable state (and hence continue the flow of ecosystem services), and avoid passing a critical threshold, or flipping into another state where the ecosystem functions and services will be (potentially greatly) diminished (see Chapter 3 for critical thresholds, and TEEB Foundations (2010) for wider discussion on insurance value). In addition, Box 4.4 highlights that a cautious approach to land-use conversion might also be justifiable in light of the high costs associated with reversing past conversion decisions.

Box 4.4 The inherent value residing in the preserving options for the future: River restoration in Denmark

The decision to develop or convert land is often irreversible in practical terms: even where restoration may be technically possible it can involve very high costs and long delays. The Skjern River in Denmark provides an interesting illustration of this: the high costs of restoring the river to a natural course were incurred only a generation after the original decision to canalize the river (see Dubgaard, 2004). The restoration involved creating outflows from the river to the fjord in order to form a delta of ca. 220 hectares, creating a lake of ca. 160 hectares, and permitting periodic floods on land within the project area, requiring the conversion of 1550 hectares of arable land to extensive grazing.

Costs and benefits of Skjern River restoration (DKK million, 2000 prices, at 5 per cent discount rate and exchange rate of DKK8.08:$1)

Costs	149 ($18m)	Project costs (survey, design and construction work)
	27 ($3.3m)	Nature monitoring, information and education programmes
	(–32) (–$4.0m)	Grant from European Union (EU) towards above costs
	14.9 ($1.8m)	Operation and maintenance
	52.5 ($6.5m)	Opportunity cost of land (over 20 years)
Benefits	70.7 ($8.8m)	Improved outdoor recreation
	9.0 ($1.1m)	Improved hunting
	52.4 ($6.5m)	Improved fishing
	50.6 ($6.3m)	Non-use value of biodiversity
	29.2 ($3.6m)	Cost savings (land allocation, pumping costs, flood protection etc.)
	61.0 ($7.6m)	Nutrient and metal reduction
	5.0 ($0.6m)	Reed harvesting

The 'bottom line' results suggested NPVs of 228 million DKK ($36 million) at 3 per cent discounting, falling to 67 million ($8 million) at 5 per cent and break even at 7 per cent. This sensitivity to the discount rate is typical for projects with front-loaded costs and long-term benefits.

> The EU grant of 32 million DKK ($4 million) was counted as a benefit in the study because from the Danish perspective this was (arguably) additional funding that would not otherwise accrue to Denmark. From the European perspective, of course, this represents a transfer payment that should not appear in the CBA.
>
> The fact that this restoration decision was taken relatively soon after the original decision to canalize the river highlights a major asymmetry. Decisions to protect, conserve, or delay development are generally reversible in the sense that the development or conversion option will probably remain open in future, whereas decisions to develop or convert land may be costly or impossible to reverse. This asymmetry is reflected in economic value frameworks through option value. This is the value associated with keeping open the option of making currently unplanned use of resources in future, and it arises because of uncertainty about future conditions and preferences. This is particularly important in the context of biodiversity loss, which is irreversible, and where uncertainties about future possible uses and ecosystem service impacts are significant, making the option values associated with conservation potentially very large.
>
> *Source:* Dubgaard, 2004

The above approach(es) are all part of 'anthropocentric' valuation, and it is important to underline that biodiversity also has intrinsic values, i.e. value independent from human appreciation. While this chapter (and indeed the whole book) is mainly focused on ecosystem services flow – a human-centred approach to natural capital – we should never lose sight of biodiversity's wider ecological values.

Although in theory TEV could cover all benefits to the economy, people and society, in practice only a subset of the ecosystem services will be assessed in monetary terms; several benefits are still understood only in a partial way and some values have yet to be understood. As noted above, the TEV should therefore be seen as a partial estimate of the total system value (TSV) that combines all benefits, whether monetized, quantified or simply understood qualitatively.

2 Expanding monetary valuation of ecosystem services

2.1 How do common valuation methods work?

There are a number of methods for determining the monetary value of ecosystem services, all linked to 'willingness to pay' (WTP). Annex 1 provides a more detailed description of these methods and shows how they can be applied to different ecosystem services (see also Chapter 5 of TEEB Foundations, 2010).

Market analysis

Market analysis (i.e. revealed WTP) is valuable for measuring a range of benefits and costs where data on prices, quantities and costs associated with actual markets is available. These include market price-based approaches (where linked to prices of goods or services on the market) and cost-based approaches (e.g. related to avoided costs, replacement costs and mitigation or restoration costs) (see Annex 1 and TEEB Foundations, 2010). Examples include explicit revenues generated from services (e.g. forest products, fish) and a range of avoided costs, such as those of expenditure (e.g. water purification and provision), of replacement (e.g. artificial pollination), of insurance payments (e.g. for impacts of natural hazards) and of damage (e.g. from flooding).

Non-market valuation techniques

Where market values are not directly available or usable, we can use two well-recognized groups of non-market valuation techniques:

- 'Revealed preference methods' (i.e. imputed WTP) is demonstrated through e.g. increased house prices near parks, forests and beaches. These can lead to increased local government receipts.
- 'Stated preference methods' (e.g. expressed WTP) can be used in relation to e.g. improving water quality (linked to water pricing) or protecting charismatic species (linked to funding or park entrance fees).

There are also 'production function'-based approaches that look at the change in service provision from a change in biological resource and then value the impact of changes, e.g. by looking at corresponding change in marketed output (see Annex and TEEB Foundations, 2010).

Box 4.5 shows how different valuation techniques can be combined to provide a relatively complete picture of an ecosystem's total value.

The above methods provide primary analysis for use on a case-by-case basis. The next section considers ways to adapt case-specific information for wider application.

Box 4.5 Valuing ecosystem services to inform land-use choices: Opuntia scrubland in Peru

Opuntia scrublands in Ayacucho host cochineal insects (the source of carminic acid, a natural dye used in food, textile and pharmaceutical industries) and are used by local farmers for animal grazing and food provision. They perform a major environmental role by protecting slopes against erosion and flooding, and rehabilitating marginal lands, thus improving levels of humidity and soil retention capability.

A mix of techniques from demand- and supply-side toolkits can be used to assess the values associated with these different ecological functions, as detailed below.

Valuation of provisioning services

Direct use values of Opuntia (production of food, fruit, cochineal exports, manufactured dyes, fodder, fuel and ornamental goods) can be derived using direct market prices and, if necessary, the value of the closest substitute goods. For scrubland products (e.g. cochineal and fruit), once the yearly quantity and quality of yields and the size of the collection area are calculated, market prices can be used to derive the direct use value of the products collected in a given year. The use value of scrubland as a source of fuel can be quantified by considering the wage rate as a broad approximation of the opportunity cost of time spent by households in periodic working hours to generate the supply of fuel.

Value of regulating services

The value of the cash-crop depends on a parasitic insect living on Opuntia plants: farmers collect the cochineal by removing the insect from host plants. Insects not harvested are used to repopulate the scrubs for later harvests. The value of these nursery and refugium services can be quantified using a supply-side approach (based on the costs that farmers would incur if the host plants had to be manually infested, calculated by reference to the applicable labourers' wages that represent the opportunity cost of time).

Value of supporting services

Indirect use values attach to erosion control services critical for farmers in the high-sloped Andean area. Soil loss affects crop productivity but changes only become apparent after many years of severe soil loss. Farmers' interest in soil erosion is mainly concerned with on-farm impacts, e.g. increased production costs, decreased profitability owing to soil fertility decline, cost of implementing soil conservation measures. One way to quantify such benefits is to use a Contingent Valuation method, e.g. stated preference techniques to obtain a broad monetary idea of household WTP for erosion control services provided by scrubland.

The valuation found that even if only some of the intangible benefits are considered, the value of ecosystem services provided by Opuntia scrubland is higher than computable direct financial revenues from agriculture. The proportion of farmers' income attributable to direct use value of scrubland products is as high as 36 per cent. When indirect use values (regulation of soil erosion) are included, the value of scrubland for farmers rises to over 55 per cent of income.

Source: Adapted from Rodríguez et al (2006)

2.2 Scope for extending benefits transfer methods

'Benefits transfer' is a method of estimating economic values for ecosystem services by using values already developed in other studies of a similar ecosystem. It is a pragmatic way of dealing with information gaps and resource (time and money) constraints. This is important as there are rarely enough resources available to conduct a primary (or site-specific) valuation study for every site, ecosystem or service being assessed (see also Figure 4.2 above).

Benefits transfer is not a new concept but can be considered as a practical solution to resource constraints. The basic rationale is that there may be sufficient commonalities between ecosystem services in different areas to allow values from one area to be transferred to another. However, this needs to be done with care as values can vary widely even among similar ecosystems (see Box 4.6).

Box 4.6 Use of benefits transfer of values for non-timber forest products (NTFPs)

An analysis of studies undertaken suggests a clustering of NTFP values from a few dollars per hectare/year up to about US$100/year. Suggested 'default' values have been set at US$50 to US$70 per ha/year. While it is useful to respond to these default values by seeing if local natural capital has the same value, it would be a serious error to simply extrapolate these benchmark values to all forests. Typically, higher values relate to readily accessible forests whereas values for non-accessible forests would be close to zero in net terms, due to the cost of access and extraction. The key questions to consider are whether there are sufficient commonalities to allow a benefit transfer and also what 'weighting factor' may need to be applied, in the light of any differences, to make the benefits transfer sufficiently robust.

Source: CBD (2001)

The conditions which determine whether benefits transfer can provide valid and reliable estimates include:

- the commodity or service being valued is very similar at the site where the estimates were made and the site where they are applied;
- the populations affected have very similar characteristics; and
- the original estimates being transferred must themselves be reliable (CBD Decision VIII/26).

There is some scope to factor in differences (e.g. income, environmental conditions) and a range of tools available (see also TEEB Foundations, 2010), including:

- unit benefits transfer – e.g. multiplying a mean unit value (per household or per hectare) from a similar site by the quantity of the service at the site being assessed;
- adjusted unit benefits transfer – as above, but adjusting for site characteristics (e.g. income, population levels);
- value function transfer – e.g. use a value or demand function from one site (e.g. for travel cost and value of protected area) and apply, with parameters for new site (e.g. population, average income), to obtain site-specific value;
- meta-analysis (meta-analytic function transfer) – combine value or demand functions from several sites and apply with local site parameters.

Benefits transfer is still a developing subject. Specific actions that need to be undertaken to make such methods more widely applicable include:

- Development of more primary valuation studies. The more studies we have, the greater the statistical confidence with which a transfer can be undertaken – and the greater the policy makers' confidence in the underlying techniques.
- Increased development and access to valuation study databases. Some databases have been developed to make the technique of benefits transfer easier but existing databases tend either to be incomplete in their coverage of studies or are not freely available.[2]

- Development of benefits transfer guidance. Guidance on accounting for differences between the ecosystem/site being assessed and the ecosystem/site from which the benefit value/function is used (transferred) from and their respective beneficiaries should be developed to show best practice and indicate where benefits transfer can give a reasonable value of ecosystem services.

TEEB Foundations (2010) has collated over 1000 valuation studies and is developing them into a matrix of ecosystem services values across ecosystems to help offer a publicly valuable tool (see Box 4.7).

Box 4.7 Collected evidence on the values of ecosystem services

Over 1300 values have been collected to date, covering 11 biomes and 22 ecosystem services at around 270 locations. Values are organized based on geographical and socio-economic criteria and are also influenced by the context of the valuation study.

For most ecosystem services, it is not possible to 'plug and play' values from elsewhere without first considering the local characteristics. This was highlighted in Chapter 1 for tourism from coral reefs; Figure 4.5 shows values for different ecosystem services in tropical forests.

In practice, the 'default assumption' is often that the value of forests is the timber, and that there is no value attached to the wide range of other ecosystem services. The reality is that the value of other services can be high. This shows the need to consider how an ecosystem serves people and the impacts of its loss.

Understanding the services lost is an easy first step towards understanding the value at risk. Understanding the value is the basis for due commitment to and design of instruments that then turn some of the 'valuation values' into 'real values' and hence change the practical incentives on the ground.

Database soon to be available at http://www.fsd.nl/esp

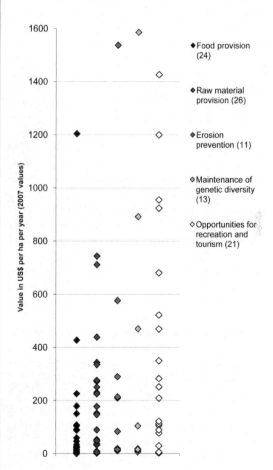

Figure 4.5 *Ecosystem services values from forests – sample from studies collected within TEEB Foundations (2010)*

Source: TEEB Foundations (2010) Appendix 3 and van der Ploeg et al (2010)

2.3 Examples of valuation in practice

The best way to demonstrate the 'value of valuation' is to show practical examples of some of the many ways in which it is already used.

Valuation can highlight the value of natural assets and help determine where ecosystem services can be provided at lower cost than man-made technological alternatives, e.g. water purification and provision, carbon storage, flood control (see Box 4.8).

Valuation can also communicate the need for and influence the size of payments for ecosystem services (PES). This can be useful for municipalities setting up PES for activities leading to clean water provision and, at international/national level, in discussions on the design and future implementation of REDD+ (Reducing Emissions from Deforestation and Forest Degradation in developing countries) (see Chapter 5).

Non-market valuation techniques can be used to evaluate damage to natural resources to determine appropriate compensation, e.g. under liability regimes in the US and the EU this has proved of particular value for court decisions on liability (see Box 4.9).

Box 4.8 Values of water provision in New Zealand

A 2006 study commissioned by the Department of Conservation found that Te Papanui Conservation Park (Lammermoor Range) provided the Otago region with water that would cost NZ$136 million (around US$96 million) to get from elsewhere. The 22,000 hectare tussock grass area acts as a natural water catchment, supplying water flows valued at NZ$31 million (around US$22 million) for hydroelectricity, NZ$93 million (around US$65 million) for the city of Dunedin's water supply and a further NZ$12 million (around US$8.5 million) for irrigating 60,000 hectares of Taieri farmland. The NZ$136 million corresponds to a one-off sum to describe the avoided cost of having to suddenly get water currently provided free of charge by Te Papanui from somewhere else.

Source: New Zealand Department of Conservation (2006)

Box 4.9 Three cases of using valuation to assess levels of compensation in legal claims

The *Exxon Valdez* oil spill

The *Exxon Valdez* oil spill (1989), which affected 200km of Alaskan coastline, provides an example of 'stated preference' being used to calculate compensation. The legal proceedings included a compensation claim for both use and non-use values, calculated through a contingent valuation study over 18 months (including field testing, work with focus groups, pilot surveys and interviews with around 1600 people). Statistical analysis of these responses gave a US$2.8 billion lower bound WTP to avoid the damages. Eventually, Exxon settled its lawsuit with the US Government for US$1 billion and agreed to spend around US$2 billion on clean-up: it later settled a class action lawsuit for additional amounts. These costs were consistent with the estimates from the valuation study. The case also:

- boosted efforts to evaluate environmental damage and helped to speed up development and use of methodologies to capture the value of biodiversity and ecosystem services;
- stimulated policy responses consistent with the polluter pays principle (i.e. compensation payments based on values of damaged biodiversity and ecosystem services);
- led to enactment of the US Oil Pollution Act 1990 and international maritime regulations;
- based on economic analysis, led to regulatory prescriptions for double-hull ship building measures. Now a great majority of oil tankers criss-crossing the globe are of double-hull design.

Indian Supreme Court and forest conversion payments

In 2006, the Indian Supreme Court set compensatory payments for the conversion of different types of forested land to non-forest use. The Court drew on an economic valuation study of Indian forests by the Green Indian States Trust (GIST, 2006) to determine the rates. This estimated for six different classes of forests the value of timber, fuelwood, non-timber forest products (NTFPs) and ecotourism, bioprospecting, ecological services of forests and non-use values for the conservation of some charismatic species (e.g. royal Bengal tiger, Asian lion).

The compensatory payments are made to a forestation fund to improve the country's forest cover. In 2009 the Supreme Court directed that Rs.10 billion (around €143 million) be released every year towards forestation, wildlife conservation and for creating rural jobs (see also Chapter 7).

Valuation of fees for damages to coral reefs in Israel

Ship groundings are frequent occurrences that damage coral reefs, impairing their ability to provide services such as fisheries and recreation. The results of a monetary valuation of coral reefs in the northern Red Sea were used to develop a protocol for estimating the size of fees for damages caused by ship groundings to coral reefs. This protocol considers the area of a coral reef that is damaged, the costs of damage assessment incurred by the environmental authorities, the costs of habitat restoration projects and their monitoring, and the rates of natural recovery of coral reefs. In the Israeli Red Sea, where coral reefs provide important recreational services, the damage of a 20m^2 area of coral reef would signify a charge of approximately US$120,000 to the party responsible for the damage (Wielgus et al, 2003; Wielgus, 2004).

Valuation can create political support for designing new fiscal instruments, e.g. to help set taxes at the level equivalent to the cost of environmental impacts of certain activities. One example is the UK landfill tax: the value of damage caused by using landfills for waste disposal (instead of incineration) was an element in setting the tax rate (EEA, 2005). In Japan, valuation was used to justify local taxes to help with forest management (see Box 4.10).

Box 4.10 Using valuation to justify payment of local tax revenues for forests in Japan

Background

About two-thirds of land in Japan is covered by forests. However, for decades local forest industries have been negatively affected by having to compete with cheaper timber imports. Many forest lands were simply abandoned without proper management, resulting in serious degradation of forest land and related ecosystem services. In 2001, the Science Council of Japan estimated that the value of ecosystem services under threat amounted to JPY70 trillion (Yen) per year or US$620 billion/year.

Table 4.1 Evaluation of multiple functions of forests

Ecosystem service	Value per year of forests for 2001 (JPY)	Billion US$/yr
Absorb carbon dioxide	1.24 trillion/year	10.8
Substitute for fossil fuel	0.23 trillion/year	2.0
Prevent surface erosion	28.26 trillion/year	245.7
Prevent loss of topsoil	8.44 trillion/year	73.4
Ameliorate flooding	6.47 trillion/year	56.2
Conserving headwater resources	8.74 trillion/year	84.7
Purify water	14.64 trillion/year	127.3
Health and recreation	2.26 trillion/year	19.6

Note: For the first seven services the replacement cost method was used; for health and recreation, household expenditures (travel costs) were used.

Source of funds

The scheme was introduced in Kochi Prefecture in 2003. By June 2009, 30 out of 47 prefectures had adopted comparable 'forest environmental taxes' or 'water and green forest management taxes'. Each prefecture levies JPY500 to JPY1000 (approximately US$5 to US$10) per inhabitant and JPY10,000 to JPY80,000 (approximately US$100 to US$800) per business every year to fund restoration and enhancement of forest ecosystem services (excluding timber production).

Use of the funds

Tax revenues are usually paid into a special fund spent on forest management activities to maintain water resources, prevent natural disasters or enrich biodiversity by altering mono-species forest to mixed species forest, etc. To ensure long-term environmental benefits, the Prefecture and forest owners usually conclude an agreement not to harvest the forest in the short term but to maintain it for a certain period of time (e.g. at least 10 years) before getting financial assistance through the scheme.

Source: Science Council of Japan (2001); MAFF Japan (2008)

The travel cost method can be used to set entry fees for e.g. national parks (see Box 4.11 and also Chapter 8).

Valuation has informed impact assessment of proposed legislation and policies. Examples include the EU Water Framework Directive and new marine legislation in the UK which provides for the establishment of Marine Conservation Zones on the basis of the ecosystem service benefits they provide.

For products not traded in conventional markets, valuation can reveal the relative importance of different ecosystem products (see Box 4.12).

Box 4.11 Entry fees for parks

Countries that face difficulties in mobilizing public money for nature conservation often resort to entrance fees to national parks, which are important revenue sources, as in the case of entry fees to the Biebrza National Park, Poland (OECD, 1999).

Charging special fees for specific activities in protected areas is also quite common, such as the fees added to diving costs in marine reserves in the Philippines (Arin and Kramer, 2002).

Evaluation exercises help to identify the range of prices that a visitor will be willing to pay for access to a natural area and recreation or other activities there. Tourists are interested in preserving the sites they visit and a small increase in the fees they pay only amounts to a small fraction of the total cost of their trip.

Box 4.12 Valuing ecosystem services at the country and regional level in the Mediterranean

A 2005 regional study valued the potential of NTFPs as a source of livelihood and sustainable development. It estimated benefits for six major NTFP groups: firewood, cork, fodder, mushrooms, honey and other products. Valuation was based on a variety of techniques, drawing on official statistics, and supplemented by local surveys.

At the regional level, NTFPs were found to provide annual benefits of about €39/ ha of forests, i.e. about 25 per cent of the total economic value of forests. The average estimate for southern countries (€54/ha) is considerably higher than for northern (€41/ ha) or eastern countries (€20/ha). The study thus reveals the importance of NTFP benefits both for specific countries and for the region as a whole.

Source: Croitoru (2005)

2.4 Limits to monetary valuation

Valuation tools that follow best practices can provide useful and reliable information on changes in the value of non-marketed ecosystem services that would result from human activities. However, monetary valuation has its limits and it would be contentious and incorrect to rely solely on this. Some key factors to bear in mind are outlined below:

- Costs and required expertise can be significant. Most assessment frameworks recognize this by recommending that scoping studies are prepared for 'light' analysis and that in-depth analysis is done later only if it provides added value.
- Valuation provides an essentially static picture, in other words what something is worth today. As ecosystem services become scarcer or support more marketed goods, then their value changes over time.
- It is only appropriate for small changes. Particular care needs to be taken where threshold effects (i.e. critical ecological thresholds passed) are possible as this can lead to abrupt changes in values (see TEEB Foundations, 2010).
- Expertise in monetary valuation is concentrated in developed countries. It is less used in developing countries, where other cultural or socio-economic challenges may also make it necessary to adapt techniques before application, e.g. incorporation of more participatory approaches and building local research capacity (Christie et al, 2008).

Overall, there are clearly reasons for optimism about using non-market valuation techniques for the valuation of ecosystem services. The thousands of studies already undertaken have led to considerable practical progress. However, valuation needs to be used judiciously. It is only one of many inputs into decision making, given the complexity of the underlying ecosystem services that are being valued. In view of current constraints on quantification and valuation, we need to see economic assessment as a tool to inform biodiversity protection, not as a precondition for taking action.

3 Integrating economic thinking into policy assessment

The role of all policy assessments[3] – including cost–benefit analysis – is to organize information in such a way that decision makers can consider trade-offs and take better-informed decisions. Valuation is an input to decision making, but does not by itself provide the decision. It has a particular role for biodiversity as the provision of ecosystem services is currently often not factored into decisions affecting ecosystems. The policy assessment techniques described in this chapter are feasible, practical and road-tested ways to correct this distortion.

3.1 What can policy assessments contribute?

A policy assessment framework is a way to improve the quality and coherence of the policy development process and better integrate biodiversity concerns.

It is hard to measure the pay-off of such a framework because, by definition, we do not know what would have happened in its absence. However, where properly conducted, assessments are generally found to be a worthwhile and often low-cost investment. The European Commission estimates that they change around two-thirds of its policies for the better: this finding is supported by broader analysis of regulatory impact assessment (Jacobs, 2006; Evaluation Partnership, 2007).

Policy assessments come in many forms, from formal to informal and from upfront to reactive (i.e. to justify decisions already taken or at least check that there are no major negative impacts). They are in place for different levels of decision making: local, regional and national. Box 4.13 describes the best-known formal procedures.[4]

Although this range may seem wide, the processes are closely related. For example RIA, sustainability impact assessments and integrated assessments can all be seen as forms of SEA applied to specific institutional contexts.

Box 4.13 The main policy assessment processes: EIA and SEA

Environmental impact assessment

Environmental impact assessment (EIA) has a project focus. It is the process of evaluating the likely environmental impacts, including impacts on biodiversity, of a proposed project prior to decision making. EIA is intended to predict environmental impacts at an early stage in project planning and design, find ways and means to reduce adverse impacts, shape projects to suit the local environment and present the predictions and options to decision makers. However, existing EIA tools often do not perform their full job as they are not applied early or thoroughly enough in the decision-making process and their insights are not always fully taken on board in subsequent project decisions.

Strategic environmental assessment

Strategic environmental assessment (SEA)[5] has a broader sustainable development (economic, social and environmental) focus. It is a systematic and comprehensive process of identifying and evaluating the environmental consequences of proposed policies, plans or programmes to ensure that they are fully included and addressed early on in decision making, along with economic and social considerations. SEA covers a wide range of activities, often over a longer time span. It may be applied to an entire sector (e.g. a national energy policy) or geographical area (e.g. a regional development scheme).

These two frameworks should complement each other. EIA is undertaken 'downstream' whereas SEA takes place 'upstream'. SEA does not usually reduce the need for project-level EIA but it can help to streamline incorporation of environmental concerns (including biodiversity) into the decision-making process, often making project-level EIA more effective.

EIA and SEA are familiar terms, but variants of SEA can be found in several contexts:

- UNEP – integrated assessment and policymaking for sustainable development;
- regulatory impact analysis (RIA) to examine and measure the likely benefits, costs and effects of proposals or amendments to policies and regulations;
- trade impact assessment – sometimes referred to as integrated assessments (IA) or sustainability impact assessment (SIA) – covers trade both in goods that can affect biodiversity and in commodities provided by biodiversity that are traded internationally.

Assessment frameworks ask common questions, tailored to the needs of the specific policy-making process. This commonality is no surprise because the broad questions that need to be asked to inform decisions are always the same, whether it is a decision on biodiversity or finance or at local or national level. What is the problem? What do we want to achieve? What are the options for addressing the problem? What are the impacts of different options? Answering these questions can change policies (see Box 4.14).

These common characteristics provide opportunities for learning from others and sharing best practice in order to understand how a wide range of policies can impact biodiversity and ecosystem services. Box 4.15 outlines ways in which SEA has been useful in one region of the world.

Box 4.14 Valuation study to determine a watershed tax rate in Japan

In Japan, around 29 local prefectures have introduced forest conservation taxes or watershed forest taxes. In Kanagawa Prefecture near Tokyo, valuation methods were used to determine the tax rate for the watershed forest tax in 2002. The valuation study was conducted at the initiative of the Kanagawa Prefecture supported by a professor. This found the WTP for a forest conservation policy to be JPY3673 per person per year (contingent valuation method) and JPY1966 per person per year (conjoint analysis). These results were fed into the Prefecture's discussions on the level of the watershed forest tax: the tax rate was finally set at around JPY950 per person per year, varied according to income level. A similar example is available from the Shiga Prefecture focused on WTP for the establishment of an environmental agriculture fund.

Source: Yoshida (2004)

Box 4.15 Has SEA helped? Lessons learned in the European Union

A review of the way the 27 EU Member States implement the SEA Directive shows that application varies from country to country, reflecting different institutional and legal arrangements. Reported SEA costs vary widely, according to the type of plan or programme being assessed, ranging from €3000 to €100,000.

Member States identify a large number of benefits of SEA, the main ones being that:

- SEA integrates environmental considerations into decision making and makes plans and programmes 'greener';
- SEA supports participation and consultation of relevant public authorities and strengthens cooperation between different (planning and environmental/health) authorities;
- SEA increases transparency in decision making through better stakeholder involvement;
- SEA makes it easier to comply with specific requirements of the policy concerned and to check coherence with other environmental policies;
- SEA helps to identify relevant issues and knowledge of an area's environmental context and to share this knowledge between different actors.

Source: COWI (2009)

All decision making relies on information, even where no formal EIA or SEA has been undertaken. In the area of biodiversity and ecosystem services, information demands are complex. Common difficulties relate to measurement, data availability, lack of scientific certainty, the unidentified value of biodiversity, and uncertainty over the relationship between biodiversity and ecosystem services. Moreover, impacts are often felt in the future or in distant places, and even expert knowledge can be uncertain or conflicting.

In practice, often the question is essentially a choice between uncertain value (biodiversity and ecosystem services) and the relative certainty of an alternative land use. This choice will almost always be weighted towards the alternative land use.

The need to better incorporate biodiversity into mainstream sectoral policy assessments is now receiving high-level attention. Box 4.16 provides an example of work being carried out at the agriculture–trade–biodiversity interface.

3.2 How can we make better use of available information?

Good progress is now being made to develop indicators for biodiversity and ecosystem services (see Chapter 3). However, we also know that information needed is often available but not accessed. Involving the stakeholders who do have information at hand is fundamental – not least because they may ultimately be the people most affected.

Box 4.16 Making a case for biodiversity in mainstream policy assessment

A synthesis of assessment frameworks used to identify the impact of trade liberalization on agricultural biodiversity revealed several common challenges with respect to integrating biodiversity into trade-related assessments.[6]

The frameworks analysed offer entry points to explicitly integrate biodiversity into assessments as a way to move the issue up the policy agenda. However, their practical application shows that final recommendations tend to focus on wider environmental issues (deforestation, soil degradation, pesticide use or water quality) where impacts are obvious and information more easily available. Particular challenges for ensuring proper consideration of biodiversity within the assessment include:

- difficulties in establishing cause–effect chains of trade liberalization on agricultural biodiversity;
- the multidimensional concept of biodiversity makes it harder to develop aggregated indicators that could be included in economic models;
- insufficient data availability and comparability;
- insufficient methodologies to measure biodiversity impacts;
- shortage of reliable scientific information.

Building on its earlier work on integrated assessment of trade-related policies (UNEP, 2009a), UNEP has developed step-by-step guidance for incorporating biodiversity-related issues and actions at each stage of the assessment process (UNEP 2009b, see Annex 2).

Sources: UNEP (2009a, 2009b)

Decisions are always taken in the absence of perfect information. In practice, this is a question of degree. The reality in both developing and developed countries is that there are data gaps and more systematic collection of biodiversity data is needed. However, this lack of information should not be taken as an argument to delay action to protect ecosystem services, rather the opposite. A small amount of analysis can often allow decision makers to protect biodiversity and ecosystem services in ways that can benefit the majority.

The strength of a policy assessment process is to provide a structured framework for systematically asking standard questions and requiring collection of necessary information. Table 4.2 shows how standard questions can be given a biodiversity-specific dimension.

3.3 Best practices for more effective assessment frameworks

This section sets out 'building blocks' to improve assessment frameworks and shows how and when information on the economics of ecosystems and biodiversity can be fed into the process.

Table 4.2 Adapting standard questions to cover biodiversity and ecosystem services

Standard question	Biodiversity and ESS-specific questions
What is the problem?	• How do we measure biodiversity? • How do we measure biodiversity loss? • How does loss of biodiversity translate into lost ESS? • Are there threshold effects, including critical thresholds, that might be breached? • What are the relationships between biodiversity in this site and elsewhere?
What are the objectives?	• Are there national biodiversity objectives? • Is there a national biodiversity strategy?
What are the main policy options?	• How could biodiversity loss be mitigated?
What are the economic, social and environmental impacts of those options?	• How much biodiversity would be lost or gained with a particular action? • What is the value of ESS? • How do we account for loss of biodiversity far into the future? • How do we take account of distributional impacts? • How do we account for the fact that biodiversity loss may affect people in other areas or countries? • How do we value ESS that have only 'option value' or have not even been identified so far?
What is the most favourable option?	• How do we ensure decisions take into account the lack of certainty over biodiversity? • How do we balance potential biodiversity impacts against other potential impacts (balancing various policy options)?
How will it be monitored and evaluated in the future?	• How do we monitor and ensure implementation of 'conservation area' or rules (e.g. management practices)?

Best practice 1: Understand changes in ecosystem services

We need to understand what is currently happening (sometimes called 'problem definition'). This means understanding the state of existing biodiversity and the ecosystem services that it provides. There is also a need to understand what is driving current trends, including the degradation or loss of biodiversity (see Box 4.17).

For any policy, there is ultimately a need to understand what ecosystem services will be lost and what this means for different stakeholders and what actions will tackle the problem.

Best practice 2: Undertake an integrated analysis

Information is of little use if it does not influence decisions. Similarly, having information on biodiversity and ecosystem services impacts is of little use if it is not considered with information on other economic, social and environmental impacts (see Box 4.18). The best approach is always a fully integrated assessment. EIA and SEA are the best-known processes for delivering such integration. They can be extremely effective but current EIA implementation is often weak, which leads to problems on the ground.

Box 4.17 Example of analysis of drivers of biodiversity loss

Understanding the combination of direct and indirect factors leading to biodiversity loss allows for better targeted and more cost-efficient policies to be put in place. In this example, a mixture of economic, institutional, political, natural and social factors constitute the drivers of deforestation and degradation. The first step in designing a policy response is to appreciate that the reasons for continued conversion of tropical forest land are interrelated as well as their relative importance in a specific country.

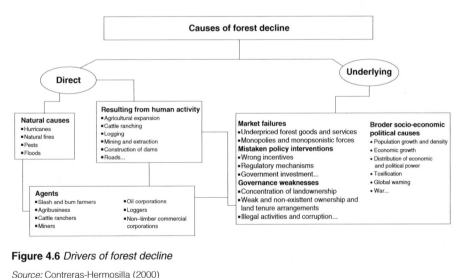

Figure 4.6 *Drivers of forest decline*

Source: Contreras-Hermosilla (2000)

Box 4.18 Implementing an integrated landscape approach in India

Social and environmental issues are addressed together through the Biodiversity Conservation and Rural Livelihood Improvements Project, currently being implemented by the Government of India with the support of the Global Environment Facility. The project is designed at a landscape level which encompasses protected areas (PAs), non-PA forests and other land uses. It signals a shift from PA-based conservation approaches, which largely managed PAs as 'islands' surrounded by other land uses which were rarely compatible with conservation goals and outcomes.

Through its integrated approach, the project influences development and conservation in lands surrounding the PAs by promoting rural livelihoods and addressing biodiversity concerns. This has strengthened the management and viability of core PAs, thus expanding conservation efforts to the landscape level (see also Chapter 8).

Source: BCRLIP (2009)

For assessment processes focused on other types of impact, one way to force biodiversity impacts to be considered is to require environmental assessments or more specific biodiversity assessments.

Best practice 3: Quantify and monetize ecosystem service impacts where possible

Decision making is always based on a broad comparison of costs and benefits, even in cases where these are not all monetized (i.e. balancing pros and cons). However, biodiversity and ecosystem services are too often left out of the decision when they cannot be quantified or monetized.

We therefore need a framework that begins by identifying all costs and benefits. This can then be developed, first by including qualitative information on their nature and scale and then through quantification and valuation. Where only partial quantification and valuation is possible, this still helps to highlight which relevant costs and benefits have been included and which omitted.

Once we have quantification and valuation in monetary terms (see Section 2), we usually have to compare costs and benefits both now and over time by using a 'discount rate'. Discounting is the practice of attaching a lower weight to future costs and benefits than to present costs and benefits (e.g. a social discount rate of 4 per cent means that society values €1 today as equivalent to €1.04 in a year's time).[7] There are different views about what an appropriate discount rate should be (see Box 4.19).

Best practice 4: Compare pros and cons (or costs and benefits)

When considering an option, we need to consider all the relevant positive and negative impacts together. What are the trade-offs? What ecosystem services might be lost and what would we gain in their place?

Box 4.19 The choice of the discount rate

Discounting is important to the analysis of long-term projects. For instance, a hundred-year project, yielding benefits of €22,000 on completion, is worth around €8000 today at a 1 per cent discount rate but only €1 at a 10 per cent discount rate.

In general, a lower discount rate will favour ecosystem services as they are expected to continue into the far future and this increases the weighting placed on them. However, this is not always the case as a low discount rate will also favour any project with large upfront costs and benefits further in the future, including for example road building, which could adversely impact on biodiversity and ecosystem services.

Practice varies considerably. An OECD survey of its Member Countries found that the social discount rate used was usually around 4 to 5 per cent but varied from 3 per cent in Denmark to 10 per cent in Australia. Some countries allowed for declining rates (usually after 30 years). In practice, what is most surprising is how infrequently the benefits of ecosystem services are recognized, quantified and monetized. This – rather than the choice of discount rate – may well be the biggest analytical bias against the preservation of ecosystem services.

Some argue that the social discount rate should be lower. The Stern Review on the Economics of Climate Change argued for a discount rate lower than any of those used currently used by a government, though this is challenged by a number of mainstream economists (see TEEB Foundations, 2010).

Source: OECD (2006a)

Comparing trade-offs is simple enough when there is a full financial cost–benefit analysis: all economic, social and environmental impacts are expressed in monetary terms and can be easily added up or subtracted. However, this is rarely possible. In practice, we have to consider positive and negative impacts, only some of which will be quantified (see Box 4.20 for a case where a high degree of monetization was possible).

Box 4.20 An integrated valuation approach for the Scheldt (Belgium–Netherlands)

Major infrastructural works were planned in the Scheldt estuary, flowing from Belgium into The Netherlands, including the deepening of the fairway to the harbour of Antwerp and complementary measures to protect the land from storm floods coming from the North Sea.

A cost–benefit analysis was carried out, taking into account ecosystem services and using a contingent valuation study to value the recreational value of new floodplains. It shows that an intelligent combination of dikes and floodplains can offer more benefits at lower cost than more drastic measures such as a storm surge barrier near Antwerp. The hydrodynamic modelling also shows that floodplains are the best way to reduce future flooding risks.

The initial results showed that the benefits of floodplains were highest and that floodplains with reduced tidal areas (RTA) were more attractive than floodplains with a controlled inundation area (CIA). Based on these results, the Dutch and Flemish governments approved an integrated management plan consisting of the restoration of approximately 2500ha of intertidal and 3000ha of non-tidal areas, the reinforcements of dikes and dredging to improve the fairway to Antwerp.

Table 4.3 Different alternatives for flood protection in the CBA (Phase One: Different measures; Phase Two: Optimization)

Measurements	Phase One: Different measures					Phase Two: Optimization
	Storm surge barrier	Over-Schelde	Dikes (*340km*)	Floodplains (CIA, *1800ha*)	Floodplains (RTA, *1800ha*)	Floodplains (*1325ha*) + dikes (*24km*)
Investment and maintenance costs	387	1,597	241	140	151	132
Loss of agriculture				16	19	12
Flood protection benefits	727	759	691	648	648	737
Ecological benefits				8	56	9
Other impacts:						
Shipping	−1					
Visual intrusion				−3	−3	−5
Total net benefits	339	−837	451	498	530	596
Payback period (years)	**41**		**27**	**17**	**14**	**14**

Note: Figures are net present values in €/million (2004), based on central estimates for economic growth and discounting (4 per cent). Non-use values for nature development are not included in the figures.

Source: De Nocker et al (2004), Meire et al (2005), Broekx et al (2010)

As discussed above, there is a strong case for quantifying and valuing in monetary terms more systematically than we do now. Even where this happens, there will still be questions about the impact on different groups and on distributional impacts. This reminds us that policy assessment serves to inform decision makers and help them weigh up the pros and cons of different options, but not to take the actual decision in their place.

A partial cost–benefit analysis can often be performed where some elements are quantified and monetized. The identified net benefits can then be compared with the qualitative assessment of remaining costs and benefits. Several analytical frameworks can help in such cases, including multi-criteria analysis. All methods are designed to ensure that the main impacts have been identified and then compare their pros and cons.

Best practice 5: Identify who wins and who loses from changes in ecosystem services

Knowing what the impacts are is not enough: we also need to understand who is affected and when. If the loss of ecosystem services affects one group disproportionately, this needs to be taken into account: it might lead to measures to protect that group or the biodiversity they depend on. Different actions could leave existing inequalities unchanged, aggravate them or help to reduce them.

Table 4.4 uses the example of forestry to show how different elements of total economic value may vary in their importance to different groups.

Distributional analysis can reveal areas where we need to align local decisions with social benefits at the national or even international level, using mechanisms such as REDD-plus. Under current systems, incentives for different groups are often incompatible. For example, deforestation may be in the interests of a regional community, but against those of an indigenous community and the international community.

Best practice 6: Involve and engage stakeholders

One of the best ways to understand who wins and loses is to involve all potentially affected groups in the appraisal process (see Box 4.21). As highlighted in Chapter 2, stakeholders are a source of expertise, data and opinions. The traditional knowledge

Table 4.4 Distributing total economic value from forestry between stakeholders

Stakeholders	Extractive direct use values	Non-extractive direct use values	Indirect use values	Preservation values
Forest land users	Forest and agricultural products, including sale, subsistence and inputs into the farming system, (e.g. fodder, litter, etc.)	Cultural and spiritual values	Microclimate, hydrological, soil conservation and nutrient cycling	Preserving use values for descendants
Commercial interests	Timber, commercial NTFPs, genetic material for pharmaceutical development	Tourism	Downstream irrigation/water benefits to commercial farmers, water and electricity companies, and other businesses	Undiscovered commercial potential of biodiversity
National and forestry department interests	Forest revenue and foreign exchange	Recreation, tourism, education, science	A range of watershed protection services	Future biodiversity values
Global society interests	Globally traded products	Science (especially medical, education)	Global environmental services, e.g. carbon sinks	Existence values, future medicinal discoveries

of indigenous people who are the stewards of biodiversity is immensely rich and should be seen as an essential complement to the generation of technology-based data (GIS, remote sensing, etc.).

Developing stakeholders' sense of ownership and building trust in the people undertaking the policy assessment makes it easier to feed their perceptions and knowledge into the decision-making process. This has many advantages, particularly because biodiversity issues are often hidden to all but a few expert or local stakeholders.

As Chapter 3 emphasized, it is often the poorest in society who depend most on biodiversity and ecosystem services and are most vulnerable to changes in such services (e.g. availability of fuel or water for private use). Consulting such groups presents challenges but neglecting them in decision making can undermine the effectiveness of adopted policies (e.g. resistance, weak implementation and/or adverse social side-effects).

The need for better participatory practices and more transparency is now widely acknowledged (see Box 4.22): this book highlights many examples of good practice in both developing and developed countries. Where done well, these are a relatively easy way to improve decision-making processes and understanding of final policy choices.

Box 4.21 Identifying the three different levels of stakeholders

Beneficiaries

Beneficiaries are target groups that make use of or put value on known ecosystem services which will be deliberately enhanced by the policy, plan or programme under consideration.

Affected people

Affected (groups of) people experience intended or unintended changes in the ecosystem services they value as a result of the policy, plan or programme.

General stakeholders

General stakeholders can be:

- national or local government institutions having formal responsibility for management of defined areas (town and country planning departments, etc.) or ecosystem services (fisheries, forestry, water supply, coastal defence, etc.);
- formal and informal institutions representing affected people (water boards, trade unions, consumer organizations, civil rights movements, ad hoc citizens committees, etc.);
- formal and informal institutions representing (the intrinsic value of) biodiversity (non-governmental nature conservation organizations, park management committees, scientific panels, etc.);
- the general public, which wants to be informed on new developments in their direct or indirect environment (linked to transparency of democratic processes); and
- stakeholders of future generations who may rely on the biodiversity under consideration.

Source: CBD and NCEA (2006)

Box 4.22 International backing for public participation in environmental decision making: Aarhus Convention (1998)

The UNECE Convention on Access to Information, Public Participation in Decision making and Access to Justice in Environmental Matters ('Aarhus Convention') establishes legally binding rights and obligations with regard to government decision-making processes on matters concerning the local, national and transboundary environment. It has so far been signed by around 40 (primarily European and Central Asian) countries and the European Community and described by Kofi Annan, former Secretary-General of the United Nations (1997–2006), as 'the most ambitious venture in the area of environmental democracy so far undertaken under the auspices of the United Nations' (see Aarhus Convention website: www.unece.org/env/pp/).

Box 4.23 Valuing keystone species: The case of the Asian elephant, India

In the Western Ghats biodiversity hotspot in Karnataka, India, a valuation study was conducted among a cross-section of local communities (coffee growers, tribal people, farmers and pastoralists living in or near national parks and wildlife sanctuaries). It used the Asian elephant as a case study in order to assess the opportunity costs of biodiversity conservation, local community attitudes and their willingness to pay for biodiversity conservation and wildlife protection.

The study revealed that despite the high local opportunity costs of biodiversity conservation, the local communities had a pro-environmental attitude and were willing to pay about US$139.40 per household/year (1999 prices) in terms of spending time on participatory conservation activities. The hotspot provides valuable ecosystem services, including drinking water from the Cauvery River for Bangalore, Mysore and other towns as well as irrigation water for farmers in the Cauvery Delta.

The study recommended imposition of a watershed protection charge on the city residents and on farmers in order to reward forest dwellers who conserve this important ecosystem service: the funds collected are paid towards development and forestation works in the forest areas. The Western Ghats Task Force, set up by the Government of Karnataka (India), accepted this recommendation.

Source: Ninan (2007)

Stakeholder consultation and transparency, alongside good governance (see Chapter 2), are essential to limit abuse or non-use of available information (e.g. in cases where decision makers benefit from a situation that has negative impacts for the majority). Well-designed processes can promote effective public participation (see Box 4.23) provided that they specifically address common constraints such as:

- poverty (involvement means time spent away from income-producing tasks);
- rural settings (distance makes communication more difficult and expensive);

- illiteracy or lack of command of non-local languages can inhibit representative involvement if print media are used;
- local behavioural norms or cultural practice can inhibit involvement of groups who may not feel free to disagree publicly with dominant groups (e.g. women versus men);
- languages (in some areas a number of different languages or dialects may be spoken, making communication difficult);
- legal systems may be in conflict with traditional systems and cause confusion about rights and responsibilities for resources;
- interest groups may have conflicting or divergent views and vested interests;
- confidentiality (this can be important for the proponent, who may be against early involvement and consideration of alternatives) (CBD and NCEA, 2006).

Best practice 7: Implement the ecosystem approach

Assessment processes can be linked to the ecosystem approach, a paradigm for the integrated management of land, water and living resources that promotes conservation and sustainable use in an equitable way. The ecosystem approach can be applied to a specific sector (e.g. by the FAO for fisheries) or in a more generic way as under the Convention on Biological Diversity.[8]

The ecosystem approach is based on the application of appropriate scientific methodologies focused on levels of biological organization which encompass the essential processes, functions and interactions among organisms and their environment. Box 4.24 provides an example of how human uses, cultural diversity and established economic practices can be recognized through an ecosystem-based approach to assessment.

Box 4.24 Applying ecosystem-level SEA in the Sperrgebiet Land Use Plan, Namibia

The Sperrgebiet is a biodiversity-rich desert wilderness in southwest Namibia which includes a diamond mining area. In 1994, recognizing conflicting demands on the fragile ecosystem, an agreement was reached between the government, Namdeb (the mining licence holder) and NGOs to formulate an integrated land-use plan to safeguard the region's long-term economic and ecological potential. An SEA-type approach was used, involving several steps:

- a literature review with gaps filled through consultations with specialists;
- development of sensitivity maps for various biophysical and archaeological parameters;
- extensive public consultation (public workshops, information leaflets, feedback forms, land-use questionnaires)
- identification of different land-use options for the area and their evaluation in terms of environmental opportunities and constraints;
- formulation of a vision (declaration of the entire Sperrgebiet as a protected area);
- development of an interim zoning plan to guide immediate decisions, followed by a technical specialist workshop to refine the final zoning plan;
- a preliminary economic analysis of the main land-use options;

- development of an administrative framework covering land proclamation, management advisory committee, ecotourism models, zoning, future access control, and integration into the surrounding political and economic structures;
- for each potential land use, guidelines were prepared outlining what needs to be included in a project-specific EIA and the Environmental Management Plan.

The Land Use Plan was finalized in 2001 and the Sperrgebiet proclaimed a National Park in 2004, after the Plan's recommendations were accepted.

Source: OECD (2006b)

Best practice 8: Account for risks and uncertainty

Since we know relatively little about biodiversity, there are often significant risks attached to policies that impact on it. It is important to identify these risks, their likelihood and the probable consequences (i.e. the impact, extent of the damage and costs) using different risk scenarios. Risks can rarely be reduced to zero without incurring large costs, but there are often measures to reduce them in an efficient way.

The 'precautionary principle'[9] requires decision makers to take a cautious approach where impacts on biodiversity cannot be predicted with confidence and/or where there is uncertainty about the effectiveness of mitigation measures. This obviously presents major challenges, e.g. for risks of invasive alien species impacts (species displacement, predation, lost output from agriculture), of fish stock collapse from overfishing or of loss of entire ecosystems (e.g. from coral reef loss due to pollution or climate change) (see Chapter 1).

We need to improve our understanding of the timing and scale of these impacts and, when it comes to diseases or invasive alien species spread, the pathway or pathogen involved. The biggest potential costs of biodiversity loss come from ecosystem collapse (see TEEB Climate Issues Update (2009) with regard to coral reefs), but it is extremely difficult to estimate the probability of this happening. Even at a local level, critical thresholds can mean change is unpredictable – ecosystems could be resilient but, above a certain threshold, become vulnerable to even small changes. It is important to develop indicators of critical thresholds and associated critical trends in the context of wider sets of indicators within the drivers, pressures, status, impact and responses (DPSIR) framework (see Chapter 3).

Risks from natural hazards, on the other hand, are well known – such as risks of flooding, storm surges on coasts, fires or drought – and there is also fairly good understanding, based on historical precedents, of where the areas most at risk are located, although now there is increasing uncertainty due to climate change.

It is increasingly clear that natural capital can significantly reduce the risk and scale of impact and damage (see Chapters 8 and 9). A valuable tool to manage the risk involves creating 'risk maps' to identify at-risk zones (e.g. for flooding). Looking to the future, identifying where natural capital (e.g. wetlands, mangroves, protected areas) can play a role in mitigating risks will be fundamental to risk maps and risk mitigation strategies. This can also contribute directly to strategies to adapt to climate change and reduce the risk of impacts. Links to spatial planning tools and policies will be of critical importance to help reduce the risks.

4 Next steps: The need to build assessment capacity

Throughout the world, policy-making processes are closely tied to social structures, cultures and established political, legal and administrative systems. These all have their own built-in rigidities. The priority now is to establish a culture of analysis and data collection and to institutionalize it. This is challenging, but it is possible; it is already happening in several countries.

The best way forward often involves step-by-step improvements. Even though the most detailed policy assessment frameworks can seem daunting in terms of effort, there are often 'low-hanging fruit', in other words a small amount of analysis can quickly pay dividends. We already have good examples that can be replicated and frameworks that can be adopted – most importantly some form of SEA.

Box 4.25 Capacity building for integrated assessment by UNEP

UNEP guidance for integrating assessment of trade-related policies and biodiversity in the agricultural sector (see Box 4.16) is built on the practical experiences of six African, Pacific and Caribbean (ACP) countries (Cameroon, Jamaica, Madagascar, Mauritius, Uganda and Papua New Guinea).

Between 2005 and 2009, these countries received support to design and undertake an integrated assessment of a trade policy affecting the agricultural sector and, based on the results, to implement policy recommendations and adjust tools and techniques to country-specific contexts. Pilot projects were designed and led through national institutions (a core team of researchers and decision makers, supported by national steering committees and stakeholders invited for consultations and review). In-country learning was complemented by international workshops for core team members (acting as multipliers) and by expert input at key stages.

Efforts to monetize biodiversity and ecosystem services through the UNEP programme fell short of initial expectations, due to lack of easily accessible data and insufficient resources under the projects to fill the gap. However, positive results of the initiative can be seen at different levels:

- collection of baseline data, development of biodiversity indicators, identification of data gaps and commitment to fill these gaps;
- establishment of government–research partnerships and a formalized process for stakeholder consultation, including those that represent biodiversity;
- commitment to more systematic screening of policies, decrees, laws and existing assessment procedures to better incorporate biodiversity considerations;
- enhanced promotion of farming systems that support conservation and/or sustainable use of biodiversity, e.g. through training in management practices, development of strategic sectoral plans, land-use plans and/or sustainability standards;
- initiation of further training in integrated assessment for national policy makers;
- expressed interest to apply the integrated assessment to other policies and sectors.

Source: UNEP (2009b)

A successful assessment process needs support and resources. Capacity-building programmes need to be country-specific and tailored to cultural, socio-economic and legal characteristics on the ground (see example in Box 4.25).

Capacity is most likely to develop if there is an accepted, functional and supported policy assessment framework that creates a demand for it. Ad hoc assessments may be good some of the time, but are unlikely to be systematically good or to allow for institutional learning.

Notes

1   Even with such a structured analysis, there is a risk of undervaluing the benefits of biodiversity. For example, there is a question as to whether secondary benefits of an ecosystem that favour another ecosystem are always properly covered.
2   Three of the best-known databases for ecosystem valuation are: the EVRI database www.evri.ca/; the RED database www.isis-it.net/red/; and the Ecosystem Services Database or ARIES database http://ecoinformatics.uvm.edu/aries/.
3   Policy assessment is a participatory process of combining, interpreting and communicating knowledge. It usually involves setting out a cause–effect chain – involving environmental, social and economic factors – associated with a proposed public policy to inform decision making. Including information on biodiversity and ecosystem services in this process means it is considered in decisions (UNEP, 2009a, p5).
4   This is not meant to be a full list. There are other tools (e.g. life cycle analysis which compares the environmental and social impacts of products and services) that are not mentioned but which are also a form of policy assessment targeted at a particular need.
5   See, for example, UNECE protocol for SEA at www.unece.org/env/eia/sea_protocol.htm.
6   The Synthesis included the assessment frameworks used by the OECD, UNEP, The North American Commission for Environmental Cooperation and the European Commission, the Canadian National Framework for Conducting Environmental Assessments of Trade Negotiations and the US Guidelines for Environmental Review of Trade Agreements. See www.cbd.int/doc/meetings/cop/cop-07/information/cop-07-inf-15-en.pdf.
7   The social discount rate is the weight placed on *all* estimates of costs and benefits. When environmental impacts are monetized and included in a cost–benefit analysis, they are discounted using the same discount rate applied to all other costs and benefits.
8   See www.cbd.int/ecosystem/.
9   As expressed in the Preamble to the CBD, this provides that 'where there is a threat of significant reduction or loss of biological diversity, lack of full scientific certainty should not be used as a reason for postponing measures to avoid or minimize such a threat'.
10 For example, the contribution of a given ecosystem service (e.g. regulating service) to the value of another service (e.g. provisioning service) or commodity which is in turn associated with a price in the marketplace.

Acknowledgements

The authors wish to thank Samuela Bassi, IEEP, Belgium; Rudolf de Groot, Wageningen University, The Netherlands; Deanna Donovan, Joint Nature Conservation Committee (JNCC), UK; Helen Dunn, Government Department for Environment, Food and Rural Affairs (Defra), UK; Sonja Gantioler, IEEP, Belgium; Clive George, University of Manchester, UK; Pablo Gutman, World Wide Fund for Nature (WWF), International; Julian Harlow, Natural England, UK; Peter Hjerp, IEEP, UK; Benjamin Kushner, World Resources Institute, US; Markus Lehmann, Secretariat of the Convention on Biological Diversity (SCBD), International; Paul Morling, Royal Society for the Protection of Birds, International; Alastair Morrison, Department of Conservation, New Zealand; Rosimeiry Portela, Conservation International, International; Matt Rayment, GHK, UK; Alice Ruhweza, Katoomba Group, Uganda; James Vause, Defra, UK; Madhu Verma, Indian Institute of Forest Management, India; Richard Waite, World Resources Institute, US; Jaime Webbe, SCBD, Canada; Sander van der Ploeg, Wageningen University, The Netherlands and Vera Weick, United Nations Environmental Programme (UNEP), International.

References

Annan, K. (1998) Aarhus Convention 1998, www.unece.org/env/pp/

Arin, T. and Kramer, R. A. (2002) 'Divers' willingness to pay to visit marine sanctuaries: An exploratory study', *Ocean and Coastal Management*, vol 45, pp171–183

Balmford, A., Rodrigues, A. S. L., Walpole, M., ten Brink, P., Kettunen, M., Braat, L. and de Groot, R. (2008) *The Economics of Biodiversity and Ecosystems – Scoping the Science*, Report for the European Commission (contract ENV/070307/2007/486089/ETU/B2), Cambridge

Batker, D., Barclay, E., Boumans, R. and Hathaway, T. (2005) *Ecosystem Services Enhanced by Salmon Habitat Conservation in the Green/Duwamish and Central Puget Sound Watershed*, Asia Pacific Environmental Exchange

BCRLIP (Biodiversity Conservation and Rural Livelihood Improvement Project) (2009) 'Draft executive summary environment and social assessment and indigenous development plan', www.envfor.nic.in/mef/SEIA_report.pdf, accessed 23 October 2009

Broekx S., Smets S., Liekens I., Bulckaen D. and De Nocker L. (2010) 'Designing a long-term flood risk management plan for the Scheldt estuary using a risk-based approach', *Natural Hazards*, online first, September

CBD (Convention on Biological Diversity) (2001) *The Value of Forest Ecosystems*, CBD Technical Series No 4, CBD, Montreal

CBD and NCEA (Convention on Biological Diversity and Netherlands Commission for Environmental Assessment) (2006) *Biodiversity in Impact Assessment, Background Document to CBD Decision VIII/28: Voluntary Guidelines on Biodiversity-Inclusive Impact Assessment*, CBD Technical Series No 26, www.cbd.int/doc/publications/cbd-ts-26-en.pdf, accessed 23 October 2009

Christie, M., Fazey, D., Cooper, R., Hyde, T., Deri, A., Hughes, L., Bush, G., Brander, L. M., Nahman, A., de Lange, W. and Reyers, B. (2008) 'An evaluation of economic and non-economic techniques for assessing the importance of biodiversity to people in developing countries', Report to the Department for Environment, Food and Rural Affairs, London

Contreras-Hermosilla, A. (2000) *The Underlying Causes of Forest Decline*, Occasional Paper No 30, Center for International Forestry Research, Indonesia

Cooper, E., Burke, L. and Bood, N. (2008) *Coastal Capital: Belize. The Economic Contribution of Belize's Coral Reefs and Mangroves*, World Resources Institute, Washington, DC, http://pdf.wri.org/working_papers/coastal_capital_belize_wp.pdf, accessed 8 November 2010

COWI (Consultancy Within Engineering, Environmental Science and Economics) (2009) *Study Concerning the Report on the Application and Effectiveness of the SEA Directive (2001/42/EC)*, www.ec.europa.eu/environment/eia/pdf/study0309.pdf, accessed 23 October 2009

Croitoru, L. (2005) *Valuing Mediterranean Forests: Towards Total Economic Value*, CABI, Wallingford, UK

Defra (Department for the Environment, Food and Rural Affairs) (2007) *Introductory Guidance for Valuing Ecosystem Services*, Defra, London

De Nocker L., Broekx S. and Liekens I. (2004) *Maatschappelijke kosten-batenanalyse voor de actualisatie van het Sigmaplan, Conclusies op hoofdlijnen, Tussentijds rapport in opdracht van Ministerie van de Vlaamse Gemeenschap, LIN AWZ, Afdeling Zeeschelde, door Vito i.s.m. Tijdelijke Vereniging RA-IMDC*, Vito, September, available from www.sigmaplan.be

Dubgaard, A. (2004) 'Cost-benefit analysis of wetland restoration', *Journal of Water and Land Development*, vol 8, pp87–102

EEA (European Environment Agency) (2005) *Market-Based Instruments for Environmental Policy in Europe*, EEA Technical Report No 8/2005, Copenhagen, Denmark

Emerton, L., Erdenesaikhan, N., de Veen, B., Tsogoo, D., Janchivdorj, L., Suvd, P., Enkhtseteg, B., Gandolgor, G., Dorjsuren, Ch., Sainbayar, D. and Enkhbaatar, A. (2009) *The Economic Value of the Upper Tuul Ecosystem, Mongolia*, The World Bank, Washington, DC

Evaluation Partnership (2007) *Evaluation of the Commission's Impact Assessment System*, The Evaluation Partnership, UK, www.ec.europa.eu/governance/impact/key_docs/docs/tep_eias_final_report.pdf, accessed 22 October 2009

GIST (Green India States Trust) (2006) *The Value of Timber, Carbon, Fuelwood, and Non-Timber Forest Products in India's Forests*, TERI Press, New Delhi, www.gistindia.org/pdfs/GAISPMonograph.pdf, accessed 19 August 2009

Humes, A. (2010) 'Owners of ship Westerhaven must pay $11.5 million for damage to Barrier Reef caused by negligence', *Amandala*, Belize, www.amandala.com.bz/index.php?id=9757, accessed 19 August 2010

Jacobs, S. (2006) 'Current trends in regulatory impact analysis: The challenge of mainstreaming RIA into policy making', Jacobs and Associates, Washington, DC, www.regulatoryreform.com/pdfs/Current%20 Trends%20and%20Processes%20in%20RIA%20-%20May%202006%20Jacobs%20and%20 Associates.pdf, accessed 23 October 2009

Kettunen, M., Bassi, S., Gantioler, S. and ten Brink, P. (2009) *Assessing Socio-Economic Benefits of Natura 2000: A Toolkit for Practitioners*, Institute for European Environmental Policy, London and Brussels

Kniivillä, M., Ovaskainen, V. and Saatamoinen, O. (2002) *Journal of Forest Economics*, vol 8, pp131–150

MAFF (Forestry Agency, Ministry of Agriculture, Forestry and Fisheries of Japan) (2008) *Annual Report on Trends in Forests and Forestry*, MAFF, Japan

Meire, P., Ysebaert, T., van Damme, S., van den Bergh, E., Maris, T. and Struyg, E. (2005) 'The Scheldt estuary: a description of a changing ecosystem', *Hydrobiologia*, vol 540, nos 1–3, pp1–11

New Zealand Department of Conservation (2006) *The Value of Conservation: What Does Conservation Contribute to the Economy?* NZDC, New Zealand

Ninan, K. N. (2007) *The Economics of Biodiversity Conservation: Valuation in Tropical Forest Ecosystems*, Earthscan, London

Ninan, K. N., Jyothis, S., Babu, P. and Ramakrishnappa, V. (2007a) 'Nagarhole – The Context of Tribal Villages Located Within and Near a National Park', in K. N. Ninan (ed) *The Economics of Biodiversity Conservation: Valuation in Tropical Forest Ecosystems*, Earthscan, London

Ninan, K. N., Jyothis, S., Babu, P. and Ramakrishnappa, V. (2007b) 'Uttar Kannada: The context of agricultural cum pastoral villages located within and near a wildlife sanctuary', in K. N. Ninan (ed) *The Economics of Biodiversity Conservation: Valuation in Tropical Forest Ecosystems*, Earthscan, London

OECD (Organisation for Economic Co-operation and Development) (1999) *Handbook of Incentive Measures for Biodiversity: Design and Implementation*, OECD, Paris

OECD (2006a) *Use of Discount Rates in the Estimation of the Costs of Inaction with Respect to Selected Environmental Concerns*, OECD, Paris

OECD (2006b) *Applying Strategic Environmental Assessment Good Practice Guidance for Development Co-Operation*, OECD/DAC Guidelines and Reference Series

Office of the President, Republic of Guyana (2008) 'Creating incentives to avoid deforestation', available at http://gina.gov.gy/booklet%20on%20avoided%20deforestationf.pdf, accessed 4 November 2010

O'Gorman, S. and Bann, C. (2008) *Valuing England's Terrestrial Ecosystem Services*, Defra, UK

Rodríguez, J. P., Beard, T. D. Jr., Bennett, E. M., Cumming, G. S., Cork, S., Agard, J., Dobson, A. P. and Peterson, G. D. (2006) 'Trade-offs across space, time and ecosystem services', *Ecology and Society*, vol 11, no 1

Science Council of Japan (2001) 'Evaluation of the multiple functions of agriculture and forests that concern the global environment and the human living environment', Report and appendices

Supreme Court of Belize (2010) 'Westerhaven Decision', Belize (26 April 2010), Claim No 45

TEEB (2009) *The Economics of Ecosystems and Biodiversity: Climate Issues Update*, www.teebweb.org, accessed 22 September 2010

TEEB Foundations (2010) *The Economics of Ecosystems and Biodiversity: Ecological and Economic Foundations* (ed P. Kumar), Earthscan, London

UNEP (United Nations Environment Programme) (2009a) 'Integrated assessment: Mainstreaming sustainability into policymaking: A guidance manual', www.unep.ch/etb/areas/IntTraRelPol.php, accessed 23 October 2009

UNEP (2009b) *Agriculture, Trade and Biodiversity: A Policy Assessment Manual*, www.unep.ch/etb/areas/ biodivAgriSector.php, accessed 23 October 2009

van der Ploeg, S., de Groot, R.S. and Wang, Y. (2010) *The TEEB Valuation Database: Overview of Structure, Data and Results*, Foundation for Sustainable Development, Wageningen, The Netherlands

Wielgus, J. (2004) *General Protocol for Calculating the Basis of Monetary Legal Claims for Damages to Coral Reefs by Vessel Groundings, and an Application to the Northern Red Sea*, Israel Nature and National Parks Protection Authority, Jerusalem

Wielgus, J., Chadwick-Furman, N. E., Zeitouni, N. and Shechter, M. (2003) 'Effects of coral reef attribute damage on recreational welfare', *Marine Resource Economics*, vol 18, pp225–237

Yoshida, K. (2004) *Utilization of Environmental Valuation as a Public Participation Tool for the Introduction of a Local Environmental Tax in Japan*, Annual Report of Society for Environmental Economics and Policy Studies No 9, Tokyo (in Japanese)

Annex 1 Overview of methodologies used in assessing value of ecosystem services

This annex provides information on the most commonly used valuation methods (economic and non-economic) to assess the value of ecosystem services.

Market analysis

Market valuation methods are divided into three main approaches:

1. price-based approaches;
2. cost-based approaches which are based on estimates of the costs if ecosystem service benefits had to be recreated through artificial means; and
3. production function-based approaches that value the environment as an input.[10]

Their main advantage is that they are based on data associated with actual markets, thus on actual preferences or costs by individuals. Moreover such data – i.e. prices, quantities and costs – are relatively easy to obtain. Examples include where a product is traded, such as timber or fish, or where ecosystem services contribute to marketed products, such as the value of clean water that is used as an input to local companies.

Revealed preference methods

Revealed preference methods use data from actual (past) behaviour to derive values. They rely on the link between a market good and the ecosystem service and the fact that demand for the market good is influenced by the quality of the ecosystem service. People are 'revealing' their preferences through their choices. The two main methods are the travel cost method and the hedonic pricing approach.

The travel cost method

The travel cost method is mostly used for determining the recreational values related to biodiversity and ecosystem services. It is based on the rationale that recreational experiences are associated with a cost (direct expenses and opportunity costs of time). It is most commonly used to measure the recreational value of a site, and to assess the value that might be at risk if the site were to be damaged.

Hedonic pricing

Hedonic pricing uses information about the implicit demand for an environmental attribute of marketed commodities. For instance, houses or property in general consist of several attributes, some of which are environmental in nature (e.g. proximity of a house to a forest or the view of a nice landscape). It would most commonly be used to measure the prices of houses near, for example, a forest, and to compare them with those further away.

Stated preference methods

Stated preference techniques are based on the demand for a given ecosystem service (or a change in its provision) measured by means of a hypothetical market simulated through the use of surveys. These methods require people to rate or rank trade-offs. Typically, the responses are collected using survey questionnaires of a representative sample of people. These valuation techniques can be used in situations where use and/ or non-values are to be estimated and/or when no surrogate market exists from which value can be deduced.

However, there are difficulties in constructing hypothetical markets. Criticism of valuation techniques is greatest for stated preference techniques where some feel that it can often be unclear exactly what people are valuing (one service, all services, etc.) and whether they were making strategic responses.

The main forms of stated preference techniques are:

- **Contingent valuation method:** This method uses questionnaires to ask people how much they would be willing to pay to protect or enhance ecosystems and the services they provide, or alternatively how much they would be willing to accept for their loss or degradation.
- **Choice modelling:** Individuals are faced with two or more alternatives with shared attributes of the services to be valued, but with different levels of attribute (one of the attributes being the money people would have to pay for the service).
- **Group valuation:** A newer and rarer form of technique that combines stated preference techniques with elements of deliberative processes, to explore value, such as value pluralism, incommensurability, non-human values, or social justice.

Table 4.A1 below sets out in more detail the methods used, and their applicability to different ecosystem services.

Table 4.A1 Valuation methods in more detail (adapted from Defra, 2007)

Economic valuation methods	Description	Ecosystem services valued
Revealed preference methods		
Market prices	These can be used to capture the value of ecosystem services that are traded, e.g. the market value of forest products. Even where market prices are available, however, they may need to be adjusted to take account of distortions such as subsidies. Market prices can act as proxies for direct and indirect use values but do not capture non-use values; the price will be a minimum expression of the willingness to pay.	Ecosystem services that contribute to marketed products, e.g. timber, fish, genetic information, value of clean water that is an input to local companies.
Averting behaviour	This approach focuses on the price paid by individuals to mitigate against environmental impacts.	Depends on the existence of relevant markets for the ecosystem service in question. For instance, the cost of water filtration may be used as a proxy for the value of water pollution damages; or costs of buying pollution masks to protect against urban air pollution (although this will only represent part of the damage value).
Production function approach	This focuses on the relationship that may exist between a particular ecosystem service and the production of a market good. Environmental goods and services are considered as inputs to the production process and their value is inferred by considering the changes in production process of market goods that result from an environmental change.	Regulating and supporting services that serve as input to market products e.g. effects of air or water quality on agricultural production and forestry output.
Hedonic pricing	This assumes that environmental characteristics (e.g. a pleasant view or the disamenity of a nearby landfill site), as well as other property features, are reflected in property prices. The value of the environmental component can therefore be captured by modelling the impact of all possible influencing factors on the price of the property.	Ecosystem services (e.g. regulating cultural and supporting services) that contribute to air quality, visual amenity, landscape, quiet, in other words attributes that can be appreciated by potential buyers.
Travel cost method	This is a survey-based technique that uses the costs incurred by individuals taking a trip to a recreation site (e.g. travel costs, entry fees, opportunity cost of time) as a proxy for the recreational value of that site.	All ecosystem services that contribute to recreational activities.
Random utility models	This is an extension of the travel cost method and is used to test the effect of changing the quality or quantity of an environmental characteristic at a particular site.	All ecosystems services that contribute to recreational activities.

Table 4.A1 Valuation methods in more detail (adapted from Defra, 2007) (*Cont'd*)

Economic valuation methods	Description	Ecosystem services valued
Stated preference methods		
Contingent valuation	This is a survey-style approach that constructs a hypothetical market through a questionnaire. Respondents answer questions regarding what they are willing to pay for a particular environmental change.	All ecosystem services.
Choice modelling	This is a survey-style approach that focuses on the individual attributes of the ecosystem in question. For example, a lake may be described in terms of water quality, number of species, etc. Participants are presented with different combinations of attributes and asked to choose their preferred combination or rank the alternative combinations. Each combination of attributes has a price associated with it and therefore the respondents reveal their 'willingness to pay' or 'willingness to accept' for each attribute.	All ecosystem services.
Cost-based approaches	These approaches consider the costs in relation to provision of environmental goods and services and only provide 'proxy' values. Examples of cost-based approaches are those that infer a value of a natural resource by how much it costs to replace or restore it after it has been damaged.	
Opportunity cost	This method considers the value forgone in order to protect, enhance or create a particular environmental asset (e.g. opportunity cost of agricultural production lost if land is retained as forest).	Depends on the existence of relevant markets for the ecosystem service in question. Examples include man-made defences being used as proxy for wetlands storm protection; expenditure on water filtration as proxy for value of water pollution damages.
Cost of alternatives/ substitute goods	This approach considers the cost of providing a substitute good that has a similar function to the environmental good. For example, wetlands that provide flood protection may be valued on the basis of the cost of building man-made defences of equal effectiveness. Given that wetlands provide a range of ecosystem services, this costing would be a minimum estimate of the value of a wetland.	
Replacement cost method	This technique looks at the cost of replacing or restoring a damaged asset to its original state and uses this cost as a measure of the benefit of restoration. The approach is widely used because it is often easy to find estimates of such costs.	

Table 4.A1 Valuation methods in more detail (adapted from Defra, 2007) (*Cont'd*)

Economic valuation methods	Description	Ecosystem services valued
Focus groups, in-depth groups	Focus groups aim to discover the positions of participants regarding, and/or explore how participants interact when discussing, a pre-defined issue or set of related issues. In-depth groups are similar in some respects, but they may meet on several occasions, and are much less closely facilitated, with the greater emphasis being on how the group creates discourse on the topic.	All ecosystem services.
Citizens' juries	Citizens' juries are designed to obtain carefully considered public opinion on a particular issue or set of social choices. A sample of citizens is given the opportunity to consider evidence from experts and other stakeholders and they then hold group discussion on the issue at hand	All ecosystem services.
Health-based valuation approaches	The approaches measure health-related outcomes in terms of the combined impact on the length and quality of life. For example, a quality-adjusted life year (QALY) combines two key dimensions of health outcomes: the degree of improvement/deterioration in health and the time interval over which this occurs, including any increase/decrease in the duration of life itself.	All ecosystem services.
Q-methodology	This methodology aims to identify typical ways in which people think about environmental (or other) issues. While Q-methodology can potentially capture any kind of value, the process is not explicitly focused on 'quantifying' or distilling these values. Instead it is concerned with how individuals understand, think and feel about environmental problems and their possible solutions.	All ecosystem services.
Delphi surveys, systematic reviews	The intention of Delphi surveys and systematic reviews is to produce summaries of expert opinion or scientific evidence relating to particular questions. Delphi relies largely on expert opinion, while systematic review attempts to maximize reliance on objective data. Delphi and systematic review are not methods of valuation but, rather, means of summarizing knowledge (which may be an important stage of other valuation methods).	All ecosystem services.

Annex 2

Table 4.A2 Stages of a policy assessment, proposed actions and ways to address biodiversity (UNEP, 2009b)

Stages	Actions proposed	How to address biodiversity and related aspects
A Understanding the policy context	A1 Identify the purpose of the integrated assessment	Define the purpose, main objectives and sectoral focus. Define objectives in terms of original assessment and influencing decision makers to maximize positive outcomes on biodiversity and other sustainability issues.
	A2 Review the proposed policy and context	Identify environmental and biodiversity-oriented policy objectives, commitments or agreements relevant for the study focus (area, commodity). Understand the policy process that is being assessed.
	A3 Identify participants and stakeholders	Identify relevant stakeholders and biodiversity specialists, and ensure they are involved in the study.
	A4 Identify and review available information	Identify and make an overview of relevant (biodiversity- and trade-related) documents for the country/region concerned.
B Determining the focus	B1 Develop a conceptual framework	Make a summary of key issues and create a conceptual framework. Include critical biodiversity components and ecosystem services, social and economic issues, and cause–effect chains.
	B2 Identify priority sustainability issues	Identify the main sustainability issues (related to problems and opportunities) as associated with the conceptual framework.
C Assessing the impacts	C1–3 Identify criteria relevant to the main issues, develop economic, social and environmental indicators and determine the baseline	Identify objectives or criteria and associate indicators to assess baselines and trends. Assessment of trends should be done using selected indicators. Define the status and trends of the most important indicators for the focal sectors of the assessment. Scenarios can be developed for expected changes. This is followed by a causality analysis to identify specific drivers of change and explaining possible outcomes for biodiversity and ecosystem services.
	C4 Identify policy options including most likely option	Identify policy options for which to assess impacts. There may be three policy options: baseline, existing policy measures (subject of the assessment) and proposed positive policy.
	C5 Analyse impacts using appropriate tools and techniques	Analyse the impacts of defined policy options on biodiversity, as well as social and economic indicators. Assess the likely impacts of policy options with the baseline scenario. If possible, quantify expected (positive or negative) changes in biodiversity and ecosystem services.
D Developing policy recommendations	D1 Finalize assessment of trade-offs and draw conclusion	Draw conclusions as regards the most desirable and realistic policy options. Consider alternative trade policy options to maximize overall positive sustainability outcomes. These are preferred over policy measures for mitigation or compensation of impacts on biodiversity and ecosystem services.
	D2 Develop policy recommendations	Define policy recommendations in line with the assessment results. Consider the most effective mechanisms for communicating results, using stakeholder input.

Part III

Available Solutions: Instruments for Better Stewardship of Natural Capital

Chapter 5
Rewarding Benefits through Payments and Markets

Coordinating lead author
Patrick ten Brink

Lead authors
Section 1 Payments for ecosystem services (PES)
Patrick ten Brink, Samuela Bassi, Joshua Bishop, Celia A. Harvey,
Alice Ruhweza, Madhu Verma, Sheila Wertz-Kanounnikoff

Section 2 International PES: REDD+ and beyond
Katia Karousakis, Patrick ten Brink, Celia Harvey,
Alexandra Vakrou, Stefan van der Esch

Section 3 Redirecting tax and payment mechanisms for environmental benefit
Irene Ring

Section 4 Sharing benefits derived from genetic resources
Anil Markandya, Paulo A. L. D. Nunes

Section 5 Developing markets for green goods and services
Andrew J. McConville, Joshua Bishop, Patrick ten Brink,
Alexandra Vakrou

6 Expanding markets through green public procurement (GPP),
Stefan van der Esch, Samuela Bassi, Patrick ten Brink

Contributing authors
James Boyd, Ingo Bräuer, Leen Gorissen, Pablo Gutman, Bernd Hansjürgens,
Sarah Hodgkinson, Markus Lehmann, Katherine McCoy, Carlos Muñoz Piña, Valerie Normand,
Burkhard Schweppe-Kraft, Clare Shine, Pavan Sukhdev, Mandar Trivedi,
Kaavya Varma, Francis Vorhies

Contents

Key messages   179

Summary   181

1 Payments for ecosystem services (PES)   181
1.1 What do we mean by PES?   181
1.2 Principles and architecture of PES   182
1.3 Practical applications, benefits and lessons learned from PES   186
1.4 Opportunities and challenges   194
1.5 Moving forward on PES design and implementation   195

2 International PES: REDD+ and beyond   199
2.1 The rationale for international engagement   199
2.2 REDD+: A carbon mechanism with potentially large biodiversity co-benefits   200
2.3 Direct international payments for global ecosystem services   209

3 Redirecting tax and compensation mechanisms for environmental goals   212
3.1 Using public levies to stimulate conservation   212
3.2 Greening intergovernmental fiscal transfers   216
3.3 Public compensation schemes for wildlife damage   219

4 Sharing benefits derived from genetic resources   221
4.1 The value of genetic resources   222
4.2 Adding value through more efficient bioprospecting   224
4.3 Equitable sharing of benefits derived from genetic resources   228
4.4 Towards an international regime on ABS   230

5 Developing markets for green goods and services   231
5.1 Support for biodiversity-friendly products and services   231
5.2 Barriers to the success of certified products   238
5.3 Expanding the reach of biodiversity-friendly products   240

6 Expanding markets through green public procurement (GPP)   242
6.1 Objectives and evolution of GPP policies   242
6.2 GPP standards, criteria and costing   243
6.3 Tackling constraints on implementing GPP   244

Notes   247

Acknowledgements   249

References   249

Key messages

Markets do not fully recognize the value of biodiversity and ecosystem services, leading to decision making that ignores or understates their local to global benefits. This chapter focuses on innovative tools to provide incentives for long-term conservation through targeted payment schemes and greener tax, contract and market mechanisms, as part of a policy mix appropriate to national context and priorities.

National and international payments for ecosystem services (PES)

Public and private payments for ecosystem services (PES) schemes are flexible instruments to reward the provision of biodiversity and ecosystem services at different scales. PES offer major potential to raise new funds, target existing funds more efficiently and secure environmental benefits that underpin business profitability and community livelihoods. Effective targeting, monitoring and governance – and measures to ensure additionality (beyond 'business as usual') and minimize leakage (displacing damage elsewhere) can ensure fairness and value for money.

International PES opportunities include the financial mechanism proposed within the post-2012 regime under the United Nations Framework Convention on Climate Change: REDD+ (Reducing Emissions from Deforestation and Forest Degradation in developing countries) could offer substantial biodiversity co-benefits alongside critically needed measures to curb deforestation, which is estimated to account for up to 17 per cent of global greenhouse gas (GHG) emissions. A proposed Green Development Initiative (which aims to support the CBD in its work on innovative finance mechanisms) and other emerging initiatives could have far-reaching benefits to support direct investment in biodiversity, public goods and natural capital across a wider range of ecosystems.

Tax and public compensation mechanisms

Tax systems and intergovernment fiscal transfers can provide positive incentives for private actors and public agencies to make investment choices favouring long-term stewardship over short-term development options, building on ecological criteria and releasing funds to those responsible for on-site conservation. Public compensation programmes to cover damage by protected wildlife can also influence attitudes by providing rewards for the presence and protection of wildlife.

Sharing benefits derived from genetic resources

Historically, host countries have benefited little from the development and commercialization of products based on traditional knowledge and genetic resources sourced from their territory, weakening incentives for on-site conservation. Fairer and more efficient contractual mechanisms can recognize value, establish rights for local people and facilitate discoveries and their application across many sectors, including new opportunities linked to biomimicry.

The dedicated Access and Benefit Sharing (ABS) regime being negotiated under the CBD is essential to provide an international equitable framework and strengthen local capacity.

Greening the markets

Market push (supply-side) initiatives by producers and market pull (demand-side) changes in consumers, business and government preferences and procurement criteria can encourage biodiversity-friendly production and low-impact services and help redirect purchasing decisions. Policy makers can support certification and labelling schemes for a wider range of products and services by backing robust standards and verification systems that cover biodiversity conservation, and providing advice and capacity services for business. Cooperative measures should be put in place to enable production and export sectors in developing countries to participate effectively in the development and implementation of new market standards.

Summary

We never know the worth of water until the well is dry. (English proverb)

Earlier chapters showed how biodiversity provides ecosystem services that benefit people locally, nationally and internationally. These are supplied through natural processes but often need management to maintain, develop or protect them. As many services are unpriced or underpriced in the markets, economic signals do not reflect the true value of natural capital.

Chapter 5 focuses on tools that can reward this flow of ecosystem services. Section 1 and Section 2 discuss payments for ecosystem services (PES). Section 1 explains how PES schemes work, drawing on lessons learned to identify scope for improvement. Section 2 considers PES at the international scale, particularly proposals for REDD+ under the UN Framework Convention on Climate Change and for a Green Development Initiative to support the CBD and other biodiversity-related conventions.

Section 3 and Section 4 shows how taxes, public compensation and fairer contractual frameworks for genetic resources can provide positive incentives for conservation. Section 3 outlines use of property, income tax and compensation regimes for long-term results. Section 4 discusses specific issues for fairer sharing of benefits derived from genetic resources and summarizes progress towards an international regime on Access and Benefit Sharing (ABS), currently being negotiated under the CBD.

Section 5 and Section 6 consider more familiar tools to stimulate and target market supply and demand for 'greener' goods and services, including eco-labelling and certification schemes (5) and green public procurement policies (6).

1 Payments for ecosystem services (PES)

Men do not value a good deed unless it brings a reward. (Ovid, BC43–18AD, Roman poet)

This section describes how governments and private entities can pay resource owners/ users to protect natural ecosystems or adapt management practices to enhance provision of ecosystem services (Section 1.1). It describes basic PES principles and architecture (Section 1.2) and gives concrete examples with lessons learned (Section 1.3). It identifies remaining constraints and new opportunities (Section 1.4) before setting out practical steps to improve PES design and implementation (Section 1.5).

1.1 What do we mean by PES?

PES is a generic name for a variety of arrangements through which the beneficiaries of ecosystem services pay the providers of those services (Gutman, 2006). The term covers payments for sustainable management of water resources and/or agricultural land, biodiversity conservation, and storage and/or sequestration of carbon in biomass.

PES programmes operate in both developed and developing countries and may focus on single or multiple services. Common goals of land management are to ensure water quality for nearby cities (e.g. Saltillo City, Mexico/Zapalinamé mountains);

Box 5.1 Definition of PES

PES can be defined as *voluntary* transactions where a *well-defined* ecosystem service (ESS) (or land use likely to secure that service) is 'bought' by at least one ESS *buyer* from at least one ESS *provider,* if – and only if – the ESS provider secures ESS provision (*conditionality*).

Source: Adapted from Wunder (2005)

---

cleanse coastal waters (e.g. Sweden, see Zanderson et al, 2009); protect groundwater (e.g. many parts of Europe and Japan, see Porras et al, 2008); reward carbon sequestration (via farms in New Zealand and forests in Costa Rica and Uganda); and conserve biodiversity (Bushtender programme in Victoria, Australia).[1] The EU and US use agri-environment payments to maintain additional ecosystem services (Baylis et al, 2004; Wunder et al, 2008; Zanderson et al, 2009) and South Africa pays for management of external threats (invasive alien species) (Turpie et al, 2008).

Multi-service PES schemes to combine improved groundwater quality with increased biodiversity are found, for example, in Germany (see Box 5.6) and Bolivia (Los Negros watershed, see Asquith et al, 2008). The US Conservation Reserve Programme has a set of mutually reinforcing objectives (increasing wildlife habitat, reducing soil erosion, enhancing water supplies, improving water quality and reducing damage from floods and natural disasters).[2]

PES are highly flexible and can be established by different actors. Some schemes are managed by national governments (e.g. Costa Rica, Ecuador, Mexico, China, EU Member States and the US). Others are run by water companies or user associations (e.g. in the Catskill Mountains/Delaware watershed to meet federal water quality standards for New York City, and in Bolivia, Ecuador and Mexico). PES can also be purely private in cases where companies reliant on specific services pay the providers (e.g. payments by Perrier-Vittel to French farmers – see Box 5.4; also payments by the beer brewer Rochefort to Belgian farmers). NGOs can also play a key role (e.g. by collaborating with the municipal water company in Quito: see Wunder et al, 2008).

PES can be applied at different spatial scales, ranging from the very local (e.g. 496 hectares in an upper watershed in Ecuador) to large regions (e.g. 4.9 million ha of reforested farmland in China; see Bennett (2008) and Chapter 9).

1.2 Principles and architecture of PES

Rationale for investing in PES

The overarching principle of PES is to ensure that those who benefit from a particular ecosystem service compensate those who provide it, giving them an incentive to continue doing so. Direct beneficiaries or 'users' of ecosystem services – such as water companies, irrigation authorities, aquaculture operations or hydroelectric power companies – are often willing to pay to secure the services that underpin their businesses (e.g. water purification). Private beneficiaries who make voluntary PES contracts with providers can thus internalize (some) environmental externalities without investing in more expensive remediation.

PES aim to change the economics of ecosystem service provision by improving incentives for land-use and management practices that supply such services. In situations where trade-offs exist between private and societal benefits from different land uses, PES can tip the balance and make conservation-focused land use more profitable for the private owner/user with additional benefits for society (see Figure 5.1). Without such PES, the owner/user would probably not choose the social optimum unless other regulations or tax incentives are in place or socio-cultural norms or customs support this optimum without the need for payment.

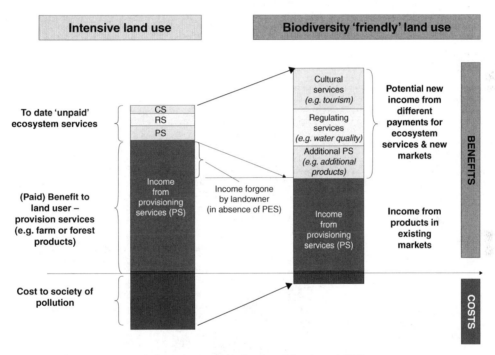

Figure 5.1 *Increasing rewards for ecosystem services provision through PES*

Source: Bassi and ten Brink, own representation adapted from Bassi et al (2008)

Baselines and additionality

Most PES schemes assume that a resource owner will choose management practices to maximize private net benefits under existing regulations and market incentives. Privately optimal choices will evolve in line with adjustments to relevant requirements or norms (e.g. to reduce pollution) if these are properly enforced. The situation may vary in some developing countries where enforcement of environmental regulation is a major challenge.

The usual point of departure for PES is the level aligned with existing regulation and norms, in other words PES are intended to reward good management practices that go beyond what is legally compulsory (the 'reference level' in Figure 5.2 below). At this stage there may be scope to gain further environmental benefits at reasonable cost by paying the resource owner to undertake specified actions. Governments may find that it is less expensive or more consistent with other policy objectives (e.g. poverty reduction) to offer incentives rather than imposing management obligations. Other beneficiaries may find that the reference level of service provision does not meet their needs and therefore make voluntary payments to resource owners.

In countries with weak law enforcement, routine management practices can fall well below minimum regulatory levels. Using PES in this type of situation can bring results as it involves a reward instead of an obligation but it can also undermine enforcement efforts. Where governments choose to use PES as an incentive to bring practice up to the legal standard, it effectively operates as a subsidy (see Chapter 6) and is not consistent with the polluter pays principle (PPP). This cannot be seen as a long-term solution, given concerns related to cost, budgets, governance, equity and efficiency. In other cases, governments may find it more appropriate to raise standards, strengthen enforcement and implement the PPP more fully. However, it is generally politically easier for the government to subsidize good behaviour than to tax bad behaviour.

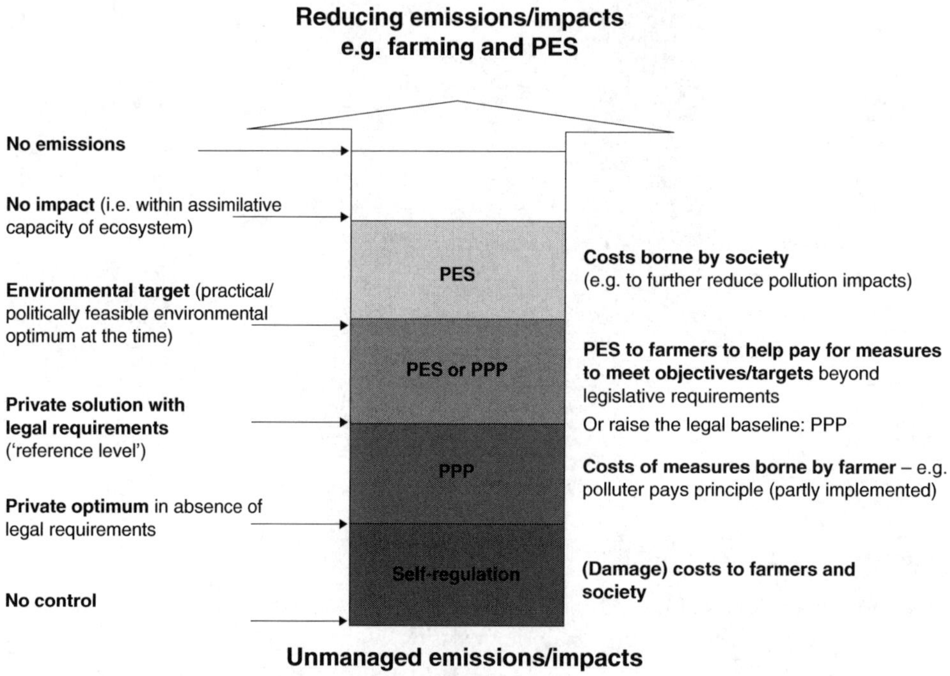

**Reducing emissions/impacts
e.g. farming and PES**

No emissions

No impact (i.e. within assimilative capacity of ecosystem)

Environmental target (practical/politically feasible environmental optimum at the time)

PES

Costs borne by society
(e.g. to further reduce pollution impacts)

PES or PPP

PES to farmers to help pay for measures to meet objectives/targets beyond legislative requirements

Or raise the legal baseline: PPP

Private solution with legal requirements ('reference level')

PPP

Costs of measures borne by farmer – e.g. polluter pays principle (partly implemented)

Private optimum in absence of legal requirements

Self-regulation

No control

(Damage) costs to farmers and society

Unmanaged emissions/impacts

Figure 5.2 *PES and the polluter pays principle (PPP)*

Source: Patrick ten Brink, own representation building on Scheele (2008)

Even where legal standards are combined with incentives, there will often be residual adverse impacts when compared with undisturbed ecosystems. These are ultimately borne by society unless cost-effective means or technological solutions are found to avoid such damage (e.g. pesticide or fertilizer use may be reduced through rules and incentives but there will still be impacts if legislation and targets do not demand zero impact, i.e. use levels that remain within the ecosystem's assimilative or regenerative capacity) (see Figure 5.2).

For the above reasons, PES effectiveness and feasibility are closely tied to the regulatory baseline and its enforcement (see Chapter 7). The main challenge is to determine the appropriate reference level, in other words to distinguish between what resource owners/managers can reasonably be expected to do at their own cost and what else they might agree to undertake on the basis of PES.

The answer will depend on how environmental rights and duties are allocated between beneficiaries and providers (formally or through de facto established practices). This varies between different legal systems and social contexts. Where downstream populations have a right to clean water, this implies that upstream landowners should pay to reduce pollution in line with the polluter pays principle. Conversely, where landowners have unrestricted rights to choose how they manage their land, service beneficiaries downstream may bear the burden of persuading them to modify their practices (Johnstone and Bishop, 2007).[3]

PES is often criticized as a 'second best' solution by those who believe beneficiaries have a right to enjoy ecosystem services that would have been freely available in the absence of damaging activities; based on this argument, PES is less ethically satisfactory than strengthening the law to make polluters pay. Others suggest that PES is often just a disguised subsidy to encourage compliance with existing laws and can unfairly burden the public purse (i.e. when government-financed).

In response to such concerns, the justification for PES is that it can be more cost-effective than strict enforcement, more progressive (where providers are relatively poor land users) and/or that it secures additional benefits beyond minimum legal requirements. PES can also be seen as a temporary measure to stimulate adoption of new management practices and technologies which may eventually become economically justifiable in their own right (Johnstone and Bishop, 2007).

Defining reference levels in terms of business-as-usual (BAU) scenarios carries a risk that resource owners exaggerate the level of environmental threat in order to win more payments for conservation: this could lead to instruments having lesser 'additionality' than they could ideally have. This risk can be minimized by e.g. investing in robust information on the status of biodiversity/land use and ecosystem services (see Chapter 3 on indicators).

The structure of PES

There are many ways to structure PES schemes, depending on the specific service, scale of application and context for implementation. Some are based on legal obligations (e.g. PES linked to carbon markets with binding emission targets) whereas private schemes tend to be voluntary with little government involvement. Sources and mechanisms for payments vary as do the providers and the beneficiaries. Figure 5.3 provides a generic outline of basic structure and stakeholder relationships for most PES.

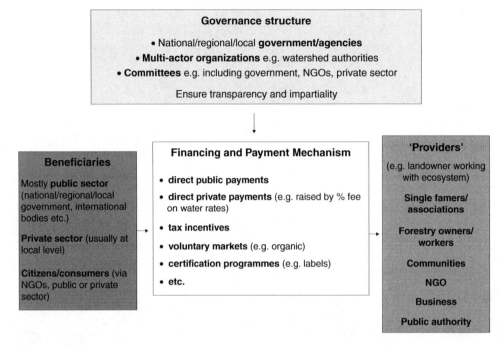

Figure 5.3 *PES stakeholders and their interactions*

Source: Adapted from Pagiola (2003)

1.3 Practical applications, benefits and lessons learned from PES

Application of PES to different contexts

PES can be implemented at different scales, depending on the beneficiaries, the providers and the spatial relationship between them. If a site provides a mainly local service (e.g. crop pollination), a local PES makes sense. However, if it provides national benefits (e.g. pest control), it is arguably for national government to initiate the appropriate PES or use legal measures to secure a public good or service. Where it provides global benefits (e.g. carbon services), an internationally coordinated approach may be needed (see Section 2).

The first national PES schemes in developing countries were pioneered in Costa Rica (see Box 5.2) and Mexico (see Box 5.3). The Costa Rican programme is very well known and well studied: landowner requests to participate outstrip available funding and the programme is periodically reviewed and adjusted. Particularly interesting features of the Mexican programme include a prioritized approach and hierarchy of ambitions, design criteria for cost-effectiveness and explicit synergies between biodiversity, water and poverty reduction.

PES schemes can also be piloted at local level and subsequently rolled out on a wider scale. In Japan, the combination of serious forest degradation and the findings of a national valuation of forest ecosystem services shifted the policy landscape. The resulting estimates of monetary values helped generate sufficient political support to change local tax systems in over half the country's prefectures (see Box 5.4 and also Box 4.10 in Chapter 4 on the importance of valuation).

Box 5.2 An evolving nationwide scheme: The Pagos por Servicios Ambientales (PSA), Costa Rica

Background and objectives

The national PSA programme pays landholders for providing carbon sequestration and hydrological services (watershed protection) and conserving biodiversity and landscapes. From 1997 to 2004, Costa Rica invested some US$200 million, protecting over 460,000ha of forests and forestry plantations and providing additional income to over 8000 forest owners. By 2005, the programme covered 10 per cent of national forest areas.

Payments and funding

US$64 per ha/year were paid for forest conservation in 2006 and US$816 per hectare over ten years for forest plantations. The programme is based on national and international partnerships, contributing to long-term financial sustainability. The main revenue source is a national fossil fuel tax (US$10 million/year) with additional grants from the World Bank, Global Environment Facility and the German aid agency (Kreditanstalt für Wiederaufbau, KFW). Funds are also provided through individual voluntary agreements with private water users (US$0.5 million/year) which will increase with the gradual introduction of a new water tariff and potential new opportunities from carbon finance.

Results and lessons learned

The PSA programme has helped slow deforestation, added monetary value to forests and biodiversity, increased understanding of the socio-economic contribution of natural ecosystems and is generally considered a success. However, recent assessments suggest that many areas within PSA would have been conserved even without payments, for three main reasons: deforestation pressures were already much reduced by the time PSA was introduced; the use of uniform payments (fixed prices); and limited spatial targeting of payments in the early stages of implementation. PSA is being adjusted in response to these lessons.

Source: Portela and Rodriguez (2008); Pagiola (2008); Wunder and Wertz-Kanounnikoff (2009); and personal communication, Carlos Manuel Rodríguez, former Minister of Environment of Costa Rica

Box 5.3 Mexico's programme for the Payment of Hydrologic Environmental Services of Forests (PSAH)

Background

Mexico's federal government created a voluntary PES scheme in 2003 with the aim of linking those benefiting from the forests' water-related environmental services with their providers in the watersheds and aquifers recharge areas of the country. The link was achieved by reforming the Mexican Federal Fees Law to earmark a portion of the federal water fee revenues (approximately 2 per cent of total) to finance the programme. Within a multi-criteria eligibility area, participants are selected among the pool of applicants and signed into five-year contracts to conserve their forests. The rate paid varies between US$28 and US$38 per hectare per year, according to the type of forest, cloud forests being considered the most valuable. It is a performance-based programme: if satellite images show any part of the forest under contract was deforested in any given year the payment of that year is not made and the rest of the contract cancelled. This money is kept in a special Forestry Fund to give certainty to participants that no budget cut or reallocation threatens their funds during the time of the contract.

Objectives

The primary objective is to halt the deforestation threatening forests critical for watershed-related environmental services in Mexico, by paying landowners to preserve forested land and avoid its transformation for other uses, such as agriculture and cattle ranching. The ecosystem services which are meant to be preserved through this scheme are:

- aquifer recharge, especially the vulnerable, over-exploited ones;
- improved surface water quality: less suspended particles and lower filtering costs;
- reduced frequency of and damage from flooding in short steep watersheds.

Targeting

The programme by-laws are open to modifications each year. That has had the advantage of introducing flexibility to learn from experience, but also opens a gap for rent-seeking behaviour. Among the particularly valuable selection criteria contributing to improved targeting of the programme are the level of marginality of forest communities and owners, and the degree of aquifer over-exploitation. However, introduction of additional criteria, such as participation in other government programmes or being within natural protected areas despite little impact on water scarcity, reduced the relative importance of the hydrological criteria over time. Hence the importance of a criteria introduced in 2007 following a series of econometric analysis which mapped the predicted deforestation patterns: the criteria of *level of economic risk of deforestation* made an important contribution to ensuring effectiveness of the programme, with the result that the funds more effectively reduced forest loss. Despite the advances, mistargeting problems remain significant, so current policy discussions seek to order priorities by classifying application evaluation criteria into primary ones (hydrological importance, poverty, deforestation risk) leaving the rest as secondary, tie-breaking, criteria.

Size and scope

The PSAH has been a developing scheme with increasing participation, area coverage and payments. The table below provides an overview of the first six years of operation.

Year in which forest is signed into the programme	2003	2004	2005	2006	2007	2008	2009	Total
Surface incorporated into the programme (1000 hectares)	127	184	169	118	546	654	567	**2365**
Forest owners participating (individuals and collectives)	272	352	257	193	816	765	711	**3366**
Total payment to be made over 5 years (million US$)	17.5	26.0	23.5	17.2	84.2	100.9	87.4	**303**

Results

By comparing statistically equivalent forests between 2000 to 2007, Muñoz et al (2010) conclude the PSAH reduced the rate of deforestation from 1.6 per cent to 0.6 per cent. This was achieved even under conditions in which signed forests had a lower than average risk of deforestation and where PSAH had contracts with an average of two years under operation. This translates into 18,300 hectares of avoided deforestation with three more years of contract to go. Expressed in avoided greenhouse gas (GHG) emissions this equates to 3.2 million tonnes CO_2e.

An improved targeting mechanism could increase the effect on reduced deforestation, reduced emissions and greater protection of watersheds and aquifers of the programme, giving fee-payers more environmental value for their money.

Key insights include:

- three times as many applications as funds;
- the choice of objectives and prioritization significantly affects the focus and allocation of funds: this is directly reflected in the final outcomes;
- GIS, hydrological and census data were valuable elements in setting up the programme as they helped identify areas of deforestation, aquifer over-exploitation and poverty.

Source: Muñoz-Piña et al (2008); Muñoz et al (2010)

Box 5.4 PES incentives to conserve agricultural ecosystem services in Japan

National and prefectoral governments in Japan reward local communities or small groups of farmers in hilly and mountainous areas for conserving agricultural ecosystem services:

- Direct payments are made to local groups of farmers to motivate them not to abandon farmlands and to conserve the associated ecosystem services.
- Direct payments are also made to local communities to conserve land, water and the environment (28,757 community agreements in 1028 cities in 2008).
- To conserve paddy field ecosystem services, PES operate to improve landscape amenity, species and ecosystem diversity and land conservation and to prevent water pollution by encouraging less use of chemical inputs for agriculture.

Source: Yoshida (2010)

Regulatory baselines and additionality

Regulatory baselines and additionality are addressed in two cases on improving groundwater quality, involving private and public beneficiaries (see Boxes 5.5 and 5.6). In both cases, existing regulations were not stringent enough to prevent pollution of groundwater with nitrates and pesticides or to make the polluters pay for avoidance. In response to product quality and cost concerns (Vittel) and broader health and biodiversity concerns (both cases), a pragmatic approach was adopted. These agreements can be characterized either as PES (provision of public goods through increased biodiversity) or as a subsidy for environmental services (contribution to reducing pollution) (see Chapter 6).

A well-documented case of PES as value for money comes from the Catskills Mountains, in the US. A comprehensive PES programme for this 200km² watershed cost around US$1 billion to US$1.5 billion over ten years, significantly less than the estimated cost of a water filtration plant (one-off costs of US$4 billion to US$6 billion and operational and maintenance costs of US$300 million to US$500 million). Nearly all (93 per cent) farmers in the region participate and water bills have been raised by 9 per cent instead of doubling in the case of new filtration capacity (Wunder and Wertz-Kanounnikoff, 2009; see also Chapter 9).

Using water rates to fund PES can be done in different ways. One study analysed 17 local PES schemes where fees are charged to domestic water users. Seven make the additional costs visible in water bills: percentage premiums are added to final water bills in Pimampiro, Ecuador (20 per cent) and in Cuenca, Quito (5 per cent); a flat rate per cubic metre is used in Heredia, Costa Rica; and in Zapalinamé, Mexico, contributions are voluntary and users can choose the level, helping to address social concerns (Porras et al, 2008).

PES with multiple co-benefits

PES schemes can be designed to create or support other socio-economic objectives such as employment related to the provision of ecosystem services. The type and

---

Box 5.5 Private sector contracts for PES: The example of Vittel mineral water, France

Background and objectives

Since 1993, Vittel has conducted a PES programme in its 5100ha catchment in the Vosges Mountains to maintain high water quality. 26 farmers ('sellers of ecosystem services') in the watershed are paid to adopt best low-impact practices in dairy farming (no agrochemicals; composting animal waste; reduced stocking rates).

Payments and funding

The programme combines cash payments (conditional upon the adoption of new farming practices) with technical assistance, reimbursement of incremental labour costs and arrangements to take over lands and provide usufruct rights[4] to farmers. Average payments are €200/ha/year over a five-year transition period and up to €150,000 per farm to cover costs of new equipment. Contracts are long-term (18 to 30 years) with payments adjusted according to opportunity costs on a farm-by-farm basis. Land use and water quality are monitored over time: this provides evidence of improvement in relevant ecosystem services compared to an otherwise declining baseline, clearly making the investments profitable.

Results and lessons learned

The Vittel scheme built on a four-year research programme by the French National Institute for Agricultural Research (INRA) and took ten years to become operational. It is implemented through Agrivair, a buyer-created intermediary agency that helps to mediate between parties. Total costs in 1993 to 2000 (excluding intermediary transaction costs) were almost €17 million (US$25 million). The tenacity of Vittel in securing an agreement reflects the fact that it was simply much cheaper to pay for a solution with farmers than to move the sourcing of water elsewhere (in France, natural mineral waters are not allowed pre-treatment).

Sources: Perrot-Maître (2006); Wunder and Wertz-Kanounnikoff (2009)

---

number of jobs will obviously depend on the scale of the scheme and the nature of the activity involved. A large-scale example is the Working for Water (WfW) public works programme in South Africa which protects water resources by stopping the spread of invasive plants. WfW has more than 300 projects in all nine South African provinces. It has employed around 20,000 people per year, 52 per cent of them women,[5] and also provided skills training, health and HIV/AIDS education to participants. WfW is best understood as a PES-like programme as it does not pay landowners to provide continued services but consists of the municipal government contracting workers to manage public land sustainably (Wunder, 2008; see also Chapter 9).

Box 5.6 Public water quality contracts for PES: The example of farmers in Germany

Nitrates in drinking water are a health hazard but their removal is very costly. It is economically more efficient to prevent them entering water supplies in the first place.

Payments and funding

The Bundesländer (federated states) combine mandatory 'groundwater extraction charges' and voluntary measures. Water utility companies pay a charge to the relevant Land (state) for every m³ of groundwater extracted, part of which is used to pay farmers to reduce use of fertilizers and pesticides: in some cases this is complemented by EU funds. In Baden-Württemberg, payments to farmers for water-related measures in 2007 to 2013 will be around €107 million. Nitrate concentrations fell by approximately 16 per cent in 1994 to 2008 (Fuhrman, 2010).

Results and lessons learned

The Länder increasingly use this money to fund voluntary projects between local water utilities and farmers, which makes it easier to protect groundwater with little additional effort or loss of agricultural output. Nationally, around 435 projects took place in 2002, involving 33,000 farmers over 850,000ha (5 per cent of all farmland): in Lower Saxony, projects covered 50 per cent of groundwater extraction areas. This cooperation also helped to protect biodiversity by preserving species-rich grasslands and creating new grassland areas and provides a model for PES for other conservation objectives.

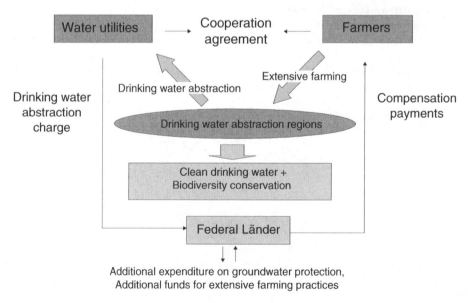

Figure 5.4 *Public water quality contracts for PES – A schematic*

Source: Niedersächsisches Umweltministerium, Niedersächsisches Landesamt für Ökologie (2002)

Box 5.7 Recent large-scale PES to alleviate poverty and reduce deforestation in Ecuador

Background and objectives

Ecuador's deforestation rate is one of the highest in South America (around 200,000ha each year out of a total 10 million ha of native forest cover). This emits about 55 million tonnes CO_2e and entails a huge loss of ecosystem services and subsistence for local people.

In 2008, the Programa Socio Bosque (Forest Partners Programme) was launched under the National Development Plan to combine development and conservation objectives and directly benefit poor farmers and indigenous communities.

Payments and funding

Landowners receive a direct annual payment per hectare of native forest conserved. Participation is voluntary and compliance is monitored regularly through interpretation of satellite images and field visits. Programme goals for the first six years are:

- to protect over 4 million hectares of forest to conserve globally important biodiversity, protect soils and water and mitigate natural disasters;
- to reduce GHG emissions as an integral part of the national REDD strategy, supported by stronger enforcement of illegal logging and a national reforestation plan;
- to increase income in the poorest rural areas (about 1 million beneficiaries).

Criteria to prioritize implementation areas may include high deforestation threat, high value for ecosystem services and high levels of poverty.

Results and lessons learned

By May 2009, about 23,000 beneficiaries had been registered, covering 320,000ha of forest. A dedicated trust fund has been established to assure long-term financial sustainability and transparent use of resources. The government intends to complement its own resources with international cooperative funds, national/international PES schemes and carbon markets.

Sources: Ministerio del Ambiente del Ecuador: personal correspondence with Marcela Aguiñaga, Manuel Brav, Tannya Lozada; Conservación Internacional Ecuador: Free de Koning and Luis Suárez. Background information available at: www.ambiente.gov.ec/contenido.php?cd=278

On the other hand, some PES schemes can reduce rural employment if land is completely taken out of production or dedicated to less labour-intensive management practices to secure environmental benefits. Although such a strategy has been used in EU and US agri-environmental programmes with few inequitable impacts, this could pose a much greater problem in developing country contexts, e.g. for landless households that rely on selling labour to farmers as a source of cash income (Zilberman et al, 2006).

Poverty concerns are addressed through Ecuador's ambitious Socio Bosque Programme which combines protection for a wider set of ecosystem services, including carbon storage and sequestration (see Box 5.7). This is of particular interest because climate change-related payments are expected to be a major driver of PES in coming years. Schemes of this type could offer win–win opportunities if targeted at areas of high biodiversity value offering additional non-carbon ecosystem services, as well as at areas of high poverty.

Non-monetary benefits of PES

In some cases PES involve non-monetary benefits. For example, protected area managers are increasingly exploring collaborative management models to reduce tension across park boundaries and better integrate protected areas into broader regional development. In Kulekhani, Nepal, local PES-like schemes to regulate water or reduce erosion provide communities with development assistance in the form of medical services and education, rather than cash payments. In east and southern Africa, communities living near protected areas are sometimes granted limited access to the ecosystem in return for supporting conservation action. However, the effectiveness of such indirect approaches may be questioned (Ferraro and Kiss, 2002).

1.4 Opportunities and challenges

PES can make the value of ecosystem services more explicit and thus modify or even reverse incentives for users to over-exploit or convert them. Although demand for some services is currently low, this may well rise as services become increasingly scarce (e.g. due to population growth or loss of other areas providing similar services). To determine whether PES could help secure future benefits, it is important to assess the level of ecosystem service provision and how this could change in the future and affect demand.

The voluntary aspect of PES is a key feature, although legal/regulatory underpinning is essential to realize their full potential. There is potential to scale up PES (from local initiatives to national coverage), to implement PES in more countries and to make PES more cost-effective.

It is estimated that there are already more than 300 PES programmes in existence (Wunder et al, 2008; Blackman and Woodward, 2009), through which approximately US$6.53 billion are paid out in China, Costa Rica, Mexico, the UK and the US alone (OECD, 2010). The scale of PES is increasing by 10 to 20 per cent per year (Ecosystem Marketplace, 2008).

PES involving the private sector offer the potential to raise additional finance and thus complement public conservation funding. As public and private PES may operate differently, it is important to explore the relative benefits of voluntary and regulatory approaches. While private actors can play a role in PES, the willingness to pay (WTP) of existing beneficiaries is often not enough to cover start-up or operating costs. This may be due to 'free rider' problems or simply to a lack of knowledge about the benefits provided by the ecosystem concerned. In such cases, governments may need to provide extra incentives or find alternative solutions. One approach could be to make a scheme obligatory once a certain percentage of beneficiaries agrees to it, mitigating the free-rider problem.

PES schemes also face several constraints. They require significant investments in information and capacity building. Priorities include mapping the supply and demand of ecosystem services, understanding current and expected future use of resources, engaging relevant stakeholders and training administrators.

High transaction costs can create a barrier to developing PES. Depending on the value of the ecosystems concerned, there may be a justification for states (or international agencies) to subsidize start-up or transaction costs to facilitate progress, e.g. by paying for mapping ecosystem services or for stakeholder participation processes.

PES are not appropriate everywhere. They can be particularly difficult to implement where tenure or use rights are poorly defined or enforced, e.g. the high seas and some mangroves, coral reefs, floodplains and forests. Where institutional capacity and transparency are lacking or resource access and ownership are in dispute, PES 'buyers' have little incentive to participate because they have few guarantees that the activities paid for will actually be implemented – or even that a legitimate service provider can be identified.

PES design and implementation can also be compromised where there is unequal bargaining power between service providers and beneficiaries. This can affect who is included in the scheme, the way the money is shared, the rate of payment and the conditions set for service provision and access (see Figure 5.5 below).

In some cases, a PES targeting a single service will not be enough to halt degradation or loss as the payment will be less than the opportunity costs of alternative resource uses. However, PES schemes can be part of a broader mix of policy instruments that addresses the full range of ecosystem services from an area. This holistic approach is particularly important wherever potential trade-offs are involved. A PES focused on a single ecosystem service may have negative impacts on the provision of other services (e.g. promoting plantation of exotic species for rapid carbon sequestration at the expense of more biodiverse natural grasslands).

More generally, proper sequencing is important for achieving effective and coherent policies. Introducing PES without the prior or simultaneous removal or reform of policies that damage ecosystems and biodiversity will lead to waste and inconsistency. This has been repeatedly underlined by the Organisation for Economic Co-operation and Development (OECD), particularly with regard to environmentally harmful subsidies (see Chapter 6).

The ability to quantify, monetize and communicate ecosystem service values to key stakeholders – from politicians to industry to local communities – can build support. However, PES are still feasible without a biophysical assessment and economic valuation of an ecosystem service (Wunder, 2007). Some of the most valuable services may be those that are most difficult to measure and, in some cases, precise quantification would be prohibitive (e.g. for small watershed schemes). In these cases, arguments based on the precautionary principle may be enough to justify starting PES. Nevertheless, economic valuation should be used as and when new information is available to adjust payments, targeting or conditions.

1.5 Moving forward on PES design and implementation

Experience to date underlines the importance of careful design and preparation to ensure that PES schemes are effective and appropriate for local conditions. Information on the social, economic and ecological context and the legal and institutional context needs to be taken into account. Ideally, PES should be targeted, cost-effective, accountable, enforceable, coordinated with other instruments, responsive to community needs and fair. In practice, the reality can be very different.

Supportive legal and institutional context

PES schemes require rules and institutions to function effectively, including mechanisms to enforce contracts. This can have equity implications as new rules will change the distribution of rights and responsibilities over ecosystems and their services. Institutions are needed to:

- Facilitate transactions and reduce transaction costs. Most ecosystems provide a range of services, even if only one or a subset are recognized by a PES scheme. Payment can be made for a specific 'bundle' of services from large numbers of providers or there may be different instruments or different buyers for different services, evolving over time (see Figure 5.5). In some cases one ecosystem service will be a free co-benefit, alongside another service that is paid for.

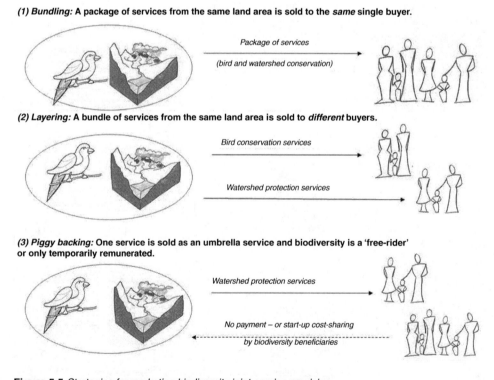

(1) Bundling: A package of services from the same land area is sold to the *same* single buyer.

(2) Layering: A bundle of services from the same land area is sold to *different* buyers.

(3) Piggy backing: One service is sold as an umbrella service and biodiversity is a 'free-rider' or only temporarily remunerated.

Figure 5.5 *Strategies for marketing biodiversity joint service provision*

Source: Wunder and Wertz-Kanounnikoff (2009)

- Set up insurance or other mechanisms to manage risks.
- Provide business support, e.g. for beneficiaries to be willing to pay for ecosystem services, methods to measure and assess biodiversity in working landscapes must be improved.

Identification of services, buyers and sellers

Enabling conditions for PES include economic, technical, governance and practical factors:

- On the demand side, where the supply of a valuable service is threatened, its beneficiary needs to be aware of the threat, willing to pay to maintain the service and able to do so.
- On the supply side, the opportunity costs of changing resource management practices must not be too high. It must be possible to improve the supply of the service through a change in use, e.g. land set aside, switch to organic production, water-saving irrigation (see also Wunder, 2008).
- Technical information is needed to understand the service, who provides it and how, who benefits (using spatial mapping), historical and expected future trends in demand and supply, and other contextual factors (this makes it possible to target payments to those who can actually deliver the desired service).
- In terms of governance, trust between beneficiaries and suppliers (or the potential to build trust) is essential, along with appropriate legal and institutional support for monitoring and contract enforcement, clarity on resource tenure and mechanisms for redress.

Negotiation of PES deals

In principle, PES initiatives should be financially self-sustaining to secure services over the long term. However, where continuous payments by beneficiaries are not feasible, it may be possible to convert a one-off payment (e.g. a grant) into long-term flows by setting up trust funds or to pool payments from different beneficiaries (see 'layering' strategy in Figure 5.5).

As PES have distributional consequences, it is critical to address issues of ownership and reward explicitly to ensure that they do not aggravate existing inequities and to monitor cost–benefit distribution consistently. Wide participation in PES-related decisions can help ensure transparency and acceptance and avoid covert privatization of common resources. Participatory resource assessments and valuation can enable PES schemes to take account of traditional knowledge and practices and all stakeholder interests. Capacity building and, where needed, adequate institutional measures are important to help weaker stakeholders participate in negotiations and share their insights on ecosystem conservation. In Costa Rica and Mexico, 'collective contracting' was introduced to facilitate the participation of poorer small farmers, once it was realized that they would otherwise be excluded.

PES schemes are not primarily designed to reduce poverty but can offer new opportunities for the rural poor to earn additional income (see Box 5.8). Many rural people earn their living from activities such as forestry and farming in which income fluctuates by season and year. PES based on ecosystem restoration or improved land management can provide a stable source of additional income and employment in rural areas.

Box 5.8 Phased performance payments under PES schemes on Mafia Island, Tanzania

A two-part payment scheme was set up to encourage the mainly poor local population to conserve sea turtles. It consists of, first, a fixed payment for finding and reporting a nest and, second, a variable payment linked to the nest's hatching success. The initial payment provides immediate recompense for not harvesting nests (important as poor residents apply high discount rates to future payments) and makes the overall payment scheme less risky for poor residents than if all payment depended on successful hatchings. The post-hatching variable payment then provides an incentive not to poach eggs once the nest has been reported.

The island has around 150 turtle nests and 41,000 residents. Participation is agreed directly between volunteers and villagers, and based on oral agreements. Most payments go to about half a dozen individuals actively searching for nests. The scheme reduced poaching rates of turtle nests dramatically, from 100 per cent (2001, year of introduction) to less than 1 per cent in 2004. From 2001 to 2004, the number of hatchlings increased in both absolute terms (from about 1200 to a little over 10,000) and relative terms (from 55 per cent to 71 per cent of the eggs remaining at hatching time).

Source: Ferraro (2007)

Overarching conditions for success

Effective PES requires – and can help to strengthen – certain 'enabling conditions' such as:

- reliable scientific information (e.g. sources of ecosystem services, their spatial distribution and beneficiaries);
- economic data (start-up and implementation costs, including opportunity costs of managing resources for ecosystem services, non-market values and incentive effects of alternative PES arrangements);
- identification and participation of key stakeholders.

Successful PES schemes typically demonstrate transparency, reliability (of e.g. payments), appropriate cultural conditions (e.g. acceptance of differential payments for environmental stewardship, trust) and strong commitment by all parties. Effective monitoring and enforcement is critical to ensure delivery of the intended services and their measurement. Payments must be clearly linked to service provision and may be withdrawn if resource users abandon management practices associated with the service. Monitoring data on the quality and quantity of site services can help improve the targeting of payments or make other refinements (see also Chapter 3).

As noted, PES will not work everywhere. It may be difficult to secure sufficient support for PES in situations where competing (destructive) resource uses are highly lucrative. Weak governance, unclear resource tenure and high transaction costs can also be major barriers.

As with any innovation, a critical step is to secure support from leaders at various levels who can communicate the importance of ecosystem services and the potential of PES to both providers and beneficiaries. There is also a need for careful analysis and effective communication of experiences, both positive and negative, to replicate and scale up successful initiatives.

Overall, OECD (2010) summarizes a number of prerequisites and key criteria to enhance the environmental and cost-effectiveness of PES programmes as follows:

- remove perverse incentives;
- clearly define property rights;
- clearly define PES goals and objectives;
- develop a robust monitoring and reporting framework;
- identify appropriate buyers and ensure sufficient and long-term sources of finance;
- identify sellers and target ecosystem service benefits;
- consider opportunities for bundling or layering multiple ecosystem services;
- establish baselines to ensure additionality;
- reflect ecosystem service providers' opportunity costs through differentiated payments;
- address leakage (displacement of emissions);
- ensure permanence.

2 International PES: REDD+ and beyond

This section presents the economic, social and environmental case for international payment schemes for ecosystem services that provide global public good benefits (Section 2.1). It describes the proposed mechanism for Reducing Emissions from Deforestation and Forest Degradation (REDD+) in developing countries, under the United Nations Framework Convention on Climate Change, which is intended to help address the global climate change challenge, and how this mechanism could provide co-benefits for biodiversity as well as other non-carbon-related ecosystem services (Section 2.2). Lastly, it discusses new initiatives for specific international PES for global biodiversity-related services (Section 2.3).

2.1 The rationale for international engagement

The global benefits from biodiversity – genetic information for bio-industry and pharmaceuticals, carbon storage and resilience to climate change, international hydrological services, wildlife and landscape beauty that support international tourism and non-use values – need to be recognized, and the costs of maintenance fairly shared, to halt their degradation.

Commitment to international PES can help secure rewards for a range of these benefits. These are PES where payments are transferred across international borders: they may be bilateral, regional or global. Existing PES-like instruments for biodiversity at the international level include bioprospecting, conservation concessions, international voluntary biodiversity offsets and international grants (OECD, forthcoming).

Regional and continental PES schemes – or equivalent cooperation – can address ecological functions in large transboundary ecosystems, such as the Nile, Lake Victoria

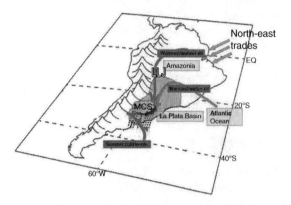

Figure 5.6 *Opportunities for regional PES: Example of the Amazonian 'water pump'*

Note: EQ: Equator; MCS: mesoscale convective system

Source: Adapted from Marengo et al (2004)

or the Amazon. Cooperating to identify interdependencies between providers and beneficiaries is likely to lead to mutually beneficial outcomes rather than acting solely in the national interest: the latter may deliver short-term gains for a few but long-term losses for all as natural capital erodes.

In Amazonia, for example, forests evaporate roughly 8 trillion tonnes of water each year (IPCC, 2007b). This falls as rain, helps maintain forests and is transported to the Andes and down to the Plata River Basin (see Figure 5.6). Agriculture and hydropower generate major economic returns for the countries in the basin (Argentina, Bolivia, Brazil, Paraguay and Uruguay) (Vera et al, 2006), which means that the entire region's food, energy and water security are underpinned by the Amazonian 'water pump'. Regional and/or international PES could help to maintain this critical service.

2.2 REDD+: A carbon mechanism with potentially large biodiversity co-benefits[6]

> If a post Kyoto climate agreement fails on avoiding tropical deforestation, the achievement of overall climate change goals will become virtually impossible. The lives and livelihoods of millions of people will be put at risk, and the eventual economic cost of combating climate change will be far higher than it needs to be. (Bharrat Jagdeo, President of Guyana; Global Canopy Programme, 2008)

The international community, under the auspices of the UNFCCC, has proposed a new financial mechanism, Reducing Emissions from Deforestation and Forest Degradation (REDD+) in developing countries, to help internalize the carbon-related ecosystem services provided by forests. As forest loss and degradation accounts for about 17 per cent of global GHG emissions (IPCC, 2007c), reaching agreement on a REDD+ mechanism could significantly contribute to meeting the UNFCCC objective 'to achieve stabilization of greenhouse gas concentrations in the atmosphere at a level that would prevent dangerous anthropogenic interference with the climate system' (Article 3).

Box 5.9 The evolution of REDD+ under the UNFCCC

In 2005, at the 11th meeting of the UNFCCC Conference of the Parties (COP-11), Papua New Guinea proposed integrating a mechanism to reduce emissions from deforestation (i.e. RED) within the post-2012 climate change regime. The proposal received widespread support and a formal process was created to examine this further.

In 2007, UNFCCC Parties adopted the Bali Action Plan (Decision 2/CP.13) which mandated negotiation of a post-2012 instrument to include, among other things, financial incentives for forest-based climate change mitigation in developing countries. By this time, the role of forest degradation in carbon emissions was also acknowledged and the Plan specifically called for 'policy approaches and positive incentives on issues relating to reducing emissions from deforestation and forest degradation in developing countries; and the role of conservation, sustainable management of forests and enhancement of forest carbon stocks in developing countries' (Decision 1/CP.13, para 1b(iii)). It was also recognized that action to support REDD 'can promote co-benefits and may contribute to achieving the aims and objectives of other relevant international conventions and agreements' (Decision 2/CP.13).

In 2008 many highlighted that forest conservation, management and enhancement were of high importance and the term 'REDD+' came into official use (COP-14; Poznan, 2008). The possible scope of forestry activities for inclusion has since been significantly enlarged since its initial conceptualization, and could reward 'enhanced positive changes' through forest restoration/rehabilitation (see Table 5.1). It is not yet clear whether forestation and reforestation activities will be eligible for REDD+.

Table 5.1 Possible scope of creditable activities in a REDD+ mechanism

Changes in:	Reduced negative change	Enhanced positive change
Forest area (hectare)	Avoided deforestation	Afforestation and reforestation (A/R)
Carbon density (carbon per hectare)	Avoided degradation	Forest restoration and rehabilitation (carbon stock enhancement)

Source: Angelsen and Wertz-Kanounnikoff (2008)

Forests play a globally important role in biodiversity provision as well as in climate change mitigation and adaptation (see Chapter 1). For example, sustaining high forest biodiversity not only improves the carbon storage capacity of forests but also their resilience to changes in climatic conditions, pollution and biological invasions. This section introduces REDD+, including how the proposed mechanism has evolved (see Box 5.9) and examines options to maximize biodiversity co-benefits in REDD+ and to avoid potential adverse impacts on biodiversity.

A REDD+ mechanism could have a substantial climate change impact because it is estimated to be a low-cost GHG mitigation option compared to many other emission abatement options (see Box 5.10). The actual amount of deforestation and degradation that could be avoided – and thus the level of emissions prevented and new carbon sequestered – will depend (among other things) on:

Box 5.10 The costs and benefits of reducing GHG emissions from deforestation

Estimated costs of reducing emissions from deforestation vary across studies, depending on models and assumptions used. In comparison to GHG mitigation alternatives in other sectors, REDD is estimated to be a low-cost mitigation option (Stern, 2007; IPCC, 2007c).

Eliasch (2008) estimated that REDD could lead to a halving of deforestation rates by 2030, cutting emissions by 1.5 to 2.7Gt CO_2/year, that it would require between US$17.2 billion/year and US$33 billion/year and have an estimated long-term net benefit of US$3.7 trillion in present value terms (this accounts only for the benefits of reduced climate change). Delaying action on REDD would reduce its benefits dramatically: waiting ten more years could reduce the net benefit of halving deforestation by US$500 billion (Hope and Castilla-Rubio, 2008).

A study from the Woods Hole Research Centre estimates that 94 per cent of Amazon deforestation could be avoided at a cost of less than US$1 per tonne of CO_2 (Nepstad et al, 2007). Olsen and Bishop (2009) find that REDD, at a carbon price of less than US$5 per tonne of CO_2 equivalent, is competitive with most land uses in the Brazilian Amazon and many land uses in Indonesia. Kindermann et al (2008) estimate that a 50 per cent reduction in deforestation in 2005 to 2030 could provide 1.5 to 2.7Gt CO_2/year in emission reductions and would require US$17.2 billion/year to US$28 billion/year (see Wertz-Kanounnikoff (2008) for a review of cost studies).

Sources: Stern (2007); IPCC (2007a); Nepstad et al (2007); Eliasch (2008); Hope and Castilla-Rubio (2008); Kindermann et al (2008); Wertz-Kanounnikoff (2008)

- how emission baselines from forestry are determined;
- the underlying incentives driving deforestation (i.e. the opportunity costs); and
- the level of finance that is mobilized to address REDD+ (discussed below).

Several technical and methodological REDD+ issues still need to be agreed through the international UNFCCC process (for an overview see Karousakis and Corfee-Morlot, 2007; Angelsen, 2008). Key REDD+ design elements with implications for biodiversity relate to scope, baselines/reference levels, financing, and monitoring and reporting methodologies (for a synopsis of REDD+ proposals, see Parker et al, 2009).

REDD+ design at the international level and implications for biodiversity

Possible scope of REDD+ in comparison to REDD

A well-designed REDD+ mechanism that delivers real, measurable and long-term emission reductions from deforestation and forest degradation in developing countries, is likely to lead to significant positive impacts on biodiversity in itself, since these emission reductions imply a decline in forest area lost, habitat destruction, landscape fragmentation and thus in biodiversity loss.

At the global scale, for example, Turner et al (2007) examine how ecosystem services (including climate regulation) and biodiversity coincide geographically and conclude that tropical forests offer the greatest synergy. These cover about 7 per cent of the world's dry land (Lindsey, 2007) but contain 80 to 90 per cent of terrestrial biodiversity (FAO, 2000).

A REDD+ mechanism could have additional positive impacts on biodiversity if achieved through appropriate restoration of degraded forest ecosystems and landscapes. Including afforestation and reforestation (A/R)[7] activities in REDD+ could provide incentives to regenerate forests in deforested areas and increase connectivity between forest habitats. However, there is a need for safeguards to avoid potential negative effects. For example, providing financial support for A/R activities that resulted in monoculture plantations could have adverse impacts on biodiversity: first, there are lower levels of biodiversity in monoculture plantations compared to most natural forest and, second, the use of alien plant species could have additional negative impacts. Conversely, planting mixed native species in appropriate locations could yield multiple benefits for biodiversity and ecosystem resilience.

National and sub-national baselines/reference levels

Baselines provide a reference level against which to assess changes in emissions and help to ensure 'additionality' (i.e. achieving emission reductions that are additional to what would have occurred under the business-as-usual scenario). Various proposals have been tabled for how these could be established for REDD+ at national and sub-national (including project)[8] level. The accounting level selected has implications for 'carbon leakage' i.e. displacement of anthropogenic emissions from GHG sources to outside the accounting boundary, due to deforestation and/or forest degradation increasing elsewhere as a result. Leakage could have adverse consequences for biodiversity if deforestation/degradation were displaced from an area with relatively low biodiversity value to one with higher value. In general, national-level emissions accounting is better able to account for leakage than sub-national and/or project level accounting.[9]

A related design element is the treatment of protected areas (PAs) in these baselines. Some high-carbon/high-biodiversity ecosystems may be located in legally defined PAs, giving the impression that the carbon they store is safe and that REDD+ finance to PAs would not offer additional sequestration benefits. While this is true for well-managed PAs, many sites remain vulnerable to degradation through encroachment, poaching and other illegal activities (Leverington et al, 2008). This reflects, among other things, the significant financing gap that exists for many PAs across the world (see Chapter 8).

About 312Gt of terrestrial carbon is stored in the existing PA network. If this were lost to the atmosphere, it would be equivalent to approximately 23 times the total global anthropogenic carbon emissions for 2004 (Kapos et al, 2008). Targeting REDD+ finance at PAs at risk of degradation/deforestation and/or with potential for improved ecological status – rather than at 'safe' PAs – could yield both high carbon and biodiversity benefits.

Gross versus net deforestation rates

A further issue under negotiation is whether gross or net deforestation rates will be considered when estimating emission reductions.[10] From a climate perspective, the most relevant figure is what the atmosphere actually experiences (net values). However, the use of net rates could hide the loss of mature (i.e. primary and modified natural) forests and their replacement with areas of new forest, either on-site or elsewhere. This could result in significant losses in biodiversity (CBD, 2008).

REDD+ financing

UNFCCC discussions at COP-15 (Copenhagen, 2010) moved towards a three-phased approach to financing:

1 voluntary funding for national REDD+ strategy development and capacity building (including monitoring and establishing a reference level);
2 implementation of policies and measures proposed in national REDD+ strategies, supported by an internationally binding financial instrument funded by e.g. auctioning assigned amount units (AAUs);
3 performance-based payments on the basis of verified emission reductions measured against agreed reference levels.

It is not yet clear, however, whether finance in Phase 3 would be delivered through the international carbon market (i.e. allowing REDD+ credits to be traded with other allowances), through a fund mechanism, or both. These options have different implications for how biodiversity co-benefits could be promoted and which stakeholders would be involved in decision making.

For example, if Phase 3 of REDD+ were financed through the regulated international carbon market, any REDD+ credits would need to be fungible (interchangeable) with existing AAUs under the Kyoto market.[11] The unit of exchange would be tonnes of carbon equivalents (t CO_2e). Demand for credits would be generated by the carbon market which would drive investment towards the least-cost mitigation options (subject to any restrictions that governments might place on market access for REDD+ credits).

Given their ability to engage the private sector, market-based approaches to REDD+ are likely to mobilize higher levels of sustainable and long-term financing, resulting in larger areas of avoided deforestation and thus larger biodiversity co-benefits. Although fund-based approaches may be more flexible in taking other objectives into account, such as biodiversity, they may not deliver such high volumes of finance in the long run.

Maximizing biodiversity co-benefits of REDD+ at the implementation level

In addition to ensuring the REDD+ design elements at the international level are conducive to promoting biodiversity co-benefits, there are large opportunities for national and local REDD+ investors to enhance biodiversity co-benefits in REDD+ at the implementation level. Notably, biodiversity co-benefits can 'piggy-back' at national

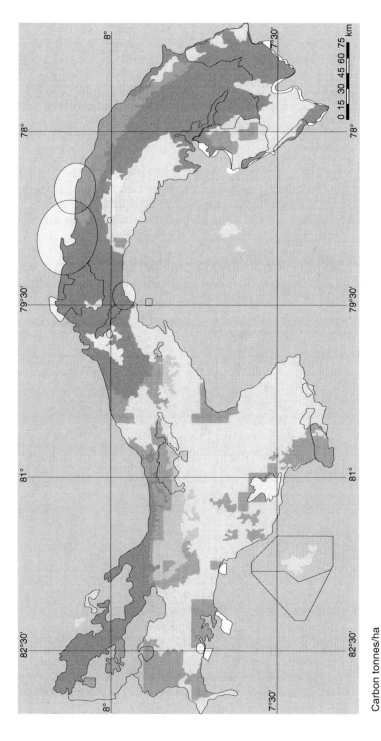

Carbon tonnes/ha

Low (0–175)

Medium (175–313)

High (313–626)

High biodiversity (>584 species)

National protected areas

Figure 5.7 *National carbon and biodiversity map for Panama*

Note: Areas of 'high biodiversity importance' are those where at least four indicators overlap, with areas in dark grey indicating a greater degree of overlap.

Source: UNEP-WCMC (2008)

and local levels if REDD+ activities are targeted towards forest areas that have high carbon potential as well as high biodiversity benefits. Identifying and geographically targeting such areas requires tools such as spatial mapping. Mapping areas where both high-carbon and high-biodiversity benefits overlap makes it possible for governments and/or private sector investors to capture two environmental services for the price of one. Such mapping tools are currently emerging and are in different stages of development. One example is the Carbon and Biodiversity Demonstration Atlas (UNEP-WCMC, 2008). It presents regional and national maps for six tropical countries that show where areas with high carbon coincide spatially with areas of biodiversity importance. To identify the latter, UNEP-WCMC used six biodiversity indicators: biodiversity hotspots, endemic bird areas, amphibian diversity, global 200 terrestrial ecoregions, global 200 freshwater ecoregions and centres of plant diversity (see Figure 5.7).

Spatial tools of this kind can help governments and potential investors to identify and prioritize REDD+ activities. However, further work is needed to establish similar maps based on national biodiversity data combined with greater spatial understanding of the economic values of biodiversity and ecosystem service benefits.

If such targeting were effectively implemented, a REDD+ finance mechanism could free up existing biodiversity funding (e.g. from official development assistance, ODA, and/or developing country government budgets) that is currently invested in high-carbon/high-biodiversity areas. These funds could then be redirected to target biodiversity conservation in areas with high-biodiversity and low-carbon benefits, allowing the delivery of greater total biodiversity benefits.

Marketing biodiversity benefits directly alongside REDD+ by bundling and layering

In addition to 'piggy-backing' biodiversity co-benefits in a REDD+ mechanism, it is also possible to jointly market (i.e. co-finance) biodiversity provision by bundling and layering biodiversity payments with carbon payments (see Figure 5.5 above). By mobilizing additional finance from those who use or benefit from the non-carbon-related ecosystem services, and co-financing REDD+ activities in areas with high-carbon and high-biodiversity benefits, deforestation can be avoided over larger areas. In the voluntary carbon market, several initiatives already bundle carbon and biodiversity benefits in forestry activities. These take the form of premiums for voluntary REDD credits that provide additional biodiversity benefits.[12] Examples include the Climate, Community and Biodiversity Alliance (CCBA) which has established voluntary standards and REDD demonstration activities for forestry projects, Plan Vivo, CarbonFix, Social Carbon and the California Climate Action Registry (see Karousakis, 2009).

The UNFCCC Bali Action Plan called for REDD demonstration activities to obtain practical experience and share lessons learned. These pilot activities are still in the fairly early stages of design and implementation but can eventually provide good practice insights and lessons for a future REDD+ mechanism.[13] Policy makers can use these pilot activities to actively promote approaches to maximize biodiversity co-benefits in REDD+.

Ongoing demonstration activities highlight the need to provide alternative livelihoods to communities dependent on forests, improve governance and clarify tenure (see Box 5.11).

Box 5.11 Example of a multiple-benefits REDD project in Madagascar

Background

Less than 15 per cent of Madagascar's land area is forested. About half the forest cover has been lost since 1953 (Hanski et al, 2007) and most coastal lowland forests have been cleared. Unprotected natural forest was lost at an annual rate of 0.65 per cent from 2000 to 2005 (MEFT et al, 2009).

Project design and goals

The Ankeniheny-Mantadia-Zahamena Corridor Project aims to protect some of the last remaining low and mid-elevation primary rainforest and deliver multiple benefits for biodiversity, livelihoods and climate change mitigation. It is structured to take advantage of carbon financing from the emerging voluntary and compliance markets through the sale of emissions reductions from REDD. It will create a new protected area and reforest target sites to restore habitat connectivity, enhance local resource management capacity (about 315,000 people live in 30 nearby communes) and conserve endemic species.

Project governance and funding

NGO backing is led by Conservation International (CI). The Environment Ministry acts as project manager, protected area administrator and 'vendor' of the carbon offsets created through REDD and reforestation activities. Communities and NGOs are organized into Local Management Units, federated within sectors, and ultimately report to the Ministry. CI and the World Bank's BioCarbon Fund (BioCF) provide technical expertise and financial support to access carbon finance mechanisms, including future application of REDD carbon accounting methodology and monitoring emissions reductions.

As carbon finance rarely covers high start-up and transaction costs in forest carbon projects, the project combined carbon-credit purchase commitments and project support from BioCF with targeted biodiversity investments (CI, government) and community development funding through USAID and the World Bank.

Source: Personal communication, Olaf Zerbock and James McKinnon, CI

Recent initiatives linked to REDD+

Current international initiatives to promote biodiversity in REDD+ activities include:

- The World Bank Forest Carbon Partnership Facility (FCPF) which has incorporated biodiversity considerations in its REDD Readiness Fund for capacity building. Country participants have to submit a Readiness Preparation Proposal that includes measures to deliver and monitor multiple benefits as part of national REDD+ strategies, including but not limited to biodiversity, poverty reduction and benefit sharing.

- The UN-REDD Programme, which also supports multiple benefits through consultations with pilot countries, spatial analyses of the relationship between carbon storage, biodiversity and ecosystem services in forests, and the development of tools to assist decision makers in promoting synergies, addressing conflicts and managing trade-offs.

Pending formal agreement on a REDD+ mechanism, several international contributions and funds have already been set up to build capacity in developing countries, indicating the growing support for combined carbon/biodiversity activities in the donor community (see Box 5.12).

Box 5.12 Examples of international funding initiatives to address deforestation

National donor activities

National donor activities include:

- the Norway Forest Fund, which has committed US$2.8 billion over five years from 2008;
- the Japanese government's Cool Earth Partnership to support adaptation to climate change and access to clean energy, which includes forest measures: US$2 billion per year out of a US$10 billion fund is allocated for adaptation measures;
- the Australian Deforestation Fund, which aims to reduce deforestation in the South-east Asia region with funds of AUS$200 million;
- the German commitment of €500 million per year for biodiversity.

Emergency funding proposal

The Prince's Rainforests Project has proposed an emergency global fund to protect rainforests, financed by a public–private partnership in developed countries which could include issuing Rainforest Bonds. The aim is to raise around £10 billion per year. An international working group was formed in April 2009 with G20 support to study a range of proposals.

Reforestation registered under the UNFCCC Clean Development Mechanism (CDM)

Eight forestry projects have been registered under the CDM. In Africa, these include the Nile Basin Reforestation Project led by Uganda's National Forestry Authority in association with local community organizations. The Rwoho Central Forest Reserve Project will generate up to 700 local jobs and receive revenues from the BioCF for planting pine and mixed native tree species on degraded grasslands. It aims to deliver co-benefits for livelihoods, climate resilience and biodiversity.

Source: Adapted from Ministry of Foreign Affairs of Japan (2008); The Prince's Rainforests Project (2010); World Bank (2010)

Most recently, decisions stemming from CBD COP-10 in Nagoya on Biodiversity and Climate Change (agenda item 5.6) in the context of REDD+ include *inter alia* a call for Parties to provide advice on the application of relevant safeguards for biodiversity (para 9 (h)) and, more generally, further work on ways and means to achieve biodiversity co-benefits.

2.3 Direct international payments for global ecosystem services

> A mechanism needs to be devised to compensate societies that preserve the global commons. (UNEP, 2009c)

This section discusses emerging initiatives that aim to help address the global public good benefits of biodiversity and create incentives to maintain global ecosystem services.

Biodiversity as a global public good

As underlined throughout this book, biodiversity and ecosystem services provide critical inputs to local communities and countries in terms of production, cultural values and recreational amenity. However, biodiversity is also a global public good which merits international cooperation on conservation, restoration and management in its own right.

We have seen that protecting the supply of public goods usually falls to government as these are by definition non-excludable and non-rival. Recognizing biodiversity as a global public good implies that all governments have a role to play, either by creating conditions for organizations, businesses and individuals to undertake larger-scale and more effective conservation or by taking on this task themselves.

There are at least three good reasons for governments to invest in natural capital and ecosystem services beyond their borders and support international PES:

1   Global benefits, including direct and indirect use and non-use values (see Chapter 4), derive from biodiversity and from ecosystem services at different levels and need to be made explicit in government policies.
2   Economic development that avoids global environmental impoverishment will require direct efforts from biodiversity-rich developing countries and significant and sustained investment support from developed countries.
3   Importing primary commodities into developed economies without internalizing their full environmental costs can be seen as exporting environmental pressure to other countries. Mechanisms to compensate or avoid negative environmental impacts abroad could decrease pressure and buy time to make the shift to more sustainable production.

Geographically, ecosystem use and provisioning are unevenly distributed throughout the world. This is the case for important use values (e.g. agricultural harvests), cultural values (e.g. charismatic species), carbon storage (see Kapos et al, 2008) and biodiversity-rich areas. This imbalance is partly a consequence of past human development paths and population movements and partly due to natural endowments and climatic conditions.

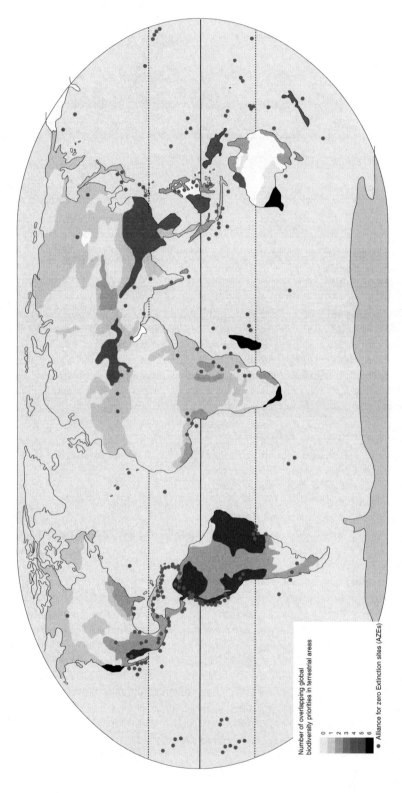

Figure 5.8a *Comparative maps of biodiversity hotspots and major wilderness areas and the UN's Human Development Index (HDI): Global Biodiversity 'priority areas' map*

Note: This map builds on Conservation International's Hotspots, WWF's Global 200 ecoregions, Birdlife International Endemic Bird Areas (EBAs), WWF/IUCN Centres of Plant Diversity (CPDs) and Amphibian Diversity Areas plus Alliance for Zero Extinction (AZE) sites

Source: Kapos et al (2008)

HDI: HDI value (2010)

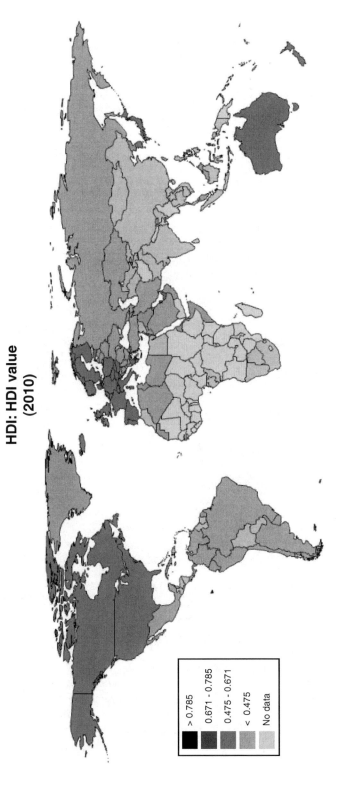

> 0.785
0.671 - 0.785
0.475 - 0.671
< 0.475
No data

Figure 5.8b *Comparative maps of biodiversity hotspots and major wilderness areas and the UN's Human Development Index (HDI): Human Development Index (HDI) map*

Source: UNDP (2009)

Box 5.13 Think PINC: The 'Proactive Investment in Natural Capital' proposal

We propose that a new mechanism of Proactive Investment in Natural Capital (PINC) is created to promote adaptation in existing protected areas and standing forests that may not benefit directly from REDD funds. (Trivedi et al, 2009)

PINC, proposed by the Global Canopy Programme, seeks to provide a complementary funding stream for large areas of standing forests that are not immediately threatened or might not benefit from a REDD mechanism (depending on its design and implementation). It recognizes the immense value of tropical forests in monetary and non-monetary terms and calls for a mechanism to reward their function as global providers of multiple ecosystem services beyond carbon storage (e.g. biodiversity protection, rainfall generation, water supply regulation and atmospheric cooling, which are likely to become increasingly important as a result of climate change).

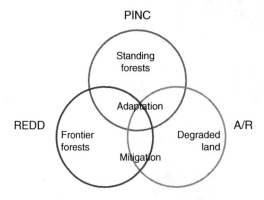

Figure 5.9 *Three mechanisms for maintaining or restoring the tropical forest eco-utility*

Source: Trivedi et al (2009)

Projected biodiversity loss is particularly high in developing countries, many of which face the greatest challenges related to economic and social development (combating poverty, providing education and jobs) (see Figure 5.8). There are often also significant opportunity costs associated with biodiversity protection (e.g. as exemplified by Ecuador's Yasuni National Park, one of the most biodiverse places on earth, which also sits on significant oil reserves). In the short term, at least, sustainable management and conservation of the world's most biodiverse areas will not take place without much more investment in those countries. Developed economies, which benefit directly and indirectly from this biodiversity and associated services, have a role in paying for its conservation and sustainable use.

Box 5.14 Stimulating international biodiversity demand through a Green Development Initiative (GDI)

The Dutch Ministry of Infrastructure and the Evironment, Earthmind, IUCN, OECD and UNEP, in cooperation with the CBD Secretariat, are facilitating expert discussions and consultations on a proposed innovative market-based financial mechanism for biodiversity, known as the Green Development Initiative, which aims to support the CBD.

The GDI aims to create enabling conditions to mobilize private sector finance for CBD implementation and to mitigate biodiversity loss. Whereas biodiversity finance has traditionally come from official development assistance and philanthropic grants, a GDI would link biodiversity supply and demand through a functional market mechanism, underpinned by standards and an accreditation/certification process.

Current thinking about the GDI is that it will facilitate the supply of biodiversity-protected hectares ('certified protected areas') in the form of GDI-accredited areas available for voluntary purchase by businesses, consumers and others. The sale would not involve the land itself but rather the biodiversity management of that land, including its conservation and the sustainable use of its biological resources.

Unlike the carbon market, biodiversity would not be traded as a commodity (e.g. tonnes of reduced emissions) but as units of land, in other words a set amount of hectares protected by a certified biodiversity management plan. In addition, the GDI would generally not support international offsets because biodiversity offsets are normally 'like-for-like' requiring localized offsets. Instead, it would support international payments for the biodiversity management of specific areas.

Sources: Swanson (2009); Swanson et al (2009); CBD (2010); Earthmind (2010)

Biodiversity's role in the global economy is clearly revealed by the interdependency of countries through regional and international trade. Many countries import a high proportion of their primary consumption products, which ultimately derive from ecosystems. Ecosystem services important for international production should be managed on a long-term basis and protected by appropriate laws (see Sections 5 and 6).

Opportunities for global investment in biodiversity

Global contenders for international PES, in addition to carbon sequestration and capture (such as REDD), include nitrogen deposition, water and rainfall regulation and global cultural services provided by species and natural areas.

Different approaches have been proposed for international biodiversity transfers and to mobilize international investment in natural capital. The common starting point is that without the means to make a global ecosystem service 'excludable', we have to find alternative ways to create demand for investment in such services. One approach is to use global targets for contributions to biodiversity conservation to determine burden-sharing (see Box 5.13). Another is market mechanisms that can help countries to deliver certain ecosystem services more cost-efficiently (see Box 5.14).

Whatever approach is taken, international agreements supported by national legislation are likely to be needed to ensure sustainable long-term financing for global biodiversity. Governments can support this international momentum and already seek ways to engage the private sector and create appropriate incentives for business to reduce adverse impacts and invest in biodiversity and ecosystem services.

3 Redirecting tax and compensation mechanisms for environmental goals

Economic instruments have a central – indeed indispensable – role to play in valuing nature's public services to society (Bräuer et al, 2006; EC, 2007). These services can be targeted by a range of public policy instruments, including taxes (Section 3.1), intergovernmental fiscal transfers (Section 3.2) and government spending (Section 3.3) (Ring, 2002).

As part of the agenda for ecological fiscal reform (Meyer and Schweppe-Kraft, 2006; Ring, 2008a), fiscal instruments could be used more widely to provide incentives for conservation and to raise funds for conservation (OECD, 1999; Emerton et al, 2006). Such tools are also central to social policy, including the redistribution of wealth and income. This makes them especially suitable for combining biodiversity and ecosystem conservation with poverty reduction (OECD, 2005; World Bank, 2005).

3.1 Using public levies to stimulate conservation

Economic instruments such as taxes, charges and fees – and targeted exemptions – are a crucial element of the policy maker's toolkit and complement PES (see Sections 1 and 2 above), certification (see Section 5), regulation (see Chapter 7) and non-binding agreements (Menzies, 2002). They can provide strong incentives for more sustainable behaviour by citizens, businesses and even governments – if well-designed and based on relevant indicators.

Land, property and income taxes have considerable potential to reward conservation and sustainable management but are rarely used for this purpose. This can be done through targeted reduction of the tax burden through credits or exemptions. Tax exemptions can function like PES to reward positive conservation efforts: the difference is that the PES is a direct payment for a service whereas the exemption is effectively a non-payment (of moneys that would otherwise be due as tax). Even if the financial outcome is similar, the instrument design is different and so, often, is public perception. Some see tax breaks as a form of 'thanks for efforts' that are preferable to payments for services rendered, although in economic terms they may be equivalent.

Tax exemptions or credits can be made available for landowners who undertake conservation or forgo future development in order to safeguard habitats (Boyd et al, 2000). Exemptions take many forms and are found in a range of jurisdictions (Shine, 2005). Familiar examples include conservation easements and tax incentives to donate land for conservation (see Box 5.15).

Tax incentives are not limited to gifts of property or interests. In The Netherlands, for example, capital gains tax exemptions can apply to specified green investment (see Box 5.16).

There are also cases where banks offer lower-interest loans to provide incentives to help borrowers to meet conservation objectives (see Box 5.17).

Box 5.15 Tax incentives for conservation easements and ecological gifts in North America

An easement is a legally binding restriction placed on a piece of property to protect its resources (natural or man-made) by prohibiting specified types of development from taking place on the land. It may be voluntarily sold or donated by the landowner.

The United States

The US has long experience of using easements to secure long-term conservation of natural areas, the rationale being that public goods arise from private lands. They are currently used by over 1260 local and regional 'land trusts' or conservancies, which act as the easements' trustees. By 2000, land trusts had already protected over 1 million ha (nearly 2.6 million acres) through conservation easements – almost 500 per cent increase on 1990 – and this figure continues to grow. By 2005, land trusts held easements on over 2.5 million ha (6.2 million acres): government agencies and non-profit organizations also had sizeable easement holdings (Land Trust Alliance, 2006).

The Nature Conservancy is the largest non-profit holder of conservation easements with 1.3 million ha (3.2 million acres). The Natural Resources Conservation Service (NRCS), funded by the US Department of Agriculture, is responsible for monitoring, managing and conducting enforcement activities on about 11,000 easements covering over 800,000ha (2 million acres) (Rissman et al, 2007).

Easements can be purchased or donated. Donations are motivated by the ability to reduce taxes and claim charitable deductions. Progressive changes in tax codes and development of practical appraisal techniques have encouraged their use while easement contracts are fairly straightforward to prepare. Part of the explanation for the popularity of easements in the US is that environmental land-use regulations are relatively weak, governed by municipalities rather than state and federal governments, yet private landowners have a suite of incentives to donate or sell the public interests in their land. There may be less need for easements in countries with tighter land-use restrictions and highly developed rights of public access, e.g. in European countries such as Germany or the UK.

Key questions when designing easement contracts include their duration (perennity), monitoring and enforcement in order to avoid challenges to use/development restrictions arising as properties change hands over generations.

Sources: TNC (2003); Boyd et al (2000)

Canada

The Ecogift Programme, introduced in 2001, provides tax benefits to owners of ecologically sensitive land if they donate it – fully or partially – to specified recipients who take responsibility for its sustainable management and conserving natural habitat. Over 800 ecological gifts valued at over CAD$500 million (approximately US$485 million) have been donated, protecting over 134,000ha of wildlife habitat. The list of possible recipients is strictly defined by legislation and includes the federal government, provincial or territorial governments, municipalities, municipal or public bodies performing government functions and charities approved by Environment Canada. The donor of the land or interest therein receives tax benefits in return:

- the total value of the ecogift from an individual donor may be used to calculate a non-refundable tax credit;
- the value of the gift can be directly deducted from taxable income of a corporate donor;
- capital gains are exempt from taxes.

Source: Environment Canada (2010)

Box 5.16 'Green Funds Scheme' in The Netherlands (Regeling groenprojecten)

The scheme was set up to encourage projects that have positive environmental effects. The government offers a tax advantage to 'green' savers and investors, and banks can offer loans at lower interest rates for projects, e.g. sustainably built houses, wind farms, developing forests or organic agricultural businesses. In the Dutch tax system, savers and investors normally pay 1.2 per cent capital gains tax over the amount saved or invested. However, green capital is exempt from such tax up to a maximum of €52,579 per person (2006).

Source: SenterNovem (2010)

Box 5.17 Using low interest rates to provide incentives for urban greening in Japan

Faced with an urgent need to stop the depletion of privately owned green space, which covers approximately two-thirds of Nagoya City in Japan, the city authority implemented the Local Greening Programme in October 2008. This requires a minimum green area in all new construction or extension on sites at or above a certain size. For example, on a 300m^2 site with building-to-land ratio restricted to 50 per cent, the equivalent of 20 per cent of site area must be covered with green. Nagoya Bank, a local private bank, launched a new housing loan scheme to lower the interest rate for customers who submit a NICE GREEN certification label, issued by the city to prove the level of greening.

Source: Sado City, Japan, www.city.sado.niigata.jp/

3.2 Greening intergovernmental fiscal transfers

Public spending includes fiscal transfers between different levels of government – which are often neglected in conservation strategies. Huge amounts of tax revenues are redistributed from national to sub-national and local governments to provide the latter with monies to build and maintain schools, hospitals and roads, and so on. These public finance mechanisms are critically important for local and regional decision makers (see TEEB in Local Policy, 2011) but are rarely considered in terms of their ecological impact (Ring, 2002).

Integrating biodiversity conservation and maintenance of ecosystem services into systems for distributing tax revenues to lower levels of government can encourage decision makers to take better care of nature while also nurturing their tax base. Currently, however, local tax incentives mainly focus on attracting more businesses, residents and construction activities. This can give rise to land uses that destroy or damage natural habitats.

Restructuring intergovernmental transfers can create win–win situations. By way of example, many federal authorities use the area of a municipality or province as one criterion for determining fiscal transfers – it is only a small step to include 'protected area' (PA) as an additional criterion for allocating tax revenues. This could help raise funds to deliver local management and conservation objectives for protected areas (see Chapter 8) and reduce their image as a fiscal burden or obstacle to development (Ring et al, 2010).

Positive effects will be even stronger if people living in and around these sites receive some of the benefits involved in ecological fiscal transfers: this could help to reduce local opposition to PAs in some cases. In addition, the prospects of stable revenues following the designation of a PA may also encourage the establishment of new PAs. If the financial means which are needed for their effective management are secured, this reduces the need to make funding available from the local authorities' own resources.

Decisions to establish PAs are often taken by higher levels of government with local decision makers having little influence on site selection. Including PAs as a criterion for intergovernmental fiscal transfers could help to reconcile local PA costs with their broader benefits, often reaching far beyond municipal boundaries.

A few countries have taken steps to introduce ecological fiscal transfers to compensate municipalities for land-use restrictions imposed by PAs. Since 1992, several states in Brazil have introduced PAs as an indicator for the redistribution of value-added tax from state level to municipalities (Grieg-Gran, 2000). In January 2007, Portugal amended its Municipal Finance Law to introduce ecological fiscal transfers to reward municipalities for designated EU Natura 2000 sites and other PAs within their territories (De Melo and Prates, 2007).

Using such criteria to redistribute tax revenues between different levels of government can help realign the incentives of public actors, as the Brazilian experience shows (see Box 5.18). However, care should be taken to ensure that such transfers are clearly linked to wider benefits and that higher levels of government do not end up paying for provision of local goods and services (e.g. sewage disposal) normally provided direct by municipalities.

As with PES schemes, spatially explicit modelling and GIS tools can help illustrate the potential consequences of ecological fiscal transfers at the planning stage. Fiscal transfer schemes are country-specific and politically sensitive, due to the substantial financial flows involved. Building on existing transfer schemes and integrating suitable ecological criteria (e.g. PA coverage in hectares as a percentage of territory covered) can help decision makers promote innovative solutions to raise funds for conservation.

For Switzerland, Köllner et al (2002) have developed a model for intergovernmental transfers to the local level, based on biodiversity indicators and cantonal benchmarking.

Box 5.18 Ecological fiscal transfers in Brazil

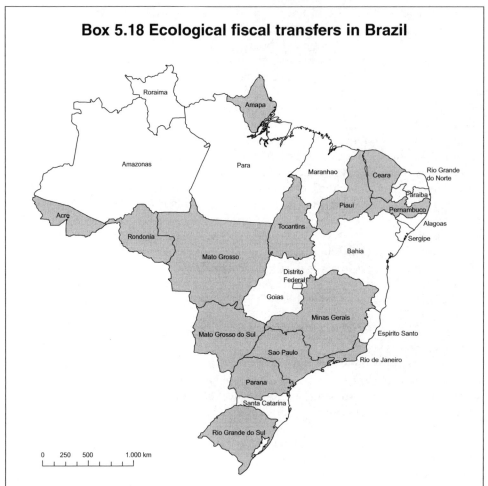

Figure 5.10 *Ecological fiscal transfers in Brazil*

Note: Shading indicates states that have adopted the tax.

Source: UFZ

The 'ICMS Ecológico' (equivalent of Ecological Value-Added Tax on goods and services) has been adopted by 14 out of 26 Brazilian states (see map) and others are preparing relevant legislation. This mechanism provides for redistributing part of ICMS revenues collected by the states to municipalities, using ecological indicators as criteria. While different states have implemented different indicators, all (except one) provide compensations for the land-use restrictions imposed following the establishment of protected areas. This has made the creation of new areas for biodiversity conservation more attractive.

Paraná was the first state to introduce the ecological ICMS, in 1992. Of the amount distributed at local level, 2.5 per cent is allocated according to the quantity and quality of PAs; another 2.5 per cent considers water protection areas within a municipality's territory. By 2000, PAs had increased by 165 per cent and municipalities with larger shares of protected areas had considerably benefited from increased revenues.

Source: May et al (2002); Ring (2008b); TNC (2010)

For Germany, Ring (2008a) suggested ways of incorporating PAs into the intergovernmental fiscal transfer system in Saxony (see Box 5.19). In Indonesia, intergovernmental fiscal transfers have been suggested as necessary tools to implement REDD+ at national level and link biodiversity conservation and climate mitigation policies (Irawan and Tacconi, 2009; Ring et al, 2010).

3.3 Public compensation schemes for wildlife damage

Compensation payments are designed to indemnify land users, mostly farmers and fishermen, for the damage caused by wildlife species that are subject to conservation measures, e.g. damage to livestock by wolves (Fourli, 1999) or to fishing gear by seals (Similä et al, 2006). These kinds of payments can be controversial but many have

Box 5.19 Modelling intergovernmental fiscal transfers for conservation in Germany

This model of Saxony's fiscal transfer system from state to local level is based on administrative, social and economic data from 2002. It has been enlarged by the conservation units (CU) indicator to take account of local ecological services whose benefits cross municipal borders. CUs are standardized areas within the borders of a municipality that belong to existing categories of PAs defined by Saxony's Nature Conservation Law (Figure 5.11). The map in Figure 5.12 shows relative changes in general lump sum transfers if CUs are used in addition to existing indicators (inhabitants and schoolchildren) to calculate the fiscal need of a Saxon municipality.

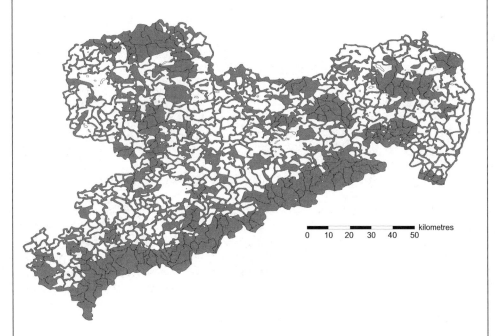

Figure 5.11 *Protected areas overlaid over municipal borders in Saxony, Germany*

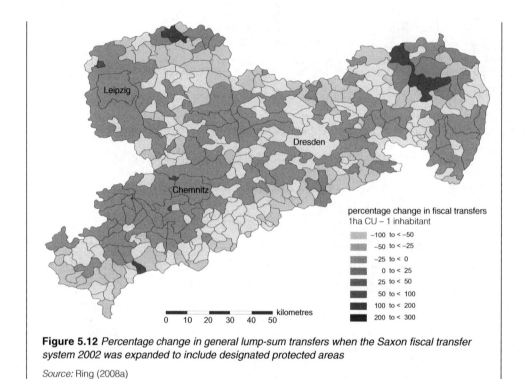

Figure 5.12 *Percentage change in general lump-sum transfers when the Saxon fiscal transfer system 2002 was expanded to include designated protected areas*

Source: Ring (2008a)

proven to be effective and are accepted by local stakeholders. Compensation schemes operate in developed and developing countries (see Box 5.20 and also Chapter 8 for an example of rewards for elephants in India).

Although compensation payments for wildlife damage are sometimes essential to prevent hunting or culling of protected and highly endangered species, they are often associated with – or may even create – a negative perception of wildlife. In many countries, perspective is shifting away from damage compensation schemes (i.e. seeing wildlife as a cost) towards developing public payments to reward the presence of wild

---

Box 5.20 Goose Management Scheme, Scotland

This scheme aims to promote conservation and a sustainable goose population by compensating farmers for crop damage by wintering wild geese. It requires a specific area on each farm to be set aside for geese, which may then be scared away from the remaining farm areas. At the start of this initiative, payments were made on the basis of geese headage which involved high transaction costs. Payments are now made on an area basis. The general (maximum) payment was around £195 or about €237 (maximum £300 or about €365) per ha of rotational grass or arable land. The payments are made by the UK government according to the five-year agreement in place.

Sources: Bräuer et al (2006); The Scottish Government (2007)

animals on private land or support measures to provide feeding habitats for protected species (i.e. seeing wildlife as positive and making related payments) (Similä et al, 2006; Suvantola, in preparation; see Box 5.21).

Box 5.21 Rewarding conservation of golden eagles by the Sami in Finland

The scheme provides compensation for losses caused by golden eagles to reindeer husbandry in Northern Finland. As recently amended, it aims to promote the conservation status of the species rather than focusing primarily on damage. Payments are now based on species nesting and reproduction and actively involve the Sami people in monitoring nesting sites. Participants have access to information on nesting sites and provide information to conservation authorities on newly discovered sites. The scheme discourages disturbance of the eagles during nesting and encourages creation of nesting sites rather than their destruction. There is ongoing follow-up to build trust between the authorities and those who are subject to the negative impacts of the species' recovery.

Source: Suvantola (in preparation)

---

4 Sharing benefits derived from genetic resources

> My father said, 'You must never try to make all the money that's in a deal. Let the other fellow make some money too, because if you have a reputation for always making all the money, you won't have many deals.' (John Paul Getty)

This section describes progress towards rewarding the value of genetic resources more fairly and efficiently through contractual mechanisms and the new Protocol on Access and Benefit Sharing adopted under the Convention on Biological Diversity. It looks at economic factors that influence the value of genetic resources (Section 4.1) and how to overcome constraints on maximizing such value (Section 4.2). We also argue (Section 4.3) that the fair and equitable sharing of benefits is desirable not only on equity grounds, but also because it is, at the end of the day, critical to ensure the more efficient management and utilization of genetic resources. These are key issues not only for the users of genetic resources (for instance, pharmaceutical or biotechnological industries), but also to those who own genetic resources or are involved in land-use decisions affecting them, who are often relatively poor farming or indigenous communities. The fair and equitable sharing of the benefits from genetic resources could improve their livelihoods and stimulate the sustainable use of the ecosystems hosting the genetic resources. Sharing benefits more fairly and more equitably has a strong North–South component – many genetic resources are located in developing countries of the South, while the bulk of the commercial utilization of genetic resources is undertaken by industries located in industrialized countries of the North.

The fair and equitable sharing of benefits arising from the utilization of genetic resources is one of the three objectives of the Convention on Biological Diversity (CBD). Following the call for action by heads of state at the World Summit for Sustainable Development (Johannesburg, 2002), negotiations under the CBD recently led to the adoption of the Nagoya Protocol on Access to Genetic Resources and the Fair and Equitable Sharing of the Benefits arising out of their Utilization. In order to support the further implementation of its relevant CBD provisions, the Protocol sets out obligations to ensure the fair and equitable sharing of benefits arising from the use of genetic resources with provider countries in exchange for clear procedures with respect to access to genetic resources (see Sections 4.3 and 4.4).

4.1 The value of genetic resources

Genetic resources provide source material for a range of commercial products from mainstream pharmaceutical to botanical medicines, new seed varieties, ornamental horticultural products, new enzymes and micro-organisms for biotechnology, crop protection products and personal care and cosmetic products. In 2006, the global market for pharmaceuticals grew 7 per cent to US$643 billion (IMS Health, 2007). Natural products continue to play a dominant role in the discovery of new leads for drug development and contribute significantly to the bottom line of large companies, e.g. between 1981 and 2006, 47 per cent of cancer drugs and 34 per cent of all small-molecule new chemical entities (NCE) for all disease categories were natural products or directly derived from them (Newman and Cragg, 2007).

Table 5.2 presents data on the estimated size of the market for key product categories and the percentage derived from genetic inputs in order to provide an indication of the economic value of activities dependent on genetic resources.

A key question from a business perspective is how much of the value of final products is attributable to genetic material and how much to other factors of

Table 5.2 Market sectors dependent on genetic resources

Sector	Size of market	Comment
Pharmaceutical	US$643 billion in 2006	A significant share derived from genetic resources (e.g. 47% of cancer drugs over period 1981 to 2006)
Biotechnology	US$70 billion in 2006 from public companies alone	Many products derived from genetic resources (enzymes, micro-organisms)
Crop protection products	US$30 billion in 2006	Some derived from genetic resources
Agricultural seeds	US$30 billion in 2006	All derived from genetic resources
Ornamental horticulture	Global import value US$14 billion in 2006	All derived from genetic resources
Personal care, botanical, and food and beverage industries	US$22 billion for herbal supplements; US$12 billion for personal care; US$31 billion for food products. All in 2006	Some products derived from genetic resources: represents 'natural' component of the market

Source: IMS Health (2007); Newman and Cragg (2007); CBD (2008)

production (labour, capital, local knowledge, etc.)? To answer this, we need to distinguish between:

- what a producer of drugs or other products has to pay to obtain the genetic material; and
- what the material is worth to the producer (i.e. the maximum that a company would pay – the so-called 'willingness to pay').

The difference between this maximum payment and the cost of obtaining the genetic material is called its 'rent'. Questions asked in the literature sometimes relate to the cost of exploitation and sometimes to the rent, but the two should not be confused. The costs of obtaining genetic material are paid to relevant parties in proportion to their effort whereas the rent can go to either party (i.e. the company that uses the material or the party that provides it). It is precisely this sharing that needs to be carried out in a way that is fair and equitable (see Section 4.3).

The economic rent is calculated by taking the value of the final product and subtracting the costs of development, production, collection and classification of the genetic material. These calculations are complex as research and development (R&D) is an uncertain activity: some return is essential to compensate for the riskiness of the venture. As most numbers involved are large and the rent is the difference between them, the calculations are obviously affected by even small errors in the numbers.

Several estimates of economic rent have been made to date. To the dismay of those who believe that genetic resources are a global resource of high value, these estimates came out rather low. A key early study (Simpson et al, 1996) calculated values of genetic resources in 1996 prices at between US$0.20 per hectare (California), and US$20.60 per hectare (western Ecuador) and argued that these estimates could be on the high side. Other studies making the same point include Barbier and Aylward (1996) and Frinn (2003). Reasons identified for values being so low included the high cost of developing the final goods and bringing them to market, the long time lags involved and inefficiencies in the systems for exploiting genetic resources.

Subsequent studies tried to improve on these estimates. Craft and Simpson (2001) argued that if we base calculations not on the price of final drugs but on the willingness to pay of those who benefit from lifesaving drugs, the rent could be two orders of magnitude higher than the above estimates. However, this raises the question of how (and whether) to capture higher use values. Massive increases in the price of drugs would exclude many poorer users and could hardly be described as a fair division of the benefits of genetic resources.

There are now far more uses of genetic resources than covered in Simpson et al (1996), which should increase their net value. Finding more effective and cost-efficient ways to collect information about and screen genetic materials can also increase the rent. Rausser and Small (2000) estimated the possible increase as equal to one order of magnitude higher than the estimates in Simpson et al (1996). Although Rausser and Small's estimate has in turn been criticized (Costello and Ward, 2006), there is no doubt that lowering transaction costs should increase the economic rent (see Section 4.2).

For developing countries, one constraint on increasing the value of genetic material is the growing importance of micro-organisms for which the tropics are not an especially important source. However, this is not always the case as companies collecting from nature continue to be interested in samples from diverse and extreme environments (CBD, 2008). Strong partnerships with providers are needed and the monitoring of developments of natural product compounds should contribute to ensuring the sharing of benefits with the providers of the genetic resources used as a basis for the development of these compounds.

Current arrangements for sharing whatever rent exists are not particularly favourable to providers of genetic resources, in particular communities living in the area where genetic resources are located. Several agreements made in the 1990s to share the benefits of products derived from such resources attracted considerable attention. Reviews of eight of the most important[14] showed that:

- most contained an element of royalty sharing;
- their duration varied from two to eleven years;
- some required the bioprospector to contribute financially to biodiversity protection in the region;
- some contained an element of technology transfer to develop local preparation and screening capabilities;
- the financial resources involved in these transactions were relatively small (see Box 5.22).

Although a comprehensive assessment of the transfers actually made is not available, it appears unlikely that they amounted to more than a few million dollars over the duration of each contract. Even if we accept the lowest estimates of the value of these resources, the total amount of economic rents paid should be higher than paid to date.

Although more socially responsible companies no longer consider genetic resources as available for free, it is very likely that a significant amount of bioprospecting still takes place without the prior informed consent of the provider and without mutually agreed terms having been established between the provider of genetic resources and the individual or institution seeking access to these resources with a view to ensuring the fair and equitable sharing of benefits arising from the use of the resources accessed, as required under the CBD. In such cases a fair share of the rent is not passed back to the owners or managers of genetic resources. It would be useful to make an estimate of the total payments actually made for access to such resources and how this figure has evolved over time. To our knowledge, no such estimate yet exists.

4.2 Adding value through more efficient bioprospecting

Considerable efforts have gone into making agreements for the exploitation of genetic resources more efficient. Contractual and institutional frameworks – partnerships between large companies and more specialized companies and universities, the creation of an intermediate market for taxonomy services and changes in the mechanisms for transferring traditional knowledge – are evolving and lessons learned from the first generation of contracts can improve the design of future agreements. This section considers ways to lift or reduce institutional and market constraints that limit the value of genetic resources, including steps to minimize transaction costs while retaining flexibility.

Box 5.22 Examples of benefit sharing and payments under bioprospecting contracts

Kenya

In May 2007 the Kenya Wildlife Service (KWS) and Novozymes, a Danish biotech company, entered a five-year partnership for the collection, identification and characterization of micro-organisms from Kenya's national parks. The agreement was not driven from a particular interest on the part of Novozymes to undertake bioprospecting in the region, but rather to negotiate a benefit-sharing agreement for the commercialization of much earlier collections that were made outside any agreement. One of these led to the development of a commercial product (pulpzyme) that reduces the amount of chlorine needed to bleach wood pulp. KWS will undertake all collections within the national parks and reserves. Since the agreement is on micro-organisms it does not lend itself to the use of traditional knowledge, which is not covered under the agreement. A microbial laboratory has been set up by Novozymes and is staffed by KWS researchers. Under the agreement KWS will receive running royalties on any commercial product developed, as well as an upfront payment to cover the costs of sample collections and laboratory work. Other benefits to KWS include training for its staff. Any intellectual property that comes out of the partnership will be co-owned by both parties.

Ethiopia

In 2004 a ten-year ABS agreement was concluded for the breeding and development of tef (*Eragrostis tef*) between the Institute for Biodiversity Conservation (IBC) in Ethiopia, the Ethiopian Agrocultural Research Organization and a small Netherlands-based company, Health and Performance Food International (HPFI). Tef is one of the most significant cereal crop species in the region. Because it is gluten free it is increasingly in demand in western markets and has various other attributes of interest to the food industry. The scope of the agreement is limited to the use of tef for food and beverage products, with HPFI having exclusive access to the materials. Benefit sharing takes the form of an agreement by HPFI to pay IBC a lump sum of profits arising from the use of tef genetic resources; royalties of 30 per cent of net profit from the sale of tef varieties; a licence fee linked to the amount of tef grown by anybody supplied seed by HPFI; and contributions by HPFI of 5 per cent net profit, no less than €20,000 per year, to a fund named the Financial Resource Support for Tef (FiRST), established to improve the living conditions of local farming communities and for developing tef business in Ethiopia. Unusually this agreement deals not only with provision of access to genetic material, but also to the trade of tef as a commodity.

India

Scientists at the Tropical Botanical Garden and Research Institute (TBGRI), a publicly funded research institute based in Trivandrum, worked with the Kani tribals of Kerala to obtain traditional knowledge about medicinal use of the plant Arogyapaacha (*Trichopus zeylanicus*). TBGRI successfully developed a drug from the plant and sold the technology to a Coimbatore-based pharmaceutical company, which agreed to pay

Rs.1 million and a 2 per cent share in the royalty. These proceeds are being shared equally by TBGRI and the tribal community.

Brazil

In 1999, Glaxo Wellcome and Brazilian Extracta jointly signed a contract where Glaxo paid US$3.2 million for the right to screen 30,000 compounds of plant, fungus and bacterial origin from several regions in Brazilian forests. This, however, relates to a payment for the permission to access, and is not strictly speaking about sharing benefits arising from the use of these compounds which may include the results of the research carried out, sharing of the technologies used for the screening or eventually the sharing of the benefits arising out of the development of products based on these resources.

Costa Rica

The best-known and most emblematic contract was signed between INBio (National Biodiversity Institute) and Merck Pharmaceutical Ltd in 1991. INBio received US$1 million over two years and equipment for processing samples and scientific training from Merck.

Source: Neto and Dickson (1999); Laird and Wynberg (2008)

Better screening of genetic materials

Asymmetric and incomplete information about genetic material of interest is still an obstacle to contract development. On the technical side, positive developments include more efficient scientific and technological tools for screening and use of specialist intermediaries to carry out these activities, leading to better upfront information and lower costs for product developers. The bioprospecting industry is steadily moving in this direction: most large companies are forming partnerships with smaller companies and universities that generate leads from research into natural products (CBD, 2008). This trend should increase the rent from genetic resources, part of which should revert to the provider countries, including communities from which those resources originated.

Technological progress should be accompanied by increased resources for collection and classification of materials. In developing countries, this is still mainly carried out by relatively inefficient public sector institutions short of funds. However, such work does not only have to be carried out by public bodies. It could be made a fee-based service involving the private sector: creation of an intermediary market for such services would improve bioprospecting efficiency and increase the net value of resources.

Better use of traditional knowledge

Reliance on traditional knowledge of properties of local plants and other species is currently small and seems to be on the decline. This may be partly due to the emphasis in drug development on disease categories that do not feature prominently in traditional medicine and partly to the increasing role of micro-organisms and the diminished role of plants in genetic discoveries (CBD, 2008, p106). Nevertheless, many researchers believe that such knowledge can help in new product development but that the process is hampered by the lack of appropriate mechanisms to document and transfer it and – important from a benefit-sharing perspective – to appropriately reward information providers.[15]

This issue could be addressed by requiring product developers to share, under mutually agreed terms, the benefits in proportion to the information provided and used. In order to address these situations, the Nagoya Protocol sets out obligations to support compliance with prior informed consent and mutually agreed terms. These include measures to encourage, monitor and enforce compliance with prior informed consent and mutually agreed terms across jurisdictions, for ensuring that these obligations are met once the genetic resources have left the country where they were collected (see Section 4.4).

Improving contract design

Typically, sellers (usually public institutions) supply screened samples, novel compounds and research leads derived from their field collections. They are responsible for obtaining permission to access genetic resources and/or traditional knowledge ('prior informed consent'), and for negotiating with source suppliers[16] the terms of access and benefits to be shared before conducting field collection ('mutually agreed terms'). Sellers also collaborate with companies on development and commercialization of these resources, which may entail separate contracts or other agreements with private companies.

Conditions of access and use, and transfer to third parties, are to be agreed with the initial provider in the country of origin/provider country. The seller needs to ensure that these terms are transferred to third-party users (in this case the private companies) and that prior informed consent from the provider country is sought if there is a change in use of the genetic resources accessed, in accordance with the mutually agreed terms. In other words, the provider country has an important role to play in setting the conditions of access and use, also with third parties.

Buyers[17] are usually engaged in industries carrying out R&D into commercial applications of genetic resources. Although these encompass several sectors, the pharmaceutical industry undoubtedly represents the largest market, invests a higher proportion of turnover in R&D than other industries and incurs higher risks in the drug discovery and development process. Pharmaceutical companies thus play a crucial steering role in driving efficiency gains in bioprospecting contracts.

The most important provisions of genetic resource contracts relate to:

- sharing of royalty revenues where the company patents a new discovery (e.g. a medicinal drug) derived from R&D using the genetic material sold in the contract;
- transfer of R&D technology and screening capabilities to local institutions and/or local capacity building and training;
- the structure of the financial agreement: in addition to royalties and technology transfer, this includes upfront payments and milestone payments;

- possible financial contribution by the buyer to protect local biodiversity e.g. through partial transfer of the royalty revenues; and
- ancillary provisions e.g. possible common use of the resource and/or whether exploitation rights are exclusive or not.

Extending the length of contracts

Bioprospecting activities, especially in the pharmaceutical industry, are characterized by:

- high asset specificity, in particular site-specificity (particular genetic materials are sited in particular locations) and dedicated assets (companies invest in bioprospecting to exploit the possibility of patenting new discoveries) (Williamson, 1979);[18]
- high uncertainty: firms investing in R&D are unsure about the probability of new discoveries (Williamson, 1979); and
- high complexity: the activity generates several (positive and negative) impacts on biodiversity exploitation, research, innovation, corporate competitiveness and wealth redistribution.

Long-term contracts represent a way to minimize transaction costs[19] linked to these factors or to bureaucratic and administrative constraints (e.g. public tender procedures, permit systems for access to biological resources). Minimizing such costs is important to provide incentives for companies to invest in R&D and to share benefits in accordance with CBD provisions. Specific areas where there may be scope for improvement include:

- building a high level of trust between the parties, given the complexity of the issue and the impossibility of monitoring all aspects related to agreements; and
- instituting facilities to track the use of genetic resources and related benefits and resolve disputes across jurisdictional boundaries to make benefit-sharing agreements enforceable, including the sharing of results arising from research and development and financial benefits, such as the sharing of royalties: this needs intergovernmental cooperation. The Nagoya Protocol, once in force, can play an important role in both regards.

4.3 Equitable sharing of benefits derived from genetic resources

Economic research shows that the fair and equitable sharing of benefits is desirable not only on equity grounds, but also because it ensures more efficient management and utilization of genetic resources. The precise terms of access and benefit sharing need to be considered on a case-by-case basis, adapted to the community context (see Box 5.23) and taking account of the broader economic context.

Traditional economics states that market institutions determine the efficient allocation of resources and the issue of equity can be left to policy makers. If applied to the context of genetic resources, this would mean that it did not matter who received what proportion of the rent from their exploitation: the market structure would ensure that materials were exploited and conserved optimally.

Box 5.23 Learning from practitioners: Benefit-sharing perspectives from enterprising communities

In 2008 representatives of 14 communities from various ecosystems were interviewed for a CBD-backed study to identify how principles of governance, ethics, equity and resource sharing were applied in community activities for development and use of biological resources and profit sharing in order to secure local and household livelihoods.

The implications of community actions on community well-being were analysed using Sen and Nussbaum's 'Capabilities Framework' and Maslow's 'Hierarchy of Human Needs'. The results showed that community well-being improved in terms of various indicators such as basic needs (i.e. food security, shelter and health), safety needs (i.e. security from natural and economic risks), belonging needs (i.e. equity in governance, access to resources and benefit) and self-esteem (i.e. of degree of autonomy to determine use of resources, economic activities, education, etc.).

The authors of the study consider it a pilot exercise in using an analytical framework to explore the links between actual community practices on distributing benefits and well-being, one of the implied mandates of the CBD.

Source: UNEP (2009b)

However, recent literature shows that the traditional divide between equity and efficiency does not hold in this field where bilateral contracting is prevalent (van Soest and Lesink, 2000; Gatti et al, 2004).[20] Genetic resource contracts negotiated between corporations and institutions in provider countries are very different from atomistic market transactions. A better way to analyse their outcomes is to learn from empirical results of game theory experiments. Results from so-called ultimatum game experiments (where one party offers a contract on a take-it-or-leave-it basis) strongly suggest that the final outcome depends on the perception of fairness by the respective parties. People appear to prefer no deal to a deal they think is unfair (based on results from ultimatum games where one party offers a contract on a take-it-or-leave-it basis). They may even opt for 'strategic destruction' when offered a bad deal (for an application to trade-related aspects of intellectual property rights and biodiversity, see Gatti et al, 2004). It is, however, not efficient to make no deal even though 'gains from trade' could be realized.

Bioprospecting and biomimicry benefits should thus be shared in such a way that provider countries and the local stewards of biodiversity – the rural and indigenous communities – receive a fair and equitable proportion of the value derived from the exploitation of the resources. This will not only contribute to improved living standards for the poor but also increase incentives to conserve remaining biodiversity.

How can this be done? Suggestions include:

- Forming a cartel to negotiate on behalf of all owners of such resources, i.e. like the Organization of the Petroleum Exporting Countries (OPEC) on behalf of global oil producers.[21] Like all cartels, this might in principle succeed in obtaining a higher share of the rent from exploitation of genetic materials, but it would also be unstable with strong incentives of individual members to undercut the agreed price (e.g. the price of crude oil has fluctuated since 1974, when the cartel started restricting supply).

• Giving providers of genetic resources and associated traditional knowledge the opportunity to obtain access to justice and appropriate remedies when access and benefit-sharing requirements are not respected or when there is a breach to mutually agreed terms. Well-designed access and including provisions for dispute resolution are encouraged.

• Increasing the share of development undertaken in provider countries, e.g. by locating the emerging partnerships between large corporations and smaller companies and universities whenever feasible, in provider countries, and by working closely with local resource providers.

Finally, we need to recognize that greater transparency and knowledge about the value derived from genetic materials will make it easier for all parties to reach an equitable accord. At present the rent derived from such materials is still somewhat obscure, with some researchers claiming that overall rent is small. No one has estimated how much goes to each of the parties. More research on what the rent is – and how it is being shared at present – should help make the case for larger transfers to provider countries.

4.4 Towards an international regime on ABS

Many activities identified above require well-coordinated international action – such as ensuring compliance with ABS contracts once the genetic resources have left the provider country. The new Nagoya Protocol is therefore very welcome and its speedy ratification and implementation by governments is important. If ratified and implemented speedily, the Protocol could make a critical contribution in the areas described below.

In the short to medium term the Protocol could:

• facilitate capacity building and resource transfer where necessary to improve efficiency in genetic resource management, e.g. by establishing transparent national access and benefit-sharing regulatory frameworks providing legal certainty for those seeking to obtain access to genetic resources;

• exchange, through an international clearing house on ABS, information on, and experiences with, national policies governing genetic resources, in order to contribute to transparency for resources users and providers, and to facilitate the identification of good practices for countries to improve effectiveness and efficiency of their policies.

• strengthen compliance and monitoring frameworks to ensure fair and equitable benefit sharing through the implementation of prior informed consent (PIC) and mutually agreed terms (MAT);

• ensure that ABS agreements cover all fields of use of genetic resources (i.e. are not focused solely on pharmaceuticals (see Box 5.25).

In the medium to long term the Protocol could:

- improve knowledge generation/exchange and dissemination of pertinent information on e.g. the accurate value of genetic resources; the rent available to be shared between resource providers and developers; analysis of the link between equitable distribution of rents and their efficient management;
- strengthen the innovation system of biodiversity-rich developing countries for R&D on genetic resources and biological resources more generally, as a contribution to the sustainable development of these countries.

5 Developing markets for green goods and services

Market mechanisms that reflect the values of biodiversity are well established for some goods and services, and growing steadily.[22] This trend reflects increasing awareness that conventional production and consumption practices threaten the long-term viability of ecosystems. This section outlines progress on certification in key sectors (Section 5.1), discusses remaining barriers for certain 'green' products and services (Section 5.2) and considers ways to expand the reach of biodiversity-friendly markets (Section 5.3).

5.1 Support for biodiversity-friendly products and services

Market niches are available for products and services that can reliably distinguish themselves from their competitors by demonstrating conservation credentials, including:

- products with reduced direct impacts on biodiversity, due to more efficient or low-impact production and processing methods (e.g. reduced impact forestry or fisheries);
- products with reduced indirect impacts on biodiversity as a result of decreased pollution load (e.g. biodegradable detergents);
- services based on sustainable use of ecosystem services and biodiversity (e.g. ecotourism).

As TEEB in Business (2011) shows, evidence from across the world shows that conservation can enhance a company's competitive position where 'green' products and services:

- attract market share or premiums for certain products and their suppliers;
- facilitate access to previously inaccessible markets or create entirely new markets;
- offer enhanced product differentiation in increasingly competitive global markets;
- improve community relations and corporate image;
- boost employee morale, retention and productivity; and
- support the poor where they are directly involved in production (Bishop et al, 2008).

Who can contribute to greening supply chains?

For most sectors and companies, conservation is still seen as a liability rather than a potential source of revenue. Drivers for investment come from regulations, environmental management systems and procurement pressures from purchashers, charitable impulses and pressure from shareholders, communities and NGOs. The business case for investment is mainly expressed in terms of protecting market share or minimizing risk to reputation.

Innovative private initiatives have already helped markets work better for the environment. When large companies choose to direct their purchasing power in a particular direction, they can have a large impact on global trade and production practices. Such initiatives need vision and commitment from the top and patience, but the paybacks in public relations and corporate social responsibility are often deemed worth the risk.

Public support for green markets can also catalyse change. In 2009, the European Commission issued a communication signalling its strong support for fair trade (EC, 2009). Fair trade focuses on social rather than environmental criteria but EU support is a positive development for the certification industry in general. Support for 'BioTrade' – production and commercialization of goods and services derived from native biodiversity under strict sustainable development criteria – has been formally expressed by e.g. CBD, the UN Conference on Trade and Development (UNCTAD), CITES and a growing number of countries. Governments can endorse such approaches through green public procurement policies (see Section 6).

NGOs have played a key role in developing voluntary standards for products and services (see Boxes 5.25 and 5.26) and some (e.g. CI, WWF) are currently involved in forums addressing biofuel production. Along with private bodies, they contribute to independent verification mechanisms to assess selected commodities against emerging biodiversity-related standards.

Certification of sustainable forestry products

The International Tropical Timber Organization (ITTO) defines sustainable forest management as forest-related activities that do 'not damage the forest to the extent that its capacity to deliver products and services – such as timber, water and biodiversity conservation – is significantly reduced. Forest management should also aim to balance the needs of different forest users so that its benefits and costs are shared equitably'.[23]

Forest certification schemes have achieved significant market penetration (see Box 5.24). Between 2001 and 2005, global coverage of certified forests expanded by about 50 million hectares per year, mainly due to a rapid increase in North America. By 2009, 325.2 million hectares worldwide (8.3 per cent of total forest area) were certified under various schemes.

However, the rate of expansion of certified roundwood production (i.e. sections of timber in raw unmanufactured state) has decreased over the last three years (total increase between May 2008 to May 2009 was under four million hectares). This may reflect the fact that most larger forest areas in the developed world are already certified. Certifying forests in developing countries presents challenges linked to lack of capacity, resources and incentives to participate, as a significant proportion of forests are owned by non-industrial and communal sectors. The geographical bias of certified forests towards the northern hemisphere inevitably limits its effectiveness as an instrument to protect biodiversity (see Table 5.3 and Section 5.2).

Certification of sustainable fisheries

This book has highlighted the level of pressure on global fish stocks (see Chapter 1). Aquaculture expansion, seen as a means to reduce pressures on wild stocks, is

Box 5.24 Forest certification schemes

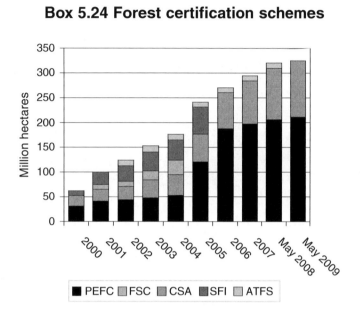

Figure 5.13 *Forest area certified by major certification schemes (2000–2009)*

Source: UNECE/FAO (2009)

PEFC (Programme for the Endorsement of Forest Certification schemes) is an international organization supporting assessment and recognition of currently 25 independent national schemes, including for small forests. These must comply with basic PEFC requirements but may adhere to stricter environmental criteria.

FSC (Forest Stewardship Council), established in 1993, has a mixed membership (environmental and social groups, timber trade, indigenous people's groups, forest product certification organizations). Certification is based on ten principles that encompass sustainable development, equity and environment. In 2009, the value of FSC-labelled sales was estimated at over US$20 billion, representing fourfold growth since 2005.

By 2008, 77 per cent of drinks cartons produced by Tetrapak, Elopak and SIG Combibloc (80 per cent of the global market) were made from certified or controlled wood fibres. The companies have pledged to purchase all paperboard from 'legal and acceptable' sources by 2015, using FSC, PEFC or equivalent standards.

Source: www.pefc.org; www.fsc.org; FSC (2009); UNECE/FAO (2009); Independent verifier ProForest, ENDS Bulletin (2009)

implicated in the loss of coastal habitat (e.g. mangroves) while farming of higher value species (e.g. salmon and prawns) still requires substantial fishmeal inputs. The fisheries sector thus has a strong rationale to commit to sustainable stock and ecosystem management to secure long-term supplies of target fish and to safeguard reputation and access to markets.

Market-based initiatives to conserve fish stocks and habitats can build on the FAO Code of Conduct for Responsible Fisheries (1995), the internationally agreed voluntary

Table 5.3 Global supply of roundwood from certified resources (2007–2009)

Region	Total forest area (million ha)	Total certified forest area (million ha)			Total forest area certified (%)		
		2007	2008	2009	2007	2008	2009
North America	470.6	164.2	181.7	180.3	34.9	38.6	38.3
Western Europe	155.5	80.8	84.2	82.2	52.0	54.1	52.8
CIS	907.4	20.6	24.6	25.2	2.3	2.7	2.8
Oceania	197.6	9.9	9.4	10.3	5.0	4.8	5.2
Africa	649.9	2.6	3.0	5.6	0.4	0.5	0.9
Latin America	964.4	12.1	15.0	14.6	1.3	1.6	1.5
Asia	524.1	1.6	2.0	3.0	0.3	0.4	0.6
World total	**3869.5**	**291.8**	**319.9**	**321.1**	**7.5**	**8.3**	**8.3**

Sources: UNECE/FAO (2009) using individual certification schemes; the Canadian Sustainable Forestry Certification Coalition; FAO and authors' compilations (2009).

framework covering sustainable practices and ecosystem approaches to fisheries management.[24] The Seafood Choices Alliance, a global association of fishers, fish farmers, wholesalers and restaurants, promotes ocean-friendly seafood[25] while the Global Tuna Conservation Initiative works to establish an ecosystem-based management approach for tuna stocks.[26] In terms of fisheries labelling, the Marine Stewardship Council operates the most widely recognized scheme with the largest geographic coverage (see Box 5.25).

Box 5.25 Volume and value of fisheries certified by the Marine Stewardship Council (MSC)

The MSC uses eco-labelling and independently verified certification to recognize sustainable fishing practices. A certified fishery must comply with three principles (sustainable fish stocks; minimizing environmental impact; effective management). MSC-certified fisheries rose by 41 per cent between 1 April and 30 September 2008.[27] By 2009, over 2300 MSC-labelled products were available in 42 countries, derived from annual catch of nearly 4 million tonnes.[28] Their retail value was around US$1.4 billion, US$400 million more than in 2008.

Source: www.msc.org

Certification of biodiversity-friendly agricultural practices

Certain impacts from intensive agricultural practices (e.g. habitat conversion and degradation, pollution) are the main drivers of terrestrial biodiversity loss (CBD and

MNP, 2007). At the same time, the agricultural sector can provide major biodiversity benefits through alternative technologies and practices. Agroforestry (combining trees and shrubs with crops and/or livestock) has long been part of traditional agriculture (Tetetay and Tegineh, 1991) and can support soil regeneration, high-quality production and key ecosystem services.[29]

Several labels and standards – e.g. 'sustainable farm certification',[30] 'organic', 'free-range' and business-to-business labels[31] – are now used to identify farms and products using environmentally favourable practices. Depending on how such standards are implemented, they could enable agri-businesses of all sizes to promote conservation and sustainable use of biological resources (Bishop et al, 2008) and can provide incentives to farmers (see Box 5.26).

Box 5.26 Using rice labelling to support habitat restoration and economic benefits in Japan

The crested ibis (*Nipponia nippon*) became extinct in Japan largely due to pesticide use and land consolidation programmes that destroyed habitat. As rice grown in Sado City in north Japan had always been sold for a premium price, farmers had no incentive to shift to environmentally friendly methods. A scheme was established to restore rice paddy habitats in order to reintroduce the crested ibis. Certified rice – grown through alternative methods, including winter flooding to restore waterbird habitat – is sold at almost twice the average market price (JPY2980 for 5kg of rice grown using half the normal amount of pesticide; JPY3700 for 5kg of organically grown rice). Farmers received government grants of JPY27,000 per 1000m² to compensate for lost profits and to promote no-tilling farming during the first three years. The growing area for '50 per cent less pesticide' certified rice doubled between 2007 (427ha) and 2009 (880ha).

Source: Sado Japanese crested ibis conservation center, www4.ocn.ne.jp/~ibis/

Organic agriculture is the largest type of certified agriculture. Over 32 million hectares were certified organic worldwide by the end of 2007, and 35 million hectares in 2008.[32] Global sales of organic food and drink have been increasing by over US$5 billion a year, reaching US$46 billion in 2007:[33] most are consumed in Europe or North America (Bishop et al, 2008). However, there is much debate about its contribution to biodiversity conservation (Bengtsson et al, 2005; Gibson et al, 2007) as different certification schemes require different biodiversity measures. The International Federation of Organic Agricultural Movements has developed a guide for farmers on biodiversity management and landscape quality in organic agriculture (Bosshard et al, 2009).

Towards ecotourism labelling

The tourism industry provides some 220 million jobs (7 per cent of total employment) and over 9 per cent of global GDP: in 2004, the nature and ecotourism market grew three times faster than the tourism industry as a whole.[34] Tourism is a key export for 83 per cent of developing countries and for the 40 poorest countries, the second most important source of foreign exchange after oil.[35] In the last decade, 23 biodiversity hotspots saw over 100 per cent tourism growth (Christ et al, 2003). Nature-based recreation (e.g. hunting, fishing and observing wildlife) accounted for nearly 1 per cent of GDP in the US in 2006 or US$122 billion (US Fish and Wildlife Service, 2007).

Maintaining natural areas in good condition is fundamental to the sector's continued growth. Reinvesting some tourism revenues in ecosystem protection can support community-based conservation and provide an alternative to more damaging development (see Box 5.27).

Box 5.27 Biodiversity benefits from nature-based tourism in the Philippines

In Olango Island reef in Cebu, most revenues received (about US$2.5 million annually) come from on- and off-site expenditures of diving tourists. It has been estimated that if reef quality and wetland stewardship were improved, the area could see a 60 per cent increase in annual net revenues not only from reef and mangrove fisheries but also from tourist expenditures.

Source: de Groot et al (2006)

Despite this growth, ecotourism – 'responsible travel to natural areas that conserves the environment and improves the welfare of local people'[36] – has lagged behind other sectors in establishing formal certification processes. However, several labelling initiatives could support higher industry standards. The new Tourism Sustainability Council (formed by a merger between the Partnership for Global Sustainable Tourism Criteria and the Sustainable Tourism Stewardship Council in September 2009) has the potential to provide a global accreditation body for ecotourism programmes. One criterion for assessing its effectiveness will be how well it meets the needs of small tourism operators, especially in the developing world.

The natural cosmetics sector

Cosmetics, care products and remedies based on natural ingredients form part of the expanding trade in biodiversity products, but no formal certification schemes are in place. A European Commission report found mainstreaming of demand, driven by growing awareness of human environmental impacts and a desire to eliminate use of products containing harsh chemicals: the sector is growing at roughly 20 per cent per year in the EU and has already achieved a 10 per cent market share in the US (Global Insight, 2007). A 2008 study estimated the global market in natural cosmetics at US$7 billion.[37]

Biomimicry

> Anyone doubting the economic and development value of the natural world need only sift through the extraordinary number of commercially promising inventions now emerging ... a result of understanding and copying nature's designs and the superior way in which living organisms successfully manage challenges from clean energy generation to re-using and recycling wastes. (Achim Steiner, UNEP Executive Director; UNEP, 2008b)

The need to develop more efficient reward frameworks that reflect nature's values more fully is particularly apparent when we consider the technological and economic opportunities associated with the rapidly emerging field of biomimicry.

Biomimicry is derived from the Greek words *bios* (life) and *mimesis* (to imitate). It is a new discipline that studies and then emulates natural forms, processes, systems and strategies to solve human problems sustainably (Benyus, 1997). It can offer industry alternatives to the 'heat, beat and treat' approach that requires enormous amounts of energy, raw material, toxic chemicals and heavy machinery to manufacture everyday products while polluting the soil, water and air (Lovins, 2008). Biomimicry brings together science, design, policy and manufacturing to tackle problems faster, smarter and with less impact on the biosphere.

The *Harvard Business Review* (2009) identified the business of biomimicry as one of the year's key breakthrough ideas. An examination of the worldwide Patent Database for 1985 to 2005 shows that the appearance of terms like 'biomimicry', 'bioinspired' and 'biomimetics' has jumped by 93 per cent compared with a 2.7 per cent increase in patents overall (Janine Benyus, cited in Freedman, 2010). Biomimicry is profitable (see examples in Box 5.28): estimated revenue from the top 100 biomimetic products in 2005 to 2008 totalled US$1.5 billion.[38]

Box 5.28 Biomimicry: Examples of economic gain linked to learning from nature

In Zimbabwe, termite architecture inspired Arup Associates to design a Harare office complex that needed no air conditioning, uses around one-tenth of the energy of ordinary buildings, saving over $3.5 million dollars in energy costs per year (UNEP, 2009c; Biomimicry Institute, 2010a). InterfaceFLOR, an international carpet tile manufacturer, designed non-directional tiles modelled on the rainforest floor: this reduces installation waste to less than 1 per cent compared to conventional tiles (BusinessGreen, 2010) and the product reached the top of the best-seller list faster than any product in the company's history (Lovins, 2008). The Whalepower company develops wind turbine blades inspired by the bumpy fins of humpback whales to increase energy efficiency (Biomimicry Institute, 2010b; see also *Nature*, 2008; van Nierop et al, 2009). Studying fish shoals may lead to the generation of ten times more energy from the same amount of space in wind farms (Whittlesey et al, 2010).

Reward structures could be designed to ensure that a part of biomimetic revenues flows back to the protection of natural habitats (e.g. as in the Innovation for Conservation Initiative of the Biomimicry Institute).

5.2 Barriers to the success of certified products

Uneven coverage, linked to the cost and complexity of certification

Despite impressive recent growth, the overall market share of certified products remains small. For example, MSC-certified seafood products have grown steadily over the past decade but still account for only 7 per cent of the FAO's total recorded global capture fisheries production (MSC, pers. comm.). Forest certification covers 8.3 per cent of the world's production forests but in regions of highest forest biodiversity (Africa, Latin America and Asia), this falls to 0.9 per cent, 1.5 per cent and 0.6 per cent respectively (UNECE/FAO, 2009: see Table 5.3 above and Figure 5.14). FSC increased its coverage in Africa by 88 per cent in the year to May 2009 and now has approximately 5.6 million certified hectares (UNECE/FAO, 2009) but has only certified just over 1 per cent of the total forest estate in Indonesia.

The expansion of certified biodiversity-friendly products and services is hampered by the cost and complexity of implementation, reflected in relatively low levels of certified production in developing countries. The direct costs of certification may be insignificant for large operators but can be a challenge for many small-scale producers and community enterprises.[39] Although the MSC does allow a small part of a fishery to be assessed and certified, this depends on the whole stock being sustainable, i.e. individual operators who adopt improved practices may incur higher costs than their competitors without any credible marketing advantage.

Difficulties in communicating biodiversity values

A more fundamental barrier to expanding voluntary green markets is limited consumer WTP. A study focusing on eight EU Member States found a low level of awareness and WTP for certified products among end-users (Forest Industries Intelligence Limited 2009, cited in UNECE/FAO, 2009). There are indications that end-user reluctance to pay the higher cost of certified products has steered importers and manufacturers sourcing from countries in the tropics away from FSC certification towards cheaper products verified as legal but not necessarily sustainable. This also seems to be the case in countries that were traditionally strong FSC supporters e.g. The Netherlands (UNECE/FAO, 2009).

A large proportion of certified wood is often not labelled as such on the market, as it is intended for business-to-business transactions rather than retail outlets. In countries such as Finland, where most forest area is certified, domestic timber markets have no incentive to differentiate between certified and non-certified wood (ITTO, 2008).

While certification systems can signal values important to some groups of people, they do not always capture aspects important to other groups e.g. the cultural values of biodiversity.

Developing a coordinated sector approach involving all relevant stakeholders is more difficult where there is a time lag between profit-generating activities and the appearance of environmental degradation (Bishop et al, 2008). For example, although

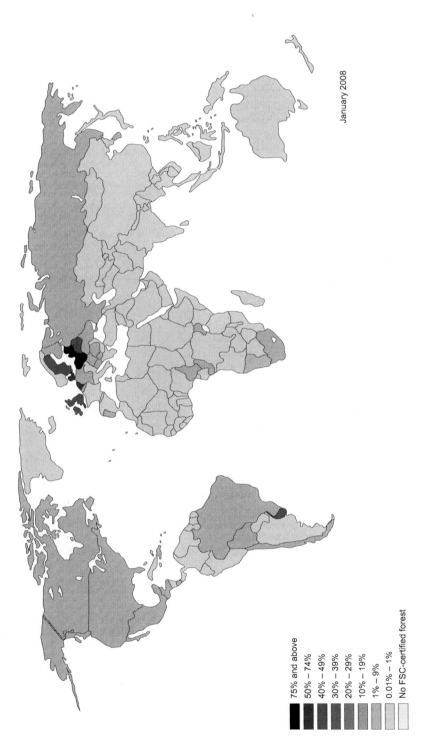

January 2008

75% and above
50% – 74%
40% – 49%
30% – 39%
20% – 29%
10% – 19%
1% – 9%
0.01% – 1%
No FSC-certified forest

Figure 5.14 *FSC-certified forest per region, as of 1 January 2008*

Source: FSC (2008a)

nature tourism depends on a healthy environment, the tourism industry may be slow to take steps to protect it. In 90 of the 109 countries where coral reefs occur, these are damaged by cruise ship anchors and sewage, by tourists breaking off chunks and by commercial harvesting for sale to tourists (Bishop et al, 2008).

Lack of biodiversity focus by certified products and services

Many certification systems do not make their relationship to biodiversity explicit. Organic farming labels, for example, have been reported to be generally beneficial but the certification does not set out to ensure biodiversity benefits and there are substantial differences in how biodiversity is treated across standards. Depending on local circumstances and the label, they can sometimes fail to prevent loss of species richness (Bengtsson et al, 2005).

Certification systems tend to rely too much on the assumption that merely adopting specified production and processing practices will yield positive biodiversity and ecosystem benefits, regardless of the producer's location in the landscape/watershed. In practice, most certified forests are not very biodiverse[40] and an organic farm located in the midst of a large agro-industrial landscape may provide few benefits to biodiversity for reasons beyond its control. Greater attention to landscape/watershed criteria in certification systems could help ensure better biodiversity outcomes although, as seen with the MSC, a broad ecosystem-based approach can weaken incentives for individual producers.

Unintended consequences of new legislation

New regulations can sometimes limit market opportunities for natural products. For example, a potential barrier to growth in natural cosmetics comes from tighter legislation in the US and the EU (Registration, Evaluation, Authorisation and Restriction of Chemicals, REACH) on the safety of chemicals in cosmetics. This could reduce research investment into potential new ingredients, making it harder for new products to meet the new criteria. The end result could be continued reliance on existing species/products already approved under the legislation, at the expense of lesser-known biodiversity-friendly options.

5.3 Expanding the reach of biodiversity-friendly products

Practical steps to improve the market penetration of certified products, consistent with rules and disciplines applicable to international trade (see Box 2.2 in Chapter 2), could be taken to:

- Review and strengthen the biodiversity element of existing and new certification systems to ensure they monitor biodiversity use and impacts. Requirements should be harmonized across labels to be more consistent with customer expectations.
- Include broader landscape considerations in certification processes to ensure that business works to improve overall regional biodiversity, e.g. landscape connectivity across agricultural regions, prioritized efforts in high biodiversity areas, etc.

- Create more supply push and market pull through increased consumer awareness and supply-chain management by large commercial buyers. This could be done through networks setting targets[41] or eco-investment funds to support companies that are certified and/or develop innovative business models. For example, HotelPlan, a Swiss company, used a US$3 levy on bookings to raise US$750,000 in 2002 to support sustainable tourism, environmental efforts and emergency one-off projects (cited in Bishop et al, 2008).
- Invest directly or indirectly in companies that market certified products, particularly from high conservation value areas, e.g. through technical assistance to improve profitability, sustainable practices and access to markets. Such investment could be leveraged through specific mechanisms (see Box 5.29) to create incentives for companies committed to purchasing biodiversity-friendly products or making biodiversity protection their key output.
- Make better use of traditional knowledge of plant (and animal) species to develop new products that could reduce the costs of complying with chemical safety legislation.
- Make global markets work better for the poor by helping provide non-timber forest products and other products suitable for BioTrade.
- Support the adoption of certification standards in developing countries, particularly in regions where they are currently non-existent or embryonic and help small to medium businesses for whom the initial investment is prohibitive (see Box 5.30).

Box 5.29 Social stock exchange for companies providing services of public benefit

The Social Stock Exchange is a way for investors to invest in businesses that deliver specific social objectives, e.g. alleviating poverty, preventing environmental destruction.[42] Allowing 'social investors' to make educated choices about the impacts organizations have on society could act as a powerful support for companies that provide a social good. Supporting this type of investment and trade can provide incentives to maintain biodiversity in the face of competition from less biodiverse alternatives.

Source: Yunus (2007)

Box 5.30 MSC risk-based support framework for smaller fisheries

The MSC *Guidelines for assessment of small-scale and data-deficient fisheries* aim to support such fisheries in carrying out the necessary assessment for certification. The MSC risk-based framework methodology provides an approach to help evaluate key environmental indicators of the MSC environmental standard for sustainable fishing. Although not limited to developing countries, it is likely to have the greatest uptake among them.

Source: MSC (2010)

6 Expanding markets through green public procurement (GPP)

> Europe's public authorities are major consumers. By using their purchasing power to choose environmentally friendly goods, services and works, they can make an important contribution to sustainable consumption and production – what we call Green Public Procurement, or GPP. (Janez Potočnik, EU Commissioner for Environment)

6.1 Objectives and evolution of GPP policies

Green public procurement (GPP) means that public purchasers take account of environmental factors when buying products, services or works. A product or service can only qualify as 'green' if it goes beyond what is required by law and beyond the performance of products commonly sold in the market.

Governments at all levels and public agencies and organizations can implement GPP policies to achieve rapid results in reducing pressures on biodiversity, driving markets and greening the supply chain. Their vast buying power – from offices and canteens to construction and transportation – can directly expand the market for products and services produced or supplied with less environmental impact (e.g. energy- and water-efficient devices and building techniques, non-hazardous or biodegradable products, organic or seasonal food, sustainably produced timber and paper). Other products and services are progressively placed at a significant disadvantage when competing for government contracts.

GPP facilitates eco-innovation because governments can take more risk when opting for new products. This can create economies of scale and help companies move up the learning curve, put new products on the market and create green-collar jobs.

GPP has developed rapidly since 2000 and is being mainstreamed by environmentally ambitious governments. The EU market for government purchases alone exceeds €1500 billon/year (16 per cent of EU Gross National Product) and the European Commission has encouraged Member States to shift 50 per cent of purchasing to GPP by 2010 (EC, 2008). Some have set more ambitious targets, e.g. The Netherlands set a GPP target of 100 per cent for national government by 2010, and 50 to 75 per cent for local and regional governments (Bouwer et al, 2006).

Box 5.31 Strengthening regulations for GPP implementation in China

Five years after China's Government Purchase Law (2003), official statistics showed that about 5.1 billion Yuan (US$630 million) had been saved in procurement costs. The original law established a 'preferential' list (public authorities could select other products if justified on cost and energy-efficiency grounds). In 2007, the State Council changed this approach and adopted a compulsory list of nine key types of products. The State Council Order 2009 provides for further strengthening of procurement rules for energy-saving products.

Source: China Daily, 14 April 2009

Many other large economies – including Japan, China, New Zealand, Korea and the US – also have formal policies to stimulate GPP (see example in Box 5.31).

6.2 GPP standards, criteria and costing

Standards and criteria are the backbone of GPP. Producers and suppliers need to know how their products are assessed and how to improve their chances of winning a contract. Making environmental criteria measurable and transparent is a challenge, given the range of products and services purchased by governments. Cooperation with relevant sectors and producers is needed to strike a balance between environmental ambition and product availability. Training purchasers is important to translate policy goals into action.

Governments can use GPP policies to target purchasing at environmentally certified or labelled products guaranteed to meet specific criteria (see Section 5 above and Box 5.32). This not only has direct environmental benefits but also raises the profile and market penetration of certification and labelling schemes.

Box 5.32 Tightening criteria for centralized procurement: Timber purchasing in the UK

The UK established a Central Point of Expertise for Timber (CPET) to guide government purchasing. The CPET advised that the five main timber certification schemes (FSC, PEFC, CSA, SFI, MTCC) complied with government criteria on legality, as did certain independent schemes. As purchases not covered by such schemes had to supply 'equivalent evidence' ('Category B' evidence), most suppliers opted to use formal certification as it simplified proof of compliance.

In April 2009, criteria were strengthened. The entry level for GPP was raised from 'Legal' to 'Legal & Sustainable', effectively limiting central government projects to fully certified timber. This high-level commitment has boosted demand for and availability of certified timber in the UK market, as measured by rapid growth in certified forest area and the number of Chain of Custody certificates.

Remaining challenges include patchy implementation of detailed compliance specifications through a complex government bureaucracy. However, the mere existence of this policy sends out a clear and powerful message of intent.

Source: www.cpet.org.uk

Some green purchases yield higher environmental benefits than others. Recent studies have focused mainly on CO_2 effects of GPP policies and not yet on direct biodiversity impacts. However, it is clear that creating demand for products with low environmental impacts is directly or indirectly beneficial for soil and water quality, ecosystem integrity and long-term sustainability of natural capital.

Because it takes time to develop comprehensive criteria for all products, the 'quick wins' can come from starting with products with the highest impacts. Products offering good opportunities to reduce biodiversity impacts – and which represent a significant share of public expenditure – include:

- Timber (used in construction, water works, furniture and paper: see Box 5.33).
- Food (canteens, schools, hospitals). One estimate suggests that if all authorities switched to organically produced foodstuffs, this would reduce phosphate release in fertilizer by 41,560 tonnes/year (PO_4-equivalent), roughly the amount currently used by 3.5 million Europeans.[43]
- Information and communications technology (ICT). Aside from energy consumption, ICT demand for metals and minerals (e.g. silver, tin, copper, gold, cadmium, lead and mercury) forms a significant part of global trade in these inputs: extraction and waste management practices can be modified to reduce impacts.

Box 5.33 Energy and water savings through green procurement in Denmark

Public procurement of virgin paper is about 22,500 tonnes per year: for each tonne of recycled paper, 3200kWh of energy and 10m³ of water can be saved. It has been estimated that if all public procurement switched to recycled paper, this would save 73,000MWh in energy and 225,000m³ of water, equivalent to the yearly energy consumption of 15,000 households.

Source: www.gronindkobsportal.dk/Default.asp?ID=262

GPP is not automatically more expensive than conventional procurement and can be a cost-saving tool for government. Price will depend on products available, market competition and the way in which costs are assessed. Assessing a purchase over its entire life cycle (whole life costing or WLC), rather than simply assessing the purchase cost, shows that energy-saving products are often worth the investment and can reduce long-term costs (see Box 5.34).

Economies of scale are available where criteria and standards can be applied across several markets and/or through joint GPP policies (see Box 5.35). Harmonizing purchasing criteria across countries could further lower costs but could involve lengthy international negotiation.

6.3 Tackling constraints on implementing GPP

GPP faces several barriers (Bouwer et al, 2006). First, there is often a perception that buying green costs the organization more: as mentioned above, this is not necessarily the case. However, the right balance must be struck between ambitious criteria and sufficient supply of goods. Strict criteria are little use if there are no or too few products available to meet them. Second, governments may lack the infrastructure to develop and implement GPP. Investment may be needed to build capacity to develop and set criteria, apply these to practical tools and assessments, and train purchasing officers. Essential components of GPP policies include third-party verification of compliance and supply chain management: the more a product combines different inputs, the more complicated it can be to trace their impacts at their respective points

Box 5.34 Cost savings identified through WLC in Germany

WLC analyses for GPP in some German cities reveal that the overall cost of green products and services is often lower than conventional products, once their entire life is considered. The table below compares green and other products, based on city experiences. Negative values indicate that GPP resulted in cost savings.

Organization	Product	Non-green Costs (in € – comparison of bids)	Green Costs (in € – comparison of bids)	Applied green criteria	Absolute difference (€)	Relative difference
Freiburg	Paper A4	205,980	171,650	Blue Angel	−34,330	−17%
	PC	64,545	65,433	Blue Angel, Energy Star 4.0	888	1%
	Thin-film transistor displays	9020	7177	Energy Star 4.0	−1843	−20%
Heidelberg	Paper A4	100,000	88,000	Blue Angel	−12,000	−12%
	Toilet paper	20,250	15,000	Blue Angel	−5250	−26%

Note: Costs are inclusive of VAT and inclusive of life cycle costs per year

Source: Öko-Institut and ICLEI (2006)

Box 5.35 Joint procurement through the EcoProcurement Service, Vorarlberg, Austria

Since 1998, 96 municipalities in one Austrian province have collaborated on GPP. In 2001, they launched the dedicated ÖkoBeschaffungs service to centralize procurement for members, offer legal and environmental advice, develop GPP guidelines for specific product groups and help municipalities to implement sustainable construction. Substantial savings have been made in administrative costs (20 to 60 per cent) and in prices paid for products (5 to 25 per cent). In 2005 total savings of about €286,500 were achieved.

Source: www.leap-gpp-toolkit.org/index.php?id=3490

of production. Third, building support at political and/or managerial level is important for efficient implementation. A phased approach can be useful, using demonstrated small-scale success to leverage support for broader roll-out (see Box 5.36).

Box 5.36 Phased implementation of green food procurement in East Ayrshire, Scotland

Between 2004 and 2007, the East Ayrshire Council transformed the school meal service to a successful model of sustainable provision supporting local and organic producers and healthier food. The programme was progressively expanded from pilot phase (one primary school providing 20,000 meals per year) and will eventually cover the 44 primary schools and 9 secondary schools in the county. It is based on the 'Food for Life' criteria for school canteens, e.g. at least 75 per cent of food ingredients must be unprocessed; at least 50 per cent of food ingredients must be locally sourced; and at least 30 per cent of food ingredients must be organic. The programme, financially supported by the Scottish Executive initiative, has reduced food miles by 70 per cent, reduced packaging waste and saved almost £100,000 in environmental costs.

Source: Sonnino (2008)

Fourth, differences in criteria and/or procedures between countries or administrations can create extra costs and uncertainties. Some countries are moving beyond GPP towards 'sustainable public procurement' which explicitly combines environmental and social criteria in purchasing decisions. Where priorities vary, procurement criteria will also vary.

In some cases, such differences have raised concerns over international competitiveness. In general terms, there is always the risk that GPP targets and criteria put strain on free trade agreements or, in the case of the EU, the internal market (e.g. criteria that give preference to national producers could distort competition and create suspicions of protectionism). Inclusion of social criteria could also lead to conflicts under trade agreements (see Chapter 2 and also Box 5.37).

Box 5.37 Compatibility of GPP with free trade rules and disciplines

The General Agreement on Tariffs and Trade (GATT) requires states to treat foreign and domestically produced goods alike ('national treatment obligation' under Article III) and prohibits discrimination against imported goods that are 'like' domestically produced goods, independent of how or where they have been produced. However, Article III.8(a) excludes all products consumed by a government in the course of its normal activity from the 'national treatment obligation', e.g. furniture, hospital material or social housing. This means that GPP policies have significant scope to explicitly promote biodiversity-friendly purchasing (e.g. by specifying FSC products or equivalents) without infringing GATT provisions.

Source: FSC (2008b)

GPP can yield broader results when combined with development cooperation efforts and where resources for capacity building and green industry development are available. Supporting greener production in countries of origin, especially developing countries, will open up new markets to providers, improve and expand a reliable supply of green products and lower the price of green procurement.

Looking to the future:

- GPP is a policy instrument with considerable environmental benefits, given the huge markets for government purchases.
- Most quantification of benefits has been based on substitution costs (e.g. replacing virgin paper with recycled), reduction in natural resource use (e.g. water) or reduced emissions (e.g. GHG, pollution). Much more work needs to be done to quantify the benefits to biodiversity from certification and labelling programmes.
- The time is right for committed governments to scale up GPP and set national goals, as first lessons have been learned and criteria are being devised and revised at an increasing rate.
- Harmonization where feasible could further lower costs and increase GPP's attractiveness.
- Transparency and clarity of processes and criteria are important for producers of all sizes to be able to adapt their offer to requirements.
- National GPP policies can be combined with development objectives to support the development of certified markets in other countries.

Notes

1   Australian Government, Department of the Environment, Water, Heritage and the Arts, www.environment.gov.au/biodiversity/incentives/tender.html.
2   United States, Department of Agriculture, www.nrcs.usda.gov/programs/CRP/.
3   There may be arguments in favour of a 'provider gets' approach rather than a 'polluter pays' approach, at least in the context of developing countries (Wertz-Kanounnikoff, 2006) where equity concerns play an additional role and where a polluter pays approach would impose the cost of environmental protection on often poorer land users rather on better-off service beneficiaries (Pagiola et al, 2005).
4   A usufruct right is the right to enjoy the use and advantages of another's property short of the destruction or waste of its substance.
5   See Republic of South Africa, Department: Water and Environmental Affairs, www.dwaf.gov.za/wfw/.
6   This section draws on Karousakis (2009) *Promoting Biodiversity Co-benefits in REDD*, OECD Paris.
7   Reforestation relates to areas previously covered in forest. Afforestation relates to areas not previously covered in forests.
8   Sub-national refers to states or provinces, or regions within countries.
9   Monitoring emission reductions from deforestation/degradation requires two types of data: changes in forest stocks and changes in carbon stocks.
10   Net deforestation (net loss of forest area) is defined in the FAO Global Forest Resources Assessment (FAO, 2006) as overall deforestation minus changes in forest area due to forest planting, landscape restoration and natural expansion of forests.
11   REDD credits could also be fungible with permits/allowances under existing (domestic) emission trading schemes such as the European Union allowances (EUAs) under the EU Emissions Trading Scheme (EU ETS).
12   These are in essence 'Green Standard' REDD credits, similar to existing Gold Standard Clean Development Mechanism (CDM) credits which are voluntary premiums for CDM credits meeting additional sustainable development criteria.
13   The UNFCCC REDD web-platform was created to share such information. As this is at an early stage, there is information on actions being undertaken but relatively little on lessons learned (see http://unfccc.int/methods_science/redd/items/4531.php).
14   More details on the agreements are available from Breibart, 1997; ICBG, 1997; Mulholland and Wilman, 1998; Neto and Dickson, 1999; ten Kate and Laird, 1999; Merson, 2000; Artuso, 2002; Greer and Harvey, 2004; Dedeurwaerdere et al, 2005; UNEP, 2009a, 2009b.

15   It should be noted that not all indigenous communities are keen on pursuing this line of development as some reject the commercial exploitation of knowledge.

16   'Source suppliers' covers source country governments, management entities, indigenous people/ communities, national organizations and/or stakeholder groups with access to traditional knowledge (for more details and key constraints, see Ding et al, 2007).

17   Note that 'buyers' can also be intermediaries, such a local research institutes and universities.

18   One reviewer noted that asset specificity may not apply so forcefully to bioprospecting, arguing that wild and so far undiscovered genetic resources collected for screening usually have no specificity. A provider country can offer their resources to any company interested in the use and companies can approach any provider country.

19   For a further discussion of how transaction costs economics apply to bioprospecting, see Gehl Sampath (2005).

20   For further discussion on the constraints on equitable sharing of benefits and related economic issues, see OECD (2003) and Richerhagen and Holm-Mueller (2005).

21   Suggestion made by Professor Vogel, University of Costa Rica (http://ictsd.net/i/environment/31517).

22   For example, see UNECE (2006) on forests: www.unece.org/timber/docs/fpama/2006/fpamr2006.pdf; and the Marine Stewardship Council for fisheries: www.msc.org/.

23   International Tropical Timber Organization: www.ITTO.int/.

24   For the Code and supporting technical guidelines for implementation, see www.fao.org/fishery/ccrf/en.

25   www.seafoodchoices.com/home.php.

26   Set up by WWF and TRAFFIC: see http://assets.panda.org/downloads/fortuna.pdf.

27   See www.msc.org/newsroom/news/sustained-growth-of-msc-labelled-products/.

28   See www.msc.org/documents/msc-brochures/MSC-FisheriesCommitments-Aug09-WEB.pdf.

29   See www.worldagroforestry.org/af/ and also www.ecoagriculture.org/index.php.

30   See www.sustainablefarmcert.com/. The Rainforest Alliance agriculture programme used this standard to protect wildlife, habitat, workers and communities (www.rainforest-alliance.org/agriculture.cfm?id=main).

31   For example GlobalGAP (Good Agricultural Practice) is a private sector body that sets voluntary agricultural standards covering biodiversity issues (www.globalgap.org/cms/front_content.php?idart= 3&idcat=9&lang=1).

32   The 2007 figures from the new World of Organic Agriculture: Statistics and Emerging Trends 2008, cited on their website: www.ifoam.org/press/press/2008/Global_Organic_Agriculture_Continued_ Growth.php. The 2008 figures from FiBL and IFOAM, Survey 2010 available on www.organic-world. net/statistics-world-area-producers.html.

33   See Organic Monitor research news www.organicmonitor.com/r3001.htm.

34   See www.wttc.org/.

35   See www.mekongtourism.org/site/uploads/media/IETS_Ecotourism_Fact_Sheet_-_Global_1__01.pdf

36   See www.ecotourism.org/site/c.orLQKXPCLmF/b.4835303/k.BEB9/What_is_Ecotourism__The_ International_Ecotourism_Society.htm (cited in Mastny, 2001).

37   See www.organicmonitor.com/r1709.htm.

38   Bharat Bhusnan, Director of Nanoprobe Laboratory for Bio and Nanotechnology & Biomimetics at Ohio State University, US (cited in Freedman, 2010).

39   See Timbmet Group Ltd (2004) 'What do we know about the costs and benefits of tropical timber certification?' Oxford.

40   Plantations are usually more productive than natural forests, and some argue that the world's timber and fibre needs should be met from plantations, thereby relieving pressure on natural forest to provide the same material.

41   For example the Global Forest and Trade Network (GFTN), brokered by WWF, enables consuming and producing companies to register and, in return for use of the GFTN logo for PR purposes, to report annually to the WWF on progress against individually agreed targets (www.gftn.panda.org/about_gftn/).

42   See www.socialstockexchange.eu/why/default.html.

43   See http://ec.europa.eu/environment/gpp/index_en.htm.

Acknowledgements

The authors wish to thank Barbara Akwagyiram, IEEP, Belgium; Arild Angelsen, Norwegian University of Life Science (UMB), Norway; Viviane André, European Commission – DG Environment, Belgium;

Jonathan Armstrong, IEEP, UK; Giles Atkinson, London School of Economics, UK; Ivan Bond, International Institute for Environment and Development (IIED), UK; Joana Chiavari, IEEP, Belgium; Bas Clabbers, Ministerie van Volkshiisvesting, Ruimetelijke Ordening en Milieubeheer (VROM), The Netherlands; Tamsin Cooper, IEEP, UK; Chris Cox, Organisation for Economic Co-operation and Development (OECD), France; Florian Eppink, UFZ, Germany; Naoya Furuta, International Union for Conservation of Nature (IUCN), Japan; Sonja Gantioler, IEEP, Belgium; Pablo Gutman, World Wildlife Fund (WWF), US; Sarah Hernandez, Centre for Ecology and Hydrology – Natural Environment Research Council, UK; David Huberman, IUCN, Switzerland; Mikkel Kallesoe, World Business Council for Sustainable Development (WBCSD), Switzerland; Sylvia Kaplan, Federal Environment Ministry, Germany; Marianne Kettunen, IEEP, Finland; Annegret Kindler, UFZ, Germany; Chris Knight, Price Waterhouse Coopers, UK; Eimear Nic Lughadha, Royal Botanic Gardens Kew, UK; Leonardo Mazza, IEEP, Belgium; Alaistair Morrison, New Zealand Department of Conservation, New Zealand; Hylton Murray, Canopy Capital, UK; Valerie Preston, Multilateral and bilateral Affairs Directorate Environment, Canada; Walter Reid, The David and Lucile Packard Foundation, North America; Ewald Rametsteiner, International Institute for Applied Systems Analysis (IIASA); Carmen Richerzhagen, German Development Institute (DIE), Germany; Mark Schauer, TEEB Secretariat, Germany; Burkhard Schweppe-Kraft, The Federal Environment Ministry, Germany; Bambi Semroc, Conservation International (CI); Monique Simmonds, Royal Botanical Gardens Kew, UK; Benjamin Simmons, United Nations Environment Programme (UNEP); Paul Smith, Royal Botanical Gardens Kew, UK; Leila Suvantola, University of Finland, Finland; Monique Simmonds, Royal Botanical Gardens Kew, UK; Giuliana Torta, European Commission – DG Environment, Belgium; Graham Tucker, IEEP, UK; Andreas Tveteraas, Norway's International Climate and Forest Initiative, Norway; Jean-Louis Weber, European Environment Agency (EEA), Denmark; Steve White, European Commission – DG Environment, Belgium; and Sven Wunder, Center for International Forestry Research (CIFOR).

References

Angelsen, A. (2008) *Moving Ahead with REDD: Issues, Options and Implications*, Center for International Forestry Research, CIFOR, Bogor

Angelsen, A. and Wertz-Kanounnikoff, S. (2008) 'What are the key design issues for REDD and the criteria for assessing options?', in A. Angelsen (ed) *Moving Ahead with REDD: Issues, Options and Implications*, CIFOR, Bogor

Artuso, A. (2002) 'Bioprospecting, benefit sharing, and biotechnological capacity building', *World Development*, vol 30, no 8, pp1355–1368

Asquith, N., et al (2008) 'Selling two environmental services: In-kind payments for bird habitat and watershed protection in Los Negros, Bolivia', *Ecological Economics*, vol 65, no 4, pp675–684, www.sciencedirect.com/science?_ob=ArticleURL&_udi=B6VDY-4RW4S2G-1&_user=10&_rdoc=1&_fmt=&_orig=search&_sort=d&view=c&_acct=C000050221&_version=1&_urlVersion=0&_userid=10&md5=da8c60544f71328bcdbf180faa3ad07d, accessed 6 November 2009

Barbier, E. B. and Aylward, B. (1996) 'Capturing the pharmaceutical value of biodiversity in a developing country', *Environmental and Resource Economics*, vol 8, pp157–181

Bassi, S., et al (2008) 'Agriculture and environment: Payments for environmental services (PES)', Presentation at the conference on Common Agriculture Policy and its Impacts in Malta (Victoria, Gozo, 7–9 November 2008)

Baylis, K., Rausser, G. and Simon, L. (2004) 'Agri-environmental programs in the United States and European Union', in G. Anania, M. E. Bohman, C. A. Carter and A. F. McCalla (eds) *Agricultural Policy Reform and WTO: Where Are We Heading?* Edward Elgar, Cheltenham, pp210–233

Bengtsson, J., Ahnström, J. and Weibull, A. (2005) 'The effects of organic agriculture on biodiversity and abundance: A meta-analysis', *Journal of Applied Ecology*, vol 42, pp261–269

Bennett, M. (2008) 'China's sloping land conversion programme: Institutional innovation or business as usual?' *Ecological Economics*, vol 65, no 4, pp699–711

Benyus, J. (1997) *Biomimicry: Innovation Inspired by Nature*, William Morrow & Co., New York

Biomimicry Institute (2010a) *Architecture: Learning from Termites How to Create Sustainable Buildings*, www.biomimicryinstitute.org/case-studies/case-studies/architecture.html, accessed 9 July 2010

Biomimicry Institute (2010b) *Energy: Learning from Humpback Whales How to Create Efficient Wind Power*, www.biomimicryinstitute.org/case-studies/case-studies/energy.html, accessed 9 July 2010

Bishop, J., Kapila, S., Hicks, F., Mitchell, P. and Vorhies, F. (2008) *Building Biodiversity Business*, Shell International Limited and the International Union for Conservation of Nature, London, and Gland, Switzerland

Blackman, A. and Woodward, T. (2009) 'User financing in a national payments for environmental services program', Discussion Paper – February 2009, RFF DP 09-04, Resources for the Future, US

Blackman, A. and Woodward, T. (2010) 'User financing in a national payment for environmental services program: Costa Rican hydropower', *Ecological Economics*, vol 69, no 8, pp1626–1638

Bosshard, A., Reinhard, B. R. and Taylor, S. (eds) (2009) *Guide to Biodiversity and Landscape Quality in Organic Agriculture*, IFOAM, Bonn

Bouwer, M., Jonk, M., Berman, T., Bersani, R., Lusser, H., Nappa, V., Nissinen, A., Parikka, K., Szuppinger, P. and Viganò, C. (2006) *Green Public Procurement in Europe 2006: Conclusions and Recommendations*, Virage Milieu & Management bv, Haarlem, The Netherlands, http://ec.europa.eu/environment/gpp/pdf/take_5.pdf, accessed 30 July 2010

Boyd, J., Caballero, K. and Simpson, R. D. (2000) 'The law and economics of habitat conservation: Lessons from an analysis of easement acquisitions', *Stanford Environmental Law Journal*, vol 19, no 1, pp393–412

Bracer, C., Scherr, S., Molnar, A., Sekher, M., Ochieng, B. O. and Sriskanthan, G. (2007) 'Organization and governance for fostering pro-poor compensation for ecosystem services', CES Scoping Study Issue Paper No 4, ICRAF Working Paper No 39, World Agroforestry Center, Nairobi, Kenya

Brand, D. (2002) 'Investing in the environmental services of Australian forest', in S. Pagiola, J. Bishop and N. Landell-Mills (eds) *Selling Forest Environmental Services: Market-Based Mechanisms for Conservation and Development*, Earthscan, London

Bräuer, I., Müssner, R., Marsden, K., Oosterhuis, F., Rayment, M., Miller, C. and Dodoková, A. (2006) *The Use of Market Incentives to Preserve Biodiversity*, Final Report, Project under Framework contract for economic analysis ENV.G.1/FRA/2004/0081, Berlin

Breibart, J. (1997) 'Bioprospecting planned for Yellowstone Park', *Albion Monitor*, www.albionmonitor.com/9709b/parkbugs.html

BusinessGreen (2010) 'Biomimicry: Hippy nonsense or corporate game-changer?' www.businessgreen.com/business-green/analysis/2264291/biomimimetics-green-business, accessed 9 July 2010

CBD (Convention on Biological Diversity) (1992) Convention on Biological Diversity Convention Text, http://biodiv.org/doc/legal/cbd-en.pdf, accessed 9 November 2009

CBD (2008) *Access and Benefit-Sharing in Practice: Trends in Partnerships Across Sectors*, Technical Series No 38, Montreal, www.cbd.int/doc/publications/cbd-ts-38-en.pdf, accessed 29 June 2010

CBD (2009) *Connecting Biodiversity and Climate Change Mitigation and Adaptation: Report of the Second Ad Hoc Technical Expert Group on Biodiversity and Climate Change*, Technical Series No 41, Montreal

CBD (2010) 'Policy options concerning innovative financial mechanisms: Draft recommendation', UNEP/CBD/WG-RI/3/INF/13, Nairobi, http://gdm.earthmind.net/2010-05-nairobi/wgri-03-L-13-en.pdf, accessed 22 September 2010

CBD and MNP (Netherlands Environmental Assessment Agency) (2007) *Cross-roads of Life on Earth: Exploring Means to Meet the 2010 Biodiversity Target*, Solution oriented scenarios for Global Biodiversity Outlook 2, Technical Series No 31, Montreal

Christ, C., Hillel, O., Matus, S. and Sweeting, J. (2003) *Tourism and Biodiversity: Mapping Tourism's Global Footprint*, Conservation International, Washington, DC

Coase, R. H. (1960) 'The problem of social cost', *Journal of Law and Economics*, vol 3, no 1, pp1–44

Costello, C. and Ward, M. (2006) 'Search, bioprospecting and biodiversity conservation', *Journal of Environmental Economics and Management*, vol 52, no 3, pp615–626

Craft, A. B. and Simpson, R. D. (2001) 'The value of biodiversity in pharmaceutical research with differentiated products', *Environmental and Resource Economics*, vol 18, no 1, pp1–17

De Melo, J. J. and Prates, J. (2007) 'EcoTerra Model: Economic instruments for sustainable land use management in Portugal', Paper presented at the 7th International Conference of the European Society for Ecological Economics, Leipzig, 5–8 June 2007

de Groot, R., Stuip, M., Finlayson, M. and Davidson, N. (2006) *Valuing Wetlands: Guidance for Valuing the Benefits Derived from Wetland Ecosystem Services*, Ramsar Technical Report No 3, CBD Technical Series No 27, www.cbd.int/doc/publications/cbd-ts-27.pdf, accessed 5 June 2009

Dedeurwaerdere, T. (2005) 'From bioprospecting to reflexive governance', *Ecological Economics*, vol 53, no 4, pp473–491

Dedeurwaerdere, T., Krishna, V. and Pascual, U. (2005) *Biodiscovery and Intellectual Property Rights: A Dynamic Approach to Economic Efficiency*, Department of Land Economy Environmental Economy and Policy Research Working Papers, 13.2005, University of Cambridge

Ding, H., Nunes, P. A. L. D. and Onofri, L. (2007) *An Economic Model for Bioprospecting Contracts*, Fondazioni Eni Enrico Mattei – Note di Lavoro, 102.07, Fondazioni Eni Enrico Mattei, Milan, Italy

Earthmind (2010) 'The website of the GDM 2010 Initiative', http://gdm.earthmind.net, accessed 22 September 2010

EC (Commission of the European Communities) (2007) 'Green Paper on market-based instruments for environment and related policy purposes', COM (2007) 140 final, Brussels

EC (2008) 'Public procurement for a better environment', Communication COM (2008) 400 final, Brussels, http://eur-lex.europa.eu/LexUriServ/LexUriServ.do?uri=COM:2008:0400:FIN:EN:PDF, accessed 27 October 2010

EC (2009) 'Contributing to sustainable development: The role of fair trade and non-governmental trade-related sustainability assurance schemes', Communication COM (2009) 215 final, Brussels

Ecosystem Marketplace (2008) *Payments for Ecosystem Services: Market Profiles*, Forest Trends/Ecosystem Marketplace, http://moderncms.ecosystemmarketplace.com/repository/moderncms_documents/PES_Matrix_Profiles_PROFOR.1.pdf

Eliasch, J. (2008) *Climate Change: Financing Global Forests. The Eliasch Review*, Earthscan, London

Emerton, L., Bishop, J. and Thomas, L. (2006) *Sustainable Financing of Protected Areas: A Global Review of Challenges and Options*, IUCN, Gland, Switzerland and Cambridge

Ends Bulletin (2009) 'Drink pack firms boost use of certified wood fibres', www.endseurope.com/index.cfm?go=22631&referrer=search, accessed 27 October 2010

Environment Canada (2010) 'Ecological Gifts Program', www.ec.gc.ca/pde-egp/default.asp?lang=En&n=FCD2A728-1, accessed 22 September 2010

FAO (Food and Agriculture Organization) (2000) *Global Forest Resource Assessment*, Food and Agriculture Organization of the United Nations, Rome, ftp://ftp.fao.org/docrep/fao/003/y1997E/frA%202000%20Main%20report.pdf, accessed 26 October 2009

FAO (2006) *Global Forest Resource Assessment 2005*, FAO, Rome, Italy

Ferraro, P. (2007) *Performance Payments for Sea Turtle Nest Protection in Low-Income Nations: A Case Study From Tanzania*, Georgia State University, www2.gsu.edu/~wwwcec/docs/doc%20updates/NOAA%20Paper%20TZ%20Final%20Draft%20June%202007.pdf, accessed 9 November 2009

Ferraro, P. J. and Kiss, A. (2002) 'Direct payments to conserve biodiversity', *Science*, vol 298, pp1718–1719

Forest Industries Intelligence Limited (2009) *The EU Market for 'Verified Legal' and 'Verified Legal and Sustainable' Timber Products*, UK Timber Trade Federation and Department for International Development

Fourli, M. (1999) *Compensation for Damage Caused by Bears and Wolves in the European Union*, Office for Official Publications of the European Communities, Luxembourg

Freedman, M. (2010) 'Nature is the model factory', *Newsweek*, www.newsweek.com/2010/05/28/nature-is-the-model-factory.html, accessed 9 July 2010

Frinn, R. D. (2003) 'Bioprospecting: Why is it so unrewarding?' *Biodiversity and Conservation*, vol 12, pp207–216

Frost, P. and Bond, I. (2008) 'The CAMPFIRE programme in Zimbabwe: Payments for wildlife services', *Ecological Economics*, vol 65, no 4, pp776–787

FSC (Forest Stewardship Council) (2008a) 'Facts and figures on FSC growth and markets: Info pack', FSC Presentation, 28 February 2008, www.fsc.org/fileadmin/web-data/public/document_center/powerpoints_graphs/facts_figures/FSC_market_info_pack-2008-01-01.pdf, accessed 27 October 2010

FSC (2008b) *Specifying FSC in Public Procurement: In Line with WTO Rules*, FSC Factsheet

FSC (2009) 'Facts and figures', www.fsc.org/facts-figures.html, accessed 15 June 2009

Fuhrman, P. (2010) *Umsetzung der Wasserrahmenrichtlinie in Baden-Wuerttember – Wege zur Reduzierung landwirtschaftlicher Eintraege in Gewaesser*, www.umweltbundesamt.de/wasser-und-gewaesserschutz/gruene-woche/2010.pdf, accessed 12 July 2010

Gatti, J., Goeschl, T., Groom, B. and Swanson, T. (2004) 'The biodiversity bargaining problem', CWPE 0447, University of Cambridge

Gehl Sampath, P. (2005) *Regulating Bioprospecting: Institutions for Drug Research, Access and Benefit-Sharing*, www.unu.edu/publications/briefs/policy-briefs/2005/bioprospecting.pdf, accessed 27 October 2010

Gibson, R. H., Pearce, S., Morris, R. J., Symondson, W. O. C. and Memmott, J. (2007) 'Plant diversity and land use under organic and conventional agriculture: A whole-farm approach', *Journal of Applied Ecology*, vol 44, pp792–803

Global Canopy Programme (2008) *The Little REDD Book,* Global Canopy Foundation, www.amazonconservation.org/pdf/redd_the_little_redd_book_dec_08.pdf, accessed 28 October 2010

Global Insight (2007) *A Study of the European Cosmetics Industry*, Prepared for European Commission, Directorate General for Enterprise and Industry, http://ec.europa.eu/enterprise/newsroom/cf/document.cfm?action=display&doc_id=4561&userservice_id=1, accessed 9 December 2009

Greer, D. and Harvey, B. (2004) *Blue Genes: Sharing and Conserving the World's Aquatic Biodiversity*, Earthscan/IDRC, London and Ottawa

Grieg-Gran, M. (2000) *Fiscal Incentives for Biodiversity Conservation: The ICMS Ecológico in Brazil*, Discussion Paper 00-01 IIED December 2000, London

Gutman, P. (2006) 'PES: A WWF perspective', Presentation given at the Workshop on Conservation Finance, Global Biodiversity Forum, Curitiba, Brazil, 25 March 2006, http://assets.panda.org/downloads/peswwfmpo.pdf, accessed 11 November 2009

Hanski, I., Koivulehto, H., Cameron, A. and Rahagalala, P. (2007) 'Deforestation and apparent extinctions of endemic forest beetles in Madagascar', *Biol. Lett.*, vol 3, no 3, pp344–347, http://rsbl.royalsocietypublishing.org/content/3/3/344.full.pdf+html, accessed 4 December 2009

Harvard Business Review (2009) 'Breakthrough ideas for 2009', http://hbr.org/web/tools/2009/01/list-toc, accessed 9 July 2010

Hope, C. and Castilla-Rubio, J. C. (2008) 'A first cost benefit analysis of action to reduce deforestation', Paper commissioned by the Office of Climate Change as background work to its report *Climate Change: Financing Global Forests* (The Eliasch Review), www.ibcperu.org/doc/isis/11462.pdf, accessed 26 July 2010

ICBG (International Cooperative Biodiversity Groups) (1997) *Report of a Special Panel of Experts on the International Cooperative Biodiversity Groups*, www.fic.nih.gov/programs/research_grants/icbg/final_report.htm, accessed 22 September 2010

IMS Health (2007) 'Intelligence 360, Global Pharmaceutical Perspectives 2006', www.imshealth.com

IPCC (Intergovernmental Panel on Climate Change) (2007a) 'Climate Change 2007: Synthesis report', Intergovernmental Panel on Climate Change Fourth Assessment Report, pp1–72

IPCC (2007b) *Climate Change 2007: The Physical Science Basis*, Contribution of Working Group I to the Fourth Assessment Report of the Intergovernmental Panel on Climate Change, Cambridge University Press, Cambridge

IPCC (2007c) *Climate Change 2007: Mitigation of Climate Change*, Contribution of Working Group III to the Fourth Assessment Report of the Intergovernmental Panel on Climate Change, Cambridge University Press, Cambridge

Irawan, S. and Tacconi, L. (2009) 'Reducing Emissions from Deforestation and Forest Degradation (REDD) and decentralized forest management', *International Forestry Review*, vol 11, pp427–438

ITTO (International Tropical Timber Organization) (2008) 'Developing forest certification towards increasing the comparability and acceptance of forest certification systems worldwide', Technical Series 29, http://illegal-logging.info/uploads/TS29.pdf, accessed 10 November 2009

Johnstone, N. and Bishop, J. (2007) 'Private sector participation in natural resource management: What relevance in developing countries?' *International Review of Environmental and Resource Economics*, vol 1, pp67–109

Kapos, V., Ravilious, C., Campbell, A., Dickson, B., Gibbs, H. K., Hansen, M. C., Lysenko, I., Miles, L., Price, J., Scharlemann, J. P. W. and Trumper, K. C. (2008) *Carbon and Biodiversity: A Demonstration Atlas*, UNEP-WCMC, Cambridge

Karousakis, K. (2009) *Promoting Biodiversity Co-benefits in REDD*, ENV Working Paper Number 11, Organisation for Economic Co-operation and Development, OECD, Paris

Karousakis, K. and Corfee-Morlot, J. (2007) *Financing Mechanisms to Reduce Emissions from Deforestation: Issues in Design and Implementation*, Organisation for Economic Co-operation and Development, OECD, Paris

Kindermann, G., Obersteiner, M., Sohngen, B., Sathaye, J., Andrasko, K., Rametsteiner, E., Schlamadinger, B., Wunder, S. and Beach, R. (2008) 'Global cost estimates of reducing carbon emissions through avoided deforestation', *PNAS*, vol 105, no 30, pp10302–10307

Köllner, T., Schelske, O. and Seidl, I. (2002) 'Integrating biodiversity into intergovernmental fiscal transfers based on cantonal benchmarking: A Swiss case study', *Basic and Applied Ecology*, vol 3, pp381–391

Laird, S. and Wynberg, R. (2008) *Access and Benefit Sharing in Practice: Trends in Partnerships Across Sectors*, CBD Technical Series No 38, Secretariat of the Convention on Biological Diversity, Montreal

Land Trust Alliance (2006) '2005 National land trust census', Land Trust Alliance, Washington, DC, www. sfbayjv.org/tools/ConservationEasementsBiodiversityProtectionandPrivateUse.pdf, accessed 6 December 2009

Leverington, F., Hockings, M. and Lemos Costa, K. (2008) *Management Effectiveness Evaluation in Protected Areas: A Global Study*, The University of Queensland, IUCN, WWF, The Nature Conservancy, Gatton, Queensland

Lindsey, R. (2007) 'Tropical Deforestation', NASA Earth Observatory, 30 March 2007, http:// earthobservatory.nasa.gov/Features/Deforestation/, accessed 12 November 2009

Lovins, H. (2008) 'Rethinking production', in *State of the World 2008: Innovations for a Sustainable Economy*, Worldwatch Institute, www.worldwatch.org/files/pdf/SOW08_chapter_3.pdf, accessed 22 September 2010

MA (Millennium Ecosystem Assessment) (2005a) *Ecosystems and Human Well-Being: Biodiversity Synthesis*, World Resources Institute, Washington, DC

MA (Millennium Ecosystem Assessment) (2005b) *Ecosystems and Human Well-Being: General Synthesis*, World Resources Institute, Washington, DC

MAFF (Forestry Agency, Ministry of Agriculture, Forestry and Fisheries of Japan) (2008) *Annual Report on Trends in Forests and Forestry*, MAFF, Japan

Marengo, J. A., Soares, W. R., Saulo, C. and Nicolini, M. (2004) 'Climatology of the low-level jet east of the Andes as derived from the NCEP-NCAR reanalyses: Characteristics and temporal variability', *Journal of Climate*, vol 17, pp2261–2280

Mastny, L. (2001) *Travelling Light: New Paths for International Tourism*, Worldwatch Paper #159, p37, www.mekongtourism.org/site/uploads/media/IETS_Ecotourism_Fact_Sheet_-_Global_1__01.pdf, accessed 13 December 2009

May, P. H., Veiga Neto, F., Denardin, V. and Loureiro, W. (2002) 'Using fiscal instruments to encourage conservation: Municipal responses to the "ecological" value-added tax in Paraná and Minas Gerais, Brazil', in S. Pagiola, J. Bishop and N. Landell-Mills (eds) *Selling Forest Environmental Services: Market-Based Mechanisms For Conservation and Development*, Earthscan, London, pp173–199

MEFT (Ministère de l'Environnement des Forêts et du Tourisme), USAID (United States Agency for International Development) and CI (Conservation International) (2009) *Evolution de la couverture de forêts naturelles à Madagascar, 1990–2000–2005*, Conservation International, Antananarivo

Menzies, D. (2002) 'Conflict or collaboration? The New Zealand Forest Accord' in P. ten Brink (ed) *Voluntary Environmental Agreements: Process and Practice, and Future Trends*, Greenleaf Publishing, Sheffield

Merson, J. (2000) 'Bio-prospecting or bio-piracy: Intellectual property rights and biodiversity in a colonial and postcolonial context', *Osiris*, vol 15, pp282–296

Meyer, C. and Schweppe-Kraft, B. (eds) (2006) *Integration ökologischer Aspekte in die Finanzpolitik*, BfN-Skripten, Bonn

Ministry of Foreign Affairs of Japan (2008) 'Financial mechanism for "Cool Earth Partnership"', Japan, www.mofa.go.jp/policy/economy/wef/2008/mechanism.html, accessed 22 September 2010

MSC (Marine Stewardship Council) (2010) 'Credibility: Access for all fisheries', www.msc.org/about-us/ credibility/all-fisheries, accessed 22 September 2010

Mulholland, D. M. and Wilman, E. A. (1998) *Bioprospecting and Biodiversity Contracts*, Working Papers in Ecological Economics 9806, Centre for Resource and Environmental Studies, Ecological Economics Program, Australian National University

Muñoz, C., Rivera, M. and Cisneros A. (2010) *Estimated Reduced Emissions from Deforestation under the Mexican Payment for Hydrological Environmental Services*, INE Working Papers No DGIPEA-0410, Mexico

Muñoz-Piña, C., Guevara, A., Torres, J. M. and Braña, J. (2008) 'Paying for the hydrological services of Mexico's forests: Analysis, negotiation, and results', *Ecological Economics*, vol 65, no 4, pp725–736

Nature (2008) 'Lifting a whale: Research highlights', *Nature*, vol 451, p868

Nepstad, D., Soares Filho, B., Merry, F., Moutinho, P., Rodrigues, H. O., Bowman, M., Schwartzman, S., Almeida, O. and Rivero, S. (2007) *The Costs and Benefits of Reducing Carbon Emissions from Deforestation and Forest Degradation in the Brazilian Amazon*, Woods Hole Research Center, Woods Hole, MA

Neto, R. B. and Dickson, D. (1999) '$3m deal launches major hunt for drug leads in Brazil', *Nature*, vol 400, p302

Newman, D. J. and Cragg, G. M. (2007) 'Natural products as sources of new drugs over the last 25 years', *Journal of Natural Products*, vol 70, pp 461–477

Niedersächsisches Umweltministerium, Niedersächsisches Landesamt für Ökologie (2002) *10 Jahre Trinkwasserschutz in Niedersachsen. Modell der Kooperation zwischen Landwirtschaft und Wasserwirtschaft*, Hannover, www.mu1.niedersachsen.de/download/6324, accessed 27 October 2010

OECD (Organisation for Economic Co-operation and Development) (1999) *Handbook on Incentive Measures for Biodiversity*, OECD, Paris

OECD (2003) *Economic Issues in Access and Benefit Sharing of Genetic Resources: A Framework for Analysis*, OECD Paris/Working Party on Global and Structural Policies/Working Group on Economic Aspects of Biodiversity

OECD (2005) *Environmental Fiscal Reform for Poverty Reduction*, OECD, Paris

OECD (2010) *Paying for Biodiversity: Enhancing the Cost-Effectiveness of Payments for Ecosystem Services*, OECD, Paris, www.oecd.org/env/biodiversity/pes, accessed October 27, 2010

OECD (forthcoming) *International Financing for Biodiversity Conservation: An Overview of Innovative Approaches and Persistent Challenges*, OECD, Paris

Öko-Institut and ICLEI (2006) *Costs and Benefits of Green Public Procurement in Europe*, Final report to DG Environment of the European Commission, Service contract number: DG ENV.G.2/SER/2006/0097r, Freiburg

Olsen, N. and Bishop, J. (2009) *The Financial Costs of REDD: Evidence from Brazil and Indonesia*, IUCN, Gland

Pagiola, S. (2003) *Paying for Water Services*, World Conservation No 1, World Bank, Washington, DC

Pagiola, S. (2008) 'Payments for environmental services in Costa Rica', *Ecological Economics*, vol 65, no 4, pp712–725

Pagiola, S. and Platais, G. (2002) *Market-Based Mechanisms for Conservation and Development: The Simple Logic of Payments for Environmental Services*, Environmental Matters Annual Review, July 2001 to June 2002 (FY 2002): 6, Environment Department, World Bank, Washington, DC

Pagiola, S., Landell-Mills, N., and Bishop, J. (2002) 'Making market-based mechanisms work for forests and people', in S. Pagiola, J. Bishop and N. Landell-Mills (eds) *Selling Forest Environmental Services: Market-Based Mechanisms for Conservation and Development*, Earthscan, London

Pagiola, S., Arcenas, A. and Platais, G. (2005), 'Can payments for environmental services help reduce poverty? An exploration of the issues and the evidence to date from Latin America', *World Development*, vol 33, no 2, 237–253.

Parker, C., Mitchell, A., Trivedi, M. and Mardas, N. (2009) *The Little REDD+ Book*, Global Canopy Programme, www.globalcanopy.org/themedia/file/PDFs/LRB_lowres/lrb_en.pdf, accessed 10 November 2009

Perrot-Maître, D. (2006) *The Vittel Payments for Ecosystem Services: A 'Perfect' PES Case?* International Institute for Environment and Development, London

PNAAPD (2007) 'Plan national d'action pour des achats publics durables', Ministère de l'Ecologie, de l'Energie, du Développement durable et de la Mer, Paris, www.ecoresponsabilite.environnement.gouv.fr/IMG/PNAAPD.pdf, accessed 27 October 2010

Porras, I., Grieg-Gran, M. and Neves, N. (2008) *All That Glitters: A Review of Payments for Watershed Services in Developing Countries*, Natural Resource Issues No 11, International Institute for Environment and Development. London

Portela, R. and Rodriguez, M. C. (2008) 'Environmental services payment in Costa Rica', unpublished manuscript, Conservation International

Prenen, E. (2008) Green and sustainable public procurement in The Netherlands: An inconvenient truth, 3rd International Public Procurement Conference Proceedings, www.ippa.ws/IPPC3/Proceedings/Chaper%2032.pdf, accessed 27 October 2010

The Prince's Rainforests Project (2010) 'Emergency package', www.rainforestsos.org/pages/emergency-package/, accessed 22 September 2010

PWC (Price Waterhouse Coopers) (2009) *Collection of Statistical Information on Green Public Procurement in the EU*, Price Waterhouse Coopers, London

Rausser, G. C. and Small, A. A. (2000) *Valuing Research Leads: Bioprospecting and the Conservation of Genetic Resources*, Berkeley Program in Law and Economics, UC Berkeley, http://escholarship.org/uc/item/4t56m5b8, accessed 9 December 2009

Richerhagen, C. and Holm-Mueller, K. (2005) 'The effectiveness of access and benefit sharing in Costa Rica: Implications for national and international regimes', *Ecological Economics*, vol 53, pp445–460

Ring, I. (2002) 'Ecological public functions and fiscal equalization at the local level in Germany', *Ecological Economics*, vol 42, pp415–427

Ring, I. (2008a) *Compensating Municipalities for Protected Areas: Fiscal Transfers for Biodiversity Conservation in Saxony, Germany*, GAIA 17(S1), pp143–151

Ring, I. (2008b) 'Integrating local ecological services into intergovernmental fiscal transfers: The case of the ecological ICMS in Brazil', *Land Use Policy*, vol 25, no 4, pp485–497

Ring, I., Drechsler, M., van Teeffelen, A. J., Irawan, S. and Venter, O. (2010) 'Biodiversity conservation and climate mitigation: What role can economic instruments play?' *Current Opinion in Environmental Sustainability*, vol 2, pp50–58

Rissman, A. R., Lozier, L., Comendant, T., Kareiva, P., Kiesecker, J. M., Shaw, M. R. and Merenlender, A. M. (2007) 'Conservation easements: Biodiversity protection and private use', *Conservation Biology*, vol 21, no 3, pp709–718

Sarr, M. and Swanson, T. (2007) *The Economics of IPR for Genetic Resources and Traditional Knowledge: North-South Cooperation in Sequential R&D*, mimeo, University College London

Saxon State Ministry for the Environment and Agriculture (2006) 'Green procurement is simpler than you think', Dresden

Science Council of Japan (2001) *Evaluation of the Multiple Functions of Agriculture and Forests that Concern the Global Environment and the Human Living Environment*, Report and Appendices, November 2008

Scheele, M. (2008) 'Common Agricultural Policy: Landscapes goods and environmental services for rural areas', Presentation at 12th Congress of the European Association of Agricultural Economists, Brussels Session 'Health check and future perspectives of the CAP: Challenges for agriculture: A day of scientific dialogue', Brussels, 28 August 2008, http://ec.europa.eu/agriculture/events/eaae/2008_en.htm, accessed 12 November 2009

The Scottish Government (2007) 'Report of the National Goose Management Review Group: Review of the National Policy Framework for Goose Management in Scotland: Response by the Scottish Executive', www.scotland.gov.uk/Publications/2007/10/30142133/0, accessed 22 September 2010

SenterNovem (2010) 'Green funds scheme', www.senternovem.nl/greenfundsscheme/index.asp, accessed 22 September 2010

Shine, C. (2005) *Using Tax Incentives to Conserve and Enhance Biodiversity in Europe*, Nature and Environment No 143, Council of Europe Publishing

Similä, J., Thum, R., Varjopuro, R. and Ring, I. (2006) 'Protected species in conflict with fisheries: The interplay between European and national regulation', *Journal of European Environmental and Planning Law*, vol 5, pp432–445

Simpson, R. D., Sedjo, R. and Reid, J. (1996) 'Valuing biodiversity for use in pharmaceutical research', *Journal of Political Economy*, vol 104, no 1, pp163–185

Sonnino, R. (2008) 'Creative public procurement: Lessons from Italy and the UK', in K. Morgan and R. Soninno (eds) *The School Food Revolution: Public Food and the Challenge of Sustainable Development*, Earthscan, London

Stern, N. (2007) *The Economics of Climate Change: The Stern Review*, Cambridge University Press, Cambridge

Suvantola, L. (in preparation) 'The Golden Eagle Compensation Scheme in Finland as an example of incentive measures: Potential for conflict management?' in R. Klenke, I. Ring, A. Kranz, N. Jepsen, F. Rauschmayer and K. Henle (eds) *Human-Wildlife Conflicts in Europe: Fisheries and Fish-Eating Vertebrates as a Model Case*, Springer, Heidelberg

Swanson, T. (2009) 'An international market based instrument to finance biodiversity conservation: Towards a Green Development Mechanism', Report from Amsterdam expert workshop by T. Swanson and K. Mullan, March 2009

Swanson, T., Mullan, K. and Kontoleon, A. (2009) 'Towards an international market-based instrument to finance biodiversity conservation', Green Development Mechanism technical background paper, http://gdm.earthmind.net/2009-02-amsterdam/Background_Paper.pdf, accessed 22 September 2010

TEEB in Business (2011) *The Economics of Ecosystems and Biodiversity in Business and Enterprise* (ed J. Bishop), Earthscan, London

TEEB in Local Policy (2011) *The Economics of Ecosystems and Biodiversity in Local and Regional Policy and Management* (ed H. Wittmer and H. Gundimeda), Earthscan, London

ten Brink, P. (ed) (2002) *Voluntary Environmental Agreements: Process and Practice, and Future Trends*, Greenleaf Publishing, Sheffield

ten Kate, K. and Laird, S. A. (1999) *The Commercial Use of Biodiversity*, Earthscan, London

Tetetay, D. and Tegineh, A. (1991) 'Traditional tree crop base agroforestry in coffee producing areas of Harerge, Eastern Ethiopia', *Agroforestry Systems*, vol 16, no 3, pp257–267

Timbmet Group (2004) 'What do we know about the costs and benefits of tropical timber certification?', Oxford, www.fwi.or.id/sertifikasi/sertifikasi13.pdf

TNC (The Nature Conservancy) (2003) *Conservation Easements: Conserving Land, Water and a Way of Life*, www.nature.org/aboutus/howwework/conservationmethods/privatelands/conservationeasements/files/consrvtn_easemnt_sngle72.pdf, accessed 25 June 2010

TNC (The Nature Conservancy) (2010) *icms ecológico*, www.icmsecologico.org.br, accessed 10 October 2010

Trivedi M. R., Mitchell, A. W., Mardas, N., Parker, C., Watson, J. D. and Nobre, A. D. (2009) REDD and PINC: A new policy framework to fund tropical forests as global 'eco-utilities', http://iopscience.iop.org/1755-1315/8/1/012005/pdf/1755-1315_8_1_012005.pdf, accessed 28 October 2010

Turner, W. R., Brandon, K., Brooks, T. M., Costanza, R., da Fonseca, G. A. B. and Portela, R. (2007) 'Global conservation of biodiversity and ecosystem services', *BioScience*, vol 57, pp868–873

Turpie, J. K., Marais, C. and Blignaut, J. N. (2008) 'The working for water programme: Evolution of a payments for ecosystem services mechanism that addresses both poverty and ecosystem service delivery in South Africa', *Ecological Economics*, vol 65, no 4, pp788–798

UNECE (United Nations Economic Commission for Europe) and FAO (Food and Agriculture Organization) (2006) *Forest Products Annual Market Review: 2005–2006*, Geneva Timber and Forest Study Paper 21, United Nations Economic Commission for Europe/FAO, New York and Geneva

UNECE and FAO (2009) *Forest Products Annual Market Review: 2008–2009*, Geneva Timber and Forest Study, United Nations Economic Commission for Europe/Food and Agriculture Organization, New York and Geneva

UNEP (United Nations Environment Programme) (2008) *Entrepreneurs of the Natural World Showcase Their Groundbreaking Solutions to the Environmental Challenges of the 21st Century*, Bonn/Geneva/Nairobi, www.unep.org/Documents.Multilingual/Default.Print.asp?DocumentID=535&ArticleID=5816&l=fr

UNEP (2009a) *Benefit Sharing in ABS: Options and Elaborations*, United Nations Environment Programme and United Nations University Institute of Advanced Studies Report, Yokohama, Japan, www.ias.unu.edu/resource_centre/UNU_ABS_Report_Final_lowres.pdf, accessed July 30, 2010

UNEP (2009b) *Learning from the Practitioners: Benefit Sharing Perspectives from Enterprising Communities*, United Nations Environment Programme and United Nations University Institute of Advanced Studies Report, Yokohama, Japan, www.ias.unu.edu/resource_centre/UNU-UNEP_Learning_from_practitioners.pdf, accessed July 30, 2010

UNEP (2009c) *Global Green New Deal*, Policy Brief, p19, www.unep.org/pdf/GGND_Final_Report.pdf, accessed 17 August 2010

UNEP–WCMC (United Nations Environment Programme World Conservation Monitoring Centre) (2008) *Carbon and Biodiversity: A Demonstration Atlas*, (eds) V. Kapos, C. Ravilious, A. Campbell, B. Dickson, H. Gibbs, M. Hansen, I. Lysenko, L. Miles, J. Price, J. P. W. Scharlemann and K. Trumper, UNEP–WCMC, Cambridge

US Fish and Wildlife Service (2007) *2006 National Survey of Fishing, Hunting, and Wildlife-Associated Recreation: National Overview*, http://wsfrprograms.fws.gov/Subpages/NationalSurvey/nat_survey2006_final.pdf, accessed 10 November 2009

van Nierop, E. A., Alben, S. and Brenner, M. P. (2008) 'How bumps on whale flippers delay stall: An aerodynamic model', *Phys. Rev. Lett.*, vol 100, 054502

van Soest, D. P. and Lesink, R. (2000) 'Foreign transfers and tropical deforestation: What terms of conditionality?' *American Journal of Agricultural Economics*, vol 88, pp389–399

Vera, C., Baez, J., Douglas, M., Emmanuel, C. B., Marengo, J., Meitin, J., Nicolini, M., Nogues-Paegle, J., Paegle, J., Penalba, O., Salio, P., Saulo, C., Dias, M. A. S., Dias, P. S. and Zipser, E. (2006) 'The South American low-level jet experiment', *Bulletin of the American Meteorological Society*, vol 87, pp63–77, www.eol.ucar.edu/projects/mesa/documentation/salljex_paper_final.pdf, accessed 30 July 2010

Wertz-Kanounnikoff, S. (2006) 'Payments for environmental services: A solution for biodiversity conservation?', Idées pour le Débat 12/2006, Institut du développement durable et des relations internationales, Paris

Wertz-Kanounnikof, S. (2008) *Estimating the Costs of Reducing Forest Emissions: A Review of Methods*, CIFOR Working Paper No 42, Bogor, Indonesia

Whittlesey, R. W., Liska, S. and Dabiri, J. O. (2010) 'Fish schooling as a basis for vertical axis wind turbine farm design', *Bioinspiration and Biomimetics*, vol 5, http://dabiri.caltech.edu/publications/WhLiDa_BB10.pdf, accessed 22 September 2010

Willer, H. and Yussefi, M. (eds) (2007) *The World of Organic Agriculture: Statistics and Emerging Trends 2007* (9th edition) IFOAM (International Federation of Organic Agriculture Movements), Bonn, Germany

Williamson, O. (1979) 'Transaction cost economics: The governance of contractual relations', *Journal of Law and Economics*, vol 22, pp233–261

World Bank (2005) *Environmental Fiscal Reform: What Should Be Done and How to Achieve It*, Washington, DC

World Bank (2010) 'Climate Change: Uganda leads in cutting global warming emissions', Press Release No: 2010/093/AFR, http://beta.worldbank.org/climatechange/news/uganda-registers-first-forestry-project-africa-reduce-global-warming-emissions, accessed 22 September 2010

Wunder, S. (2005) *Payments for Environmental Services: Some Nuts and Bolts*, Occasional Paper No 42, CIFOR

Wunder, S. (2007) 'The efficiency of payments for environmental services in tropical conservation', *Conservation Biology*, vol 21, no 1, pp48–58

Wunder, S. (2008) 'Necessary conditions for ecosystem service payments', Paper presented at the Economics and Conservation in the Tropics: A Strategic Dialogue conference, Moore Foundation/CSF/RFF, San Francisco, 31 January to 1 February 2005, www.rff.org/News/Features/Pages/ConservationStrategiesintheTropics.aspx, accessed 10 November 2009

Wunder, S. and Wertz-Kanounnikoff, S. (2009) 'Payments for ecosystem services: A new way of conserving biodiversity in forests', *Journal for Sustainable Forestry*, vol 28, pp576–596

Wunder, S., Engel, S. and Pagiola, S. (2008) 'Taking stock: A comparative analysis of payments for environmental services programs in developed and developing countries', *Ecological Economics*, vol 65, no 4, pp834–52

Yoshida, K. (2010) *Economic Valuation of Biodiversity: Japanese Case Studies*, www.iges.or.jp/jp/news/event/20100218/biodiversity/pdf/Yoshida.pdf, acessed 14 July 2010

Yunus, M. (2007) *Creating a World Without Poverty*, Public Affairs, New York

Zanderson, M., Bråten, K. G. and Lindhjem, H. (2009) 'Payment for and management of ecosystem services, issues and options in the Nordic context', TeamNord 2009:571, Nordic Council of Ministers, Copenhagen

Zilberman, D., Lipper, L. and McCarthy, N. (2006) 'When are payments for environmental services beneficial to the poor?' ESA Working Paper No 06-04 (April), FAO, Rome

Chapter 6
Reforming Subsidies

Coordinating lead author
Markus Lehmann

Lead Author
Patrick ten Brink

Contributing authors
Samuela Bassi, David Cooper, Alexander Kenny, Sophie Kuppler,
Anja von Moltke, Sirini Withana

Editing and language check
Clare Shine

See end of chapter for acknowledgements for reviews and other contributions

Contents

Key messages   261

Summary   263

1   Subsidies and their implications   263
    1.1   What are subsidies?   263
    1.2   How big are existing subsidies?   264

2   Why do some subsidies miss their mark?   265
    2.1   Distinguishing between 'good' and 'bad' subsidies   265
    2.2   How subsidies can harm or benefit the environment   267

3   Specific impacts of subsidies across sectors   270
    3.1   Agriculture   270
    3.2   Fisheries   273
    3.3   Transport   277
    3.4   Water   278
    3.5   Energy   280

4   Making reform happen   283
    4.1   Analytical tools   283
    4.2   Resistance to change   284
    4.3   Organizing reform   287

5   Targeting subsidy reform at today's priorities   290

Acknowledgements   293

References   293

Key messages

The last decade has seen increased efforts to phase out or reform subsidies in some countries. Lessons learned indicate that subsidy reform or removal can alleviate environmental pressures, increase economic efficiency and reduce the fiscal burden.

Despite reductions in some sectors and countries, overall subsidies remain remarkably high. Conservative estimates point to hundreds of billions of dollars in annual subsidies, though most sectors face conceptual and data deficiencies in making accurate assessments. Agricultural subsidies in OECD countries averaged US$261 billion/year in 2006 to 2008 while global fisheries subsidies are estimated at US$15 billion to US$35 billion per year. Energy subsidies are around US$500 billion/year worldwide and reached US$310 billion in the 20 largest non-OECD countries in 2007 (see Table 6.1).

Many production subsidies serve to reduce costs or enhance revenues (e.g. most agricultural support measures in OECD countries). Together with below-cost pricing for natural resources, these effectively provide incentives for higher use, production and consumption of subsidized resources. This not only increases environmental damage but may also restrict the development and use of more sustainable technologies and processes. Globally, agricultural and fisheries subsidies are a particular cause for concern in this respect. Analyses of other sectoral subsidies highlight substantial potential for environmental gains through their reform.

Not all subsidies are bad for the environment. Some programmes already reward ecosystem benefits, such as transfer programmes in agriculture or forestry that compensate lost revenue or make payments in return for less harmful production methods. However, even 'green' subsidies can distort economies and markets and may not be well-targeted or cost-effective.

Comprehensive subsidy reform needs to go beyond the identification of environmentally harmful subsidies to cover subsidies that have clearly outlived their purpose, are not targeted at their stated objectives or do not meet their objectives cost-effectively. Such measures have opportunity costs: phasing out ineffective subsidies frees up funds which can be redirected to areas with more pressing funding needs. From the TEEB perspective, this includes rewarding the benefits provided by ecosystem services and biodiversity.

Successful reform depends on improving the quality and comprehensiveness of available data and analytical information. Transparency is essential for a well-informed public debate on current programmes and can provide a strong driver for change. Dialogue and communication with stakeholders is needed to develop a clear set of objectives and a timetable for reform.

With a few exceptions, progress on subsidy reform is too slow and protracted. In many countries, raising levels of public debt will require stringent budgetary consolidation policies in the coming years. Subsidy reform needs to be a key element of consolidation policies in order to free up increasingly scarce public resources for priority policy interventions.

The G20's recent commitment to phase out inefficient fossil fuel subsidies in the medium term is laudable and needs not only to be implemented but also urgently expanded to other relevant subsidies. At the global level, priorities to support better ecosystem and biodiversity conservation include removing capacity- or effort-enhancing fisheries subsidies, and continuing and deepening the reform of production-inducing agricultural subsidies, still prevalent in most OECD countries. Depending on national circumstances, most OECD countries also need to prioritize reform efforts in other subsidized sectors, particularly transport, water and energy. These sectors are also interesting candidates for subsidy reform in non-OECD countries, which need to determine priorities in the light of national circumstances.

In the short run, governments should establish transparent and comprehensive subsidy inventories and assess their effectiveness against stated objectives, cost-efficiency and environmental impacts – bearing in mind that the size of a subsidy does not necessarily reflect its harmful effects. Based on these assessments, governments should develop prioritized plans of action for subsidy removal or reform for implementation in the medium term (up to 2020). Windows of opportunity for earlier subsidy reform, arising within existing policy cycles, should be proactively and systematically seized.

Summary

Subsidies are often inefficient, expensive, socially inequitable and environmentally harmful, imposing a burden on government budgets and taxpayers – all strong arguments for reforming the existing subsidy policies. (OECD, 2005)

Chapter 6 addresses the need for comprehensive reform of subsidy policies to reduce harm to biodiversity and ecosystem services and make public expenditure more effective. Section 1 outlines the terminology and scale of current subsidies. Section 2 explains how these can fall short of their stated objectives, be cost-inefficient and impact on the environment. Section 3 provides a sector-by-sector breakdown, showing how subsidies can be better designed for social and environmental goals. Section 4 presents a roadmap for reform with guidance on tackling specific obstacles. Section 5 concludes the chapter with priority actions for the way ahead.

1 Subsidies and their implications

Subsidies have figured highly on the international agenda for 20 years. Studies by major international and non-governmental organizations in the 1990s led to considerable analytical work during the last decade on the implications of subsidies for cost-effective government expenditures, social objectives and the environment.

Practical guidance is now available on identifying and reforming environmentally harmful subsidies (EHS). This builds on the significant reform efforts made in several countries – efforts which, in some cases, have been successful. Lessons learned indicate that subsidy reform or removal can increase economic efficiency and reduce the burden on government budgets while alleviating environmental pressures.

1.1 What are subsidies?

Subsidies come in many shapes and forms. They can consist of direct transfers of funds and potential direct transfers to cover possible liabilities (e.g. for nuclear accidents), income or price support (e.g. for agricultural goods and water), tax credits, exemptions and rebates (e.g. for fuel), low-interest loans and guarantees, preferential treatment and use of regulatory support mechanisms (e.g. demand quotas). They can also involve implicit income transfers in situations where natural resources or services (e.g. water, energy) are not priced at full cost.

Some subsidies are *on-budget* (clearly visible in government budgets or can be estimated from budget accounts) while others are *off-budget* (not accounted for in national budgets).

There are two internationally agreed definitions of a subsidy but other key terms and definitions are used in specific contexts (see Box 6.1). Similarly, different measurement approaches are used for different purposes and sectors (e.g. international trade), each with its own specific indicators.

Box 6.1 Subsidies: Different definitions for different contexts

A subsidy is 'government action that confers an advantage on consumers or producers in order to supplement their income or lower their cost' (OECD, 2005).

The subsidy definition provided by the United Nations Statistics Division (UNSD) is used for constructing national accounts and covers only budgetary payments to producers. The more comprehensive World Trade Organization (WTO) definition is used for subsidies that affect trade and provides that 'a subsidy is a financial contribution by a government, or agent of a government, that confers a benefit on its recipients'. This definition excludes general infrastructure provided by government.

Different definitions are used in different contexts for specific purposes. Terms like 'transfers', 'payments', 'support measures', 'assistance' and 'protection' are all common and are sometimes used interchangeably, even though they refer to instruments that partially overlap and are associated with different methods of measurement and different indicators.

Not all contexts cover all issues. For example, the WTO definition does not include transfers from consumers to producers through border protection. This is one reason why the broader term 'support' is used in some contexts (e.g. OECD support estimates for agriculture).

One issue under debate is whether to expand the formal definition of a subsidy to include the non-internalization of external costs (e.g. where a polluter does not pay for damage resulting from pollution). Those who object do so for analytical clarity (i.e. the notion of a subsidy traditionally implies an explicit government intervention rather than implicit lack of intervention) and also point to the practical challenges of computing externalities. From the TEEB perspective, however, it is clear that non-internalization of externalities – or government inaction more generally – will frequently act like a subsidy (e.g. it lowers costs to polluters in the market and thereby confers an advantage on them).

1.2 How big are existing subsidies?

The overall level of global subsidies is enormous. Despite a slightly declining trend in some instances, they add up to hundreds of billions of dollars every year. Energy subsidies are the largest at around US$557 billion/year in 2008, followed by subsidies to agriculture (estimated at over US$250 billion/year in OECD countries alone). Subsidies to other sectors are also significant – and probably underestimated due to limited data and the specific measurement methodologies used (see Table 6.1).

These estimates give a useful indication of the order of magnitude of global subsidies but are still riddled with conceptual and data deficiencies.

The agricultural sector has the most complete data in terms of comprehensiveness and methodology as well as some of the highest subsidy levels. In contrast, other sectoral coverage remains rather patchy, even though considerable progress has been made in the last 20 years to formalize measurement methodologies.

Little or no subsidy data is available for large parts of the manufacturing sector or for other environmentally significant sectors like mining and forestry: data is also less comprehensive for water. This incomplete coverage reflects a lack of transparency in subsidy reporting as well as methodological constraints (OECD, 2003a; IEEP et al,

Table 6.1 Aggregate subsidy estimates for selected
economic sectors

Sector	Region
Agriculture	OECD: US$261 billion/year (2006–2008) (OECD, 2009)
Biofuels	US, EU and Canada: US$11 billion in 2006 (GSI, 2007; OECD, 2008b)
Energy	World: US$557 billion/year in 2008 (IEA, 2010)
Fisheries	World: US$15–US$35 billion/year (UNEP, 2008a)
Transport	World: US$238–US$306 billion/year, of which EHS are estimated at US$173–US$233 billion/year (Kjellingbro and Skotte, 2005)
Water	World: US$67 billion/year, of which EHS are estimated at US$50 billion/year (Myers and Kent, 1998)

2007; Valsecchi et al, 2009). Table 6.1 arguably presents an underestimate for the
level of water subsidies. Conversely, transport subsidy data may contain elements of
over-estimation because measurement methodologies for this sector often include non-
internalized externalities. For these reasons, comparing subsidies across sectors is
often difficult or potentially biased.

2 Why do some subsidies miss their mark?

2.1 Distinguishing between 'good' and 'bad' subsidies

Subsidies are introduced or maintained for various social or economic reasons: to
promote economic growth, secure employment or stabilize incomes by helping small
producers. These are all 'good' – or at least politically rational – purposes.

All too often, however, subsidies end up as long-term rigidities that distort prices
and adversely affect resource allocation decisions, benefiting some producers to the
detriment of others (including foreign producers). For analytical purposes, it is
therefore important to distinguish between the stated objectives of subsidies and their
actual effects.

The difference between 'good' and 'bad' subsidies often comes down to their
specific design and implementation. Key questions (Pieters, 2003) include:

- Effectiveness: do they serve (or continue to serve) their intended purpose?
- Efficiency: at what cost?
- Equity: how are the costs and benefits distributed?
- Environmental impact: last but not least, are they harmful for the environment in
  general and for ecosystem services and biodiversity in particular?

Answering these questions requires a careful assessment covering all three dimensions
of sustainable development (economic, environmental and social) (De Moor and
Calamai, 1997; OECD, 2005). The assessment process can help identify priorities for
phasing out or reform (e.g. subsidies that have clearly outlived their rationale). When

a subsidy programme is launched, policy makers are often not fully aware of all its implications, including the risk of environmentally harmful effects. Strategic impact assessments based on forecasts, undertaken as an integral part of policy formulation, can help minimize or avoid such effects and many of the other pitfalls associated with subsidies (see Chapter 4). They can also help identify opportunities for better instrument design.

In reality, subsidy programmes rarely seek to implement a single clearly defined policy objective. They tend to have a long, complex and somewhat chaotic history, having been introduced and amended over decades, often under political pressure, without a long-term strategic vision and for multiple objectives (Barde and Honkatukia, 2003).

This mix of explicit and implicit objectives sometimes creates a daunting barrier to reform. It means that subsidies can too easily be presented as 'multifunctional' – the argument being that we cannot afford to remove them. Disentangling the effects and purposes of subsidies and separating myths from reality are important preconditions for successful reform. This makes the issue of cost-effectiveness in achieving stated goals a very useful test (OECD, 2003a).

We can see this clearly by looking at subsidies defended on social grounds (e.g. to support smaller marginal producers in critical sectors such as agriculture or fisheries). A careful analysis of their distributive effects reveals that many subsidies are not well targeted, which means they may not be very cost-effective. In agriculture, for example, a 2003 study showed that most subsidies in OECD countries went to larger farms (which tend to be richer) and that only 25 per cent of market price support ended up as net income gain for farmers (i.e. the bulk of the difference ended up somewhere else in the value chain) (OECD, 2003c).

Box 6.2 provides another illustration of poor targeting, this time with regard to energy subsidies in developing countries.

Whenever social objectives are presented as justification for subsidies, the general rule is that the transfer effects of such subsidies should be at least neutral or, even better, contribute towards more equal distribution of wealth or income. Put simply, subsidies

---

Box 6.2 Estimated distributional impact of energy subsidies in four developing countries (2005)

- In Bolivia, the poorest 40 per cent of households receive 15 per cent of the total benefits from fuel subsidies; the richest 60 per cent of households get 85 per cent.
- In Gabon, it is estimated that the richest 10 per cent of households capture 33 per cent of fuel subsidies, while the poorest 30 per cent (below the poverty line) receive merely 13 per cent.
- In Ghana, the poorest 40 per cent of households get 23 per cent and the richest 60 per cent capture 77 per cent of the benefits of fuel subsidies.
- In Ethiopia, the highest-income 20 per cent of the population capture 44 per cent of fuel subsidies, while the lowest-income 20 per cent get less than 9 per cent).

Source: Coady et al (2006); Rijal (2007)

should work to the benefit (or at least not the detriment) of socially marginalized populations. This is frequently not the case. Subsidies that disadvantage such populations are prime candidates to consider for prioritized removal or reform (Steenblik, 2007).

Subsidies are embedded in the policy landscape in most countries and are linked in different ways to a range of other instruments, reflecting different regulatory styles and traditions. Their effects and the potential benefits of their removal or reform – as well as the associated challenges – need to be understood in the context of these interconnections.

Since subsidies are typically funded through either taxes or deficits, they put considerable strain on governmental coffers and ultimately on taxpayers. Conversely, phasing out a subsidy frees up funds which can help smooth the transition and/or mobilize public support for wider subsidy reform. The funds released can be used for different purposes:

- for general deficit reduction or lowering taxes;
- to fund alternative policies that target the original objectives of the subsidy more cost-effectively;
- to be redirected to areas with more pressing funding needs – e.g. to reward benefits of ecosystem services and biodiversity (see Chapter 5).

2.2 How subsidies can harm or benefit the environment

An environmentally harmful subsidy (EHS) is 'a result of a government action that confers an advantage on consumers or producers in order to supplement their income or lower their costs but, in doing so, discriminates against sound environmental practices'. This definition draws on OECD definitions of a 'subsidy' (OECD, 1998, 2005).

Some subsidy types have been identified as critical drivers of activities that are harmful to ecosystems and biodiversity, resulting in losses of ecosystem services. They negatively impact the environment in two ways.

1 Underpricing the use of natural resources

Even without subsidies, the price charged for using natural resources, if any, rarely reflects their real value in terms of the ecosystem services that they provide. However, too low a price leads to over-consumption. This results from free markets that fail to incorporate negative externalities and from poorly defined property rights (see Chapters 2 and 7). Subsidies can aggravate this problem by reducing the price even further to below extraction cost. They often benefit consumers of services (e.g. provision of water and energy at low prices) which can in turn lead to increased production where subsidized resources are used as an input (e.g. irrigation subsidies to agriculture, energy subsidies to industry in general).

2 Increasing production

Many policies providing subsidies in OECD countries are implemented to support environmentally sensitive sectors, e.g. agriculture, fisheries, energy production, transport and heavy industry. Support measures that reduce costs or enhance revenue for producers provide incentives to produce in larger quantities than in the absence of the subsidy. This leads to increased use of possibly polluting inputs (e.g. pesticides, fertilizers) and higher production levels, which in turn aggravates the risk of environmental damage. Specific environmental impacts across sectors are described in Section 3.

Support that is not conditional on production or input levels tends to be less environmentally damaging than other support mechanisms, although the overall level of the subsidy is also relevant.

The size of a subsidy does not necessarily reflect the extent of its harmful effect (OECD, 2003a). Even relatively small subsidies can have a major negative impact. For example, subsidies paid to high-seas bottom-trawl fleets operating outside the Exclusive Economic Zones (EEZ) of maritime countries amount to around US$152 million/year (Sumaila et al, 2006). Bottom-trawling practices have a major impact on the habitat of deep-sea fish species which, with their long life span and low growth rate, are particularly vulnerable.

Quantifying subsidy impacts on ecosystems and biodiversity is difficult due to the complexity of the analysis:

- First, the effects of subsidies on consumption and production depend on many factors, including 'price elasticities' (the relative increase in demand or supply of a good, due to relative price changes), 'leakages' (of support away from the intended targets of the subsidy) and the specific regulatory, tax and policy system in place.
- Second, there are often several contributing factors, making it very challenging to disentangle the direct causality between subsidies and the exact extent of their environmentally harmful effects.
- Third, ecosystem functioning is not fully understood. The strain put on ecosystems by increased production and consumption affects intricate interlinkages of species in ways that are hard to predict and quantify. For instance, there may be 'threshold' levels of pollution and environmental damage beyond which adverse effects on biodiversity increase substantially.

The associated uncertainty, the possibility of irreversible damage and the alarming rate of current biodiversity loss all demonstrate the need to apply a precautionary approach. This could include reversing the burden of proof for damage, i.e. requiring potentially damaging subsidy programmes to show, where appropriate, that they are not harmful to the environment (OECD, 2003a).

All subsidies operate in the larger context of what Pieters calls a 'policy filter'. This includes a range of environmental policy tools, such as sustainability criteria (see UNEP and WWF, 2007), environmental taxes, charges or fees, production/extraction limits, emissions standards and tradable pollution quota (Pieters, 2003). These tools may counteract (some of) the adverse incentives created by subsidies but their application is not always successful. Success depends on effective monitoring and ensuring compliance, which can be too costly or beyond the institutional capacity of many states. Moreover, analysis of the political economy of subsidies suggests that, in the presence of large potential profits created by subsidies, lobbying by beneficiaries can lead to weak regulation.

It is important to stress that not all subsidies are bad for the environment. Some are used to correct specific market failures. For example, road transport and its environmentally harmful effects would further increase if public transport were not subsidized: removing or reducing support to private passenger transport, road haulage and air transport can potentially provide environmental benefits. In the energy sector, many countries have substantial programmes to support renewable energy development and production – although the claimed environmental benefits for some programmes seem unclear (see below).

Subsidy programmes are already used to generate ecosystem benefits. A prime example concerns transfers to farmers under agri-environment programmes that compensate lost revenue (income forgone) arising from adoption of less harmful production methods. In a growing number of cases – e.g. payments for watershed protection to improve water provision to cities – such transfers can be characterized as payments for ecosystem services (see Chapter 5). Where there is a specific focus on increasing ecosystem service provision to provide a public good, the term 'subsidy' is arguably not appropriate.

However, even 'green' subsidies can still distort economies and markets and may not be well-targeted or cost-effective. This is not surprising as there is no proven reason why 'green' subsidies should be superior in this respect. In some cases, they can even have unintended secondary impacts on the environment. In the fisheries sector, for example, vessel decommissioning schemes aim to reduce fishing capacity in order to reduce pressure on fish stocks, but may create additional rent that is reinvested in the same or another fishery (UNEP, 2004a). For these reasons, even 'green' subsidies, supporting public transport or renewable energies, for example, need to be examined carefully (OECD, 2005).

It is important not to limit subsidy reform to environmentally harmful subsidies alone but to aim for a more comprehensive review process because:

- The identification and reform of ineffective and inefficient subsidies, even if not EHS, can free up considerable funds which could be used for more pressing environmental needs.
- Ensuring that 'green' subsidies are targeted and cost-effective will strengthen their case in the eternal tug-of-war over scarce public resources.

As repeatedly emphasized by the OECD in the context of agricultural production (e.g. OECD, 2003b, 2009), it is the coherence of the overall policy package that matters. 'Green' subsidies will remain higher than necessary for as long as they are used to offset damage caused by support policies that stimulate harmful production. Simply introducing new 'green' subsidies without analysing and reforming the entire subsidy landscape runs a high and foreseeable risk of not being cost-effective.

Last, data gaps and lack of certainty over the specific size of subsidies should not delay action to identify and remove or reform subsidies identified as environmentally harmful and/or not cost-effective. With fisheries on the verge of collapse, CO_2 emissions on the rise and the international community having missed the CBD's target to significantly reduce the rate of loss of biological diversity by 2010, 'there is little need to calculate our precise speed when heading over a cliff' (Myers and Kent, 1998).

3 Specific impacts of subsidies across sectors

3.1 Agriculture

Agricultural subsidies are among the largest and need special attention because of the sector's critical importance for food security and development. Incentives to produce can lead to increased damage, typically by stimulating intensification and/or expansion.

Intensification

Intensification refers to an increase of agricultural production on a given area (e.g. application of more fertilizers and other chemicals, more irrigation, more mechanization). The most significant environmental impacts can include:

- loss of non-target species, including pollinators, due to direct and indirect effects of pesticides;
- reduced habitat diversity due to consolidation of holdings, removal of patches of non-farmed habitats and boundary features, and greater regional specialization;
- loss of biodiversity-rich extensive farmlands (e.g. semi-natural grasslands) due to increased fertilizer use or increased grazing;
- hydrological changes to habitats as a result of drainage or irrigation (e.g. leading to wetland loss and reductions in groundwater levels from over-abstraction);
- eutrophication of freshwater and marine ecosystems from fertilizers and nutrient-rich run-off;
- eutrophication of terrestrial ecosystems from deposition of airborne nutrients, particularly ammonia, from intensive livestock systems; and
- soil degradation and erosion.

Expansion

Expansion, linked to incentives to increase production, may encourage the conversion of more natural ecosystems into farming areas (land-use change). Conversely, subsidy removal or reform could lead to contraction of agricultural land. This could have positive impacts for ecosystems and biodiversity in areas of highly mechanized and specialized production, provided that effective long-term conservation policies are in place to restore the original non-agricultural habitats, e.g. wetlands (George and Kirkpatrick, 2003). However, contraction could have negative biodiversity impacts in extensive farming regions where traditional practices play a key role in creating site-specific biodiversity, soil properties and landscape amenities (OECD, 2003d; EEA, 2004; UNEP, 2004). High nature value (HNV) farmlands include semi-natural areas and features like hedges, walls, trees and buffer zones created as an integral part of farm management. In such regions, high agrobiodiversity depends on continuing these practices (see Box 6.3).

Extensive farming systems with high agricultural biodiversity are often located on marginal land (i.e. land that would be taken out of production first if subsidies were removed). In some cases, stopping production could therefore actually have negative effects on biodiversity with subsequent losses of related ecosystem services (OECD, 2000c).

Box 6.3 The EU Common Agricultural Policy (CAP) and its impacts on biodiversity

The CAP stimulated important structural shifts in farming, investment and technological development which led to widespread agricultural intensification in the EU, with well-documented impacts on biodiversity, including birds, since the 1970s. The Pan-European Common Bird Monitoring Scheme (2007) shows that the farmland bird index (an indicator of the health of European farmland ecosystems) has declined by almost 50 per cent in the last 25 years. Non-crop plants and invertebrates have also declined massively, mainly due to fertilizer and pesticide use.

Many of the remaining species-rich agricultural habitats are rare or much reduced. A high proportion of rare and vulnerable species of EU importance are associated with these threatened semi-natural habitats and agricultural landscapes. Many of these habitats and HNV farming systems, if not threatened by intensification, are at risk of abandonment as they are typically of marginal economic value. Their continuation depends on CAP payments designed to support farming in disadvantaged areas or to support environmentally beneficial practices (see also Box 6.5).

The close links between biodiversity and extensive farming on marginal land therefore raise a dual policy challenge:

- to keep these marginal lands under production and preserve traditional practices;
- to take infra-marginal lands out of production that could deliver significant positive impacts for biodiversity if converted into natural habitats.

This does not imply general support for production-inducing subsidies but recognizes that subsidy reduction or removal is not enough, in isolation, to meet the challenge of maintaining biodiversity-rich extensive farming systems.

As with other subsidies, production-increasing support is more environmentally harmful than support that is 'decoupled' from production. Since the 1990s, spurred on by the WTO Uruguay Agreement on Agriculture which exempts measures in the so-called 'Green Box' from its disciplines, many OECD countries have redesigned their support policies in favour of more decoupled measures (see Box 6.4).

Progress is clearly being made. In 2006 to 2008, 51 per cent of farm support measures as measured by the OECD Producer Support Estimate (PSE) took the form of output-based payments (e.g. market price support) or payments based on variable inputs (e.g. to reduce the price paid for fertilizers, feed, seeds, water, transportation, etc.). This was down from 82 per cent in 1986 to 1988. This reduction reflects a general decline in the relative level of support for production as a percentage of total farm receipts (down from 37 per cent in 1986 to 1988 to 23 per cent today) (OECD, 2009).

However, more reform efforts are needed.

First, over half of all support still directly increases production. The OECD has cautioned that progress on reform is uneven between OECD countries and notes that a significant part of the recent decline in support levels is a consequence of high world

---

Box 6.4 Reforming production subsidies: The EU CAP and the Agenda 2000 reforms

Rural development policy ('the second pillar') has become an essential component of the EU CAP, alongside the 'first pillar' of market measures. The Agenda 2000 reform foresaw gradual reductions in market price support and increasing reliance on direct payments, coupled with rural development programmes and agri-environmental measures.

In 2003, after difficult negotiations, EU farm ministers adopted a compromise providing for:

- the introduction of a single farm payment for farmers, independent of production under the CAP first pillar, whose level would be based on historical support payments;
- linkage of this payment to compliance with environmental, food safety, animal health and animal welfare standards ('cross-compliance');
- a reduction in direct payments to bigger farms ('modulation'), with this money being transferred to the European Agricultural Fund for Rural Development to finance the new rural development policy; and
- some revisions to the CAP's market policy.

The 2008 agreement pursuant to the CAP Health Check provides, among other measures, for phasing out some remaining coupled payments as well as increased modulation.

Many agri-environment programmes under the second pillar have generally positive impacts for biodiversity and ecosystems (Boccaccio et al, 2009). However, eight years after the introduction of this reform, most support still comes under the first pillar even though the second pillar is gradually approaching an equal share. Although less environmentally harmful than earlier support policies, the sheer magnitude of support under the first pillar gives reason for concern, because of the limits to decoupling as well as opportunity cost considerations. While cross-compliance and modulation do contribute to better targeting of payments for environmental and social objectives (see Alliance Environnement, 2007), it is doubtful whether these instruments currently maximize the cost-effectiveness of payments for such objectives.

---

prices for agricultural commodities, without any explicit changes in government policies (OECD, 2009).

Second, decoupling can never be complete because of real-world phenomena like market imperfections, risk and political dynamics (OECD, 2000b). Under imperfect capital markets, for instance, any kind of income support would be partially reinvested in agriculture, generating additional production in future years. If wealthier farmers are ready to assume more risks, any payment – by increasing their wealth – will affect their production decisions (OECD, 2000b). Scale also matters: even relatively small impacts can add up to a large aggregate distortion if the overall volume of the subsidy is high. These distortions may include the production decisions of potential foreign competitors.

Better targeting of decoupled support measures for specific income objectives or market failures thus remains a major challenge of ongoing policy reforms in OECD countries (OECD, 2009). This includes agri-environment payments. A 2005 analysis of such payments in the EU noted generally positive effects on habitat preservation, but called for the development of more impact-oriented monitoring, better-adapted evaluation procedures and better targeting of measures for the most problematic farms and most environmentally sensitive areas (Oréade-Breche, 2005). The OECD stresses that decoupling and targeting are policy principles that have been shown to improve effectiveness, efficiency and equity and should continue to inspire future policy design (OECD, 2009).

Support measures that encourage agricultural production are considered to distort potential trade flows and are therefore intended for 'substantial reductions' in the agricultural trade negotiations under the WTO Doha work programme. These negotiations also seek to review and clarify the Green Box criteria, which define the type of agricultural payments that are free from reduction commitments while ensuring that due account is taken of non-trade concerns, including environmental objectives (WTO, 2004). The successful conclusion of these negotiations could create synergy with ecosystem and biodiversity protection objectives but the positions of WTO members are currently still divergent and the agricultural negotiations remain one of the major stumbling blocks to the successful conclusion of the Doha work programme.

3.2 Fisheries

> More than a decade after adoption of the 1995 U.N. Code of Conduct for Responsible Fisheries, putting an end to overfishing remains a fundamental global challenge ... Progress towards improved fisheries subsidies policies has been made since 1997 ... but the real work of ending harmful fisheries subsidies has just barely begun. (Achim Steiner, UNEP Executive Director, and James P. Leape, WWF Executive Director; UNEP and WWF, 2007)

Subsidies to fisheries are significant in terms of their potential impact on the environment and also in relation to the size of the industry in several countries (e.g. in some EU Member States, fisheries subsidies are higher than the economic value of landings).

It is particularly urgent to address their negative environmental impacts as over one-quarter of global marine fisheries are close to collapse or have already collapsed. According to the 2008 Fisheries Report by the Food and Agriculture Organization of the United Nations (FAO):

- In 2007, 28 per cent of marine capture fish stocks monitored by FAO were over-exploited, depleted or recovering from depletion and were yielding less than their maximum sustainable yield.
- An additional 52 per cent were fully exploited, producing at or close to their maximum sustainable yield.
- The remaining 20 per cent were under-exploited or moderately exploited. Although this figure might imply that more could be produced, it must be borne in mind that some of these stocks are low-value species or consist of species for which harvesting may be uneconomic under current market conditions (FAO, 2008b; see also Figure 1.4 in Chapter 1).

There is universal acceptance in relevant literature that some types of fisheries subsidies can lead to increased fishing effort and thus have negative impacts on the level of fish stocks (UNEP, 2004a; von Moltke, 2010). Excessive capacity or catching power of global fishing fleets has been identified as a main cause of unsustainable fishing levels (Porter, 2001). While industrial fleets play the dominant role in overfishing due to their technology and size, the small-scale fishing sector sometimes plays a role too (see Box 6.5).

Box 6.5 The environmental impact of subsidies to the small-scale sector in Senegal

In the late 1970s, the Senegalese authorities started to provide direct support to fisheries, initially to the industrial sub-sector only, but later to small-scale fisheries as well. In consequence, the small-scale sector began to produce more for export than domestic markets. Fishing effort of small-scale units intensified, aggravating the pressure already exerted on demersal fish stocks by Senegalese and foreign trawler fleets. By 2003, factories received 60 per cent of their supply from small-scale fishing units. Most marketed species in this category are now in danger of biological collapse.

Source: UNEP (2003a)

Despite considerable overcapacity in the fishing industry, however, governments continue to subsidize the sector. This encourages further fishing effort which contributes to the decline in global stocks. Paradoxically, the industry is being undermined by the very subsidies supposed to protect incomes in the industry (OECD, 2003a; see also Box 6.6). Nowhere is the link between sustainable resource use and protection of livelihoods more visible than in former fishing regions where fisheries have already collapsed.

Box 6.6 Sunken billions

The contribution of the world's marine fisheries harvest sector to the global economy is substantially smaller than it could be. Using a stylized and simple model, a World Bank report estimates the lost economic benefits to be in the order of US$50 billion annually – representing the difference between the potential and actual net economic benefits from global marine fisheries.

Despite increased fishing effort, the global marine catch has been stagnant for over a decade. At the same time, natural fish capital – the wealth of the oceans – has declined and the margin has narrowed between the global cost of catching and the value of the catch. These lost benefits can be largely attributed to two factors. First, depleted fish stocks mean that there are simply less fish to catch and the cost of catching is therefore higher. Second, massive fleet overcapacity – 'too many fishers chasing too few fish' – means that potential benefits are also dissipated through excessive fishing effort.

Sources: World Bank (2008); FAO (2008a)

To help assess the impact of fisheries subsidies on stocks and the environment generally, we can conceptually distinguish different management regimes (though stylized, they reflect key features of real world management regimes; Hannesson, 2001; OECD, 2006b).

Under pure open access, standard economic analysis shows that over-exploitation of the resource results even without subsidies. However, it is generally agreed that introduction of some subsidies would make a bad situation worse by further increasing exploitation (OECD, 2000a; WTO, 2000; Munro and Sumaila, 2002; UNEP, 2004a). This would be true for any subsidy that:

- increases the producer price of the resource (i.e. the price for fish received by fishermen);
- reduces the operating costs per unit (i.e. per fishing vessel); or
- reduces the purchase price of vessel capital (Munro and Sumaila, 2002).

According to FAO data, it can be estimated that approximately 90 per cent of global fish production comes from within the 200 nautical mile EEZ of coastal states that, consistent with the UN Convention on the Law of the Sea (UNCLOS), comes under national jurisdiction (FAO, 2008b). If national authorities could retain tight control over the Total Allowable Catch (TAC) in their EEZ, subsidies should have very limited consequences on those fish stocks and, in many cases, would prove to be neutral provided that the TAC was fixed at sustainable levels (Munro and Sumaila, 2002; UNEP, 2004a; OECD, 2006b).

In practice, however, such tight control over TAC is very difficult to achieve and further complicated by subsidies. Fisheries with excessive capacity put strong pressure on the individual fisher's profits and increase the incentive to exceed catch limits and under-report catch. This aggravates monitoring and enforcement problems in coastal states. The value of illegal, unreported and unregulated (IUU) fishing is currently estimated at US$10 billion to US$23.5 billion per year (Agnew et al, 2009).

Furthermore, if there is no additional control on fishing effort, additional labour and capital will be attracted to the sector to the point where resource rents are competed away. The resulting overcapacity will, in turn, often generate political pressure on fishery authorities to set TAC beyond sustainable levels (WTO, 2000).

In principle, TAC control could be supplemented with additional controls over fishing effort (e.g. restrictions on the number of vessels, the amount of time they are allowed to fish and on fishing gear and techniques). However, despite the best efforts of regulators, it is not always possible to identify and control all the variables that determine fishing effort. As the fishing industry adapts to new restrictions, this can lead to a race between development and application of new regulations on the one hand and the implementation of effort-increasing measures by fishers on the other. This phenomenon aggravates the ever-present limitations in monitoring and enforcement capacity.

Given such constraints, capacity-enhancing subsidies should generally be seen as environmentally harmful. These include (see further UNEP, 2004a):

- Subsidies for fleet expansion and modernization (grants, low-interest loans, loan guarantees) as these reduce the purchase price of vessel capital.

- Payments to countries for the exploitation of fish stocks in their EEZ by foreign fishing fleets. These constitute subsidies to the relevant fishing industry if not fully recovered from the relevant companies.
- Tax preferences for intermediate inputs (e.g. fuel) which reduce operating costs per vessel. Empirical studies confirm that such tax preferences encourage the purchase of vessels with larger engines that, in turn, increase fishing range and enable larger catches.

One 2007 study has estimated global fisheries subsidies at US$30 billion to US$34 billion per year, of which at least US$22 billion contributes to overcapacity (see Box 6.7).

Box 6.7 Fisheries subsidies: The good, the bad, and the ugly

A 2007 study by the University of British Columbia classifies and analyses fisheries subsidies by their effects and impacts.

'Good' subsidies encourage the growth of fish stocks by supporting conservation activities and monitoring catch rates through management programmes, services and research.

'Bad' subsidies reduce the cost or enhance the revenue of fishing activities, thus exacerbating overcapacity.

'Ugly' subsidies are programmes that have the potential to increase capacity and result in harmful impacts, depending on the context and application (e.g. vessel buy-back schemes or fisher assistance programmes).

The study estimates the worldwide level of fisheries subsidies at US$30 billion to US$34 billion per year of which US$16 billion are bad subsidies (US$6 billion are for fuel alone). A further US$3.4 billion are characterized as 'ugly' subsidies, i.e. potentially harmful depending on the context and programme. Only US$6.6 billion are characterized as 'good' subsidies.

Source: Sumaila and Pauly (2007)

Removing subsidies will make the task of effective management easier, but in itself will not be effective in achieving conservation goals if the underlying management regime is not also fixed at the same time (see Boxes 6.8 and 6.15).

Some progress has been made in the current WTO negotiations on fisheries subsidies. There is broad support among WTO members for strong rules (or 'disciplines') on fisheries subsidies, although some developing country members wish to keep policy space for subsidies deemed necessary for diversification and development of certain industries. It is widely recognized, nevertheless, that any subsidies permitted should not lead to overcapacity and overfishing.

A key element in this respect has been the development of 'sustainability criteria' by UNEP and WWF which can help ensure that subsidies falling outside a possible WTO ban do not have harmful impacts on fisheries resources (UNEP and WWF, 2007).

Box 6.8 Removing fishery subsidies in Norway

Norway's experience shows that it is possible to drastically reduce subsidies – which had seemingly become a permanent lifeline – without destroying the industry. From a peak of US$150 million/year in 1981 (approximately 70 per cent of value added in the industry), subsidies were reduced to only US$30 million by 1994. This successful reform was probably made easier by timing and measures that smoothed the transition to a more self-supporting industry. Although the number of fishers has declined, the fisheries sector is now self-supporting and in many ways healthier than at the height of subsidies.

Norway's success was due to several factors:

- Optional employment opportunities existed for fishers who lost out in the immediate aftermath of the subsidy removals, as the reforms were undertaken during good economic times.
- The fall in oil prices in 1986 deprived the government of revenue and convinced many of the need for significant reform.
- There was external pressure in the form of various multilateral agreements.
- The transition was gradual, which helped fishers to take steps to prepare for the changes.

The government combined the transition with other social measures to lessen the impact on those who had come to depend on the subsidies.

Source: OECD (2006b)

3.3 Transport

The transport sector is a major contributor to global greenhouse gas (GHG) emissions, local air pollution and noise emissions but still benefits from large subsidies.

One group of subsidies takes the form of fuel prices kept below production cost. By increasing vehicle use and travel, these aggravate air pollution (i.e. release of noxious gases such as nitrogen oxides (NO_x), non-methane volatile organic compounds (NMVOCs) and sulphur dioxide emissions as well as particulates). Vehicles are a major source of GHG emissions: by 2020, global CO_2 emissions from motor vehicles are projected to increase by approximately 83 per cent from 1995 levels (IEA, 2005). Transport-related emissions have important direct and indirect impacts for ecosystems and biodiversity.

Another type of subsidy includes direct grants for building road infrastructure not recovered by receipts (through e.g. fuel taxes or charges) and for roads that are not deemed general infrastructure. This is a grey area as some roads ostensibly provide a general infrastructure service, even though in practice access to remote areas may disproportionately benefit specific industries such as mining or forestry.

Land-use change linked to transport infrastructure construction can threaten biodiversity where encroachment destroys habitats and affects the viability of ecosystems and species populations. Road building creates physical barriers to wildlife movement and fragments previously continuous blocks of habitat into smaller areas that may be less able to support complex communities of plants and animals (e.g. a study on forest fragmentation in six central African countries found that roads have reduced the proportion of forest in large unfragmented blocks from 83 per cent to 49 per cent of the total forest area (WRI, 2001). Removing ecological 'corridors' may isolate members of a species genetically and geographically (Fahrig, 2003; Crooks and Sanjayan, 2006; and Kettunen et al, 2007, for a European perspective). Because populations tend to decrease in smaller fragments of habitat, this will increasingly threaten species requiring large home ranges.

A recent study on deforestation patterns in 152 countries showed that road construction and improvement is one of the three main proximate causes of deforestation. By reducing transport costs, these roads promote forestry in remote areas, open up areas of undisturbed mature forests to pioneer settlement, logging and agricultural clearance, and provide access for hunters and poachers. The study recommended that a key government reform to slow tropical forest deforestation would be to reduce or eliminate expenditure on road building near priority conservation areas and to reduce fossil fuel and transport cost subsidies: in general, infrastructure expenditure would be less harmful to the environment if it were focused on already opened-up areas (CIFOR, 2006).

As noted in Section 1, subsidies to some types of transport may be beneficial to the environment (e.g. those to railways and public transport can reduce car use as well as emissions and local air pollution).

3.4 Water

Water services provision is subsidized by charging rates that do not cover operating and management costs (below-cost pricing), possibly combined with preferential treatment for some user groups (e.g. lower rates for irrigation water). In many countries, water charges have historically been – and in some cases still are – very low. This reflects the view that the provision of such basic services is a duty of government and access is considered a right.

Although water subsidies are often justified on social grounds, particularly for drinking water, they often do not reach poor consumers effectively at present. In many developing countries the poor do not have access to piped water networks and many pay considerably more for water as they have to rely on private vendors. A World Bank study on consumption subsidies for electricity and water in four African countries found that despite sizeable subsidy levels, only 20 to 30 per cent of poor households were connected to the utility networks (Komives et al, 2005).

Below-cost pricing, together with low collection rates, results in cash-strapped utilities which can lead to inadequate operation and maintenance. An estimated 40 to 60 per cent of water delivered by utilities in developing countries is lost due to leakage, theft and poor accounting (UNEP, 2003b). Moreover, such utilities rarely have the necessary funds to expand the network to the poorest neighbourhoods.

Below-cost pricing leads to over-use and wastage. Associated impacts include falling water tables, reduced availability for other user groups, additional investment needs for water provision (e.g. wells for farmers and households) and in some cases, damage to the aquifer itself (saltwater intrusion, increased pollution). Reforming water subsidies is increasingly urgent in the light of climate change: by 2050, the IPCC projects that the area of land subject to increasing water stress will be more than double the land with decreasing water stress (IPCC, 2008).

In the agriculture sector, the price of irrigation water has generally been low in many countries and its use consequently high (e.g. Spain; Bassi et al, 2010). Irrigation accounts for 75 to 90 per cent of total water use in developing countries and for over one-third of water use in many OECD countries (IISD, 2008). Once again, irrigation subsidies are often justified on social grounds (i.e. the need to support low-income farmers). However, subsidies usually benefit all farmers indiscriminately and tend to exacerbate the waste of often limited water resources and encourage cultivation of water-intensive crops.

Area-based tariffs for irrigation water are far more common than other payment schemes (e.g. charges based on volume of water used). Schemes not based on volume give less incentive to conserve water, exacerbated by subsidized tariffs. One study of irrigation projects in Brazil revealed that the single most important cause of water over-use was the excessive length of irrigation time (OECD, 2003a).

Water scarcity can be aggravated by the cultivation of water-intensive crops, especially where climate conditions and rainfall patterns should dictate otherwise, and the outright waste of water. In Europe as a whole, agriculture accounts for about 24 per cent of total water use but this reaches up to 80 per cent in parts of Southern Europe (EEA, 2009) where crops like corn and strawberries are still grown despite evidence of desertification. Water scarcity is expected to further increase in these already semi-arid or arid areas. The Mediterranean basin, together with the western US, southern Africa and north-eastern Brazil, are particularly exposed to the impacts of climate change, which is projected to further decrease their water resources (IPCC, 2007).

The negative impact of subsidized prices on water resources is increasingly recognized and several countries are moving towards full cost recovery. Mexico is often cited as an example of a country that, after wide-scale reform of the agriculture sector, has substantially reduced irrigation subsidy levels, with many schemes now achieving financial self-sufficiency (Kloezen, 2002; Cornish et al, 2004). The EU Water Framework Directive (EC, 2000) requires EU Member States to take into account the principle of full cost recovery in water pricing policies to promote more efficient use of resources (see also Boxes 6.9 and 6.10, and Chapter 7).

Box 6.9 Reforming water subsidies in the Czech Republic

Until 1990, water pricing covered only a fraction of its real cost as it was only €0.02 per m³. This low price led to indirect subsidization of water extraction, treatment and distribution. This hidden subsidy was removed in the 1990s, moving to full cost recovery. By 2004 the cost of water had reached €0.71 per m³. The reform also addressed fees for withdrawing surface and ground water and discharge of wastewater. Between 1990 and 1999, water withdrawals decreased by 88 per cent in agriculture, 47 per cent in industry and 34 per cent in public water mains.

Source: IEEP et al (2007)

Box 6.10 Targeting water pricing against social objectives

Maltese water pricing uses a 'rising block' system where at lower levels of household water use, the rate per m³ is significantly lower than for higher use. In 2000 there were nearly 13,000 accounts in the social assistance category. This group represented around 4 per cent of total water use in Malta and around 6 per cent of domestic use. The average consumption charge for the social assistance tranche was €0.56/m³, while for the general residential sector it was €0.79/m³. Rates are higher for higher levels of consumption, but no tariff is charged for 'lifeline' consumption levels below 5.5m³/person per year. Rates also vary by economic sectors with the highest charges paid by those where affordability is higher, i.e. tourist and commercial sectors (€1.98/m³) and government (€2.59/m³).

Source: GHK et al (2006)

3.5 Energy

> Much greater national and international efforts are indispensable to reduce those subsidies that enhance fossil-fuel use and thus act as a hurdle to combating climate change and achieving more sustainable development paths. (Achim Steiner, UNEP Executive Director; UNEP, 2008b)

The effects of energy subsidies on the environment vary depending on the type of energy source subsidized. Subsidies to fossil fuels are of particular concern. According to the International Energy Agency (IEA), the fossil fuel industry is among the most heavily subsidized economic sectors (IEA, 2005). A recent estimate calculates world spending on energy subsidies at US$557 billion/year in 2008 (IEA, 2010). This is equivalent to over 1 per cent of world gross domestic product, the figure that the Stern Review estimated necessary to stabilize the world temperature rise to 2°C (Stern, 2006).

Fossil fuel subsidies lead to increased noxious and GHG emissions while extraction of some fuels creates a huge ecological footprint. They act as a disincentive to use alternative technologies or introduce efficiency measures and can thus lead to a technology 'lock-in'. Several studies have attempted to estimate the GHG emissions reductions that could be achieved by reforming such subsidies. The IEA estimates that phasing out energy subsidies between 2011 and 2020 would decrease global energy demand by 5.8 per cent and reduce CO_2 emissions by 6.9 per cent: the resulting price increase would lead to improved efficiency in energy use, along with a switch to alternative energy sources (IEA, 2010).

Energy subsidies for producers, the most common form in OECD countries, usually come in the form of direct payments and tax breaks or as support for research and development. Consumption subsidies have been mostly eliminated in the OECD but remain important in many developing countries. Electricity and household heating and cooking fuels are usually the most heavily subsidized: some countries also subsidize road transport fuels (GSI, 2009b).

The reform of energy subsidies can significantly reduce GHG emissions and air pollution and be undertaken without severe social implications (see case studies in Boxes 6.2, 6.11 and 6.12).

Box 6.11 Fuel subsidy reform in Ghana

In 2004, it became apparent that Ghana could no longer maintain its policy of subsidizing petroleum products. Guided by a steering committee of stakeholders from ministries, academia and the national oil company, the government launched a poverty and social impact assessment (PSIA) for fuel, completed in less than a year. By the time the government announced 50 per cent price increases in February 2005, it was able to use the PSIA findings to make its case for liberalizing fuel prices to the public – including the fact that existing price subsidies most benefited the better-off. The Minister of Finance launched a public relations campaign with a broadcast and series of interviews explaining the need for the price increases and announcing measures to mitigate their impact. These measures, which were transparent and easily monitored by society, included the immediate elimination of fees at government-run primary and junior secondary schools and a programme to improve public transport. While the trade unions remained opposed to the price increases, the public generally accepted them, and no large-scale demonstrations occurred.

Sources: Bacon and Kojima (2006); ESMAP (2006)

Against this background, the recent G20 commitment (Pittsburgh 2009, reiterated at the Toronto Summit in June 2010) to phase out inefficient fossil fuel subsidies is highly welcome and should be replicated by others (G20, 2009, 2010). In some cases, subsidy reform may have direct positive impacts for ecosystems and biodiversity, e.g. peat mining is still subsidized in some countries as a major indigenous energy source even though it destroys biodiversity-rich bogs (Kirkinen et al, 2007).

Some consumer energy subsidies may be justified on environmental or social grounds. For instance, switching away from wood and other traditional energy sources (straw, crop residue and dung) can reduce deforestation caused by wood burning and reduce indoor air pollution. The argument that these subsidies are pro-poor is most pertinent where institutional preconditions for potentially more efficient social policies are poor or absent (e.g. for redistribution of income through progressive income taxation systems).

Even here, there is often substantial scope for reform. This is particularly true where the poor do not benefit from the subsidy because they have no access to the service (e.g. where the poorest are not connected to the electricity grid, it is the medium to high income groups who tend to benefit from consumer subsidies). One way of reducing harmful subsidy impacts is to set 'lifeline' rates limiting subsidies to low consumption levels and to target spending on expanding grids into poorer neighbourhoods (see Box 6.12).

Subsidies are also used to encourage the development and use of renewable energy sources to fight global warming and achieve long-term energy security. However, these may have other environmental consequences. For instance, hydroelectric dams can result in the loss of wildlife habitat and reduce biodiversity (McAllister et al, 2001);

Box 6.12 Removing fuel subsidies in Indonesia

Before raising fuel prices in October 2005, the government of Indonesia put into place a cash transfer scheme targeting 15.5 million poor and near-poor households (some 28 per cent of the population). The transfers (quarterly payments of about US$30 per household) lasted for one year. The scheme was widely publicized through newspapers, village notice boards, television talk shows and pamphlets with answers to frequently asked questions.

Though prepared quickly, the programme has performed well. The rapid roll-out was followed by many media reports about initial problems, including mistargeting and leakage. The government responded quickly, commissioning an early assessment of the programme which pointed to satisfactory results overall, with transfers made on time and beneficiaries expressing satisfaction.

For poor recipients the cash transfers easily compensate for the fuel price increase. Even with moderate mistargeting – with cash benefits randomly distributed to the poorest 40 per cent rather than the targeted 28 per cent – the programme was expected to prevent a related increase in poverty.

As a consequence, the sharp rise in fuel prices passed without major public protest.

Source: Bacon and Kojima (2006)

---

batteries for solar home systems can leak toxic heavy metals; and wind farms can have significant biodiversity impacts, especially if inappropriately located (UNEP, 2005; Drewitt and Langston, 2008). These impacts need to be carefully assessed and considered in decision making on renewable energy development.

Biofuels illustrate the complex relationship between renewable energy subsidies and environmentally damaging impacts. Various subsidies are used to encourage production and consumption of biofuels which are promoted as a way to simultaneously increase energy security, reduce GHG emissions and encourage rural development. These subsidies are provided at different points in the supply chain and include support for intermediate inputs and value adding factors, output linked subsidies, subsidies to distribution infrastructure, consumption incentives and high import tariffs. Several countries have also introduced targets and mandatory requirements that encourage biofuel development.

These subsidies have contributed to the rapid global expansion in biofuel production and use. By 2006 government support to biofuels in the US, the EU and Canada was estimated to have reached US$11 billion/year (GSI, 2007; OECD, 2008b). While the cost of reducing a tonne of CO_2-equivalent through biofuels is between US$960 to US$1700 (OECD, 2008b), recent CO_2 prices in the European Emissions Trading Scheme are in the range of US$30 to US$50.

These calculations did not consider the GHG emissions from land-use change associated with conversion to biofuel. Recent analyses suggest that large-scale biofuel expansion promoted by subsidies, targets and mandates is likely to increase net GHG through direct and indirect land-use change (Searchinger et al, 2008; Fargione et al, 2008; IEEP, 2010).

While biofuels subsidies represent a significant strain on public resources, they do not therefore appear to be the most cost-effective option for reducing GHGs – in many instances, the public may actually be paying to increase GHG emissions. There is an urgent need to review these biofuel policies (FAO, 2008a).

4 Making reform happen

> People who love soft methods and hate inequity, forget this – that reform consists in taking a bone from a dog. Philosophy will not do it. (John Jay Chapman, 1862–1933, quoted in OECD, 2007a)

> We commit our agencies to support our developing country partners in the design and implementation of fiscal reforms that raise revenue, advance environmental sustainability and assist in reducing poverty. (Statement by Klaus Töpfer, then UNEP Executive Director; Ian Johnson, then Vice President World Bank; Olav Kjorven, UNDP; as well as Ministers and government representatives from Denmark, EC, Finland, Germany, Sweden, Switzerland and the UK; World Bank, 2005)

Phasing out subsidies has the potential not only to alleviate environmental pressures but also increase economic efficiency and reduce the fiscal burden. Freed funds can be used for more pressing funding needs, like rewarding those who provide biodiversity benefits (see Chapter 5). It is therefore important to look beyond EHS and also target subsidies that have clearly outlived their purpose, are not targeted at their stated objectives or do not reach their objectives cost-effectively.

There are many calls for subsidy reform and a lot of rhetorical support. There is also some policy support and action. The OECD has called for subsidy removal or reform in many forums and agricultural and fisheries subsidies are on the WTO's Doha development agenda. The 2002 Johannesburg World Summit on Sustainable Development highlighted the need to reform subsidies for agriculture, fisheries and energy: this need will be echoed by UNEP's forthcoming Green Economy Report. For energy, the G20 commitment to phase out inefficient fossil fuel subsidies, reconfirmed in June 2010, is a welcome step which needs to be implemented, replicated by others and expanded to other types of subsidy. In the realm of global environmental policy, several multilateral environmental agreements (MEAs) have drawn attention to the impacts of subsidies on the environmental assets that MEAs protect – most notably, the new Strategic Plan for Biodiversity, adopted by the tenth meeting of the Conference of the Parties to the Convention on Biological Diversity, commits its 193 Parties (192 States and the European Union) to eliminate, phase out or reform incentives, including subsidies, harmful to biodiversity by 2020 (see Box 6.13 for the exact language) (CBD, 2010).

At national level, many countries already foresee priority action on subsidy removal, possibly in the context of (environmental) fiscal reform (World Bank, 2005). A still small but increasing range of successful subsidy reforms can now be seen around the world. And yet, with few exceptions, progress is too slow and protracted. The reasons are rooted in the political economy of subsidy reform and also, in some cases, linked to technological and institutional barriers.

4.1 Analytical tools

A range of useful tools is available to help policy makers identify subsidies whose reform offers potential benefits and assess such benefits, including for the environment:

Box 6.13 The CBD's headline target for incentives, including subsidy reform

The new Strategic Plan for Biodiversity for the period 2011–2020 was adopted by the tenth meeting of the Parties to the CBD to promote the effective implementation of the Convention through a strategic approach comprising a shared vision, a mission, strategic goals and targets that will inspire broad-based action by all Parties and stakeholders. The Plan includes 20 headline targets for 2020, organized under five strategic goals. Target three reads as follows:

By 2020, at the latest, incentives, including subsidies, harmful to biodiversity are eliminated, phased out or reformed in order to minimize or avoid negative impacts, and positive incentives for the conservation and sustainable use of biodiversity are developed and applied, consistent and in harmony with the Convention and other relevant international obligations, taking into account national socio-economic conditions.

Source: CBD (2010)

- The 'quick scan' model (OECD, 1998) addresses the questions: 'Is the support likely to have a negative impact on the environment?' and 'Does the support succeed in transferring income to the intended recipient?'
- The 'checklist' (Pieters, 2003) provides some policy guidance by addressing the question: 'Is the subsidy removal likely to have significant environmental benefits?'
- Where the checklist delivers a positive result, the integrated assessment methodology (OECD, 2007a) will help create a comprehensive story on the effectiveness of the subsidy rather than a pass–fail test, and look at alternative policies.
- For 'green' subsidies, a specific checklist (UNEP, 2008b) provides minimum criteria any subsidy should fulfil to prevent it from turning perverse in the long run (see Section 5 and Box 6.17).

The assumption underlying the OECD integrated assessment approach is that better policies will result when there is an explicit understanding of the distribution of costs and benefits, and this information is made available to policy makers and the interested public. Ideally, this means full disclosure of all costs and benefits, winners and losers, intended and unintended effects (environmental, economic, social) and highlighting where trade-offs exist.

To help policy makers systematically reform their subsidies in line with tomorrow's priorities, Box 6.14 provides a checklist of useful questions.

4.2 Resistance to change

Subsidies create or maintain economic activity and foster a culture of entitlement: even if only granted for a set period of time, people come to expect their renewal. Changing income distribution between individuals, and their broader economic

Box 6.14 Developing a roadmap for subsidy reform: A checklist for policy makers

Is a subsidy causing damage to ecosystems and biodiversity?

- Is there harm to the environment?
- Is there a subsidy in place that contributes to environmental damage (e.g. by influencing consumption, production levels) and if so, what is it?
- Does it lead to significant or potentially excessive resource use (e.g. water use leading to loss from aquifers; thresholds crossed, such as salinization of aquifers; social impacts from reduced resource availability)?
- Does it actually harm the environment or do policy filters avoid such pressure/ damage? (Consider wider policy scenarios, regulations, quotas and enforcement/ legality of activities.)

Should the subsidy be the target of reform?

- Does the subsidy fulfil its objectives (social/economic/environmental)? If not, it needs reform.
- Does the subsidy lack an in-built review process and has it been in place for a long time? If so, it is likely to need reform (i.e. it has already locked in inefficient practices).
- Are there public calls for reform or removal or calls to use the funds for other purposes? (This is often an indicator for the two points following.)
- How does the subsidy distribute social welfare? If there are equity issues, it might be worth reforming it.
- Do any of the subsidy impacts lead to social or other economic losses? For example tourism loss following overfishing.
- Are there alternative less damaging technologies available, which are hindered by the subsidy's existence? If so, it might be slowing innovation and creating technological 'lock in': reform could bring benefits.
- Does it offer value for money? Where there is still a valid rationale for the subsidy, could the same or less money be used to achieve the same objectives with lesser environmental impacts?

Reform scenarios

If subsidy reform has been identified as bringing potential benefits, the following questions can be asked:

- Would the reform be understandable for policy makers and the public?
- What would the reform entail (measure changed + compensatory measures)? It is rarely a simple case of 'getting rid of the subsidy altogether'.
- What would be the costs and benefits of potential reform, covering the following six areas:
  1. Potential environmental benefits: include thinking on benefits in other countries and secondary effects, which can be perverse.
  2. Potential economic costs: for example national (tax, GDP, etc.), sector-wide, for winners and losers within the sector (including new entrants/future industry), for consumers/citizens (affordability).

3 Potential social impacts: for example jobs, skills, availability of goods/services, health.

4 Potential competitiveness and innovation benefits.

5 Potential ethical benefits, e.g. as regards fairness of income, appropriateness of support, links to future generations.

6 Is the reform practical and enforceable?

The next step: Setting priorities for the roadmap

To identify the likelihood of success and whether it is worthwhile using political capital for reform, the following questions can be useful:

- Is there a policy/political opportunity for action?
- Is there a window of opportunity? For example, policy review process, evaluation, public demand.
- Is there a potential policy champion?
- Will there be sufficient political capital for success?

Source: Chapter authors, building on the OECD tools (OECD, 1998; Pieters, 2003; OECD, 2007a; Valsecchi et al, 2009)

opportunities, is the driving force behind the political economy of subsidy reform. Those who stand to gain from the current situation or lose from the reform have a strong incentive to lobby for the retention of the existing regime.

What often makes resistance to change successful is that the benefits of subsidies tend to be concentrated in the hands of specific well-organized groups whereas costs are spread widely across (poorly organized) taxpayers and sometimes consumers (OECD, 2006a).

Subsidy removal can raise legitimate concerns regarding affordability, e.g. when this would lead to higher prices of essential goods like drinking water. However, careful design of policy reforms can mitigate affordability issues and minimize social impacts. For example, the use of progressive water tariffs allows low charges for low usage and thus addresses the needs of lower-income households (see Maltese example in Box 6.10). Transitional assistance is another option (see below).

In the long run, reform can generate new opportunities. In principle, more efficient resource allocation creates a stronger enabling environment in which economic activity can flourish. In the short run, however, individuals and communities may find it difficult to reorient economic decisions and livelihoods, especially in the absence of proactive capacity building as part of transition management. This could be due to geographical isolation (e.g. fishing, agriculture and resource-dependent areas with no immediate alternatives for employment or economic diversification). It could also be due to technological lock-in (e.g. phasing out subsidies for private transport will have little effect on car use if people have no reasonable alternative modes of transportation). Identifying and understanding the very real short-term social impacts of dismantling subsidies is one of the most difficult aspects of reform (OECD, 2006a).

Institutional barriers may also play a role. Unsurprisingly, institutions and bureaucracies that manage subsidy schemes will rarely push for their removal, either because of vested interests or because they lack the vision to do things differently. The sheer number of players can also create barriers. For instance, the exemption of aviation kerosene from excise taxes (stemming from the 1953 Chicago Convention on Civil Aviation) should clearly be removed to enable pollution charges. However, this would not only affect the vested interests of the airline companies but also require an international conference to seek new consensus among parties to the Convention or else the renegotiation of a large number of bilateral treaties (van Beers and de Moor, 2001).

4.3 Organizing reform

Experience with reforms to date shows that the design of the reform process is a critical success factor. It needs to take the political economy and other barriers into consideration and often hinges on five important conditions:

1 Policy objectives must be defined transparently and rigorously.
2 The distribution of benefits and costs must be transparently identified.
3 Government must engage broadly with stakeholders.
4 Government should set ambitious endpoints, but, depending on circumstances, timetables for reform may need to be cautious.
5 Fiscal transfers and/or other flanking measures are often required to facilitate the transition process (OECD, 2007a).

The multiple policy objectives often associated with subsidy programmes need to be analysed carefully. Disentangling explicit and implicit objectives can help identify opportunities to introduce separate, better-designed and more transparent instruments. For example, Finland recently reformed its forestry subsidies and created a specific Forest Biodiversity Programme to make regular payments for landowners in return for maintaining or improving specified forest biodiversity values. By separately targeting the biodiversity objective, the programme is more transparent, and its cost-effectiveness easier to assess, than general forestry subsidies with several objectives (OECD, 2007a).

Information from analytical frameworks (e.g. the OECD's integrated assessment) can only build the case for reform if it is understandable by the general public and widely disseminated. Increased transparency is a major factor in the push to reform environmentally harmful subsidies (see Box 6.15).

Transparency is a key precondition for well-informed public debate on current subsidy programmes and can also make reform more appealing. Identifying who benefits from subsidies and highlighting their relative bargaining power can provide a powerful motivating force for change (OECD, 2003a). By helping to debunk the myths surrounding subsidies and their reform, such assessments can also be useful to overcome resistance by vested interests.

Governments need to build alliances for change and discourage behaviour that would reduce or distort change. Practitioners regularly underline stakeholder engagement as another key precondition for durable reform. Multi-stakeholder processes based on outreach and communication can help to build consensus – or at least common understanding – on new approaches or options for reform. The overarching goal is less about convincing stakeholders who gain most from the existing situation and more about using the planning and implementation process to minimize opposition to change and maximize support (OECD, 2003a).

Box 6.15 Enhancing transparency of farm subsidies in the European Union

2006 financial regulations (EC, 2006a, 2006b) require 'adequate ex-post disclosure' of the recipients of all EU funds, with agricultural spending transparency to begin in the 2008 budget. The regulation has spurred watchdog initiatives such as the online services http://farmsubsidy.org, http://caphealthcheck.eu and www.fishsubsidy.org. These seek to monitor compliance by Member States and assess the quality of the released data. However, compliance with the regulation is still uneven.

There is also a critical need to build cooperation and horizontal analysis between government departments and agencies whose mandates, policies and programmes may overlap within the subsidized sectors. Reform often requires a whole-government approach linking relevant institutional actors to ensure policy coherence (OECD, 2003a).

Changes in the policy landscape can open windows of opportunity (see Chapter 2), even if sweeping electoral victories of parties with a strong reform agenda are rare. Even in such cases, practitioners caution against jumping straight to the 'best' solution for several reasons. These include the limited capacity of governments to undertake major reforms on many fronts at the same time and for short-term adaptation by affected communities. In practice, demonstrating actual benefits delivered through more gradual reforms can be more compelling than upfront projections of expected benefits, even if these are larger. For the same reasons, dramatic reforms may increase the likelihood of policy reversal (OECD, 2005).

Despite these words of caution, cases of fast and successful reform do exist (see Boxes 6.11, 6.12 and 6.16). One advantage of eliminating or changing subsidies immediately, without prior warning, is that recipients cannot take advantage of the phase-out period to increase their entitlements, thus leading to associated environmental damage.

Usually, however, political change is more gradual. Peer pressure, civil society and regional or international organizations can increase interest and participation. Mandatory requirements under regional or international treaties (e.g. WTO) can also provide useful leverage for change. Political leadership can use growing public and other support, wherever it exists, as a springboard to build a broad coalition for reform with ambitious endpoints and the phase-in of changes over an extended time period.

Policy packages can include transitional payments to those most affected by the reform and changes to the industry's regulatory environment to ease the adjustment process and possibly improve long-term efficiency (see Box 6.16 for lessons learned in New Zealand). When backed by a credible roadmap for reform, these may reduce opposition to change. However, designing adequate sequencing can be difficult and big reform packages are often politically difficult to sell (OECD, 2005).

Many packages include some form of transitional assistance, even where the reform of the current situation does not really justify this (it is impossible and

---

Box 6.16 Removal of agricultural and fisheries subsidies in New Zealand

New Zealand was one of the first – and is still one of the few – OECD countries to have completely dismantled its system of agricultural price supports and other farm subsidies. These reforms were driven by concerns for the economic unsustainability of the subsidy programmes rather than for the environment.

The two decades prior to 1984 had seen a gradual acceleration in agricultural production grants and subsidies. In the 1960s agricultural support amounted to just 3 per cent of farm income. By 1983 it was nearly 40 per cent in the sheep sector alone and New Zealand's general macroeconomic situation had deteriorated markedly. Increased agricultural output was generally worth less than the actual costs of production and processing.

In 1984 the new government abolished tax concessions for farmers and minimum price schemes for agricultural products. Land development loans, fertilizer and irrigation subsidies and subsidized credit were reduced and then phased out from 1987, along with assistance for flood control, soil conservation and drainage. Subsidy removal was combined with wider reforms across the economy (including floating of the currency, phased tariff liberalization to lower input prices etc.). Their removal was an important contributing factor to improvement in the sector's circumstances.

Social impacts were not as great as widely predicted. Around 1 per cent of farmers left the industry, considerably less than the projected 16 per cent. Substantial environmental improvements were observed through decreased use of agricultural chemicals and in livestock, as well as by taking marginal land out of production.

New Zealand also undertook a major reform of its fisheries policy in the early 1990s. Subsidies were eliminated virtually overnight. However, subsidy reduction alone would not have been enough to create a sustainable fishing sector and would have caused substantial financial and social distress. It would also have had a negative impact on stocks due to overfishing by fishermen increasing effort to try and cover marginal costs. For these reasons, the reduction was combined with a major change in the management regime (introduction of rights-based management and individual transferable quotas, combined with a minimum buyout of existing rights). These measures gave those remaining in the sector a good chance of creating a profitable business environment, while allowing those who wished to leave to be bought out.

Sources: Vangelis, in OECD (2005); Cox, in OECD (2007a)

---

undesirable to compensate all members of society from harm caused by economic change). In practice, political economy considerations sometimes dominate discussions about the rationale of transition support programmes. However, simply buying out those groups who lobby most effectively against reform carries the risk that the transition support will eventually replicate and perpetuate some of the initial subsidy's adverse effects. Moreover, it may actually reduce long-term public support for the reform. For these reasons, great care is needed in the design of transitional support. Those with the loudest voice are not necessarily those with the highest need.

Transitional support can increase the resilience of affected communities to economic change, e.g. by helping producers who want to leave the industry to do so with dignity and financial standing through grants, job training, buyouts or early retirement plans. It can also enhance the sector's human and social capital and thus improve the competitiveness or viability of those who stay in the sector (OECD, 2005). Investment programmes can be helpful for attracting new industries to regions affected by the reform. Firm sunset clauses can help to ensure that transitional support does not nourish a sense of permanent entitlement.

5 Targeting subsidy reform at today's priorities

Over the last two decades, we have come to understand the scale of subsidies in different sectors, the extent and mechanics of their environmentally harmful effects and how cost-effective they are (or not) in achieving their goals. Some progress has been made in removing and/or reforming subsidies but, with few exceptions, the progress is piecemeal and fragmented. Globally, subsidy reform is unfinished business.

Persistent myths surround subsidies and their reform and can block change. Many of these myths can and should be debunked; frequently made claims are investigated below.

Claim: Subsidy reform will harm competitiveness

Keeping subsidies harms a sector's long-term competitiveness as it becomes dependent on the subsidies, encourages technology lock-in, reduces incentives for innovation and puts strains on public finances.

Claim: Subsidy reform will result in job losses

In the short term, this can be the case for the sector concerned. However, compensatory measures can address some adverse impacts, and incentives can be put in place to attract investment. There are also possible employment gains from use of monies elsewhere (the net effect depends on relative labour intensities of the activity replaced compared to the new activity). In the long term, increased competitiveness through innovation (e.g. energy efficiency) or increased availability of resources (e.g. fish) should help support or create jobs.

Claim: Subsidy reform will have negative implications for social equity

This claim is often made about energy subsidies yet poorer households spend less on energy than middle-income households. There are more targeted and effective ways of helping the poor than subsidies that tend to benefit all users.

Claim: Subsidy reform will lead to a loss of livelihoods

This can include the livelihoods of, for example, poor farmers and fishermen. Empirical studies show that many existing subsidy programmes are not well-targeted at social objectives: even if the poor draw some benefit, most of it goes to the relatively rich.

Claim: Many people do not wish to change their livelihood

It is claimed that people may not wish to change their livelihood, e.g. from fishing or mining. In some cases this is indeed true, but in others there is interest in other forms of employment. Acceptability is linked to options for employment substitution, and opportunities to learn the skills required to seize these employment opportunities.

Claim: Reforming environmentally harmful subsidies is almost impossible because of vested interests

In reality, the picture is mixed. Evidence shows that reforming subsidies is possible and that negative effects on the economic and social system can be reduced, compensated or borne by people within acceptable limits.

Claim: Subsidies are good for the environment

Financial transfers that are well-targeted at environmental objectives and cost-effective can play an important role in improving incentives to conserve ecosystems and biodiversity (see Chapter 5). Yet many existing subsidies are environmentally harmful: their prior or simultaneous removal or reform will improve the cost-effectiveness of environmental incentive payments. As even 'green' subsidies may not be well-targeted and/or cost-effective, adjusting them to improve performance will ultimately make their case stronger.

The G20 Heads of State have recently committed to phase out and rationalize inefficient fossil fuel subsidies over the medium term while providing targeted support for the poorest. Moreover, with the adoption of the Strategic Plan for Biodiversity for 2011–2020, the Parties to the CBD (192 States and the European Union, as a Regional Organization) are now committed to eliminate, phase out or reform subsidies that are harmful for biodiversity. These commitments are to be commended as important steps and should be implemented forcefully.

From a global ecosystems and biodiversity perspective, priority areas for reform include the removal of capacity- or effort-enhancing fisheries subsidies and the continuing and deepened reform of production-inducing agricultural subsidies, particularly in most OECD countries. Reasons include the size of their environmentally harmful effects and/or their sheer magnitude, the resulting strain on scarce resources and high opportunity costs.

Ongoing WTO negotiations on fisheries subsidies and agricultural domestic support have significant potential to support the accelerated removal of EHS. Governments should redouble their efforts to successfully conclude the negotiations on the WTO Doha programme of work.

Most OECD countries also need to complement these global priorities with additional and prioritized reform efforts in other sectors, depending on national circumstances. In addition to energy subsidies on fossil fuels and biofuels (where these fail to encourage real CO_2 savings), these should address the following subsidies that harm biodiversity and ecosystem services:

- transport subsidies, e.g. habitat fragmentation linked to subsidies for road building;
- water subsidies which result in unsustainable water consumption.

For non-OECD countries, concrete priorities will obviously depend on national circumstances but the sectors mentioned above are also interesting candidates for subsidy removal or reform. Relevant factors include the importance of specific sectors, the existing subsidy landscape, the design of individual programmes and how these interact with the broader policy and institutional framework.

The stimulus programmes that have been implemented in many countries in the recent past require stringent budgetary consolidation in the next few years. Subsidy reform should be an important element of this process. Focusing on the short term, all countries need to:

- establish transparent and comprehensive subsidy inventories;
- assess their effectiveness against stated objectives, cost-efficiency and environmental impacts, and, based on these assessments, develop prioritized plans of action for subsidy removal or reform for medium-term implementation to 2020;
- seize windows of reform opportunity that arise within existing policy cycles.

Looking beyond budgetary consolidation, funds that become available from subsidy reform can also be used in areas of more pressing funding needs. Critical needs are to reward the unrewarded benefits of ecosystem and associated biodiversity, in particular:

- payments to biodiversity stewards for a range of ecosystem services (see Chapter 5);
- provision of funds to expand the protected area network (corridors, marine protected areas, etc.) and improve its management (see Chapter 8);
- investment in ecological infrastructure (e.g. restoration), notably where this helps in adaptation to climate change (e.g. flood control, sea-level rise, storm surges – see Chapter 9) or poverty (see Chapter 1).

Care should be taken to ensure that these new programmes do not fall into the design traps of past subsidies (see Box 6.17).

Box 6.17 Minimum criteria for subsidy programme design

- **Targeted:** Subsidies should go only to those who they are meant for and who deserve to receive them.
- **Efficient:** Subsidies should not undermine incentives for suppliers or consumers to provide or use a service efficiently.
- **Soundly based:** Subsidies should be justified by a thorough analysis of the associated costs and benefits.
- **Practical:** The amount of subsidy should be affordable and it must be possible to administer the subsidy in a low-cost way.
- **Transparent:** The public should be able to see how much a subsidy programme costs and who benefits from it.
- **Limited in time:** Subsidy programmes should have limited duration, preferably set at the outset, so that consumers and producers do not get 'hooked' on the subsidies and the cost of the programme does not spiral out of control.

Source: UNEP (2004b)

New programmes should therefore:

- be based on clear, targeted and measurable objectives and associated indicators;
- ensure cost-effectiveness, for instance by using smart economic mechanisms (e.g. reverse auctions);
- include monitoring, reporting and evaluation provisions; and
- include sunset and review clauses to help avoid their continuation beyond their useful life.

Last, many parties are involved in the reform process. Too often, short-term, national or private interests dictate the terms. Focusing on wider economic and social benefits and costs in a longer-term perspective is essential to reform the subsidy landscape and point economic signals in the right direction – to help current and future generations meet the challenges of the coming years.

Acknowledgements

The authors wish to thank David Baldock, IEEP, UK; Tamsin Cooper, IEEP, UK; Anthony Cox, Organisation for Economic Co-operation and Development (OECD); Claudia Dias Soares, Portuguese Catholic University; Marcus Gilleard, Earth Watch, UK; Bernd Hansjürgens, Helmholtz Centre for Environmental Research (UFZ), Germany; Celia Harvey, Conservation International (CI); Markus Knigge, The Pew Charitable Trusts; Indrani Lutchman, IEEP, UK; Leonardo Mazza, IEEP, Belgium; Helen Mountford, OECD, Paris; Jerzy Pienkowsky, European Commission – DG Environment, Belgium; Manfred Rosenstock, European Commission – DG Environment, Belgium; Alice Ruhweza, Katoomba Group, Uganda; Burkhard Schweppe-Kraft, The Federal Environment Ministry – Germany (BMU); Benjamin Simmons, UNEP, Switzerland; Ronald Steenblik, OECD, France; Rashid Sumaila, The University of British Columbia (UBC), Canada; Carolina Valsecchi, IEEP, UK; Koen Van Den Bossche, IEEP, Belgium; Madhu Verma, Indian Institute of Forest Management, India; Vaclav Vojtech, OECD, France; Stephen White, European Commission – DG Environment, Belgium; Peter Wooders, International Institute for Sustainable Development (IISD), Switzerland; and Heidi Wittmer, UFZ, Germany.

References

Agnew, D. J., Pearce, J., Pramod, G., Peatman, T., Watson, R., et al (2009) 'Estimating the worldwide extent of illegal fishing', *PLoS ONE*, vol 4, no 2 e4570, www.plosone.org/article/info:doi/10.1371/journal.pone.0004570, accessed 26 July 2010

Alliance Environnement (2007) *Evaluation of the Application of Cross-compliance under Regulation 1782/2003: Executive Summary*, http://ec.europa.eu/agriculture/eval/reports/cross_compliance/full_text_en.pdf, accessed 26 October 2009

Bacon, R. and Kojima, M. (2006) *Phasing Out Subsidies: Recent Experiences with Fuel in Developing Countries*, Note 310, Financial and Private Sector Development Vice Presidency, World Bank Group

Barde, J. P. and Honkatukia, O. (2003) 'Environmentally harmful subsidies', Contribution to the *ERE 2003 Handbook*, www.iddri.org/Activites/Seminaires-reguliers/barde.pdf, accessed 22 July 2010

Barniaux, J. M., Chateau, J., Dellink, R., Duval, R. and Jamet, S. (2009) 'The economics of climate change mitigation: How to build the necessary global action in a cost-effective manner', OECD, Paris, www.oecd-ilibrary.org/content/workingpaper/224074334782, accessed 22 July 2010

Bassi, S., Suarez, C. D. and Valsecchi, C. (2010) 'Reforming environmentally harmful subsidies in the water sector: Irrigation subsidies in Spain', in C. D. Soares, J. E. Milne, H. Ashiabor, L. Kreiser, K. Deketelaere (eds) *Critical Issues in Environmental Taxation – International and Comparative Perspectives – Volume VIII*, Oxford University Press, New York

Boccaccio, L., Brunner, A. and Powell, A. (2009) *Could Do Better: How is EU Rural Development Policy Delivering for Biodiversity?* BirdLife International, Sandy, UK

CBD (2010) *Decision X/2 on Updating and Revision of the Strategic Plan for the Post-2010 Period, Tenth Meeting of the Conference of the Parties to the Convention on Biological Diversity*, advance unedited text, available at www.cbd.int/nagoya/outcomes, accessed 15 November 2010

CIFOR (2006) 'Issues relating to reducing emissions from deforestation in developing countries', Submission by the Center of International Forestry Research (CIFOR) to the UNFCCC, http://unfccc.int/resource/docs/2006/smsn/igo/003.pdf, accessed 27 October 2010

Coady, D., El-Said, M., Gillingham, R., Kpodar, K., Medas, P. and Newhouse, D. (2006) 'The magnitude and distribution of fuel subsidies: Evidence from Bolivia, Ghana, Jordan, Mali, and Sri Lanka', Working Paper WP/06/247, International Monetary Fund, Washington, DC

Cornish, G., Bosworth, B. and Perry, C. (2004) *Water Charging in Irrigated Agriculture: An Analysis of International Experience*, Food and Agriculture Organization of the United Nations, Rome

Crooks, R. K. and Sanjayan, M. (eds) (2006) *Connectivity Conservation*, vol 14, Cambridge University Press, Cambridge

Danielsen, F., et al (2008) 'Biofuel plantations on forested lands: Double jeopardy for biodiversity and climate', *Conservation Biology*, vol 23, pp348–358

De Moor, A. P. G. and Calamai, P. (1997), *Subsidizing Unsustainable Development: Undermining the Earth with Public Funds*, The Earth Council, San Jose, Costa Rica, www.cbd.int/doc/case-studies/inc/cs-inc-earthcouncil-unsustainable-en.pdf, accessed 22 July 2010

Drewitt, A. and Langston, R. H. W. (2008) 'Collision effects of wind-power generators and other obstacles on birds', *Annuals of the New York Academy of Sciences*, vol 1134, pp233–266

EC (2000) 'Directive 2000/60/EC of the European Parliament and of the Council establishing a framework for the Community action in the field of water policy', *Official Journal of the European Union*, OJ L 327, 22 December 2000

EC (2006a) 'Council Regulation (EC, Euratom) No 1605/2002 applicable to the general budget of the European Communities as lately amended by Council Regulation (EG) No 1995/2006', *Official Journal of the European Union*, OJ L 390, 13 December 2006

EC (2006b) 'Commission Regulation (EC) No 1828/2006 setting out rules for the implementation of Council Regulation (EC) No 1083/2006 laying down general provisions on the European Regional Development Fund, the European Social Fund and the Cohesion Fund and of Regulation (EC) No 1080/2006 of the European Parliament and of the Council on the European Regional Development Fund', *Official Journal of the European Union*, OJ L 371, 27 December 2006

EEA (2004) *High Nature Value Farmland. Characteristics, Trends and Policy Challenges*, European Environment Agency, Copenhagen, Denmark

EEA (2009) *Water Resources Across Europe: Confronting Water Scarcity and Drought*, EEA Report No 2/2009, European Environment Agency, Copenhagen, Denmark

ESMAP (Energy Sector Management Assistance Programme) (2006) 'Coping with Higher Fuel Prices', Report 323/06, Washington, DC

Fahrig, L. (2003) 'Effects of habitat fragmentation on biodiversity', *Annual Review of Ecology, Evolution and Systematics*, vol 34, pp487–515

FAO (1992) *Marine Fisheries and the Law of the Sea: A Decade of Change*, FAO Fisheries Circular No 853 (FID/C853), Food and Agriculture Organization of the United Nations, Rome

FAO (2008a) *Biofuels: Prospects, Risks and Opportunities, The State of Food and Agriculture 2008*, Food and Agriculture Organization of the United Nations, Rome

FAO (2008b) *State of World Fisheries and Aquaculture 2008*, Food and Agriculture Organization of the United Nations, Rome

Fargione, J., Hill, J., Tilman, D., Polasky, S. and Hawthorne, P. (2008) 'Land clearing and the biofuel carbon debt', *Science*, vol 319, pp1235–1237

George, C. and Kirkpatrick, C. (2003) *Sustainability Impact Assessment of Proposed WTO Negotiations: Preliminary Overview of Potential Impacts of the Doha Agenda, Final Report*, Institute for Development Policy and Management, University of Manchester, www.sia-trade.org/wto/FinalPhase/FINAL_OVERVIEWJul2006.pdf, accessed 22 July 2010

GHK, IEEP, Ecolas and Cambridge Econometrics (2006) 'Strategic evaluation on environment and risk prevention under Structural and Cohesion Funds for the period 2007–2013', Report for the European Commission, GHK, Brussels, http://ec.europa.eu/regional_policy/sources/docgener/evaluation/pdf/evalstrat_env/el_main.pdf, accessed 22 September 2010

GSI (2007) *Biofuels: At What Costs? Government Support for Ethanol and Biodiesel in Selected OECD Countries*, Global Subsidies Initiative, International Institute for Sustainable Development (IISD)

GSI (2009a) 'Achieving the G20 call to phase out subsidies to fossil fuels', Policy Brief, Global Subsidies Initiative, International Institute for Sustainable Development (IISD)

GSI (2009b) *Relative Subsidies to Energy Sources: GSI Estimates*, International Institute for Sustainable Development (IISD), www.globalsubsidies.org/files/assets/relative_energy_subsidies.pdf and www.globalsubsidies.org/en/resources/energy, accessed 27 July 2010

G20 (2009) 'Leader's Statement', The Pittsburgh Summit, 24–25 September 2009, www.pittsburghsummit.gov/mediacenter/129639.htm

G20 (2010) 'The G20 Toronto Summit Declaration', 26–27 June 2010, www.mea.gov.in/meaxpsite/declarestatement/2010/06/27js02.pdf, accessed 27 October 2010

Hannesson, R. (2001) 'Effects of liberalizing trade in fish, fishing services and investment in fishing vessels', OECD Papers Offprint No 8, OECD, Paris

ICTSD (2006) *Fisheries Access Agreements: Trade and Development Issues*, International Center for Trade and Sustainable Development, Geneva

IEA (2005) CO$_2$ *Emissions from Fuel Combustion*, IEA, Paris

IEA (2008) *World Energy Outlook 2008*, OECD Publications, Paris

IEA (2010) *Energy Subsidies: Getting the Prices Right*, International Energy Agency, Office of the Chief Economist, Brief issued 7 June 2010

IEEP (Institute for European Environmental Policy – Valsecchi, C., ten Brink, P., Fergusson, M., Bassi, S., Skinner, I. and Pallemaerts, M.), Ecologic (Best, A., Blobel, D., Berglund, M.), FEEM (Markandya, A., Sgobbi, A., Longo, C.) and IVM (Oosterhuis, F.) (2007) *Reforming Environmentally Harmful Subsidies*, Report to the European Commission – DG Environment, available at http://ec.europa.eu/environment/enveco/others/pdf/ehs_sum_report.pdf, accessed 22 September 2010

IEEP (2010) *Anticipated Indirect Land Use Change Associated with Expanded Use of Biofuels and Bioliquids in the EU – An Analysis of the National Renewable Energy Action Plans*, Institute for European Environmental Policy, London

IFPRI (2009) *Land Grabbing by Foreign Investors in Developing Countries: Risks and Opportunities*, Policy Brief 13, International Food Policy Research Institute

IISD (2008) 'Towards a common methodology for measuring irrigation subsidies', Discussion Paper, Global Subsidies Initiative of the International Institute for Sustainable Development, Geneva, Switzerland

IPCC (2007) *AR4 Synthesis Report: Summary for Policy Makers*, IPCC Fourth Assessment Report, Cambridge University Press, New York

IPCC (2008) *Technical Paper on Climate Change and Water*, Intergovernmental Panel on Climate Change, Geneva

Kettunen, M., Terry, A., Tucker, G. and Jones, A. (2007) 'Guidance on the maintenance of landscape connectivity features of major importance for wild flora and fauna', Institute for European Environmental Policy, Brussels

Kirkinen, J., et al (2007) 'Greenhouse impact due to different peat utilization chains in Finland: A life-cycle approach', *Boreal Environment Research*, vol 12, pp221–223, www.borenv.net/BER/pdfs/ber12/ber12-211.pdf, accessed 22 July 2010

Kjellingbro, P. and Skotte, M. (2005) *Environmentally Harmful Subsidies: Linkages Between Subsidies, the Environment and the Economy*, Environmental Assessment Institute, Copenhagen, www.imv.dk/files/Filer/IMV/Publikationer/Rapporter/2005/harmful_subsidies.pdf, accessed 27 October 2010

Kloezen, W. H. (2002) *Accounting for Water. Institutional Viability and Impacts of Market-Oriented Irrigation Interventions in Central Mexico*, University of Wageningen, The Netherlands

Koh, L. P. (2007) 'Potential habitat and biodiversity losses from intensified biodiesel feedstock production', *Conservation Biology*, vol 21, pp1373–1375

Komives, K., Foster, V., Halpern, J. and Wodon, Q. (2005) *Water, Electricity, and the Poor: Who Benefits from Utility Subsidies?* World Bank, Washington, DC

Larson, B. and Shah, A. (1992) 'World energy subsidies and global carbon dioxide emissions', *World Development Report 1992*, Background Paper No 25, World Bank, Washington, DC

McAllister, D., Craig, J. F., Davidson, N., Delany, S. and Seddon, M. (2001) *Biodiversity Impacts of Large Dams*, IUCN, UNEP and WCD, http://intranet.iucn.org/webfiles/doc/archive/2001/IUCN850.PDF, accessed 22 September 2010

Munro, G. S. and Sumaila, U. S. (2002) 'The impact of subsidies upon fisheries management and sustainability: The case of the North Atlantic', *Fish and Fisheries*, vol 3, pp233–290

Myers, N. and Kent, J. (1998) *Perverse Subsidies: Tax Dollars Undercutting our Economies and Environments Alike*, International Institute for Sustainable Development, Winnipeg, Canada

OECD (Organisation for Economic Co-operation and Development) (1998) *Agricultural Policies in OECD Countries (I and II)*, OECD, Paris

OECD (2000a) *Transition to Responsible Fisheries: Economic and Policy Implications*, OECD, Paris

OECD (2000b) *Decoupling: A Conceptual Overview*, OECD, Paris

OECD (2000c) *Domestic and International Environmental Impacts of Agricultural Trade Liberalization*, OECD, Paris, http://129.3.20.41/eps/it/papers/0401/0401010.pdf, accessed 22 July 2010

OECD (2003a) *Subsidy Reform and Sustainable Development: Economic, Environmental and Social Aspects*, OECD, Paris

OECD (2003b) *Agricultural Policies in OECD Countries: Monitoring and Evaluation*, OECD, Paris

OECD (2003c) *Farm Household Incomes: Issues and Policy Responses*, OECD, Paris

OECD (2003d) 'Perverse Incentives in Biodiversity Loss', Document submitted to the ninth meeting of the Subsidiary Body on Scientific, Technical and Technological Advice (SBSTTA) of the Convetion on Biological Diversity, UNEP/CBD/SBSTTA/9/INF/34, www.oecd.org/dataoecd/50/17/19819811.pdf, accessed 12 July 2010

OECD (2005) *Environmentally Harmful Subsidies: Challenges for Reform*, OECD, Paris

OECD (2006a) *Subsidy Reform and Sustainable Development: Economic, Environmental and Social Aspects*, OECD, Paris

OECD (2006b) *Financial Support to Fisheries: Implications for Sustainable Development*, OECD, Paris

OECD (2007a) *Subsidy Reform and Sustainable Development: Political Economy Aspects*, OECD, Paris

OECD (2007b) *Agricultural Policies in OECD Countries*, OECD, Paris

OECD (2008a) *Environmentally Harmful Subsidies in the Transport Sector*, Paper ENV/EPOC/WPNEP/T(2007)1/FINAL, OECD, Paris

OECD (2008b) *Biofuel Support Policies. An Economic Assessment*, OECD, Paris

OECD (2009) *Agricultural Policies in OECD Countries: Monitoring and Evaluation*, OECD, Paris, www.cbd.int/doc/case-studies/inc/cs-inc-oecd-agriculturalpolicies2009-en.pdf, accessed 27 July 2010

Oréade-Brèche (2005) *Evaluation of Agri-Environmental Measures in the European Union*, Executive Summary, Auzeville, France, www.cbd.int/doc/case-studies/inc/cs-inc-eur-agrienv-execsum-workshop2009-en.pdf, accessed 22 September 2010

Pan-European Common Bird Monitoring Scheme (2007) *State of Europe's Common Birds 2007*, CSO/RSPB, Prague

Pieters, J. (2003) 'When removing subsidies benefits the environment: Developing a checklist based on the conditionality of subsidies', in OECD (2003) *Environmentally Harmful Subsidies: Policy Issues and Challenges*, www.oecdbookshop.org/oecd/display.asp?lang=en&sf1=DI&st1=5LMQCR2K1QXR, accessed 27 July 2010

Porter, G. (2001) *Fisheries Subsidies and Overfishing: Towards a Structured Discussion*, United Nations Environment Programme, Geneva, www.unep.ch/etu/etp/acts/manpols/fishery.pdf, accessed 22 July 2010

Rijal, K. (2007) 'Energy subsidies in developing countries: Can we make it for those whom it is intended?' Presentation at the Joint UNEP and UNECE Expert Meeting on Energy Subsidies, 15–16 November 2007, Geneva, Switzerland, United Nations Development Programme, New York, www.unep.ch/etb/events/EnergySubsidiesPresentations1516Nov07/Kamal_14Nov'07_Energy%20Subsidies_Draft.ppt#418,33,Slide 33, accessed 22 July 2010

Scharlemann, J. P. W. and Laurance, W. F. (2008) 'How green are biofuels?', *Science*, vol 319, pp43–44

Searchinger, T., Heimlich, R., Houghton, R. A., Dong, F., Elobeid, A., Fabiosa, J., Tokgoz, S., Hayes, D., Yu, T.-H. (2008) 'Use of US croplands for biofuels increases greenhouse gases through emissions from land-use change', *Science*, vol 319, pp1238–1240

Steenblik, R. (2007) *Biofuels: At What Cost? Government Support for Ethanol and Biodiesel in Selected OECD Countries*, Global Subsidies Initiative, International Institute for Sustainable Development (GSI/IISD), Geneva

Stern, N. (2006) *Stern Review: The Economics of Climate Change*, HM Treasury, London

Sumaila, U. R., Khan, A., Teh, L., Watson, R., Tyedmers, P. and Pauly, D. (2006) 'Subsidies to high seas bottom trawl fleet and the sustainability of deep sea benthic fish stocks', in U. R. Sumaila and D. Pauly (eds), *Catching More Bait: A Bottom-Up Re-Estimation of Global Fisheries Subsidies*, Fisheries Centre Research Reports, vol 14, no 6, Fisheries Centre, University of British Columbia, Vancouver, pp49–53

Sumaila, U. R. and Pauly, D. (eds) (2007) *Catching More Bait: A Bottom-up Re-estimation of Global Fisheries Subsidies*, Fisheries Centre Research Reports, vol 14, no 6, University of British Columbia, Vancouver, www.fisheries.ubc.ca/sites/default/files/FCRR-14-16(2).pdf, accessed 27 July 2010

Sumaila, U. R., Khan, A., Watson, R., Munro, G., Zeller, D., Baron, N. and Pauly, D. (2007) 'The World Trade Organization and global fisheries sustainability', *Fisheries Research*, vol 88, pp 1–4

UNEP (2003a) 'Fisheries subsidies and marine resources management: Lessons learned from studies in Argentina and Senegal', in *UNEP/ETB Fisheries and the Environment Series* (Vol 2), Geneva, www. unep.ch/etu/etp/acts/capbld/rdtwo/FE_vol_2.pdf, accessed 22 July 2010

UNEP (2003b) *Integrated Urban Resources Management: Water*, UNEP and International Environment Technology Centre (IETC), Geneva, www.unep.or.jp/ietc/focus/iuwrm.doc, accessed 22 July 2010

UNEP (2004a) *Analyzing the Resource Impact of Fisheries Subsidies: A Matrix Approach*, UNEP, Geneva, www.unep.ch/etb/publications/fishierSubsidiesEnvironment/AnaResImpFishSubs.pdf, accessed 22 July 2010

UNEP (2004b) *Energy Subsidies: Lessons Learned in Assessing Their Impact and Designing Policy Reforms*, UNEP, Geneva

UNEP/Eurobats (2005) 'Report of the Intersessional Working Group on wind turbines and bat populations', 10th Meeting of the Advisory Committee, 25–27 April 2005, Bratislava, Slovak Republic

UNEP (2008a) *Fisheries Subsidies: A Critical Issue for Trade and Sustainable Development at the WTO: An Introductory Guide*, UNEP, Geneva, www.unep.ch/etb/areas/pdf/UNEP-ETB%20Brochure%20 on%20Fisheries%20Subsidies_May2008.pdf, accessed 22 July 2010

UNEP (2008b) *Reforming Energy Subsidies: Opportunities to Contribute to the Climate Change Agenda*, UNEP, Geneva

UNEP (forthcoming) *Green Economy Report*, UNEP, Geneva, available at www.unep.org/greeneconomy/ GreenEconomyReport/tabid/1375/Default.aspx, accessed 27 October 2010

UNEP and WWF (2007) *Sustainability Criteria for Fisheries Subsidies: Options for the WTO and Beyond*, UNEP, Geneva, www.unep.ch/etb/publications/fishierSubsidiesEnvironment/UNEPWWF_FinalRevi 09102007.pdf, accessed 22 July 2010

Valsecchi, C., ten Brink, P., Bassi, S., Withana, S., Lewis, M., Best A., Oosterhuis F., Dias Soares C., Rogers-Ganter H. and Kaphengst T. (2009) *Environmentally Harmful Subsidies (EHS): Identification and Assessment*, Report to the European Commission's DG Environment by IEEP (Institute for European Environmental Policy), Ecologic and IVM, http://ec.europa.eu/environment/enveco/taxation/pdf/ Harmful%20Subsidies%20Report.pdf, accessed 22 September 2010

van Beers, C. and de Moor, A. (2001) 'Public subsidies and policy failure: How subsidies distort the natural environment, equity and trade and how to reform them', *Ambio*, vol 38, no 6, pp339–341

von Moltke, A. (2010) *Fisheries Subsidies, Sustainable Development and the WTO*, Earthscan, London

World Bank (2005) *Environmental Fiscal Reform: What Should be Done and How to Achieve It*, International Bank for Reconstruction and Development, Washington, DC, http://siteresources. worldbank.org/INTRANETENVIRONMENT/Publications/20712869/EnvFiscalReform.pdf, accessed 22 July 2010

World Bank (2008) *Sunken Billions: The Economic Justification for Subsidies Reform*, International Bank for Reconstruction and Development, Washington, DC

WRI (World Resources Institute) (2001) *Earthtrends 2001: Forest Fragmentation by Roads in Central Africa*, WRI Environmental Information Portal, http://earthtrends.wri.org/pdf_library/maps/9_m_ ForFragCentralAf.pdf, accessed 27 July 2010

WTO (World Trade Organization) (2000) *Environmental Benefits of Removing Trade Restrictions and Distortions: The Fisheries Sector*, WT/CTE/W/167, World Trade Organization, Geneva

WTO (World Trade Organization) (2004) 'Doha Work Programme: Decision Adopted by the General Council on 1 August 2004', Document WT/L/578, World Trade Organization, Geneva

WWF (World Wide Fund for Nature) (Endangered Seas Campaign) (1998) *The Footprint of Distant Water Fleets on World Fisheries*, WWF, Godalming, Surrey

Chapter 7
Addressing the Losses through Regulation and Pricing

Coordinating lead authors
Bernd Hansjürgens, Christoph Schröter-Schlaack

Lead authors
Graham Tucker, Alexandra Vakrou

Contributing authors
Samuela Bassi, Patrick ten Brink, Ece Ozdemiroglu,
Clare Shine, Heidi Wittmer

Editing and language check
Clare Shine

See end of chapter for acknowledgements for reviews and other contributions

Contents

Key messages   **301**

Summary   **303**

1   Basic principles for halting ongoing losses   **303**

2   Regulating to avoid damage: Environmental standards   **305**
    2.1   Importance of a strong regulatory baseline   305
    2.2   Using economic analysis in standard setting   309

3   Compensating for losses: Offsets and biodiversity banks   **310**
    3.1   Why do we need compensation instruments?   310
    3.2   Ways to maximize biodiversity benefits and minimize risks   314
    3.3   Experience of biodiversity offsets and banking to date   316

4   Setting more accurate prices: Market-based instruments   **317**
    4.1   Changing incentives in decision making   317
    4.2   What can market-based instruments contribute?   320
    4.3   Limitations of market-based instruments   326
    4.4   Role of economic information in instrument design   328

5   Monitoring, enforcement and criminal prosecution   **330**
    5.1   Environmental crime: A local and global problem   330
    5.2   New approaches to tackle crime   334

6   Making it happen – Policy mixes to get results   **336**

Acknowledgements   **338**

References   **338**

Key messages

Existing policies have not managed to stop ongoing losses and degradation of biodiversity and ecosystem services. For the reasons outlined in this book, the associated costs are still hidden or distorted. Polluters and resource users rarely meet the real costs of the damage they cause and sometimes pay nothing at all.

Rewarding benefits and reforming subsidies (Chapters 5 and 6) are important components of policy reform but will never be enough on their own. Coherent actions to make the full costs of loss visible and payable should form the backbone of new biodiversity policies.

Basic principles for halting ongoing losses

Policy design should be based on two key principles: polluter pays and full cost recovery. Many tools already exist and more are coming on stream, but their potential could be much better exploited. They can encourage private and public actors to incorporate biodiversity values in decisions and investments, and stimulate efficiency and technical innovation. They can improve social and distributional equity as well as policy credibility and acceptability.

Regulating to avoid damage: Environmental standards

Environmental regulation will remain central to addressing pressures on biodiversity and ecosystems. Using prohibitions, standards and technical conditions has a proven track record and delivers major benefits. A well-defined and comprehensive regulatory framework provides the essential baseline for introducing complementary compensation mechanisms and market-based instruments. It should also guide private sector efforts to develop efficient approaches to damage prevention and remediation by responsible parties.

Setting more accurate prices through market-based instruments

A systematic proactive approach is needed to send accurate price signals about the true value of ecosystem services. Incentives can be adjusted by applying standards and/or introducing taxes, charges, fees, fines, compensation mechanisms, tradable permits or liability rules. This should be part of a wider fiscal reform in favour of biodiversity (see also Chapters 5, 6 and 9).

Designing smart policy mixes

It is crucial to communicate the benefits of regulation and market-based instruments to overcome political/social opposition. Policy mixes can target different actors, taking account of institutional background, capacity, traditions, affordability and the specific resource or service in question. Flexible approaches can:

- stimulate efficiency through price signals and least-cost solutions to problems;
- use compensation tools to support 'no net loss' in policies or even create 'net-gain' solutions;
- generate extra public revenues that, if earmarked, can support pro-biodiversity measures. ·

Monitoring, enforcement and criminal prosecution

Effective enforcement is critical to give policies teeth and demonstrate the gravity of environmental crimes. Adequate funding for technical equipment and trained staff is essential to show policy makers' commitment to tackling biodiversity and ecosystem losses.

Summary

If we were running a business with the biosphere as our major asset, we would not allow it to depreciate. We would ensure that all necessary repairs and maintenance were carried out on a regular basis. (Professor Alan Malcolm, Chief Scientific Adviser, International Union of Pure and Applied Chemistry, no date)

Chapter 7 focuses on ways to increase accountability for the cost of damage to biodiversity and ecosystem services in order to curb further losses. Section 1 sets out key concepts that should underpin all policies, aligned with the polluter pays principle. Section 2 describes the role of environmental regulation and shows how economic information can be used to inform and target regulatory standards. Section 3 analyses compensation schemes to ensure no net loss or a net gain of biodiversity and ecosystem services. Section 4 discusses the scope and limitations of market-based instruments in delivering additional conservation gains and encouraging innovative approaches. Section 5 addresses the critical need to improve enforcement and international cooperation on environmental crime. Section 6 provides design indicators for a smart policy mix.

1 Basic principles for halting ongoing losses

If we refuse to take into account the full cost of our fossil fuel addiction – if we don't factor in the environmental costs and national security costs and true economic costs – we will have missed our best chance to seize a clean energy future. (President Barack Obama, 2010)

As highlighted throughout this book, policies to date have not managed to halt the loss or degradation of ecosystems and biodiversity. To turn this situation around, we need instruments that incorporate the cost of such losses. Many promising tools are available and can be more widely shared but their potential is not yet fully exploited.

Chapters 5 and 6 showed how payments for ecosystem services (PES) and reformed subsidies can help build up natural capital and create positive incentives for biodiversity action. However, their contribution will be undercut if economic activities continue to generate pollution and degrade ecosystems. Targeted prevention measures are therefore a core component of the policy mix.

Decision makers and resource users will only take such losses into account if confronted with their real costs. This book has already stressed the factors that conceal such costs: lack of information and appropriate incentives, incomplete property rights, relatively few markets or regulation. We face market failure because most markets do not signal the true value of biodiversity and ecosystem services or show what their losses cost us.

This chapter discusses a range of policy tools to incorporate these costs, showing their respective advantages and disadvantages and providing guidance to improve instrument design. This can have several advantages for policy makers:

- Using values transparently can justify environmental regulation and help overcome political resistance (see Chapter 2). Showing what and how much society is losing can strengthen the hand of policy makers arguing for improved policies. Confronting those who cause damage with the associated costs can stimulate prevention efforts and boost efficiency (e.g. less water-intensive production, less fertilizer use, more use of biodegradable products, low-carbon energy sources).
- Making the polluter pay is more equitable: it is not fair that a few benefit while society pays for the damage (see Box 7.1). Signalling that those causing damage are also responsible for addressing it improves governance and the credibility of the regulatory system.
- Applying the full cost recovery principle to the user/polluter/emitter can set appropriate incentives and reduce burdens on public budgets (see Box 7.1).
- Some instruments (e.g. taxes, fees and charges, auctioned licences) can generate revenues for conservation (see PES/REDD in Chapter 5, protected areas in Chapter 8 and investment in natural capital in Chapter 9).

Box 7.1 Fundamental principles for incorporating costs of biodiversity loss

Together with equity and social considerations, three closely related principles should guide the choice and design of policy instruments:

The polluter pays principle

The polluter pays principle (PPP) is anchored in the 1992 Rio Declaration on Environment and Development (UNEP, 2009a) and embedded in many national environmental policies (e.g. most OECD countries and EU Member States). It requires environmental costs to be 'internalized' and reflected in the price of goods and services. The polluter has to take prevention or reduction measures and in some cases pay taxes or charges and compensate for pollution impacts. For ecosystem degradation, the polluter should pay directly for clean-up and restoration or pay a fine to help offset damage costs.

The user/beneficiary pays principle

The user/beneficiary pays principle is a variant of the PPP. Recipients of a benefit (e.g. use of natural resources) should pay for the cost of providing it (e.g. users of a clean beach should contribute towards beach cleaning expenses).

The full cost recovery principle

The full cost recovery principle provides that the full costs of environmental services should be recovered from the entity benefiting from a service. There is a growing international trend to apply this principle to energy, electricity and water pricing to pass full costs on to consumers.

Source: Adapted from ten Brink et al (2009)

---

2 Regulating to avoid damage: Environmental standards

> It is bad policy to regulate everything ... where things may better regulate themselves and can be better promoted by private exertions; but it is no less bad policy to let those things alone which can only be promoted by interfering social power. (Friedrich List, German economist, 1789–1846; List, 1996, p85)

2.1 Importance of a strong regulatory baseline

Regulation has long been – and still is – the most widely used instrument for environmental protection. It is used to establish protection objectives, reduce pollution and hazardous events and trigger urgent environmental improvements.

A clearly defined regulatory framework provides orientation for the private sector. Regulation needs to be conducive to business, compatible with commercial activities and it should set a level playing field to encourage capacity building, training and compliance with best professional standards (see TEEB in Business, 2011).

A strong system of regulation and governance is also essential to establish market-based policies such as trading schemes, biodiversity offsets and banking (see Section 3). It provides the reference point for such instruments (see Section 4) and needs to be underpinned by monitoring and enforcement (see Section 5).

Environmental regulation sets rules and standards across a range of areas (see Box 7.2).

A tight regulatory framework defining the scope and extent of resource use is essential to halt losses. Because biodiversity has a public good character, it is the

---

Box 7.2 Scope and flexibility of environmental regulation

As in many other fields of law, the regulatory toolkit includes a battery of prohibitions, restrictions, mandatory requirements, standards and procedures that directly authorize or limit certain actions or impacts. The generic terms 'regulation' and 'command-and-control' are often used for instruments promulgated by a (government) authority (compared to self-regulation and social norms).

There are three main types of regulatory instruments for biodiversity and ecosystem services:

1. Regulation of emissions involves standards for emissions, ambient quality and technical practice (e.g. best available techniques, BAT); performance (e.g. air quality management) or management practice (e.g. in agriculture).
2. Regulation of products sets restrictions on product use (e.g. illegally logged timber, activities damaging to endangered species, etc.) or establishes production standards (certification, best practice codes, etc.).
3. Spatial planning regulates land uses with direct implications for ecosystem services or habitats (see Box 7.3). Decisions are usually devolved to local or regional planning boards (see TEEB in Local Policy, 2011). Designation and establishment of protected areas is a specific regulatory tool based on spatial planning (see Chapter 8).

responsibility of politicians to define relevant targets and set up an adequate framework to ensure such targets are met.

We often underestimate the contribution that sectoral regulations can make to safeguarding biodiversity. In agriculture, for example, regulating fertilizer use can reduce nutrient run-off into soils and water, eutrophication in river systems, lakes and coastal areas and algae build-up on beaches. This in turn supports multiple ecosystem services and benefits (aesthetic, tourism and cultural values, reduced health impacts, provisioning and regulating services) and improves carbon storage in the soil (see examples in Table 7.1).

Box 7.3 Agro-ecological zoning to consolidate ecosystem service provision in Brazil

Faced with increasing domestic and international scrutiny of its sugarcane biofuels programme, the Brazilian government introduced the world's first agro-ecological zoning system in 2009. These regulations guide sustainable crop sowing by coupling government subsidies and credits to support crops appropriate to the climatic, hydrological and soil conditions in different regions and biomes, and prohibiting expansion into sensitive areas like the entire Amazon region and Pantanal hydrographic basin.

By matching sugar production to appropriate conditions and non-sensitive regions, Brazil's programme supports the retention and improvement of several provisioning and regulating ecosystem services, especially soil health, carbon sequestration and energy production. It also makes creative use of the 'bottlenecks' of lending institutions and processing plants, through which all sugarcane producers must pass, to place significant responsibility for oversight in the hands of an easily observable and controllable part of the private sector.

Source: Leopold and Aguilar (2009)

Table 7.1 Examples of sectoral regulations that can benefit ecosystem services

Regulated activity	Type of regulation	Affected ecosystem service
Water use	Drinking water	Fresh water
	Water/groundwater extraction	Food
	Wastewater treatment	Water purification
	Water body condition	Water regulation
	Water pollution and quality	Natural hazard regulation
		Recreation and ecotourism
		Aesthetic values
		Water cycling
		Nutrient cycle
Air pollution	Ambient air quality standards	Food
	Emission standards	Fresh water
	Off-gas treatment	Air quality regulation
	Fuel efficiency standards	Climate regulation
	Lead ban motorfuels	Natural hazard regulation
	Exhaust emission standards	Recreation and ecotourism

Table 7.1 Examples of sectoral regulations that can benefit ecosystem services (*Cont'd*)

Regulated activity	Type of regulation	Affected ecosystem service
Land use	Spatial planning/zoning Mineral extraction Soil protection and contamination	Food Fibre Fresh water Biochemicals Water regulation Climate regulation Natural hazard regulation Erosion control Air quality regulation Aesthetic Values Cultural diversity Recreation and ecotourism Soil formation Water cycling Nutrient cycle
Agriculture	Required minimum practices Best practices Fertilizers Regulation on transgenic crops	Food Fibre Climate regulation Erosion control Pest control Disease regulation Recreation and ecotourism Soil formation Nutrient cycling
Forestry	Afforestation/reforestation Best practices Timber harvest regulation Forest product licensing Hunting licensing Abstraction of non-timber forest products	Food Fibre Biochemicals Climate regulation Erosion control Natural hazard regulation Water regulation Aesthetic values Recreation and ecotourism Inspiration Water cycling Nutrient cycle
Fisheries	Catch licensing Nursery protection Mesh size	Food Genetic resources Climate regulation Recreation and ecotourism Nutrient cycle
Nature Protection	Protected areas Protected Species Act Habitat Directive Birds Directive	Fresh water Genetic resources Biochemicals Natural hazard regulation Aesthetic values Inspiration Educational value Spritual and religious values
Key:	Provisioning Services Regulating Services	Cultural Services Supporting Services

Source: Christoph Schröter-Schlaack, own representation

Regulation has already catalysed real environmental improvements by reducing the release of pollutants that damage ecosystem status and functions. Management of air quality, water and soils rely heavily on such rules (see Box 7.3) whereas regulations for chemicals address risks associated with producing, distributing and using certain products or compounds.

Box 7.4 Regulatory success stories: Tackling air pollution and promoting sustainable forestry

Germany

Forest damage from 'acid rain' – mainly caused by SO_2 emissions from energy-producing combustion plants (*Waldsterben*) – created huge pressure on politicians in the early 1980s. A tight SO_2-emission standard was set at 400mg/m^3, binding all plants from 1993. Following its enactment, the electricity sector started a major reduction programme that led to a sharp decline in emissions (see table).

Year	1980	1982	1985	1988	1989	1990	1992	1995
SO_2-emissions (mg/m^3)	2154	2160	1847	582	270	290	250	154

Sweden

Forest decline in the 1980s and 1990s led to updating of the Swedish Forestry Act in 1994, under which forests 'shall be managed in such a way as to provide a valuable, sustainable yield and at the same time preserve biodiversity'. The Act provides for new standards to be established (i) after felling, (ii) if forest land is unused, and (iii) if the forest condition is clearly unsatisfactory. It sets quotas for maximum annual allowable cut to promote even age distribution of forest stands. Recent statistics demonstrate positive results, especially the increase in the number of old or deciduous trees recovered in the last 20 years (10 to 90 per cent, depending on diameter).

Sources: RRV (1999); Wätzold (2004); Swedish Forestry Act; Berggren (2009)

The higher the potential hazard to human health or the environment, the stricter the necessary regulations will be. In practice, however, these are often adopted reactively after a catastrophe (e.g. the US Oil Pollution Act 1990 followed the *Exxon Valdez* oil spill, see Chapter 4).

Regulation is not expensive for public budgets in itself but it carries administrative costs for monitoring and enforcement (see Section 5). Costs of implementation and compliance mainly fall on private resource users who have to pay for abatement or equivalent measures to reach the required standard. Monitoring activities (e.g. of wastewater effluent or river water quality downstream) can be funded by the emitting source, consistent with the polluter pays principle.

Decision makers and administrators are very familiar with these regulatory tools. Where institutional capacity for implementation is already in place, it is often easier to expand regulation than to set up market-based approaches. For example, emission limits for power stations and industrial plants can be tightened over time to respond to new environmental or health needs. Existing BAT standards for specific technologies or techniques and monitoring can be easily adapted to local conditions, building on lessons learned and precedents from other countries.

Regulation forms the baseline and catalyst for additional complementary measures. Emissions trading instruments, for example, emerged against a background of air quality standards in the US (Hansjürgens, 2000). The first generation of instruments in the 1970s (i.e. netting, offset, bubble and banking policy) was based on credits that could be created if abatement went beyond a certain standard. Only the additional emissions 'saved' by over-compliance could be used for compensation or trading. Similar rules apply for biodiversity offsets and/or banking (see Section 3).

2.2 Using economic analysis in standard setting

Economic valuation of ecosystem services can inform the regulatory framework for biodiversity. It can support arguments in favour of policies to avoid net losses and increase the credibility and acceptance of tighter standards.

When regulatory instruments were first designed, cost–benefit considerations were often ignored or only implicit. This balancing act was rarely needed because the imperative was to tackle urgent concerns of human life and health. This is still true for some well-known hazards, e.g. carcinogenic substances, air quality standards for particulates.

Including costs and benefits in decision making has become essential for several reasons:

- Many countries have unseen potential for regulation. Where institutions are weak and administrative capacities underdeveloped, identifying and valuing ecosystem services can feed information into national and local planning processes and reveal where better regulation may be needed (see Box 7.5).
- Many countries now apply the precautionary principle even where environmental risks are not hazardous to human life. Balancing costs and benefits is critical to provide justification for possible regulation. Stricter controls are often only accepted by stakeholders and the general public once the benefits are clearly shown to outweigh the costs.

Box 7.5 Feeding catchment assessment data into the regulatory process, South Africa

The municipality of uMhlathuze was confronted with the classic 'development versus conservation' dilemma for a local biodiversity hotspot – with the poor socio-economic climate making development a tempting option. The municipality undertook a Strategic Catchment Assessment to identify the ecosystem services provided free of charge by the catchment. The estimated value of these services (e.g. nutrient cycling, waste management and water regulation) was found to be nearly US$200 million/year. 'Biodiversity averse' politicians reacted positively to this concrete information on ecosystem economic values and identified management actions to ensure sustainable use of the ecosystem and its resources.

Source: Slootweg and van Beukering (2008)

3 Compensating for losses: Offsets and biodiversity banks

3.1 Why do we need compensation instruments?

Developments linked to economic growth often lead to habitat loss and fragmentation, pollution and disturbance. These impacts can often be avoided or substantially reduced through measures at the design stage (see Chapter 4) and during operations (mitigation and remediation measures supported by monitoring and adaptive management). Even so, many developments will inevitably have significant residual biodiversity impacts.

Compensation for these impacts is essential to stop ongoing cumulative losses of biodiversity and ecosystem services (compensation in this context refers to comparable biodiversity outcomes and not monetary compensation: it is sometime called 'compensatory mitigation'). Offsets and biodiversity banks are the main instruments for this purpose (see Box 7.6). They play a key role in delivering explicit 'no net loss' policies (Bean et al, 2008) and are implicitly required as part of the policy mix to achieve targets to halt biodiversity loss, e.g. in the EU.

Offsets and habitat banking work by triggering new actions that provide additional measurable biodiversity benefits (credits) compared to the damage (debits). This equivalence can involve the same kind of habitat or species (like-for-like) or different kinds of equal or higher importance or value. Offset benefits arise from actions to protect habitats at risk (i.e. risk aversion offsets) or to restore degraded or destroyed habitats.

Biodiversity banks create a market-based instrument by turning offsets into tradable assets (credits) (see Box 7.6). Offsets in isolation involve actions that typically follow a sequential logic: planning a specific project or activity; identifying likely residual damage; offsetting for residual damage. Biodiversity banking allows these

---

Box 7.6 Biodiversity compensation mechanisms

Biodiversity offsets

Biodiversity offsets are 'measurable conservation outcomes resulting from actions designed to compensate for significant residual adverse biodiversity impacts arising from project development and persisting after appropriate prevention and mitigation measures have been implemented. The goal of biodiversity offsets is to achieve no net loss, or preferably a net gain, of biodiversity on the ground with respect to species composition, habitat structure and ecosystem services, including livelihood aspects.'

Biodiversity banking

Biodiversity banking is a market system, based on biodiversity offsets, for the supply of biodiversity credits and demand for those credits to offset damage to biodiversity (debits). Credits may be produced in advance of – and without predicted links to – the debits they compensate and be stored over time. Often known as conservation banks, they can include habitat banks and species banks.

Source: BBOP (2009)

---

actions to take place without prior connection and in any order. The credit can be created before the scale of the debit has been assessed and be stored until needed to compensate for a damaging project. This involves speculation over credit demand and supply over time and discounting of values. In some respects biodiversity banking resembles carbon trading but is more complex because:

- there is no such thing as a 'unit of biodiversity' as there is for carbon;
- the location of biodiversity damage and/or compensation material can present constraints;
- whereas policy instruments are in place to support carbon trading, regulations to control biodiversity loss are weak in most countries and demand for biodiversity trading usually low.

Some offset demands result from voluntary commercial considerations (e.g. managing business risks and liabilities; securing access to investments; accreditation requirements; public relations; and corporate social responsibility goals). For example, one mining company uses offsets to compensate for unavoidable residual impacts and thereby meet its 'aim to have a net positive impact on biodiversity' (Rio Tinto, 2004). As voluntary demand is usually low, however, the following drivers are needed to create sufficient demand for compensation mechanisms to support viable biodiversity banking markets:

- Clear policy requirements for no net loss or a net gain of biodiversity.
- Legislation requiring compensation for residual impacts to achieve no net loss or a net gain of biodiversity (e.g. for Natura 2000 sites under the EU Habitats Directive). Such measures are normally strictly regulated and must be project-specific like-for-like offsets, usually within or close to the project development site.
- Planning and impact assessment procedures (e.g. the EU EIA and SEA Directives, see Chapter 4) that identify mitigation requirements and significant residual impacts from projects and programmes. The impact compensation requirement varies considerably depending on national and local policies (especially regarding no-net-loss obligations), the importance of the impacted biodiversity and the magnitude of the predicted impacts.

We should always remember that many biodiversity components and ecosystem services are unique and irreplaceable and cannot be effectively compensated. Offsets and banks are best suited to addressing moderate residual impacts on biodiversity components that are replaceable and can be conserved or restored using known techniques within a reasonable time frame (see Box 7.7 and Figure 7.1). They are also appropriate for impacts that seem minor in isolation but are cumulatively significant. For impacts on widespread biodiversity, trading up (i.e. activities to protect more important biodiversity) is likely to be acceptable in most cases. However, where impacts are relatively small, project-specific compensation can have prohibitive transaction costs. In such cases, it may be possible to develop simple schemes, such as standard in-lieu payments to independent but regulated trusts that reflect biodiversity offset costs. The trusts can then distribute funds to biodiversity banks or projects according to conservation priorities and stakeholder concerns.

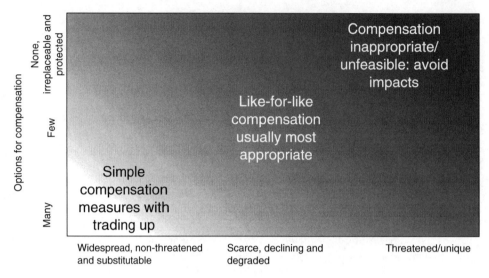

Figure 7.1 *Appropriateness of compensation in relation to the importance of impacted biodiversity and availability of reliable compensation options*

Source: adapted from BBOP (2009)

Box 7.7 Offsetting deforestation in Flanders, Belgium

With a forest index of only 10.8 per cent, Flanders is one of Europe's most heavily deforested regions. The Flemish government has therefore prioritized forest protection and preservation. To prevent further decrease in valuable forest areas, three main principles apply:

1   Deforestation is in principle prohibited.
2   When permitted, an authorization is required.
3   An authorization may not be delivered without compensation (Afdeling Bos and Groen, 2002).

Compensation consists of paying a 'forest preservation contribution' of €1.98/m² for coniferous forest and €3.96/m² for indigenous deciduous forest. The Flemish authority uses the revenues to buy land for afforestation (Vlaamse Regering, 2001).

By 2007, deforestation was almost completely balanced with official afforestation measures (VBV, 2008). In 2008, 156 hectares were deforested under permit but only 152 hectares were created through afforestation. As the annual afforestation target of 769 hectares has not been met in recent years (VBV, 2009), the Flemish authority has committed itself to revive and broaden the scope of the forest preservation fund (Commissie voor Leefmilieu, Natuur, Ruimtelijke Ordening, 2010).

Potential benefits of offsets and biodiversity banking

Well-designed biodiversity offsets and banks can provide additional benefits beyond no net loss from individual developments. Net biodiversity gains are most feasible in regions where past impacts have created landscapes dominated by artificial or cultural habitats with relatively low biodiversity and where remaining areas of semi-natural or natural habitats are small, fragmented and degraded. In such cases, offsets can:

- balance development and conservation, and deliver more conservation efforts than the 'status quo';
- generate extra funds for conservation, and mainstream biodiversity into business and regional planning;
- reverse some past losses of restorable threatened habitats and increase the size of remaining small habitat patches, thereby increasing the viability of species populations and resilience to pressures such as climate change;
- reduce habitat fragmentation by recreating habitats in appropriate locations to restore connectivity;
- in some cases, secure more reliable biodiversity outcomes than potential mitigation measures, especially if biodiversity banks are established in advance;
- be more cost-effective than avoidance and mitigation measures, especially where banks benefit from economies of scale and competitive market forces; cost reductions may encourage measures to be implemented beyond strict legal requirements;
- provide a mechanism to address the cumulative impacts of low-level impacts in a cost-effective and practical manner.

Constraints and potential risks of offsets and biodiversity banking

Significant constraints need to be considered to avoid risks to biodiversity if compensation measures are inappropriately applied (EFTEC and IEEP, 2010). The most fundamental one is probably that such measures must provide long-term added value (i.e. not just benefits that would have occurred anyway). Measures must also be based on outcomes above and beyond what is already required under existing/foreseen policy and legislation.

In some cases, significant biodiversity benefits can be obtained by stopping ongoing degradation and avoiding losses from e.g. agricultural improvement, deforestation, wetland drainage and pollution. Agreements (e.g. contracts or covenants) can be made with individuals who give up the right to convert habitat in return for payments or other benefits. However, offsets of this kind can only deliver benefits where there are significant areas of remaining habitat that are:

- worth maintaining;
- unprotected and likely to remain so in the future (to ensure additionality);
- subject to significant and predictable levels of loss or degradation.

In practice, options for risk aversion compensation may be limited in areas where protection levels for important habitats are already high. Furthermore, even when protecting one area of habitat succeeds, this can simply lead to the threat being displaced to another area and thus have no impact on the overall rate of loss (often referred to as 'leakage').

Given these constraints, many offsets and biodiversity banks focus instead on habitat restoration or recreation (see Chapter 9). In practice, this is extremely difficult particularly for natural and ancient habitats that have developed over thousands of years. A key principle is that reliability of compensation outcomes should increase in relation to the importance of the habitat/species affected (Figure 7.1). Stringent and reliable avoidance and mitigation measures should therefore be taken to avoid residual impacts on very rare or otherwise valuable habitats.

Offset proposals need to provide a high level of certainty of achieving their conservation objectives (or at least high compared to alternative mitigation measures). In this respect, biodiversity banks have a distinct advantage if they store credits (restored or enhanced habitats) ahead of possible impacts: this reduces uncertainty and concerns over the feasibility and likely quality of compensation, even if some long-term uncertainty remains. However, the commercial risks and long time scales involved in creating many habitat banks can discourage their establishment and the development of a supply of credits.

These issues highlight the need for strong regulation of biodiversity offsets and banks. Without this, there are significant risks that project proponents will use compensation to avoid more costly measures and/or project delays. They have a financial incentive to underestimate potential impacts, overestimate the reliability and benefits of compensation (or other mitigation measures with lower costs) and avoid implementation of agreed measures. It is therefore critical to develop these systems alongside appropriate regulation and adequate administrative capacities. A robust regulatory framework can ensure that biodiversity impacts of programmes or projects are properly assessed and that appropriate compensation measures are properly implemented, monitored and managed for at least the period of residual impacts – which often means in perpetuity.

3.2 Ways to maximize biodiversity benefits and minimize risks

The potential benefits and risks of offsets and biodiversity banking have been widely recognized (e.g. ten Kate et al, 2004; Carroll et al, 2007; Bean et al, 2008). The Biodiversity and Business Offsets Programme (BBOP) has developed a set of design principles in consultation with stakeholders to maximize benefits and minimize risks (see most recent version in Box 7.8).

These principles are generally applicable to all compensation measures but need to be carefully interpreted and applied. Principle 3, in particular, is often misinterpreted. A key objective of the mitigation hierarchy is to reduce the risk of biodiversity loss from developers taking easy least-cost actions, i.e. using offsets and biodiversity banking as a 'licence to trash'. However, some expensive mitigation measures (e.g. tunnels or viaducts) may not represent good value for money in terms of biodiversity outcomes. Moreover, it is clearly inappropriate to expect project proponents to take preventive measures for low-level impacts if much greater benefits could be obtained by simple compensation measures traded up to provide higher biodiversity benefits.

The term 'appropriate' is therefore central to the mitigation hierarchy. The specific aim should be to compare the respective conservation benefits of the potential

Box 7.8 BBOP Principles on Biodiversity Offsets

1. **No net loss:** A biodiversity offset should be designed and implemented to achieve on-site measurable conservation outcomes that can reasonably be expected to result in no net loss and preferably a net gain of biodiversity.
2. **Additional conservation outcomes:** A biodiversity offset should achieve conservation outcomes above and beyond results that would have occurred if the offset had not taken place. Offset design and implementation should avoid displacing activities harmful to biodiversity to other locations.
3. **Adherence to the mitigation hierarchy:** A biodiversity offset is a commitment to compensate for significant residual adverse impacts on biodiversity identified after appropriate avoidance, minimization and on-site rehabilitation measures have been taken according to the mitigation hierarchy.
4. **Limits to what can be offset:** There are situations where residual impacts cannot be fully compensated for by a biodiversity offset because of the irreplaceability or vulnerability of the biodiversity affected.
5. **Landscape context:** A biodiversity offset should be designed and implemented in a landscape context to achieve the expected measurable conservation outcomes, taking into account available information on the full range of biological, social and cultural values of biodiversity and supporting an ecosystem approach.
6. **Stakeholder participation:** In areas affected by the project and by the biodiversity offset, the effective participation of stakeholders should be ensured in decision making about biodiversity offsets, including their evaluation, selection, design, implementation and monitoring.
7. **Equity:** A biodiversity offset should be designed and implemented in an equitable manner, which means the sharing among stakeholders of the rights and responsibilities, risks and rewards associated with a project and offset in a fair and balanced way, respecting legal and customary arrangements. Special consideration should be given to respecting both internationally and nationally recognized rights of indigenous peoples and local communities.
8. **Long-term outcomes:** The design and implementation of a biodiversity offset should be based on an adaptive management approach, incorporating monitoring and evaluation, with the objective of securing outcomes that last at least as long as the project's impacts and preferably in perpetuity.
9. **Transparency:** The design and implementation of a biodiversity offset, and communication of its results to the public, should be undertaken in a transparent and timely manner.
10. **Science and traditional knowledge:** The design and implementation of a biodiversity offset should be a documented process informed by sound science, including an appropriate consideration of traditional knowledge.

Source: BBOP (2008)

mitigation and compensation measures to identify the combination that delivers the highest reliable benefit (EFTEC and IEEP, 2010). The question of reliability must be considered in accordance with the precautionary principle. Uncertainty can affect all types of mitigation and compensation measures depending on the circumstances: some mitigation measures may be more reliable than compensation measures or vice versa. The weight given to reliability should increase with the importance and irreplaceability of the habitats and species that may be impacted. For biodiversity of high conservation importance, measures should focus on avoidance actions (assuming they are most likely to be reliable) rather than risky compensation options.

As noted, one advantage of established biodiversity banks is to reduce uncertainty over the amount and quality of compensation that will be obtained, given that credits already exist and can be measured directly in terms of their ecological value and ecosystem benefits. However, it is still important to assess the ongoing value of these benefits (e.g. in relation to climate change or other external pressures) as well as their additionality.

3.3 Experience of biodiversity offsets and banking to date

A recent ecosystem marketplace review found at least 39 biodiversity compensation programmes around the world (and another 25 in development), ranging from active biodiversity banking to programmes channelling development impact fees to policies that drive one-off offsets (Madsen et al, 2010). It estimates that there are over 600 biodiversity banks worldwide.

Countries with legal requirements for offsets include Brazil, South Africa, Australia and the US, which probably has the most advanced biodiversity banking market (Carroll et al, 2007; Bean et al, 2008). Box 7.9 provides examples of practice to date in two of these countries. Although the EU has strict legal requirements for compensation measures for 'unavoidable impacts' on protected areas of European importance (Natura 2000 sites), the types of habitat involved and the need for like-for-like compensation restricts the potential to use biodiversity banks (EFTEC and IEEP, 2010). However, some EU Member States (e.g. France and Germany) have additional legislation and policies requiring or enabling offsets and habitat banking.

Box 7.9 Biodiversity compensation and offsets in Australia and the US

Australia's BioBanking system provides that where land-use conversion and associated biodiversity loss are inevitable, alternative sites can be restored or put in conservation. This provides an incentive to encourage conservation on private land and provide compensation for biodiversity loss at other locations. No economic data are available yet as the programme is still in an early stage.

In the United States more than 400 wetland banks have been established, creating a market for wetland mitigation worth more than US$3 billion/year. There are also more than 70 species banks which can trade between US$100 million and US$370 million in species credits each year.

Sources: Bayon (2008); DECC (2009)

Many biodiversity banks have been developed by businesses and public–private partnerships that have mobilized private funds. The financial sector has spotted opportunities for further business creation and development of 'green' investment products targeted to this niche market. However, many schemes are expensive and can entail high upfront and long-term investment. Involvement of public or financial stakeholders is therefore sometimes needed to provide support for complicated and large-scale projects.

In conclusion, experience to date shows that while there have been some problems, well-designed and regulated offsets and biodiversity banks can be efficient market-based instruments to help businesses compensate for the residual unavoidable harm from development projects. A decisive element of successful schemes is a strong regulatory baseline upon which they can build.

4 Setting more accurate prices: Market-based instruments

Taxes are what we pay for civilized society. (Oliver Wendell Holmes Jr., American jurist, US Supreme Court, 1927, paragraph 19)

Maybe environmental tax reform is the price of a sustainable society? (Jacqueline McGlade, EEA, Speech at the 8th Global Conference on Environmental Taxation, Munich, 2007)

4.1 Changing incentives in decision making

Market-based instruments (MBIs) can change the incentives available to private actors when deciding upon resource use and contribute to more effective and efficient management of biodiversity and ecosystem services.

MBIs (e.g. taxes, charges, fees and fines; commercial licences, tradable permits, quotas; liability rules) send out economic signals. They can be adjusted to discourage harmful activities by increasing the cost of using certain services, requiring users to buy tradable permits and/or mandating consideration of risks within decision making. Targeted reinforcement of this kind can catalyse a shift to more environmentally friendly alternatives.

In principle, the same is true for direct environmental regulation (see Section 2 above). However, MBIs give private actors more choice in selecting the most cost-efficient option (i.e. to pay the higher price or find an alternative).

MBIs work in three ways: controlling prices, controlling quantities or setting liability rules.

Price-based instruments

Taxes, fees and charges determine the price that has to be paid for using an ecosystem, e.g. charges for water abstraction, sewage fees, entry fees to national parks, a carbon tax, deposit–refund systems or waste fees (see Box 7.10).

Box 7.10 Use of volume-based waste fees to reduce waste generation in Korea

In 1995, Korea introduced a volume-based waste fee (VBWF) where residents pay for solid waste services by purchasing standard waste bags. In principle, the full cost of collection, transport and treatment should be included in the VBWF bag price. However, to avoid negative side effects of a sudden increase in waste treatment costs (e.g. illegal dumping), each municipality sets a different rate depending upon its financial circumstances and treatment costs. Disposal of waste without using VBWF bags or illegally burning waste is subject to the €1 million (US$1000) negligence fine.

The VBWF programme has had far-reaching effects. From 1994 to 2004, it led to a 14 per cent reduction in the quantity of municipal solid waste generated (corresponding to a 20 per cent decline in waste generation per capita) and an increase of 15 per cent in the quota of recycled waste (up to 49 per cent).

Categories	1994	1996	1998	2000	2002	2004
Total waste generation (tons/day)	58,118	49,925	44,583	46,438	49,902	50,007
– of which waste is recycled	8927	13,085	15,566	19,167	21,949	24,588
– of which waste is land-filled	47,116	34,116	25,074	21,831	20,724	18,195
Per person (kg/day)	1.30	1.10	0.96	0.98	1.04	1.03

Source: Korean Ministry of Environment (2006)

Quantity-based instruments

Tradable permit schemes place an absolute limit on use of a resource and create an artificial market by:

- determining the number of rights to use the resource (e.g. tons of timber to be cut per year);
- allocating these rights (e.g. to cut one tonne of timber) to the users (e.g. logging companies or local landholders) by auction or free of charge; and
- facilitating the trading of rights between potential users (e.g. between different logging companies) or the sale of rights (e.g. from local landholders to commercial loggers).

The tradable permit price emerges through supply and demand. The best-known example is to control air pollution (e.g. CO_2 or SO_2) but the concept has been successfully adapted to a range of resources and goods, e.g. to manage fish stocks (see Box 7.11), regulate water abstraction (see Box 7.13) or limit urban sprawl and preserve open space (see Box 7.15). Further applications are being discussed, especially for trading forest carbon (see REDD+, Chapter 5), water quality or habitats (for an overview, see Hansjürgens et al, 2011).

Box 7.11 Experience with tradable fishery quotas in New Zealand

New Zealand's fishing industry has grown exceptionally fast in the last century: by 2004 the seafood sector was the fifth largest export earner occupying over 10,000 workers. To ensure sustainable fish stock management, the Fisheries Act 1986 introduced a system of tradable fishing quotas. The Fisheries Ministry sets an annual total allowable catch (TAC), based on biological stock assessment, which is handed out as 'individual tradable quotas' to fishing companies. Companies are free to decide whether to use their quota (catch fish) or to sell or buy remaining quotas depending on their profits per catch.

The results are so far quite positive: most fish stocks have been rebuilt and the country's fishing grounds are some of the very few in the world to achieve less than 10 per cent stock collapse, the conservation target set in New Zealand.

Sources: Ministry of Fisheries NZ (2005); Yandle and Dewees (2008); Worm et al (2009)

Box 7.12 Scope of environmental liability rules

Legal regimes provide for two main variations:

1 Strict liability does not require proof of culpability (i.e. fault or negligence) for damage. This is used for inherently risky activities that present specific hazards e.g. the International Convention on Civil Liability for Oil Pollution Damage, nuclear accidents and, in some countries, damage caused by genetically modified organisms. Tightly limited exceptions may be provided in the relevant legislation, e.g. for situations where the operator proves that the activity/emission was authorized by the competent authority and carried out to the required technical standard without fault.
2 Fault-based liability depends on the operator being proven to be negligent or at fault. This is usually the standard retained for other occupational activities that cause damage to the environment and its components.

Regulatory instruments can combine these approaches to cater for the different levels of risk presented by different types of activity. A prominent example of this dual approach is the EU Environmental Liability Directive 2004 which focuses on damage to EU-protected habitats and species, EU water resources and land contamination that presents hazards to human health. It excludes matters regulated under international liability regimes and interests covered by traditional liability regimes (personal injury and damage to goods and property), which vary between countries.

Liability regimes may also confer rights on civil society, including environmental NGOs, to request competent authorities to take action and to apply to the courts for review of administrative action or inaction.

Liability-based instruments

These create a process by which responsibility for the cost of damage (prevention and remediation) is explicitly assigned to those who cause that damage. Liability rules are based on the polluter pays principle and provide economic incentives to developers/users to incorporate the risk of a potential hazard and the value of remediation into their decisions.

Environmental liability regimes operate by reference to regulatory frameworks that set standards for resource use. The basic rule is that those who damage the environment beyond a defined limit must pay for necessary clean-up and/or restoration. Depending on the regime, they may also have to pay for the continued losses of ecosystem services pending restoration (or in perpetuity if restoration is not possible).

The early systems concentrated on pollution but several laws now address broader environmental damage in recognition of its public good character. Box 7.12 outlines the two main types of liability.

Liability rules provide economic incentives to reduce risk and can directly stimulate technical improvements. The potential polluter balances risks (paying for the impacts of potentially hazardous activities) and costs (of avoidance measures) to decide what measures are most appropriate. Options include abatement (e.g. better filters), recycling, less hazardous production techniques, risk management procedures and standards (e.g. international environmental management ISO standards, the European Eco-Management and Audit Scheme) and insuring against potential claims (if insurance is available).

MBIs can be designed to address very different environmental concerns (see examples in Table 7.2). Depending on the ecosystem or ecosystem service, there are different entry points for pricing resource use. Prices can be levied on:

- input goods (e.g. water charges, stumpage fees, fuel taxes, land conversion fees);
- processes and associated emissions (emission trading for pollutants like SO_2, NO_x or CO_2); or
- output (e.g. mineral oil tax; waste fees; wastewater charges or pollution taxes; fertilizer or pesticide taxes).

Economics suggests that prices work best if directly based on emissions or harmful products because abatement measures can be effectively tailored to quantitatively mitigate these damaging processes (Hansjürgens, 1992).

The term 'MBI' is sometimes used for other instruments that may improve market conditions, including market friction reduction policies, information programmes and labelling (Chapter 5) or subsidies (Chapter 6).

4.2 What can market-based instruments contribute?

MBIs to price resource use have particular strengths in four areas. If set at sufficient rates they:

1 make the polluter pay more explicitly than regulation does;
2 put the full cost recovery principle into effect;
3 enable environmental goals to be reached more efficiently with potential for cost savings (although actual savings depend on instrument design and implementation as well as the ecosystem service in question);
4 generate public revenues which can be used to finance biodiversity-friendly policies.

Table 7.2 Examples of different uses of MBIs to protect biodiversity and ecosystems

Name	Country	Object	Purpose	Mechanics	Success	Further Information
Landfill tax credit scheme	UK	Terrestrial ecosystems	Repricing	Tax scheme and funding	£1 billion paid from landfill operators to environmental projects	ENTRUST (2009)
Acid rain programme	US	Air quality management	Repricing	Tradable permits for emission of sulphur	Reduction of SO_2 by 52% compared to 1990	US EPA (2009)
Garbage collection fee	Japan	Waste reduction	Repricing	Garbage fee (e.g. in Tokyo US$0.43 per 10 litres)	Significant reduction of garbage in participating cities	UNESCAP (2003)
Reforestation charge	Liberia	Forest protection	Repricing	Charges on felled trees (US$5 per m³ reforestation charge)	Helps to prevent unsustainable use of forests	FAO (2009)
Tradable hunting permit	Mexico	Protection of specific sheep	Repricing	Hunting quotas for big-horned sheep in every community	Hunting for animals does not endanger the existence of the whole population	Biller (2003)
Nitrogen oxide charge	Sweden	Air quality management	Repricing	Charge of SEK40 (€3.9) per emitted kilogram NO_2	Emissions reduced from just over 300 tonnes (1990) to 200 tonnes in 2003	Naturvardsverket (2006)
Taxes on pesticides	Sweden	Groundwater management	Repricing	Tax of SEK20/kg (in 2002) on pesticides	65% reduction in use of pesticides	Sjöberg (2007)
Taxes on fertilizer	The Netherlands, Finland	Soil and water management	Repricing	Taxes on fertilizers and excess nutrients to promote efficiency in fertilizer use for crops	Decrease in product use and subsequent reduction of pollution levels in soil and water (20% to 30% in The Netherlands, 11% to 22% in Finland)	Ecotec (2001)
Tradable permits on water pollution, Hunter River	Australia	Catchment	Repricing	Each mine is allowed to discharge a percentage of the total allowable salt load, calculated in relation to conductivity levels	Exceeding permitted quotas decreased from 33% to 4% after implementation	Kraemer et al (2003b)
Environmental taxes and water taxes	Colombia	Catchment	Repricing	Pollution and water use is taxed	BOD (amount of oxygen required to biologically decompose organic matter) dropped by two-thirds in four years	Kraemer et al (2003a)

Table 7.2 Examples of different uses of MBIs to protect biodiversity and ecosystems (*Cont'd*)

Name	Country	Object	Purpose	Mechanics	Success	Further Information
Guabas River water user association	Colombia	Watershed management	Repricing/revenue-raising	Water users downstream pay fees (per litre of water received) to a fund for watershed management activities	Revenues (about US$600,000 annually) used for projects to protect/regenerate degraded forests, to reforest with native species and for community organization	Landell-Mills (2002); Echavarría (2002)
Plastic bag tax	Ireland	Waste reduction	Repricing/revenue-raising	€0.33 per bag to be paid at checkout	Plastic bag consumption dropped by 80% in 2002 to 2003; revenues (US$9.6 million) earmarked for a green fund	Rosenthal (2008)
Fees for mountain gorilla tracking	Uganda	Forest habitat protection	Revenue-raising	Visitors have to pay a US$500 permit to go gorilla tracking	Population of gorillas is slowly increasing, also due to improved management (e.g. more guards)	Zeppel (2007); Uganda Wildlife Authority (2009);
Water conservation fund	Ecuador	Biosphere park management/ financing	Revenue-raising	Self-financing of watershed reservoir	Over US$301,000 were spent on water management projects in 2005, securing the important functions of the reservoir	TNC (2007)
Entrance fees for Galapagos Islands	Ecuador	Protected area management/ financing	Revenue-raising	Entrance fee: US$6 for Ecuadorians/ US$100 for other tourists	Revenues (>US$3 million annually) help to improve the management of the National Park	Vanasselt (2000)

Implementation of the polluter/user pays principle

Direct regulation and use of MBIs both support the polluter pays principle but only MBIs make visible the values attached to resource use. They confront actors with at least part of the environmental and social costs of their actions (i.e. previously externalized costs that were not considered in private decision making) and lead to explicit payments. Tax bills and permit prices are more transparent and easier to mainstream into private accounts than investments in technical adaptations to comply with environmental regulations (see Box 7.13).

Box 7.13 Experience of water use rights in reducing water consumption in China

China's first water use rights system with tradable water use quotas was launched early in 2002 (Zhangye City, Ganzhou District, Gansu Province) as part of a national water saving project. Water use in the pilot area was readjusted based on local ecological and social conditions: high-efficiency users were given preference for distribution of use rights and per capita use was determined based on proximity to water resources.

Water use rights certificates were distributed to county irrigation districts and subsequently to townships, villages and households. In Minle County, each district distributed certificates to households based on land area and a water resource deployment scheme which was checked, ratified and strictly enforced. Water used for irrigation was reduced to 1500–1800m³/ha/year, significantly lower than the previous year.

Source: Forest Trend (2009)

Designing MBIs for full cost recovery

MBIs can make the polluter/user carry the full cost of pollution/resource use, provided that charge/tax rates are set high enough or the number of permits is adequately restricted. This is a key difference with regulatory approaches which require compliance to a set standard but leave resource use below this limit free of charge (i.e. there is no incentive to reduce pollution below the standard). MBIs impose the charge/tax on all emissions (e.g. every tonne of carbon, every litre of discharged water) and thus increase incentives for reduction. However, tax rates, fees or charges will only reflect the true economic value of the resource if MBIs are explicitly designed and set at an adequate level to secure full cost recovery.

Experience gained in using this approach is mainly derived from the water sector. In some countries water charges have historically been – and in some cases still are – very low. This reflects the view that provision of basic services is a government duty with access considered a right. In such cases, end-users often pay less than full cost. This has led to over-use, wastage, groundwater depletion, pollution, soil salinization and biodiversity loss.

Adequate water pricing to end-users can improve price signals and promote increased efficiency (OECD, 2006), leading to reduced investment needs for infrastructure (water supply and downstream wastewater treatment) and lower overall costs. Both effects can significantly reduce environmental pressures. Under a

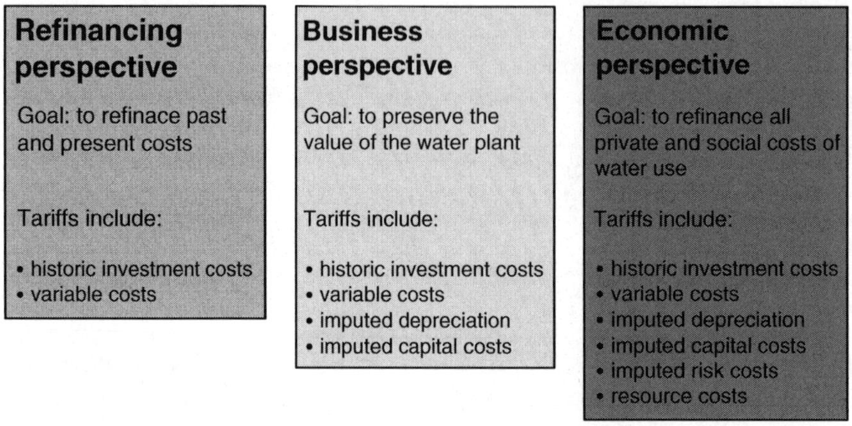

Refinancing perspective

Goal: to refinace past and present costs

Tariffs include:

• historic investment costs
• variable costs

Business perspective

Goal: to preserve the value of the water plant

Tariffs include:

• historic investment costs
• variable costs
• imputed depreciation
• imputed capital costs

Economic perspective

Goal: to refinance all private and social costs of water use

Tariffs include:

• historic investment costs
• variable costs
• imputed depreciation
• imputed capital costs
• imputed risk costs
• resource costs

Figure 7.2 *Cost recovery in water pricing: Towards an economic perspective*

Source: Hansjürgens (2004)

full cost recovery approach to water, users should pay for the full cost of abstraction, supply infrastructure, preservation of plant value and all private and social costs associated with its provision (see Figure 7.2 and Box 7.14).

Box 7.14 Full cost recovery as a tool to reduce over-exploitation: Water pricing examples

Many EU Member States (e.g. The Netherlands and the UK) have moved towards full cost recovery, involving significant changes for most newer Member States. In the Czech Republic, water pricing gradually increased from €0.02/m³ before 1990 to €0.71/m³ in 2004. From 1990 to 1999, water withdrawals decreased by 88 per cent (agriculture), 47 per cent (industry) and 34 per cent (public water mains). All houses were provided with metering: consumption of drinking water decreased by about 40 per cent from 171 litres per person/day in 1989 to 103 litres in 2002 (Government of the Czech Republic, 2003). In 2003 it was about 10 per cent below the EU average (Naumann, 2003). It should be emphasized that there was no sudden imposition of full cost recovery: implementation was gradual in order to avoid social impacts and take affordability issues into account.

Sources: Naumann (2003); Government of the Czech Republic (2003); OECD (2006); IEEP et al (2007)

In Mexico, annual water withdrawal represents only 43 per cent of the average total renewable water per year, but availability varies by region and water scarcity has increased in most areas over the last ten years. A pricing system with two different tariffs was therefore introduced. The first tariff involves a fixed price per cubic metre used, which varies between water supply zones. The second uses an increasing block-rate structure to take account of different forms of water use and previously unmet infrastructure costs. Prior to this programme, water prices covered only about 20 per cent of operation, maintenance and replacement costs. Water tariffs now cover more than 80 per cent of these costs, contributing to a more sustainable use of water by irrigation, industrial and municipal water use (see also the Mexican PES scheme in Chapter 5).

Sources: Dinar (2000); Guerrero and Howe (2000)

Potential cost savings through MBIs

Incorporating costs and using market forces has the potential to make MBIs more cost-effective than standard setting by direct regulation. This arguably opens up opportunities to set and reach more ambitious conservation goals (using a given budget) or to achieve substantial cost savings.

In the area of land development, a well-known example for achieving conservation goals without public expenditure concerns local tradable development rights programmes implemented across the US (see Box 7.15). Similar programmes are run in New Zealand, Italy and France (OECD, 1999a).

Box 7.15 Tradable development rights to control urban sprawl and preserve open space: The case of Montgomery County (Maryland, US)

The rural and mainly agricultural northern part of Montgomery County has cultural and environmental significance beyond its base economic importance. It enhances the quality of life for residents and visitors in the densely developed Washington, DC/ Baltimore corridor by providing opportunities for access to locally grown produce and recreation. A combination of low building density and adapted farming and forestry practices have protected the natural air and water filtration abilities of this ecologically diverse landscape.

In 1981, a tradable development rights (TDR) scheme was introduced to prevent urban sprawl and preserve contiguous blocks of open space. Landowners in a 'sending zone' in the rural north are given rights in exchange for downsizing the authorized development density of their land. TDR can be bought by developers in 'receiving zones' who face high development pressure and want to exceed the authorized development density of such zones.

This TDR scheme is considered one of the most successful in the US. By 2008 it had preserved over 50,000 acres of prime agricultural land and open space by transferring more than 8000 development rights, accounting for 75 per cent of all preserved agricultural land in the county (Pruetz and Standridge, 2009). The programme is fully private: savings in public expenditure for the amount of land preserved are estimated at nearly US$70 million (Walls and McConnel, 2007).

Other areas of environmental protection may also provide opportunities for potential cost savings. Projections are mainly available for tradable emission rights to regulate air pollutants. Studies based on econometric estimates and survey methods found savings of 43 to 55 per cent compared to use of a uniform standard to regulate facility emissions (Carlson et al, 2000; Ellerman et al, 2000; Burtraw and Szambelan, 2010). The European Emissions Trading Scheme is expected to cut the cost of meeting Kyoto targets for EU Member States. At global level, potential cost savings of an emissions trading scheme compared to a protocol without trade have been estimated as significant: 84 per cent at world level and 56 per cent for the EU (Gusbin et al, 1999). However, any assessment of cost-effectiveness is of course specific to the instrument, problem and context. Some MBIs have been set at very low rates and cannot subsequently be scaled up, due to public opposition or lack of political will.

Generation of public revenue through MBIs

Public revenues can also be generated through tradable permit schemes where the state auctions the rights. These can amount to quite a substantial percentage of public budgets: estimates for the Seychelles show that biodiversity-related taxes, levies and permits made up one-third of total public revenues in 1997 (Emerton, 1997). Revenues generated can provide extra funds for protective measures, e.g. payments for environmental services or tax incentives to enhance pro-biodiversity practices by landowners (see Chapter 5).

Examples can be found in many countries that earmark environmental taxes for biodiversity policies or use taxes to set up funds (see Box 7.16).

Box 7.16 Creating synergies: Using MBI revenues to finance biodiversity policies

Pricing systems to generate revenues to restore/manage biodiversity can take many forms:

- Australia introduced a water extraction levy for the Murray River Basin and earmarked the revenues for wetland restoration and salt interception schemes (Ashiabor, 2004).
- Mexico increased gasoline tax by 5.5 per cent in October 2007. Of the proceeds, 12.5 per cent will go to support investments in the environment sector, including protected area management (Watkins et al, 2008).
- Entrance fees to national parks are important revenue sources for countries with limited public money for nature conservation, e.g. fees to the Biebrza National Park in Poland (OECD, 1999b).
- Charging special fees for specific activities in protected areas is also common, e.g. diving fees in marine reserves in the Philippines (Arin and Kramer, 2002). Tourists are interested in preserving sites they come to visit: the increase in fees paid is only a small fraction of their trip's total cost.
- In the US, duck hunters are required to purchase Federal Duck Stamps. Of the revenue generated, 98 per cent goes directly to the purchase/lease of wetlands, targeting vital breeding habitats within the National Wildlife Refuge system. The system raises around US$50 million/year (see www.fws.gov/duckstamps; Dunbar, no date).

MBI revenues can also play a key role in helping countries to meet their Millennium Development Goal commitments. Governments can consider using taxes to finance social and physical infrastructure, promote growth and fairly share the costs and benefits of development. Stable and predictable fiscal policy and administration provide a favourable context for economic activity and investment. Consultation on taxation between governments, citizens and other stakeholders can contribute to improved efficiency, accountability and governance.

4.3 Limitations of market-based instruments

Despite their potential, resource-pricing tools to safeguard biodiversity and ecosystem services are underdeveloped in most countries. There are many market-based approaches globally but the share of environmental taxes as a percentage of total tax receipts is small and even decreasing in some countries (see Figure 7.3). Fully implemented levies on harmful products are rare. Receipts from environmental taxes were about 6.4 per cent of GDP in the EU in 2006; this could be significantly increased (Bassi et al, 2009), but political resistance is still substantial.

At pan-European level, a comparative study by the Council of Europe of tax systems specifically targeting biodiversity suggests that tax incentives are underdeveloped as a mechanism and do not make a targeted contribution to strengthening ecological networks. They are also generally fragmented and poorly integrated into biodiversity policy toolkits (Shine, 2005).

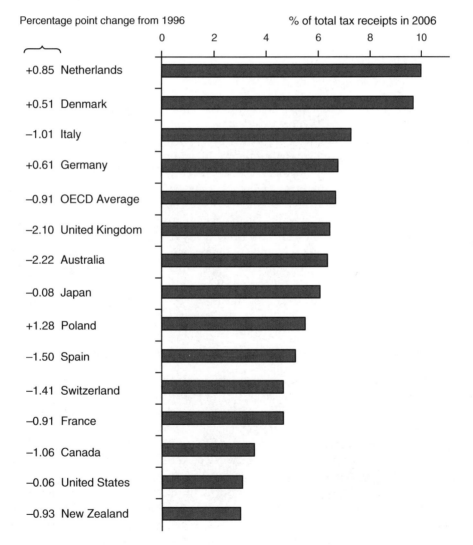

Figure 7.3 *Environmental taxes as a percentage of total tax receipts in 2006*

Source: own representation, building on OECD database on economic instruments

MBIs are not appropriate in every situation and for every ecosystem. As they leave actors free to choose between reducing resource use or paying the price, they cannot be relied on to secure site-specific goals to safeguard threatened ecosystems or species. Moreover, since inflation may erode the dissuasive effect of taxes, fees or charges over time, rates have to be continuously reviewed and adapted. For permit trading schemes, determining the 'safe load' (i.e. number of permits to be issued) requires a detailed analysis of the ecosystem at stake. Experience suggests that incentive-based approaches rely on trying one thing, failing and then trying another (Bayon, 2004). For these reasons, MBIs should only be applied where trial-and-error is acceptable, i.e. where failures do not lead to severe or even irreversible damage.

Liability regimes face additional constraints. Problems often arise when the operator responsible for damage caused by accidents cannot be traced ('orphan liability' cases or sites). Other problems relate to damage generated by repetitive actions that lead to significant cumulative damage (e.g. diffuse pollution) for which transaction costs for assessing natural resource damage can be substantial. When apportioning responsibility between individual polluters, conventional liability rules may not apply, e.g. the individual polluter's share of the damage is not enough to trigger liability. In such cases, it often makes sense for the state to provide directly for damage restoration (see Chapter 9).

Introducing MBIs is often associated with high political costs. In many countries, raising taxes is likely to raise more political resistance from affected interest groups than complex technical requirements set by environmental standards. Administrative requirements are also quite high, especially to operate permit markets. There may be also ethical and equity issues at stake. Some see a charge, tax or quota as a paid right to pollute or degrade the environment which may be ethically questionable. These instruments can be perceived as unfair as the rich can more easily pay than the poor.

Policy makers and public agencies therefore play a vital role in creating the legal framework for MBIs, to operate effectively. This means that tradable permit markets for use of ecosystem services are difficult – if not impossible – to implement in countries with weak institutions and regulatory regimes. The aim should not be to develop MBIs, as a substitute for direct regulation but to provide more flexibility for targeted actors to achieve more ambitious conservation goals by minimizing abatement costs (see Section 6).

4.4 Role of economic information in instrument design

Economic values can feed into MBI design, e.g. to set the rates or number of permits necessary to address the loss of ecosystems and biodiversity.

Understanding the costs of loss can trigger new pricing instruments. Valuation provides facts and evidence of ongoing damage and sheds light on negative effects of current consumption patterns. These cost calculations can help policy makers to establish user-pays instruments as they justify the need for price-based approaches and support awareness-raising.

This type of information can also improve the design of price instruments to capture the values of public goods. To implement full cost recovery for associated environmental costs, the full costs obviously need to be known. Economic assessments will play an increasingly important role in e.g. future water pricing policies.

Economic information can be used directly to determine the tax rate or price, e.g. for fees, charges and trading rules to enable tradable permit markets to run properly. The case study from India (see Box 7.17) provides a good example of using economic valuation to calculate compensation for forest conversion.

Box 7.17 Using economic valuation to determine mandatory compensation rates in India

In 2006 the Indian Supreme Court set compensation rates for conversion of different types of forested land to non-forest use. Much higher damage assessment multiples were applied to conversion of biodiversity-rich protected areas (5x for sanctuaries, 10x for national parks). This ruling drew on an economic valuation study of Indian forests by the Green Indian States Trust (GIST, 2006) which estimated the value for six different classes of forests (see table below) of timber, fuelwood, non-timber forest products (NTFPs) and ecotourism, bioprospecting, ecological services of forests and non-use values (conservation of charismatic species like the royal Bengal tiger or the Asian lion). Converters pay compensation to an afforestation fund to improve national forest cover. In 2009 the Supreme Court directed Rs.10 billion (~US$215 million) to be paid out of the fund every year for afforestation, wildlife conservation and creating rural jobs (*Thaindian News*, 2009).

Eco-value class	Forest type	Very dense forest	Dense forest	Open forest
I	Tropical wet evergreen and semi-evergreen; tropical moist deciduous	22,370	20,100	15,700
II	Littoral and swamp	22,370	20,100	15,700
III	Tropical dry deciduous	19,000	17,200	13,400
IV	Tropical thorn and tropical dry evergreen	13,400	12,100	9400
V	Subtropical broadleaf hill, subtropical pine and subtropical dry evergreen	20,100	18,100	14,100
VI	Montane wet temperate, Himalayan moist and dry temperate, sub alpine, moist and dry alpine scrub	21,300	19,200	15,000

Note: All values per hectare, transformed to US$ and rounded

Non-market valuation studies can help set an adequate price level for entrance fees. Visitors' willingness to pay may be higher than first thought by protected area (PA) administrators. One study provided support for sustainably financing the Bonaire National Marine Park in the Caribbean (see Box 7.18). Another study – focused on the Polish Baltic Sea – showed that a substantial number of coastal users were

---

Box 7.18 Analysing willingness to pay (WTP) to adjust fee structures in the Antilles

The National Parks Foundation is a non-governmental non-profit foundation commissioned by the island government to manage the Bonaire National Marine Park (BNMP), one of the world's premier diving sites. The Foundation gets its income from park admission fees, users of commercial and private moorings, donations and grants, including a government grant for the education coordinator's salary. A successful visitor and user fee system, introduced in the early 1990s, was amended in the light of economic valuation studies and now provides more than 90 per cent of self-generated revenues for BNMP. A contingent valuation survey (Dixon et al, 1993) showed that the WTP of scuba divers for annual BNMP dive tags far exceeded the modest US$10 fee instituted in 1992. This led to a tag price increase to US$25 in 2005: in addition, all users now have to pay entrance fees.

Sources: Dixon et al (1993); Slootweg and van Beukering (2008); STINAPA Bonaire (2009)

---

willing to support the idea of a tax to protect the Baltic Sea from eutrophication (Zylicz et al, 1995).

To summarize, experience suggests that MBIs can be powerful tools to manage and protect ecosystem goods and services if properly designed, implemented, monitored and enforced. As environmental pricing regimes and permit markets develop, it is important to learn lessons from their implementation – and to study how far existing markets for a resource could be applied more widely within and between countries (e.g. under what institutional and regulatory conditions). Showing what works in a neighbouring country is sometimes the best argument for launching the instrument at home.

5 Monitoring, enforcement and criminal prosecution

Building awareness across society and political commitment at all levels is fundamental to improving environmental performance and compliance.

In parallel, monitoring, enforcement and prosecution of non-compliant behaviour are essential for any environmental policy to become effective. Environmental crimes often yield high profits for perpetrators yet risks of detection and available penalties are too low to deter illegal practices. Turning this situation around will require adequate funding for monitoring, international cooperation on law enforcement and the provision of viable and legal alternatives for certain groups.

5.1 Environmental crime: A local and global problem

Individuals and businesses will be more likely to comply with a standard, meet a compensation requirement or pay a tax if positive incentives and meaningful deterrents are in place. Weak government efforts to track down crimes may be taken by some as a tacit acceptance that environmental requirements do not need to be respected. Good governance and credibility are therefore critical to compliance and enforcement.

Box 7.19 outlines the range of activities and sectors concerned by environmental crime.

Box 7.19 What are environmental crimes?

Environmental crimes include any actions – or failure to act – that breach relevant legislation. They can range from relatively minor to serious offences causing or risking significant harm to the environment and/or human health. The best-known categories include emissions or discharges in breach of permitted thresholds, illegal trade in ozone-depleting substances and protected wildlife, shipment or dumping of banned waste and illegal logging and fisheries, but there are others like unauthorized building, land conversion and water extraction.

Impacts of environmental crime can be felt at very local up to global levels. Offences with trade or pollution aspects are more likely to have a cross-border dimension which can widen the number of impacted people. Overlooking this question can have implications for a country's trading status and the ability of its businesses to develop new opportunities. Several initiatives to improve international governance, collaboration on monitoring and enforcement, and attitudes are therefore under way.

Many drivers need to be considered, from poverty (i.e. lack of alternatives) to corruption and organized crime. The economics of wildlife crime show that trade in illegally harvested biodiversity is extremely profitable, generating billions of dollars. The same magnitude of profits can be made by polluters who defy environmental standards and permit conditions.

Pollution and other damaging activities

Serious offences include the handling, transport, trading, possession and disposal of hazardous waste or resources in breach of national and/or international law. These have a clear and direct impact on human health, biodiversity and provision of ecosystem services due to the inherently hazardous nature of the substances. They can also have knock-on transboundary or wider impacts, with consequences going beyond the damage caused by the initial act, often over a considerable period of time. Businesses that violate applicable laws (i.e. do not invest in prevention and avoidance measures) have an unfair economic advantage over law-abiding ones.

We easily overlook 'minor' offences but these too have significant cumulative impacts, e.g. destruction of breeding places or nests, ongoing chronic pollution and non-compliance with conditions laid down by administrative permits (see Box 7.20).

Regulatory frameworks set rules and standards to avoid or minimize the risk of damage and are reflected in environmental management procedures and best practices implemented by reputable operators around the world. While accidents can always happen, negligence and/or deliberate non-compliance recognizably increase the likelihood of damage. This is particularly true for the oil storage and transport sector, oil distilleries, chemical manufacturing and storage, waste treatment and water services as well as agriculture.

Environmental liability rules provide a mechanism for relating the harmful activity to the polluter (where identified) and securing restoration and compensation (see Section 4). Environmental criminal law goes a step further by defining what constitutes illegal conduct, the standard applied (deliberate/negligent) and available penalties (monetary, imprisonment or both). However, enforcement is always cumbersome as relevant activities are often widespread and surveillance on the spot cannot reliably

---

Box 7.20 Wider impacts of pollution and dumping

Oceans are fast becoming a garbage dump. In Australia, surveys near cities indicate that up to 80 per cent of marine litter comes from land-based sources (becoming sea-based sources in more remote areas). Cigarette products, paper and plastic bags headed the Top 10 List of Marine Debris items for 1989 to 2007. Plastic, especially plastic bags and polyethylene terephthalate (PET) bottles, is the most pervasive type of marine litter around the world, accounting for over 80 per cent of all litter collected in several regional seas assessed.

One key step is to review the level of fines for ocean dumping to increase the level of deterrent where necessary. In the US, for example, the cruise ship *Regal Princess* was fined US$500,000 in 1993 for dumping 20 bags of garbage at sea (UNEP, 2009b).

Dumping of mining waste is another major problem. The Panguna copper mine in Papua New Guinea used to dump 150,000 tons per day of tailings into the Kawerogn/Jaba River system (Brown, 1974). The damage spread over 30km from the source and all life disappeared from the river due to the metal and leach acids. The conflict over the mine inflamed a civil war, which led to its eventual closure (Young, 1992). Although this particular case has been dealt with, mining remains one of the most polluting and controversial activities with potentially severe effects on biodiversity and ecosystem services.

Sources: Young (1992); UNEP (2009b); ten Brink et al (2009)

---

take place. Corruption in certain countries further adds to this problem. Too often monitoring comes into play only after the damage has occurred and its effects on the ecosystem are apparent. Such monitoring rarely makes it possible to trace a polluting incident back to the polluter with the degree of certitude required for penal actions.

Illegal use of resources and wildlife crime

Offences related to natural resource use and wildlife take many forms at many levels. Most countries have long regulated direct taking, trade and other activities affecting valued resources, species and their derivatives where these could collectively lead to over-exploitation or irreversible damage. Bans and permit systems (e.g. to prevent over-collection of wild plants and poaching of animals) are very familiar to environmental administrations even if detection and enforcement present major logistical difficulties.

We should not neglect the fact that some illegal activity is generated by poverty in developing countries. Illegal hunting can be triggered by increasing demand for bush meat from poor and indigenous people who sell on to collectors and restaurants, meat suppliers and poachers.

This book has emphasized how many rural and indigenous populations depend on ecosystem goods and services for their livelihoods, cultural identity and even survival. Access to common resources and harvesting is a right. Conflicts of interest are often inevitable and foreseeable where restrictions or bans are extended to resources used by such groups.

The guiding principles for policy makers (see Chapter 2) are critical when negotiating new controls affecting vulnerable populations. In parallel, environmental crime needs to be addressed by providing income-producing alternatives and education. Linking conservation strategies with poverty alleviation is an absolute must for developing countries.

Global illegal trade in wildlife species has grown into a multi-billion dollar business. Species most at risk are plants of edible, medicinal or decorative use; emblematic animal species for their skins and trophies; and exotic species (e.g. reptiles, amphibians, fish/ corals and birds) collected as pets, ornamentals and for their eggs or venom. Existing black markets, problematic as they are, mirror the values underlying biodiversity and specific ecosystem services (see Box 7.21).

Box 7.21 The economics behind environmental crimes

A whole economy is associated with illegal poaching and hunting. Related profits can be substantial and easily exceed the financial penalties imposed were the crime to be detected. By way of example:

- Cambodian farmers can get 250 times their monthly salary for selling one dead tiger.
- In Papua Province, Indonesia, a shipload of illegal timber for which the penalty is US$6.47 yields profits of roughly US$92,000: the rewards are over 14,000 times greater than the risks.
- In Brazil, illegal loggers in the Atlantic Forest can make $75 per tree they harvest but face a deterrent of only US$6.44.
- In Mexico's Selva Maya Forest, poachers obtain a net average of US$191.57 per trip but face a deterrent of only US$5.66.
- In the Philippines, illegal dynamite and cyanide fishing in the Calamianes Islands earn fishermen an average of US$70.57 per trip. The value of the deterrent is only US$0.09.

Smuggling wildlife, including many endangered species, is the third largest and most profitable illegal cross-border activity after arms and drugs. Increasing demand for animal parts has driven a drastic decline in tiger and other big animal populations (elephants, rhinos) since 1950. For example, through the black market in Asia, ivory now sells for US$750 per kilogram, up from US$100 in 1989 and US$200 in 2004.

Source: Akella and Cannon (2004)

International treaties can leverage agreement on stronger frameworks to protect endangered and threatened species. The 1973 CITES treaty (Convention on International Trade in Endangered Species of Wild Flora and Fauna) protects 900 species from being commercially traded and restricts international trade for 29,000 species that may become threatened. However, a major constraint on global implementation is that even though over 170 countries are party to CITES, enforcement remains inadequate at national level and penalties are insufficient deterrants.

5.2 New approaches to tackle crime

The economic value of biodiversity and wildlife that drives illegal activities can shed light on possible policy responses. Public spending for improved monitoring and detection may be a worthwhile investment and provide viable alternatives of livelihoods for local people. Being a global problem, international collaboration to fight environmental crimes is essential to get better results.

Stronger enforcement of existing regulations is key to stopping illegal activities. This can be assisted by high-tech tools that facilitate crime detection and identify the source (detection of illegal logging activities, DNA tests on poached animals, remote pollution alerts and monitoring, satellite tracking of fishing vessels). However, detection is not the same as actual enforcement. A study by Akella and Cannon (2004) suggests that strengthening crime detection in isolation has often been ineffective. It is more promising to address the entire enforcement chain – detection, arrest, prosecution, conviction and penalties – in an integrated way.

Only if penalties are high enough to be meaningful will they deter some people and businesses from illegal conduct. In EU Member States, environmental offences are subject to similar penalties as traditional crimes (fines, prison, community sentences) but in practice, fines are by far the most common sanction and it is extremely rare to see prison sentences imposed. However, there is now a general trend towards more severe sentencing and a recent study has revealed that the number of prosecutions for environmental crimes is increasing (Huglo Lepage and Partners, 2003, 2007).

Engaging citizens in monitoring and management activities is a promising avenue for further progress. Environmental NGOs are often in a good position to monitor conditions on the ground, investigate breaches of legislation and raise the alarm about environmental crimes at local, national or global level. Several do this very effectively in cases of e.g. forest destruction, dumping from minefields or marine pollution. Other NGOs provide technical support for tracing, detecting and investigating wildlife trade crimes.

There are now good examples of how citizens can engage actively in protecting wildlife and reporting bad practices, which can also help with improving prosecution rates (see Box 7.22).

Box 7.22 Investigating bat crime in the UK

All UK bats and their roosts are protected by law. The Bat Conservation Trust (BCT) established a two-year Investigations Project in 2001 in collaboration with the Royal Society for the Protection of Birds to monitor bat-related crime. A total of 144 incidents were reported to the Investigations Project but it was acknowledged that this was likely to be only a small proportion of actual offences. Building development and maintenance accounted for 67 per cent of incidents. In addition, 87 per cent of all incidents involved destruction or obstruction of a roost threatening the bat population of an area. The BCT's work led to criminal prosecution and penalization of several offenders (e.g. recent fines of £3500 for a developer who destroyed two roosts).

Source: Bat Conservation Trust (2009)

As part of a coherent approach to address drivers of illegal activities, creating income alternatives and reforming unjust laws will help to improve compliance.

To prevent illegal poaching, a starting point is to educate local people about the hunting rules in force while also providing viable alternatives for jobs and livelihoods. Experience with ex-poachers in Thailand suggests that they now make more money taking ecotourists into the forest (and protecting bird populations against poachers) than they did by poaching hornbills themselves (Cribb, 2003; *Wildlife Extra*, 2009).

Sustainable use of wildlife has also been recognized as a possible solution (see Box 7.23). Safari hunting could offer a significant and durable source of financing to offset some of the costs of maintaining Africa's wild lands and protected areas. However, some scientists have called for a better quantitative assessment of whether trophy hunting is both ecologically sustainable and economically competitive over the long term relative to other land uses (Wilkie and Carpenter, 1999).

Box 7.23 Enforcement at Serengeti National Park

Scientists from the University of Washington have shown that in the Serengeti, which has a 50-year record of arrests and patrols, a precipitous decline in enforcement in 1977 resulted in a large increase in poaching and decline of many species. Conversely, expanded budgets and anti-poaching patrols since the mid-1980s have significantly reduced poaching and allowed populations of buffalo, elephants and rhinoceros to rebuild. After the improved patrols in the Serengeti proved effective, Tanzania initiated a community conservation programme in 2000. Outside established reserves, using tourism or hunting expeditions to generate economic benefits for local communities is the cornerstone to enlisting their help in protecting wildlife.

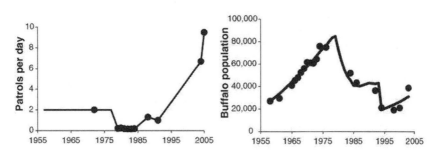

Figure 7.4 *Patrols and buffalo populations*

Sources: Wildlife Extra (2008); Hilborn et al (2006)

Demand for illegal wildlife products needs to be halted. We urgently need to change people's perceptions and help consumers understand the scale of the catastrophe in terms of population declines (see TEEB for Citizens, no date, for more details). Trade bans and efforts to control borders and customs are frequently suggested tools. However, these are controversial: it has been argued that proactive management of trade in endangered wildlife makes more sense than last-minute bans that can inadvertently stimulate demand (Rivalan et al, 2007).

In today's global economy, there is more need than ever for an international strategy to deal with environmental crime. Continued cooperation under international treaties to harmonize standards and monitor requirements is indispensable, together with mutually supportive collaboration on criminal prosecution. The Interpol Working Groups on Pollution Crime and on Wildlife Crime (Interpol, 2009) provide an excellent example of what can be done.

6 Making it happen – Policy mixes to get results

Policies and instruments to recover full costs from polluters are a key element of responses to the biodiversity challenge. Policy mixes are crucial: they can combine the advantages of regulatory and voluntary approaches (see also ten Brink, 2002) and deliver added value if properly designed with consideration of institutional and cultural factors.

Stopping ongoing losses must form the backbone of the policy response. This means minimizing emissions from point sources (e.g. factories) and diffuse sources (e.g. pesticides) and tackling resource over-use.

Policy makers already have a useful toolkit at their disposal. Strong regulatory frameworks and standard setting (e.g. to control pollution control, over-use of resources and damaging development) has achieved great successes. Many environmental problems that were pressing in the past (e.g. contaminated water bodies, high concentrations of pollutants in the atmosphere) have been significantly reduced. There is considerable scope for further use of regulation to address environmental problems directly.

However, a strong regulatory framework can deliver wider benefits. It is the basic precondition for introducing other instruments such as offset requirements, biodiversity banking or ecological taxes. Such taxes and charges are already used widely, often to address a specific concern (e.g. NO_x emissions to air, or water scarcity) and sometimes as part of a wider strategy to make the transition to ecological tax reform (see Box 7.24).

No single policy instrument is enough to tackle the wide range of activities, sources and sectors affecting biodiversity and ecosystem services provision. Smart policy mixes combining the advantages of regulation and flexible MBIs are critical to reach the full potential of the polluter pays and full cost recovery principles. The optimal policy mix will depend on the state of the resource or ecosystem in question, and the number and variety of actors affected. By way of example:

- for hazard prevention, strong environmental regulation is important (e.g. banning highly toxic substances that may be released into the environment);
- for sustainable management of renewable resources, market-based solutions such as permit trading merit serious consideration;
- for a single resource, a combined approach is often suitable, e.g. in fisheries policies, no-take zones might be appropriate to provide undisturbed spawning grounds while fish catch might best be managed through individual tradable quotas.

MBIs can deliver significant social benefits by stimulating development of least-cost abatement solutions among resource users. However, these need careful design to be sensitive to distributional concerns and to take the needs of the poor and vulnerable into account. Governments around the world already use a significant share of their revenues to equalize incomes and regulate market activity to safeguard access by these

---

Box 7.24 Environmental/ecological tax reform

Environmental tax reform (ETR) involves a progressive reform of the national tax system to shift the burden of taxation from conventional taxes (e.g. on labour) to environmentally damaging activities (e.g. unsustainable resource use, pollution). The burden of taxes should fall more on 'bads' than 'goods' to send out appropriate signals to consumers and producers, and to better distribute tax burdens across the economy from a sustainable development perspective.

The economic rationale is that welfare gains are generated by reducing taxes on labour or capital and increasing taxes on externalities, thus helping to avoid 'welfare-reducing' activities that impact on employment. The tax shift potentially leads to a 'double dividend' of environmental improvement and employment. ETR can be an important tool in helping directly confront today's and tomorrow's environmental challenges relating to climate change, water scarcity, energy security and general resource limits. There is therefore significant scope to address the indirect drivers of biodiversity loss. At the moment there is less experience with using ETR to address biodiversity directly (Bassi et al, 2010).

Ecological fiscal reform (EFR) is a broader approach, which focuses not just on shifting taxes and tax burdens but also on reforming economic subsidies (see also Chapter 6). The pioneering countries in the EFR field were Finland, Sweden, Denmark and The Netherlands. 'Green tax commissions' were used to guide the progress of fiscal reform in Norway, The Netherlands, Sweden and Belgium: these are high-level panels mandated to discuss and recommend possible developments and can include cross-ministry representation as well as wider stakeholder groups. Denmark and Ireland have set up interministerial committees.

The ongoing financial crisis in Ireland has led to the government embracing environmental fiscal reform. One of the green fiscal measures launched was that of water charges for households to cover local authorities' operational costs. These are expected to raise €500 million. Other changes include carbon taxes and property taxes.

Sources: EEA (2005); GreenBudgetEurope (2010)

---

groups to goods and services. Smart policy mixes therefore need to go beyond simple cost recovery mechanisms to include appropriate distributional measures.

Policy design also needs to consider the institutional conditions necessary for implementation (see also Chapter 2). Setting up an emissions trading market is much more ambitious than requiring a minimum standard for filtering emissions at every smokestack. Tax regimes or charging systems (e.g. to reduce water consumption) will only work if payments can actually be collected and at reasonable administrative cost. Offsets (e.g. for environmental impacts caused by urban development) will only secure no net loss if their criteria and effectiveness are monitored and kept under review over the long term.

Information on the economic costs of biodiversity loss and ecosystem service degradation can help policy makers wishing to propose a new instrument, reform an existing one or build capacity to better implement an existing instrument that is not yet reaching its potential. Economic insights can also help with instrument choice (i.e. which combination is more likely to create cost-effective solutions) and in policy implementation (e.g. high damage costs suggest high penalties). Building on local knowledge and cultural and institutional contexts can stimulate new innovative approaches (see TEEB in Local Policy, 2011).

Every country is different and what works in one country will not automatically work in another. On the other hand, learning from success stories and experience elsewhere provides opportunities to adjust and adapt policy tools to national conditions. Combined regulatory and market-based solutions should be actively promoted alongside the recommendations and guidance in Chapters 5, 6, 8 and 9. These can build on a policy commitment to implement the polluter/user pays and full cost recovery principles, and complement incentives to reward positive behaviour and shift market signals in favour of natural assets. A gradual shift in the tax burden to encourage wise stewardship of natural resources will be a critical part of this in most countries.

Creative thinking should guide national and international policy makers in their future efforts to design smart policy responses to the tremendous biodiversity challenge confronting us and the generations to come.

Acknowledgements

The authors wish to thank Jonathan Armstrong, IEEP, UK; Burkhard Schweppe-Kraft, Federal Environment Ministry, Germany; Thomas Kretzschmar, UFZ, Germany; Dorit Lehr, UFZ, Germany; Hylton Murray Philipson, Canopy Capital, UK; Manfred Rosenstock, European Commission, Belgium; Jo Treweek, Treweek Environmental Consultants, UK; Koen van der Bosch, IEEP, Belgium; and Frank Wätzold, UFZ, Germany.

References

Afdeling Bos & Groen, Administratie Milieu-, Natuur-, Land- en Waterbeheer (AMINAL) (2002) *Regelgeving bij het Ontbossen*, Ministerie van de Vlaamse Gemeenschap, www.boscompensatie.be/files/brochure_regelgeving_ontbossen.pdf, accessed 14 August 2010

Akella, A. S. and Cannon, J. B. (2004) *Strengthening the Weakest Links: Strategies for Improving the Enforcement of Environmental Laws Globally*, Centre for Conservation and Government at Conservation International, www.oecd.org/dataoecd/18/37/33947741.pdf, accessed 24 September 2009

Arin, T. and Kramer, R. A. (2002) 'Divers' willingness to pay to visit marine sanctuaries: An exploratory study', *Ocean and Coastal Management*, vol 45, pp171–183

Ashiabor, H. (2004) 'Taxation and the fostering of biodiversity conservation in Australia', *Bulletin for International Fiscal Documentation*, vol 58, no 7, pp315–325

Barroso, J. M. D. (2009) *Biodiversity: Giving Proper Value to a Priceless Asset*, Speech at 'Biodiversity Protection: Beyond 2010' conference, Athens, 27 April 2009, www.eu-un.europa.eu/articles/en/article_8673_en.htm, accessed 14 September 2009

Bassi, S., ten Brink, P., Pallemaerts, M. and von Homeyer, I. (2009) 'Feasibility of implementing a radical ETR and its acceptance', Report under task C of *Study on Tax Reform in Europe over the Next Decades: Implication for the Environment, for Eco-Innovation and for Household Distribution*, European Environment Agency, Brussels

Bassi, S., ten Brink, P. and Pallemaerts, M. (2010) 'Exploring the potential of harmonizing environmental tax reform efforts in the European Union', in C. D. Soares, J. E. Milne, H. Ashiabor, L. Kreiser and K. Deketelaere (eds) *Critical Issues in Environmental Taxation – International and Comparative Perspectives – Volume VIII*, Oxford University Press, New York

Bat Conservation Trust (2009) *Bats: The Real Stars of the Night*, www.bats.org.uk/, accessed 16 October 2009

Bayon, R. (2004) *Making Environmental Markets Work: Lessons from Early Experience with Sulphur, Carbon, Wetlands, and Other Related Markets*, Forest Trend, Washington, DC

Bayon, R. (2008) 'Banking on Biodiversity', in *2008 State of the Environment Report: Innovations for a Sustainable Economy*, The Worldwatch Institute, pp123–137

BBOP (Business and Biodiversity Offsets Programme) (2008) *Principles on Biodiversity Offsets Supported by the BBOP Advisory Committee*, http://bbop.forest-trends.org/guidelines/principles.pdf, accessed 16 October 2009

BBOP (2009) *Biodiversity Offsets*, http://bbop.forest-trends.org/offsets.php, accessed 14 September 2009

Bean, M., Kihslinger, R. and Wilkinson, J. (2008) *Design of US Habitat Banking Systems to Support the Conservation of Wildlife Habitat and At-Risk Species*, The Environmental Law Institute, Washington, DC

Berggren, U. (2009) 'Elk grazing damage, hunting and wildlife', Swedish Forestry Statistics, www.svo.se/minskog/Templates/EPFileListing.asp?id=16685, accessed 16 October 2009

Biller, D. (2003) *Harnessing Markets for Biodiversity: Towards Conservation and Sustainable Use*, OECD, Paris

Brown, M. J. F. (1974) 'A development consequence — Disposal of mining waste on Bougainville, Papua New Guinea', *Geoforum*, vol 5, pp19–27

Burtraw, D. and Szambelan, S. (2010) 'US emissions trading markets for SO_2 and NO_x', in B. Hansjürgens, R. Antes and M. Sterk (eds) *Permit Trading in Different Applications*, Routledge, Oxford

Carlson, C. P., Burtraw, D., Cropper, M. and Palmer, K. (2000) 'SO_2 control by electric utilities: What are the gains from trade?' *Journal of Political Economy*, vol 108, pp1292–1326

Carroll, N., Fox, J. and Bayon, R. (2007) *Conservation and Biodiversity Banking: A Guide to Setting Up and Running Biodiversity Credit Trading Systems*, Earthscan, London

Commissie voor Leefmilieu, Natuur, Ruimtelijke Ordening en Onroerend Erfgoed (2010) Vergadering (2010) 'Vraag om uitleg van mevrouw Michèle Hostekint tot mevrouw Joke Schauvliege, Vlaams minister van Leefmilieu, Natuur en Cultuur, over het bosuitbreidingsbeleid en de evolutie van het bosareaal in Vlaanderen', Vlaams Parlement, www.vlaamsparlement.be/Proteus5/showVIVerslag.action?id=578796, accessed 14 August 2010

Cribb, J. (2003) 'Thai poachers become animal protectors', *Wildlife Extra*, www.wildlifeextra.com/go/news/thailand-hornbills783.html#cr, accessed 24 September 2009

DECC (Department of Environment and Climate Change of the Government of New South Wales) (2009) *BioBanking*, www.environment.nsw.gov.au/biobanking/, accessed 16 October 2009

Dinar, A. (2000) *The Political Economy of Water Pricing Reforms*, A World Bank Publication, Oxford University Press, Oxford

Dixon, J. A., Fallon Scura, L. and van't Hof, T. (1993) 'Meeting ecological and economic goals: Marine parks in the Caribbean', *Ambio*, vol 22, pp117–125

Dunbar, S. G. (no date) 'Paying for biodiversity', Loma Linda University, CA, http://resweb.llu.edu/rford/courses/BIOL549/docs/Lecture9PayingForBiodiversity.pdf, accessed 19 August 2009

Echavarría, M. (2002) *Land-Water Linkages in Rural Watersheds*, Case Study Series, FAO, Rome, www.rlc.fao.org/Foro/psa/pdf/water.pdf, accessed 25 August 2009

Ecotec (2001) *Study on the Economic and Environmental Implications of the Use of Environmental Taxes and Charges in the European Union and its Member States*, http://ec.europa.eu/environment/enveco/taxation/pdf/ch9_fertilisers.pdf, accessed 19 August 2009

EEA (European Environment Agency) (2005) *Market-Based Instruments for Environmental Policy in Europe*, EEA Technical Report No 8/2005, Copenhagen, Denmark

EFTEC, IEEP, et al (2010) *The Use of Market-Based Instruments for Biodiversity Protection: The Case of Habitat Banking*, Technical Report for European Commission DG Environment. EFTEC and IEEP, London, http://ec.europa.eu/environment/enveco/pdf/eftec_habitat_technical_report.pdf, accessed 1 July 2010

Ellerman, A. D., Joskow, P. L., Montero, J. P., Schmalensee, R. and Bailey, E. M. (2000) *Markets for Clean Air: The US Acid Rain Program*, Cambridge University Press, New York

Emerton, L. (1997) *Seychelles Biodiversity: Economic Assessment*, www.cbd.int/doc/external/countries/seychelles-eco-assessment-1997-en.pdf, accessed 19 August 2009

Emerton, L. (2001) *National Biodiversity Strategies and Action Plans: A Review of Experiences, Lessons Learned and Ways Forward*, IUCN (The World Conservation Union), Regional Environmental

Economics Programme for Asia, Karachi, www.unep.org/bpsp/Economics/Synthesis%20(Economic).pdf, accessed 19 August 2009

ENTRUST (2009) 'How the LCF works', www.entrust.org.uk/home/lcf/how-it-works, accessed 15 September 2009

FAO (2009) 'Description of the Forest Revenue System', *The Forest Revenue System and Government Expenditure on Forestry in Liberia*, Forestry Department, FAO, www.fao.org/docrep/007/ad494e/AD494E06.htm

Forest Trend (2009) *Markets for Ecosystem Services in China: An Exploration of China's 'Eco-compensation' and Other Market-Based Environmental Policies*, www.forest-trends.org/documents/files/doc_2317.pdf, accessed 19 August 2009

GIST (Green India States Trust) (2006) *The Value of Timber, Carbon, Fuelwood, and Non-Timber Forest Products in India's Forests*, www.gistindia.org/pdfs/GAISPMonograph.pdf, accessed 19 August 2009

Government of the Czech Republic (2003) 'A case study on commitments: Related best practice or lessons learned', *Water in the Czech Republic*, UNDP (United Nations Development Programme), http://waterwiki.net/index.php/A_Case_Study_on_Commitments-Related_Best_Practice_or_Lessons_Learned_in_Water_in_the_Czech_Republic, accessed 9 September 2009

GreenBudgetEurope (2010) *GreenBudgetNews: European Newsletter on Environmental Fiscal Reform*, no 27, December, www.foes.de/pdf/GreenBudgetNews27.pdf, accessed 11 February 2011

Guerrero, H. and Howe, C. (2000) *Water Pricing in Mexico: Principles and Reality*, www.soc.uoc.gr/calendar/2000EAERE/papers/PDF/D1-Howe.pdf, accessed 16 October 2009

Gusbin, D., Klaassen, G. and Kouvaritakis, K. (1999) 'Costs of a ceiling on Kyoto flexibility', Presentation at the IAEA Workshop: The clean development mechanism and nuclear power, http://r0.unctad.org/ghg/background.htm, accessed 19 August 2009

Hansjürgens, B. (1992) 'Umweltabgaben im Steuersystem. Zu den Möglichkeiten einer Einfügung von Umweltabgaben in das Steuer- und Abgabensystem der Bundesrepublik Deutschland', Nomos, Baden-Baden

Hansjürgens, B. (2000) 'Effizienzsteigerungen in der Umweltpolitik durch Policy-Mix – Umweltordnungsrecht und handelbare Umweltnutzungsrechte', in E. Gawel and G. Lübbe-Wolff (eds) *Effizientes Umweltordnungsrecht*, Nomos, Baden-Baden, pp251–275

Hansjürgens, B. (2004) 'Cost recovery and water pricing', Presentation at Wageningen University, 26 May 2004

Hansjürgens, B., Antes, R. and Strunz, M. (eds) (2011) *Permit Trading in Different Applications*, Routledge, Oxford

Hilborn, R., Arcese, P., Borner, M., Hando, J., Hopcraft, G., Loibooki, M., Mduma, S. and Sinclair, A. R. E. (2006) 'Effective enforcement in a conservation area', *Science*, vol 314, no 5803, pp1266

Huglo Lepage and Partners Counsel (2003) *Criminal Penalties in EU Member States' Environmental Law: Final Report*, Study Contract ENV.B.4-3040/2002/343499/MRA/A, http://ec.europa.eu/environment/legal/crime/pdf/criminal_penalties2.pdf, accessed 19 August 2009

Huglo Lepage and Partners (2007) 'Criminal penalties in EU Member States' environmental law', Study on Environmental Crime in the 27 Member States, Contract JLS/D3/2006/05, EC, http://ec.europa.eu/environment/legal/crime/pdf/report_environmental_crime.pdf, accessed 19 August 2009

IEEP (Institute for European Environmental Policy) et al (2007) *Reforming Environmentally Harmful Subsidies*, Final report to the European Commission DG Environment, http://ec.europa.eu/environment/enveco/others/pdf/ehs_sum_report.pdf, accessed 22 September 2010

Interpol (2009) 'Environmental crime', www.interpol.int/Public/EnvironmentalCrime/Default.asp, accessed 19 August 2009

Korean Ministry of Environment (2006) *Current Status of Waste Disposal*, http://eng.me.go.kr/content.do?method=moveContent&menuCode=pol_rec_sta_disposal, accessed 19 August 2009

Kraemer, R. A., Guzmán, Z., Ronaldo C., da Motta, S. and Russell, C. (2003a) *Economic Instruments for Water Management: Experiences from Europe and Implications for Latin America and the Caribbean*, Inter-American Development Bank, Washington, DC, http://ecologic.eu/download/projekte/1850-1899/1872/1872-01_final_publication.pdf, accessed 19 August 2009

Kraemer, R. A., Kampa, E. and Interwies, E. (2003b) *The Role of Tradable Permits in Water Pollution Control*, Ecologic, Berlin, and IEEP, Brussels, http://ecologic.eu/download/projekte/1850-1899/1872-03/1872-03_tradable_permits.PDF, accessed 25 August 2009

Landell-Mills, N. (2002) *Marketing Forest Environmental Services: Who Benefits?* Gatekeeper Series No 104, IIED, London, www.iied.org/pubs/pdfs/9217IIED.pdf, accessed 25 August 2009

Leopold, A. and Aguilar, S. (2009) 'Brazil', in E. Morgera, K. Kulovesi and A. Gobena (eds) *Case Studies on Bioenergy Policy and Law: Options for Sustainability*, FAO Legislative Study 102, FAO Rome, www.fao.org/docrep/012/i1285e/i1285e00.htm, accessed 20 July 2010

List, F. (1996) *Outlines of American Political Economy*, Wiesbaden, Böttiger

Madsen, B., Carroll, N. and Moore Brands, K. (2010) *State of Biodiversity Markets Report: Offset and Compensation Programs Worldwide*, Ecosystem Marketplace, Washington, DC, www.ecosystemmarketplace.com/documents/acrobat/sbdmr.pdf, accessed 4 July 2010

Malcolm, A. (no date) Quote on the Natural Capital Initiative, Chief Scientific Adviser, Society of Biology, International Union on Pure Applied Chemistry, www.naturalcapitalinitiative.org.uk/34-quotes/, accessed 10 October 2010

McGlade, J. (2007) Speech of the morning plenary session on 18 October 2007 at the 8th Global Conference on Environmental Taxation, Munich, Germany, 18–20 October 2007, www.eea.europa.eu/pressroom/speeches/eco-innovation-and-climate-change-the-role-of-fiscal-instruments, accessed 16 October 2009

Ministry of Fisheries New Zealand (2005) 'Characteristics of the fishing sectors', www.fish.govt.nz/en-nz/Publications/Ministerial+Briefings/Ministerial+Briefing+05/Annex+1+-+Fisheries+Management+in+New+Zealand/Characteristics+of+the+fishing+sectors.htm, accessed 19 August 2009

Naturvardsverket (2006) *The Swedish Charge on Nitrogen Oxide*, Stockholm, Sweden, www.naturvardsverket.se/Documents/publikationer/620-8245-0.pdf, accessed 25 August 2009

Naumann, M. (2003) 'Current status of water sector in the Czech Republic', Working Paper, www.irs-net.de/forschung/forschungsabteilung-2/intermediaries/WP1_CzechRepublic.pdf, accessed 10 October 2010

Obama, B. (2010) 'Remarks by the President on the Economy at Carnegie Mellon University, Pennsylvania', Office of the Press Secretary, The White House, www.whitehouse.gov/the-press-office/remarks-president-economy-carnegie-mellon-university, accessed 22 September 2010

OECD (Organisation for Economic Co-operation and Development) (1999a) *Implementing Domestic Tradable Permits for Environmental Protection*, OECD, Paris

OECD (1999b) *Handbook of Incentive Measures for Biodiversity: Design and Implementation*, OECD, Paris

OECD (2006) 'Improving water management: Recent OECD experience', Policy Brief, February 2006, www.oecd.org/dataoecd/31/41/36216565.pdf, accessed 16 October 2009

Pruetz, R. and Standridge, N. (2009) 'What makes transfer of development rights work? Success factors from research and practice', *Journal of the American Planning Association*, vol 75, no 1, pp78–87

Rio Tinto (2004) *Rio Tinto's Biodiversity Strategy*, www.riotinto.com/documents/CorpPub_BiodiversityStrategy.pdf, accessed 14 September 2009

Rivalan, P., Delmas, V., Angulo, E., Bull, L. S., Hall, R. J., Courchamp, F., Rosser, A. M. and Leader-Williams, N. (2007) 'Can bans stimulate wildlife trade?' *Nature*, vol 447, pp529–530

Rosenthal, E. (2008) 'Motivated by a tax, Irish spurn plastic bags', *New York Times*, www.nytimes.com/2008/02/02/world/europe/02bags.html, accessed 16 October 2009

RRV (Swedish National Audit Office) (1999) *The Work Done by the Swedish Forestry Organization in order to put the Environmental Goal on an Equal Footing with the Production Goal*, www.eurosaiwgea.org/Environmental%20audits/Natural%20Resources/Documents/1999-Sweden-Swedish%20Forestry.pdf, accessed 10 October 2010

Shine, C. (2005) *Using Tax Incentives to Conserve and Enhance Biodiversity in Europe*, Nature and Environment No 143, Council of Europe

Sjöberg, P. (2007) *Taxation of Pesticides and Fertilizers*, Department of Business Administration and Social Sciences, Luleå University of Technology, http://epubl.ltu.se/1404-5508/2005/101/LTU-SHU-EX-05101-SE.pdf, accessed 25 August 2009

Slootweg, R. and van Beukering, P. (2008) *Valuation of Ecosystem Services and Strategic Environmental Assessment: Lessons from Influential Cases*, Netherlands Commission for Environmental Assessment, www.indiaenvironmentportal.org.in/files/cs-impact-nl-sea-valuation-en.pdf, accessed 16 October 2009

STINAPA Bonaire (Stichting Nationale Park Foundation Bonaire) (2009) STINAPA Bonaire website, www.stinapa.org/, accessed 16 October 2009

Swedish Forestry Act, www.svo.se/episerver4/templates/SNormalPage.aspx?id=12677, accessed 16 October 2009

TEEB for Citizens (no date) www.teeb4me.com, accessed 10 October 2010

TEEB in Business (2011) *The Economics of Ecosystems and Biodiversity in Business and Enterprise* (ed J. Bishop), Earthscan, London

TEEB in Local Policy (2011) *The Economics of Ecosystems and Biodiversity in Local and Regional Policy and Management* (ed H. Wittmer and H. Gundimeda), Earthscan, London

ten Brink, P. (ed) (2002) *Voluntary Environmental Agreements: Process and Practice, and Future Trends*, Greenleaf Publishing, Sheffield

ten Brink, P., Lutchman, I., Bassi, S., Speck, S., Sheavly, S., Register, K. and Woolaway, C. (2009) *Guidelines on the Use of Market-Based Instruments to Address the Problem of Marine Litter*, Institute for European Environmental Policy (IEEP), Brussels and Sheavly Consultants, Virginia, US

ten Kate, K., Bishop, J. and Bayon, R. (2004) *Biodiversity Offsets: Views, Experience, and the Business Case*, IUCN and Insight Investment, Gland, Switzerland and Cambridge, UK

Thaindian News (2009) 'Apex court provides funds for afforestation, wildlife conservation', www.thaindian.com/newsportal/enviornment/apex-court-provides-funds-for-afforestation-wildlife-conservation_100216356.html, accessed 19 August 2009

TNC (The Nature Conservancy) (2007) 'Watershed valuation as a tool for biodiversity protection', www.nature.org/initiatives/freshwater/files/watershed_report_02_02_07_final.pdf, accessed 25 August 2009

Uganda Wildlife Authority (2009) 'Gorilla permit booking', www.uwa.or.ug/gorilla.html, accessed 25 August 2009

UNEP (United Nations Environmental Programme) (2009a) *Rio Declaration on Environment and Development*, www.unep.org/Documents.Multilingual/Default.asp?DocumentID=78&ArticleID=1163&l=en, accessed 9 September 2009

UNEP (2009b) *Marine Litter: A Global Challenge*, www.unep.org/pdf/UNEP_Marine_Litter-A_Global_Challenge.pdf, accessed 16 October 2009

UNESCAP (2003) 'Good practices suite examples: Japan's garbage collection fee', www.unescap.org/drpad/vc/conference/ex_jp_14_jgc.htm, accessed 22 September 2010

US EPA (US Environmental Protection Agency) (2009) *Emission, Compliance, and Market Data*, www.epa.gov/airmarkets/progress/ARP_1.html, accessed 25 August 2009

US Supreme Court (1927) 'Compania General De Tabacos De Filipinas v. Collector of Internal Revenue, 275 U.S. 87' (decided 21 November 1927), http://bulk.resource.org/courts.gov/c/US/275/275.US.87.42.html, accessed 10 October 2010

Vanasselt, W. (2000) 'Ecotourism and conservation: Are they compatible?' in *World Resources 2000–2001*, http://earthtrends.wri.org/features/view_feature.php?theme=7&fid=29, accessed 25 August 2009

VBV (Vereniging voor Bos in Vlaanderen vzw) (2008) *Bosbarometer 2008*, http://vbv.be/bosbarometer/2008/VBV_Bosbarometer_2008.pdf, accessed 14 August 2010

VBV (2009) *Bosbarometer 2009*, http://vbv.be/bosbarometer/2009/VBVBosbarometer2009.pdf., accessed 14 August 2010

Vlaamse Regering (2001) 'Besluit van de Vlaamse regering van 16 februari 2001 tot vaststelling van nadere regels inzake compensatie van ontbossing en ontheffing van het verbod op ontbossing', Belgisch Staatsblad, www.emis.vito.be/sites/default/files/actuele_wetgeving/sb230301-1.pdf, accessed 10 October 2010

Walls, M. and McConnel, V. (2007) 'Transfer of development rights in US communities: Evaluating program design, implementation, and outcomes', RFF, Washington, DC, www.rff.org/rff/News/Features/upload/30347_1.pdf, accessed 19 August 2009

Watkins, S., Ervin, J., Salem, R., Flores, M., Weary, R. and Spensley, J. (2008) 'Supporting national implementation of the programme of work on protected areas: Lessons learned and ingredients of success', www.cbd.int/doc/meetings/pa/wgpa-02/information/wgpa-02-inf-07-en.doc, accessed 18 July 2010

Wätzold, F. (2004) 'SO₂ emissions in Germany: Regulations to fight Waldsterben', in W. Harrington, D. Morgenstern and T. Sterner (eds) *Choosing Environmental Policy: Comparing Instruments and Outcomes in the United States and Europe*, RFF Press, Washington, DC, pp23–40

Wildlife Extra (2008) 'Serengeti patrols cut poaching of buffalo, elephants, rhinos', www.wildlifeextra.com/go/news/serengeti-poaching.html#cr, accessed 24 September 2009

Wildlife Extra (2009) 'Hornbill conservation in Thailand: Poacher to gamekeeper', www.wildlifeextra.com/go/news/thailand-hornbills783.html#cr, accessed 24 September 2009

Wilkie, D. S. and Carpenter, J. (1999) 'The potential role of safari hunting as a source of revenue for protected areas in the Congo Basin', *Oryx*, vol 33, no 4, pp340–345

Wilkinson, C. R. (ed) (2004) *Status of the Coral Reefs of the World: 2004*, Vols 1 and 2, Australian Institute for Marine Sciences, Townsville, Australia

Worm, B., et al (2009) 'Rebuilding global fisheries', *Science*, vol 325, pp578–585

Yandle, T. and Dewees, C. M. (2008) 'Consolidation in an individual transferable quota regime: Lessons from New Zealand 1986–1999', *Environmental Management*, vol 41, no 6, pp915–928

Young, J. E. (1992) *Mining the Earth*, Worldwatch Paper 109, Worldwatch Institute, Washington, DC

Zeppel, H. (2007) *Indigenous Ecotourism: Sustainable Development and Management*, CABI, Cairns, Australia

Zylicz, T., Bateman, I., Georgiou, S., Markowska, A., Dziegielewska, D., Turner, K., Graham, A. and Langford, I. (1995) *Contingent Valuation of Eutrophication in the Baltic Sea Region*, CSERGE Working Paper GEC 95-03, www.uea.ac.uk/env/cserge/pub/wp/gec/gec_1995_03.pdf, accessed 19 September 2009

Chapter 8
Recognizing the Value
of Protected Areas

Coordinating lead author
Marianne Kettunen

Lead authors
Augustin Berghofer, Aaron Bruner, Nicholas Conner, Nigel Dudley,
Sarat Babu Gidda, Marianne Kettunen, Kalemani Jo Mulongoy,
Luis Pabon-Zamora, Alexandra Vakrou

Contributing authors
Meriem Bouamrane, Patrick ten Brink, Stuart Chape,
Paul Morling, Andrew Seidl, Sue Stolton

Editing and language check
Clare Shine

See end of chapter for acknowledgements for reviews and other contributions

Contents

Key messages   347

Summary   348

1   Protecting areas for biodiversity and people   348
    1.1   The value of protected areas   348
    1.2   The diversity and range of protected areas   349
    1.3   Challenges and opportunities for policy makers   353

2   Weighing the benefits and costs of protected areas   355
    2.1   Protected area benefits   355
    2.2   Protected area costs   360
    2.3   Comparing the benefits and costs of protected areas   361

3   Improving effectiveness through economic evaluation   368
    3.1   Valuing ecosystem services for advocacy   368
    3.2   Valuing ecosystem services for decision support   369
    3.3   Valuing ecosystem services to address social impacts   371

4   Securing sustainable financing for protected areas   373
    4.1   Is there a financing gap for protected areas?   373
    4.2   Mobilizing funds: Existing sources and innovative mechanisms   375
    4.3   A framework for successful financing   377

5   Strengthening policy and institutional support   385
    5.1   Major policy initiatives on protected areas   385
    5.2   Institutional requirements for protected areas   385
    5.3   Key elements for successful management   387
    5.4   Promoting coherence and synergies: The example of climate change   388

6   Creating a workable future for protected areas   388

Notes   390

Acknowledgements   391

References   391

Annex 1 Key elements for successful implementation and relevant policy provisions   399

Key messages

Protected areas already cover 12.9 per cent of the Earth's land surface. Marine protected areas only cover 6.3 per cent of territorial seas and a tiny proportion of the high seas (IUCN and UNEP-WCMC, 2010) but are increasing rapidly in number and area. Ecosystems inside protected areas provide a multitude of benefits and the global benefits of protection far outweigh costs. However, benefits from protection are often broadly disbursed, long-term and non-market while the costs of protection and the earning potential from non-protection choices are often short-term and concentrated. Policy actions are needed to address this unequal distribution of benefits and costs. This is vital to make protected areas a socially and economically attractive choice and to maximize their contribution to human well-being at all scales.

Completing comprehensive, representative and effectively managed coherent systems of national and regional protected areas and – as a matter of urgency – establishing marine protected areas are essential to conserve biodiversity and maintain ecosystem services. Well-designed and well-managed protected areas can play an important role in supporting the maintenance and recovery of fish stocks as well as many other services.

Integrating protected areas into the broader landscape and seascape, and enhancing/ restoring ecological connectivity between sites and with their wider environment can increase ecosystem resilience. Improved capacity to recover from disturbance, including climate-related pressures, can support ecosystem-based adaptation to climate change.

Economic valuation should be used to help establish effective policies and mechanisms for equitable sharing of costs and benefits arising from protected areas (e.g. payment for environment services) and incentives created to overcome opportunity costs for affected stakeholders where this is justified by the broader benefits.

Stable financial resources need to be secured to implement and manage protected areas, e.g. though innovative funding instruments and adequate international funding, particularly to support the needs of developing countries. We need to understand better the scale and implications of the current protected area financing gap.

Greater policy coherence can create 'win–win' situations and establish an enabling environment for effective protected areas. Important synergies with other policies include:

- recognizing the role of protected areas in ecosystem-based adaption to climate change;
- demonstrating how marine protected areas can help in fish stock recovery, increase food security and enhance coastal protection; and
- investing in protected areas to reduce risks related to natural hazards, including water scarcity.

It is critical to ensure the participation of local communities and support local livelihoods, e.g. by using appropriate governance models and ensuring that appropriately established and managed protected areas contribute to poverty reduction and local livelihoods and build on local knowledge of the ecosystems.

Summary

Chapter 8 focuses on the role of protected areas in underpinning global human welfare and ways to improve their effectiveness. Section 1 provides an overview of their current status (definition, categories, coverage) and outlines the value and socio-economic potential of ecosystems preserved by protected areas. Section 2 analyses specific benefits and costs associated with protected areas and presents the results of comparisons at global, national and local levels. Sections 3 and 4 provide insights on how economic valuation of protected area costs and benefits can provide useful tools to support their implementation, e.g. by building an attractive case for protection and helping to obtain sustainable and long-term financing. Section 5 addresses the broader context and the importance of multi-level policy support and effective institutional frameworks to secure lasting results. Section 6 draws together key conclusions and presents an enabling framework for protected areas in the future.

Please note that this chapter focuses on the relevance of protected areas to international and national decision makers. For detailed information on their importance to local policy makers, readers should consult Chapter 7 in TEEB in Local Policy (2011).

1 Protecting areas for biodiversity and people

> Protected areas promise a healthier future for the planet and its people. Safeguarding these precious areas means safeguarding our future. (Nelson R. Mandela and HM Queen Noor; UNEP, 2003)

1.1 The value of protected areas

Protected areas, often considered as the last safe haven for nature's jewels, are central to global efforts to conserve biodiversity. Yet they not only safeguard our invaluable natural capital but also play a key role in maintaining our economic and social well-being (Balmford and Whitten, 2003; Dudley et al, 2008; Mulongoy and Gidda, 2008; Kettunen et al, 2009).

Ecosystems help underpin global human welfare, for example by maintaining food security, mitigating environmental risks and helping adaptation to climate change (see Section 2.1). Establishing protected areas (PAs) can help maintain or even increase the provision of ecosystem services from the ecosystems inside their boundaries (see Figure 8.1). This in no way means that the area concerned loses its socio-economic significance – quite the opposite. PA designations help to prevent degradation of ecosystems and can increase the already valuable services provided by natural sites.

Some ecosystem services are obviously likely to continue, whether or not a site is formally designated. A PA's total ecosystem service value can therefore be divided into two main components:

1   The added value of designation:

- value of protected area status (e.g. increased ecotourism interest);
- value of subsequent avoided degradation due to measures on and off site;
- increased value due to management and investment;

2   The value of services maintained even without designation (see Figure 8.1).

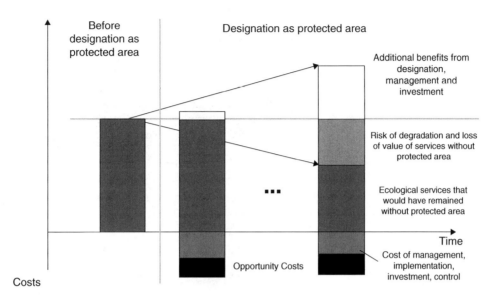

Figure 8.1 *Schematic for analysing the value of protected areas over time*

Source: Patrick ten Brink, own representation

In practice, it can be difficult to distinguish the added value of designation from a PA's total ecosystem value, especially over time, as this depends not only on the specific designation and management measures but also on what would have happened in their absence. If non-designation and associated measures were to lead to ecosystem degradation and loss of services, then designation and effective protection would obviously offer significant value added. Conversely, if there is only a low threat of degradation anyway, PA designation offers fewer additional benefits. This chapter presents concrete examples of how marginal or additional protected area values have been calculated (where only total values are available, this is made explicit).

Costs – of management, investment, implementation and control – can also increase with PA designation in order to meet conservation objectives: there will also be a range of opportunity costs (see Section 2).

It is important to underline that PAs also have unique intrinsic values in addition to the benefits they provide to people, society and the economy. Even if this chapter (indeed the whole book) is mainly focused on ecosystem services flow – a human-centred approach to natural capital – we should never lose sight of biodiversity's wider ecological values.

1.2 The diversity and range of protected areas

Protected areas already cover 12.9 per cent of the Earth's land surface. Marine protected areas (MPAs) only cover 6.3 per cent of territorial seas and a tiny proportion of the high seas (IUCN and UNEP-WCMC, 2010) but are increasing rapidly in number and area. Box 8.1 presents the two most widely used definitions.

Box 8.1 Definitions of protected areas

There are two PA definitions, one from the Convention on Biological Diversity (CBD) and one from the IUCN World Commission on Protected Areas. Both convey the same general message. These definitions encompass several other international classifications, such as natural world heritage sites and biosphere reserves established by the United Nations Educational, Scientific and Cultural Organization (UNESCO).

- **The CBD definition:** 'A geographically defined area which is designated or regulated and managed to achieve specific conservation objectives.'
- **The IUCN definition:** 'A clearly defined geographical space, recognized, dedicated and managed, through legal or other effective means, to achieve the long-term conservation of nature with associated ecosystem services and cultural values.'

Source: Dudley et al (2008)

PAs are a flexible mechanism that can be designed to deliver multiple benefits for biodiversity and people (see Section 2). There are six internationally recognized categories (see Table 8.1 below) which show just how diverse their management objectives and structures may be.

Although most people associate PAs mainly with nature conservation and tourism, well-managed PAs can provide vital ecosystem services, such as water purification and retention, erosion control and reduced flooding and unnatural wild fires (e.g. Dudley and Stolton, 2003; Stolton et al, 2006; Mulongoy and Gidda, 2008; Stolton et al, 2008a; Stolton and Dudley, 2010; see also Chapter 9 of this book and TEEB in Local Policy, 2011, Chapter 7). They buffer human communities against different environmental risks and hazards, and support food and health security by maintaining crop diversity and species with economic and/or subsistence value. They also play an important role in ecosystem-based approaches to climate change adaptation and contribute to mitigation by storing and sequestering carbon (see Section 1.3).

PAs are often an important part of local cultural heritage and identity in addition to their recreation, education, health and tourism benefits. Conferring protected area status gives formal recognition to these values and creates favourable conditions for their conservation and long-term management.

As many rural communities depend on protected forests, pastures, wetlands and marine areas for subsistence and livelihoods, PAs contribute directly to the global agenda for sustainable development, poverty reduction and maintaining cultures (Dudley et al, 2008; Mulongoy and Gidda, 2008). Many existing and proposed PAs, particularly in developing countries, overlap with areas of high rural poverty (Redford et al, 2008). They increasingly feature in national poverty reduction programme strategies as potential sources of economic development that can also contribute to human well-being (subsistence, cultural, spiritual and environmental benefits) (e.g. Blignaut and Moolman, 2006). PAs have become important vehicles for supporting self-determination: many indigenous peoples and local community movements have either self-declared or worked with governments to develop PAs to secure traditional lands and protect biodiversity.

Table 8.1 *Internationally recognized system of PA categories*

IUCM category (primary management objective)	A. Governance by governments			B. Shared governance			C. Private governance			D. Governance by indigenous peoples and local communities	
	Federal or national ministry or agency in charge	Local ministry or agency in charge	Management delegated by the government (e.g. to an NGO)	Transboundary protected area	Collaborative management (various pluralist influences)	Collaborative management (pluralist management board)	Declared and run by private individual	Declared and run by non-profit organizations	Declared and run by for-profit individuals	Declared and run by indigenous peoples	Declared and run by local communities
I – Strict nature or wilderness protection			H								
II – Ecosystem protection and recreation		A		G							
III – Protection of natural monument or feature	I										
IV – Protection of habitats and species			E	G	B					C	
V – Protection of landscapes or seascapes								D			
VI – Protection and sustainable resource use					F						

Source: The authors, building on Dudley et al (2008)

Notes:

The IUCN typology of protected area management types and governance approaches distinguishes six categories of management objective and four governance types (Dudley, 2008).

The examples below give an idea of their sheer diversity (letters correspond to those in the matrix above).

A: Girraween National Park, Queensland, Australia

Owned and managed by the state government of Queensland to protect ecosystems and species unique to the area.

B: Dana Nature Reserve and Biosphere Reserve, Jordan

Managed by the state in cooperation with local communities to reduce grazing and restore desert species.

C: Alto Fragua Indiwasi National Park, Colombia

Proposed by the Ingano people on their traditional forest lands and managed according to shamanic rules.

D: Sečovlje Salina Natural Park, Slovenia

Important area of salt works and wetland, funded as a private reserve by Slovenia's largest mobile phone company. The park also forms part of the EU Natura 2000 network.

E: Sanjiangyuan Nature Reserve, China

Since 2006 part of the reserve has been managed by villagers from Cuochi, who patrol and monitor an area of 2440km^2 in exchange for a commitment to help ensure that resource use is sustainable (Basanglamao and He Xin, 2009).

F: Rio Macho Forest Reserve, Costa Rica

An extractive reserve under mixed ownership (70 per cent government, 30 per cent private) zoned for protection, tourism and sustainable use of forest products and agriculture.

G: Maloti-Drakensberg Transboundary Protected Area

Includes the Natal-Drakensberg Park (Kwazulu Natal, South Africa, category II) and the Maloti-Sehlabthebe National Park (Kingdom of Lesotho, category IV).

H: The Strict Nature Reserve of Aldabra Atoll in the western Indian Ocean

Managed by the Seychelles Islands Foundation, a public trust established by the government.

I: Monterrico Multiple Use Area, Guatemala

This government-managed PA protects the largest remaining block of mangrove in the country and is managed for protection and artisanal fishing.

Depending on their category and design (see Table 8.1), PAs may allow for some controlled economic activities to take place within the designated area. Some, particularly private reserves and state national parks, may function as profit-making entities in their own right. Several PA types, notably UNESCO biosphere reserves and protected landscapes, can act as models for sustainable development in rural areas. Not all PAs are expected to generate income to help local communities, but where the opportunity exists they can make an important contribution to livelihoods (e.g. Mmopelwa and Blignaut, 2006; Mmopelwa et al, 2009; and see examples in Section 3).

PAs also impose costs on society where access to resources is restricted and economic options forgone (e.g. James et al, 2001; Colchester, 2003; Chan et al, 2007; Dowie, 2009). These costs must be recognized alongside the benefits (see Sections 2 and 4 below).

1.3 Challenges and opportunities for policy makers

PA agencies need to prove that the benefits from PAs justify the costs, convince stakeholders of these benefits and ensure that costs are equitably distributed. The potential to deliver such benefits depends on the mechanisms chosen to meet the agreed objectives. Planning, design, legal basis, management, orientation, skills, capacity and funding are all key.

Although the aim is usually to protect PAs from unsustainable human use, in practice they face many challenges and many perform at suboptimal levels. Pressures come both from distant sources (e.g. long-range pollution, climate change) and from near or inside the site (e.g. poaching, encroachment, inappropriate tourism, abandonment of traditional management) (see Box 8.2). Economic valuation of benefits and costs, used in conjunction with an understanding of social and cultural issues, can provide information needed to overcome some of these challenges (see Section 3).

Many legally designated PAs are 'paper parks', i.e. there are no means of enforcing the intended protection. While designation can itself provide a measure of protection and is a valuable first step, PAs without appropriate management are often vulnerable. Lack of capacity and resources, weak political support, poor understanding of social interactions, absence of community consultation, and problems in empowering stakeholders can reduce their effectiveness, undermining the supply of ecosystem services as well as conservation.

Some pressures stem from the way that a PA is set up. If local communities or indigenous peoples lose substantial rights to their territories and resources without agreement or compensation, they may have little choice but to continue 'illegal' activity in the new PA. Other pressures arise because natural resources like timber and bush meat attract criminal activity. Weak management capacity often hinders adequate responses.

The type and level of threats varies enormously with national or regional socio-economic conditions: pressures from encroachment and collection of natural resources can be particularly high in areas of poverty. Building effective PAs in a poor country is particularly challenging and needs different approaches to those possible in countries where most people are relatively wealthy. In developed countries, many PAs are dominated by semi-natural or even highly human-influenced ecosystems (e.g. arable farmland): in such cases, maintaining low-intensity land-use practices is often the key

---

Box 8.2 Main direct pressures posing risks to protected areas

A global meta-study coordinated by the University of Queensland examined over 7000 assessments of PA management effectiveness (Leverington et al, 2008) and identified the following key direct pressures on PAs (in descending importance):

* hunting and fishing;
* logging, wood harvesting and collection of non-timber forest products (NTFPs);
* housing and settlement;
* recreation (mostly unregulated tourism);
* activities nearby, including urbanization, agriculture and grazing;
* grazing and cropping;
* fire and fire suppression;
* pollution;
* invasive alien species;
* mining and quarrying.

The study does not identify underlying causes, e.g. hunting may be driven by poverty or inequality in land tenure. It also does not address the implications of climate change which will increase pressures on many PAs and may eliminate viable habitat for some species or shift it outside current reserve boundaries (Hannah et al, 2007).

Most identified pressures stem from economic activity, demonstrating the value of resources found in PAs. In some but not all cases, different management models might allow some exploitation of these resources within PA management models.

---

requirement for biodiversity conservation. Because such land uses are threatened by intensification or sometimes by land abandonment (Stoate et al, 2001; EEA, 2006), funding is often required to maintain such practices.

We still have no comprehensive global picture of pressures on PAs but a major study focusing on direct pressures is being undertaken for this purpose (see Box 8.2). In addition, the World Heritage Committee draws up the *World Heritage in Danger* list for UNESCO world heritage sites at most risk.

Protected area systems are not yet necessarily representative of the biodiversity within a country: numerous gaps in species and ecosystem protection remain (Rodrigues et al, 2004). In some countries PAs are disproportionately located in areas where there are less likely to be conflicts with economic uses, such as polar regions, deserts and mountains, leaving more biodiverse ecosystems and habitats largely unprotected (e.g. only 2 per cent of lake systems are in PAs; see Abell et al, 2007).

Despite increasing threats to the marine environment, progress in establishing marine protected areas (MPAs) has been very slow, particularly for the high seas (0.5 per cent coverage; Coad et al, 2009). Yet research shows that MPAs can be an effective conservation strategy for a range of species, particularly fish (see examples in Section 2.1). It has been estimated that conserving 20 to 30 per cent of global oceans through MPAs could create a million jobs, sustain fish catch worth US$70–80 billion/year and ecosystem services with a gross value of roughly US$4.5–6.7 trillion/year (Balmford et al, 2004). However, the extent to which MPAs can deliver benefits for biodiversity and fisheries will again obviously depend on careful design and effective management. Predicted recovery of fish populations may also take time so that benefits become visible only after a number of years.

For PAs to function as ecological networks, a more systematic and spatially integrated approach to their establishment and management is needed. The CBD Programme of Work on Protected Areas (see Section 5 below) recognizes that this requires a more holistic way of viewing PAs and highlights opportunities for PA agencies and managers to work with other stakeholders to incorporate PAs into broader conservation strategies.

Well-managed PA networks also offer critical opportunities to adapt to and mitigate climate change. Climate change will put new pressures on biodiversity and increasingly modify ecosystems outside PAs, adding to the demands on PA systems and resources and giving them an even more important role in the maintenance of resilient and viable populations, e.g. species of economic importance. Some plants and animals will need to move their range, calling for more connectivity between PAs than is currently available. Ways to achieve this connectivity include changing management in the wider landscape and seascape, restoring ecological connections between PAs and expanding the protected area system itself (IUCN, 2004; Huntley, 2007; Taylor and Figgis, 2007; Harley, 2008; CBD AHTEG, 2009).

PAs often contain carbon-rich soils and habitats (e.g. store forests, peatlands, wetlands and marine ecosystems like mangroves, seagrass and kelp) that sequester and store carbon (mitigation). They also help people adapt to climate change by maintaining ecosystem services that reduce natural disaster impacts (coastal and river protection, control of desertification), stabilize soils and enhance resilience to changing conditions. PAs support human life by protecting fish nurseries and agricultural genetic material and providing cheap, clean drinking water from forests, and food during drought or famine. These can all create significant win–wins for biodiversity conservation and socio-economic resilience to climate change (Dudley and Stolton, 2003; Stolton et al, 2006, 2008a; Dudley et al, 2009b; see also Chapter 9).

2 Weighing the benefits and costs of protected areas

This section draws on state-of-the-art research to examine two sets of questions fundamental to the impact of PAs on human well-being:

- **Do benefits outweigh costs?** If so, in which contexts and at what scales? These questions address the rationale for investing in effective management and potential global expansion of PAs.
- **Who benefits and who bears the costs?** Over what time frame are benefits and costs experienced? For which benefits do markets exist and where can they be created? These questions address equity concerns and can guide decisions on siting and managing PAs by governments and private actors on the ground.

We have chosen examples for their clarity and methodological rigour in quantifying particular services or costs (see Sections 2.1 and 2.2). The main focus is on examples that capture marginal rather than total benefits (i.e. they quantify the additional service flows from protection, rather than the total value of services). All examples are case-specific and do not indicate average levels of benefits or costs across all PAs.

Box 8.3 Protected areas support for local livelihoods

Lao PDR: Nam Et and Phou Loei National Parks

The 24,000 people who live in and around the parks use them for wild plants, fodder for animals, wild meat, construction materials and fuel. In 2002 these uses amounted to 40 per cent of total production per family, with a total value of nearly US$2 million/year (Emerton et al, 2002).

Zambia: Lupande Game Management Area

In 2004 two hunting concessions earned the 50,000 residents revenues of US$230,000 per year, which was distributed in cash and to projects such as schools (Child and Dalal-Clayton, 2004).

Nepal: Royal Chitwan National Park

A Forest User Group in the buffer zone earned US$175,000 in ten years through wildlife viewing and used this to set up biogas plants. It operates a microcredit scheme providing loans at low interest rates (O'Gorman, 2006).

Cambodia: Ream National Park

Fish breeding grounds and other subsistence goods from mangroves were worth an estimated US$600,000 per year in 2002, with an additional US$300,000 in local ecosystem services such as storm protection and erosion control (Emerton et al, 2002).

India: Buxa Tiger Reserve

Of families living in and around Buxa, 54 per cent derive their income from NTFPs harvested in the reserve (Das, 2005).

Vietnam: Hon Mun Marine Protected Area

About 5300 people depend on the reserve for aquaculture and near-shore fishing. Gross fisheries value is estimated at US$15,538/km^2 (Pham et al, 2005).

Costa Rica: The coastal/marine Ostional Wildlife Refuge

In 2001, the revenue from legally collected and sold turtle eggs from the reserve, benefiting local villagers and broader businesses alike, was estimated as US$1 million (Troëng and Drews, 2004).

To understand how benefits and costs compare (Section 2.3), we rely on two other sources of information to make appropriate comparisons: (i) a smaller set of site- and country-level studies that evaluate the benefits and costs of PAs together; and (ii) global evaluations of protection benefits/costs that provide average or summary values. Last, Section 2.4 describes additional factors that influence whether protection will be perceived as a good choice, independent of purely economic considerations.

2.1 Protected area benefits

Section 1 provided an overview of the importance of PAs for human livelihoods and well-being. This section gives concrete examples of some of the most important PA beneficial functions, while noting that specific benefits from individual sites will vary depending on location, ecosystem and management strategy.

PAs are a supply of clean water

Well-managed natural forests provide higher-quality water with less sediment and fewer pollutants than water from other catchments. PAs are a key source of such water worldwide. One-third of the world's hundred largest cities draw a substantial proportion of their drinking water from forest PAs, e.g. this has cumulatively saved the city of New York at least US$6 billion in water treatment costs (Dudley and Stolton, 2003). In Europe, freshwater supply to several residential areas in Sofia depends on protected high mountain peat bog areas situated within Vitosha National Park (Dudley and Stolton, 2003). Venezuela's national PA system prevents sedimentation that would reduce farm earnings by around US$4 million/year (based on Gutman, 2002).[1]

PAs reduce risk from unpredictable events and natural hazards

PAs can reduce risks such as landslides, floods, storms and fire by stabilizing soil, providing space for flood waters to disperse, blocking storm surges and limiting illegal activity in fire-prone areas. In Vietnam, following typhoon Wukong in 2000, areas planted with mangroves remained relatively unharmed while neighbouring provinces suffered significant losses of life and property (Brown et al, 2006). In Sri Lanka, flood attenuation provided by the 7000ha Muthurajawella Marsh near Colombo has been valued at over US$5 million/year (Schuyt and Brander, 2004; for other examples, see Chapter 9). In Europe, the value of forests managed for protective functions in the Alps is estimated at several billion dollars a year (International Strategy for Disaster Reduction, 2004; see further Chapter 7 and TEEB in Local Policy, 2011).

PAs maintain food security by increasing resource productivity and sustainability

PAs provide habitat and breeding grounds for pollinating insects and other species with economic and/or subsistence value (e.g. game, fish, fruit, natural medicines, biological control agents) and can also support food and health security by maintaining crop genetic diversity (Box 8.4). In the US, the agricultural value of wild native pollinators sustained by natural habitats adjacent to farmlands is estimated at billions of dollars per year (adapted from Daily et al, 2009).

Box 8.4 Maintaining food security: Crop wild relatives and protected areas

Recognition of wider benefits can influence choices about location and management of protected areas. Conservation of crop wild relatives (CWR) in their natural environment helps to provide fresh crop breeding material and maintain food security (Stolton et al, 2008a; see examples on map). CWR are concentrated in relatively small regions often referred to as 'centres of food crop diversity'. Habitat protection in 34 ecoregions containing such centres is significantly lower than average: 29 had less than 10 per cent protection and six had less than 1 per cent protection (Stolton et al, 2008b). Some are also undergoing rapid losses in natural habitat, thus putting CWR at risk.

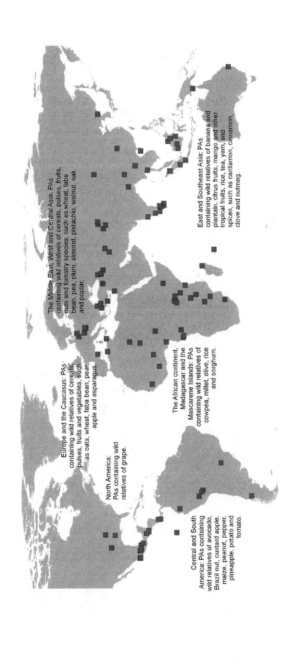

The Middle East, West and Central Asia: PAs containing wild relatives of cereals, pulses, fruits, nuts and forestry species, such as wheat, faba bean, pea, plum, almond, pistachio, walnut, oak and poplar.

East and Southeast Asia: PAs containing wild relatives of banana and plantain, citrus fruits, mango and other tropical fruits, rice, tea, yam, and spices, such as cardamon, cinnamon, clove and nutmeg.

Europe and the Caucasus: PAs containing wild relatives of cereals, pulses, fruits and vegetables, such as oats, wheat, faba bean, pear, apple and asparagus.

North America: PAs containing wild relatives of grape.

The African continent, Madagascar and the Mascarene Islands: PAs containing wild relatives of cowpea, millet, olive, rice and sorghum.

Central and South America: PAs containing wild relatives of avocado, Brazil nut, custard apple, maize, peanut, pepper, pineapple, potato and tomato.

Figure 8.2 *Food security and protected areas*

Source: Stolton and Dudley (2010).

Well-designed 'no-take' zones in MPAs can function similarly (Gell and Roberts, 2003). A review of 112 studies in 80 MPAs found that fish populations, size and biomass all dramatically increased inside reserves, allowing spillover to nearby fishing grounds (Halpern, 2003). Various studies have reported fish catch increases in the vicinity of MPAs a few years after their establishment (McClanahan and Mangi, 2000; Gell and Oberts, 2003; Russ et al, 2003). MPAs can also rebuild resilience in marine ecosystems and provide insurance against fish stock management failures (Pauly et al, 2002).

PAs support nature-based tourism

Natural and cultural resources in PAs (e.g. biodiversity, landscape and recreational values, scenic views and open spaces) are an important driver of tourism. Over 40 per cent of European travellers surveyed in 2000 included a visit to a national park (Eagles and Hillel, 2008). This can be an important source of local earnings and employment:

- In Finland the total annual revenue linked to visitor spending in national parks and key recreation areas (total of 45 areas) has been estimated as €87 million/ year, generating €20 return for every €1 of public investment (Metsähallitus, 2009).
- In Scotland, the Cairngorms National Park receives around 1.4 million visitors a year, each spending on average £69 (US$100) per day on accommodation, food, transport and entertainment (Cairngorms National Park Authority, 2005).
- In New Zealand, economic activity from conservation areas on the west coast of South Island created an extra 1814 jobs in 2004 (15 per cent of total jobs) and extra spending in the region of US$221 million/year (10 per cent of total spend), mainly from tourism (Butcher Partners, 2005).
- In Bolivia, tourism related to PAs and wider nature-based tourism is estimated to generate around 20,000 jobs, indirectly supporting close to 100,000 people (Pabon-Zamora et al, 2009).

The importance of biodiversity in attracting visitors will vary between sites and visitor groups. 'Charismatic' or 'flagship' species are often the main attraction but some are drawn to the more complex biodiversity web. In other PAs open space, landscapes or beaches may drive most interest. Where specific insights are available on the particular driver of tourism (e.g. elephant- or tiger-based tourism), this is noted in the case studies.

PAs contribute to climate change mitigation and adaptation

PAs contain 15 per cent of global terrestrial carbon stock, with a value understood to be in the trillions of dollars (Campbell et al, 2008). With deforestation accounting for an estimated 17 per cent of global carbon emissions (IPCC, 2007), maintenance of existing PAs and strategic expansion of the global PA system can play an important role in controlling land-use-related emissions. Intact ecosystems inside PAs may also be more robust to climatic disturbances than converted systems.

PAs protect cultural and spiritual resources

These values are poorly accounted for by markets[2] but can nonetheless be immensely important to society. In Brazil's Saõ Paulo municipality, residents have expressed willingness to pay more than US$2 million/year to preserve the 35,000ha Morro do Diablo State Park, which protects a key fragment of Brazil's Atlantic forest (Adams et al, 2007). Visitors to South Korea's Chirisan National Park value the conservation of a single species – the Manchurian black bear – at more than US$3.5 million/year (Han and Lee, 2008). Sacred sites are probably humanity's oldest form of habitat protection, representing a voluntary choice to forgo other land uses in favour of larger spiritual benefits (Dudley et al, 2009a). In Spain, for example, monks in an ancient monastery in Montserrat National Park manage some of their land as a nature reserve: this practice is becoming increasingly common with monastic orders in Europe (Dudley et al, 2009a). Lastly, indigenous groups and other traditional owners living in PAs often have fundamental ties to traditional lands and resources (Beltran, 2000).

PAs preserve future values

PAs are crucial if future generations are to enjoy the natural places that exist today. Equally important, the rate at which society is now recognizing previously unappreciated ecosystem services suggests that nature's currently unknown option value may be immense. For example, the contribution of standing forests to controlling climate change was little appreciated outside scientific circles just a decade ago – today, as noted above, we understand how colossal their carbon storage may be. When we include the potential for important new discoveries, e.g. in medicine, crop resilience, biomimicry and other areas, preservation of option values is a significant argument in its own right for creating and managing PAs on a major scale.

2.2 Protected area costs

Ensuring the provision of benefits from PAs requires society to incur costs. These can include financial costs of management; social and economic costs, e.g. of human–wildlife conflict, restricted access to resources, displacement from traditional lands; and opportunity costs of economic options forgone. As with benefits, costs depend significantly on location, planning processes and management strategy (see Sections 2.3 and 3). The main categories of cost are outlined below.

Management costs

Designation confers some protection on the site and its ecosystem services (Bruner et al, 2001; Adeney et al, 2009) but appropriate management is essential to ensure effective provision of benefits (WWF, 2004; Leverington et al, 2008).[3] Spending on PA management is inadequate at the global level (James et al, 2001; Esteban, 2005; Pearce, 2007). In developing countries few costs are covered, leaving many PAs attempting to address complex contexts without basic equipment or staff (e.g. Wilkie et al, 2001; Vreugdenhil, 2003; Galindo et al, 2005; see Section 4). In developed countries, funding is often required for payment schemes to maintain low-intensity land-use practices (see Section 1.3). Expanding and strategically integrating PAs into the wider landscape to maintain key services will further increase management needs (Balmford et al, 2002; CBD AHTEG, 2009).

Human–wildlife conflict

These can be significant where wildlife is found in areas used for human activities. Costs can range from frequent low-level crop raiding by monkeys to loss of entire harvests and significant property damage by elephant herds to actual loss of life (Distefano, 2005). In Zimbabwe, livestock predation by carnivores from PAs was estimated to generate losses of approximately 12 per cent of household income (Butler, 2000). In India, wildlife damages accounted for 7 to 15 per cent of the discounted costs of coffee cultivation (Ninan and Satyapalan, 2005). The need to defend crops can trigger further costs in the form of forgone activities, e.g. farming, children's school attendance.

Loss of access to natural resources

PA creation and management can reduce or block access to economically and culturally important resources, bringing significant losses. In Cameroon, use restrictions imposed on residents by the creation of Bénoué National Park led to the loss of about 30 per cent of agricultural income and 20 per cent of livestock-derived income (Weladji and Tchamba, 2003; see also Harper, 2002).

Displacement

Many people have been directly displaced by PAs. While there is debate about scope, it is clear that displacement has been a real problem in several cases and that its social and economic costs can be disastrous (Brockington and Igoe, 2006; Adams and Hutton, 2007; Agrawal and Redford, 2007). This was the case in the Democratic Republic of Congo when the Bambuti Batwa people were evicted from their ancestral lands during the creation of the Kahuzi-Biega National Park (Nelson and Hossack, 2003).

Opportunity costs

Choosing to create and manage PAs requires forgoing alternative uses. For private actors, key opportunity costs include the potential profit from legitimate resource uses. For national governments, such costs come from forgone tax revenues and revenues from state-run extractive enterprises. Governments also have an obvious interest in the private opportunity costs borne by their citizens.

Even though PAs tend to occupy land with lower agricultural potential (Gorenflo and Brandon, 2005; Dudley et al, 2008) their opportunity costs often remain significant. The private opportunity cost for all strictly managed PAs in developing countries has been estimated at US$5 billion/year (James et al, 2001). PA expansion to safeguard a range of services and adapt to climate change would also involve significant opportunity costs, probably more than US$10 billion per year for at least the next 30 years (James et al, 2001; Shaffer et al, 2002).

2.3 Comparing the benefits and costs of protected areas

Benefits and costs of protection vary significantly depending on geographic scale (see Table 8.2 and Figure 8.4). This section compares benefits to costs at three scales: to the global community from all PAs worldwide; to countries from their national PA systems (noting significant differences between developed and developing countries, as highlighted above); and to local actors living in and around individual sites. As mentioned, we base our analysis on two types of study suitable for evaluating net benefits: (i) studies that quantify benefits and costs for the same site or region using comparable methodologies and (ii) studies that present global average or total values.

Global benefits vs. costs

Starting with a word of caution, global values necessarily rely on assumptions, generalizations and compilations of findings from valuation methodologies that are not perfectly comparable. Their conclusions should be regarded as indicative rather than precise. On the other hand, significant methodological progress has been made in addressing some major challenges (e.g. Balmford et al, 2002; Rayment et al, 2009). Furthermore, the scale of the difference between benefits and costs appears to be so large globally that even if the analyses are incorrect by an order of magnitude, the basic conclusions would be unchanged. Such a degree of inaccuracy is unlikely.

According to the most widely cited estimates, an expanded PA network covering 15 per cent of the land and 30 per cent of the sea would cost approximately US$45 billion per year, including effective management, compensation for direct costs and payment of opportunity costs for acquiring new land. The ecosystems within that PA network would deliver goods and services with a net annual value greater than US$4.4 trillion. This suggests that investment in PAs would help maintain global ecosystem

Table 8.2 Examples of protected area benefits and costs accruing at different scales

	Benefits	Costs
Global	• Dispersed ecosystem services (e.g. climate change mitigation/ adaptation) • Nature-based tourism • Global cultural, existence and option values	• PA management* (global transfers to developing countries) • Alternative development programmes* (global transfers to developing countries)
National	• Dispersed ecosystem services (e.g. clean water for urban centres, agriculture or hydroelectric power) • Nature-based tourism • National cultural values	• Land purchase* • PA management (in national PA systems)* • Compensation for forgone activities* • Opportunity costs of forgone tax revenue
Local	• Consumptive resource uses • Local ecosystem services (e.g. pollination, disease control, natural hazard mitigation) • Local cultural and spiritual values	• Restricted access to resources • Displacement • PA management (private landowners, municipal lands) • Opportunity costs of forgone economic activities • Human-wildlife conflict

Notes: *These cost categories in effect transfer costs from the local to national level, or from the national or international level. Section 3 provides more information on these and related options.

service benefits worth 100 times more than the costs of designating and managing the network (Balmford et al, 2002).[4]

As noted earlier, some of these services would flow without major investment – especially where there are few pressures on the ecosystem. On the other hand, where there is a risk of land-use conversion or degradation, designation and investment can be essential to avoid the loss of ecosystem services. Any comparison between the costs of protection and the benefits of action should ideally take this into account, paying careful attention to the portion of the total ecosystem service flow at risk and other issues related to comparing marginal costs to marginal benefits. This means that the 100 to 1 ratio could be smaller in practice, depending on the approach to ecosystem service valuation (see Note 4) as well as specific threats to services. It should therefore be seen as a motivating context setter, which highlights how maintenance and investment in these natural assets can make good economic sense (Balmford et al, 2002; see also Chapter 9 on investing in natural capital). However, specific PA investment decisions should focus on the site context to ensure that proposed measures do offer appropriate added value and also take opportunity costs into account (see further examples below).

A complementary perspective is available from the findings of the Stern Review on the economics of climate change (Stern, 2006) and other recent works that enable us to compare PA benefits to costs in areas of active deforestation in developing countries:

- Stern estimates that for areas being actively cleared, the average annual opportunity cost from forgone agricultural profits and one-off timber harvests is approximately US$95/ha (Grieg-Gran, 2006).
- Seven studies of human–wildlife conflict reviewed by Distefano (2005) show average income losses of around 15 per cent, suggesting additional direct costs of perhaps US$15/ha per year.[5]
- Average management costs are reported to be around US$3/ha per year (James et al, 1999), yielding an estimate of total annual costs of perhaps US$115/ha per year.
- On the other hand, average total benefits per hectare per year from a wide range of ecosystem services provided by tropical forests are estimated at around US$2,800/ha per year[6] (Rayment et al, 2009).[7]

Taken together, these studies suggest that even in areas of active deforestation, global PA benefits have the potential to greatly outweigh costs.[8]

It is also useful to compare total benefits from protected ecosystems with those from converting natural ecosystems to agriculture, aquaculture or other primary production. Balmford et al (2002), Papageorgiou (2008) and Trivedi et al (2008) synthesize findings from eight studies that compare the benefits delivered by intact ecosystems with benefits from conversion (Figure 8.3). All studies include market goods and ecosystem services provided by both conservation and conversion, to ensure that production landscapes are not unfairly disadvantaged by the over-simplified assumption that they provide no ecosystem services. This comparative analysis again suggests that protection can be an excellent investment globally. Including major market and non-market values, the global benefits from retaining intact ecosystems appear to be on average 250 per cent greater than benefits from conversion.[9]

National benefits vs. costs

Some key benefits from protection accrue largely to the global community (e.g. carbon sequestration, existence or option values; see Balmford and Whitten, 2003) or to companies and individuals from other countries (nature-based tourism; see Walpole and Thouless, 2005). In contrast, PA costs are mostly national or local.

Even if carbon sequestration, existence values and tourism values are assumed to accrue only to the global community and are completely removed from the comparisons in the studies reviewed above (Figure 8.3), remaining national benefits still average more than 150 per cent of total benefits from conversion.[10] This suggests that, at the national scale, ecosystem service benefits continue to greatly outweigh the cost of protecting them, making national investment in PAs on balance a sound economic choice. A substantial body of case evidence also supports this conclusion. For instance:

• In the Amazon, Brazil, ecosystem services from PAs provide national and local benefits worth over 50 per cent more than the return to smallholder farming,

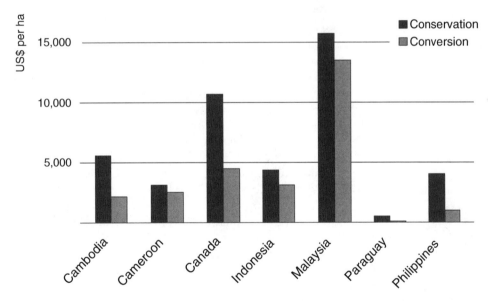

NPV of benefits from conservation and conversion
(Value of US$ in 2007)

Figure 8.3 *Total benefits of conservation compared to benefits from conversion for seven case study sites in different countries*

Notes: The original values from these case studies have been inflated to reflect values in 2007. A case from Thailand (Sathirathai, 1998) is excluded from the graph for purposes of scale. 'Conservation' includes sustainable production of market goods and services including timber, fish, NTFPs and tourism. 'Conversion' refers to replacement of the natural ecosystem with a system dedicated to agriculture, aquaculture or timber production. Both scenarios include ecosystem services.

Sources: Bann (1997), Yaron (2001), van Vuuren and Roy (1993), van Beukering et al (2003), Kumari (1994), Naidoo and Ricketts (2006) and White et al (2000), as reviewed by Balmford et al (2002), Papageorgiou (2008) and Trivedi et al (2008).

including (reduced) ecosystem service flows following conversion (based on Portela and Rademacher, 2001). They can draw three times more money into the economy at the regional level than extensive cattle ranching, the most likely alternative use for PA land (Amend et al, 2007).

*   In Madagascar, investment in managing the national PA system and providing compensation to local farmers for the opportunity costs of forgone farm expansion would pay for itself and generate an additional return of 50 per cent from tourism revenues, watershed protection and international financial support to biodiversity (Carret and Loyer, 2003).
*   In Scotland, the ecosystems protected by Natura 2000 sites provide benefits to the Scottish public worth more than three times their associated costs, including direct management and opportunity costs (based on Jacobs et al, 2004).

On the other hand, it may not be in the national best interest to protect some globally valuable areas in the absence of markets or other transfers to support provision of key services. In Paraguay's Mbaracayu Biosphere Reserve, for instance, 85 per cent of benefits are generated by carbon sequestration. Although the Reserve is of net benefit globally, the value of ecosystem services that accrue nationally[11] is significantly lower than potential income from forgone agricultural conversion (Naidoo and Ricketts, 2006), making the reserve a net cost to the country.

Local benefits vs. costs

Many key services from PAs benefit local actors most, from sustainable resource use to disease control to local cultural or spiritual values. Values like watershed protection are of benefit locally, but often also at a larger scale. Although management costs are mainly paid at national or international level (Balmford and Whitten, 2003), costs of lost access to resources and wildlife conflict are often extremely localized (Naughton-Treves, 1997; Shrestha et al, 2006). The opportunity cost of conversion to non-natural systems tends to be borne in part locally (e.g. where PAs prevent local actors from clearing land) and in part by commercial, typically non-local actors who clear land for shrimp farms, large-scale ranching and similar uses (see Figure 8.4).

As with the larger-scale comparisons, there is evidence that local benefits provided by ecosystems within PAs can outweigh costs. In Costa Rica, communities affected by PAs have less poverty, better houses and better access to drinking water than communities living farther away (Andam et al, 2008). However, there are also cases where local costs clearly outweigh benefits, particularly where groups are displaced or lose access to key resources (e.g. Harper, 2002; Colchester, 2003).

Particularly at the local scale, whether or not PAs are a net benefit or a net cost depends significantly on their design, management and policies to share costs and benefits, as well as the site's service provision and the local socio-economic context and opportunity costs (see Section 3 below). The following general points on local benefits and costs therefore include reference to different management choices.

Ecosystem services can underpin local economies

Clean water, pollination and disease control are often fundamental to local well-being. In Indonesia, people living near intact forests protected by Ruteng Park have fewer illnesses from malaria and dysentery, children miss less school due to sickness and

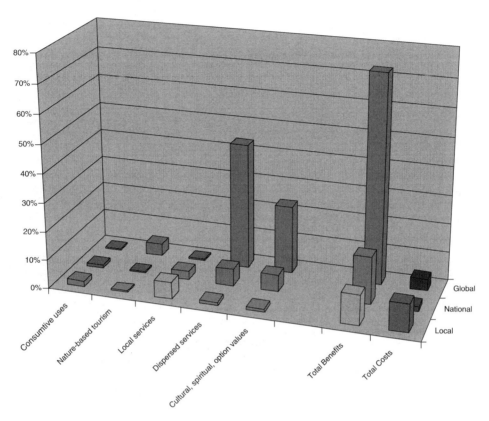

Figure 8.4 *Schematic distribution of benefits and costs of conserving PAs in developing countries as a percentage of the value of total benefits*

Note: Scale is illustrative

Source: Authors' own representation, building on the distribution of benefits and costs from Balmford and Whitten (2003)

there is less hunger associated with crop failure (Pattanayak et al, 2005; Pattanayak and Wendland, 2007).

Protected areas can support sustainable local use

In Cambodia's Ream National Park, estimated benefits from sustainable resource use, recreation and research are worth 20 per cent more than benefits from current destructive use. The distribution of costs and benefits favours local villagers, who earn three times more under a scenario of effective protection than under a scenario without management (De Lopez, 2003).

Sustainability frequently brings short-term local costs

St Lucia's Sufriere MPA has significantly increased fish stocks since its creation, providing a sustainable local benefit. However, this required 35 per cent of fishing grounds to be placed off-limits, imposing a short-term cost on local fishermen in the form of reduced catch (Lutchman, 2005).

Locally created PAs can protect values defined by local people

Community PAs can conserve resources and services locally defined as being worth more than the opportunity cost of their protection. Local people and governments can also collaborate to create PAs to maintain key values at both levels. In Indonesia, the 100,000ha Batang Gadis National Park was created by local initiative in response to flash flooding caused by upland deforestation (Mulongoy and Gidda, 2008).

Failure to recognize local rights and uses can result in major costs

Evicting people to make way for PAs can be devastating. Lost access to natural resources can also have serious negative impacts. Conversely, real participation in PA planning and management can help ensure local rights are respected, benefits are maintained or enhanced and effective conservation is achieved (Potvin et al, 2002). Such involvement has not been systematically sought but there is growing evidence of its importance. In Fiji, for instance, the participatory creation and management of Navakavu Locally Managed Marine Area led to higher sustainable fish consumption by local families and more community cooperation in resource management (Leisher et al, 2007).

Why are costs often perceived as greater than benefits?

If PAs can provide such important benefits to society at all levels, why are they under threat of degradation and why are they often perceived mainly in terms of costs? Key reasons include the following:

Costs are more palpable than benefits

Resource degradation typically offers clear and immediate returns in the form of marketable products, tax revenues or subsistence goods. Crop raiding or livestock predation can also cause sudden palpable losses. In contrast, many benefits from conservation have no market value, are less well understood and therefore poorly appreciated and deliver benefits to a wider and more dispersed group of beneficiaries over a longer time period.

Private benefits from production make protection unattractive for local decision makers

For private actors, converting natural areas to production frequently offers net benefits even if conversion represents a net local cost (Chan et al, 2007). In Thailand, for instance, the total private return from converting mangroves to shrimp farms has been estimated at US$17,000/ha. This makes deforestation attractive to individual decision makers despite losses to local society of more than US$60,000/ha in terms of decreased fisheries productivity, reduced storm protection and loss of a key source of timber, fuel and other forest products (Sathirathai, 1998). While the benefit–cost comparison depends on the specific ecosystem, socio-economic context, market prices, subsidy levels and other factors, similar results are found in a range of contexts (see also Sathirathai and Barbier, 2001; Barbier, 2007; Hanley and Barbier, 2009; and Chapters 1 and 9).

Beneficiaries do not adequately share costs

Globally, PAs have not yet taken full advantage of fee-charging mechanisms to help cover costs (Emerton et al, 2006; see Chapter 7). More significantly, most benefits they provide are classic 'public goods' from which people benefit independently of their own actions and which receive little support from society without specific policy interventions. At national level, the most common solution – government support for PAs using tax revenue – is often hampered by an inadequate appreciation of benefits. At international level, there is even less appreciation of the imperative to share costs even though distribution analysis of benefits suggests that global cost sharing is economically rational. Large-scale mechanisms to facilitate such cost sharing are lacking.

3 Improving effectiveness through economic evaluation

As outlined in Section 1, a key challenge for PAs is to ensure that they can actually meet their objectives. Hundreds have been designated in recent decades but many fail to provide effective conservation and lack functioning management structures to secure support from administrators and neighbouring communities. External pressures, local conflicts, lack of financial resources and poor capacity are frequent obstacles. Inappropriate institutional structures and unclear land rights often exacerbate the problem.

At the national level, policy makers can promote an enabling framework for effective PAs in several ways:

- shaping funding priorities for PA conservation and funding mechanisms to ensure these provide the right incentives and sufficient financial stability for effective management;
- ensuring that the legal framework, operational goals and administrative structure of national PA systems supports local flexibility in management arrangements and resource-use regimes to reduce the risk of conflicts;
- raising their political profile to influence public perceptions and encourage business involvement in conservation;
- sharing information and best practices internationally and facilitating coordination and cooperation between government agencies and other stakeholders.

An economic perspective on ecosystem services can make this task easier for policy makers as regards advocacy, decision support and handling social impacts (see below).

Results of economic valuation need to be appropriately interpreted and embedded in sound management processes. Valuation studies are always based on a number of underlying assumptions (see Section 3.2 below) which must be clearly understood to use and correctly interpret their results. This is particularly important where the results are employed for decision support, e.g. to decide the best framework and tools for managing PAs. While monetary values can help to translate ecological concerns into economic arguments, the latter should always be considered within the bigger picture of sound PA governance and management (e.g. participation of local communities and engagement of broader public) which requires political support.

3.1 Valuing ecosystem services for advocacy

Ecosystem service valuations can be a powerful tool to communicate protection as an attractive choice central to sustainable development strategies.

Globally, it has been estimated that every US$1 invested in PA management can help ensure that ecosystems within PAs (continue to) deliver US$100 worth of services – partly by maintaining existing provision and partly by increasing the delivery of services from (degraded) ecosystems (adapted from Balmford et al, 2002). More precise estimates can be developed at national and local level (see also Chapter 9 and TEEB in Local Policy, 2011).

It is particularly important to demonstrate the importance of ecosystem services that sustain economic growth and/or broader public benefits. Where rapid industrial development based on exploitation of natural resources is a high national priority, valuations can illustrate that functioning ecosystems are critical to this long-term growth. Conversely, degrading ecosystems and vital services jeopardizes economic development by raising costs and customer concerns. In Ethiopia, the remaining mountain rainforests host the last wild relatives of *Coffea arabica* plants: the high economic value of their genetic diversity is a strong argument for strengthening conservation efforts in these landscapes undergoing rapid transformation (Hein and Gatzweiler, 2006). In western Ireland, the combined public and private (i.e. tourism) benefits of protecting the traditional rural landscape in the Burren are estimated to be significantly higher than the associated costs, with 235 per cent minimum rate of return on government support to conservation activities in the area (van Rensburgh et al, 2009). Demonstrating the economic value of these benefits is considered to have played a role in successfully securing future financing to protect the Burren landscape (Dr B. Dunford, pers. comm.). Similar evidence is available from the Leuser National Park, Indonesia (Box 8.5; see TEEB in Local Policy, 2011, for further information).

3.2 Valuing ecosystem services for decision support

Valuing ecosystem services can support sound decision making by helping to assess the costs and benefits of different options, e.g. where a PA should be located, comparison between different resource-use regimes. It can also provide useful answers to broader questions such as: what are the cost-effective choices for enlarging our national networks? What sectoral policies, use regimes and general regulations do we need for landscapes surrounding PAs and for resource use inside their borders? What priorities should national conservation strategies focus on? Answers to these and similar questions can benefit from even partial/selective valuation (Box 8.6).

Valuations can inform debate between those responsible for PAs and those affected by them, making visible the real trade-offs and economic consequences involved in alternative options. They support transparent estimates of the consequences of different conservation strategies in terms both of costs incurred and ecosystem services secured. Valuations can at least partly translate ecological considerations into more widely understood, less technical arguments and substantially contribute to a more informed public debate about conservation priorities.

Valuation studies do not provide ready solutions to difficult questions. They should inform, not replace, critical debate that draws on a broader range of ecological and political information based on research and experience. Where trade-offs entail strong conflicts among key actors, these cannot be resolved by valuation studies.

Box 8.5 Using economic arguments to support conservation in Indonesia

Aceh Province (northern Sumatra) has one of the largest continuous forest ecosystems remaining in South-east Asia. The forest sustains local community livelihoods by retaining water in the rainy season, providing continuous water supply throughout the dry season, mitigating floods and erosion and providing timber and non-timber products. Since 1980, the Leuser National Park has sought to protect this rich natural heritage. However, illegal logging is threatening the Leuser ecosystem.

Faced with the Park's rapid degradation, the managers of the National Park commissioned a valuation study of the impact of biodiversity loss on the province's potential for economic development (van Beukering et al, 2003). This analysed the benefit of the Park's ecosystems for production of timber, food and fibre, water provisioning, flood prevention, carbon storage, tourism and supply of hydropower as well as the allocation of these benefits among stakeholders and their regional distribution.

The study found that conserving the forest and its biodiversity would provide the highest long-term economic return for the Province (US$9.5 billion at 4 per cent discount rate) as well as benefits for all stakeholders, particularly local communities. Continued deforestation would cause ecosystem service degradation and generate lower economic return for the Province (US$7 billion). There would be short-term benefits mainly for the logging and plantation industry but long-term negative impacts for most other stakeholders. It is now hoped that the results of this valuation will help to ensure more effective protection of the Leuser National Park.

Source: van Beukering et al (2003); *Jakarta Post* (2004)

The scope and design of valuation studies affects their outcomes. Valuation can only ever assess a subset of benefits associated with PAs. This is a point of concern: by focusing on what we can easily measure, we may neglect what we cannot assess, e.g. cultural and spiritual values. Valuations require several choices to be made, e.g. about the ecosystem services we focus on, the number of years we consider and the assumptions we make concerning the future state of the ecosystem. Such choices imply that we can have two different study designs producing different results, without one being wrong and the other right.

Valuations imply value judgements, so policy makers need to agree on the design of a study and be aware of its implications when considering its possible use for decision support. To overcome such challenges, some agencies – such as the New Zealand Department of Conservation – have chosen to focus on ecological measurements as a surrogate for measuring ecosystem services. This alternative method is based on the assumption that ecosystem maintenance and restoration works, based on ecological criteria, will lead to maintained and restored services. There is evidence that this method works for at least some ecosystem services (McAlpine and Wotton, 2009; see also Chapter 3, Section 2, which shows how a combination of qualitative, quantitative and monetary values can most usefully present the value of a given site).

Box 8.6 Valuation for decision support: Regional conservation planning in Chile

In western Patagonia, 47 per cent of the territory is under legal protection – raising the question of whether such areas are in the right place to protect the region's biodiversity and natural heritage.

Chilean researchers assessed the capacity of territorial units to provide a broad range of ecosystem services and generated an ecosystem value per unit (Map 1). They overlaid this map with the current boundaries of Patagonia's PAs (Map 2) and also analysed factors threatening the provision of ecosystem services, drawing on multi-criteria evaluation and expert judgement, to construct a spatially explicit analysis of threat intensity (Map 3). These threats ranged from global issues (e.g. reduction of the ozone layer) to impacts of local salmon farming.

The comparison of all three maps indicated that:

- despite their vast extent, existing PAs covered only a very limited percentage of territory with high ecosystem value;
- the highest threat level was found in areas with high ecosystem value outside PAs.

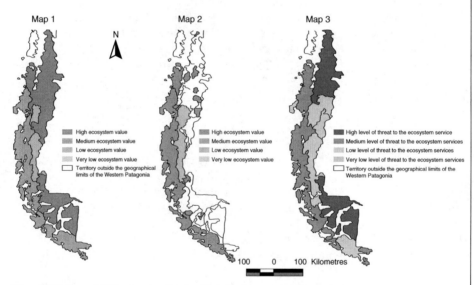

Figure 8.5 *Map of Chile showing PAs and threats to ecosystem*

Source: Martínez-Harms and Gajardo (2008)

The study enables regional conservation planners to examine the assumptions that underlie the composite variables of ecosystem value and threat intensity. If they agree with the authors' approach, they can draw on these insights to complement and/or correct their approach, e.g. to reallocate conservation funds and prioritize management actions appropriately at regional level.

3.3 Valuing ecosystem services to address social impacts

Valuation helps to analyse the social impacts of conservation by helping us track the distribution of costs and benefits associated with providing ecosystem services and maintaining ecosystem functions. Studies can make visible the situations where benefits are partly global but costs (maintenance effort, use restrictions) are borne by the local population and thus highlight a PA's equity implications (see Box 8.7). Scaled up to national system level, such studies can help policy makers orient conservation efforts according to social impacts and set different objectives for different areas. This enhanced transparency and comparative analysis can improve negotiation efforts and compensation schemes, even if dedicated anthropological studies are better suited to describe the complex social dimension of conservation efforts and how they affect people's livelihoods.

Making local costs visible stimulates efforts to increase local benefits. Many PAs have considerable scope to enhance local benefits and minimize local costs. Local

---

Box 8.7 Compensation through insurance against elephant damage in Sri Lanka

Rapid population growth and several decades of violent conflict have increased poverty and exacerbated one of Sri Lanka's major rural problems – the human–elephant conflict (HEC). With elephants consuming 150kg of food every day, crop raiding is a serious problem. In densely inhabited areas, defence strategies like watchtowers and firecrackers have not led to acceptable long-term solutions.

To explore alternative possibilities for solving this conflict a survey was carried out to estimate the local residents' willingness to accept compensation for the damage incurred (e.g. level of compensation required). An additional survey revealed that the residents' willingness to pay (WTP) for elephant conservation exceeded the level of funding needed to compensate damage in rural areas.

The surveys led to the first insurance scheme covering elephant damage in Sri Lanka. In 2007, Ceylinco Insurance presented a scheme that is partly corporate social responsibility and partly profit-driven. It charges a small addition to the premium payments of existing life/vehicle policy-holders, which is paid into a trust to fund compensation payments. This effectively transfers the financial burden of conservation to urban residents who do not have to risk their lives and livelihood living in areas with large numbers of elephants.

Farmers pay a nominal fee to participate in the scheme. In addition to compensation of elephant damage, other benefits include built-in child policies and educational cover for farmers' children. The scheme's most progressive element is that landownership is not a consideration for qualification as many farmers suffering elephant damage are slash-and-burn (shifting) cultivators who encroach on government lands.

Valuing conservation costs in terms of affected rural livelihoods has made the social implications of protecting elephants visible. Valuing WTP (willingness to pay) for elephant conservation has led to the development of a concrete insurance scheme to address the problem.

Source: PREM (2006); Indian Environment Portal (2007)

losses can be greatly reduced by sharing new and traditional techniques to deter crop/livestock raiding, e.g. physical enclosures to protect livestock at night, use of guard dogs and planting of repellent crops (Distefano, 2005). Finding alternative sources of local income to compensate for use restrictions is more challenging but essential for the long-term success of any PA. These may include conservation easements, payments for ecosystem services (see Chapter 5) and tourism. These funding sources not only need significant start-up funds but also strong political leadership and continued high-level support.

Valuations support the use of cost-efficient compensation mechanisms. Where local costs of PAs cannot be met by alternative sources of income, well-designed compensation programmes can fill the gap (Box 8.7). Identifying costs, benefits and their distribution at a finer scale reduces the risk of compensating either too little (questionable conservation outcomes) or too much (wasting scarce resources). All compensation mechanisms need functioning governance structures and simple procedures to limit fraud risk and administrative costs. Successful schemes also need to ensure that associated transaction costs do not exceed the level of compensation, making them ineffective. For instance, a study in India showed that the compensation payments to farmers were exceeded by the costs of processing the compensation claims (e.g. travel costs to local forest offices, opportunity costs of time lost) (Ninan and Satyapalan, 2005).

4 Securing sustainable financing for protected areas

This section focuses on financing PAs and the role of ecosystem service valuation in fundraising. In most countries, information on financial needs and available funds for PA planning, design, establishment and effective management is fragmentary. However, it is generally accepted that creation and management costs can be substantial and that there is a considerable shortfall between PA needs and the financial resources allocated (see Section 2 above). This is particularly true for developing countries where most biodiversity is concentrated and conservation demands are high.

Economics and valuation can play a very important role in improving PA financing. Better awareness of financial gaps can help mobilize resources through existing and new mechanisms to improve and expand PA system coverage and stabilize future funding.

4.1 Is there a financing gap for protected areas?

Cost estimations for global PAs vary significantly between different studies. They depend on assumptions used, e.g. elements included in total costs; type of management required (strict scientific reserves and wilderness areas may require less investment than national parks or habitat/species management areas);[12] size and location (terrestrial/marine, developed/developing country, due to differences in labour, opportunity costs and land acquisition costs); and whether resources are for managing existing PAs or expanding the network.

Cost estimates identified in the literature range from US$1.2 billion/year for a fully efficient (existing) PA network in developing countries only (James et al, 1999) to US$45 billion/year (global network covering 30 per cent of marine area and 15 per cent of terrestrial area[13] (Balmford et al, 2004; for projected benefits of this expansion, see

RECOGNIZING THE VALUE OF PROTECTED AREAS 373

Section 2.3). Values within this range have been calculated by other researchers (e.g. James et al, 1999, 2001; Vreugdenhil, 2003; Bruner et al, 2004; European Commission, 2004, Gantioler et al, 2010) under various scenarios of PA expansion and for different regions. For example according to the latest estimate by Gantioler et al, the annual costs of managing the EU Natura 2000 Network are estimated to be €5.8 billion for the EU-27 Member States. For developing countries, Bruner et al (2004) suggest that a system covering some of the highest global priority land sites could increase annual management costs in these countries to US$4 billion/year and incur land acquisition costs of up to US$9 billion/year over a 10-year period, depending on the level of ambition and acquisition opportunities.

Turning to actual expenditure, an estimated US$6.5–US$10 billion/year is currently spent on supporting the global PA system (Gutman and Davidson, 2007). This breaks down into US$1.3–US$2.6 billion of public expenditure by developing countries for biodiversity protection; US$1.2–US$2.5 billion of official development assistance from developed countries for PAs in developing countries, NGO contributions and business spending; and US$4–US$5 billion allocated by developed countries to support their own PA networks. However, more recent estimates by the CBD report a rise in PA assistance to developing countries, including bilateral agreements, to US$3.5 billion in 2008 (CBD, 2010). Country-specific examples highlight the scale of the financing gap for existing PAs. In Cameroon, Ghana, Ecuador, Peru and Bolivia, for example, current spending has been estimated to account for 20 to 70 per cent of funding needs (Culverwell, 1997; Wilkie et al, 2001; Ankudey et al, 2003; Molina et al, 2003; Galindo et al, 2005; Ruiz, 2005). In monetary terms, the estimated annual gap in six South American countries – Brazil, Bolivia, Colombia, Chile, Ecuador (Galapagos) and Peru – totalled US$261 million in 2006. In Indonesia, the gap was around US$100 million/year (Watkins et al, 2008). A recent study by the UNDP (see Box 8.8) covering Latin America and the Caribbean gives an update, with the total financing gap assessed at 45 per cent of needs, with the largest gaps between actual funding and needs seen in Paraguay, Uruguay and Nicaragua, and the smallest in Bolivia and Costa Rica (UNDP and TNC 2010).

If we consider the available medium-range cost estimate for efficient functioning of the existing global network of US$14 billion/year (James et al, 1999, 2001) and compare them with current levels of available global funding for biodiversity (Gutman and Davidson, 2007), we can say that the world community is investing 60 to 75 per cent of what would be needed to effectively manage the existing PA network. However, this general statement is no longer valid if broken down by world region (Figure 8.6). The figures then show that PA systems in more developed regions (North America, Australia/New Zealand) receive far more support compared with the gaps in poorer and less developed regions (developing Asia, Africa). The percentage would be even lower if the need to fund an expanded global PA system to cover representative ecosystems were taken into account. However, while this is the most recent estimate available, the numbers will have changed since publication, particularly in Europe as the Natura 2000 network has been established.

4.2 Mobilizing funds: Existing sources and innovative mechanisms

Biodiversity financing from different international sources and funds is estimated to be around US$4–US$5 billion a year, with some 30 to 50 per cent going to finance

Box 8.8 Financial sustainability of protected areas (PAs) in Latin America and the Caribbean

A recent study on PA financial sustainability in Latin America and the Caribbean reveals the level of financial gap in the region but also suggests that reducing this gap is both achievable and affordable.

Official data from 19 countries show that available resources for PA systems in the region are around US$402 million per year. The basic management needs for national PA systems are estimated to range from US$3–US$5 million for countries such as Uruguay or El Salvador to over US$120 million for Mexico and US$300 million for Brazil. Aggregated for the region, the PA financing gap (i.e. financial needs minus available funds) amounts to US$314 million per year just for basic management activities: for more rigorous management (optimal needs), the gap is approximately US$700 million/year.

The study points out that the basic management costs could be met if the annual government allocation to PA budgets in the region increased by a factor of three. However, this is the average factor, derived from the 18 countries reporting their funding gaps. The factors applicable in individual countries vary considerably (e.g. in Argentina and Colombia about 80 per cent of financial needs are covered whereas countries such as Paraguay, Nicaragua and Uruguay cover less than 30 per cent of financial needs).

Source: UNDP and TNC 2010

PAs (Gutman and Davidson, 2007). Official development assistance (ODA) from high-income countries provides up to US$3.5 billion/year: this is mostly in the form of country-to-country bilateral aid, with the rest as multilateral aid managed by the Global Environment Facility (GEF), other UN agencies, the International Development Agency and multilateral development banks. The percentage spent on biodiversity conservation has remained consistently low over the past 15 years (2.4 to 2.8 per cent of total bilateral ODA; see UNEP and CBD, 2005; OECD, 2009) despite awareness-raising efforts within the CBD and through the IUCN. Severe competition for available funds with other aid demands (e.g. poverty alleviation, rural infrastructure, water provision, education and health) is obviously a constraint for increasing expenditure on biodiversity-related activities.

Funding by non-profit organizations (mainly channelled through international conservation NGOs, private and business foundations) probably contributes more than US$1 billion/year to international biodiversity protection but relevant information and data are fragmentary (Gutman and Davidson, 2007). Information on NGO spending suggests that funds allocated to PAs and biodiversity may be even higher. As with ODA, non-profit funding for biodiversity conservation has grown sluggishly during the past decade. Constraints include levels of public awareness, the state of the economy and competition between different environmental priorities, e.g. the international focus on climate change which has gained higher political and business support, and created the impression that biodiversity is losing ground.

Market-based sources of PA income could contribute US$1–US$2 billion annually (Gutman and Davidson, 2007). These include international tourism, especially

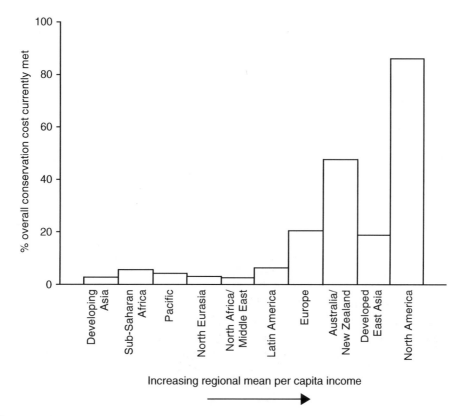

Figure 8.6 *Financing gaps by region for existing protected areas*

Source: Balmford et al (2003)

ecotourism, and markets for environmentally friendly products such as organic, certified and fair-trade products (see Chapter 5). These funding sources have grown quickly in the last 20 years and raised high expectations but their direct contribution to PAs needs to be determined.

The three categories of funding listed above can come from public and private sources, be generated within or outside the PA (Emerton et al, 2006) and be targeted at actions at the local, national, regional or global level.

Financing for PAs can also be obtained through new innovative mechanisms and instruments. These additional sources could be based on licensing and concessions, establishment of trust funds, benefits transfer through the creation and deployment of a Green Development Initiative, payments for ecosystem services and creating international markets for ecosystem services through offsetting schemes or trading (see Chapters 5 and 7). Transnational and international PES for global public goods (e.g. carbon sequestration through the proposed REDD scheme under UNFCCC) are among the most prominent recent proposals for financing schemes: others include environmental taxes and public–private partnerships that link businesses, NGOs, public bodies and communities.

Table 8.3 lists the main existing funding mechanisms for PAs, both traditional and innovative, with an assessment of their strengths and weaknesses. Most funds available today come from traditional methods of income generation such as entry and use fees, tourism charges or funds from NGOs, foundations, private and business sources, ODA or trust funds. Between 1991 and 2006, donor countries invested more than US$1.6 billion through the GEF in 1600 PAs around the world, spanning 360 million hectares (an area equivalent to Mongolia and Greenland together). This investment leveraged an additional US$4.2 billion in co-financing. As a result, very few countries lack PA systems at the national level. However, some of the traditional mechanisms (e.g. debt-for-nature swaps) have proved cumbersome and require specific operational conditions. In the last 15 years, the total generated by commercial debt-for-nature swaps was only US$112 million according to figures compiled by the WWF's Centre for Conservation Finance.

Despite increased resources, such mechanisms have failed to provide the funds needed to establish the comprehensive and ecologically representative PA system to fulfil CBD objectives (see Section 5 below). At the ninth meeting of the CBD Conference of the Parties in May 2008, the world community reiterated concerns that insufficient resources were still a key obstacle to PA planning, design, establishment and effective management, particularly for developing countries and countries with economies in transition.

The same meeting also noted that innovative mechanisms, including market-based approaches, could complement (but not replace) public funding and development assistance (CBD, 2008a; see also UNEP and CBD, 2006, on public–private partnerships). Table 8.3 lists several such mechanisms (e.g. bioprospecting fees and contracts, green lotteries). Many are still being tested and will need capacity building for their design and use. However, some like PES and REDD have already begun to gather significant support due to their design flexibility and are attracting political backing for their further development. Other ideas – like the reform of the financing system and international environmental taxation – are still met with caution (Verweij and de Man, 2005).

4.3 A framework for successful financing

Traditionally, financial planning for PAs has focused on the priorities of international donors and lacked an enabling regulatory framework or incentives for behavioural change. Plans have rarely been supported by accurate assessments of financial needs and gaps, cost reduction strategies, assessment and diversification of income sources, business plans or a framework to prioritize revenue allocation. As a result, only a few countries have completed financial plans that incorporate such elements at system level: these include Ecuador, Costa Rica, Peru, Brazil, Colombia, Grenada and the EU (European Commission, 2004).

This section outlines four steps to secure more successful financing for PAs.

Creating markets and promoting market-based tools

Economic incentives that bridge the gap between private and public values of biodiversity can provide some solutions to the problem of the global commons and improve the rationale for actions to protect biodiversity (see Box 8.9). Building on the discussion in Chapter 5, creating markets for goods or services derived from PAs calls for the removal of trade-related barriers and enhanced public knowledge of their

Table 8.3 Existing funding mechanisms for protected areas, including lessons learned concerning their effectiveness

Source of funds	Available Instruments	Geographic area			Strengths	Weaknesses/needs for improved performance
		L/R	Nat	Int		
Private	Protected area entrance and use fees	X			Core component of PA funding	Better calculation of prices; introduce ecological sustainability when extractive/harvesting uses
Private	Tourism-related incomes	X	X	X	Can recover resource costs; can capture WTP from the visitors; diversification of tourism markets; rural/local development; can be used to manage demand	Investments to improve facilities; expertise to provide and market these services; calculation of prices and charges
Private	Markets for sustainable rural/local products	X	X		Can promote and communicate the value of the resource; can assist in branding a PA; work in combination with local/rural development; moneys are distributed to local communities; certification is a top-up	Investment needed for certification; developing markets/marketing
Private	Innovative goodwill fundraising instruments (Internet-based, etc)	X	X	X	Very innovative source of funds that seek to reach global 'small' contributors; additionality is key	Need for making it policy-specific and targeting; mainstream the instruments in policy; need for new creative ideas and marketing
Private	Green lotteries	X	X	X	New tool to mobilize funds; appeal to consumers and wider public; works better when associated with biodiversity of high value	Need for publicity and marketing
Private/Public	Non-profit organization (NGOs, foundations, trusts and charities) funding	X	X	X	Important source of funds overall, provided at PA level or species level; can help in mobilizing actors to donate	Need to sustain and increase donor and public interest in PAs; increase interaction with donors/public; develop new approaches and marketing of PAs

Table 8.3 (*Cont'd*)

Source of funds	Available Instruments	Geographic area			Strengths	Weaknesses/needs for improved performance
		L/R	Nat	Int		
Private/Public	(International) Markets for all type of ecosystem services (PES) and green markets		X	X	Use has increased recently; opportunity to generate revenues for services and not just extractive use; can provide compensation to landowners who adhere to PA management	Need for developing design guidelines, supportive policy and legislative frameworks; improved methodologies for establishing the biophysical links; set prices; monitor delivery of services
Private/Public	Bioprospecting		X	X	Immediate link with PA; can develop significant potential and mobilize additional funds	R&D and administrative costs; need for highly specialized knowledge; need to work together with access and benefit sharing (ABS)
Private	Public–private partnerships and business–public–NGO partnerships	X	X	X	Can evolve in the context of business CSR; measure included in the menu of many international financing efforts (climate change, poverty, etc); experiences exist; flexibility and adaptability can be applied	Tendency to 'move on'; local/regional implementation can be more stable
Private	Business voluntary standards		X	X	Can be developed for PAs and sustainable practices; although not bringing actual money into the PA system, they can contribute to sustainable management of PAs and local development	Not all business can follow, as standards are costly even for those who introduce/are leaders
Private	Businesses' goodwill investments (e.g. corporate social responsibility – CSR)	X	X	X	Potential for increasing corporate support/sponsoring to PAs	Need to sustain and increase interest in PAs, increase interaction with private sector, develop new approaches and marketing of PAs
Private	Venture capital and portfolio (green) investments		X	X	Potential for mobilizing corporate funds in a sustainable way; sponsoring PAs and species; can support environmental business from SMEs near the PA	High administrative costs; may generate low returns and loose support from capital/investors; providing for corporate tax relief associated with these mechanisms may further support their uptake

Source of funds	Available Instruments	Geographic area			Strengths	Weaknesses/needs for improved performance
		L/R	Nat	Int		
Public/ Private	Biodiversity cap-and-trade schemes and market-based instruments (MBIs) (e.g. offsets, habitat banking)			X	Instrument that can help in, but mostly around, PAs; can mobilize significant funds; can create markets for biodiversity and their services	Costs for administration; implementation at global level and registration/monitoring; further work on equivalency methods and their application may be needed
Public/ Private	Carbon emission permits (use part of the auctions)		X	X	Can provide complementary funds for PAs; some synergies can be strengthened between climate change adaptation and ecosystem financing needs	Competition for distribution of the revenue from auctions/permits between different environmental purposes
Public	Government budgetary allocations	X	X	X	Core component of PA funding, but are not enough on their own	Some evidence of PA funding decline; resources often driven to compete with other priorities, strengthening policy integration and mainstreaming PAs is needed
Public	Earmarking public revenues		X	X	Can potentially provide sufficient resources that will go to PA and biodiversity conservation	Quite difficult to achieve: if resources earmarked for environmental purposes there is competition between different environmental goals/policies
Public	Environment-related taxes (national or international)		X	X	Introducing or increasing taxation linked to international trade; some products are related to nature (timber, etc); others (aviation, shipping) are of environmental nature but already can be accepted	Competition about the distribution of revenues between different environmental causes
Public	Environmental tax reform		X	X	Reforming taxation of international currency transactions can bring important resources for environmental purposes (climate and biodiversity)	Political will is needed for environmental tax reform; internationally this requires more efforts
Public	Reforming subsidies (rural production, fisheries, etc.)		X	X	Can help provide subsidies for landowners and users of PA that will allow sustainable use of the resource or even enable implementation of PA management	Better calculation of prices/subsidies, design of subsidies to be more green (agri-environmental measures), but quite difficult to achieve consensus and harmonized approach at global level
Public	Benefit sharing and revenue sharing	X	X		Integral component of PA funding; potential to offset local opportunity costs; increase availability of local funds; tap into development sources; improving benefit sharing	Need for design and communication with local/national authorities; monitoring of implementation to demonstrate benefits

Table 8.3 (*Cont'd*)

Source of funds	Available Instruments	Geographic area			Strengths	Weaknesses/needs for improved performance
		L/R	Nat	Int		
Public	Reforms in the international monetary system			X	Reforming taxation of international currency transactions can bring important resources for environmental purposes (climate and biodiversity)	Political will is needed for agreeing the introduction of such taxes internationally
Public	Bilateral and/or multilateral aid (and GEF)			X	Core component of PA funding; source of direct budgetary support to PAs	Some evidence of funding decline; major reorientation to poverty reduction and sustainable development may drive resources to other priorities; strengthening integration and mainstreaming of PA is needed
Public	Debt-for-nature swaps		X	X	Can provide large and secure amounts for PAs or specific sites; funding PAs through sustainable development and poverty reduction	Instrument in decline, due to difficulties in persuading donors/government to release large amounts of funds; difficulties in persuading PA agencies to invest large amounts for the future
Public	Development banks and agencies		X	X	Big number of agencies, lots of funds, but no increase there	Biodiversity priorities mixed with other environmental objectives/Millennium Development Goals (MDG); bureaucracy; increased spending on start-up but not so much on recurring costs
Public	Long-term ODA commitments through a Green Development Initiative (GDI)	X	X	X	Help transfers from developed/developing countries to less developed countries, GDI can implement MDG and assist local needs too	Need for developing guidelines, legislative frameworks at global level, improved methodologies for establishing the biophysical links, set prices, monitor delivery of services, evaluate the efficiency of transfers

Abbreviations: Private (Pri), Public (Pub), Local (L), Regional (R), National (Nat), International (Int), Small and medium sized businesses (SME)

Sources: Compilation of information within Emerton et al (2006); UNEP and CBD (2005); Bräuer et al (2006)

Box 8.9 Using tourism revenue to support the protection of dolphins at Samadi Reef

The Samadi Reef, situated in the Red Sea by the Egyptian coast, is an area famous for its spinner dolphins (*Stenella longinostris*). The reef is therefore an important destination for tourism operators in the area (e.g. diving). In 2004, a management plan was adopted to ensure sustainable use of the Samadi Reef, with foreseeable long-term benefits to both conservation and tourism activities. Its implementation resulted in higher dolphin activity in the area and increased growth of coral reefs within the site. The number of visitors was kept within the carrying capacity (200 individuals/day) yet revenues generated by visitor fees still exceeded US$500,000/year. This income is used to maintain the site and improve its conservation, which has greatly improved the local tourism business. The attitude of tourists and the tourism experience have also been improved by raising public awareness.

Source: Fouda (2010)

---

importance and special characteristics. One important precondition is to establish and assign well-defined and stable property and/or use rights. Another is to create information instruments for the products and services that PAs provide.

Market creation is based on the premise that holders of rights derived from a resource (landowners, people with use permits, etc.) will maximize the value of their resources over long time horizons, thus optimizing biodiversity use, conservation and restoration (OECD, 2008). Translated into simple terms, this means that there needs to be:

- an understanding that a PA produces ecosystem services and benefits of value to the public (whether local communities or a global constituency);
- a clear understanding of the property rights involved;
- a commitment to efficient management to reduce pressure on the PA so that it will continue to provide the services;
- identification of global and local beneficiaries and communication of the value of the services they gain; and
- last but not least, an efficient mechanism to collect the fees/support from global and local beneficiaries and allocate them to efficient management of the resource.

Addressing funding instability and creating a diverse income portfolio

Even if funding is obtained and appropriate mechanisms make the transfers from the beneficiary to the resource, there is not always a guarantee of long-term success. Often projects begin well and raise expectations but are then discontinued for various reasons. A common scenario is that donors only finance initial phases of the PA management plan and then move on to other areas, or else enabling conditions change significantly and finance stagnates. In other cases, the upward trend in the financial flow collapses; when this is totally unexpected, there can be big consequences for the stability of any conservation project. Sometimes, government backing or any public authority support may not be strong enough to provide funds needed over time.

These risks reinforce the need to develop a diverse portfolio of sources of income for PAs to the widest extent possible. This requires committed management efforts and good relations with the range of possible donors and sectors that may wish to operate in the area. Keeping links with all potential funding sources can at times involve a high risk of conflicts between actors with different interests in the PA.

Bringing different finance sources together under a common umbrella is not always easy, but can be a solution when there is a higher risk that independent efforts and mechanisms will fail to deliver, mainly due to institutional conditions in the country concerned. For these reasons, the possibility of establishing trust funds to manage the income generated directly by the PA and funds from international donors may often be a better solution (see Box 8.10).

It is likely that any individual funding source and mechanism may experience changes over time (e.g. limitations to available resources and changes in funding priorities). A diverse portfolio of funding sources, including public and private mechanisms, can therefore increase the long-term sustainability of PA financing and management.

Addressing possible social impacts of protected area financing

Ecotourism is widely promoted as a conservation tool and actively practised in PAs worldwide. Theoretically, support from different stakeholders inside and outside PAs

---

Box 8.10 Options for financing a new network of protected areas in Sierra Leone

The Sierra Leone government applied for GEF funding to create a national network of PAs. The issue of sustainable financing for this network is of paramount importance. A study prepared by the Royal Society for the Protection of Birds, the National Commission for the Environment of Sierra Leone and the Conservation Society of Sierra Leone demonstrated that although there are several potential mechanisms to generate income for PAs (debt swaps, a hypothecated airport departure tax, sale of carbon credits, donations from the mining industry, GEF, support from NGOs), the creation of a trust fund would be the optimum solution for establishing sustainable financial security. This would help to bring together various possible income streams and ensure their effective coordination.

The reason behind this proposal was the serious constraints on generating dependable ongoing revenue in Sierra Leone and the vulnerability that arose from dependence on a series of one-off injections of funds.

Source: RSPB et al (2006)

Box 8.11 Inequalities in benefit distribution in China's Wolong Nature Reserve

Research on the distribution of benefits derived from ecotourism in the Wolong Nature Reserve for giant pandas revealed two types of uneven distribution of economic benefits among four major groups of stakeholders. This created conflict and eventually failure in reaching the reserve's conservation objectives.

Significant inequalities exist between local rural residents and other stakeholders. The former, along with farmers, bear most of the costs of conservation but most economic benefits (investment, employment, goods/services) in three key ecotourism sectors (infrastructure construction, hotels/restaurants, souvenir sales) go to stakeholders outside the reserve. Moreover, the distribution of benefits is also unequal even between reserve residents. Most rural households benefiting from ecotourism are located near the main road and have less negative impacts on panda habitat than households located and exercising activities far from the road in natural areas. This distribution gap is likely to discourage conservation support from the second group of households, yet their activities are the main forces degrading panda habitats. The problem can be addressed by enhancing local participation, increasing the use of local goods and encouraging the relocation of rural households closer to ecotourism facilities.

Source: He et al (2008)

---

is maximized if they benefit in proportion to the opportunity costs they bear. Conversely, unbalanced distribution of benefits between stakeholders can erode their support for – or even lead to the failure of – ecotourism and conservation initiatives (see Box 8.11).

Making available funds work better

Securing adequate financial resources does not of itself guarantee effective management of PAs. Compliance is critical – pressure on valuable and scarce resources will always exist and must be addressed by enforcing existing restrictions on PA use (see Chapter 7).

To strengthen appropriate PA management, good monitoring mechanisms are needed to report on site-specific pressures, measure progress towards set objectives, assess efficiency of funds used and identify what else needs to be done (see Chapter 3). Many researchers and practitioners have long identified the lack of monitoring as a key reason for conservation failures in PAs, along with inadequate community/public participation in decision making (see Box 8.12). Building capacity within the park and in local or regional administrations can help make implementation more efficient and protection more meaningful.

5 Strengthening policy and institutional support

Successful establishment and management of PAs, and the delivery of associated benefits, requires multi-level policy support and effective institutional frameworks. This section broadens the analysis in Sections 1 to 4 to discuss the broader policy,

---

Box 8.12 The importance of monitoring in forest protected areas, Panama

PAs are cornerstones in forest conservation and may play a significant role in reducing deforestation rates. Research in nine PAs in Panama illustrates that coupling monitoring measures with greater funding and strong governance is essential to reduce deforestation, but these factors alone are not enough to protect forests. Conservation approaches that complement effective monitoring with community participation and equitable benefit sharing will be best placed to address wider issues of leakage and permanence under potential REDD implementation.

Source: Oestreicher et al (2009)

---

institutional and stakeholder context needed to ensure that PAs achieve their goals and provide societal benefits.

5.1 Major policy initiatives on protected areas

Many international and regional agreements, treaties and programmes focus on PA establishment, management, funding and general importance. In parallel, organizations like IUCN, with its regular global conferences and World Commission on Protected Areas, help create a global consensus on key PA issues. In the EU, the Natura 2000 Network forms a policy cornerstone for the conservation of Europe's most valuable species and habitats.

In February 2004, the international community agreed the most comprehensive and specific PA commitments ever made by adopting the CBD Programme of Work on Protected Areas (PoWPA) (see Box 8.13). This builds on resolutions from the Fifth World Parks Congress (the Durban Accord) and enshrines the principle of developing comprehensive PA systems sustainably financed and supported by society. The PoWPA, by emphasizing equitable sharing of costs and benefits, recognizing different governance types and giving prominence to management effectiveness and multiple benefits, provides a comprehensive global plan of action for implementation. It can therefore be considered the 'blueprint' for PAs for decades to come (Stolton et al, 2008c; Chape et al, 2008).

5.2 Institutional requirements for protected areas

Successful institutional structures for PAs typically include a commitment to the following elements:

- a common set of goals across a portfolio of diverse PAs;
- a culture of learning, capacity building and adaptive management;
- collaboration between and among key PA actors and stakeholders;
- full recognition of PA ecological, economic, social, cultural values and benefits; and

- the ability to adequately monitor and adapt to ecological and social conditions (Slocombe, 2008).

PA institutions also need the authority, ability and willingness to promote sustainable resource use, facilitate equitable distribution of costs and benefits, and support different governance types (Barrett et al, 2001).

Successful PA establishment and management requires coordination mechanisms between institutional levels (e.g. different sectors, stakeholders and government

---

Box 8.13 The CBD Programme of Work on Protected Areas

The Programme of Work on Protected Areas (PoWPA), adopted by 188 CBD Parties in 2004, is one of the most ambitious environmental strategies in history and aimed to establish comprehensive, effectively managed and ecologically representative national and regional systems of PAs by 2010 (terrestrial) and 2012 (marine). It is generally judged to have been a success, even though these goals will not be completed by the target dates (see phased timetable below). In the future, PoWPA will be updated, to reflect the new global biodiversity targets and timetable agreed by the CBD's tenth Conference of the Parties (COP in 2010).

Potential main outcomes of PoWPA Phase I (2004–2006)

- **'Master plan' for protected areas.** Completing, in effect, a 'master plan' for the system of protected areas (key elements include, for example: plans for filling ecological gaps; securing financial resources; building capacity; promoting governance arrangements; and addressing policy, legislative and institutional barriers).
- **Studies and assessments** for input into 'master plans', covering, for example, socio-economic contributions of protected areas, ecological gaps in protected area systems and types of governance arrangements.
- **New protected areas**: Establishment of new protected areas where urgent action is required.

Potential main outcomes of PoWPA Phase II (2007–2008)

- **Threats**: Mechanisms in place to address key threats.
- **Financial resources**: Sufficient financial resources secured.
- **Standards**: Standards adopted for all major aspects of protected areas.

Potential main outcomes of PoWPA Phase III (2009–2015)

- **Effective systems of protected areas**: Comprehensive, ecologically representative and effectively managed systems of protected areas.
- **Integration** of protected areas into wider land and seascapes.

Source: Dudley et al (2005)

agencies). This contributes to well-informed management planning and significantly improves the efficiency and effectiveness of conservation spending. Communication and exchange of information is an important part of this process (e.g. stakeholder forums, inter-agency groups).

Improved monitoring is another key component of institutional transparency (see Section 4.3). This needs to be based on clear objectives and measurable targets, agreed with stakeholders, that address pressures to PAs and aim to improve the state of biodiversity and ecosystem services. Efficient monitoring helps to demonstrate that PAs do indeed provide benefits to biodiversity and people – and are therefore worth the investment.

5.3 Key elements for successful management

Six elements have been identified as critical to focus concerted efforts and combine the strengths of all sectors of society (policy makers, civil society, indigenous and local communities, business). These can be thought of as 'The Six Cs' and should be embedded in PA policy and institutional structures at local, national, regional and global levels and translated into practical actions on the ground.

Box 8.14 shows how these elements can be effectively incorporated, using the example of PAs in Micronesia. Annex 1 illustrates how certain decisions under the CBD, Ramsar Convention on Wetlands, World Heritage Convention and UN Convention to Combat Desertification (UNCCD) address these key elements.

5.4 Promoting coherence and synergies: The example of climate change

Policy makers need to align PAs with other policies to ensure broad policy coherence and build on opportunities for synergies. One example of this is making explicit linkages between PAs and climate change adaptation. Better-managed, better-connected, better-governed and better-financed PAs are recognized as key to both climate change mitigation and adaptation.

PAs are critical to preventing further carbon emissions from degradation and development, and can make an important contribution to an overall strategy for climate change mitigation. A total of 312Gt of terrestrial carbon is currently stored in the existing PA network: if lost to the atmosphere, this would be equivalent to approximately 23 times the total global anthropogenic carbon emissions for 2004 (Kapos et al, 2008). In the future, their contribution will certainly increase as governments continue to designate new PAs in the Arctic, tropical rainforests and boreal forests.

However, PAs are generally not considered in current REDD discussions and strategies, given the impression that carbon in PAs is safe and that such areas would not offer additional carbon sequestration. Yet PAs remain vulnerable to degradation: a significant number of the world's PAs are poorly or inadequately managed (Leverington et al, 2008). A comprehensive network of effectively designed and managed PAs would ensure that this stored carbon is protected into the foreseeable future: it should therefore be considered as a primary REDD strategy. Formal linkage to REDD would need to respect the need for additionality in order to ensure real, measurable and long-term emission reductions.

Box 8.14 Micronesia Challenge commitment to protected area implementation

The Micronesia Challenge is a commitment by the Chief Executives of the Federated States of Micronesia, the Republic of the Marshall Islands, the Republic of Palau, the US Territory of Guam and the US Commonwealth of the Northern Mariana Islands to effectively conserve at least 30 per cent of near-shore marine resources and 20 per cent of terrestrial resources across Micronesia by 2020. It serves as a model for conservation initiated by a coalition of regional governments, endorsed at international level and implemented on the ground with local communities.

The Micronesia Challenge demonstrates six critical elements:

1 **Capacity:** A regional technical support team includes a wide range of partners, supported by a technical working group to ensure that there is adequate capacity among all member countries.
2 **Capital:** The Nature Conservancy and Conservation International have jointly pledged US$6 million to leverage an additional US$12 million for the first phase of the Challenge. The leaders and their partners are working to secure matching funds for this pledge: GEF has promised a US$6 million contribution as part of a new 'Pacific Alliance for Sustainability' initiative. These developments have coincided with the establishment of the Micronesia Conservation Trust Fund.
3 **Coordination:** The Micronesia Challenge steering committee and partners have developed a comprehensive strategic plan to ensure coordination by clearly defining the roles and responsibilities of each partner.
4 **Cooperation:** There is a high level of cooperation among all partners, including participating governments, NGOs and local communities.
5 **Commitment:** Each government has made a strong public commitment. There is also clear commitment among stakeholders at sub-national levels, including local communities and in locally managed marine areas.
6 **Communication:** A dedicated working group has developed a regional communications strategy, local communication plans and a regional inventory of outreach materials to gain publicity at a global level.

Source: http://micronesiachallenge.org

The UN Framework Convention on Climate Change (UNFCCC) recognizes the value of ecosystem resilience (Article 2) and introduced the term 'ecosystem-based adaptation' at its COP14. However, it has not yet explicitly recognized the contribution of PAs to ecosystem resilience and ecosystem-based adaptation. Climate adaptation on the ground cannot and should not be solely addressed through human-made infrastructure (see for example CBD AHTEG, 2009; Campbell et al, 2009): on the contrary, climate-resilient development should include ecosystem-based adaptation where appropriate. Well-designed coherent networks of appropriately managed and ecologically connected PAs are one of the most cogent responses to climate change and should be an explicit component of an ecosystem-based adaptation strategy (e.g. Kettunen et al, 2007).

6 Creating a workable future for protected areas

Increased support for PAs is in society's best interest, with their global benefits (i.e. total benefits provided by ecosystems within PAs) generally far outweighing costs. Globally, the scale of the difference between benefits and costs appears to be so significant, even allowing for inevitable imprecision in analyses, that these basic conclusions would be unchanged even if analyses were incorrect by more than an order of magnitude. At the local level, benefits can be greater than the costs even without any national or international payments for broader ecosystem service benefits – although the ratio is of course very site-specific. Payments for the provision of services from these sites can increase the economic attractiveness of PAs and help them to be engines of local development.

Support can take the form of new designations where this would benefit ecosystems of particular value in terms of species and habitats. There is still a large untapped potential for new marine PAs which currently cover only 5.9 per cent of territorial seas and 0.5 per cent of the high seas (see Section 1 above). Support can also include increased investment in – or payment for the management of – existing PAs to address the funding gap and help them fulfil their potential to protect biodiversity and deliver important ecosystem services locally, nationally and internationally.

Policy actions for more equitable distribution of benefits and costs are fundamental. The benefits of protection are often broadly disbursed, long-term and non-market, whereas the costs of protection are more immediate and the earning potential from conversion options more short-term and concentrated. At the local and sometimes national levels, whether PAs represent net benefits or net costs will depend on recognizing local rights, ensuring meaningful participation, managing PAs to maximize benefits and minimize costs, and creating mechanisms to make beneficiaries pay for or invest in what they receive. Policies of this kind will increase the perceived fairness of PAs and optimize their contribution to human well-being.

Policy makers can strengthen the effectiveness of PAs through an enabling national framework (e.g. clear legislative basis, policy consistency, cooperation between stakeholders) and by ensuring that funding models provide the right incentives and sufficient financial stability for effective management. They play a key role in raising the profile of PAs in both national and international forums and in encouraging positive stakeholder engagement.

Valuation of benefits and costs provided by ecosystems within PAs can deliver multiple benefits for biodiversity and people. It can support decision making and fundraising (e.g. by showing that biodiversity conservation can often be a socio-economically attractive choice) but results need to be appropriately interpreted and embedded in sound management processes. Monetary values can help to translate ecological concerns into economic arguments, but these arguments must always be considered within the bigger picture of PA governance. It must be stressed that sustainable use and expanded compensation programmes will not make protection attractive for everyone. Enforcement of regulations to ensure respect for jointly agreed PA rules is therefore vital.

Current expenditure on PAs does not match funding needs. There is a clear need for an integrated multi-level policy response and a long-term vision for financing PAs to bridge the current funding gap. Steps towards this goal include better communication to build public understanding of the positive returns from funding PAs and support innovative mechanisms and instruments.

Although practitioners are still refining the figures on PA financing needs, the CBD and the conservation community should consider setting a fundraising target for global biodiversity conservation and mobilize all relevant actors. The CBD's Ninth COP (Bonn, 2008) called for national financial targets to support implementation of the CBD Programme of Work on Protected Areas: Decision IX/18 (CBD, 2008a). This decision should pave the way for consolidated action.

To achieve future funding targets, the financing gap needs to be addressed in a strategic way. Efforts to increase PA funding have already shown considerable success: the global network continues to expand and dedicated PA programmes now exist in nearly all countries. In 2008, CBD Parties adopted a general strategy to mobilize resources to implement CBD objectives, including improving PA financing (CBD, 2008b). This strategy addresses key obstacles to achieving adequate biodiversity funding but needs concerted efforts to translate it into practical actions for individual stakeholders.

Stronger cooperation, both North–South and South–South, is essential to expand the funding base for PAs. The establishment of a dedicated global fund or financial mechanism could help mobilize and focus resources effectively. Reducing existing demands on public financing by reforming harmful subsidies could also help generate additional resources for PAs (see Chapter 6). Identified financial needs could be further integrated into existing and emerging financial instruments for the environment, e.g. the REDD discussions highlight potential synergies between climate change and biodiversity objectives (see Chapter 5). Market-based instruments can significantly contribute to generating additional funds for PAs, e.g. from consumers and the business sector (see Chapter 7).

There is clear international policy commitment and institutional support for PAs – this should now be translated into concrete actions on the ground in a coherent and mutually supporting manner. The current global financial crisis may provide an opportunity to devise a new economic system connected to the Earth's natural systems in place of a system that is disconnected and runs down natural capital. A suite of long-term economic measures is needed that fully accounts for the true benefits and costs of ecosystem protection. Investment in the network of global PAs is one such measure.

Notes

1   Updated by authors to account for inflation and increase in land under irrigated agriculture.
2   An important exception involves visits to well-known culturally important sites such as Machu Picchu in Peru or Angkor Wat in Cambodia.
3   Management costs can usefully be divided into recurrent costs (e.g. staff salaries, fuel, maintenance of equipment, community engagement/participation, monitoring and evaluation, site level administration), upfront establishment costs (e.g. stakeholder consultations, scientific studies, boundary demarcation, land/equipment purchase, construction) and subsequent investments to upgrade management and also the PA itself (e.g. through infrastructure, restoration or other improvements). It should be stressed that key establishment activities have not been carried out in many existing PAs.
4   The valuations of ecosystem goods and services underlying these estimates have been criticized, e.g. see Toman (1998). On the other hand, the study makes an important methodological advance in calculating marginal rather than total benefit of protection, by comparing the goods and services provided by intact versus converted forms of each biome.
5   Countries included were Zimbabwe, Kenya, Zanzibar, Uganda, India, Mongolia and China.
6   While an average is given for illustrative purposes, in reality values will vary significantly from site to site, depending on the state of ecosystem, the services it provides, its spatial relation with beneficiaries and their socio-economic status (see Chapters 1 and 4 for further discussion).
7   Not all ecosystem services are covered, given the limits to what valuation studies have covered. In addition, the average has excluded some high outliers to avoid undue influence on the illustrative average. These values are arguably conservative.

8   The difference in the ratio of benefits to costs here, compared to Balmford et al (2002), might reasonably be expected given that PAs have on balance been created on less agriculturally valuable lands and further from transportation infrastructure, which implies significantly lower opportunity costs than those found in areas of active deforestation (Gorenflo and Brandon, 2005; Dudley, 2008).
9   This perspective (net benefits from competing scenarios) and these ratios are not directly comparable to the two previous assessments (benefit/cost of conservation) and would be expected to yield a much lower ratio. The figures are lower than the broad 100-to-1 figure, due to the inclusion of ongoing service provision in the calculation and also to the explicit integration of opportunity costs (these are the core part of the potential benefits of conversion). In addition, the studies reviewed in this section include a smaller set of ecosystem goods and services than do the benefit/cost assessments, suggesting that benefits of conservation are estimated conservatively.
10 Calculations made by modifying the global ratio of benefits to costs reported by Balmford et al (2002) according to the percentage of benefits accruing at the national level in the studies reviewed in Figure 8.4.
11 Existence and carbon sequestration are assumed to be purely global values.
12 See IUCN management categories. Categories I–IV (strictly protected areas and national parks) require US$60–240/ha/year in land and over US$1000/ha/year in small marine parks.
13 Includes management and opportunity costs.

Acknowledgements

The authors wish to thank Sarah Andrews, Ceredigion, UK; Giles Atkinson, London School of Economics, UK; Tim Badman, IUCN, Global; David Baldock, IEEP, UK; Basanglamao, Sanjiangyuan Nature Reserve, China; Peter Bridgewater, JNCC, UK; Deanna Donovan, JNCC, UK; Brendan Dunford, Teagasc, Ireland; Moustafa Fouda, Egyptian Environmental Affairs Agency, Egypt; Ninan Karachepone, Institute for Social and Economic Change, India; Jairo Escobar Llanos, Inter-American Development Bank, Bolivia; Jean-Pierre Revéret, Université du Québec à Montréal; Alice Ruhweza, Katoomba Group, Uganda; Rania Spyropoulou, EEA, Denmark; Peter Torkler, WWF, Germany; Graham Tucker, IEEP, UK; Francies Vorhies, Earth Mind, Switzerland; He Xin, Shan Shui Conservation Center, China; Heidi Wittmer, UFZ, Germany; and many others.

References

Abell, R., Allan, J. D. and Lehner, B. (2007) 'Unlocking the potential of protected areas for freshwaters', *Biological Conservation*, vol 134, pp48–63
Adams, C., Seroa da Motta, R., Arigoni Ortiz, R., Reid, J., Ebersbach Aznar, C. and de Almeida Sinisgalli, P. A. (2007) 'The use of contingent valuation for evaluating protected areas in the developing world: Economic valuation of Morro do Diabo State Park, Atlantic Rainforest, São Paulo State', *Ecological Economics*, vol 66, pp359–370
Adams, W. M. and Hutton, J. (2007) 'People, parks and poverty: Political ecology and biodiversity conservation', *Conservation and Society*, vol 5, no 2, pp147–183
Adeney, J. M., Christensen Jr., N. L. and Pimm, S. L. (2009) 'Reserves protect against deforestation fires in the Amazon', *PLoS ONE*, vol 4, no 4, e5014.
Agrawal, A. and Redford, K. (2007) 'Conservation and displacement: An overview', in K. H. Redford and E. Fearn (eds) *Protected Areas and Human Displacement: A Conservation Perspective*, Working Paper 29, Wildlife Conservation Society, New York, pp4–15
Amend, M., Gascon, G. and Reid, J. (2007) 'Beneficios economicos locais de areas protegidas na regiao de Manaus, Amazonas', *Megadiversidade*, vol 3, no 60
Andam, K. S., Ferraro, P. J., Holland, M. B. and Sanchez-Azofeifa, G. A. (2008) *Measuring the Social Impacts of Protected Areas: An Impact Evaluation Approach*, Prepared for the Global Environment Facility Evaluation Office
Ankudey, N., Volta-Tineh, B. and Howard, P. (2003) 'Protected area management costs in Ghana: Requirements and reality', Paper presented at the Fifth World Parks Congress, 8–17 September 2003, Durban, South Africa
Balmford, A. and Whitten, T. (2003) 'Who should pay for tropical conservation, and how could the costs be met?' *Oryx*, vol 37, pp238–250

Balmford, A., Bruner, A., Cooper, P., Costanza, R., Farber, S., Green, R. E., Jenkins, M., Jefferiss, P., Jessamy, V., Madden, J., Munro, K., Myers, N., Naeem, S., Paavola, J., Rayment, M., Rosendo, S., Roughgarden, J., Trumper, K. and Turner, R. K. (2002) 'Economic reasons for conserving wild nature', *Science*, vol 297, pp950–953

Balmford, A., Gaston, J. J., Blyth, S., Simon, A. and Kapos. V. (2003) 'Global variation in terrestrial conservation costs, conservation benefits and unmet conservation needs', *PNAS*, vol 100, no 3, pp1046–1050

Balmford, A., Gravestock, P., Hockley, N., McClean, C. J. and Roberts, C. M. (2004) 'The worldwide costs of marine protected areas', *PNAS*, vol 101, pp9694–9697, www.pnas.org/content/101/26/9694.full. pdf+html, accessed 2 August 2010

Bann, C. (1997) *An Economic Analysis of Alternative Mangrove Management Strategies in Koh Kong Province, Cambodia*, Economy and Environment Program for Southeast Asia, International Development Research Centre

Barbier, E. B. (2007) 'Valuing ecosystem services as productive inputs', *Economic Policy*, vol 49, pp177–229

Barrett, C. B. K., Brandon, K., Gibson, C. and Gjertsen, H. (2001) 'Conserving tropical biodiversity amid weak institutions', *BioScience*, vol 51, pp497–502

Basanglamao and He Xin (2009) Collaborative management of the Sanjiangyuan Nature Reserve, China – A case study prepared for TEEB. Based on personal communication

Beltran, J. (2000) *Indigenous and Traditional Peoples and Protected Areas: Principles, Guidelines and Case Studies*, World Commission on Protected Areas Best Practice Protected Area Guidelines Series No 4. IUCN, Gland, http://data.iucn.org/dbtw-wpd/edocs/PAG-004.pdf, accessed 10 November 2009

Blignaut, J. and Moolman, C. (2006) 'Quantifying the potential of restored natural capital to alleviate poverty and help conserve nature: A case study from South Africa', *Journal for Nature Conservation*, vol 14, pp237–248

Bräuer, I., Müssner, R., Marsden, K., Oosterhuis, M., Rayment M., Miller, C., ten Brink, P. and Dodoková, A. (2006) *The Use of Market Incentives to Preserve Biodiversity*, A study under the Framework contract ENV.G.1/FRA/2004/0081, http://ec.europa.eu/environment/enveco/biodiversity/pdf/mbi.pdf, accessed 10 November 2009

Brockington, D. and Igoe, J. (2006) 'Eviction for conservation: A global overview', *Conservation and Society*, vol 4, pp424–470

Brown, O., Crawford, A. and Hammill, A. (2006) *Natural Disasters and Resource Rights: Building Resilience, Rebuilding Lives*, International Institute for Sustainable Development, Manitoba, Canada

Bruner, A. G., Gullison, R. E., Rice, R. E. and da Fonseca, G. A. B. (2001) 'Effectiveness of parks in protecting tropical biodiversity', *Science*, vol 291, pp125–128

Bruner, A. G., Gullison, R. E. and Balmford, A. (2004) 'Financial costs and shortfalls of managing and expanding protected area systems in developing countries', *Bioscience*, vol 54, no 12, pp1119–1126

Butcher Partners (2005) 'Regional economic impacts of West Coast conservation land', www.doc.govt.nz/ conservation/threats-and-impacts/benefits-of-conservation, accessed 10 November 2009

Butler, J. (2000) 'The economic costs of wildlife predation on livestock in Gokwe communal land, Zimbabwe', *African Journal of Ecology*, vol 38, no 1, pp23–30

Cairngorms National Park Authority (2005) *Tourism and the Cairngorms National Park: Introducing the Park's Sustainable Tourism Strategy and Survey of Visitors*, Granton on Spey, UK

Campbell, A., Miles, L., Lysenko, I., Hughes, A. and Gibbs, H. (2008) *Carbon Storage in Protected Areas: Technical Report*, UNEP-WCMC, www.unep-wcmc.org/climate/pdf/Carbon%20storage%20in%20 protected%20areas%20technical%20report.pdf, accessed 10 November 2009

Campbell, A., Kapos, V., Chenery, A., Kahn, S. I., Rashid, M., Scharlemann, J. and Dickson, B. (2009) *The Linkages Between Biodiversity and Climate Change Adaptation: A Review of the Recent Scientific Literature*, UNEP-WCMC

Carret, J. C. and Loyer, D. (2003) *Madagascar Protected Area Network Sustainable Financing: Economic Analysis Perspective*, World Bank, Washington, DC

CBD (Convention on Biological Diversity) AHTEG (2009) 'Draft findings of the Ad Hoc Technical Expert Group on Biodiversity and Climate Change', CBD, Montreal

CBD (2008a) 'Decision IX/18: Protected areas', COP 9, Bonn, Germany, 19–30 May 2008, www.cbd.int/ decision/cop/?id=11661, accessed 22 September 2010

CBD (2008b) 'Decision IX/11: Review of implementation of Articles 20 and 21 – In-depth review of the availability of financial resources', COP 9, Bonn, Germany 19-30 May 2008, www.cbd.int/doc/ decisions/cop-09/cop-09-dec-11-en.pdf, accessed 28 October 2010

CBD (2010) *Resource Mobilization Strategy in Support of the Achievement of the Convention's Three Objectives* (UNEP/CBD/COP/10/INF), CBD, Montreal

Chan, K. M. A., Pringle, R. M., Ranganathan, J., Boggs, C. L., Chan, Y. L., Ehrlich, P. R., Haff, P., Heller, N. E., Al-Khafaji, K. and MacMynowski, D. (2007) 'When agendas collide: Human welfare and biological conservation', *Conservation Biology*, vol 21, no 1, pp59–68

Chape, S., Spalding, M. and Jenkins, M. (eds) (2008) *The World's Protected Areas*, UNEP-WCMC, University of California Press, Berkeley, CA

Child and Dalal-Clayton (2004) 'Learning from the Luangwa experience, Zambia', in T. O. McShane and M. P. Wells (eds) *Getting Biodiversity Projects to Work*, Columbia University Press, New York

Coad, L., Burgess, N. D., Bombard, B. and Besançon, C. (2009) 'Progress towards the Convention on Biological Diversity's 2010 and 2012 targets for protected area coverage', A technical report for the IUCN international workshop 'Looking at the Future of the CBD Programme of Work on Protected Areas', Jeju Islad, Republic of Korea, 14–17 September 2009, UNEP-WCMC, Cambridge

Colchester, M. (2003) *Salvaging Nature: Indigenous Peoples, Protected Areas and Biodiversity Conservation*, World Rainforest Movement and Forest Peoples' Programme, www.wrm.org.uy/subjects/PA/texten.pdf, accessed 10 November 2010

Culverwell, J. (1997) *Long-Term Recurrent Costs of Protected Areas Management in Cameroon: Monitoring of Protected Areas, Donor Assistance and External Financing, Ecological and Management Priorities of Current and Potential Protected Area System*, WWF Cameroon/Ministère de l'Environnement et des Forêts (Project 33.06.01)

Daily, G. C., Alexander, S., Ehrlich, P. R., Goulder, L., Lubchenco, J., Matson, P. A., Mooney, H. A., Postel, S., Schneider, S. H., Tilman, D. and Woodwell G. M. (2009) 'Ecosystem services: Benefits supplied to human societies by natural ecosystems', *Issues in Ecology*, vol 2, pp1–16

Das, B. K. (2005) 'Role of NTFPs among forest villagers in a protected area of West Bengal', *Journal of Human Ecology*, vol 18, pp129–136

De Lopez, T. T. (2003) 'Economics and stakeholders of Ream National Park, Cambodia', *Ecological Economics*, vol 46, pp269–282

Distefano, E. (2005) *Human-Wildlife Conflict Worldwide: Collection of Case Studies, Analysis of Management Strategies and Good Practices*, FAO, Rome, www.fao.org/SARD/common/ecg/1357/en/HWC_final.pdf, accessed 10 November 2009

Dowie, M. (2009) *Conservation Refugees: The Hundred-Year Conflict Between Global Conservation and Native Peoples*, MIT Press, MA

Dudley, N. and Stolton, S. (2003) *Running Pure: The Importance of Forest Protected Areas to Drinking Water*, World Bank/WWF Alliance for Forest Conservation and Sustainable Use, WWF, Gland, Switzerland

Dudley, N., Mulongoy, K. J., Cohen, S., Stolton, S., Barber, C. V. and Gidda, S. B. (2005) *Towards Effective Protected Area Systems: An Action Guide to Implement the Convention on Biological Diversity Programme of Work on Protected Areas*, CBD Technical Series No 18, CBD, Montreal, www.cbd.int/doc/publications/cbd-ts-18.pdf, accessed 10 November 2009

Dudley, N., Mansourian, S., Stolton, S. and Suksuwan, S. (2008) *Safety Net: Protected Areas and Poverty Reduction*, WWF, http://assets.panda.org/downloads/safety_net_final.pdf, accessed 10 November 2009

Dudley, N., Higgins-Zogib, L. and Mansourian, S. (2009a) 'The links between protected areas, faiths and sacred natural sites', *Conservation Biology*, vol 23, pp568–577

Dudley, N., Stolton, S., Belokurov, A., Krueger, L., Lopoukhine, N., MacKinnon, K., Sandwith, T. and Sekhran, N. (eds) (2009b) *Natural Solutions: Protected Areas Helping People Cope with Climate Change*, IUCN–WCPA, The Nature Conservancy, UNDP, Wildlife Conservation Society, The World Bank and WWF, Gland, Switzerland and Washington, DC

Eagles, P. and Hillel, O. (2008) 'Improving protected area finance through tourism in protected areas', in SCBD (Secretariat of the Convention on Biological Diversity) *Protected Areas in Today's World: Their Values and Benefits for the Welfare of the Planet*, CBD Technical Series No 36, CBD, Montreal, www.cbd.int/doc/publications/cbd-ts-36-en.pdf, accessed 10 November 2009

EEA (European Environment Agency) (2006) 'Integration of environment into EU agriculture policy: The IRENA indicator-based assessment report', EEA, Copenhagen, Denmark

Emerton, L., Philavong, O. and Thanthatep, K. (2002) *Nam Et-Phou Loei National Biodiversity Conservation Area, Lao PDR: A Case Study of Economic and Development Linkages*, IUCN, Gland

Emerton, L., Bishop, J. and Thomas L. (2006) *Sustainable Financing of Protected Areas*, IUCN, Gland

Esteban, A. (2005) 'Estimating Natura 2000 funding needs', Royal Society for the Protection of Birds Discussion Paper, RSPB, Sandy, UK

European Commission (2004) 'Financing Natura 2000', Communication from the Commission to the Council and the European Parliament, EC, http://ec.europa.eu/environment/nature/natura2000/financing/index_en.htm, accessed 10 November 2009

Fernández, M., Moreno, V., Picazo, I., Torres, A. and Martínez, B. (2008) 'Valoración de los costes indirectos de gestión de la Red Natura 2000 en España', Dirección General de Medio Natural y Política Forestal, Ministerio de Medio Ambiente y Medio Rural y Marino, Madrid (Unpublished)

Fouda, M. M. (2010) Sustainable Use of Samadi Dolphins, South Marsa Alam, Red Sea, Egypt, available at www.egyptchm.org/chm/implementation/pdf/marine/sustainable_use_samadi_dolphins.pdf, accessed 23 November 2010

Galindo, J., Calvopiña, J., Baus, C., Ayllón, M.-F. and Vela, S. (2005) Análisis de Necesidades de Financiamiento del Sistema Nacional de Áreas Protegidas (SNAP) del Ecuador, Mentefactura, Quito, Ecuador

Gantioler, S., Rayment, M., Bassi, S., Kettunen, M., McConville, A., Landgrebe, R., Gerdes, H. and ten Brink, P. (2010) Costs and Socio-Economic Benefits associated with the Natura 2000 Network, Final report to the European Commission, DG Environment on Contract Number ENV.B.2/SER/2008/0038, Institute for European Environmental Policy/GHK/Ecologic, Brussels, http://ec.europa.eu/environment/nature/natura2000/financing/docs/natura2000_costs_benefits.pdf, accessed 27 October 2010

Gell, F. R. and Roberts, C. M. (2003) 'Benefits beyond boundaries: The fishery effects of marine reserves', TRENDS in Ecology and Evolution, vol 18, no 9, pp448–455

Gorenflo, L. J. and Brandon, K. (2005) 'Agricultural capacity and conservation in forested portions of biodiversity hotspots and wilderness areas', Ambio, vol 34, pp199–204

Grieg-Gran, M. (2006) 'Is tackling deforestation a cost-effective mitigation approach?' Sustainable Development Opinion, International Institute for Environment and Development (IIED), www.iied.org/pubs/display.php?o=11058IIED, accessed 28 July 2010

Gutman, P. (2002) 'Putting a price tag on conservation: Cost benefit analysis of Venezuela's National Parks', Journal of Latin American Studies, vol 34, no 1, pp43–70

Gutman, P. and Davidson, S. (2007) A Review of Innovative International Financial Mechanisms for Biodiversity Conservation – with a Special Focus on the International Financing of Developing Countries' Protected Areas, WWF–MPO Washington, DC

Halpern, B. S. (2003) 'The impact of marine reserves: Do reserves work and does reserve size matter?' Ecological Applications, vol 13, no 1, pp117–137

Han, S.-Y. and Lee, C.-K. (2008) 'Estimating the value of preserving the Manchurian black bear using the contingent valuation method', Scandinavian Journal of Forest Research, vol 23, no 5, pp458–465

Hanley, N. and Barbier, E. B. (2009) 'Valuing ecosystem services', in N. Hanley and E. B. Barbier (eds) Pricing Nature: Cost-Benefit Analysis and Environmental Policy, Edward Elgar, London

Hannah, L., Midgeley, G., Andelman, S., Araújo, M., Hughes, G., Martinez-Meyers, E., Pearson, R. and Williams, P. (2007) 'Protected area needs in a changing climate', Frontiers in Ecology and the Environment, vol 5, no 3, pp131–138

Harley, M. (2008) 'Review of existing international and national guidance on adaptation to climate change with a focus on biodiversity issues', Convention on the Conservation of European Wildlife and Natural Habitats, Standing Committee 28th meeting, Strasbourg, 24–27 November 2008, Council of Europe, Strasbourg

Harper, J. (2002) Endangered Species: Health, Illness and Death among Madagascar's People of the Forest, Carolina Academic Press, Durham, NC

He, G., Chen, X., Liu, W., Bearer, S., Zhou, S., Yeqing Cheng, L., Zhang, H., Ouyang, Z. and Liu, J. (2008) 'Distribution of economic benefits from ecotourism: A case study of Wolong Nature Reserve for Giant Pandas in China', Environmental Management, vol 42, pp1017–1025

Hein, L. and Gatzweiler, F. (2006) 'The economic value of coffee (Coffea arabica) genetic resources', Ecological Economics, vol 60, no 1, pp176–185

Huntley, B. (2007) 'Climatic change and the conservation of European biodiversity: Towards the development of adaptation strategies', Convention on the Conservation of European Wildlife and Natural Habitats, Standing Committee 27th meeting, Strasbourg, 26–29 November 2007, Council of Europe, Strasbourg

Indian Environment Portal (2007) Press Release, March 2007, www.indiaenvironmentportal.org.in/node/7613, accessed 10 November 2009

IPCC (Intergovernmental Panel on Climate Change) (2007) 'The physical science basis', in S. Solomon, D. Qin, M. Manning, Z. Chen, M. Marquis, K. B. M. Tignor and H. L. Miller (eds) Contribution of Working Group I to the Fourth Assessment Report of the IPCC, Cambridge University Press, Cambridge and New York

International Strategy for Disaster Reduction (2004) *Living with Risk: A Global Review of Disaster Reduction Initiatives*, UN/ISDR, Geneva, Switzerland

IUCN (International Union for Conservation of Nature) (2004) 'Global action for nature in a changing climate', Conclusions of a Meeting of IUCN's Climate Change Adaptation Working Group Convened by Conservation International, English Nature, IUCN, The Nature Conservancy, RSPB, Woodland Trust, WWF, IUCN, Gland, Switzerland

IUCN and UNEP-WCMC (2010) *The World Database on Protected Areas (WDPA): January 2010*, UNEP-WCMC, Cambridge, www.wdpa.org/Statistics.aspx, accessed 28 July 2010

Jacobs, NFO WorldGroup, Gibson, H., Hanley, N., Wright, R., Coulthard, N. and Oglethorpe, D. (2004) *Environment Group Research Report: An Economic Assessment of the Costs and Benefits of Natura 2000 Sites in Scotland*, Final Report, The Scottish Government, www.scotland.gov.uk/Resource/Doc/47251/0014580.pdf, accessed 10 November 2009

Jakarta Post (2004) 'Officials blamed for deforestation in Leuser', *Jakarta Post*, Jakarta, 30 July 2004

James, A. N., Gaston, K. J. and Balmford, A. (1999) 'Balancing the Earth's accounts', *Nature*, vol 401, pp323–324

James, A. N., Gaston, K. J. and Balmford, A. (2001) 'Can we afford to conserve biodiversity?' *BioScience*, vol 51, pp43–52

Kapos, V., Ravilious, C., Campbell, A., Dickson, B., Gibbs, H. K., Hansen, M. C., Lysenko, I., Miles, L., Price, J., Scharlemann, J. P. W. and Trumper, K. C. (2008) *Carbon and Biodiversity: A Demonstration Atlas*, UNEP-WCMC, Cambridge

Kettunen, M., Terry, A., Tucker, G. and Jones, A. (2007) 'Guidance on the maintenance of landscape connectivity features of major importance for wild flora and fauna', Guidance on the implementation of Article 3 of the Birds Directive and Article 10 of the Habitats Directive, http://ec.europa.eu/environment/nature/ecosystems/index_en.htm#art10, accessed 10 November 2009

Kettunen, M., Bassi, S., Gantioler, S. and ten Brink, P. (2009) *Assessing Socio-Economic Benefits of Natura 2000: A Toolkit for Practitioners* (November 2009 edition), Output of the European Commission project Financing Natura 2000: Cost estimate and benefits of Natura 2000, IEEP, Brussels

Kumari, K. (1994) 'Sustainable forest management in Peninsular Malaysia: Towards a total economic valuation approach', PhD thesis, University of East Anglia, UK

Leisher, C., van Beukering, P. and Scherl, L. M. (2007) *Nature's Investment Bank: How Marine Protected Areas Contribute to Poverty Reduction*, The Nature Conservancy, Arlington, VA

Leverington, F., Hockings, M. and Lemos Costa, K. (2008) *Management Effectiveness Evaluation in Protected Areas: A Global Study*, The University of Queensland, IUCN, WWF, The Nature Conservancy, Gatton, Queensland

Lutchman, I. (2005) *Marine Protected Areas: Benefits and Costs for Islands*, Icran, TNC, WCPA and WWF, http://icran.org/pdf/mpa_cost.pdf, accessed 10 November 2009

Martínez-Harms, M. J. and Gajardo, R. (2008) 'Ecosystem value in the Western Patagonia protected areas', *Journal for Nature Conservation*, vol 16, pp72–87

McAlpine, K. G. and Wotton, D. M. (2009) 'Conservation and the delivery of ecosystem services: A literature review', *Science for Conservation* 295, Department of Conservation, Wellington, New Zealand, www.doc.govt.nz/upload/documents/science-and-technical/sfc295entire.pdf, accessed 10 November 2009

McClanahan, T. R. and Mangi, S. (2000) 'Spillover of exploitable fishes from a marine park and its effect on the adjacent fishery', *Ecological Applications*, vol 10, no 6, pp1792–1805

Metsähallitus (2009) Kansallispuistojen ja retkeilyalueiden kävijöiden rahankäytön paikallistaloudelliset vaikutukset, Report 3017/52/2009, Metsähallitus (luontopalvelut) and Metla, available at www.metsa.fi/sivustot/metsa/fi/Eraasiatjaretkeily/Virkistyskaytonsuunnittelu/suojelualueidenmerkityspaikallistaloudelle/Documents/Kavijoiden%20paikallistaloudelliset%20vaikutukset.pdf, accessed 29 November 2010

Mmopelwa, G. and Blignaut, J. (2006) 'The Okavango Delta: The value of tourism', *SAJEMS*, vol 9, no 1, pp113–127

Mmopelwa. G., Blignaut, J. N. and Hassan, R. (2009) 'Direct use values of selected vegetation resources in the Okavango Delta wetland', *SAJEMS*, vol 12, no 2, pp242–255

Molina, F., Z'ophelan, C., Argandoña, J. and Campos, F. (2003) 'Planificación estratégica financiera para la gestión integral del las áreas protegidas del SNAP', Ministerio de Desarrollo Sostenible y Planificación, Servicio Nacional de Áreas Protegidas, La Paz, Bolivia

Mulongoy, K. J. and Gidda, S. B. (2008) *The Value of Nature: Ecological, Economic, Cultural and Social Benefits of Protected Areas*, CBD, Montreal

Naidoo, R. and Ricketts, T. H. (2006) 'Mapping the economic costs and benefits of conservation', *PLoS Biology*, vol 4, no 11

Naughton-Treves, L. (1997) 'Farming the forest edge: Vulnerable places and people around Kibale National Park, Uganda', *Geographical Review*, vol 87, no 1, pp27–46

Nelson, J. and Hossack, L. (2003) *From Principles to Practice: Indigenous Peoples and Protected Areas*, Forest Peoples Programme, Moreton-in-Marsh, UK

Ninan, K. N. and Satyapalan, J. (2005) 'The economics of biodiversity conservation: A study of a coffee growing village in the Western Ghats of India', *Ecological Economics*, vol 55, no 1, pp61–72

OECD (Organisation for Economic Co-operation and Development) (2008) *OECD Environmental Outlook to 2030: Executive Summary*, OECD Publishing, www.oecd.org/dataoecd/29/33/40200582.pdf, accessed 10 November 2009

OECD (2009) 'Biodiversity conservation: Financing needs and gaps', Presentation by H. Mountford, OECD, WGEAB Workshop, 2 July 2009, www.oecd.org/dataoecd/2/32/43311222.pdf, accessed 27 October 2010

Oestreicher, J. S., Benessaiah, K., Ruiz-Jaen, M.-C., Sloan, S., Turner, K., Pelletier, J., Guay, B., Clark, K. E., Roche, D. G., Meiners, M. and Potvin, C. (2009) 'Avoiding deforestation in Panamanian protected areas: An analysis of protection effectiveness and implications for reducing emissions from deforestation and forest degradation', *Global Environmental Change*, vol 19, no 2, pp279–291

O'Gorman, T. L. (2006) *Species and Poverty: Linked Futures*, WWF International, Gland, Switzerland

Pabon-Zamora L., Escobar, J. and Emerton L. (2009) *Valuing Nature: Why Bolivia's Protected Areas Matter for Economic and Human Well-Being*, The Nature Conservancy, Arlington, VA

Papageorgiou, S. (2008) 'Is it the money stupid! Is market environmentalism primarily a financing mechanism with scant regard for equity issues?', Essay for the option course in 'Ecosystems, Markets and Development', Environmental Change Institute, University of Oxford Centre for the Environment, Oxford

Pattanayak, S. K. and Wendland, K. J. (2007) 'Nature's care: Diarrhea, watershed protection and biodiversity conservation in Flores, Indonesia', *Biodiversity and Conservation*, vol 16, no 10, pp2801–2819

Pattanayak, S., Corey, C., Lau, Y. and Kramer, R. (2005) 'Forest malaria: A microeconomic study of forest protection and child malaria in Flores, Indonesia', RTI Working Paper 0505, Research Triangle Institute, Research Triangle Park, NC, http://nicholas.duke.edu/solutions/documents/forest-malaria.pdf, accessed 10 November 2009

Pauly, D., Christensen, V., Guénette, S., Pitcher, T. J., Rashid Sumaila, U., Walters, C. J., Watson, R. and Zeller, D. (2002) 'Towards sustainability in world fisheries', *Nature*, vol 418, pp689–695

Pearce, D. (2007) 'Do we really care about biodiversity', *Environmental Resource Economics*, vol 37, pp313–333

Pham, K. N., Tran, V. H. S., Cesar, H. and Pollnac, R. (2005) 'Financial sustainability of the Hon Mun Marine Protected Area: Lessons for other marine parks in Vietnam', Poverty Reduction and Environmental Management, Institute for Environmental Studies, The Netherlands

Portela, R. and Rademacher, I. (2001) 'A dynamic model of patterns of deforestation and their effect on the ability of the Brazilian Amazonia to provide ecosystem services', *Ecological Modelling*, vol 143, pp115–146

Potvin, C., Revéret, J.-P., Patenaude, G. and Hutton, J. (2002) 'The role of indigenous peoples in conservation actions: A case study of cultural differences and conservation priorities', in P. le Prestre (ed) *Governing Global Biodiversity: The Evolution and Implementation of the Convention on Biological Diversity*, Ashgate Publishing, Brookfield

PREM (Poverty Reduction and Environmental Management) (2006) Policy Brief No 11, June 2006, www.prem-online.org/archive/14/doc/11%20Sri%20Lanka%20policy%20brief.pdf, accessed 10 November 2009

Rayment, M., Bräuer, I., Chiabai, A., Gerdes, H. and ten Brink, P. (2009) 'The cost of policy inaction: The case of not meeting the 2010 biodiversity target. Database of ecosystem values – working draft', in P. ten Brink, M. Rayment, I. Bräuer, L. Braat, S. Bassi, A. Chiabai, A. Markandya, P. Nunes, M. van Oorschot, H. Gerdes, N. Stupak, V. Foo, J. Armstrong, M. Kettunen and S. Gantioler (eds) *Further Developing Assumptions on Monetary Valuation of Biodiversity Cost of Policy Inaction (COPI)*, European Commission project: Final report, Institute for European Environmental Policy (IEEP), London and Brussels

Redford, K. H., Levy, M. A., Sanderson, E. W. and de Sherbinin, A. (2008) 'What is the role for conservation organizations in poverty alleviation in the world's wild places?', *Oryx*, vol 42, pp516–528

Rodrigues, A. S. L., Andelman, S. J., Bakarr, M. I., Boitani, L., Brookes, T. M., Cowling, R. M., Fishpool, L. D. C., da Fonseca, G. A. B., Gaston, K. J., Hoffmann, M., Long, J. S., Marquet, P. A., Pilgrim, J. D., Pressey, R. L., Schipper, J., Sechrest, W., Stuart, S. N., Underhill, L. G., Waller, R. W., Watts, M. E. J. and Yan, X. (2004) 'Effectiveness of the global protected area network in representing species diversity', *Nature*, vol 428, pp640–643

RSPB (The Royal Society for the Protection of Birds), National Commission for Environment and Forestry (Sierra Leone) and the Conservation Society of Sierra Leone (2006) 'Sustainable financing for protected areas in Sierra Leone: A contribution towards developing the proposed World Bank GEF project', in M. Davies (ed) *Wildlife Protection and Biodiversity Conservation in Sierra Leone*

Ruiz, J. V. (2005) *Análisis de las Necesidades de Financiamiento del SINANPE 2005–2014*, PROFONANPE, Lima, Peru

Russ, G. R., Alcala, A. C. and Maypa, A. P. (2003) 'Spillover from marine reserves: The case of Naso Vlaingii at Apo Island, The Philippines', *Marine Ecology Progress Series*, vol 264, pp15–20, http://eprints.jcu.edu.au/6836/, accessed 28 July 2010

Sathirathai, S. (1998) 'Economic valuation of mangroves and the roles of local communities in the conservation of natural resources: Case study of Surat Thani, South Thailand', Economy and Environment Program for SE Asia, Singapore, unpublished report

Sathirathai, S. and Barbier, E. (2001) 'Valuing mangrove conservation in Southern Thailand', *Contemporary Economic Policy*, vol 19, no 2, pp109–122

Schuyt, K. and Brander, L. (2004) *The Economic Values of the World's Wetlands*, WWF, Gland, Switzerland

Shaffer, M. L., Scott, J. M. and Casey, F. (2002) 'Noah's options: Initial cost estimates of a national system of habitat conservation areas in the United States', *BioScience*, vol 52, no 5, pp439–443

Shrestha, R. K., Alavalapati, J. R. R., Siedl, A. F., Weber, K. E. and Suselo, T. B. (2006) 'Estimating the local cost of protecting Koshi Tappu Wildlife Reserve, Nepal: A contingent valuation approach', *Environment, Development and Sustainability*, vol 9, pp413–426

Slocombe, D. S. (2008) 'Forty years of institutional change and Canadian protected areas: Are things getting better or just more complicated?', Paper Commissioned for Canadian Parks for Tomorrow: 40th Anniversary Conference, 8–11 May 2008, University of Calgary, Canada, http://hdl.handle.net/1880/46879, accessed 10 November 2009

Stern, N. (2006) *Stern Review on the Economics of Climate Change*, Cambridge University Press, Cambridge

Stoate, C., Boatman, N. D., Borralho, R. J., Carvalho, C. R., de Snoo, G. R. and Eden, P. (2001) 'Ecological impacts of arable intensification in Europe', *Journal of Environmental Management*, vol 63, pp337–365

Stolton, S. and Dudley, N. (eds) (2010) *Arguments for Protected Areas: Multiple Benefits for Conservation and Use*, Earthscan, London

Stolton, S., Maxted, N., Ford-Lloyd, B., Kell, S. and Dudley, N. (2006) *Food Stores: Using Protected Areas to Secure Crop Diversity*, WWF and University of Birmingham, Gland, Switzerland and Birmingham, UK

Stolton S., Dudley, N. and Randall, J. (2008a) *Natural Security: Protected Areas and Hazard Mitigation*, WWF and Equilibrium, Gland, Switzerland, http://assets.panda.org/downloads/natural_security_final.pdf, accessed 10 November 2009

Stolton, S., Boucher, T., Dudley, N., Hoekstra, J., Maxted, N. and Kell, S. (2008b) 'Ecoregions with crop wild relatives are less well protected', *Biodiversity*, vol 9, pp52–55

Stolton, S., Ervin, J. and Dudley, N. (2008c) 'Editorial', *Parks*, vol 11, no 7, pp1–3

Taylor, M. and Figgis, P. (eds) (2007) *Protected Areas: Buffering Nature against Climate Change*, Proceedings of a WWF and IUCN World Commission on Protected Areas symposium, 18–19 June 2007, Canberra, WWF Australia, Sydney

TEEB in Local Policy (2011) *The Economics of Ecosystems and Biodiversity in Local and Regional Policy and Management* (ed H. Wittmer and H. Gundimeda), Earthscan, London

Trivedi, M., Papageorgiou, S. and Moran, D. (2008) *What Are Rainforests Worth? And Why It Makes Economic Sense to Keep Them Standing*, Forest Foresight Report 4, Global Canopy Programme, www.globalcanopy.org/files/what_are_rainforests_worth_1aug08.pdf, accessed 10 November 2009

Troëng, S. and Drews, C. (2004) *Money Talks: Economic Aspects of Marine Turtle Use and Conservation*, WWF, Gland, Switzerland, http://assets.panda.org/downloads/moneytalks.pdf, accessed 23 July 2010

Toman, M. (1998) 'Why not to calculate the value of the world's ecosystem services and natural capital', *Ecological Economics*, vol 25, no 1, pp 57–60

UNDP and TNC (The Nature Conservancy) (authors A. Bovarnick, J. Fernandez-Baca, J. Galindo and H. Negret) (2010) *Financial Sustainability of Protected Areas in Latin America and the Caribbean: Investment Policy Guidance*, United Nations Development Programme and TNC

UNEP (2003) *Our Planet – The Magazine of the United Nations Environment Programme*, vol 14 no 2, www.unep.org/ourplanet/imgversn/142/images/Our_Planet_14.2_english.pdf, accessed 27 October 2010

UNEP and CBD (2005) 'Options for mobilizing financial resources for the implementation of the Programme of Work by developing countries and countries with economies in transition', UNEP/CBD/WG-PA/1/3, Ad Hoc Open-Ended Working Group on Protected Areas, First meeting, Montecatini, Italy, 13–17 June 2005, www.cbd.int/doc/meetings/pa/pawg-01/official/pawg-01-03-en.pdf, accessed 10 November 2009

UNEP and CBD (2006) 'Managing national parks: How public-private partnerships can aid conservation', *World Bank Public Policy Journal*, UNEP/CBD/COP/8/INF/21, Note No 309, http://rru.worldbank.org/documents/publicpolicyjournal/309Saporiti.pdf, accessed 10 November 2009

UN Millennium Project (2005) *Environment and Human Well-Being: A Practical Strategy – Report of the Task Force on Environmental Sustainability*, Earthscan, London

van Beukering, P. J. H., Cesar, H. J. S. and Janssen, M. A. (2003) 'Economic valuation of the Leuser National Park on Sumatra, Indonesia', *Ecological Economics*, vol 44, pp43–62

van Rensburgh, T., Kelley, H. and Yadav, L. (2009) *Socio-Economics of Farming for Conservation in the Burren*, Prepared for the BurrenLIFE Project, www.burrenlife.com/Userfiles/socio-economic-report-burrenlife.1.pdf, accessed 28 July 2010

van Vuuren, W. and Roy, P. (1993) 'Private and social returns from wetland preservation versus those from wetland conversion to agriculture', *Ecological Economics*, vol 8, pp289–305

Verweij, P. A. and de Man, M. (2005) 'We cannot afford more biodiversity loss: The urgency of protected area financing', Greenpeace International, Amsterdam, www.greenpeace.org/protected-areas-financing, accessed 10 November 2009

Vreugdenhil, D. (2003) 'Modeling the financial needs of protected area systems: An application of the "minimum conservation system" design tool', Paper presented at the Fifth World Parks Congress, 8–17 September 2003, Durban, South Africa

Walpole, M. J. and Thouless, C. R. (2005) 'Increasing the value of wildlife through non consumptive use? Deconstructing the myths of ecotourism and community-based tourism in the tropics', in R. Woodroffe, S. Thirgood and A. Rabinowitz (eds) *People and Wildlife: Conflict or Co-existence?* Cambridge University Press, Cambridge, pp122–139

Watkins, S., Jamison, E., Salem, R., Flores, M., Weary, R. and Spensley, J. (2008) 'Supporting national implementation of the Programme of Work on Protected Areas: Lessons learned and ingredients of success', UNEP/CBD/WG-PA/2/INF/7, Paper submitted and discussed at the Second Meeting of the Ad Hoc Open-Ended Working Group on Protected Areas, FAO, Rome, 11–15 February 2008

Weladji, R. B. and Tchamba, M. N. (2003) 'Conflict between people and protected areas within the Bénoué Wildlilfe Conservation Area, North Cameroon', *Oryx*, vol 37, no 1, pp72–79

White, A. T., Vogt, H. P. and Arin, T. (2000) 'Philippine coral reefs under threat: The economic losses caused by reef destruction', *Marine Pollution Bulletin*, vol 40, no 7, pp598–605

Wilkie, D. S., Carpenter, J. F. and Zhang, Q. (2001) 'The under-financing of protected areas in the Congo Basin: So many parks and so little willingness to pay', *Biodiversity and Conservation*, vol 10, pp691–709

WWF (World Wide Fund for Nature) (2004) 'Are protected areas working? An analysis of forest protected areas by WWF', http://assets.panda.org/downloads/areprotectedareasworking.pdf, accessed 10 November 2009

WRI (World Resources Institute) in collaboration with UNDP (United Nations Development Programme), UNEP (United Nations Environment Programme) and World Bank World Resources (2005) *The Wealth of the Poor: Managing Ecosystems to Fight Poverty*, Washington, DC, http://population.wri.org/worldresources2005-pub-4073.html, accessed 10 November 2009

Yaron, G. (2001) 'Forest, plantation crops or small-scale agriculture? An economic analysis of alternative land use options in the Mount Cameroun Area', *Journal of Environmental Planning and Management*, vol 44, no 1, pp85–108

Annex 1

Table 8.A1 Key elements for successful implementation and relevant policy provisions

Key elements for successful implementation of protected areas	Relevant paragraphs of CBD COP Decision IX/18 on Protected Areas, some Ramsar resolutions, World Heritage Convention and UN Convention to Combat Desertification decisions
Capacity	• Establish or strengthen regional/sub-regional forum (para.A.6f) • Establish regional technical support networks (para.A.12) • Strengthen capacity of national PA professionals (para.A.13) • Convene regional capacity building workshops (para.A.15) • Further develop and make available a range of implementation tools (para.A.16) • Develop a user-friendly and comprehensive central website (para.A.17) • IUCN to further contribute to capacity building for implementation • Provide developing countries with assistance, including capacity building, in order to help reverse the factors leading to consideration of deletion or restriction of a Ramsar site: Ramsar Resolution IX.6, 12 • Promote the training of personnel in the fields of wetland research, management and wardening: Ramsar Article 4, 5 • Identify the training needs of institutions and individuals concerned with wetland conservation and wise use, and implement appropriate responses: Ramsar Strategic Plan 2003–2008, Operational Objective 20.1 • Include risk preparedness as an element in world heritage site management plans and training strategies: WHC Decision 28 COM 10B, 4 • Promote gender-sensitive capacity building to enable stakeholders to carry out specific participatory and synergistic programmes as part of their national action programmes to combat land degradation and mitigate the effects of drought, protect biodiversity, facilitate the regeneration of degraded forests, while promoting sustainable livelihoods at local level: UNCCD Decision 1/COP.6, 17
Capital	• Recognized the urgency for mobilizing adequate financial resources (preamble para.B.4) • Urged developed countries and others to provide adequate, predictable and timely financial support (para.B.1) • Parties to develop and implement sustainable financing plans based upon needs assessment and diversified portfolio (para.B.3 a, b and d) • Urged donor countries to enhance financial resources and technical support for implementation of the programme of work and ensure better alignment of PA funding with aid delivery mechanisms in the Paris Declaration on Aid Effectiveness (para.B.4d) • Invited GEF to continue to provide adequate funding including supporting protected areas under climate change (para.B.9 a and b) • Explore funding opportunities for PAs in the context of climate change (para.B.3h) • Provide developing countries with assistance to help reverse the factors leading to consideration of deletion or restriction of a Ramsar site: Ramsar Resolution IX.6, 12 • Increase support to States Parties for the identification of cultural, natural and mixed properties of potential outstanding universal value, as well as in the preparation of nomination dossiers: WHC Decision 28 COM 13.1, 11 (a) • Strengthen support for reforestation and forest conservation to combat desertification caused by drought, deforestation due to population increase, overgrazing, logging or fires; building on self-help efforts by developing countries: UNCCD Decision 21/COP.4, 2 and Decision 21/COP.4, Annex

Table 8.A1 Key elements for successful implementation and relevant policy provisions (*Cont'd*)

Key elements for successful implementation of protected areas	Relevant paragraphs of CBD COP Decision IX/18 on Protected Areas, some Ramsar resolutions, World Heritage Convention and UN Convention to Combat Desertification decisions
Coordination	• Establishment of multisectoral advisory committees (para.A.5b) • Designate a national focal point for PoWPA for coordinated development and implementation (para.A.21) • Parties, relevant intergovernmental organizations, ILCs, NGOs, donors, research institutions to establish regional support networks and enhance partnerships (para.A.12) • Mainstream and integrate PAs with development agendas (para.B.3e) • Promote international coordination of measures to further public awareness of wetland values in reserves: Ramsar Recommendation 5.8 • Collaborate with IUCN and provide support to the strategic implementation of the Global Framework Programme for Capacity Building on Natural Heritage: WHC Decision 29 COM 10, 6
Commitment	• Parties to finalize the ecological gap analysis not later than 2009 and give special attention to the implementation of programme element 2 and improving management effectiveness including monitoring (para.A.3, 4b and c) • Parties to improve, diversify and strengthen PA governance types and recognize co-managed areas and community-conserved areas through acknowledgement in national legislation. • Develop national and regional mechanisms to ensure consultation with local and indigenous people in management planning for Ramsar sites: Ramsar Recommendation 6.3, 15 • Involve local communities and indigenous peoples in restoring and maintaining wetlands: Ramsar Resolution VIII.16, 19 • Continue implementing the Regional Programme and the Action Plans adopted in Abu Dhabi to be developed into operational national work plans, and establish a fundraising strategy to provide the necessary financial and human resources: WHC Decision 30 COM 11C.1
Communication	• Recognized limited availability of information on implementation (para.A.1) • Increase public awareness on PA benefits in poverty eradication and achieving sustainable development (para.A.22) • Review and report national implementation (para.A.25a) • Promote valuation of PA goods and services including socio-economic costs and benefits of PAs (para.B.3d) • Develop facilities for promoting public awareness of wetland values at wetland reserves: Ramsar Recommendation 5.8 • Strengthen appreciation and respect for cultural and natural heritage, particularly by educational and information programmes: WHC Article 27, 1 • Develop initiatives at all levels to promote dialogue that will increase national and regional understanding for the protection of World Heritage: WHC Decision 27 COM 20B.6, 9

Chapter 9
Investing in Ecological Infrastructure

Coordinating lead author
Carsten Neßhöver

Lead authors
James Aronson, James Blignaut

Contributing authors
Florian Eppink, Alexandra Vakrou, Heidi Wittmer

Editing and language check
Clare Shine

See end of chapter for acknowledgements for reviews and other contributions

Contents

Key messages		403
Summary		404
1	**Is natural capital a worthwhile investment?**	404
	1.1 The ecological feasibility of natural capital enhancement	404
	1.2 Potential costs of ecosystem restoration	408
	1.3 Comparing costs and benefits of ecosystem restoration	412
	1.4 An indispensable role for governments	414
2	**Providing benefits beyond the environmental sector**	416
	2.1 Benefits for natural resource management	419
	2.2 Benefits for natural hazard prevention	422
	2.3 Benefits for human health	423
3	**Investing in ecosystems for climate change adaptation**	425
4	**Proactive strategies for making investment happen**	430
	4.1 Turning catastrophes and crises into opportunities	430
	4.2 Putting precaution into practice through green investment	431
Acknowledgements		433
References		433
Annex 1 Direct costs and potential benefits of restoration: Selected examples by ecosystem		442

Key messages

- Investing in 'ecological infrastructure' makes economic sense in terms of cost-effectiveness and rates of return, once we consider the full range of benefits provided by the maintained, restored or increased ecological services. Well-documented examples include investing in mangroves, other wetland ecosystems and watersheds, instead of man-made infrastructure like dikes or wastewater treatment plants, in order to sustain or enhance the provision of ecosystem services.

- It is usually much cheaper to avoid degradation than to pay for ecological restoration. This is particularly true for biodiversity: species that go extinct cannot be brought back. Nonetheless, there are many cases where the expected benefits from restoration far exceed the costs. If transformation of ecosystems is severe, true restoration of pre-existing species assemblages, ecological processes and the delivery rates of services may well be impossible. However, some ecosystem services can often be recovered by restoring simplified but well-functioning ecosystems modelled on the pre-existing local system.

- Investments in ecosystem restoration can benefit multiple policy sectors and help them to achieve their policy goals. This applies – but is not limited to – urban development, water purification and wastewater treatment, regional development, transport and tourism, as well as protection from natural hazards and policies for public health.

- In the light of expected needs for significant investment in adaptation to climate change, investment in restoring degraded ecosystems is directly relevant to many affected policy sectors. Key priorities are to maintain and enhance the productive capacity of agricultural systems under conditions of increased climate fluctuations and unpredictability and also providing buffering services against extreme weather events.

- Investment in natural capital and conservation of ecosystems can help to avoid crises and catastrophes or to mitigate their consequences. However, if catastrophes do strike, they should be regarded as opportunities to rethink policy and to incorporate greater investments in natural capital into new programmes and rebuilding efforts – e.g. mangrove or other coastal ecosystem restoration and protection following a tsunami or hurricane, wetland restoration and protection after flooding in coastal areas, forest restoration after a catastrophic mudslide.

- Direct government investment is often needed, since many returns lie in the realm of public goods and interests and will be realized only over the long term, but opportunities exist and can be expanded to create public–private partnerships. This applies especially to degraded sites and ecosystems such as post-mining areas, brownfield sites, converted forests, dredged wetlands and areas prone to erosion or desertification.

- Proactive strategies for investment in natural capital need to be further developed and implemented and to link natural capital explicitly with natural hazard risks. Systematic assessments of natural capital, creating natural capital accounting systems and maps pave the way for combining environmental risk reduction with economically efficient investment.

Summary

More and more, the complementary factor in short supply (limiting factor) is remaining natural capital, not man-made capital as it used to be. For example, populations of fish, not fishing boats, limit fish catch worldwide. Economic logic says to invest in the limiting factor. That logic has not changed, but the identity of the limiting factor has. (Herman Daly, former chief economist with the World Bank, 2005; cited in Aronson et al, 2006)

If we were running a business with the biosphere as our major asset, we would not allow it to depreciate. We would ensure that all necessary repairs and maintenance were carried out on a regular basis. (Professor Alan Malcolm, Chief Scientific Advisor, Institute of Biology, IUPAC, 2009)

This chapter focuses on ways to augment renewable natural capital – upon which our economies ultimately depend – by investing in the maintenance, restoration and rehabilitation of damaged or degraded ecosystems. Such investments can promote many different policy goals, including secure delivery of clean drinking water, natural disaster prevention or mitigation and climate change adaptation.

Section 1 shows how investments in renewable natural capital are worthwhile. Building on Chapter 8 (Protected Areas), it discusses the **costs and benefits of restoration** and identifies specific situations in which policy makers should consider directly investing public money in natural capital. Section 2 highlights the **benefits of ecosystem restoration beyond the environmental sector,** particularly for water management, natural hazard prevention and mitigation, and protection of human health. Section 3 explores the potential of ecosystem investments to deliver **concrete benefits for climate change mitigation and adaptation** policies. Section 4 concludes the chapter with proposals for **proactive investment strategies**, based on precaution, to provide benefits across a range of sectors.

1 Is natural capital a worthwhile investment?

Does investing in natural capital make economic sense? To answer this we have to determine:

- whether it is ecologically feasible to restore degraded natural capital or to invest in ecological infrastructure;
- whether restoring the natural capital in question is expected to generate significant benefits; and
- if investment is both possible and a high priority, what might it cost?

Only a few studies have comprehensively addressed these questions to date. However, they provide encouraging examples that illustrate the potential for a positive economic outcome. The following section highlights and synthesizes these results.

1.1 The ecological feasibility of natural capital enhancement

There is a lively debate between ecologists, planners and economists about the extent to which building 'designer' or engineered ecosystems – such as artificial wastewater treatment plants, fish farms at sea or roof gardens to help cool cities – can adequately respond to the huge problems facing humanity today. Increasingly, ecological restoration – and more broadly, the restoration of renewable natural capital – are seen as important targets for public and private spending to complement man-made engineering solutions.

True restoration to prior states is rarely possible, especially at large scales, given the array of global changes affecting biota everywhere and the fact that 'novel' ecosystems with unprecedented assemblages of organisms are increasingly prevalent (see Hobbs et al, 2006; Seastedt et al, 2008). Nevertheless, the growing body of available experience on the restoration and rehabilitation of degraded ecosystems suggests that this is a viable and important direction in which to work, provided that the goals set are pragmatic and realistic (Jackson and Hobbs, 2009).

Success stories do exist, such as providing nurseries for fish in mangroves, reconstructing natural wetlands for water storage, restoring entire forest ecosystems after centuries of over-use and reintroducing valuable species, e.g. sturgeon in the Baltic Sea to replenish fisheries. As catastrophic destruction of the world's coral reefs accelerates, effective restoration techniques are at last being developed (Normile, 2009).

Over the last 30 years, considerable progress has been made in our know-how both in fundamental (e.g. Falk et al, 2006) and practical realms (e.g. Clewell and Aronson, 2007). Ways and means to integrate restoration into society's search for global sustainability are moving forward quickly (Aronson et al, 2007; Goldstein et al, 2008; Jackson and Hobbs, 2009; Nellemann and Corcoran, 2010).

Box 9.1 shows how the concept and focus of restoration has gradually been broadened in recent years to encompass natural capital in order to better integrate ecological, environmental, social and economic goals and priorities.

Different restoration strategies

Depending on an ecosystem's level of degradation, different strategies can be applied to improve its state, or change its development trajectory altogether, and thereby enhance or increase its capacity to provide services in the future (Figure 9.1). The following ecosystem- and landscape-based framework for determining restoration strategies covers the three main scenarios.

Restoration

Where the spatial scale of damage is small and the surrounding environment is healthy in terms of species composition and function, it may be sufficient to implement measures for 'passive restoration' so that the ecosystem can regenerate itself to a condition resembling its pre-degradation state, or trajectory, in terms of its 'health, integrity, and self-sustainability' (SER, 2004, definition). This of course requires a series of decisions and trade-offs and thus is ultimately not a passive process at all (Clewell and McDonald, 2009).

If spontaneous or self-regeneration is not possible in a reasonable time period, active interventions may be necessary to 'jump-start' and accelerate the restoration process (e.g. by bringing in seeds, planting trees, removing polluted soil, adjusting the hydrological conditions of a body of water or reintroducing keystone species).

In both the above cases, reduction, modification and/or rationalization of human uses and pressures can lead to full or at least partial recovery of resilient, species-rich ecosystems that provide a reliable flow of ecosystem services valued by people. In both

Box 9.1 Key definitions and the expanding focus of restoration

Ecological restoration is defined as 'the process of assisting the recovery of an ecosystem that has been degraded, damaged, or destroyed' and is 'intended to repair ecosystems with respect to their health, integrity, and self-sustainability' (*Primer on Ecological Restoration*, published by the Society for Ecological Restoration International (SER, 2004). In a broader context, the *Primer* states that its ultimate goal is to recover resilient ecosystems that are not only self-sustaining with respect to structure, species composition and functionality but also integrated into larger landscapes and congenial to 'low-impact' human activities.

The concept of restoring natural capital is broader still.

'Natural capital' refers to the components of nature that can be linked directly or indirectly with human welfare. It includes biodiversity, endangered species and the ecosystems which perform ecological services in addition to traditional natural resources such as timber, water, and energy and mineral reserves. The Millennium Ecosystem Assessment (MA, 2003) considers natural capital as one of four types of capital along with manufactured capital, human capital and social capital (which includes networks that people can draw upon to solve common problems and plan for future generations) (see Figure 1.6, Chapter 1; Chapter 3; and TEEB Foundations (2010) Chapter 1).

'Ecological infrastructure' refers to the spatial context and describes any area which delivers services such as fresh water, microclimate regulation, recreation, etc., to a large proximate population, usually cities. This is sometimes referred to as green infrastructure.

Restoring renewable and cultivated natural capital (RNC) includes 'any activity that integrates investment in and replenishment of natural capital stocks to improve the flows of ecosystem goods and services, while enhancing all aspects of human wellbeing' (Aronson et al, 2007). Like ecological restoration, RNC aims to improve the health, integrity and self-sustainability of ecosystems for all living organisms. However, it also focuses on defining and maximizing the value and effort of ecological restoration and related activities for the benefit of people, thereby helping to mainstream RNC into routine social, cultural and economic activities.

RNC activities may include, but are not limited to:

- restoration and rehabilitation of terrestrial and aquatic ecosystems;
- ecologically sound improvements to arable lands and other lands or wetlands that are managed for production and other useful purposes (i.e. cultivated ecosystems);
- improvements in the ecologically sustainable utilization of biological resources on land, at sea and in wetlands; and
- establishment or enhancement of socio-economic activities and behaviour that incorporate knowledge, awareness, conservation and sustainable management of natural capital into daily activities, norms, markets and laws.

Put succinctly, RNC focuses on achieving replenishment of natural capital stocks and improvement in human welfare at both landscape and regional scales.

Source: Modified from Aronson et al (2007)

cases it is important to clarify objectives and priorities ahead of time (SER, 2004; Clewell and Aronson, 2006, 2007).

Rehabilitation

If transformation is severe and ecosystems have crossed one or more thresholds of irreversibility (Aronson et al, 1993), ecological rehabilitation may be a more realistic and adequate alternative than restoration. This aims to repair some ecosystem processes at a site and help recover the flow of certain ecological services, but not to fully reproduce pre-disturbance conditions or species composition. It is typically done on post-mining sites as well as grazing lands (Milton et al, 2003) and in wetlands used by people for production (see example in Box 9.4).

Reallocation

Where profound and extensive transformations of ecosystem structure and composition have taken place, it may be advisable to implement measures for reallocation of the most degraded areas. This means assigning them a new – usually economic – main function, which is generally unrelated to the functioning of the original ecosystem, e.g. farmland reallocated to housing and road construction.

Figure 9.1 illustrates this conceptual decision-making framework within the broader context of integrated ecosystem management at the landscape scale.

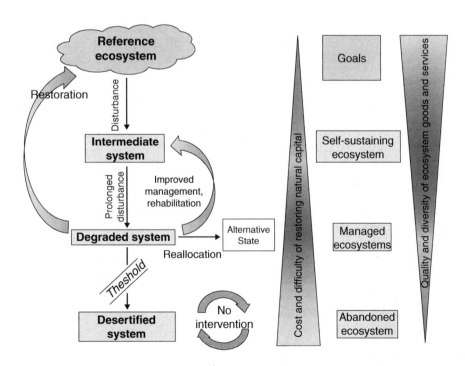

Figure 9.1 *Conceptual framework for restoration, rehabilitation and reallocation at the landscape level*

Source: Adapted after Aronson et al (2007)

As part of a holistic planning approach, various interventions can be undertaken simultaneously within appropriate landscape units of a given landscape. This type of integrated programme, if conceived and carried out effectively in close collaboration with all stakeholders, can provide the much-needed bridge between biodiversity conservation objectives, restoration priorities, and local, regional or national economic development needs (Aronson et al, 2006, 2007).

Restoration time scales

The time scale required for ecosystem restoration varies considerably (see Table 9.1). As noted, full restoration is not feasible for many ecosystems destroyed or degraded beyond a certain point. Even the less ambitious goal of rehabilitation (i.e. recovery to an acceptable state of ecosystem resilience, productivity and performance) tends to be a slow process though recovery may be quick in some instances (Jones and Schmitz, 2009). As the full benefits from restoration or rehabilitation may only become obvious at some time in the future, this reinforces the need to protect functioning ecosystems to maintain current levels of native biodiversity and flows of ecosystem goods and services.

However, the flow of some goods and services may increase from the early stages of a restoration programme (Rey Benayas et al, 2009), even if the optimum is only reached much later. Detailed information remains scarce but recent reviews show clearly that when done well, restoration across a wide range of ecosystem types can achieve enhancement of services even if full recovery is rarely possible (Janzen, 2002; Rey Benayas et al, 2009; Palmer and Filoso, 2009).

The modern approach for ecological restoration and RNC is therefore pragmatic. Jackson and Hobbs (2009, p568) state, for example, that 'restoration efforts might aim for mosaics of historic and engineered ecosystems, ensuring that if some ecosystems collapse, other functioning ecosystems will remain to build on. In the meantime, we can continue to develop an understanding of how novel and engineered ecosystems function, what goods and services they provide, how they respond to various perturbations, and the range of environmental circumstances in which they are sustainable.'

In summary, many restoration processes take considerable time but can often have rapid effects with respect to at least partial recovery of some key functions. From an ecological perspective, a strategy to avoid damage and maintain ecosystem functions and services should be preferred. However, given the scale of current damage, ecological restoration is increasingly required and understood to play an important role in bridging conservation and socio-economic goals, linked to better appreciation of the values of natural capital (see Aronson et al, 2007; Goldstein et al, 2008; Rey Benayas et al, 2009). Its crucial role is further illustrated by the fact that billions of dollars are currently being spent on ecological restoration around the world (Enserink, 1999; Zhang et al, 2000; Doyle and Drew, 2007; Stone, 2009).

1.2 Potential costs of ecosystem restoration

Thousands of projects are carried out each year to improve the ecological status of damaged ecosystems. Unfortunately and surprisingly, cost–benefit analyses of those projects are scarce. Even simple records of restoration costs are rare in the peer-reviewed literature, let alone a full discussion of the benefits to society (Aronson et al, 2010).

Table 9.1 Feasibility and time scales of restoring or rehabilitating different types of ecosystems: Examples from Europe

Ecosystem type	Time scale	Notes
Temporary pools	1–5 years	Even when rehabilitated, may never support all pre-existing organisms.
Eutrophic ponds	1–5 years	Rehabilitation possible provided adequate water supply. Readily colonized by water beetles and dragonflies but fauna restricted to those with limited specializations.
Mudflats	1–10 years	Restoration dependent upon position in tidal frame and sediment supply. Ecosystem services: flood regulation, sedimentation.
Eutrophic grasslands	1–20 years	Dependent upon availability of propagules. Ecosystem services: carbon sequestration, erosion regulation and grazing for domestic livestock and other animals.
Reedbeds	10–100 years	Will readily develop under appropriate hydrological conditions. Ecosystem services: stabilization of sedimentation, hydrological processes.
Saltmarshes	10–100 years	Dependent upon availability of propagules, position in tidal frame and sediment supply. Ecosystem services: coastal protection, flood control.
Oligotrophic grasslands	20–100 years +	Dependent upon availability of propagules and limitation of nutrient input. Ecosystem services: carbon sequestration, erosion regulation.
Chalk grasslands	50–100 years +	Dependent upon availability of propagules and limitation of nutrient input. Ecosystem services: carbon sequestration, erosion regulation.
Yellow dunes	50–100 years +	Dependent upon sediment supply and availability of propagules. More likely to be restored than recreated. Main ecosystem service: coastal protection.
Heathlands	50–100 years +	Dependent upon nutrient loading, soil structure and availability of propagules. No certainty that vertebrate and invertebrate assemblages will arrive without assistance. More likely to be restored than recreated. Main ecosystem services: carbon sequestration, recreation.
Grey dunes and dune slacks	100–500 years	Potentially restorable, but in long time frames and depending on intensity of disturbance. Main ecosystem service: coastal protection, water purification.
Ancient woodlands	500–2000 years	No certainty of success if ecosystem function is sought – dependent upon soil chemistry and mycology plus availability of propagules. Restoration possible for plant assemblages and ecosystem services (water regulation, carbon sequestration, erosion control) but questionable with respect to rare invertebrates, and other groups.
Blanket/raised bogs	1000–5000 years	Probably impossible to restore quickly but will gradually reform themselves over millennia if given the chance. Main ecosystem service: carbon sequestration.
Limestone pavements	10,000 years	Impossible to restore quickly but will reform over many millennia if a glaciation occurs.

Source: Based on Morris and Barham (2007)

Over 20,000 case studies and peer-reviewed papers were reviewed for this chapter (and for TEEB Foundations, 2010, Chapter 7), yet only 96 studies were found to provide meaningful cost data on restoration (Aronson et al, 2010). The breadth and quality of information that is available varies from study to study. Some only provide aggregate costs, others only capital or labour costs. Some restoration activities are conducted on a small scale for research purposes only.

An analysis of the relevant studies gives an overview of restoration project costs and outcomes. They cover a wide range of different efforts in different ecosystem types as well as very different costs, ranging between several hundreds to thousands of dollars per hectare (grasslands, rangelands and forests) to several tens of thousands (inland waters) to millions of dollars per hectare (coral reefs) (see Figure 9.2). Costs

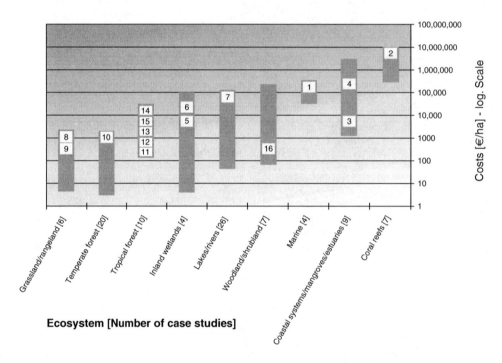

Figure 9.2 *Summary of cost ranges of restoration efforts*

Note: Bars represent the range of observed costs in a set of 96 studies reviewed for this study. The numbers refer to specific studies identified and listed below as illustrative examples of the studies in which cost data have been reported in sufficient detail to allow analysis and comparison. For further details, see Annex 1.

Sources: Aronson et al (2010) and additional studies: (1) Eelgrass restoration in harbour (Leschen et al, 2007); (2) Restoration of coral reefs in South-east Asia (Fox et al, 2005); (3) Restoration of mangroves, Port Everglades, US (Lewis Environmental Services, 2007); (4) Restoration of the Bolsa Chica Estuary, California, US (Francher, 2008); (5) Restoration of freshwater wetlands in Denmark (Hoffmann and Baattrup-Pedersen, 2007); (6) Control of phosphorus loads in stormwater treatment wetlands (Juston and DeBusk, 2006); (7) Restoration of the Skjern River, Denmark (Skovognatur, 2007); (8) Re-establishment of eucalyptus plantation, Australia (Dorrough and Moxham, 2005); (9) Restoring land for bumblebees, UK (Pywell et al, 2006); (10) Restoration in Coastal British Columbia Riparian Forest, Canada (GRN, 2007); (11) Masoala Corridors Restoration, Masoala National Park, Madagascar (Holloway et al, 2009); (12) Restoration of Rainforest Corridors, Madagascar (Holloway and Tingle, 2009); (13) Polylepis forest restoration, tropical Andes, Peru (Jameson and Ramsey, 2007); (14) Restoration of old-fields, NSW, Australia (Neilan et al, 2006); (15) Restoration of Atlantic Forest, Brazil (Instituto Terra, 2007); (16) Working for Water, South Africa (Turpie et al, 2008).

also vary as a function of the degree of degradation, the goals and specific circumstances in which restoration is carried out and the methods used.

One way to decide whether investments are worthwhile from an economic perspective is to compare the benefits of services provided by ecosystems with those of technically supplied services – and the costs to provide them. The most famous example of this type of cost-effectiveness estimation is New York City's decision to protect and restore the Catskill–Delaware Watershed (see Box 9.2 and also Chapter 5).

Cost-effectiveness analysis often focuses only on one particular ecosystem service. In the example discussed in Box 9.2, watershed protection and restoration costs were more

---

Box 9.2 Cost-effectiveness of protection and restoration over engineered solutions: Example of a US watershed

It represents a commitment among all of the parties – the city, state and federal government – to focus on the challenges of protecting the source water supply rather than pursue a costly and gargantuan construction project. (Eric A. Goldstein, senior lawyer for the Natural Resources Defense Council, quoted in DePalma, 2007)

Even in industrialized countries, such as the US, restoration of watersheds is an increasingly attractive alternative. The decision summarized below sustainably increased the supply of drinking water and saved several billion dollars that would have otherwise have been spent on engineering solutions (Elliman and Berry, 2007). A similar project is under way on the Sacramento River Basin in northern California (Langridge et al, 2007).

About 90 per cent of the more than 1 billion gallons of fresh water used daily in New York City comes from huge reservoirs in the adjacent Catskill and Delaware watersheds, located approximately 120 miles north of the city. The remaining 10 per cent are drawn from the nearer Croton reservoirs in Westchester County (these are surrounded by development and thus have to be filtered). A US$2.8 billion filtration plant for the Croton water supply is under construction in the Bronx and scheduled to be operational by 2012.

In April 2007, after a detailed review lasting several years, the US federal Environment Protection Agency concluded that the Catskill and Delaware water supplies were still so clean that they did not need to be filtered for another decade or longer and extended the City's current exemption from filtration requirements. This means that at least until 2017, the City will not have to spend approximately US$10 billion to build an additional filtration plant that would cost many millions of dollars a year to operate.

In return for this extended exemption, the City agreed to set aside US$300 million per year until 2017 to acquire upstate land to restrain development causing run-off and pollution. It will purchase land outright or work with non-profit land trusts to acquire easements that would keep land in private hands but prohibit their development (see Chapter 5, Section 3.1). The City also committed itself to reduce the amount of turbidity (cloudiness) in certain Catskill reservoirs by erecting screens, building baffles and using other technology to allow sediment to settle before water enters the final parts of the drinking water system.

Sources: DePalma (2007); Elliman and Berry (2007); Langridge et al (2007)

than compensated for by a single service (water purification). However, investing in natural capital enhancement becomes even more economically attractive if the multitude of services that healthy ecosystems provide are taken into account, e.g. climate regulation, food and fibre provision, hazard regulation. This calls for identification and valuation of the broad range of benefits of natural capital investment in order to adequately compare costs and benefits of ecosystem restoration approaches.

1.3 Comparing costs and benefits of ecosystem restoration

As noted above, few studies analysing the costs of restoration exist to date, and even fewer provide values or detailed analysis of the achieved or projected benefits. This section explores the findings of two studies on the benefits and costs of mangrove restoration and then provides a synthesis of findings across a range of studies, adding calculations of potential benefits from the work of TEEB (TEEB Foundations, 2010).

Following the 2004 Asian Tsunami disaster, there is now considerable interest in rehabilitating and restoring 'post-shrimp-farming' mangroves in Southern Thailand as natural barriers to future coastal storm events (see also Chapter 9, Section 4.1). Yields from commercial shrimp farming sharply decline after five years, after which shrimp farmers usually give up their ponds to find a new location. One study found that the abandoned mangrove ecosystems can be rehabilitated at a cost of US$8240 per hectare in the first year (replanting mangroves) followed by annual costs of US$118 per hectare for maintenance and protecting of seedlings (Sathirathai and Barbier, 2001, p119). Benefits from the restoration project comprise the estimated net income from collected forest products of US$101 per hectare/year, estimated benefits from habitat–fishery linkages (mainly the functioning of mangroves as fish nursery) worth US$171 per hectare/year and estimated benefits from storm protection worth US$1879 per hectare/year (Barbier, 2007, p211).

In order to compare costs and benefits of restoration, we need to recognize that rehabilitating mangroves takes time and that associated ecosystem services may never fully reach pre-degradation levels. Benefits were therefore accounted for in TEEB calculations on a gradual basis, starting at 10 per cent in the second year and increasing every year until eventually capped in the sixth year at 80 per cent of pre-degradation levels (TEEB Foundations, 2010).

Applying these assumptions, and a 10 per cent discount rate, the rehabilitation project would pay off after 13 years. If lower discount rates (as argued for in TEEB Foundations (2010) Chapter 6) are applied, the cost–benefit ratio of the restoration project improves. At a discount rate of 1 per cent, the project would pay off after nine years. If one extends the calculation to 40 years, the project generates a benefit/cost ratio of 4.3 and a social rate of return of 16 per cent (instead of 'internal rate of return' we use 'social rate of return' to highlight that some of the public benefits have been considered besides private benefits). It should be noted that these calculations still do not account for the wide range of other ecosystem services that may be attached to the presence of mangroves, ranging from microclimate effects and water purification to recreational values. If properly taken into account, this would increase the total benefits much further.

The example mentioned above is one of the few cases where decisions can be taken on the basis of solid data. For cases in other biomes, where only cost data was available, the TEEB team estimated potential benefits based on a 'benefits transfer' approach, i.e. taking results from valuation studies in similar ecosystems as a basis for estimating potential benefits for the biomes concerned. The estimation of benefit values was based on the results of 104 studies with 507 values covering up to 22 different ecosystem services for nine major biomes. These documented values were the basis to estimate the benefit of a restored or rehabilitated ecosystem. Recognizing that projects take time to restore flows of benefits, an appropriate accreting profile was modelled for annual benefits, growing initially and then stabilizing at 80 per cent of undisturbed ecosystem benefits (see TEEB Foundations, 2010). This approach makes it possible to carry out an illustrative comparison. Clearly, careful site-specific analysis of costs and benefits is required before any investment decision: the example listed below should therefore be seen simply as indicating the scope for potential benefits.

When calculating the potential benefits for individual biomes, we found high potential social rates of return for all biomes. These calculations are rough first estimates for two reasons: they do not include opportunity costs of alternative land use (which can be expected to be rather low in many degraded systems) and the value base on which the benefit transfer is based is small for some of the services considered. A detailed analysis is therefore recommended before investing in restoration. Nevertheless, these values indicate that in many situations high returns can be expected from restoration of ecosystems and their services within very attractive time frames.

For example, a study by Dorrough and Moxham (2005) found that cost for restoring eucalyptus woodlands and dry forests in south-east Australia, on land previously used for intensive cattle farming, would range from €285/ha for so-called passive restoration to €970/ha for active interventions aimed at restoration (currency converted from AUD on 2007 basis). Restoration of tree cover yields numerous benefits including reversing the loss of biodiversity, halting land degradation due to dryland salinization and thereby increasing land productivity. Using a benefit transfer approach and a discount rate of 1 per cent over 40 years, these services may constitute a net present value (NPV) of more than €13,000/ha.

Along the Mata Atlantica in Brazil, the Instituto Terra non-profit organization undertakes active restoration of degraded stands of Atlantic Forest by establishing tree nurseries to replant denuded areas (Instituto Terra, 2007). The costs for this approach are estimated at €2600/ha as a one-off investment. Benefits include biodiversity enhancement, water regulation, carbon storage and sequestration as well as preventing soil erosion. Using the benefit transfer approach, a 40-year NPV of tropical forests may reach €80,000/ha (1 per cent discount rate).

In South Africa the government-funded Working for Water (WfW) programme (see also Box 9.5) clears mountain catchments and riparian zones of invasive alien plants in order to restore natural fire regimes, the productive potential of land, biodiversity and hydrological functioning. WfW uses a special kind of payments for ecosystem services (PES) scheme (see Chapter 5, Section 1): previously unemployed individuals tender for contracts to restore public or private lands. By using this approach, costs to rehabilitate catchments range from €200 to €700 per hectare (Turpie et al, 2008) while benefits may reach a 40-year NPV of €47,000/ha (using the benefit transfer approach described above and a 1 per cent discount rate).

As these case studies and benefits transfer analysis show, restoration can pay. However, the costs are also quite high and many ecosystems cannot be effectively restored within reasonable time scales (see Table 9.1 above). For these reasons, it is much better to conserve these ecosystems rather than letting them degrade and then trying to undertake restoration. Moreover, systematic estimation of the potential costs and economic benefits of preservation and restoration needs to be better incorporated into the projects themselves.

Valuation of ecosystem services can help by enabling policy makers to decide which investments are worthwhile from an economic point of view and to make informed choices (TEEB Foundations, 2010). It is particularly important as many ecosystems currently have unrecognized economic and social benefits (see Milton et al, 2003; FAO, 2004; Bullock et al, 2007; de Groot et al, 2007; Blignaut et al, 2008; Blignaut and Aronson, 2008).

1.4 An indispensable role for governments

In spite of the potentially high internal rates of return, investment in natural capital seems to be a story of unrealized potential. This is largely because the benefits of such investments often lie far in the future or accrue over long periods of time which means that, with some exceptions, private investment is unlikely to occur unless it is supported or required by governments. Governments can provide incentives for this purpose by paying for or subsidizing private activities such as reforestation with native trees (see Chapters 5 and 6) and/or by prescribing mandatory offsets to mitigate wetland, coastal or terrestrial ecosystem degradation or destruction caused by human activities (see Chapter 7).

There are several good reasons why governments should also consider directly investing public funds in natural capital and its restoration. The first relates to large-scale and complex interrelated ecosystems where the costs of restoration can be very high, due to the size of the restoration site, the level of degradation and/or uncertainties about the technical efforts needed, e.g. potentially contaminated brownfields, mining areas or other heavily degraded areas. An interesting example in this regard is the Aral Sea (Box 9.3) which has suffered from catastrophic environmental damage.

Box 9.3 A natural capital 'mega-project': Example of the Aral Sea restoration

The Aral Sea was the world's fourth largest freshwater lake 50 years ago; it supported a large and vibrant economy based on fisheries, agriculture and trade in goods and services. In the 1960s, however, the two main rivers flowing into the Aral Sea were massively diverted for cotton cultivation and the Sea began to shrink and to split into smaller pieces – the 'Northern Aral' and 'Southern Aral' seas. Although large amounts of cotton were grown and exported in subsequent decades, thousands of jobs were lost in other sectors, the surrounding environment was severely degraded and the health of local people deteriorated. By 1996, the Aral Sea's surface area was half its original size and its volume had been reduced by 75 per cent. The southern part had further split into eastern and western lobes, reducing much of the former sea to a salt pan.

Against this background, neighbouring countries initiated several interventions intended to 'restore' the Aral Sea. In 2005, Kazakhstan built the Kok-Aral Dam between the lake's northern and southern portions to preserve water levels in the north. The Northern Aral actually exceeded expectations with the speed of its recovery, but the dam ended prospects for a recovery of the Southern Aral. According to Badescu and Schuiling (2009), there are now three main restoration options:

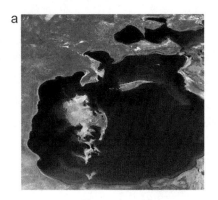 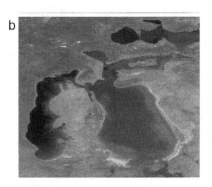

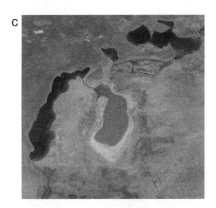

Figure 9.3 *Images of the Aral Sea: (a) 1989; (b) 2003; and (c) 2009*

Source: NASA (2008)

1   halting cotton production and letting the waters of the two feed rivers (Amu Darya and Syr Darya) flow naturally into the Aral Sea;
2   diverting waters from the Ob and other major Siberian rivers to the Aral Sea; or
3   building a new inter-basin water supply canal, including a long tunnel from Lake Zaisan to the Balkhash Lake.

All three options involve very high costs and there are considerable uncertainties about the ultimate restoration benefits.

To further illustrate the scale and complexity of the problem and its possible solutions, the implications for climate regulation also need to be considered. The discharge of major Siberian rivers into the Arctic Ocean appears to be increasing. This could affect the global oceanic 'conveyor belt' with potentially severe consequences for the climate in western and northern Europe. By diverting part of this river water towards the Aral Sea, a 'mega' restoration project could have potential beneficial effects on climate, human health, fishery and ecology in general (Badescu and Schuiling, 2009).

Sources: Micklin and Aladin (2008); Badescu and Schuiling (2009); World Bank (2009a)

Typically, large-scale and complex restoration projects involve costs that exceed the benefits identified by private parties – even though the public benefits of restoration are likely to be higher. It may therefore be necessary for governments to invest in such efforts, on behalf of the common interest in those countries. Opportunities to develop public–private restoration partnerships are increasing and need not only to be considered but also to be fostered by forward-looking government agencies.

The second justification for direct government investment relates to situations where early action is likely to be the most cost-effective approach. Here policy makers need to understand the close relationship between prevention and response. Upfront precautionary measures to avoid damage are the best way to minimize long-term socio-economic and environmental costs (see the example of invasive species in Box 9.4).

Innovative and integrated regional or landscape-scale programmes to restore or rehabilitate degraded natural systems can make use of PES-type instruments (Blignaut et al, 2008; see also Chapter 5).

Government investment may also be called for in situations where potential beneficiaries are unable to afford restoration costs. Box 9.5 illustrates how livelihoods can be improved alongside degraded ecosystems.

In Ecuador, two PES-funded restoration programmes include the 6-year-old Pimampiro municipal watershed protection scheme and the 13-year-old PROFAFOR carbon-sequestration programme (Wunder and Albán, 2008). Pimampiro is mostly focused on forest conservation but has also led to some abandonment of marginal farmland that landowners have allowed to revert to forest and then enrolled within the scheme. PROFAFOR is a voluntary programme for afforestation and reforestation, mainly on degraded lands, that received carbon credit certification. Many more are under way elsewhere in Latin America, Asia and, with some lag time, Africa and Madagascar. Countries making significant strides in this area include Costa Rica (Morse et al, 2009), Indonesia (Pattanayak, 2004; Pattanayak and Wendland, 2007) and South Africa (Holmes et al, 2007; Mills et al, 2007; Blignaut and Loxton, 2007; Turpie et al, 2008; Koenig, 2009).

In summary, there is growing evidence of a positive correlation between investment and benefits from ecological restoration, both in terms of biodiversity and ecosystem services (Rey Benayas et al, 2009). However, the funds available are far less than what is needed. It is critical to plan and budget investments at the landscape and regional scales so as to maximize returns on investments in ecological, social and economic terms.

2 Providing benefits beyond the environmental sector

Investing in natural capital does not only concern the environmental sector. Other policy sectors can also reap benefits from public investment to ensure or enhance the delivery of services provided by natural capital. Considering all benefits provided by ecosystems can make investments worthwhile, whereas approaches focused on single sectors and services may not.

A wide range of sectors – especially those dealing with natural hazard prevention, natural resource management, planning, water provision, alternative energy sources, waste management, agriculture, transport, tourism or social affairs – can gain from explicitly considering and valuing the services provided by natural capital. Investing in natural capital can thus create additional values, especially where natural capital has itself become the limiting factor to economic development (Herman Daly, quoted in Aronson et al, 2006).

2.1 Benefits for natural resource management

The limits of natural capital are most obvious in natural resource management. Fisheries, agriculture, forestry and water management directly depend on its maintenance in a healthy state. Ecological degradation (e.g. soil erosion, desertification, reduced water supply, loss of wastewater filtering) impacts on productivity, livelihoods and economic opportunities (see Box 9.5).

Increased investments in ecological infrastructure to harness and optimize freshwater resources can complement or replace technical infrastructure systems (Londong et al, 2003). Optimizing microbial activity in rivers through renaturalization of riverbeds has been shown to improve water quality at lower costs than by clean-up through water treatment plants. Big cities like Rio de Janeiro, Johannesburg, Tokyo, Melbourne, New York and Jakarta all rely on protected areas to provide residents with drinking water, which offer a local alternative to piping water from further afield and cost less than building filtration plants (see also Box 9.2). Further examples include:

- In Venezuela, only 18 national parks cater to the freshwater needs of 19 million people (83 per cent of the country's population inhabiting large cities). About 20 per cent of the country's irrigated lands depend on protected areas for their irrigation water (Pabon-Zamora et al, 2008).

Box 9.5 Valuation of livelihood benefits arising from ecosystem rehabilitation in South Africa

The Manalana wetland (near Bushbuckridge, Mpumalanga) was severely degraded by erosion that threatened to consume the entire system if left unchecked. The wetland supports around 100 small-scale farmers, 98 of whom are women. Approximately 70 per cent of local people make use of the wetland in some way, with about 25 per cent depending on it as their sole source of food and income. The wetland was thus considered to offer an important safety net, particularly for the poor, contributing about 40 per cent of locally grown food.

The 'Working for Wetlands' public works programme intervened in 2006 to reduce the erosion and improve the wetland's ability to continue providing its beneficial services. An economic valuation study completed in 2008 revealed that:

- the value of livelihood benefits derived from the degraded wetland was just 34 per cent of what could be achieved after investment in ecosystem rehabilitation;
- the rehabilitated wetland now contributes provisioning services conservatively estimated at a net return, i.e. after making provision for costs, of €297/household per year;
- the total economic value of the livelihood benefits (€182,000) provided by the rehabilitated wetland is more than twice what it cost to undertake the rehabilitation works (€86,000), indicating a worthwhile return on investment by 'Working for Wetlands';
- the Manalana wetland acted as a safety net that buffered households from slipping further into poverty during times of shock or stress.

Source: Pollard et al (2008)

Box 9.4 The economic case for government-led rapid response to invasive species

Invasive species are widely recognized to be one of the major threats to biodiversity and ecosystem functioning (Vitousek et al, 1997; Mack et al, 2000; van der Wal et al, 2008). Several economic studies estimate the scale of damage and management costs they impose on society (e.g. van Wilgen, 2001; Turpie, 2004; Turpie et al, 2008). A well-known assessment of environmental and economic costs in the US, UK, Australia, South Africa, India and Brazil, carried out in 2001 (Pimentel et al, 2001), estimated the costs of invasive species across these six countries to exceed US$314 billion/year, equivalent to US$240 per person. An update in 2005 estimated the costs for the US at US$120 billion/year (Pimentel et al, 2005). Assuming similar costs worldwide, Pimentel et al (2001) estimated that invasive species damage costs global society more than US$1.4 trillion per year, representing nearly 5 per cent of world GDP. A recent review by Kettunen et al (2009) suggests that damage and control costs of invasive alien species in Europe are at least €12 billion/year. Table 9.2 presents examples of the costs of single invasive species in European countries (Vilà et al, 2009).

A biological invasion is a dynamic, non-linear process and, once initiated, is largely self-perpetuating (Richardson et al, 2000; Kühn et al, 2004; Norton, 2009). In the majority of cases, invasions are only reversible at high cost (Andersen et al, 2004). An introduced species may appear harmless for a long time, and only be identified as harmful after it has become difficult and costly – or impossible – to eradicate, control or contain (Ricciardi and Simberloff, 2008). For these reasons, prevention should always be the preferred management option where feasible, and consistent with CBD provisions and guiding principles (CBD, 1993; Bertram, 1999; CBD, 2002; Finnoff et al, 2006). Delayed intervention increases the cost of intervention and thus the period required before the benefits potentially outweigh the costs. For example, Japanese knotweed (*Fallopia japonica*) is invasive in several EU Member States and elsewhere. It is estimated that in Wales, a three-year eradication programme would have cost about €59 million (£53.3 million) if started in 2001 but around €84 million (£76 million) if started in 2007 (Defra, 2007).

Table 9.2 *Alien species in Europe generating some of the highest costs*

Species	Biome/taxa	Country	Extent	Cost item	Period	Cost (million €/year	Reference
Carpobrotus spp.	Terrestrial plant	Spain	Localities	Control/eradication	2002–2007	0.58	Andreu et al (2009)
Anoplophora chinensis	Terrestrial invertebrate	Italy	Country	Control	2004–2008	0.53	van der Gaag (2007)

Table 9.2 Alien species in Europe generating some of the highest costs (*Cont'd*)

Species	Biome/taxa	Country	Extent	Cost item	Period	Cost (million €/year	Reference
Cervus nippon	Terestrial vertebrate	Scotland	Localities	Control		0.82	White and Harris (2002)
Myocastor coypus	Terestrial vertebrate	Italy	Localities	Control/damages	1995–2000	2.85	Panzacchi et al (2007)
Sciurus carolinensis	Terestrial vertebrate	UK	Country	Control	1994–1995	0.46	White and Harris (2002)
Azolla filiculoides	Freshwater plant	Spain	Protected area	Control/eradication	2003	1.00	Andreu et al (2009)
Eichhornia crassipes	Freshwater plant	Spain	River basin	Control/eradication	2005–2007	3.35	Andreu et al (2009)
Oxyura jamaicensis	Freshwater vertebrate	UK	Country	Eradication	2007–2010	0.75	Scalera and Zaghi (2004)
Chrysochromulina polylepis	Marine algae	Norway	Country	Toxic bloom		8.18	Hopkins (2002)
Rhopilema nomadica	Marine invertebrate	Israel	Coast	Infrastructure damage	2001	0.04	Galil and Zenetos (2002)

Note: Values are actual expenditures and not estimates or Extrapolations

Source: Vilà et al (2009)

Box 9.6 Socio-economic benefits from grassland restoration projects, South Africa

In the Drakensberg mountains, local communities depend heavily on various ecosystem services for their livelihoods. By restoring degraded grasslands and riparian zones and changing the regimes for fire management and grazing, early results suggest that it may be possible to increase base water flows during low-flow periods (i.e. winter months when communities are the most vulnerable to not having access to any other source of water) by an additional 3.9 million m^3. Restoration and improved land-use management should also reduce sediment load by 4.9 million m^3/year.

While the sale value of the water is approximately €250,000/year, the economic value added of the additional water is equal to €2.5 million/year. The sediment reduction saves €1.5 million per year in costs, while the value of the additional carbon sequestration is €2 million/year. These benefits are a result of an investment in restoration that is estimated to cost €3.6 million over seven years and which will have annual management costs of €800,000/year. The necessary ongoing catchment management will create 310 permanent jobs, while about 2.5 million person-days of work will be created during the restoration phase.

Source: MDTP (2008)

- Venezuela has a potential for generating hydroelectricity equivalent to the production of 2.5 million barrels of oil per day (it currently produces 3.2 million barrels of oil per day). Of course careful planning is required in order to minimize negative ecological impacts of any new dams that might be built (Pabon-Zamora et al, 2008).
- In Peru, around 2.7 million people use water that originates from 16 protected areas with an estimated value of US$81 million/year (Pabon-Zamora et al, 2009).

Like sponges, forests soak up water and release it slowly, limiting floods when it rains and storing water for dry periods. Watershed and catchment protection near cities is therefore a matter of economic, ecological and social common sense (Benedict and McMahon, 2008); as noted above, it may justify payments for environmental services (see Chapter 5).

These benefits are attributable not only to protected areas but also to wider ecosystems. Sound management is needed to maintain and ensure the continuous provision of these ecosystem services. Restoration can help to keep ecosystems functioning at levels that can in principle be calculated and managed. Boxes 9.6 (above) and 9.7 and 9.8 (across) present some examples of costed approaches.

Box 9.7 Multiple benefits from wetland restoration in the Everglades, Florida

Much of the unique Everglades ecosystem, which is of enormous natural beauty and the region's primary source of water, was drained in the early 1900s to make way for the cities of Miami and Fort Lauderdale. The remaining wetlands (outside the 600,000km² Everglades National Park) have suffered heavily from pollution and further drainage in the last two decades (Salt et al, 2008).

To improve the quality and secure the supply of drinking water for south Florida and protect dwindling habitat for about 69 species of endangered plants and animals (including the emblematic Florida panther, of which only 120 individuals survive in the wild) the US Congress enacted the Comprehensive Everglades Restoration Plan (CERP) in 2000. The total cost of the 226 projects to restore the ecosystem's natural hydrological functions is estimated at close to US$20 billion (Polasky, 2008).

The return on this investment, generally lower than the costs, relates to different sectors and concerns, including agricultural and urban water supply, flood control, recreation, commercial and recreational fishing and wildlife habitat protection (Milon and Hodges, 2000). However, many benefits – especially as regards the cultural value of the intact ecosystem – can only be measured indirectly as there are no markets for these non-use values. For the Everglades, a study covering non-use values shows that the overall benefits are in a similar range to the costs of restoration, depending on the discount rate used (Milon and Scroggins, 2002).

Box 9.8 Reducing poverty by investing in floodplain restoration in Cameroon

The Waza floodplain (8000km²) is a high-productivity area and critical for biodiversity maintenance in Cameroon. While it is extremely important for the human population, it is also very fragile with fluctuating levels of rainfall, widespread poverty and precarious living conditions. Around 125,000 people depend on services provided by this floodplain ecosystem for their subsistence livelihoods, and the floodplain in turn depends to a large extent on annual flooding of the Logone River. In 1979, construction of a large irrigated rice scheme reduced flooding by almost 1000km² which had devastating effects on the region's ecosystems, biodiversity and human populations (UNDP-UNEP Poverty-Environment Initiative, 2008).

Engineering works to reinstate the flooding regime have the potential to restore up to 90 per cent of the floodplain area at an estimated capital cost of approximately US$11 million (Loth, 2004). The same study found the socio-economic effects of flood loss to be significant, incurring livelihood costs of almost US$50 million over the 20 years since the scheme was constructed. Local households suffer direct economic losses of more than US$2 million/year through reduced dry season grazing, fishing, natural resource harvesting and surface water supplies (see Table 9.3 below). The affected population, mainly pastoralists, fishers and dryland farmers, represent some of the poorest and most vulnerable groups in the region.

By bringing around US$2.3 million dollars additional income per year to the region, the economic value of floodplain restoration, and return on investment, would be significant in development and poverty alleviation terms. The benefits of restoring the pre-disturbance flood regime would cover initial investment costs in less than five years. Investment in flood restoration measures was predicted to have an economic net present value of US$7.8 million and a benefit:cost ratio of 6.5:1 (over a period of 25 years and using a discount rate of 10 per cent). Ecological and hydrological restoration would thus have significant benefits for local poverty alleviation, food security and economic well-being (Loth, 2004).

Table 9.3 Effects of land conversion in the Waza floodplain and costs and benefits of restoration

Losses of floods to local households		Measures of economic profitability	
Pasture	US$1.31 million/year	Net present value	US$7.76 million
Fisheries	US$0.47 million/year	Benefit:cost ratio	6.5:1
Agriculture	US$0.32 million/year	Payback period	Five years
Grass	US$0.29 million/year		
Surface water supply	US$0.02 million/year	**Costs and benefits of flood restoration**	
Total	US$2.40 million/year	Capital costs	US$11.26 million
Physical effects of flood restoration		Net livelihood benefits	US$2.32 million/year
Additional flow	215m³/sec		
Flood recovery	90%		

Sources: Loth (2004); UNDP-UNEP Poverty-Environment Initiative (2008)

2.2 Benefits for natural hazard prevention

The damage potential of storms for coastal areas, floods from rivers and landslides can be considerably reduced by a combination of careful land-use planning and ecosystem maintenance or restoration to enhance buffering capacity. In Vietnam, for example, mangrove restoration by volunteers cost US$1.1 million but saved US$7.3 million annual expenditure on dike maintenance and benefited the livelihoods of an estimated 7500 families in terms of planting and protection (IFRC, 2002). The reduction of the impact of cyclones was also one of the main motivations for Bangladesh to invest in its coastal green belt. Since 1994 a continuous effort has been made to implement reforestation along the coastal plain: with an overall budget of US$23.4 million, the programme also helps local farmers to use the newly reclaimed areas in a sustainable way (Iftkehar and Islam, 2004; ADB, 2005).

The success of this type of project is closely linked to integrated planning and implementation. A huge amount of money was wasted in the Philippines when two decades of replanting of mangroves, including very intensive post-tsunami reforestation, were not based on sound science (see Box 9.9).

Box 9.9 Restoration failures: An example from coastal protection in the Philippines

Over the past century, the islands that make up the Philippines have lost nearly three-quarters of their mangrove forests. These provide key habitats for fish and shellfish but were routinely cleared for development and fish-farming ponds. To reverse the trend, conservation groups started replanting projects across the archipelago two decades ago, planting 44,000 hectares with millions of mangrove seedlings.

In practice, one of the world's most intensive programmes to restore coastal mangrove forests has produced poor results, largely because trees were planted in the wrong places. A survey of 70 restoration sites in the archipelago (Samson and Rollon, 2008) found mostly dead, dying or 'dismally stunted' trees because seedlings were planted in mudflats, sandflats or seagrass meadows that could not support the trees. Some of these areas have inadequate nutrients; in other places, strong winds and currents batter the seedlings. Ironically, the failed restoration effort may sometimes have disturbed and damaged otherwise healthy coastal ecosystems, thus entailing a double ecological and economic cost.

To get mangrove restoration back on track, Samson and Rollon (2008) suggest that planters need better guidance on where to place the seedlings and that the government needs to make it easier to convert abandoned or unproductive fishponds back to mangrove swamps. However, the study recognizes that this is a thorny legal and political issue as landowners are reluctant to consider the 'voluntary surrender' of potentially valuable shorefront back to nature.

Sources: Malakoff (2008); Samson and Rollon (2008)

Letting ecosystems degrade can exacerbate the devastating impact of natural disasters. Many examples have shown that deforestation, destruction of mangroves and coral reefs or wetland drainage have significantly increased the vulnerability of regions to natural hazards and the level of damage caused (Harakunarak and Aksornkoae, 2005; Barbier, 2007).

Haiti is a tragic example of this. Following steady forest degradation and deforestation for firewood and charcoal, over many decades, in 2004 Hurricane Jeanne caused 1800 deaths in Haiti, mainly by mudslides from deforested slopes. On the other side of the island, in the Dominican Republic (which was equally hard hit by Hurricane Jeanne, but where deforestation is less severe) very few deaths were reported (IUCN, 2006; see also Chapter 3, Box 3.8).

2.3 Benefits for human health

Healthy ecosystems are recognized as essential for maintaining human health and well-being in the Health Synthesis report of the Millennium Ecosystem Assessment (WHO, 2006). Despite this, collapsing ecosystems around the world pose increasing risks for human health (Rapport et al, 1998).

The spread of many infectious diseases can be accelerated by converting natural systems into intensively used ones (e.g. following deforestation or agricultural development) and the concurrent spread of invasive harmful species (for examples, see Molyneux et al, 2008; Pongsiri et al, 2009). Interconnections exist between damage or disruption to aquatic ecosystems and watershed management and water-borne diseases, as shown for example in watershed-level analyses in South-east Asia (Pattanayak and Wendland, 2007). Another example is the spreading of schistosomiasis (a disease caused by a parasitic trematode that develops in freshwater snails) due to overfishing of cichlids that feed on molluscs (Stauffer et al, 2006) (see also Box 9.10).

In terrestrial ecosystems, the destruction of forest habitat can also result in common vector species being replaced by more effective disease vectors, e.g. when an *Anopheles* species (the vector for malaria; see WHO, 2006) replaces a more benign native mosquito. This has occurred following deforestation in some parts of South-east Asia and Amazonia (Walsh et al, 1993). Not only does deforestation create new breeding sites for these mosquitoes but changes in microclimates can lead to higher water temperatures as well as more available sunlight which can in turn lead to changing community dynamics by improving breeding condition for larval mosquitoes (Tuno et al, 2005). This of course leads to accelerated feeding and increased reproduction rates of adult mosquitoes (Afrane et al, 2006). In Amazonian Peru, for instance, observed deforested sites showed a higher density of *A. darlingi* and higher biting rates for humans (Vittor et al, 2006) than intact forest areas, thus increasing public health costs significantly.

Conversely, species diversity seems to provide benefits for human health (Pongsiri et al, 2009). The bacterium that causes Lyme disease (*Borrelia burgdorferi*) is transmitted to humans by ticks that feed from blood of many different vertebrate

---

Box 9.10 Dams, irrigation and the spread of schistosomiasis in Senegal

In the 1980s, the Diama Dam on the Senegal River was constructed to prevent intrusion of salt water into the river during the dry season. While it succeeded in reducing salinity, it also dramatically altered the region's ecology. One organism that made its appearance and prospered after the dam was built was the snail *Biomphalaria pfeifferi*, an important intermediate host for *Schistosoma mansoni*, which is the parasite that causes intestinal schistosomiasis. *Bulinus globosus*, the main snail species that *B. pfeifferi* replaced in many areas around the river, is not a *S. mansoni* host.

Previously unknown to the region, *S. mansoni* quickly spread in the human population. By the end of 1989, almost 2000 people tested positive for *S. mansoni*. By August 1990, 60 per cent of the 50,000 inhabitants of the nearby town of Richard-Toll were infected.

Since 1990, schistosomiasis has continued to spread in the Senegal River Basin upstream from the Diama Dam. This provides a cautionary tale about the potential effects of dam construction and human-caused changes of ecosystems on the spread of vector-borne diseases and illustrates the complexity of human–ecosystem interactions.

Source: Adapted from Molyneux et al (2008)

species. However, white-footed mice (*Peromyscus leucopus*) are reported to be the most competent reservoir for the bacterium whereas most other tick-hosting species do not actually infect the ticks (Lo Giudice et al, 2003). White-footed mice tend to reach higher abundances in small forest fragments with low species diversity (Nupp and Swihart, 1998), leading to high probability of prevalence of infected ticks (Allan et al, 2003). This means that risks to humans from the vector-borne Lyme disease is actually reduced by high vertebrate diversity (Allan et al, 2003).

A similar connection was found in Panama where higher rodent diversity apparently reduces the density of reservoir hosts infected with hantaviruses that cause the hantavirus pulmonary syndrome (HPS) (Suzán et al, 2009). In Louisiana, US, there seems to be evidence for reduced spreading rates of the mosquito-borne West Nile virus in the various vectors where there is a higher number of non-passerine bird species (Ezenwa et al, 2006).

Negative impacts of ecosystem change and degradation on human health can also occur much more directly. At the species level, livestock and game form a key link in a chain of disease transmission from animal reservoirs to humans – as recently seen in the bird flu pandemic outbreak. At the ecosystem level, the degradation of agricultural areas can lead to decreased harvests and thus contribute to malnutrition in many areas of the world (Hillel and Rosenzweig, 2008; IAASTD, 2008). Mental health can also be affected: environmental degradation in western Australia in the form of dryland salinity was associated with cases of depression in the resident rural population (Speldewinde et al, 2009).

For these reasons, the loss or degradation of species and ecosystem diversity also directly compromises efforts to achieve several Millennium Development Goals (WHO, 2006; UNDP-UNEP Poverty-Environment Initiative, 2008). There is consequently an urgent need to further explore the relationships between healthy ecosystems and human health in order to better incorporate these considerations into ecosystem and landscape management and restoration planning (WHO, 2006; Crowl et al, 2008) and thus reduce the costs induced by ecosystem degradation in the public health sector.

3 Investing in ecosystems for climate change adaptation

> We cannot solve biodiversity loss without addressing climate change and vice versa. We therefore need to look for the 'triple win' of biodiversity that can actively contribute to climate mitigation and adaptation. (ECCHM, 2009)

Protecting biodiversity and ecosystems – and using them sustainably in the case of culturally modified systems – is the best way to preserve and enhance their resilience and one of the most cost-effective defences against the adverse impacts of climate change. An ecosystem-based approach to adaptation is crucial to ensure ecosystem services under conditions of climate change.

Climate adaptation is a challenge to many different sectors (see, for example, Adger et al, 2007; EEA et al, 2008; World Bank, 2010). Benefits from investment in natural capital may provide cost-effective solutions across multiple policy areas by focusing on the maintenance and enhancement of the joint provision of ecosystem services. All ecosystems provide a set of services and this creates opportunities to streamline policy making. Flood protection, water provision and water quality regulation (including reduction of infectious diseases) may be provided by one and the same wetland area and thus buffer the effects of changing climate regimes (see Box 9.11).

Proper coordination of climate adaptation and water provision policies can thus make it possible to minimize implementation costs while maximizing the appropriated flow of services or dividends from relevant natural capital (World Bank, 2009b) as shown in watershed-level analyses in South-east Asia (Pattanayak and Wendland, 2007).

There is clearly also a need to address biodiversity loss and climate change in an integrated manner and to develop strategies that achieve mutually supportive outcomes for both policy challenges (e.g. Campbell et al, 2009). One way to achieve this is by promoting sustainable adaptation and mitigation based on ecosystem approaches (e.g. World Bank, 2009b). Ecosystem-based approaches seek to maintain ecological functions at the landscape scale in combination with multifunctional land uses. They represent potential triple-win measures: they help to preserve and restore natural ecosystems; mitigate climate change by conserving or enhancing carbon stocks or by reducing emissions caused by ecosystem degradation and loss; and provide cost-effective protection against some of the threats resulting from climate change (for discussion, see Paterson et al, 2008).

The CBD AHTEG (2009) on biodiversity and climate change supports this way forward. This expert group concluded that 'maintaining natural ecosystems (including their genetic and species diversity) is essential to meet the ultimate objective of the

---

Box 9.11 The restoration of wetlands and lakes in the Yangtze River Basin

The extensive lakes and floodplains along the Yangtze River in China form large water retention areas which attenuate floods during periods of heavy precipitation and provide a continued flow of water during dry periods. The conversion of the floodplains to polder has reduced the wetland area by 80 per cent and the flood retention capacity by 75 per cent. This has increased flood risk: conversely, during dry periods, the reduction in water flow increases the concentration of pollutants in the remaining water bodies, thereby causing a decline in fish stocks. It is anticipated that under continued climate change the frequency of extreme events with heavy precipitation and droughts will increase, having negative consequences for the livelihoods of the 400 million people living in the basin of the Yangtze River.

In 2002 WWF initiated a programme in Hubei Province to reconnect lakes and restore wetlands – so far 448km^2 of wetlands have been rehabilitated which can store up to 285 million/m^3 of flood waters. On one hand this is expected to significantly contribute to flood prevention; on the other, increased water flow, better management of aquaculture and improved agricultural practices has enhanced the water quality to drinking water levels. This has contributed to an increase in the diversity and population of wild fish species in recent years, leading to an increase in catches of more than 15 per cent. The restoration of the wetlands thus not only reduces the vulnerability of local communities to extreme events but also improves their living conditions.

Source: WWF (2008)

UNFCCC because of their role in the global carbon cycle and because of the wide range of ecosystem services they provide that are essential for human well-being'; it stressed that ecosystem-based adaptation is key to long-term successful strategies (Campbell et al, 2009). Wider ecosystem challenges can be addressed appropriately in climate change negotiations under UNFCCC, for example by establishing a REDD+ mechanism and by including ecosystem-based approaches in the Framework for Climate Change Adaptation Action (see Chapter 5.2 and TEEB Climate Issues Update, 2009).

Given the uncertainties surrounding future rates and impacts of climate change, as well as the gaps in our knowledge and uncertainty of responses to policy initiatives, a precautionary approach is necessary (IPCC, 2007). Strong emissions-cutting policies need to be complemented with plans to adapt to major environmental, social and economic changes during the period when we are likely to overshoot safe levels of global warming, as suggested in recent IPCC reports (IPCC, 2007; Adger et al, 2007).

This will require much more investment in adaptation than is currently planned (Parry et al, 2009; TEEB Climate Issues Update, 2009). Specifically, mitigation activities need to be designed to create synergies with adaptation, biodiversity conservation and sustainable development (Paterson et al, 2008; Galatowitsch, 2009). Where such activities have potentially negative impacts on biodiversity, such as biofuel production, they need to be carefully planned and controlled and their impacts continuously assessed (e.g. Fargione et al, 2008; Searchinger et al, 2008). This type of 'mal-adaptation' should be avoided and remedial measures implemented. Conversely, mitigation measures with positive outcomes represent opportunities that should be sought and promoted.

Ecosystem-based approaches can be applied to virtually all types of ecosystems, at all scales from local to continental, and have the potential to reconcile short- and long-term priorities (see for example, Blumenfeld et al, 2009). Green structural approaches – e.g. ecosystem-based adaptation – contribute to ecosystem resilience. They not only help to halt biodiversity loss and ecosystem degradation and restore water cycles, but also enable ecosystem functions and services to deliver a more cost-effective and sometimes more feasible adaptation solution than can be achieved solely through conventional engineered infrastructure. Such approaches also reduce the vulnerability of people and their livelihoods in the face of climate change. Many pilot projects in this area are under way (see Box 9.12 and for a summary of important initiatives, World Bank, 2009b). The experience gained needs to be mainstreamed across countries and regions.

Analysis of measures targeting emission reductions illustrate that there are 'low cost co-benefit' measures which can add significantly to biodiversity conservation and sustainable use (GTZ and CBD, 2009, Campbell et al, 2009). These include restoring degraded forest land and wetlands, increasing organic matter in soils, reducing pastureland conversion and the use of 'slash and burn' practices, and improving grassland management, as well as ecosystem-based management approaches to marine systems (Levin et al, 2009). These ecosystem-based approaches and land management practices also help to maintain services important for human well-being and vital to reinforce nature's adaptive capacity in the face of climate change (Campbell et al, 2009). The costs of such actions may be much lower than those of major technological actions, although complete cost–benefit analyses of such approaches are still scarce (Fischlin et al, 2007). As a start, they may require policy incentives (e.g. positive subsidies and bonds) or longer-term research and development, thus supporting the longer-term development of such measures (see example in Box 9.13).

Box 9.12 Climate change adaptation in Bolivia

In Bolivia the frequency of natural disasters such as floods and forest fires has increased over the past years and is expected to rise further as climate change continues. This has negative impacts on rural communities dependent on agricultural production. In the Altiplano, farmers have always had to cope with the risks from natural climate variability but over past decades the depletion of vegetation, soil erosion, desertification and the contamination of water bodies decreased their resilience. Climate change puts additional stress on the agricultural sector and exacerbates the living conditions for such communities. Attempts to adapt crop management to changing climate conditions are often insufficient and migration of farmers to cities is rising.

As the agricultural sector contributes 20 per cent to national GDP and employs 65 per cent of the workforce, climate change poses a real threat to the national economy. The government has therefore identified key adaptation strategies important for national development:

- sustainable forest management;
- enhancing the efficiency of industrialization processes;
- reducing habitat fragmentation;
- improving soil and water resource management, agriculture research and technology transfer;
- identifying pastures resistant to climate change and improving livestock management; and
- coordinating water use and water conservation.

Five of these six strategies are directly related to ecosystem management which highlights the significance of ecosystem services for human well-being and development under climate change.

The World Bank has initiated a study on the Economics of Adaptation to Climate Change (EACC) and is assessing the costs of adaptation within a broader national and international context. Similar efforts to identify adaptation strategies and their costs are being undertaken in Bangladesh, Ethiopia, Ghana, Mozambique, Samoa and Vietnam.

Source: World Bank (2010)

Ecosystems needing special attention in this respect are wetlands and other freshwater ecosystems (e.g. Palmer et al, 2009), forests (e.g. Bonan, 2008; see also Chapter 5, Section 2) and agricultural systems, where the link between climate change, ecosystem services and human livelihoods is explicit. Agricultural productivity is affected by rising temperatures and increased drought (IPCC, 2007). Agricultural resilience is therefore a key part of adaptation, especially in countries with large populations dependent upon subsistence farming (IAASTD, 2008; Herrero et al, 2010; see for example Box 9.14).

In the context of nature conservation, adaptation strategies within (e.g. local and regional level) and across countries (e.g. bilateral or multilateral cooperation) will also be needed and could be cost-effective compared to purely national approaches (e.g. Balmford et al, 2003; Vos et al, 2008; Hannah, 2009). Such approaches will need to be combined with adaptation activities in other sectors (EEA et al, 2008, for an example in agriculture; see Berry et al, 2006).

Box 9.13 Restoration and conservation strategy of mires and peatlands in Germany

The degradation of mires and peatlands has led to considerable losses of these habitats and their function to store carbon in recent decades in Europe (Schäfer, 2009). In the northern German federal land of Mecklenburg-West Pomerania, this has led to a situation where greenhouse gas (GHG) emissions from converted peatlands are considered to be higher than from other anthropogenic sources (peatlands and mires: 6.1Mt CO_2e; traffic 3.1Mt CO_2e; energy 3.9Mt CO_2e; industry 0.4Mt CO_2e).

Mecklenburg-West Pomerania has now set up a programme to reduce these emissions using a mix of policy tools: setting incentives for changing agricultural practices, supporting alternative land-use practices and restoring peatlands. To fund the restoration of peatlands, it plans to establish a 'peatland bond' for business and private persons. A bond of €5000 will allow the restoration of approximately one hectare of peatland and would be equivalent to about ten tonnes of avoided CO_2 emissions.

Additional benefits are expected in terms of water retention (in the context of a warming climate) and for biodiversity conservation, as peatlands are one of the most valuable habitats for species in the region.

Sources: Ministerium für Landwirtschaft, Umwelt und Verbraucherschutz Mecklenburg-Vorpommern (2009), Schäfer (2009)

Box 9.14 Ecosystem gains from sustainable agricultural practices

Agricultural sustainability centres around the world respond to the need to develop best practices and deliver technologies that improve yields and livelihoods without damaging the supply of environmental goods and services. A study of 286 recent best practice initiatives in 57 developing countries covering 37 million hectares (3 per cent of cultivated area in developing countries) across 12.6 million farms showed how productivity increased along with improvements to the supply of ecosystem services (e.g. carbon sequestration and water quality). The average yield increase was 79 per cent, depending on crop type, and all crops showed gains in efficiency of water use. Examples of these initiatives included:

* pest management: ecosystem resilience and diversity to control pests, diseases and weeds;
* nutrient management: controlling erosion to help reduce nutrient losses;
* soil and other resources management: using conservation tillage, agroforestry practices, aquaculture and water-harvesting techniques, to improve soil and water availability for farmers.

Source: Pretty et al (2006)

4 Proactive strategies for making investment happen

TEEB findings, as presented in this book and other volumes, show that a proactive strategy to maintain natural capital and ecosystem services, especially regulating services, needs to be a high priority for decision makers. Reactive restoration efforts are generally the fall-back option for severe cases where ecosystem degradation has already taken place. However, both natural and man-made catastrophes and crises provide opportunities to rethink political practice and procedures and to undertake major public–private or all-public investments in natural capital.

4.1 Turning catastrophes and crises into opportunities

When natural crises strike, the necessary rebuilding can be designed to allow future economic development and protection from disasters to go hand-in-hand (SER-IUCN, 2004). After Hurricane Katrina devastated New Orleans, the federal government allocated US$1 billion to the city's reconstruction. The goal was to restore and revitalize the region to make it less vulnerable to future hurricanes and other natural disasters. The US Army Corps of Engineers initiated a massive Hurricane and Storm Damage Risk Reduction System that has focused on repairing and rebuilding the artificial levees along the Gulf of Mexico seafront. However, environmental engineers and restoration ecologists pointed out that over the past century, large wetland areas surrounding the city and providing barriers against storms had been lost to urban sprawl: in the wake of Katrina, the opportunity existed to restore them in conjunction with reconstructing the city's built environment by using high-performance green buildings (Costanza et al, 2006a). It was argued that New Orleans could become a model of how to move towards a sustainable and desirable future after a series of severe shocks (Costanza et al, 2006b). To date, this wetland restoration has unfortunately not been undertaken and the rebuilding of seafront levees has been favoured instead.

Other opportunities include coastal area restoration activities implemented after the catastrophic 2004 tsunami in the Indian Ocean, and Cyclone Nargis in 2008. The goal is to improve the buffering function of coral reefs and mangroves for future events (UNEP-WCMC, 2006; IUCN, 2006). In 2005 the Indonesian Minister for Forestry announced plans to reforest 600,000 hectares of depleted mangrove forest throughout the nation over the next five years. The governments of Sri Lanka and Thailand, among others, have launched large programmes to recover the natural barriers provided by mangrove areas, largely through reforestation (Harakunarak and Aksornkoae, 2005; Barbier, 2007).

Another example is provided by China's land conservation programme launched after severe flooding of the Yangtze River (see Box 9.15).

Current interest in – and increased funding opportunities for – climate change adaptation and mitigation provide new possibilities for integrating a natural capital perspective into projects and programmes. The result should be to reduce the future vulnerability of societies to new catastrophes, not only by reducing the impact of future events but also by increasing the ability of local people to cope with the effects of climate change and ensure their livelihoods in a changing world (IUCN, 2006).

Lastly, financial crises, like all major upheavals, should be regarded as an opportunity for major investments in natural capital. The financial crisis of 2008/2009 led to multi-billion dollar investment in 'stimulus packages' in many countries. If this money were

---

Box 9.15 Launch of the Sloping Land Conversion Programme after flooding in China

In 1998, the Yangtze River overflowed causing severe floods. The protection capacities of nearby dams were hindered because of the river's heavy sedimentation, leading to worse damage occurring along the river. After the flood, the river's high sediment yield was linked to the erosion from intensively farmed sloping land (Tallis et al, 2008).

As a consequence, the Chinese government implemented the Sloping Land Conversion Programme which aims to reduce soil erosion in key areas of 24 provinces by converting farmland back into forest land (Sun and Liqiao, 2006). Farmers are offered cash incentives, or quantities of grain, to abandon farming and restore forests on their land on steep slopes along key rivers. By the end of the programme in 2010, the aim is to have reconverted 14.6 million hectares into forest (Tallis et al, 2008).

The cost of the overall investment in this project, undertaken mainly by the Chinese government, is ¥337 billion (about US$49 billion; see Bennett, 2009). The government aims to combine soil protection activities with activities for socio-economic improvement of underdeveloped regions along the Yangtze River to improve local living standards by helping families to create new means for earning their livelihoods.

Sources: Sun and Liqiao (2006); Tallis et al (2008); Bennett (2009)

---

used for investing in natural capital, it would present a unique opportunity for the environment and for redirecting economic growth towards sustainability. Some governments realize that investments in green infrastructure can lead to multiple benefits such as new jobs in clean technology and clean energy businesses (see Box 9.16). Investment in natural capital in the broader sense could secure the sustainable flow of ecosystem services and provide additional jobs in sustainable agriculture and conservation-based enterprises.

4.2 Putting precaution into practice through green investment

Do we have to wait for crises to occur or natural disasters to strike or should we invest in securing our common future before severe damage occurs? The World Bank (2004) supports a precautionary approach and estimates that every dollar invested in disaster reduction measures saves seven dollars in losses from natural disasters. In other words, investment in natural capital pays – not only to improve environmental conditions and livelihoods but also in economic terms.

When tackling the many challenges we face (widespread environmental degradation, climate change and major threats of catastrophes), an integrated economic perspective can and should be developed by national governments to improve our capacity to identify and address the benefits of maintaining and restoring our limited and increasingly threatened stocks of renewable natural capital (see examples in Box 9.15 above).

A crucial step towards more proactive strategies is to develop overviews of ongoing losses of and threats to natural capital. All countries require more detailed information at regional and national scales on ecosystem services and the factors that threaten their provision, as well as better accounting systems that reflect the importance of

---

Box 9.16 Investing in the environment during the financial crisis: The case of South Korea

Although most G20 countries have missed the Global Green New Deal target of 1 per cent GDP investments in green technologies (Barbier, 2010), some countries have made substantial investments in green recovery programmes in recent years as the example of South Korea shows: the government is linking its strategy to revitalize its national economy under the current crisis with green growth (Hyun-kyung, 2009). In early 2009, President Lee Myung-bak announced that US$10 billion would be invested in restoration of four major degraded rivers to build dams and protect water reservoirs. The aim is to prevent neighbouring areas from flooding and to create 200,000 new jobs. 'Our policies of green development will benefit the environment and contribute to the fight against climate change, but it is not only an environmental plan: it's primarily a plan for economic development' (Statement of Korea's Permanent Representative to the OECD, Kim Choong-Soo).

Sources: Hyun-kyung (2009); LWEC (2009)

---

natural capital (see Chapter 3). This information will enable policy makers to develop investment strategies that include schemes to maintain or restore ecosystems that provide key services, e.g. through targeted payment schemes (see Chapter 5) or other tools, including the designation of protected areas (see Chapter 8).

Achieving this transition will require much closer links between different actors in development and restoration projects, especially in developing countries. Too often, academic institutions, government forestry and agricultural research partners, communities and commercial operators are not adequately connected and do not make best use of opportunities to work closely together. Environmental agencies and institutions have a critical role to play in promoting strong cross-sectoral policy and project coordination, facilitating the development of efficient and cost-effective actions and ensuring that the benefits of such actions are fairly shared across different stakeholder groups.

To pave the way for combining environmental risk reduction with economically efficient investment, TEEB recommends that each country carries out a systematic assessment of their national stocks of natural capital by creating natural capital accounting systems and maps (see also Chapters 3, 4 and 10). These tools will enable restoration needs to be identified in different ecosystem types, especially with regard to endangered biodiversity and the services that ecosystems provide to people, and should be developed at local up to national scales. High priorities should include:

- water provision and purification for cities;
- climate change adaptation and associated natural hazard management, risk management and augmenting natural capital stocks in the ways identified in this chapter;
- carbon storage and sequestration; and

- protecting biodiversity hotspots and all ecosystems considered valuable or essential from the perspectives of conservation, landscape planning and resource management.

A structured science-based framework for natural capital accounting will open up new possibilities for decision makers to systematically and proactively invest in the protection and restoration of ecological infrastructure. This will not only protect communities and societies against natural hazards – including those most exposed to environmental risk – but also make economic sense by providing a positive return on investment in the mid term (see e.g. World Bank, 2004) and across different sectors. Such investments in a resource-efficient economy are fundamental to help humanity move towards a sustainable future in the long term, including fairer sharing of nature's social and ecological benefits.

Acknowledgements

The authors wish to thank Jonathan Armstrong, IEEP, UK; Tim Besser, University of Bayreuth, Germany; Patrick ten Brink, IEEP, Belgium; Johannes Förster, Helmholtz Centre for Environmental Research (UFZ), Germany; Rudolf de Groot, Wageningen University, The Netherlands; Philip James, University of Salford, UK; Marianne Kettunen, IEEP, Finland; Dorit Lehr, University of Bonn, Germany; Sander van der Ploeg, Wageningen University, The Netherlands; Monique Simmonds, Royal Botanic Gardens, Kew, UK; Paul Smith, Royal Botanic Gardens, Kew, UK; Johannes Timaeus, UFZ, Germany; and Graham Tucker, IEEP, UK.

References

ADB (2005) *Coastal Greenbelt Project (Loan 1353-BAN[SF]) in the People's Republic of Bangladesh*, Project Completion Report, Asian Development Bank, www.adb.org/Documents/PCRs/BAN/pcr-ban-25311.pdf, accessed 3 December 2009

Adger, W. N., Agrawala, S., Mirza, M. M. Q., Conde, C., O'Brien, K., Pulhin, J., Pulwarty, R., Smit, B. and Takahashi, K. (2007) Chapter 17: 'Assessment of adaptation practices, options, constraints and capacity', in 'Climate Change 2007: Impacts, Adaptation and Vulnerability', A report of Working Group II to the Fourth Assessment Report of the Intergovernmental Panel on Climate Change, M. L. Parry, O. F. Canziani, J. P. Palutikof, P. J. van der Linden and C. E. Hanson (eds) Cambridge University Press, Cambridge, pp717–743

Afrane, Y. A., Zhou, G., Lawson, B. W., Githeko, A. K. and Yan, G. (2006) 'Effects of microclimate changes caused by deforestation on the survivorship and reproductive fitness of *Anopheles gambiae* in western Kenya highlands', *American Journal of Tropical Medicine and Hygiene*, vol 74, pp772–778

Allan, B. F., Keesing, F. and Ostfeld, R. S. (2003) 'Effects of habitat fragmentation on Lyme disease risk', *Conservation Biology*, vol 17, pp267–272

Andersen, M. C., Adams, H., Hope, B. and Powell, M. (2004) 'Risk assessment for invasive species: General framework and research needs', *Risk Analysis*, vol 24, no 4, pp787–793

Andreu, J., Vilà, M. and Hulme, P. E. (2009) 'An assessment of stakeholder perceptions and management of noxious alien plants in Spain', *Environmental Management*, vol 43, pp1244–1255

Aronson, J., Floret, C., Le Floc'h, E., Ovalle, C. and Pontanier, R. (1993) 'Restoration and rehabilitation of degraded ecosystems: A view from the South', *Restoration Ecology*, vol 1, pp8–17

Aronson, J., Blignaut, J. N., Milton, S. J. and Clewell, A. F. (2006) 'Natural capital: The limiting factor', *Ecological Engineering*, vol 28, pp1–5

Aronson, J., Milton, S. J. and Blignaut, J. N. (2007) 'Restoring natural capital: Definitions and rationale', in J. Aronson, S. J. Milton and J. N. Blignaut (eds) *Restoring Natural Capital: Science, Business and Practice*, Island Press, Washington, DC

Aronson, J., Blignaut, J. N., Milton, S. J., Le Maitre, D., Esler, K. J., Limouzin, A., Fontaine, C., de Wit, M. P., Mugido, W., Prinsloo, P., van der Elst, L. and Lederer, N. (2010) 'Are socioeconomic benefits of restoration adequately quantified? A meta-analysis of recent papers (2000–2008) in *Restoration Ecology* and 12 other scientific journals', *Restoration Ecology*, vol 18, pp143–154

Badescu, V. and Schuiling, R. D. (2009) 'Aral Sea: Irretrievable loss or Irtysh imports?', *Water Resource Management*, vol 24, no 3, pp597–616

Balmford, A., Gaston, K. J., Blyth, S., James, A. and Kapos, V. (2003) 'Global variation in terrestrial conservation costs, conservation benefits and unmet conservation needs', *Proceedings of the National Academy of Sciences of the United States of America*, vol 100, pp1046–1050

Barbier, E. (2007) 'Valuing ecosystem services as productive inputs', *Economic Policy*, vol 22, no 49, pp178–229

Barbier, E. (2010) 'How is the global green new deal doing?' *Nature*, vol 464, pp832–833.

Benedict, M. A. and McMahon, E. T. (eds) (2008) *Green Infrastructure: Linking Landscapes and Communities*, Island Press, Washington, DC

Bennett, M. T. (2009) 'Markets for ecosystem services in China: An exploration of China's "eco-compensation" and other market-based environmental policies', Forest Trends, www.forest-trends.org/documents/files/doc_2317.pdf, accessed 20 November 2009

Berry, P. M., Rousewell, M. D. A., Harrison, P. A. and Audsley, E. (2006) 'Assessing the vulnerability of agricultural land use and species to climate change and the role of policy in facilitating adaptation', *Environemntal Science and Policy*, vol 9, pp189–204

Bertram, G. (1999) *The Impact of Introduced Pests on the New Zealand Economy: A Blueprint for Action*, New Zealand Conservation Authority, Wellington

Blignaut, J. N. and Aronson, J. (2008) 'Getting serious about maintaining biodiversity', *Conservation Letters*, vol 1, pp12–17

Blignaut, J. N. and Loxton, C. E. (2007) 'An approach to quantify the economic value of restoring natural capital: A case from South Africa', in J. Aronson, S. J. Milton and J. N. Blignaut (eds) *Restoring Natural Capital: Science, Business, and Practice*, Island Press, Washington, DC

Blignaut, J. N., Aronson, J., Mander, M. and Marais, C. (2008) 'Investing in natural capital and economic development: South Africa's Drakensberg Mountains', *Ecological Restoration*, vol 26, pp143–150

Blumenfeld, S., Lu, C., Christophersen, T. and Coates, D. (2009) *Water, Wetlands and Forests: A Review of Ecological, Economic and Policy Linkages*, CBD Technical Series No 47, Convention on Biological Diversity and the Ramsar Convention on Wetlands, Montreal and Gland

Bonan, G. B. (2008) 'Forests and climate change: Forcings, feedbacks, and the climate benefits of forests', *Science*, vol 320, pp1444–1449

Bullock, J. M., Pywell, R. F. and Walker, K. J. (2007) 'Long-term enhancement of agricultural production by restoration of biodiversity', *Journal of Applied Ecology*, vol 44, pp6–12

Campbell, A., Kapos, V., Scharlemann, J. P. W., Bubb, P., Chenery, A., Coad, L., Dickson, B., Doswald, N., Khan, M. S. I., Kershaw, F. and Rashid, M. (2009) *Review of the Literature on the Links between Biodiversity and Climate Change: Impacts, Adaptation and Mitigation*, Technical Series No 42, Convention on Biological Diversity, Montreal

CBD (1993) *Convention on Biological Diversity (with annexes)*, United Nations Treaty Series, UN, concluded at Rio de Janeiro on 5 June 1992, registered ex officio on 29 December 1993, www.cbd.int/doc/legal/cbd-en.pdf, accessed 28 October 2010

CBD (2002) 'Review and consideration of options for the implementation of article 8(h) on alien species that threaten ecosystems, habitats or species', Convention of the parties to the Convention on Biological Diversity, www.cbd.int/doc/meetings/cop/cop-06/official/cop-06-18-en.pdf, accessed 28 October 2010

CBD AHTEG (2009) 'Draft findings of the Ad Hoc Technical Expert Group on Biodiversity and Climate Change', Convention on Biological Diversity Ad Hoc Technical Expert Group, Montreal, www.cbd.int/doc/meetings/cc/ahteg-bdcc-01/other/ahteg-bdcc-01-findings-en.pdf, accessed 20 November 2009

Chen, L. Y. (2001) 'Cost savings from properly managing endangered species habitats', *Natural Areas Journal*, vol 21, pp197–203

Clewell, A. F. and Aronson, J. (2006) 'Motivations for the restoration of ecosystems', *Conservation Biology*, vol 20, pp420–428

Clewell, A. F. and Aronson, J. (2007) *Ecological Restoration: Principles, Values, and Structure of an Emerging Profession*, Island Press, Washington, DC

Clewell, A. F. and McDonald, T. (2009) 'Relevance of natural recovery to ecological restoration', *Ecological Restoration*, vol 27, pp122–124

Costanza, R., Mitsch, W. J. and Day, J. W. Jr. (2006a) 'Creating a sustainable and desirable New Orleans', *Ecological Economics*, vol 26, pp317–320

Costanza, R., Mitsch, W. J. and Day, J. W. Jr. (2006b) 'A new vision for New Orleans and the Mississippi delta: Applying ecological economics and ecological engineering', *Frontiers in Ecology and the Environment*, vol 4, pp465–472

Crowl, T. A., Crist, T. O., Parmenento, R. R., Belovsky, G. and Lugo, A. E. (2008) 'The spread of invasive species and infectious disease as drivers of ecosystem change', *Frontiers in Ecology and the Environment*, vol 6, pp238–246

Defra (2007) 'Impact assessment of the order to ban sale of certain non-native species under the Wildlife & Countryside Act 1981', Department for Environment, Food and Rural Affairs, London

de Groot, R., de Wit, M., Brown, E. J., Brown, G., Kousky, C., McGhee, W. and Young, M. D. (2007) 'Making restoration work: Financial mechanisms', in J. Aronson, S. J. Milton and J. N. Blignaut (eds) *Restoring Natural Capital: Science, Business, and Practice*, Island Press, Washington, DC

DePalma, A. (2007) 'City's Catskill Water Gets 10-Year Approval', *New York Times*, 13 April 2007, available at www.nytimes.com/2007/04/13/nyregion/13water.html, accessed 28 July 2010

Dorrough, J. and Moxham, C. (2005) 'Eucalypt establishment in agricultural landscapes and implications for landscape-scale restoration', *Biological Conservation*, vol 123, pp55–66

Dorrough, J., Vesk, P. A. and Moll, J. (2008) 'Integrating ecological uncertainty and farm-scale economics when planning restoration', *Journal of Applied Ecology*, vol 45, pp288–295

Doyle, M. and Drew, C. A. (eds) (2007) *Large-Scale Ecosystem Restoration*, Island Press, Washington, DC

ECCHM (European Biodiversity Clearing House Mechanism) (2009) 'Message from Athens on the Future of Biodiversity Policies: April 2009', Conference: Biodiversity protection beyond 2010: priorities and options for future EU policy, http://biodiversity-chm.eea.europa.eu/stories/european-message-athens-future-biodiversity, accessed 22 September 2010

EEA, JRC and WHO (2008) *Impacts of Europe's Changing Climate: 2008 Indicator Based Assessment*, EEA Report No 4/2008, European Environment Agency, Joint Resource Centre European Commission, World Health Organization

Elliman, K. and Berry, N. (2007) 'Protecting and restoring natural capital in New York City's watersheds to safeguard water', in J. Aronson, S. J. Milton and J. N. Blignaut (eds) *Restoring Natural Capital: Science, Business, and Practice*, Island Press, Washington, DC

Enserink, M. (1999) 'Plan to quench the Everglade's thirst', *Science*, vol 285, no 5425, p180

Ezenwa, V. O, Godsey, M. S., King, R. J. and Guptill, S. C. (2006) 'Avian diversity and West Nile virus: Testing associations between biodiversity and infectious disease risk', *Proceedings of the Royal Society B*, vol 273, pp109–117

Falk, D. A., Palmer, M. A. and Zedler, J. B. (eds) (2006) *Foundations of Restoration Ecology*, Island Press, Washington, DC

FAO (2004) 'Payment schemes for environmental services in watersheds', Land and Water Discussion Paper No 83, Food and Agriculture Organization, Rome

Fargione, J., Hill, J., Tilman, D., Polasky, S. and Hawthorne, P. (2008) 'Land clearing and the biofuel carbon debt', *Science*, vol 319, pp1235–1237

Finnoff, D., Shogren, J. F., Leung, B. and Lodge, D. M. (2006) 'Take a risk: Preferring prevention over control of biological invaders', *Ecological Economics*, vol 62, no 2, pp216–222

Fischlin, A., Midgley, G. F., Price, J. T., Leemans, R., Gopal, B., Turley, C., Rounsevell, M. D. A., Dube, O. P., Tarazona, J. and Velichko, A. A. (2007) Chapter 4: 'Ecosystems, their properties, goods, and services.', in 'Climate Change 2007: Impacts, Adaptation and Vulnerability', A report of Working Group II to the Fourth Assessment Report of the Intergovernmental Panel on Climate Change, M. L. Parry, O. F. Canziani, J. P. Palutikof, P. J. van der Linden and C. E. Hanson (eds) Cambridge University Press, Cambridge

Fox, H., Mous, P., Pet, J., Muljadi, A. and Caldwell, R. (2005) 'Experimental assessment of coral reef rehabilitation following blast fishing', *Conservation Biology*, vol 19, no 1, pp98–107

Francher, J. (2008) 'California: Restoring Bolsa Chica Wetlands', www.bolsachicarestoration.org/admincms/lib/fckeditor/uploads/file/ERAPRandFAQ.pdf, www.bolsachicarestoration.org/project.php, accessed 28 October 2010

Galatowitsch, S. M. (2009) 'Carbon offsets as ecological restorations', *Restoration Ecology*, vol 17, pp563–570

Galil, B. S. and Zenetos, A. (2002) 'A sea change – exotics in the eastern Mediterranean Sea', in E. Leppäkoski, S. Gollasch and S. Olenin (eds) *Invasive Aquatic Species of Europe: Distribution, Impacts and Management*, Kluwer Academic Publishers, Dordrecht, Netherlands

Goldstein, J. H., Pejchar, L. and Daily, G. C. (2008) 'Using return-on-investment to guide restoration: A case study from Hawaii', *Conservation Letters*, vol 1, pp236–243

GRN (Global Restoration Network) (2007) *British Columbia: Restoration in Coastal British Columbia Riparian Forests*, Society for Ecological Restoration International, www.globalrestorationnetwork.org/database/case-study/?id=102

GTZ and CBD (2009) *Biodiversity and Livelihoods: REDD Benefits*, Gesellschaft für Technische Zusammenarbeit and the Convention on Biological Diversity, Eschborn, Germany

Hannah, L. (2009) 'A global conservation system for climate-change adaptation', *Conservation Biology*, vol 24, pp70–77

Harakunarak, A. and Aksornkoae, S. (2005) 'Life-saving belts: Post-tsunami reassessment of mangrove ecosystem values and management in Thailand', *Tropical Coasts*, July, pp48–55

Herrero, M., Thornton, P. K., Notenbaert, A. M., Wood, S., Msangi, S., Freeman, H. A., Bossio, D., Dixon, J., Peters, M., van de Steeg, J., Lynam, J., Parthasanthy Rao, P., Macmillan, S., Gerard, B., McDermott, J., Seré, C. and Rosegrant, M. (2010) 'Smart investments in sustainable food production: Revisiting mixed crop-livestock systems', *Science*, vol 327, pp822–827

Hillel, D. and Rosenzweig, C. (2008) 'Biodiversity and food production', in E. Chivian and A. Bernstein (eds) *Sustaining Life: How Human Health Depends on Biodiversity*, Oxford University Press, Oxford

Hobbs, R. J., Arico, S., Aronson, J., Baron, J. S., Bridgewater, P., Cramer, V. A., Epstein, P. R., Ewel, J. J., Klink, C. A., Lugo, A. E., Norton, D., Ojima, D., Richardson, D. M., Sanderson, E. W., Valladares, F., Vilà, M., Zamora, R. and Zobel, M. (2006) 'Novel ecosystems: Theoretical and management aspects of the new ecological world order', *Global Ecology and Biogeography*, vol 15, pp1–7

Hoffmann, C. and Baattrup-Pedersen, A. (2007) 'Re-establishing freshwater wetlands in Denmark', *Ecological Engineering*, vol 30, pp157–166

Holloway, L. L. and Tingle, C. C. D. (2009) 'Direct costs of Tetik'asa Mampody Savoka (TAMS)', Ankeniheny-Zahamena-Mantadia Biodiversity Conservation Corridor and Restoration Project, Madagascar, http://wbcarbonfinance.org/Router.cfm?Page=BioCF&FID=9708&ItemID=9708&ft=Projects&ProjID=9638, accessed 20 November 2009

Holloway, L. L., Andrianjara, A. H. and Zafindrandalana, J. M. (2009) 'Direct costs of Masoala Corridors Restoration Project', Masoala National Park, Madagascar

Holmes, P. M., Richardson, D. M. and Marais, C. (2007) 'Costs and benefits of restoring natural capital following alien plant invasions in fynbos ecosystems in South Africa', in J. Aronson, S. J. Milton and J. N. Blignaut (eds) *Restoring Natural Capital: Science, Business, and Practice*, Island Press, Washington, DC

Holmes, T., Bergstrom, J., Huszar, E., Kask, S. and Orr III, F. (2004) 'Contingent valuation, net marginal benefits, and the scale of riparian ecosystem restoration', *Ecological Economics*, vol 49, pp19–30

Hopkins, C. C. E. (2002) 'Introduced marine organisms in Norwegian waters, including Svalbard', in E. Leppäkoski, S. Gollasch and S. Olenin (eds) *Invasive Aquatic Species of Europe: Distribution, Impacts and Management*, Kluwer Academic Publishers, Dordrecht, Netherlands

Hyun-kyung, K. (2009) '"Green Growth" project to start', Green Growth, www.greengrowth.org/articles-etc/articles-etc-1.asp, accessed 20 November 2009

IAASTD (2008) *Global Report*, International Assessment of Agricultural Knowledge, Science and Technology for Development, Island Press, Washington, DC

IFRC (2002) *World Disasters Report 2002*, International Federation of Red Cross and Red Crescent Societies, Eurospan-London, www.ifrc.org/publicat/wdr2002, accessed 28 October 2010

Iftekhar, M. S. and Islam, M. R. (2004) 'Managing mangroves in Bangladesh: A strategy analysis', *Journal of Coastal Conservation*, vol 10, pp139–146

Instituto Terra (2007) 'Restoration of the Atlantic Forest (Mata Atlântica)', www.unep-wcmc.org/forest/restoration/docs/Brazil.pdf, www.globalrestorationnetwork.org/database/case-study/?id=93, accessed 28 October 2010

IPCC (2007) 'The physical science basis', in S. Solomon, D. Qin, M. Manning, Z. Chen, M. Marquis, B. B. M. Tignor and H. L. Miller (eds) *Contribution of Working Group I to the Fourth Assessment Report of the Intergovernmental Panel on Climate Change*, Cambridge University Press, Cambridge and New York

IUCN (2006) 'Ecosystems, livelihoods and disasters: An integrated approach to disaster risk management', Ecosystem Management Series No 4, International Union for the Conservation of Nature, p57

Jackson, S. T. and Hobbs, R. (2009) 'Ecological restoration in the light of ecological history', *Science*, vol 325, pp567–569

Jameson, J. and Ramsay, P. (2007) 'Changes in high-altitude *Polylepis* forest cover and quality in the Cordillera de Vilcanota, Peru, 1956–2005', *Biological Conservation*, vol 138, pp38–46

Janzen, D. H. (2002) 'Tropical dry forest: Area de Conservacion Guancaste, northwestern Costa Rica', in M. R. Perrow and A. J. Davy (eds) *Handbook of Ecological Restoration*, Cambridge University Press, Cambridge

Jones, H. P. and Schmitz, O. J. (2009) 'Rapid recovery of damaged ecosystems', *Public Library of Science One*, vol 4, no 5

Juston, J. and DeBusk, T. (2006) 'Phosphorus mass load and outflow concentration relationships in stormwater treatment areas for Everglades restoration', *Ecological Engineering*, vol 26, pp206–223

Kettunen, M., Genovesi, P., Gollasch, S., Pagad, S., Starfinger, U., ten Brink, P. and Shine, C. (2009) *Technical Support to EU Strategy on Invasive Species (IS): Assessment of the Impacts of IS in Europe and the EU (Final Module Report for the European Commission)*, Institute for European Environmental Policy (IEEP), Brussels

Kil-Dong, P. (2007) 'Cheonggyecheon Restoration Project', www.wfeo.org/documents/download/ Cheonggeycheon%20Restoration%20Project_%20Korea.pdf, accessed 28 October 2010

Koenig, R. (2009) 'Unleashing an army to repair alien-ravaged ecosystems', *Science*, vol 325, no 5940, pp562–563

Kühn, I., Brandenburg, M. and Klotz, S. (2004) 'Why do alien plant species that reproduce in natural habitats occur more frequently?' *Diversity and Distributions*, vol 10, pp417–425

Langridge, S., Buckley, M. and Holl, K. (2007) 'Overcoming obstacles to restoring natural capital: Large-scale restoration on the Sacramento River', in J. Aronson, S. J. Milton and J. N. Blignaut (eds) *Restoring Natural Capital: Science, Business, and Practice*, Island Press, Washington, DC

Leschen, A., Kessler, R. and Estrella, B. (2007) 'IVA: Eelgrass restoration project', The Commonwealth of Massachusetts, Boston, www.mass.gov/dfwele/dmf/programsandprojects/hubline/hubline_5yr_eelgrass_restoration.pdf, accessed 20 November 2009

Levin, P. S., Fogarty, M. J., Murawski, S. A. and Fluharty, D. (2009) 'Integrated ecosystem assessments: Developing the scientific basis for ecosystem-based management of the ocean', *Public Library of Science Biology*, vol 7, no 1, pp23–28

Lewis Environmental Services (2007) *Florida: Mangrove Restoration at West Lake (Broward County)*, www.lewisenv.com/html/mangrove_restoration.html, accessed 20 November 2009

Lo Giudice, K., Ostfeld, R. S., Schmidt, K. A. and Keesing, F. (2003) 'The ecology of infectious disease: Effects of host diversity and community composition on Lyme disease risk', *Proceedings of the National Academy of Sciences*, vol 100, pp567–571

Londong, J., Kolisch, G., Wulf, G. and Borchardt, D. (2003) 'Measures and costs of integrated river basin management: The Wupper case study', *Water Science Technology*, vol 46, no 6–7, pp47–53

Loth, P. (ed) (2004) *The Return of the Water: Restoring the Waza Logone Floodplain in Cameroon*, IUCN, Gland, Switzerland and Cambridge

LWEC (Living With Environmental Changes) (2009) '£100 million for UK's environmental challenges', Press Release, Living With Environmental Changes, www.lwec.org.uk/sites/default/files/LWEC_pr_08-06-09.pdf, accessed 20 November 2009

MA (Millennium Ecosystem Assessment) (2003) *Ecosystems and Human Well-Being: A Framework for Assessment*, Millennium Ecosystem Assessment, Island Press, Washington, DC

Mack, R. N., Simberloff, D., Lonsdale, W. M., Evans, H., Clout, M. and Bazzaz, F. (2000) 'Biotic invasions: Causes, epidemiology, global consequences and control', *Issues in Ecology*, vol 5, pp1–20

Malakoff, D. (2008) 'Massive mangrove restoration backfires', *ScienceNOW Daily News* (17 July 2008), http://sciencenow.sciencemag.org/cgi/content/full/2008/715/1, accessed 20 November 2009

Malcolm, A. (2009) cited in '34 Quotes', Natural Capital Inititive website, www.naturalcapitalinitiative. org.uk/34-quotes/, accessed 6 December 2009

MDTP (Maloti Drakensberg Transfrontier Project) (2008) 'Payment for ecosystem services: Developing an ecosystem services trading model for the Mnweni/Cathedral Peak and Eastern Cape Drakensberg areas', in M. Mander (ed) *INR Report IR281*, Development Bank of Southern Africa, Department of Water Affairs and Forestry, Department of Environment Affairs and Tourism, Ezemvelo KZN Wildlife, South Africa, www.futureworks.co.za/PES%20FINAL%20REPORT%206%20MARCH%2008.pdf, accessed 20 September 2010

Micklin, P. and Aladin, N. V. (2008) 'Reclaiming the Aral Sea', *Scientific American*, vol 298, pp64–71

Mills, A. J., Turpie, J. K., Cowling, R. M., Marais, C., Kerley, G. I. H., Lechmere-Oertel, R. C., Sigwela, A. M. and Powell, M. (2007) 'Assessing costs, benefits, and feasibility of restoring natural capital in subtropical thicket in South Africa', in J. Aronson, S. J. Milton and J. N. Blignaut (eds) *Restoring Natural Capital: Science, Business, and Practice*, Island Press, Washington, DC

Milon, J. W. and Hodges, A. W. (2000) 'Who wants to pay for Everglades restoration?' *Choices*, vol 15, pp12–16

Milon, J. W. and Scroggins, D. (2002) 'Heterogeneous preferences and complex environmental goods: The case of ecosystem restoration', in J. List and A. de Zeeuw (eds) *Recent Advances in Environmental Economics*, Edward Elgar, Chelterham

Milton, S. J., Dean, W. R. J. and Richardson, D. M. (2003) 'Economic incentives for restoring natural capital in southern African rangelands', *Frontiers in Ecology and the Environment*, vol 1, pp247–254

Ministerium für Landwirtschaft, Umwelt und Verbraucherschutz Mecklenburg-Vorpommern (2009) *Konzept zum Schutz und zur Nutzung der Moore: Fortschreibung des Konzeptes zur Bestandsicherung und zur Entwicklung der Moore*, Schwerin, http://service.mvnet.de/_php/download.php?datei_id=11159, accessed 25 June 2010

Molyneux, D. H., Ostfeld, R. S., Bernstein, A. and Chivian, E. (2008) 'Ecosystem disturbance, biodiversity loss and human infectious disease', in E. Chivian and A. Bernstein (eds) *Sustaining Life: How Human Health Depends on Biodiversity*, Oxford University Press, Oxford

Morris, R. K. A. and Barham, P. (2007) 'The Habitats Directive as a driver for sustainable development in the coastal zone: The example of the Humber estuary', in B. A. Larson (ed) *Sustainable Development Research Advances*, Nova Science Publishers, New York

Morse, W. C., Schedlbauer, J. L., Sesnie, S. E., Finegan, B., Harvey, C. A., Hollenhorst, S. J., Kavanagh, K. L., Stoian, D. and Wulfhorst, J. D. (2009) 'Consequences of environmental service payments for forest retention and recruitment in a Costa Rican biological corridor', *Ecology and Society*, vol 14, no 1, p23

NASA (2008) 'Image of the day: Aral Sea', Earth Observatory, http://earthobservatory.nasa.gov/IOTD/view.php?id=9036, accessed 22 September 2010

Neilan, W., Catterall, C., Kanowski, J. and McKenna, S. (2006) 'Do frugivorous birds assist rainforest succession in weed dominated oldfield regrowth of subtropical Australia?' *Biological Conservation*, vol 129, pp393–407

Nellemann, C. and Corcoran, E. (eds) (2010) *Dead Planet, Living Planet: Biodiversity and Ecosystem Restoration for Sustainable Development. A Rapid Response Assessment*, United Nations Environmental Programme, GRID-Arendal, www.grida.no/_res/site/file/publications/dead-planet/RRAecosystems_screen.pdf, accessed 22 September 2010

Normile, D. (2009) 'Bringing coral reefs back from the living dead', *Science*, vol 325, no 5940, pp559–561

Norton, D. A. (2009) 'Species invasions and the limits to restoration: Learning from the New Zealand experience', *Science*, vol 325, no 5940, pp569–571

Nupp, T. E. and Swihart, R. K. (1998) 'Effects of forest fragmentation on population attributes of white-footed mice and eastern chipmunks', *Journal of Mammalogy*, vol 79, pp1234–1243

Pabon-Zamora, L., Fauzi, A., Halim, A., Bezaury-Creel, J., Vega-Lopez, E. Leon, F., Gil, L. and Cartaya, V. (2008) 'Protected areas and human well-being: Experiences from Indonesia, Mexico, Peru and Venezuela', in *Protected Areas in Today's World: Their Values and Benefits for the Welfare of the Planet*, CBD Technical Series No 36, Convention on Biological Diversity, Montreal

Pabon-Zamora, L., Escobar, J., Calvo, L. M. and Emerton, L. (2009) *Valuing Nature: Why Bolivia's Protected Areas Matter for Economic and Human Well-Being*, The Nature Conservancy, Arlington, VT

Palmer, M. A. and Filoso, S. (2009) 'Restoration of ecosystem services for environmental markets', *Science*, vol 325, no 5940, pp575–576

Palmer, M. A., Lettemaier, D. P., Poff, N. L., Postel, S. L., Richter, B. and Warner, R. (2009) 'Climate Change and river ecosystems: Protection and adaptation options', *Environmental Management*, vol 44, pp1053–1068

Panzacchi, M., Bertolino, S., Cocchi, R., et al (2007) 'Population control of coypu *Myocastor coypus* in Italy compared to eradication in UK: A cost–benefit analysis', *Wildlife Biology*, vol 13, pp159–71

Parry, M., Lowe, J. and Hanson, C. (2009) 'Overshoot, adapt and recover', *Nature*, vol 458, no 30, pp1102–1103

Paterson, J. S., Araújo, M. B., Berry, P. M., Piper, J. M. and Rounsevell, M. D. A. R. (2008) 'Mitigation, adaptation and the threat to biodiversity', *Conservation Biology*, vol 22, pp1352–1355

Pattanayak, S. K. (2004) 'Valuing watershed services: Concepts and empirics from Southeast Asia', *Agriculture, Ecosystems and Environment*, vol 104, pp171–184

Pattanayak, S. K. and Wendland, K. J. (2007) 'Nature's care: Diarrhea, watershed protection, and biodiversity conservation in Flores, Indonesia', *Biodiversity and Conservation*, vol 16, pp2801–2819

Pimentel, D., McNair, S., Janecka, J., Wightman, J., Simmonds, C., O'Connell, C., Wong, E., Russel, L., Zern, J., Aquino, T. and Tsomondo, T. (2001) 'Economic and environmental threats of alien plant, animal, and microbe invasions', *Agriculture, Ecosystems and Environment*, vol 84, pp1–20

Pimentel, D., Zuniga, R. and Morrison, D. (2005) 'Update on the environmental and economic costs associated with alien-invasive species in the United States', *Ecological Economics*, vol 52, pp273–288

Polasky, S. (2008) 'Rivers of plans for the rivers of grass', in M. Doyle and C. A. Drew (eds) *Large-Scale Ecosystem Restoration*, Island Press, Washington, DC

Pollard, S. R., Kotze, D. C. and Ferrari, G. (2008) 'Valuation of the livelihood benefits of structural rehabilitation interventions in the Manalana Wetland', in D. C. Kotze and W. N. Ellery (eds) *WET-Outcome Evaluate: An Evaluation of the Rehabilitation Outcomes at Six Wetland Sites in South Africa*, WRC Report No TT 343/08, Water Research Commission, Pretoria

Pongsiri, M. J., Roman, J., Ezenwa, V. O., Goldberg, T. L., Koren, H. S., Newbold, S. C., Ostfeld, R. S., Pattanayak, S. K. and Salkeld, D. J. (2009) 'Biodiversity loss affects global disease ecology', *BioScience*, vol 59, pp945–954

Pretty, J. N., Noble, A. D., Bossio, D., Dixon, J., Hine, R. E., Penning de Vries, F. W. T. and Morison, J. I. L. (2006) 'Resource-conserving agriculture increases yields in developing countries', *Environmental Science and Technology*, vol 40, pp1114–1119

Pywell, R., Warman, E., Hulmes, L., Hulmes, S., Nuttall, P., Sparks, T., Critchley, C. and Sherwood, A. (2006) 'Effectiveness of new agri-environment schemes in providing foraging resources for bumblebees in intensively farmed landscapes', *Biological Conservation*, vol 129, pp192–206

Rapport, D. J., Costanza, R. and McMichael, A. J. (1998) 'Assessing ecosystem health', *Trends in Ecology and Evolution*, vol 13, pp397–402

Rey Benayas, J. M., Newton, A. C., Diaz, A. and Bullock, J. M. (2009) 'Enhancement of biodiversity and ecosystem services by ecological restoration: A meta-analysis', *Science*, vol 325, no 5944, pp1121–1124

Ricciardi, A. and Simberloff, D. (2008) 'Assisted colonization is not a viable conservation strategy', *Trends in Ecology and the Environment*, vol 24, pp248–252

Richardson, D. M., Pysek, P., Rejmanek, M., Barbour, M. G., Panetta, F. D. and West, C. J. (2000) 'Naturalization and invasion of alien plants: Concepts and definitions', *Diversity and Distributions*, vol 6, p93

Salt, T., Langton, S. and Doyle, M. (2008) 'The challenges of restoring the Everglades Ecosystem', in M. Doyle and C. A. Drew (eds) *Large-Scale Ecosystem Restoration*, Island Press, Washington, DC

Samson, M. S. and Rollon, R. N. (2008) 'Growth Performance of Planted Mangroves', *Development*, vol 33, no 2, pp237–253

Sathirathai, S. and Barbier, E. B. (2001) 'Valuing mangrove conservation in southern Thailand', *Contemporary Economic Policy*, vol 19, no 2, pp109–122

Scalera, R. and Zaghi, D. (2004) *Alien Species and Nature Conservation in the EU: The Role of the LIFE Program*, European Commission, Brussels

Schäfer, A. (2009) 'Moore und Euros – die vergessenen Millionen', *Archiv für Forstwesen und Landschaftsökologie*, vol 43, no 4, pp156–159

Searchinger, T., Heimlich, R., Houghton, R. A., Dong, F., Elobeid, A., Fabiosa, J., Tokgoz, S., Hayes, D. and Yu, T.-H. (2008) 'Use of US croplands for biofuels increases greenhouse gases through emissions from land-use change', *Science*, vol 319, pp1238–1240

Seastedt, T. R., Hobbs, R. J. and Suding, K. N. (2008) 'Management of novel ecosystems: Are novel approaches required?' *Frontiers in Ecology and the Environment*, vol 6, pp547–553

SER (2004) *The SER International Primer on Ecological Restoration*, International Science and Policy Working Group, Society for Ecological Restoration International, Tucson, www.ser.org/pdf/primer3.pdf, accessed 28 Octber 2010

SER-IUCN (2004) *Ecological Restoration: A Means of Conserving Biodiversity and Sustaining Livelihoods*, Society for Ecological Restoration, Tuscon and IUCN, Gland, Switzerland

Skovognatur (2007) 'Skjern River restoration', www.skovognatur.dk/common/404.htm, accessed 22 September 2010

Speldewinde, P. C., Cook, A., Davies, P. and Weinstein, P. (2009) 'A relationship between environmental degradation and mental health in rural Western Australia', *Health and Place*, vol 15, pp865–872

Stauffer Jr., J. R., Madsen, H., McKaye, K., Konings, A., Bloch, P., Ferreri, C. P., Likongwe, J. and Makaula, P. (2006) 'Schistosomiasis in Lake Malawi: Relationship of fish and intermediate host density to prevalence of human infection', *EcoHealth*, vol 3, pp22–27

Stone, R. (2009) 'Nursing China's ailing forests back to health', *Science*, vol 325, pp557–558

Sun, C. and Liqiao, C. (2006) *A Study of Policies and Legislation Affecting Payments for Watershed Services in China*, Research Centre of Ecological and Environmental Economics Beijing and International Institute for Environment and Development, London

Suzán, G., Marcé, E., Giermakowski, J. T., Mills, J. N., Ceballos, G., Ostfeld, R. S., Armién, B., Pascale, J. M. and Yates, T. L. (2009) 'Experimental evidence for reduced rodent diversity causing increased hantavirus prevalence', *Public Library of Sciences ONE*, vol 4, p5461

Tallis, H., Kareiva, P., Marvier, M. and Chang, A. (2008) 'An ecosystem services framework to support both practical conservation and economic development', *Proceedings of the National Academy of Sciences*, vol 105, no 28, pp9457–9464

TEEB (2009) *The Economics of Ecosystems and Biodiversity: Climate Issues Update*, September 2009, www.teebweb.org, accessed 20 November 2009

TEEB Foundations (2010) *The Economics of Ecosystems and Biodiversity: Ecological and Economic Foundations* (ed P. Kumar), Earthscan, London

Tuno, N., Wilberforce, O., Minakawa, N., Takagi, M. and Yan, G. (2005) 'Survivorship of *Anopheles gambiae* sensu stricto (Diptera: Culicidae) larvae in western Kenya highland forest', *Journal of Medical Entomology*, vol 42, pp270–277

Turpie, J. (2004) 'The role of resource economics in the control of invasive alien plants in South Africa', *South African Journal of Science*, vol 100, pp87–93

Turpie, J., Marais, C. and Blignaut, J. (2008) 'The Working for Water programme: Evolution of a payments for ecosystem services mechanism that addresses both poverty and ecosystem service delivery in South Africa', *Ecological Economics*, vol 65, pp788–798

UNDP-UNEP Poverty-Environment- Initiative (2008) *Making the Economic Case: A Primer on the Economic Arguments for Mainstreaming Poverty-Environment Linkages into National Development Planning*, United Nations Development Programme and United Nations Environment Programme

UNEP-WCMC (2006) *Shoreline Protection and Other Ecosystem Services from Mangroves and Coral Reefs*, UNEP-WCMC Biodiversity Series No 24, United Nations Environment Programme and World Conservation Monitoring Centre, www.unepwcmc.org/resources/publications/UNEP_WCMC_bio_series/24.cfm, accessed 20 November 2009

van der Gaag, D. J. (2007) Report workshop management of Anoplophora, 22–24 November 2006, Wageningen, Netherlands, available at www.minlnv.nl/cdlpub/servlet/CDLServlet?p_file_id=22662, accessed 28 October 2010

van der Wal, R., Truscott, A.-M., Pearce, I. S. K., Cole, L., Harris, M. P. and Wanless, S. (2008) 'Multiple anthropogenic changes cause biodiversity loss through plant invasion', *Global Change Biology*, vol 14, pp1428–1436

van Wilgen, B. W. (2001) 'The economic consequences of alien plant invasions: Examples of impacts and approaches to sustainable management in South Africa', *Environment, Development and Sustainability*, vol 3, p145

Vilà, M., Basnou, C., Pysek, P., Josefsson, M., Genovesi, P., Gollasch, S., Nentwig, W., Olenin, S., Roques, A., Roy, D., Hulme, P. E. and DAISIE partners (2009) 'How well do we understand the impacts of alien species on ecosystem services? A pan-European, cross-taxa assessment', *Frontiers in Ecology and the Environment*, vol 8, no 3, pp135–144, www.ufz.de/data/Vila-DAISIE_Frontiers-Ecology-201012676.pdf, accessed 28 October 2010

Vitousek, P. M., D'Antonio, C. M., Loope, I. L. Westbrooks, R. (1997) 'Biological invasions as global environmental change', *American Scientist*, vol 84, pp468–478

Vittor, A. Y., Gilman, R. H., Tielsch, J., Glass, G., Shields, T., Lozano, W. S., Pinedo-Cancino, V. and Patz, J. A. (2006) 'The effect of deforestation on the human-biting rate of *Anopheles darlingi*, the primary vector of falciparum malaria in the Peruvian Amazon', *American Journal of Tropical Medicine and Hygiene*, vol 74, pp3–11

Vos, C. C., Berry, P., Opdam, P., Baveco, H., Nijhof, B., O'Hanley, J., Belle, C. and Kuipers, H. (2008) 'Adapting landscapes to climate change: Examples of climate-proof ecosystem networks and priority adaptation zones', *Journal of Applied Ecology*, vol 45, pp1722–1731

Walsh, J. F., Molyneux, D. H. and Birley, M. H. (1993) 'Deforestation: Effects on vector disease', *Parasitology*, vol 106, pp55–75

White, P. C. L. and Harris S. (2002) 'Economic and environmental costs of alien vertebrate species in Britain', in D. Pimentel (ed) *Biological Invasions: Economic and Environmental Costs of Alien Plant, Animal and Microbe Species*, CRC Press, Boca Raton, FL

WHO (2006) *Ecosystems and Human Well-Being: Health Synthesis*, A report of the Millennium Ecosystem Assessment, World Health Organization, Geneva

World Bank (2004) *Natural Disasters, Counting the Costs*, http://web.worldbank.org/WBSITE/EXTERNAL/NEWS/0,,contentMDK:20169861~menuPK:34457~pagePK:34370~piPK:34424~theSitePK:4607,00.html, accessed 20 November 2009

World Bank (2009a) 'The sea is coming back', http://go.worldbank.org/DR6H6N4GQ0, accessed 20 November 2009

World Bank (2009b) *Convenient Solutions to an Inconvenient Truth: Ecosystem-Based Approaches to Climate Change*, Environmental Department, World Bank, Washington, DC

World Bank (2010) 'The economics of adaptation to climate change: A synthesis report', (final consultation draft), World Bank, Washington, DC, http://siteresources.worldbank.org/EXTCC/Resources/EACC_ FinalSynthesisReport0803_2010.pdf, accessed 5 August 2010

Wunder, S. and Albán, M. (2008) 'Decentralized payments for environmental services: The cases of Pimampiro and PROFAFOR in Ecuador', *Ecological Economics*, vol 65, pp685–698

WWF (2008) *Water for Life: Lessons for Climate Change Adaptation from Better Management of Rivers for People and Nature*, World Wide Fund for Nature International, Gland, Switzerland, http://assets. panda.org/downloads/50_12_wwf_climate_change_v2_full_report.pdf, accessed 2 December 2009

Zhang, P., Shao, G., Zhao, G., Le Master, D. C., Parker, G. R., Dunning Jr., J. B. and Li, Q. (2000) 'China's forest policy for the 21st century', *Science*, vol 288, pp2135–2136

Annex 1

Direct costs and potential benefits of restoration: Selected examples by ecosystem

Restoration effort and context	Type of restoration and cost items	Source or link	Ecosystem	Last year of data collection	Cost: €/ha	Benefits of restoration
(1) Eelgrass restoration in harbour (seabed) following the installation of an oil pipeline	Growing shoots and the transplantation of shoots using volunteer workers	Leschen et al (2007)	Seagrass meadows	2007	170,000	Habitat improvement to support the proliferation of juvenile marine resources and other forage species.
(2) Restoration of coral reefs following blast fishing in South-east Asia	Construction of new reef using special cement (all inclusive) Establishment of EcoReefs, i.e. branching ceramic stoneware modules (materials only) Placement of stones (from terrestrial sources) Comparison with Florida Keys restoration Comparison with restoration in Maldives	Fox et al (2005)	Coral reef	2002	11,000,000 500,000 50,000 5,000,000–80,000,000 300,000–1,200,000	Dynamite fishing destroys corals and habitat, which leads to reduced fishing and income from tourism. In Indonesia, lost income from this cause ranges from €410 million to €2.2 billion. Restoration attempts to restore value, both economically and biologically.
(3) Restoration of mangroves in West Lake estuary (Port Everglades, US)	The restoration of 500ha of mangrove forest through hydrologic improvements to blocked mangroves, and the removal of 80ha of historical dredged material fill and various pine species	Lewis Environmental Services (2007)	Mangroves and estuaries	1995	7148	Habitat creation to restore fish populations and to develop nature-based tourism through construction of a nature centre and outdoor classroom, multi-use boardwalks, fishing facilities, small boat launching site, public observation areas and hiking trails.

Restoration effort and context	Type of restoration and cost items	Source or link	Ecosystem	Last year of data collection	Cost: €/ha	Benefits of restoration
(4) Restoration of the Bolsa Chica estuary, California	Restoration to form part of the offset programme to mitigate large industrial-scale development	Francher (2008)	Mangroves and estuaries	2006	325,000	Creation of habitat to: provide food for fish, crustaceans, shellfish, birds and mammals; absorb pollutants; reduce erosion of the marine shore; and provide an opportunity to observe nature.
(5) Restoration of freshwater wetlands in Denmark	Wetland restoration through hydrological manipulation	Hoffmann and Baattrup-Pedersen (2007)	Inland wetland	2005	8,375	The reduction of nitrogen loads to downstream recipients and to enhance the resource value.
(6) Control of phosphorus loads in stormwater treatment wetlands	Wetland construction and hydrological manipulation	Juston and De Busk (2006)	Inland wetland	2005	25,000	The removal of phosphorus loads from open water bodies.
Restoration of the little Tennessee River, North Carolina	Riparian buffer costs, without fencing cost	Holmes et al (2004)	Rivers and riparian zones	2000	2302 (€/km)	Restoration benefits are: • abundance of game fish;
	Riparian buffer costs, with fencing cost				7341 (€/km)	
	Average cost of revetments where on-site trees were available				36,348 (€/km)	• water clarity; • wildlife habitat; • allowable water uses; and
	Average cost of revetments where on-site trees were not available				47,670 (€/km)	• ecosystem naturalness.
	Average cost of establishing a riparian buffer in a 'Representative' restoration				4825 (€/km)	The benefit:cost ratio for riparian restoration ranged from 4.03 (for two miles of restoration) to 15.65 (for six miles of restoration).
	Average cost of establishing a representative mix of restoration activities				17,870 (€/km)	

Restoration effort and context	Type of restoration and cost items	Source or link	Ecosystem	Last year of data collection	Cost: €/ha	Benefits of restoration
(7) Restoration of the Skjern River, Denmark	Construction and restoration of watercourses	Skovognatur (2007)	Rivers and riparian zones	2002	130,000	Benefits are to: • reinstate flow conditions of the Skjern River and remove unnatural barriers; • improve the aquatic environment of Ringkøbing Fjord and allow the river, fjord and sea to function as a single biological entity; • enhance conditions for migratory fish; recreate a natural wetlands habitat of international importance; and • develop the leisure and tourist potential of the Skjern River Valley.
Restoration of the Cheonggyecheon River, Seoul	Flood mitigation and channelling of the river	Kil-Dong (2007)	Rivers and riparian zones	2005	120,000	Benefits are to: • improve environmental conditions in the downtown area; • create a focal point of both historical significance and aesthetic appeal; • trigger long-term economic growth by attracting tourists and investors; and • aid in making Seoul a financial and commercial hub in the East Asian region.

Restoration effort and context	Type of restoration and cost items	Source or link	Ecosystem	Last year of data collection	Cost: €/ha	Benefits of restoration
(8) Re-establishment of native eucalyptus trees in former grassy woodland, south-east Australia	Revegetation after intensive grazing and farming: active restoration Revegetation after intensive grazing and farming: passive restoration	Dorrough and Moxham (2005)	Grasslands and rangelands	2003	970 285	Benefits are to stop and reverse: the loss of biodiversity, land degradation, land productivity loss and dryland salinization.
(9) Restoring land to increase forage for bumblebees in intensively farmed landscapes in UK	Reseeding of study area with a mixture of grass seeds	Pywell et al (2006)	Grasslands and rangelands	2003	101	Pollination services for semi-natural ecosystems and a wide range of agricultural and horticultural crops, and many garden plants.
(10) Restoration in Coastal British Columbia Riparian Forests	Thinning treatments, conifer planting. Structures were made using surplus conifer and alder trees removed at streamside to release existing site conifers.	GRN (2007)	Temperate forests	2002	2200	Management aims to improve streamflow integrity (bank stability, water quality, shade) and provision of downed trees (large woody debris) for stream channels. Large woody debris is crucial for healthy salmon and trout habitat: by creating pools and cover, it retains nutrients and stabilizes the stream.

Restoration effort and context	Type of restoration and cost items	Source or link	Ecosystem	Last year of data collection	Cost: €/ha	Benefits of restoration
(11) Masoala Corridors Restoration, Masoala National Park, Madagascar	Tree and plant nurseries Plantation Forest maintenance	Holloway et al (2009)	Tropical forests	2008	11–223 19–372 15–670	Communities depend on the ecosystem services delivered by the forests and the establishment of corridors between existing clumps of forests are essential to ensure the survival of these and the ongoing delivery of ecosystem services to communities.
(12) Restoration of rainforest corridors, Andasibe area, Toamasina Region, Madagascar (Tetik'asa Mampody Savoka, TAMS)	Sourcing and planting of trees	Holloway and Tingle (2009)	Tropical forests	2008	570–1250	Enhancement of native biodiversity, human and ecosystem well-being through restoring degraded wasteland to a mosaic of integrated, diverse natural forest and productive ecosystems.
(13) Polylepis forest restoration, Peru	Restoration and revegetation of landscape	Jameson and Ramsey (2007)	Tropical forests	2005	760	Regulation of water supplies in a seasonally dry climate: the importance of this is likely to increase as tropical glaciers retreat and dry season meltwater declines in volume.

Restoration effort and context	Type of restoration and cost items	Source or link	Ecosystem	Last year of data collection	Cost: €/ha	Benefits of restoration
						The forest floor, with a high coverage of shaded mosses, also regulates the flow of water into the rivers and the reduction of soil erosion during heavy rain on the shallow soils of the steep Andean slopes.
(14) Restoration of old-fields, New South Wales, Australia	Restoration and enhancement of natural succession of old-growth tropical plantations	Neilan et al (2006)	Tropical forests	2004	16,000	Soil productivity, biodiversity, reduced vulnerability and exposure to the invasion by alien species, and the reduction of soil erosion.
(15) Restoration of the Atlantic Forest (Mata Atlântica), Brazil	Aroeira trees (*Lithraea molleoides*) were thinned as needed, tree seedlings of other native species were planted on degraded sites and natural regeneration in these areas is being monitored	Instituto Terra (2007)	Tropical forests	1999	2600	Besides biodiversity, water from the Bulcão stream and other springs is beginning to return. A dam that had previously been silted up, along with two other springs, have been recovered. During the dry season, these recovered springs have outflows of around 20 litres/minute.

Restoration effort and context	Type of restoration and cost items	Source or link	Ecosystem	Last year of data collection	Cost: €/ha	Benefits of restoration
(16) Working for Water, South Africa	Clearing of invasive alien plants	Turpie et al (2008)	Woodland and shrubland	2008	200–700	Improved water supply, carbon sequestration and fire protection.
(17) Mangrove restoration from former shrimp farms	Replanting mangrove trees and other rehabilitation measures	Barbier (2007)	Mangroves	2007	8800–9300	Improved coastal protection, fisheries and forest products from mangroves.

Part IV

The Road Ahead

Chapter 10

Transforming our Approach to Natural Capital: The Way Forward

Coordinating lead author
Patrick ten Brink

Lead authors
Markus Lehmann, Clare Shine

Contributing authors
Arthur Eijs, Leonardo Mazza, Alice Ruhweza

Editing and language check
Clare Shine

See end of chapter for acknowledgements for reviews and other contributions

Contents

Key messages   453

Introduction   456

1   Future vision: Working with the value of nature   456
   1.1   Building visibility and appreciation of natural capital   456
   1.2   Accounting for natural values in decision making   458
   1.3   Pathways to a realistic vision to underpin future development   459

2   A framework for sustainable action   462
   2.1   Common and differentiated responsibilities and interests:
       Who can do what?   462
   2.2   Opportunities for action at the international level   464
   2.3   Opportunities for action at national (domestic) level   468

3   Delivering change   472
   3.1   Priorities for the next five years   472
   3.2   Practical tools for an alternative development path   474

Acknowledgements   478

Notes   478

References   478

Key messages

Natural capital – from invisibility to growing awareness

Ecosystems and their biodiversity underpin the global economy, society and human well-being. They need to be valued and protected. The world's natural capital is not a luxury for the rich but a necessity for all. The value of nature has long been overlooked in economic signals, policy instruments, public investments and national accounts. This has contributed to unprecedented erosion of natural capital, causing economic loss and social hardship and undermining prospects for long-term prosperity and quality of life. Now, however, awareness of these many values is growing and policy makers are beginning to change their approach to natural capital.

Future vision: Working with the value of nature

Biodiversity in all its complexity – the diversity, quality and quantity of genes, species and ecosystems – needs to be preserved for its intrinsic value and the benefits it provides to present and future generations. We have to live within the Earth's means and respect the regenerative capacity of ecosystems. This includes avoiding critical ecological thresholds, beyond which deterioration increases rapidly, and disruption and damage can be irreversible or hugely expensive to repair.

Working within the limits of nature protects not only biodiversity but also our own economic, social and personal interests. It calls for engagement by all actors, public and private, across sector policies, and at all geographic levels, from global to local.

A framework for sustainable action

International opportunities

Globally agreed frameworks for action like the Convention on Biological Diversity's (CBD) new Strategic Plan for the period 2011 to 2020 already recognize the key economic role of biodiversity and ecosystem services and urgently need effective implementation at national level. Multilateral and bilateral agencies, foundations and non-governmental organizations all have a role to play in this process, such as through capacity building in developing countries. Closer cooperation is required between international and regional environmental treaties, organizations and processes to maximize biodiversity synergies – including opportunities under the UN 'sister' conventions on desertification (UNCCD) and climate change (UNFCCC). The latter provides critically important mechanisms through the REDD+ instrument and investment in ecosystem-based mitigation and adaptation.

National opportunities

National opportunities will inevitably be country- and context-specific. Every country has a different starting point but some steps will be common across countries:

- Step 1: Assess the country's natural capital and the services it provides.

- Step 2: Understand opportunities to respond.

- Step 3: Identify where the greatest benefits of action lie and where the greatest resistance to action will come from.

- Step 4: Develop solutions that work within national context and lead by example.

Delivering change

Five global priorities should be targeted over the next five years that build on the evidence on the value of nature, address biodiversity goals and link with other priority objectives – of improved food and water security, climate change, livelihoods and job opportunities:

1. Fisheries need to respect regenerative and ecological limits for the sector's long-term viability, livelihoods and jobs, cost-effectiveness, food security and biodiversity.

2. Forest loss and degradation needs to be slowed and halted for the sake of biodiversity, the vast range and values of ecosystem services provided, peoples' livelihoods and continued storage and sequestration of globally vital quantities of carbon dioxide.

3. Coral-reef degradation and destruction needs urgent attention if they are to continue to help mitigate natural hazard impacts in coastal zones, maintain fish nurseries, support local development and provide vast potential for research.

4. Stable financial resources need to be secured to implement and manage protected areas (PAs) and incentives created to invest in restoration of degraded lands.

5. Climate–nature synergies can efficiently combine climate change and biodiversity objectives through ecosystem-based mitigation and adaptation to meet both objectives more cost-effectively.

Tools for change

Practical tools are required to help recognize, demonstrate and respond to the value of nature and transform our approach to natural capital. While each country will have its own priorities, and experiences, a common list of achievable actions and tools includes steps to:

- Integrate the evidence base for better measurement and monitoring – from biodiversity and ecosystem services indicators to natural capital accounts and more comprehensive national income accounts (as in Chapter 3).

- Develop a culture of assessment taking wider ecosystem values over longer time periods into account, as well as the range of costs and benefits across affected parties, public and private, national and international (Chapter 4).

- Adjust incentives in line with environmental impacts, positive and negative – rewarding benefits through prices payments and markets, and applying the polluter pays principle to address losses (Chapters 5, 6 and 7).

- Green the markets and the supply chain – developing and regulating markets, setting standards, supporting labelling and leading by example through green public procurement (Chapter 5).

- Reform environmentally harmful subsidies (Chapter 6).

- Use regulation and good governance to 'raise the baseline' – i.e. improve the minimum level of environmental standards or performance (Chapters 7 and 2).

- Improve the implementation and enforcement of legal frameworks (Chapter 7).

- Improve protected area networks and invest in wider ecosystems for climate change adaptation and to meet other objectives cost-effectively, including natural hazard management, poverty alleviation and other MDGs (Chapters 8 and 9).

- Invest in understanding and awareness of the value of nature to stimulate and harness policy responses for business, communities and citizens (Chapters 3 and 4).

These are all key steps to transform our approach to natural capital and move towards a development path that integrates economic, social and environmental concerns in a resource-efficient economy that works within the planet's ecological capacities.

Introduction

> I believe that the great part of miseries of mankind are brought upon them by false estimates they have made of the value of things. (Benjamin Franklin, 1706–1790; Farrand, 1993)

> There is a renaissance underway, in which people are waking up to the tremendous values of natural capital and devising ingenious ways of incorporating these values into major resource decisions. (Gretchen Daily, Stanford University; Daily and Ellison, 2002)

Biodiversity provides a range of ecosystem services that support livelihoods and underpin the global and local economy. The examples in this book show how often these values go unrecognized in the markets and in decision making by policy makers, administrators, businesses and individuals. Because nature is almost invisible in the choices we make at every level, we have been steadily drawing down our natural capital – without understanding either what it really costs to replace services provided free by nature or that man-made alternative solutions are sometimes far too expensive for these services to be replaced or substituted.

However, new momentum is under way to gather evidence and develop tools for more balanced and accountable approaches based on nature's values. *The Economics of Ecosystems and Biodiversity in National and International Policy Making* is full of examples and best practices from around the world that point to emerging solutions.

This book started with the scientific and social context for urgent action (Chapter 1) and the role of policy and governance (Chapter 2). It highlighted the critical need to measure what we manage (Chapter 3) and to integrate such values into accounting systems and policy assessment (Chapter 4). Chapters 5 to 9 discussed the rich toolkit of policy responses that can be adapted to different national circumstances, capacity and priorities. This final chapter pulls together key messages from these chapters to focus on practical ways forward. What role can policy makers play in helping to respond to the value of nature? How? At what level? Who else should be involved?

Section 1 outlines progress to date and presents a vision for working with nature. Section 2 proposes a framework for sustainable action that recognizes differentiated roles and responsibilities, and sets out concrete steps for institutions and their partners. Section 3 identifies priorities for implementation, including target actions for the next five years and key tools to achieve lasting results.

1 Future vision: Working with the value of nature

1.1 Building visibility and appreciation of natural capital

Ignorance of the value of natural capital contributes to its loss

Our 'natural capital' stocks include ecosystems, biodiversity and natural resources, and underpins our economies, societies and individual well-being. Nature provides humanity with the essentials of life – food, water, fuel, materials for construction, and genetic diversity that supports food security and development of new medicines.

Healthy ecosystems help purify water, waste and air, regulate climate, provide natural pest control and mitigate natural hazards such as flooding, fires and avalanches. The natural world creates opportunities for recreation and tourism, frames our identity and cultural and spiritual values, and stores vast information at the genetic, organism, species and ecosystem level.

Biodiversity loss has particularly severe implications for poor societies that depend on ecosystem goods and services for health, nutrition and a safety net in the face of natural disasters. Unlike the rich, the poor are often unable to replace ecosystem services with technological fixes or substitute products. Biodiversity loss undermines efforts to reduce poverty and development opportunities. At the same time, some causes of this loss stem from under-development.

For all these reasons, the world's natural capital is not a luxury for the rich but a necessity for all. Working with nature can be more cost-effective and sustainable than technological solutions available only to certain sections of society. However, the values of biodiversity and natural solutions have long been largely invisible and are still overlooked, poorly understood or difficult to capture in the market economy. Of course markets do recognize the value of some natural resources but many others are not accurately reflected in economic signals, day-to-day decisions or society's accounting systems.

This pervasive undervaluation has contributed to the steady loss of forests, soils, wetlands and coral reefs as well as wild species and productive assets like fisheries. We are running down our stock of natural capital without understanding the value of what we are losing.

Current rates of loss of biodiversity and its associated ecosystem services demonstrate not just a biological crisis. Losses in the natural world have direct economic repercussions that we systematically underestimate. Using our growing evidence base to make the value of natural capital visible will pave the way to targeted and cost-effective solutions.

Progress is being made to improve understanding

The good news is that attitudes and priorities are changing. Better estimates are increasingly available to decision makers to provide guidance on these different natural values (see TEEB Foundations, 2010).

Explicit values are already available for marketed fish, timber, agricultural commodities and tourism and wherever specific markets have been created. Implicit values can be calculated in some other cases, like the cost of man-made technology to replace some services provided free by ecosystems. Promising valuation techniques and markets are developing for services like carbon storage and water provision. In innovative areas like biomimicry, which offers great hope for the future, we are only just beginning to understand the potential values.

Some of these services are or could be important motors of development. However, progress will require improved understanding (science and economics), well-designed instruments (regulatory, market, information) and sustained political commitment.

1.2 Accounting for natural values in decision making

The short-term focus can be overcome

Decision making is still biased towards private and immediate economic benefits. The long-term value of ecosystem services is poorly understood and we still do not fully account for their public benefits, let alone their benefits for third countries and future generations.

Understanding the whole picture is essential to inform trade-offs in decision making. Modern policies that seek to integrate the three pillars of environmental, economic and social concerns need more accurate assessment of the value of natural services. When available, this information often highlights the rationale for engagement to secure long-term benefits from public goods at risk.

We also need to appreciate the opportunities and responsibilities linked to these values. Improved indicators can assess the status of biodiversity in order to set specific and measurable targets, and to design and monitor the application of policy instruments. This calls for investment in scientific understanding of biodiversity (e.g. taxonomy). Managing risks efficiently depends on understanding how ecosystems function, the relationship between their biotic and abiotic components and how they react to stresses like climate change, pollution, landscape fragmentation or invasive species.

Core tools for a fuller evidence base now include expanded biodiversity and ecosystem service indicators, spatial mapping of natural capital and assessment of the relationship between natural, economic and social systems. These can help policy makers by combining qualitative, quantitative, spatial and monetary information for integration into impact assessments and policy deliberations. Familiar policy instruments, like environmental impact assessments (EIAs) and cost–benefit analysis, can be strengthened in the process.

Understanding the limited substitution potential of ecosystem services – and the scale of socio-economic impacts from loss or degradation of natural capital – is essential. A robust evidence base can support more balanced and transparent decision making on spatial planning, land-use permits, use rights and regulations. Sound investment decisions also need to consider the link between different land uses and the services they provide.

It is arguably hard for policy makers to run economies without knowing whether the natural asset base is appreciating or depreciating and how productive it is. Investing in the development of 'natural capital accounts' – spatially articulated and value-linked ecosystem service accounts at different levels – should be prioritized in the longer term, as should the development of more comprehensive national income accounts. This represents a paradigm shift in the indicators and information that policy makers have at their disposal.

Economic insights can guide actions

Working with nature can often be cheaper than man-made solutions for flood control, water purification and provision, carbon storage and sequestration, city cooling and so on. Ecosystem-based adaptation to climate change, for example, can offer cost-effective strategies to help tackle risks ranging from degradation, desertification and erosion to species loss and biological invasions. Investing in ecological infrastructure not only makes economic sense but can also help to alleviate poverty and address commitments under the Millennium Development Goals.

Economic analysis also shows that early action is nearly always cheaper than a delayed response. Evidence on invasive species, for example, systematically shows that early detection and rapid response can avoid far larger and often generalized costs of lost agriculture or forestry output, infrastructure damage and investments in control and management. Avoiding degradation in the first place is cheaper than paying for attempted ecological restoration, which rarely guarantees a return to the earlier state.

1.3 Pathways to a realistic vision to underpin future development

In much of the world, the current development pathway involves running down natural assets in the pursuit of rapid economic growth even though this erosion of natural capital undermines the foundations of social and economic prosperity and well-being. If not curbed, this trajectory of rising consumption and production to cater for a growing and more prosperous population will inevitably go beyond natural resource limits and breach critical ecosystem thresholds. Several of these resource limits and thresholds have already been breached.

A new global vision needs to encompass the value of nature and support a shift to development pathways compatible with the planet's capacities. As a priority this must address the challenge to increase the effective net productivity of agricultural production to feed a world population of 9 billion people by 2050 while also delivering effective strategies for conservation and sustainable use of the world's natural resources. Similarly, fish stocks need to be managed in a sustainable manner if they are to offer an important source of nutrition and livelihoods in the long term.

Several proposals for components of a vision have been developed to engage people and policies concerned with biodiversity (see Box 10.1). These vary in emphasis but all seek to capture common principles and to:

- safeguard biodiversity for its intrinsic value and its benefits to mankind;
- halt and reverse biodiversity loss (no net loss or net positive gain of biodiversity);
- preserve and restore natural capital to support prosperity and human well-being;
- meet peoples' needs within the generative and regenerative capacities of ecosystems;
- avoid critical thresholds (environmental, economic and/or social tipping points);
- consider future generations, wider equity issues and ethics; including the fair and equitable sharing of benefits;
- ensure that biodiversity conservation and restoration measures support food and water needs and social goals on poverty and health (e.g. Millennium Development Goals);
- build public recognition of the value of biodiversity;
- deliver positive behaviour change through sustainable production and consumption.

Box 10.1 Visions for the future: Variations on a theme

The vision of the CBD Strategic Plan is a world of 'living in harmony with nature' where 'by 2050, biodiversity is valued, conserved, restored and wisely used, maintaining ecosystem services, sustaining a healthy planet and delivering benefits essential for all people'. (CBD; 2010)

Biodiversity and the ecosystem services – the world's natural capital – are preserved, valued and, insofar as possible, restored for their intrinsic value, enabling them to support economic prosperity and human well-being, and averting any catastrophic changes linked to biodiversity loss. (Janez Potočnik, European Commissioner for the Environment, 2010)

Nature is the basis of our existence. A natural environment with a rich biological diversity adapts easier to changes such as a warmer climate. Biodiversity is a basis for sustainable development and human well-being. Biodiversity is our life insurance. (Heidi Sørensen, Norwegian State Secretary, 2007)

Concrete progress is being made on possible new development paths to underpin the future vision. Historical patterns of eroding natural capital in pursuit of growth and prosperity are beginning to be replaced by approaches focused on decoupling growth, greening the supply chain, responsible risk management, proactive investment in natural capital and eco-innovation. These have implications for policy design, integration and implementation across many sectors as well as the management and use of biodiversity.

The path to a resource-efficient economy involves 'decoupling' (reducing the environmental impacts of economic activities so that growth in output does not imply a growth in natural resource use or pollution) (see EU, 2010). Efficiency gains (in production processes), innovation and new solutions will all be important drivers of decoupling and offer significant scope to contribute to halting biodiversity loss. However, given the projected growth and increasing wealth of the world's population by 2050, efficiency gains through relative decoupling (unit savings) will probably not be enough on their own to deliver absolute decoupling (reducing overall resource use or pollution pressure) (Jackson, 2009). However much we innovate and commit to efficiency gains, ever-growing demand risks outstripping this potential.

Complementary measures and approaches are needed to move to a resource-efficient economy as swiftly as possible. These include getting prices right (adjusting economic signals and reforming incentives like taxes, charges, fees, fines, subsidies and standards to guide producer and consumer responses) and 'greening' the supply chain by engaging supply-side solutions and demand-side encouragement for less polluting products or truly green products and services (see TEEB in Business, 2011). A green economy needs market prices and signals to take account of the value of nature. Consumption patterns also need to be made sustainable. Part of this can be addressed by pricing; consumption policy measures, social norms and habits, and consumer choices will also be critical.

An operating culture based on understood, managed and acceptable risks will require us to adjust development paths to avoid critical resource and ecosystem thresholds. Improved risk management means identifying risks (to biodiversity, ecosystem functions, service flows and impacts on people, society, infrastructure and business), investing to minimize them and planning for appropriate responses. This approach spans everything from spatial planning and natural hazards to invasive species prevention and directly relates to liability regimes and standards.

Proactive investment in natural capital will mean treating natural capital in the same way as man-made capital. Evidence of cost savings in water purification and supply, carbon capture and storage, flood control, erosion control and pollination, and of economic opportunities for bioprospecting (pharmaceuticals), biomimicry, recreation and tourism, underlines the value of natural capital. Healthy and diverse ecosystems are expected to be more resilient in the face of climate change and to help buffer human populations from its adverse impacts. Proactive investment strategies are needed to capture the value of naturally provided services and provide incentives to maintain them. One step is to reward those who help provide these ecosystem services (Chapter 5) or protect areas of particular value (Chapter 8). Another involves targeted ecological restoration either as a public investment for public goods or as a private investment to realize opportunities or meet responsibilities and liabilities (Chapters 7 and 9).

21st-century economic innovation calls for investment in whole new sectors and activities. Biomimicry – learning from nature to find nature-based engineering, architectural, material and scientific solutions to problems and challenges – is a prime example. Emerging opportunities of this kind will require research, capacity building and integration through cross-disciplinary work. They are closely linked to the concept of 'responsible citizens, responsible business' where actors understand their interactions (direct and indirect) with nature and assume responsibilities through their choice of activities (see TEEB for Citizens website).

Good governance needs to underpin all these components of a future vision, where policies and incentives across government departments and between levels of government are coordinated and complementary. This will involve due public participation and engagement (e.g. of local peoples) in decision making, a high level of transparency (e.g. on subsidies) and accountability, clear and appropriate property rights, legal certainty, implementation, and enforcement of non-compliance. This can be reinforced by a strong culture of assessment that considers the 'whole picture' across ecosystem services, peoples, geographical locations and time.

Equally important is the ethical dimension of a new global vision supporting a fair and equitable society where costs and benefits are shared, where people participate in decisions affecting their livelihoods, and concerns of poverty, health and education are addressed. This links directly to the Millennium Development Goals and is founded on the relationship between peoples and ecosystems. It is also linked to what Amartya Sen calls 'capabilities for flourishing' – those multidimensional goods, both physical and less tangible, which are essential to preserve people's capabilities to exercise their freedom (Sen, 1999). The availability of functioning ecosystems and access to their services is increasingly recognized as a prerequisite for social well-being and personal fulfilment. Mutual understanding of rights and responsibilities includes drawing a qualitative distinction between meeting people's basic needs on the one hand and facilitating ever higher levels of consumption on the other. Resource efficiency may well require us to redefine sufficiency. Future efforts and solutions will need to be determined in the light of past responsibilities if agreements are to be perceived as fair and capable of effective implementation, whether within societies or between countries. This reflects the basic respect and trust needed to underpin successful collaborative action at all levels of governance.

These visions are fundamentally interconnected and complementary. Different stakeholders will want and will be able to take forward different aspects. All contribute to the original Brundtland (WCED, 1987) definition of sustainable development:

> Sustainable development is development that meets the needs of the present without compromising the ability of future generations to meet their own needs.

2 A framework for sustainable action

2.1 Common and differentiated responsibilities and interests: Who can do what?

Partnerships and champions for change

There are many potential champions of solutions at different geographic levels and in different groups. We need to understand their respective interests, incentives, opportunities and responsibilities in order to harness their potential. Good governance can encourage these groups to contribute to the common goal of halting biodiversity loss and enable them to benefit from working sustainably with nature.

Partnerships can generate actions at the appropriate scale and mainstream biodiversity within all sectors of government, society and the economy. Cooperation between the programmes, funds and specialized agencies of the United Nations system, other agencies and foundations, NGOs and local partners (in particular women's groups, indigenous and local communities) is essential for effective action at the national level.

At the international level, policy makers can develop, and commit to, common targets, and strengthen implementation frameworks under the six biodiversity-related treaties that cooperate through the Biodiversity Liaison Group.[1] The CBD[2] arguably provides the main motor for global action, following the adoption in October 2010 of the new CBD Strategic Plan and the Nagoya Protocol on Access to Genetic Resources and the Fair and Equitable Sharing of Benefit Arising out of their Utilization, and the creation of the Intergovernmental Platform on Biodiversity and Ecosystem Services (see Section 2.2 below). The work of the UNEP Resource Panel also offers positive potential for progress.

Stronger partnerships are needed between the CBD and its two sister conventions – on climate change (UNFCCC) and desertification (UNCCD) – and associated international institutions and processes, the private sector and civil society. Meeting the Millennium Development Goals also calls for collaboration with organizations promoting health, education and human rights and addressing poverty.

Regional and bilateral efforts are another important part of the solution and can be tailored to context and priorities, building on existing frameworks for collaboration (see Section 2.2 below).

The bedrock of progress will be countries developing their own natural capital assessments and accounting for natural values in their policy frameworks and decisions on the ground. National success stories can be shared and provide models for other countries to learn from (see Section 2.3 below).

Engagement of business

Halting biodiversity loss cannot be done without the private sector. This is also often in its best short- and long-term interest and can serve to increase profitability, create new markets and help avoid liabilities.

Business opportunities already exist in certified products, nature-based pharmaceuticals and a range of markets. New opportunities will arise from REDD+, other PES schemes and biomimicry. Green public procurement should increase market pull for products and services.

Business responsibilities with regard to the environment are linked to the polluter pays principle. Its increased application in many countries will require this to be factored into business operations by ascertaining future risks and liabilities, and taking steps to minimize these. Changes in resource pricing, subsidies and cost recovery mechanisms will also feed into this process and change the overall economic signals in the market. Improved corporate governance will involve fuller disclosure of risks, investment in avoidance strategies and setting aside funds for possible compensation demands. Progressive companies are already exploring and starting to build sustainable business models that more deeply integrate and account for the value of biodiversity, opportunities and responsibilities (see also TEEB in Business, 2011).

Policy makers need to combine encouragement and support for business with targeted regulation, standards, monitoring and reporting/disclosure requirements and enforcement to achieve the above objectives. Positive and negative incentives (support vs. fines) and public–private partnerships all have a role to play.

Communities, NGOs, citizens and scientists

Community-based management of natural resources has a long and strong tradition, highlighted in this book with regard to fisheries, forests, traditional knowledge and protected areas. As Elinor Ostrom underlines, common property can be successfully managed by the groups who use it and, in some cases, is actually better managed than if privatized or managed by government (Ostrom, 1990). In the future, engaging communities will be particularly important for the acceptance, operation and performance of PES/REDD+ instruments as well as for the management of other community goods (e.g. fish, forests, reefs). Policy makers can involve communities in EIA processes and permit decisions, instrument design, protected area management, definition and protection of communal property rights, monitoring and capacity building.

NGOs are another key player. They can raise funds, purchase land, get PES schemes started, offer volunteers to help with monitoring, science and restoration, and contribute arguments and evidence to policy formation. They also provide a bridge to citizens, helping to build awareness and motivate their engagement.

Citizens, through their actions and purchasing decisions, can lower their consumption impacts out of responsibility or self-interest. This is particularly important with a growing and wealthier global population adopting western-style consumption habits (e.g. meat, goods). Policy makers can support these trends through driving changes in social habits and norms (e.g. via infrastructure and campaigns for recycling), improved information (labelling, online data, school curricula, university research and development), standards and spatial planning (see TEEB for Citizens website). However, we need to acknowledge that many consumers, faced with complicated issues like biodiversity, are reluctant to take the initiative to achieve a more sustainable consumption pattern: they expect policy makers to make the choices for them through appropriate standard setting and regulation, and by changing incentives.

Scientists and academics can provide critical insights and discoveries to help the above groups benefit from nature's extraordinary potential. This needs to be accelerated and backed by capacity building to make the most of new solutions, along with efforts to develop indicators for ecosystem services to better manage natural assets and support economic valuation and improved policy design. Opportunities to improve our knowledge base – through additional investments in taxonomy and field research for bioprospecting and biomimicry – are open-ended. Only a fraction of nature's solutions to current challenges (health, energy, pollution, food production, hazard management) have been found. Discoveries in this area can help us create the green economy of the future and to engage new motors of growth in biodiversity-rich countries.

2.2 Opportunities for action at the international level

The CBD Strategic Plan

The new Strategic Plan to implement the Convention on Biological Diversity, unanimously adopted at the tenth meeting of the Parties in October 2010, is a globally agreed framework for national implementation to 2020. It places strong emphasis on economic analysis and valuation and the application of economic tools.

The Plan sets out five strategic goals and 20 headline targets to guide national strategies and efforts to preserve biodiversity. These are reproduced in Box 10.2.

Targets 1 to 3 make explicit links to the values of biodiversity, the need for awareness, integration of these values into decision making and planning and in economic signals. The other 17 targets each have resonance with the discussions in this book which presents examples of practice that can provide insights for future implementation of CBD targets.

Other global processes offering opportunities for immediate action

The new Protocol on Access and Benefit Sharing related to Genetic Resources, also adopted in October 2010 in Nagoya, Japan, provides a global framework for more sustainable as well as fair and equitable use of this key component of biodiversity. Policy makers need to prioritize its ratification to enable the Protocol to enter into force as rapidly as feasible.

Under the UN Framework Convention on Climate Change (UNFCCC), the initiative for Reducing Emissions from Deforestation and Degradation (REDD+) may provide the opportunity for important synergies between climate and biodiversity policies. REDD+ has the potential to become one of the most important instruments available, if designed, implemented and funded to:

- ensure additionality, conditionality and verifiability;
- support due engagement by local peoples;

- cover the full range of forest ecosystem services;
- avoid detrimental impacts on biodiversity, e.g. from intensive forestry management or inappropriate afforestation.

The need to adapt to climate change and the promise of major funding for this purpose offers a way to redirect monies to ecosystem-based adaptation. Key investment opportunities and needs include mangroves and coastal planting to address coastal erosion/realignment, land management to reduce flood risks, green infrastructure in cities for cooling, and investment in protected areas and their connectivity to enhance ecosystem resilience.

Actions under the UN Convention to Combat Desertification (UNCCD) as well as actions linked to LULUCF (Land Use, Land-Use Change and Forestry) under the UNFCCC will be critically important for dryland habitats that have suffered from overgrazing and are vulnerable to climate change. Investing in their restoration and

---

Box 10.2 The CBD Strategic Plan for the period 2011–2020

Strategic goal A

Address the underlying causes of biodiversity loss by mainstreaming biodiversity across government and society

Target 1: By 2020, at the latest, people are aware of the values of biodiversity and the steps they can take to conserve and use it sustainably.

Target 2: By 2020, at the latest, biodiversity values have been integrated into national and local development and poverty reduction strategies and planning processes and are being incorporated into national accounting, as appropriate, and reporting systems.

Target 3: By 2020, at the latest, incentives, including subsidies, harmful to biodiversity are eliminated, phased out or reformed in order to minimize or avoid negative impacts, and positive incentives for the conservation and sustainable use of biodiversity are developed and applied, consistent and in harmony with the Convention and other relevant international obligations, taking into account national socio-economic conditions.

Target 4: By 2020, at the latest, governments, business and stakeholders at all levels have taken steps to achieve or have implemented plans for sustainable production and consumption and have kept the impacts of use of natural resources well within safe ecological limits.

Strategic goal B

Reduce the direct pressures on biodiversity and promote sustainable use

Target 5: By 2020, the rate of loss of all natural habitats, including forests, is at least halved and where feasible brought close to zero, and degradation and fragmentation is significantly reduced.

Target 6: By 2020 all fish and invertebrate stocks and aquatic plants are managed and harvested sustainably, legally and applying ecosystem based approaches, so that overfishing is avoided, recovery plans and measures are in place for all depleted species, fisheries have no significant adverse impacts on threatened species and vulnerable ecosystems and the impacts of fisheries on stocks, species and ecosystems are within safe ecological limits.

Target 7: By 2020 areas under agriculture, aquaculture and forestry are managed sustainably, ensuring conservation of biodiversity.

Target 8: By 2020, pollution, including from excess nutrients, has been brought to levels that are not detrimental to ecosystem function and biodiversity.

Target 9: By 2020, invasive alien species and pathways are identified and prioritized, priority species are controlled or eradicated, and measures are in place to manage pathways to prevent their introduction and establishment.

Target 10: By 2015, the multiple anthropogenic pressures on coral reefs, and other vulnerable ecosystems impacted by climate change or ocean acidification are minimized, so as to maintain their integrity and functioning.

Strategic goal C

To improve the status of biodiversity by safeguarding ecosystems, species and genetic diversity

Target 11: By 2020, at least 17 per cent of terrestrial and inland water, and 10 per cent of coastal and marine areas, especially areas of particular importance for biodiversity and ecosystem services, are conserved through effectively and equitably managed, ecologically representative and well connected systems of protected areas and other effective area-based conservation measures, and integrated into the wider landscapes and seascapes.

Target 12: By 2020 the extinction of known threatened species has been prevented and their conservation status, particularly of those most in decline, has been improved and sustained.

Target 13: By 2020, the genetic diversity of cultivated plants and farmed and domesticated animals and of wild relatives, including other socio-economically and culturally valuable species, is maintained, and strategies have been developed and implemented for minimizing genetic erosion and safeguarding their genetic diversity.

Strategic goal D

Enhance the benefits to all from biodiversity and ecosystem services

Target 14: By 2020, ecosystems that provide essential services, including services related to water, and contribute to health, livelihoods and well-being, are restored and safeguarded, taking into account the needs of women, indigenous and local communities, and the poor and vulnerable.

Target 15: By 2020, ecosystem resilience and the contribution of biodiversity to carbon stocks has been enhanced, through conservation and restoration, including restoration of at least 15 per cent of degraded ecosystems, thereby contributing to climate change mitigation and adaptation and to combating desertification.

Target 16: By 2015, the Nagoya Protocol on Access to Genetic Resources and the Fair and Equitable Sharing of Benefits Arising from their Utilization is in force and operational, consistent with national legislation.

Strategic goal E

Enhance implementation through participatory planning, knowledge management and capacity building

Target 17: By 2015 each Party has developed, adopted as a policy instrument, and has commenced implementing an effective, participatory and updated national biodiversity strategy and action plan.

Target 18: By 2020, the traditional knowledge, innovations and practices of indigenous and local communities relevant for the conservation and sustainable use of biodiversity, and their customary use of biological resources, are respected, subject to national legislation and relevant international obligations, and fully integrated and reflected in the implementation of the Convention with the full and effective participation of indigenous and local communities, at all relevant levels.

Target 19: By 2020, knowledge, the science base and technologies relating to biodiversity, its values, functioning, status and trends, and the consequences of its loss, are improved, widely shared and transferred, and applied.

Target 20: By 2020, at the latest, the mobilization of financial resources for effectively implementing the Strategic Plan 2011–2020 from all sources and in accordance with the consolidated and agreed process in the Strategy for Resource Mobilization should increase substantially from the current levels. This target will be subject to changes contingent to resource needs assessments to be developed and reported by Parties.

Source: CBD (2010)

creating green belts to prevent desert encroachment will be needed to preserve these ecosystems from further deterioration.

Future opportunities to strengthen the scientific and economic evidence base and integrate natural capital considerations into policy making can be provided by:

• the Intergovernmental Science-Policy Platform on Biodiversity and Ecosystem Services (IPBES) which offers a global forum for scientific debate and will produce regular high-level reports on the state and prospects for biodiversity and ecosystem services;

- ongoing work to develop the UN System of Environmental and Economic Accounting (SEEA, see Chapter 3);
- ongoing WTO negotiations and commitments for subsidy reform.

Multilateral efforts are already under way to create a framework to help raise and channel private money to reverse biodiversity loss and conserve our valuable ecosystems and their services where likely to prove most effective. The Green Development Initiative aims to secure global consensus on the need to further develop modalities to enhance private investments in biodiversity. One option could be the certification of types of land management that deliver both biodiversity and development outcomes and the sale of biodiversity credits derived from such management. A pilot phase is currently under development.

If established, this mechanism could help fill the funding gap to reverse biodiversity loss – much as the well-known Clean Development Mechanism (CDM) has done for climate change mitigation. These could complement transfers through international payments for transboundary ecosystem services as well as payments between private companies and local communities under a new international ABS regime.

As noted, global processes alone will not offer comprehensive solutions. It is vital to have progress at all levels so that if progress at one level is slow, action at another can prevent loss of momentum.

The regional multi-country level also offers solutions to biodiversity. Collaboration between nations provides opportunities to address regional challenges in areas of need that are beyond the domestic and outside global agreements. Multilateral frameworks are already well established for international rivers and river basins that deliver benefits to several countries, such as the Amazon, the Nile and the Danube. The same is true for marine areas managed under the framework of the UNEP Regional Seas Programme which now covers 13 seas and involves over 140 States. Strategic management programmes tailored to the needs of large marine ecosystems have been developed through some of these regional processes, notably for the Mediterranean.

Bilateral cooperation can pioneer new approaches and kick-start broader progress, possibly at regional or even global level. For example, Norwegian and German funding for activities to combat deforestation and protect biodiversity play a valuable role in highlighting European commitment to global solutions and create momentum and capacity to support REDD+ instruments. Target areas for bilateral support to launch tomorrow's green economies could include financing for ecosystem-based adaptation, accreditation of markets for certified goods, capacity building (taxonomy, bioprospecting, biomimicry) and support for developing natural capital accounts, indicators, datasets and baselines.

2.3 Opportunities for action at national (domestic) level

National governments (and also many regional and local governments: see TEEB in Local Policy, 2011) have the power and the tools to bring about lasting change. In addition to passing legislation, they can lead by example by creating markets, green procurement and direct investment in natural capital. Exploiting the multiple synergies between biodiversity and other policy goals may further enhance their legitimacy. Legislators demonstrating country (or regional or city) level commitment through action will also acquire greater influence in international forums.

It is critical that states which lack the technical expertise and institutions to realize this vision be provided with adequate support.

Every country is different in terms of its traditions, culture, geography and natural assets, infrastructure, income levels and priorities. Locally developed solutions can cater for these characteristics and maximize buy-in from affected groups. The varied cases presented in this book provide resources that can be flexibly adapted to national needs and preferences.

Recognizing this diversity does not mean that there are no common pointers for progress. The CBD's National Biodiversity Strategy and Action Plan (NBSAP) process offers a globally agreed framework for coherent biodiversity policy planning at national level. Countries can use their NBSAP revision process to improve common understanding and agreement on steps needed locally.

The following four steps can help put natural capital at the heart of national policy making and help demonstrate the value of natural capital, and in turn respond to the new understanding of the value, either by 'capturing value' (e.g. by market creation or adjusted price signals) or by regulatory policy response (e.g. by setting standards or increased enforcement).

- Step 1: Assess the nation's natural capital and the services it provides.
- Step 2: Set objectives that are ambitious and that inspire innovation, participation and identify opportunities to respond.
- Step 3: Identify where the greatest benefits of action lie and where the greatest resistance to action will come from.
- Step 4: Develop solutions that work and lead by example.

Building on this framework, the following section outlines priorities and tools for effective and achievable action.

Box 10.3 Four steps to put natural capital at the heart of national policy making

Step 1: Assess the nation's natural capital and the services it provides

1a: Assess and map ecosystems, their services and how these flow to beneficiaries

The ecosystem assessment should ideally be carried out at national level but this will depend on existing resources and opportunities (e.g. ongoing regional or local assessments) and which bodies are most interested (e.g. national, regional, local government). Assessments should include:

- State and trends of biodiversity and ecosystem services. Spatial mapping and indicators will be useful here (see Chapter 3), as would geographic information system (GIS) tools.

- Identification of potential threats (e.g. areas at risk from floods, desertification, salinization of soils and other ecosystem tipping points) and areas considered for conservation/development (see Chapters 8 and 9).
- Identification of links between biodiversity, the flow of ecosystem services and those who benefit and where. This is most usefully done in a spatial perspective and should specify, where possible, where a service is of local, national or international/global benefit.
- Synergies and trade-offs between ecosystem services and potential development.

It makes sense to start with already available information and focus on the most promising/ important sources of services. However, the longer-term aim should be to develop a full picture that covers all ecosystem services (integrated approach) and the entire country. This information would provide a valuable input to developing natural capital accounts.

1b: Target valuation where it matters

Valuations are critical to inform policy and investment decisions. The goal should be to develop a complete picture across all services. However, starting with one to two high-profile studies on critical national (or local) services can go a long way to raise awareness of the importance of these assets for the national economy and well-being and the helpful role of economic analysis. The following are examples of useful areas for valuation:

- water purification services and water supply for cities;
- natural solutions to flooding and other natural hazards;
- green infrastructure and health benefits for cities;
- ecotourism, especially in protected areas;
- marine protected areas and fisheries benefits;
- carbon storage and sequestration value of trees, soil, grasslands, wetlands, etc.;
- ecosystem-based solutions for climate adaptation (afforestation, soil formation, connectivity);
- value lost through pollution (eutrophication, oil spills and reduced water/soil quality);
- benefit of preventive action to avoid invasive species damage and lost output.

1c: Work towards natural capital accounts and extended income accounts

Including the value of natural assets in extended income accounts will provide a valuable long-term tool for policy makers. Regular reporting on the state of natural capital will make it easier to target priorities for action and intervene more rapidly.
Two types of accounts need to be developed over time:

- accounts of the physical stock;
- flow accounts that link the flow of services from physical stock to economic accounts through depreciation/appreciation of natural capital, and the lost/accrued value of services.

Step 2: Set objectives that are ambitious and that inspire innovation, participation and identify opportunities to respond

2a: Set objectives with quantified long-term targets:

- Ensure certainty for a longer period for stakeholders; create an environment where the private sector knows what it is expected to do or to adhere to and provide stability that allows for innovation and investments.

- Develop a sustained, transparent communication strategy on the ultimate goals, the reasons for setting the targets and the need for action at all levels by every stakeholder.
- Develop a coherent framework for environmental education, starting with primary school: today's children are tomorrow's voters.

2b: Identify differentiated responsibilities, roles and potential to respond:

- Identify who in the country has a strong incentive and/or capacity for action. Build on existing international processes, national and local programmes and authorities.
- Review institutional roles and needs for collaboration to help with cross-sector integration, policy coherence and good governance.
- Engage the interests and responsibility of the private sector, as well as potential liabilities.
- Engage communities and citizens through information and participation, and stimulate biodiversity action plans that link to the provision of ecosystem services at local levels (e.g. with respect to opportunities for multiple ecosystem benefits).
- While identifying differentiated responsibilities, acknowledge dilemmas that actors face – first mover advantage, the prisoner's dilemma (where two people might not cooperate even if it is in both their best interests to do so), free riders – and stand ready to solve these issues (e.g. free consumer choice versus standards).

2c: Review existing policy instruments that can help to mainstream biodiversity objectives:

- Assess strengths, gaps and weaknesses and opportunities to improve governance, synergies and coherence.
- Assess how far policies take the value of nature into account and identify priority areas for reform.
- Identify scope for 'biodiversity proofing' of government investments or funding (e.g. development aid, regional development monies, rural development, agricultural and fisheries support schemes).

2d: Seize opportunities for action

Some windows will be planned and foreseeable, others difficult to forecast. They include:

- high-level international events or processes – meetings of the CBD, UNFCCC, UNCCD, CITES, UNCSD (Rio+20) – which offer a platform for commitments and progress;
- (new) national initiatives, e.g. green tax reform commissions, evaluation of and reporting on subsidies, national capital and income accounts reports;
- periodic budget and strategy reviews;
- crises and catastrophes, e.g. oil spills, species extinctions, stock collapse and flooding, which can also act as an urgent motivating force to find solutions.

Step 3: Identify where the greatest benefits of action lie and where the greatest resistance to action will come from

To design, negotiate and implement change effectively, it is important to understand:

- the scale, location and time scale of the benefits of action, taking into account the range of services, the different stakeholders and future perspectives;
- the links to the political agendas of the day – e.g. food, water and fuel security, unemployment, health and natural hazards, climate change, economic development, budget crisis and of course biodiversity itself;
- who will be the winners and losers, including the social dimension (impacts on livelihoods and vulnerable groups);
- the trade-offs of any decision across the four capitals (man-made, environmental, social and human) and across time;
- possible synergies and trade-offs across ecosystem services (avoid solving one problem and creating another one in exchange);
- the possible need for transition management while stakeholders adjust to costs (e.g. in protected area dialogue and subsidy reform).

Step 4: Develop solutions that work and lead by example

Each country has a different context, different experience with policy tools and different political appetite for action. Leading by example where initiatives have worked nationally is central to the global solution as this will facilitate and motivate other countries to action.

Some countries might start with a focus on marine protected areas and fish – demonstrating the value and responding by due designation, management and enforcement. Others may focus on water purification and provision benefits to cities from nearby green infrastructure, and set up a PES scheme to 'capture the value'. Some may choose to focus on landscape or seascape management and invest in the assets to attract tourism and foreign earnings. Whatever the starting point, it is also important to keep an eye on the bigger picture in order to spot emerging opportunities for new initiatives.

3 Delivering change

It is increasingly evident that our current economic pathway cannot and should not be sustained. Continued erosion of our natural capital will undermine future prospects for growth, prosperity and well-being. It is therefore critical to address the most urgent ecological threats before damage is irreparable (see Section 3.1). This calls for us to put tools in place to support an alternative development path based on the vision for a sustainable future (see Section 3.2).

3.1 Priorities for the next five years

Priorities obviously depend on location, scale and urgency of the challenges: each will have different champions to plead their cause. Food security will top the list for some countries, water scarcity and climate adaptation for others, employment and livelihoods for others still.

However, although a short list can never do full justice to all needs, there are a few common issues of major concern supported by the evidence on the value of nature, which address biodiversity goals and link with other priority objectives. The following five priorities are arguably those most likely to have global resonance, either because of where the impact is felt or because of where contributions to the solution can come from.

Fisheries

Fisheries demand urgent action because of overfishing, fish stock collapse, environmental damage and impacts on food and job security and economic efficiency. The ecological limits of marine ecosystems need to be better integrated into management frameworks, with incentives reformed to discourage destructive practices and encourage investment in maintenance of fish stocks and ecosystems offering a range of key services.

Forests

Forests contain the largest share of terrestrial biodiversity, store and sequester globally vital quantities of carbon dioxide and provide a vast range of additional ecosystem services as well as homes and livelihoods for many peoples. Concerted action and collaboration is vital to slow and halt the current rate of deforestation and degradation.

Coral reefs

Coral reefs – the tropical forests of the seas – are at risk from pollution, fishing, tourism, shipping and climate change. They are essential to help mitigate natural hazard impacts in coastal zones, maintain fish nurseries, support local development and provide vast potential for research. Direct investment in their protection and increased resilience is needed as benefits from climate change commitments and engagements will take time to materialize.

Climate–nature synergies

Climate–nature synergies – measures to mitigate climate change (e.g. protecting forests and carbon-rich soils) and to promote ecosystem-based adaptation – can efficiently combine climate change and biodiversity objectives. Key steps in this approach include the protection and appropriate management of protected areas (PAs), measures to increase the ecological coherence of protected area networks and actions to reduce environmental pressures and restore degraded ecosystems in the wider environment. PAs and other ecological assets and infrastructures (rivers and floodplains, canals, buffer zones, forests and agricultural lands, parks) need to be integrated within a mutually reinforcing connected network.

Funding for biodiversity

Stable financial resources need to be secured to implement and manage protected areas, e.g. though innovative funding instruments and adequate international funding, particularly to support the needs of developing countries. Key strategies comprise an increase in core funding for biodiversity, the greening of budgets in other policy domains relevant to biodiversity and the facilitation of private investments in biodiversity conservation and sustainable use. However, it is not all about more money. We need to understand better the scale and implications of the current protected area financing gap and how to close it by reducing pressure on protected areas: appropriate measures getting prices right, reducing subsidies, making the polluter pay, good governance, and implementation and enforcement and increased awareness of the benefits of protected areas.

3.2 Practical tools for an alternative development path

The starting point of this book was the concern that erosion of the natural capital base will lead not only to biodiversity losses but also reduce the prospects of economic prosperity and social well-being (see Figure 10.1 below). Many valuable services – whether provisioning, regulatory, supporting or cultural – are at threat if the providing ecosystems deteriorate and underlying biodiversity is lost.

This book has provided evidence that we are currently running down our natural capital at an alarming rate. This is expected to have important implications for the flows of ecosystem services and negative economic repercussions, given that the number of sectors benefiting from natural capital represents a far larger share of the economy than many policy makers appreciate.

The assumption that economic 'growth' will continue even as natural capital is eroded and that GDP growth automatically leads to increased well-being, are in the authors' view over-simplistic, and even dangerous, for at least two reasons. First, we could expect an ever larger share of GDP to be taken up with 'defensive costs' to – repair

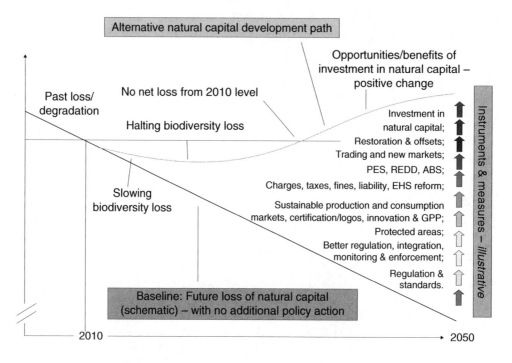

Figure 10.1 *Eroding natural capital base and tools for an alternative development path*

Source: Patrick ten Brink, own representation

(some of) the environmental harm. Second, societal and individual well-being will probably be eroded with the loss of natural capital: the use of GDP as a welfare indicator (doubtful in the first place), will become more and more meaningless. Livelihoods and quality of life are not helped by fisheries collapse, desertification or the loss of access to clean water or fuelwood.

A key question, which merits further exploration, is the way which economic growth will itself be affected by resource scarcity, limits to the availability of natural resources and critical ecological thresholds (such as fish stock collapse, major eutrophication events and extensive deforestation and degradation resulting in changed ecological functions: see Chapters 1 and 3). The links between economic development, natural capital erosion and persistence of poverty also merit further attention. Additional analysis, both at micro- and macro-economic level is needed. This can feed into discussions on the SEEA and revision of the SNA and macro-economic indicators going beyond GDP (Chapter 3), green economy and green new deal debates (UNEP's Green Economy Initiative;[3] UNEP, 2009), work on the Millennium Development Goals (MDGs), and wider economic and public policy debates.

Most of this book has focused on the range of tools that can help redirect our development path. Figure 10.1 contrasts two pathways in schematic form. One is based on continuing erosion of natural capital. The other leads to a gradual halt in biodiversity loss, followed by a reversal of such loss through restoration and investment in natural capital: recognition of the value of natural capital potentially leads to a net appreciation of the natural capital base through improved stewardship, protection and investment.

Figure 10.1 puts the milestone for halting the loss at 2020. It then envisages a gain so that no net loss relative to current levels is achieved by 2030 and a new paradigm of positive natural capital is entered thereafter. Unfortunately this appears grossly optimistic, given the current rate of biodiversity loss and increasing rather than decreasing pressures from production and consumption. The lack of integration of biodiversity concerns and ecosystem service values into the market and sector policies also adds to the pessimism. Biodiversity policy alone will not be enough to halt biodiversity loss, let alone move to the new needed paradigm of investment in natural capital and appreciation of the interconnections and interdependency of economic and social systems with our ecosystems.

However, as the evidence base in this book has shown, progress has been made in many countries and many tools are already proving their merits. Global commitments can also contribute significantly. To maintain and broaden this momentum towards a resource-efficient and green economy, policy frameworks need to make the economics of ecology a greater part of the solution. Actors of all types and at all levels need to be engaged, and committed with urgency, creativity and resilience.

Tools that can help us make the transition to a new development path include:

Integrating the evidence base for better measurement, monitoring and accounting

Developing biodiversity and ecosystem service indicators and measurable targets, and investing in natural capital accounts will make it possible to assess the status, risks to and values of natural assets and systematically consider this information in decision making (as in Chapter 3). The new Intergovernmental Science-Policy Platform on Biodiversity and Ecosystem Services (IPBES) will provide important support for national and regional action and can support capacity building.

Developing a culture of assessment that takes the wider and ecosystem values over longer time periods into account

Timely and transparent assessment of the impact on ecosystem services of policies and decisions is essential to provide policy makers – across different areas of thematic responsibility – with the evidence base needed (Chapter 4). This is a key tool for the needed integration of biodiversity into other sector policies.

Adjusting incentives in line with positive and negative environmental impacts

Payments to reward providers of ecosystem benefits (PES instruments) are one potential growth area, particularly for carbon and water-related services. REDD+ offers a significant new source of payments, but will require major global transfers of funds as well as investment in learning, monitoring and verification to be credible. It should also factor in wider ecosystem services (Chapter 5). Conversely, disincentives for destruction of natural capital are needed by strengthening the application of the polluter and user pays principles (Chapter 7). There is already an ongoing paradigm shift from an assumed right to pollute to making polluters pay: this will have complex implications for decisions on prices, regulation and compensation for damage.

Getting prices right, greening the markets and greening the supply chain

This involves a phased shift from underpriced goods and services to paying for their full cost (within the bounds of affordability and equity). It will require a careful search for opportunities and investment in markets that work. Some green markets are already operational and can progress quickly: green products (organic foods, certified timber and fish) and services (ecotourism) have moved from niche and are gaining scale and leverage (Chapter 5). Government action through green public procurement policies and quality standards (Chapter 5), combined with citizen demand and proactive business efforts, can help to mainstream less damaging products and processes (see also TEEB in Business, 2011). However, government also needs to play a strong direct role in standard setting as well as helping consumers find their way through a thick forest of certificates. Shared responsibility is fundamental to progress – but it very often needs to be catalysed by government.

Reforming subsidies

A phased transition from harmful and inefficient subsidies to ones that protect or enhance biodiversity and associated ecosystem services can accelerate the transition to a resource-efficient economy (Chapter 6). To this end, transparent inventories and reporting of subsidies can also help to refocus the direction of money flows.

Using regulation and good governance to raise the baseline

The rule of law and proper oversight and compliance remain critical to any policy framework. Core tools for use throughout the world include 'traditional' instruments like product, process and emission standards, waste management requirements, EIA and SEA procedures, spatial planning and permit systems, compensation and liability rules for damage and designation of protected areas followed by effective enforcement. These can be supported – for example, through 'no net loss' policies like offsets and habitat banking – to ensure maximum gains for biodiversity and ecosystem services (Chapters 2, 4 and 7).

Expanding and managing protected area networks on land and at sea

Steps to protect the 'crown jewels' of biodiversity for their intrinsic value, maintain key services and increase ecosystem resilience are essential for climate change adaptation and to safeguard genetic diversity for food security. In parallel, increased investment is needed in wider ecological infrastructure to maintain and restore the ecological condition and coherence of ecosystems and re-establish ecosystem service provision. Protected area 'patches' need to be integrated into the wider landscape as part of a connectivity policy that incorporates ecological corridors (links to rivers and river floodplains, green infrastructure, buffer zones and species refugia). The objective is to be able to ensure resilience to climate change and other pressures, and offer a continued flow of ecosystem services to the regions (Chapters 8 and 9).

Putting these tools in place will mean changing the mindset from 'nature as a bountiful resource to be exploited' to 'working with nature's assets and within nature's limits'. It does not have to cost more. The current economic crisis provides opportunities to look harder at subsidy and also tax reform, to find cost-effective solutions and to invest in natural capital where there are positive returns.

Being able to measure where nature offers cheaper solutions than man-made infrastructure can help save government and private budgets and contribute to halting biodiversity loss. Staying on the right side of ecological tipping points can avoid costly restoration or the impacts of irreparable damage. Stimulating new and more sustainable markets with due sharing of benefits can support jobs and livelihoods. Taken together, these approaches can help address global challenges – climate change, water security, food security and poverty.

As this book shows, policy makers at national and international levels can show leadership and foresight in their actions to support public goods provided by nature. Such actions are needed at all levels of governance and across all key sectors (biodiversity, agriculture, fish, water, forestry, pharmaceuticals, tourism, energy, food and drink, transport, etc.) and should harness the energies of markets, business, citizens and communities. Coordination at higher levels will be necessary to ensure equitable and practical sharing of burdens and benefits.

Many states, especially developing countries, will need support to develop and implement these activities. Upscaling existing or new capacity-building programmes can provide effective and timely technical support and facilitate peer-to-peer exchange. Activities at national level can be strengthened through enhanced cooperation between the programmes, funds and specialized agencies of the UN system, other multilateral and bilateral agencies, regional processes, NGOs, and indigenous and local communities.

Positive progress is clearly under way. But as the man-made and natural disasters of 2010 (oil spills, forest fires and floods) remind us, careful planning and risk management are essential to avoid catastrophic impacts linked to our current development path. It remains to be seen whether the new momentum to make polluters pay will address burning but neglected issues such as the 405 'dead zones' in the sea caused by agricultural and wastewater run-off – and whether policy makers will take new initiatives without waiting for more ecological disasters.

At the same time as major catastrophes are capturing wider public attention, a quiet revolution is paving the way for ambitious planned responses that will transform our approach to natural capital. Systematic efforts to understand the value of nature are adding to the evidence base and fuelling policy responses. The many existing initiatives and emerging solutions being launched and implemented around the planet offer constructive ways to embark upon a more sustainable development path. There is major scope to learn from these rich and diverse experiences and to respond to existing success stories. Opportunities rather than disasters should be our motivation.

> It is not enough to know, one should also use; it is not enough to want, one should also act (Johann Wolfgang von Goethe, 1749–1832)[4]

Acknowledgements

The authors wish to thank Doreen Fedrigo-Fazio, IEEP, Belgium; Marianne Kettunen, IEEP, Finland; Hugh Laxton, Joint Nature Conservation Committee (JNCC), Belgium; Keti Medarova, IEEP, Belgium; Matthew Quinn, Welsh Assembly, Wales; Graham Tucker, IEEP, UK; Stephen White, European Commission – DG Environment, Belgium; Alexandra Vakrou, European Commission – DG Environment, Belgium; and James Vause, Defra, UK.

Notes

1   See www.cbd.int/blg/
2   The Convention on Biological Diversity (CBD) entered into force on 29 December 1993. It has three main objectives:
    • the conservation of biological diversity;
    • the sustainable use of the components of biological diversity;
    • the fair and equitable sharing of the benefits arising from the utilization of genetic resources.
    See www.cbd.int/convention/about.shtml for details.
3   For more information on the Green Economy Initiative see www.unep.org/greeneconomy/Home/tabid/1350/Default.aspx, accessed 21 August 2010
4   Johann Wolfgang von Goethe (1749–1832), quote from *Wilhelm Meister's Years of Travel* (work by Goethe), first edition published 1821

References

CBD (2010) *Decision X/2 on Updating and Revision of the Strategic Plan for the Post-2010 Period, Tenth Meeting of the Conference of the Parties to the Convention on Biological Diversity*, advance unedited text, available at www.cbd.int/nagoya/outcomes, accessed 15 November 2010

Daily G. C. and Ellison K. (2002) *The New Economy of Nature: The Quest to Make Conservation Profitable*, Island Press, Washington, DC

Fargione, J., Hill, J., Tilman, D., Polasky, S. and Hawthorne, P. (2008) 'Land clearing and the biofuel carbon debt', Science, vol 319, pp1235–1237

EU (2010) 'Europe 2020: A strategy for smart, sustainable and inclusive growth', European Commission, Brussels, http://ec.europa.eu/eu2020/pdf/COMPLET%20EN%20BARROSO%20%20%20007%20-%20Europe%202020%20-%20EN%20version.pdf, accessed 16 July 2010

Farrand, M. (ed.) (1993) 'Benjamin Franklin autobiography and other writings', Oxford University Press, New York

Jackson, T. (2009) *Prosperity Without Growth? The Transition to a Sustainable Economy*, Sustainable Development Commission, UK

MA (Millennium Ecosystem Assessment) (2005) *Ecosystems and Human Well-Being, Summary for Decision Makers*, Island Press, Washington, DC

Ostrom, E. (1990) *Governing the Commons: The Evolution of Institutions for Collective Action*, Cambridge University Press, Cambridge

Potočnik, J. (2010) 'Where next for the EU Commission's biodiversity policy?' Speech for WWF Evening Dialogue on Biodiversity, Brussels, 2 March 2010, http://ec.europa.eu/commission_2010-2014/potocnik/headlines/news/pdf/2010%2003%2002%20SPEECH%20WWF%20Biodiversity.pdf, accessed 22 September 2010

Sen, A. (1999) *Development as Freedom*, Oxford University Press, Oxford

Sørensen, H. (2007) quoted in Djoghlaf, A. 'CB statement: The Sixth Trondheim Conference on Biodiversity, Norway', UNEP, Montreal, www.cbd.int/doc/speech/2010/sp-2010-02-01-trondheim-en.pdf, accessed 22 September 2010

TEEB (2008) 'The economics of ecosystems and biodiversity: an interim report', European Commission, Brussels, www.teebweb.org

TEEB (2009) 'The economics of ecosystems and biodiversity for national and international policy makers – Summary: Responding to the value of nature', www.teebweb.org

TEEB for Citizens website, www.teebweb.org

TEEB Foundations (2010) *The Economics of Ecosystems and Biodiversity: Ecological and Economic Foundations* (ed P. Kumar), Earthscan, London

TEEB in Local Policy (2011) *The Economics of Ecosystems and Biodiversity in Local and Regional Policy and Management* (ed H. Wittmer and H. Gundimeda), Earthscan, London

TEEB in Business (2011) *The Economics of Ecosystems and Biodiversity in Business and Enterprise* (ed J. Bishop), Earthscan, London

UNEP (United Nations Environment Programme) (2009) Global Green New Deal Policy Brief, UNEP, www.unep.org/pdf/A_Global_Green_New_Deal_Policy_Brief.pdf, accessed 21 August 2010

WCED (World Commission on Environment and Development) (1987) *Our Common Future*, Oxford University Press, Oxford, p43

Index

Aarhus Convention 161
ABS *see* Access and Benefit Sharing
absolute decoupling 460
access
    energy subsidies 281
    genetic resources 224, 227
    information 112, 161
    justice 230, 161
    protected areas 360, 366
access and benefit sharing (ABS) 180, 230–231
accountability 2, 461
accounting
    investing in ecological infrastructure
        403, 431–433
    natural capital 2, 79–128, 458–459, 468, 470,
        475–476
    REDD+ 203
Aceh, Indonesia 369
action 1, 3, 5–75, 453–454, 462–472
adaptation *see* climate change adaptation
additionality 183–184, 190, 203
adjusted disposable national income (ADNI) 110
adjusted net savings 105
adjusted unit benefits transfer 144
ADNI *see* adjusted disposable national income
adverse incentives 268
advocacy 368
afforestation/reforestation (A/R) 203
Africa 39, 70
agriculture
    climate change adaptation 428
    ecosystem services 98, 134
    efficiency 459
    fertilizer regulation 306
    indicators 98
    integrated policy assessment 164
    losses 15, 19–20
    PES 190
    productivity 22
    regulations 307
    subsidies 261–262, 264, 266, 269–273, 279,
        289, 291
    sustainable 234–235, 429, 466
    trade liberalization 153
agri-environment payments 98, 182, 272–273
agro-ecological zoning 306
agroforestry 235
air pollution 306, 308
air quality 97, 309
alternative development pathways 474–478
Amazonian water pump 16, 200
Amazon region 21, 67, 202, 363–364
anthropocentric valuation 141
Antilles 330
aquaculture 232–233, 466
aquifer recharge 188

A/R *see* afforestation/reforestation
Arab countries 70
Aral Sea 414–415
artificial infrastructure 104
Asian elephant 161
assessment
    culture of 454, 476
    economic analysis 58
    integrated 284
    national biodiversity indicators 90
    natural capital 469–470
    policy 129–173
    subsidies 265–266
asset valuation 111
atmospheric cleansing capacity 97–98
Australia 99, 316, 332, 413
Austria 245
averting behaviour method 170
aviation kerosene 287
awareness 63, 231, 241, 334, 453, 455, 465

Bali Action Plan, UNFCCC 201, 206
Balmford, A. 90
Bangladesh 422
baselines 101, 183–184, 190, 203, 305–309, 455,
    476–477
bat crime 334
BAU *see* business-as-usual scenarios
Belgium 157–158, 312
Belize 133
below-cost pricing 278
beneficiaries 114, 160, 185
beneficiary pays principle 304
benefits
    ecosystem services 29, 54–55, 134–135
    enhancing 466–467
    natural capital 403, 416–425, 471–472
    offsets and biodiversity banking 313–316
    PES 186–194, 209
    policy 51, 471–472
    protected areas 347, 368, 383, 388
    REDD+ 204–206
    restoration 417, 421
    sharing 2, 179–180, 221–231, 461
    subsidies 269
    see also costs and benefits
benefits transfer approaches 143–145,
    412–413
best practices 154–163
big picture approaches 87
bilateral approaches 229, 374, 468
biodiversity banks 310–317
biodiversity definitions 10–13
biofuels 15, 21, 282
biomimicry 12, 237–238, 461
bioprospecting 224–228

BioTrade 232
BNMP *see* Bonaire National Marine Park
Bolivia 266, 428
Bonaire National Marine Park (BNMP),
    Antilles 330
bottom-trawling practices 268
Brazil 117, 125, 127, 218, 226, 306,
    363–364, 413
bumblebees 445
bundling services 196, 206
burden-sharing targets 213
business-as-usual (BAU) scenarios 21, 185
business engagement 463

Cameroon 421–422
Canada 215–216
CAP *see* Common Agricultural Policy
capacity
    building 164–165, 207–208, 453, 464, 467, 477
    protected areas 387, 398
capacity-enhancing subsidies 275–276, 291
capital 26, 39, 103–104, 108, 111, 387
    see also natural capital
capital gains tax 214
carbon
    conservation and restoration 467
    protected areas 354, 358–359, 386
    REDD+ 200–209
    sequestration 97, 187, 193–194, 363, 416
    sinks 14, 64
    see also emissions; greenhouse gases
Carbon and Biodiversity Demonstration Atlas,
    UNEP–WCMC 206
carbon capture and storage (CCS) 30–31
the Caribbean 374
cartels 229–230
catastrophes 65, 403, 430–431, 477–478
    see also natural disasters
catchment assessment 309
Catskill–Delaware Watershed, US 411
Catskills Mountains, US 190
CBD *see* Convention on Biological Diversity
CCS *see* carbon capture and storage
CDM *see* Clean Development Mechanism
Central Asia 70
centralized procurement 243
cereals 225
certification 180, 232–236, 238–241, 243, 468
champions 61–62, 462–463
checklist approaches 284
Chile 370
China 68, 106, 242, 323, 383, 426, 430–431
Chinchiná River Basin, Colombia 64
Chinese Environmental Award 62
choice modelling 169, 171
CI *see* Conservation International
CITES *see* Convention on International Trade in
    Endangered Species
citizens' juries 172
citizens' responsibilities and interests 463–464
Clean Development Mechanism (CDM) 208
climate change
    biodiversity loss 24
    coral reefs 17
    ecological infrastructure investment 403

ecosystem service indicators 97
    forests 115, 201
    mitigation 22, 163, 310, 314–316, 358, 454
    protected areas 354, 358–359, 386–387
    vulnerability 36
    water subsidies 278–279
climate change adaptation
    ecological infrastructure investment 403, 425–430
    future 454, 465
    protected areas 354, 358, 386–387
climate–nature synergies 454, 473
coastal areas 16, 133, 422–423, 430, 445
co-existence, right to 64–65
coherence 386–387
Colombia 64
Common Agricultural Policy (CAP), EU 271–272
common and differentiated responsibilities 462–464
common property 463
communication 238–240, 261, 387, 399
community level 38–39, 229, 347, 352, 463–464
compensation
    biodiversity losses 2, 310–317
    elephant damage 371
    public mechanisms 179
    redirecting for environmental goals 214–221
    spatial distribution 136–138
    subsidy reform 289
    valuation 146–147, 329, 372
    see also rewards
competition between regions scenarios 20
competitiveness 231, 246, 290
complementary measures 309, 460
compliance 62–63, 383
conservation
    carbon 467
    climate change adaptation 428–429
    forests 369
    incentives 179–257
    planning 370
    policy 50
    restoration contrast 413–414
    revenues 304
conservation banks 310
Conservation International (CI) 207
consumption
    aggregates 81–82
    biodiversity loss 1, 24–25
    choices 463–464
    fixed capital 111
    price corrections 105
    resource limits 459
    SNA 109
    subsidies 267–268, 280, 282
    sustainable 465
    water use rights 323
contingent valuation methods (CVM) 58, 169, 171
contracts 227–229
conventional markets scenarios 20
Convention on Biological Diversity (CBD)
    ABS 180
    climate change adaptation 426–427
    GDI 179, 213, 468
    greening national accounts 112
    indicators 87–89
    invasive species 419

monitoring   93
protected areas   350, 354, 373, 376, 384–385,
    388–389
REDD+   209
SBSTTA   93
sharing of benefits   221–222
strategic plans   52–53, 283–284, 291, 453, 460,
    462, 464–467, 469
subsidy reform   284, 291
Convention on International Trade in Endangered
    Species (CITES)   333
conventions   52–54, 161
cooperation   180, 247, 287–288, 387, 389, 453,
    462, 477
coordination   52–59, 238–240, 385–387, 399, 432, 477
coral reefs   16–17, 29, 147, 442, 454, 466, 473
cosmetic sector   236, 240
Costa Rica   186–187, 226, 364
cost and benefits, land-use change   31–33
costs
    biodiversity loss   12, 303–304
    certification   238
    climate change adaptation   427
    ecosystem-based approaches   458–459
    ecosystem damages   9, 163, 301
    genetic resources   223, 228
    GPP   243–245
    invasive alien species   24, 419–420
    MBIs   325, 328
    monitoring   92–93
    natural capital   30–31
    PES   195–196, 198–199
    policy   51, 337
    protected areas   349, 352, 359–360, 364–367,
        372–373, 388
    regulations   308
    restoration   408–412
    subsidies   261, 293
    substitution potential   37
    valuation   150, 171
    see also costs and benefits; transaction costs
costs and benefits
    ecosystem services value   135–138, 371–372
    good governance   69
    policy assessment   156–158
    protected areas   347, 354–368, 371–372
    REDD+   202
    restoration   140–141, 412–414, 416, 442–448
    sharing   221–231, 461
    standard setting   309
    subsidy reform   284
    valuation   31–35
    see also benefits; costs
cotton production   414–415
country level
    ecosystem services valuation   149
    environmental taxes   327
    GDP of the poor   124–127
    market-based instruments   321–322
    policy   338
    protected areas   353, 373
    SEA   152
Craft, A. B.   223
crested ibis   235
criminal prosecution   302, 330–336

critical ecological tipping points   21–22
critical thresholds   85–87, 101, 163, |
    460–461
crop wild relatives (CWR)   357
cultural level
    assessment   454, 476
    ecosystem service indicators   96, 101
    policy   49, 62–63
    protected areas   350, 358–359
cumulative impacts   328, 331
CVM see contingent valuation methods
CWR see crop wild relatives
Czech Republic   279

Daly River catchment, Australia   55
dams   424
debt   108, 261
decision making   31, 50–52, 56–58, 77–173,
    317–320, 458–459
decoupling   271–272, 460
defensive costs   474–475
deforestation
    biodiversity loss   14
    carbon sinks   64
    compensation   137
    diseases   424
    natural disasters   423
    offsetting   312
    PES   188–189, 193
    protected areas   362
    REDD+   200–209
    subsidies   278, 281
    vulnerability   116
    see also forests
Delphi surveys   172
demand side   112, 180, 197, 335
demonstration activities   206–207
Denmark   140–141, 244
design
    MBIs   328–330
    PES   194–199
    smart policy mixes   301–302
    subsidies   265, 287–290, 292
designer ecosystems   404–405
developing countries
    biodiversity loss   212
    capacity building   453
    certification   232, 241
    dependency on resources   113–114
    energy subsidies   266
    genetic resources   223–224
    greening the markets   180
    GPP   247
    investment   432
    natural capital   9, 10, 432, 463
    PES   186
    protected areas   359, 362, 365, 372–373
    sharing benefits   221
    supporting   477
    sustainable agricultural practices   429
    trade   54, 103
    valuation   150
    see also Reducing Emissions from Deforestation
        and Forest Degradation in developing
        countries

development
    benefit-sharing   230
    benefits transfer methods   144–145
    economic   54, 112, 209, 350, 368, 416, 430,
        475
    GPP   247
    land tradable rights   325
    pathways   459–462, 474–478
    policies   60
diet changes   22
differentiated responsibilities   462–464, 471
direct drivers of biodiversity loss   23–24, 155
direct government investment   403, 416
direct international payments   209–214
direct transfers of funds   263
direct use values   139
discount rates   156–157, 412
diseases   424
displacement   360, 364
distributional issues
    decision making   31
    ecosystem services value   135, 371
    MBIs   336–337
    PES   197
    policy   63, 66, 159
    poverty and biodiversity links   114
    property rights   68–69
    protected areas   347, 371, 383, 388
    provisioning   209
    subsidies   266, 284–286
diverse funding portfolios   381–382
diversity
    genetic   18–19, 89–90, 466
    species   18–19, 424–425
Doha Work Programme, WTO   273, 283, 291
dolphin protection   381
domesticated animals   19
Dominican Republic   116
donors   208, 374, 376
Dorrough, J.   413
DPSIR see drivers, pressures, status, impact and
    responses framework
Drakensberg mountains, South Africa   420
drinking water   97, 192, 356
drinks cartons   233
drivers of biodiversity loss   23–26, 155
drivers, pressures, status, impact and responses
    (DPSIR) framework   85–86, 92–93, 163

early warning systems   85
easements   215–216
East Ayrshire, Scotland   246
ecological fiscal reform (EFR)   337
ecological level
    connectivity   347, 354
    corridors   278, 446, 477
    fiscal transfers   217–219
    footprints   68, 81, 83, 99, 103
    indicators   89–90
    infrastructure investment   401–448
    measurements   368
    tax reform   337
    tipping points   21–22, 477

economic development   54, 112, 209, 350, 368,
    416, 430, 475
economic growth   107, 310, 368, 459, 474–475
economic thinking   150–163
EcoProcurement Service, Austria   245
ecotourism   235–236, 375, 382–383
Ecuador   193, 416
EEA see European Environment Agency
eelgrass restoration   442
EEZ see exclusive economic zones
efficiency   224–229, 283, 459–462
EFR see ecological fiscal reform
EHS see environmentally harmful subsidies
EIA see environmental impact assessment
elephant damage   371
Eliasch, J.   202
emissions   305, 309, 325, 427
    see also carbon; greenhouse gases
employment   190–193, 290
enabling conditions   198–199, 367, 388
endogenous poverty   114
energy   21, 244, 261, 264, 266, 269, 280–282, 291
enforcement   57, 67, 184–185, 302, 330–336, 352, 388
engagement   38–39, 159–162, 199–200, 287, 334,
    461, 463
    see also participatory approaches
engineered ecosystems   404–405
engineered solutions   411
entrance fees   329–330
entry fees   149, 367
environmental impact assessment (EIA)   151, 155
environmental level
    crime   302, 330–336
    decision making   161
    incentives   476
    liability rules   319
    policy   52, 62–63, 97
    poverty   114–117
    products   375
    satellite accounts   109
    standards   301, 305–309
    subsidies   261, 263, 267–282, 291–293
    taxes   214–221, 327
    trade links   54
    vulnerability   116
environmentally harmful subsidies (EHS)   263, 267,
    269, 291, 455
environmental tax reform (ETR)   337
equity
    GDP   102, 127
    MBIs   328
    policy   63–69
    polluter pays   304
    protected areas   347
    sharing costs and benefits   221–231, 461
    subsidy reform   290
estuaries   157–158, 443
Ethiopia   225, 266, 368
ETR see environmental tax reform
EU see European Union
eucalyptus woodlands   413, 445
Europe   70, 279, 327, 419–420
European Commission   99, 151

European Environment Agency (EEA)   109–110
European Union (EU)
    Beyond GDP process   81
    biodiversity loss   88
    Common Agricultural Policy   271–272
    emissions trading   325
    environmental crime   334
    full cost recovery   324
    GPP   242
    liability rules   319
    natural cosmetic sector   236
    offsets and biodiversity banking   316
    protected areas   384
    SEA   152
    subsidies   279, 288
eutrophication   22
evaluation   57, 293, 367–372
Everglades, Florida, US   421
evidence-based policy making   84
exclusive economic zones (EEZ)   268, 275–276
exogenous poverty   114
explicit values   457
extensive farming systems   270–271
extinction   9–10, 18–19, 69, 91, 403, 466
Exxon Valdez disaster   58, 146–147

fairness   63–69, 108, 221–231, 461
    see also equity
fair trade   232
FAO see Food and Agriculture Organization
farmland bird index   271
farm subsidies   288–289
fault-based liability   319
FCPF see Forest Carbon Partnership Facility
fees   147, 329–330, 367
fertilizer regulation   306
FES see final ecosystem services indicators
final ecosystem services (FES) indicators   100
finance
    A/R activities   203
    CBD   213, 467
    MBI   326
    monitoring   92–93
    offsets and biodiversity banking   317
    PES   187, 191–194
    private sector   213, 468
    protected areas   347, 368, 372–383, 388–389,
        454
    public   216–219, 379–380
    REDD+   204, 206–208
    stable   473–474
    subsidy reform   283, 292
    turning crisis into opportunities   430–432
    valuation   148–149
    see also investment; revenues
Finland   137, 221, 238, 287
fiscal approaches   148, 214–221, 283
fisheries
    certification   232–234
    exploitation   18, 21
    indicators   83–87
    long-term viability   454
    mangrove restoration   412
    MPAs   353–354, 358

    protection and natural capital   30
    regulations   307
    risk-based support   241
    subsidies   261, 268–269, 273–277, 289, 291
    substitution potential   37–38
    sustainable   232–234, 459, 466
    tradable quotas   319
    urgent ecological threats   473
fixed capital consumption   111
flagship species   358
Flanders, Belgium   312
floodplains   157–158, 421–422
food   15, 31, 244, 350, 356–357
Food and Agriculture Organization (FAO)   273
footprints, ecological   68, 81, 83, 99, 103
Forest Carbon Partnership Facility (FCPF), World
    Bank   207
forests
    air pollution   308
    certification   232–234, 238–239
    climate change   115, 201
    conservation   369
    costs and benefits   137
    diseases   424
    ecosystem services   28–29, 138, 145
    livelihoods   13, 35–36
    loss   13–14, 19, 21, 155, 454
    natural capital   30, 420
    PES   186–189
    PINC   212
    protected areas   362, 384
    REDD+   200–209
    regulations   307
    restoration   413, 431, 445–447
    road building   278
    rural communities   35–36
    subsidy reform   287
    sustainable   232–234, 466
    urgent ecological threats   473
    valuation   147–149, 159, 329
    vulnerability   115
    water quality   97
    see also deforestation
Forest Stewardship Council (FSC)   233, 238–239
fossil fuel subsidies   261–262, 277, 280–282, 291
Framework for Climate Change Adaptation   427
France   191
free trade   246
freshwater resources   15–16, 21–22, 414–415,
    417–420, 428, 443
FSC see Forest Stewardship Council
fuel subsidies   277, 280–282
fuelwood alternatives   36–37
full cost recovery   279, 301, 304, 320, 323–324
future aspects   69, 194, 247, 388–389, 449–479

G20 countries   208, 261–262, 281, 283, 291, 432
Gabon   266
game theory   229
GATT see General Agreement on Tariffs and Trade
GBO-3 see Global Biodiversity Outlook 3
GDI see Green Development Initiative
GDP see gross domestic product
GDP of the poor   2, 82, 113–118, 124–127

geese   220
GEF *see* Global Environment Facility
General Agreement on Tariffs and Trade
   (GATT)   246
genetic resources   18–19, 89–90, 179–180, 221–231,
   466
genuine savings   105, 113
GEO-4 *see* Global Environment Outlook 4
Germany   192, 219–220, 245, 308, 429
GFCF *see* gross fixed capital formation
Ghana   266, 281
GHGs *see* greenhouse gases
giant pandas   68
gifts   215
Global Biodiversity Outlook 3 (GBO–3)   20, 21–22
Global Canopy Programme   212
Global Environment Facility (GEF)   374, 376, 382
Global Environment Outlook 4 (GEO–4)   20
global headline indicators   88
global level
   accounting   110
   biodiversity crisis   7–46
   emissions trading scheme   325
   environmental crime   330–333
   indicators   88, 90
   protected areas   361–362, 372–373, 389
   public goods   209–213
   strategic plans   52–53
   subsidies   262, 264, 280
golden eagles   221
good governance   49, 69–70, 330, 455, 461–462,
   476–477
goods and services
   biodiversity loss   24, 35
   ecosystem restoration   408, 412
   green   2, 72, 181, 231–241
   natural capital   83–84, 103
governance
   baselines   476–477
   capital   108
   compensation   372
   environmental crime   330
   future vision   455, 461
   PES   197
   policy   49, 69–70
   protected area   351
   REDD+   207
   standards   305
   sustainable action   462–463
government
   GPP   242–244
   invasive species   419–420
   investment   209, 403, 414–416, 431
   leadership   477
   mainstreaming biodiversity   465
   PES   182, 184
   stakeholders and interests   61
   subsidies   262, 287–288
GPP *see* green public procurement
grasslands   14, 420
green approaches
   accounts   113
   goods and services   2, 72, 181, 231–241
   infrastructure   103–104

investment   431–433
   subsidies   261, 269, 284, 291
   tax commissions   337
Green Development Initiative (GDI)   179, 213, 468
Green Funds Scheme, The Netherlands   216
greenhouse gases (GHGs)   200, 202, 277, 280, 282
   see also carbon; emissions
green public procurement (GPP)   59, 242–247, 476
gross deforestation rates   204
gross domestic product (GDP)   27, 81, 102,
   105–106, 124–127, 474–475
   see also GDP of the poor
gross fixed capital formation (GFCF)   105
groundwater   190
Guyana   136

habitat banking   310, 477
habitats   23–24, 235, 314, 466
habitat services definition   11
Haiti   115–116, 423
hantavirus pulmonary syndrome (HPS)   425
HDI *see* Human Development Index
headline indicators   90–91, 99–100
health   35, 98, 172, 308, 350, 423–425
hedonic pricing   168, 170
high nature value (HNV)   270
high-seas bottom-trawl fleets   268
HNV *see* high nature value
holistic approaches   2, 408
hotspots of biodiversity   210–211, 236
HPS *see* hantavirus pulmonary syndrome
human capital   26, 104
Human Development Index (HDI)   113, 210–211
human dimensions   35–39
human well-being   12, 35, 84–85, 102–103, 229,
   364–365, 461, 475
human–wildlife conflict   360
Hurricane Katrina   430

IAS *see* invasive alien species
ICT *see* information and communications technology
IEA *see* International Energy Agency
illegal activities   275, 278, 332–336, 352
impact assessments   149, 151, 173, 311
implicit values   107, 457
incentives
   changing   317–320, 455
   environmental impacts   476
   long-term conservation   179–257
   protected areas   375–376
   reforms   465
   setting   72
   sharing of benefits   2
   tax   214–216
income
   accounting   82, 470
   diverse portfolios   381–382
   GDP of the poor   118, 124–127
   indicators   81–82
   national accounting   82, 107–113
   PES   197
   protected areas   352, 372
   subsidies   263, 284–286
   sustainable measurement tools   105–106

India
    bioprospecting 225–226
    compensation 137, 147, 329
    GDP of the poor 117–118, 124–125, 127
    integrated landscape approaches 156
    valuation 147, 161, 329
indicators 2, 79–128, 293, 458, 464
indirect use values 139
Indonesia 58, 117, 126–127, 282, 369
inequality 383
information
    biodiversity costs 337
    consumer choices 464
    decision making 77–173
    genetic materials 226–227
    good governance 69
    MBIs 328–330
    PES 197–198
    policy 49, 52–59, 71, 153–154, 458
    subsidies 261, 287
information and communications technology
    (ICT) 244
infrastructure 103–104, 277–278, 401–448, 459
inherent value 140–141
innovation 375–376, 461, 470–471
institutional level
    PES 195–197
    policy 49, 62–63, 337
    protected areas 383–387
    regulations 308–309
    subsidy reform 286–287
insurance 140, 371
integrated approaches
    accounting 107–113
    assessment 284
    biodiversity values 465
    capacity 164–165
    climate change 426
    economic thinking 131, 150–163
    evidence base 475–476
    monitoring 90–92
    natural capital 467–468
    protected areas 347, 354
    restoration 408
    tax revenues 217
    valuation 157–158
intensification of agriculture 20, 134, 270–271
interests 49, 61–62, 462–464
intergovernmental fiscal transfers 216–219, 219–220
Intergovernmental Panel on Climate Change
    (IPCC) 427
Intergovernmental Platform on Biodiversity and
    Ecosystem Services 462
Intergovernmental Science-Policy Platform on Biodiversity
    and Ecosystem Services (IPBES) 467, 476
International Energy Agency (IEA) 280
international level
    access and benefit sharing 230–231
    environmental crime 333, 336
    good governance 69–70
    GPP 246
    mainstreaming targets 52–53
    PES 179, 186, 199–214
    policy mechanisms 49
    protected areas 367, 373–374, 384, 389

    public participation 161
    REDD 202–204
    standards 82
    subsidies 263
    sustainable action 453, 462, 464–468
International Tropical Timber Organization
    (ITTO) 232
International Union for the Conservation of Nature
    (IUCN) 350–351, 384
intrinsic value 141, 349, 453, 477
invasive alien species (IAS) 22, 24, 191,
    419–420, 459, 466
investment
    certified products 241
    climate change adaptation 465
    government 209, 403, 414–416, 431
    GPP 244
    infrastructure 401–448, 459
    monitoring 92
    natural capital 209, 212, 414, 461
    PES 182–183, 195, 213–214
    private sector 468
    protected areas 361–362, 368, 376, 388, 477
    science 458
    social 241
    subsidy reform 290, 292
    value of nature 455
    see also finance
IPBES *see* Intergovernmental Science-Policy Platform
    on Biodiversity and Ecosystem Services
IPCC *see* Intergovernmental Panel on Climate
    Change
Ireland 368
irrigation 279, 424
island ecosystems 22
Israel 147
ITTO *see* International Tropical Timber Organization
IUCN *see* International Union for the Conservation
    of Nature

Japan 148–149, 152, 186–187, 190, 216, 235
joint procurement 245
joint service provision 196
justice 230

Kampala, Uganda 58
Kenya 225
keystone species 161
knowledge 62–63, 230, 464, 467
    see also information; traditional knowledge
Korea 318

labelling 180, 235–236
    see also certification
lake restoration 426
land
    accounting 109
    ecological fiscal transfers 217
    regulation 305, 307
    SEA 162–163
    tradable development rights 325
    valuing ecosystem services 142–143
landfill taxes 148
landscapes 156, 240, 445
land-use change

cost and benefits   31–33
floodplain restoration   422
forests   14
protected areas   362–363
subsidies   270–273, 277–278, 282
value   134
Land Use, Land-Use Change and Forestry
    (LULUCF)   465
Latin America   374
layering services   196–197, 206
leadership   61–62, 472, 477
leakages   203, 268, 278, 313–314
learning from nature   12, 237–238, 461
learning from practitioners   229
legal level
    action opportunities   468
    implementation and enforcement   455, 476–477
    liability rules   319
    MBIs   328
    offsets and biodiversity banking   316
    PES   196–197
    valuation   146–147
    see also regulation
Leopold, Aldo   87
Leuser National Park, Indonesia   34–35
levees   430
liability   58, 319–320, 328, 331, 477
livelihoods
    fisheries   274
    forests   13, 35–36
    marine ecosystem services   38
    poverty and biodiversity links   114
    protected areas   350, 355
    rehabilitation   417
    sharing benefits   221
    subsidy reform   290–291
loans   214, 216
    see also finance
local level
    accounting   110–112
    benefits   29
    ecological fiscal transfers   217
    engagement   38–39
    environmental crime   330–333
    knowledge   62–63
    PES   186–187
    protected areas   347, 350, 352, 355, 361,
        364–367, 371–372, 388
    REDD+   206
    solutions   469
    substitution potential   37
long-term issues
    accounting for   458
    assessment   476
    conservation incentives   179–257
    discounting   157
    fisheries   454
    indicators   101–102
    offsets and biodiversity banking   313
    protected areas   347, 381
    targets   470–471
    trade and environment   54
    value   132

low interest rates   214, 216
LULUCF see Land Use, Land-Use Change and
    Forestry
Lyme disease   424–425

MA see Millennium Ecosystem Assessment
macroeconomic indicators   81, 102–107, 475
Madagascar   207, 364
Mafia Island, Tanzania   198
mainstreaming biodiversity   52–54, 465, 471
malaria   424
Malta   280
management   67, 359, 364, 367, 386–388
Manalana wetland, South Africa   417
mangroves   16, 30, 32–33, 412, 422–423, 430, 442, 448
man-made capital   26, 104
man-made disasters   477–478
manufactured capital   26, 104
mapping approaches   87, 205–206, 469–470
marginal costs   106
marginal land   270–271
marine protected areas (MPAs)   347, 349, 353–354,
    358, 365, 388
Marine Stewardship Council (MSC)   234, 238, 241
marine systems   17–18, 38, 61, 332, 468
market-based instruments (MBIs)   301, 317–330,
    336–337, 376–381, 389
markets
    accounting   107–108
    analysis   141–142, 168
    biodiversity banking   310–311
    ecosystem services   51, 55, 132
    greening   180, 231–241, 455, 476
    prices approaches   170
    protected areas   374–375
    rewarding benefits   177–257
    sustainable   477
Mata Atlantica, Brazil   413
MBIs see market-based instruments
MEAs see multilateral environmental agreements
Mediterranean region   149
Mediterranean wetlands ecosystem accounting
    109–113
mental health   425
meta-analysis   144
Mexico   186, 188–189, 324
micro level ecosystem degradation   117
Micronesia   387
Millennium Development Goals   87–88, 326, 425,
    461–462
Millennium Ecosystem Assessment (MA)   20, 55, 94
mindset changes   477
mineral water   191
mining waste   332
minority rights   68
mires   429
mitigation   163, 310, 314–316, 358, 454
monetary valuation   131, 133–135, 141–150, 156,
    158, 367–368, 388
    see also valuation
Mongolia   137
monitoring
    biodiversity framework   90–93

existing approaches 89
improving 81
natural capital 454, 475–476
protected areas 383–384, 386
regulation 302, 330–336
subsidies 293
monoculture plantations 203
Montgomery County, Maryland, US 325
mosquitoes 424
Moxham, C. 413
MPAs *see* marine protected areas
MSC *see* Marine Stewardship Council
multifunctional subsidies 266
multilateral approaches 61, 374, 468
multilateral environmental agreements (MEAs) 54, 283
multiple benefits 190–194, 207, 208, 421
multiple values 55
multi-service payments for ecosystem services 182
multi-stakeholder processes 287

Nagoya, Japan 112, 209, 216
Nagoya Protocol 112–113, 209, 222, 230–231, 462, 464, 467
Namibia 162–163
National Biodiversity Strategy and Action Plans (NBSAPs), CBD 53, 469
national income 105
national level
baselines 203
benefits 29
collaboration 468
cooperation 477
donor activities 208
income accounting 82–83, 107–113
indicators 90, 100
international agreements 213–214
leadership 62
PES 179, 186–187
protected areas 361, 363–364, 367, 371, 388
REDD+ 204–206
SNA 83, 100, 105, 108–109, 475
subsidies 262, 275, 283
sustainable action 453–454, 468–472
national net savings 105
national parks 137, 149, 330, 369
natural assets 3
natural capital
accounting 2, 79–128, 458–459, 468, 470, 475–476
costs 30–31
definition 11
economic prosperity 26–27
economic sectors 12
improving stewardship 175–448
loss of 1, 13–19
maintaining and investing 3
reliance on 9
risks 163
social capital linking 39
transforming approaches 451–479
value 131
natural cosmetic sector 236
natural disasters 423, 428, 430–431, 477–478
see also catastrophes

natural fish capital 274
natural grasslands 14
natural hazards 16, 65, 163, 356, 422–423
natural infrastructure 104
natural products 222
natural resources
benefits pyramid 134–135
community-based management 39
consumption 459
efficiency 461–462
illegal use of 332–333
natural capital investment 417–420
protected areas 360, 366
rights to 66–67
smart policy mixes 336
subsidies 267
nature-based tourism 236, 240, 358
nature value 132–133, 453, 455–462, 478
NBSAPs *see* National Biodiversity Strategy and Action Plans
NCE *see* new chemical entities
net biodiversity gains 313
net deforestation rates 204
the Netherlands 157–158, 213, 216, 242
net present value (NPV) 137, 140, 363
new chemical entities (NCE) 222
New Orleans, US 430
New Zealand 146, 289, 319
NGOs *see* non-governmental organizations
nitrates 192
non-governmental organizations (NGOs) 232, 334, 374, 463–464
non-market valuation 142–143, 146, 150, 329
non-monetary benefits of PES 194
non-profit organizations 374
non-timber forest products (NTFPs) 35, 137, 144, 149, 241, 329
non-use values 139–141
North America 215–216
North Wind's Weir, US 136
Norway 277
no-take zones 358
NPV *see* net present value
NTFPs *see* non-timber forest products

oceans 22, 332
ODA *see* official development assistance
OECD *see* Organisation for Economic Co-operation and Development
official development assistance (ODA) 373–374
offsets 310–317, 335, 337
old-fields restoration 447
open spaces 325
opportunities 463, 470–471
opportunity costs 171, 360, 364
option use values 139
Opuntia scrublands 142–143
organic agriculture 235
organic farming labels 240
Organisation for Economic Co-operation and Development (OECD) 70, 261–262, 266, 271–273, 280, 291
orphan liability 328
Ostrom, Elinor 67, 463

over-consumption   24–25, 81–82, 107–108, 267
over-exploitation
    aquifers   188
    biodiversity loss   9–10, 16, 18
    disaster impacts   116
    ESS indicators   101
    fisheries   24, 273–275
    full cost recovery   324
    illegal activities   332
    water pricing   324
ownership   160, 197

paddy fields   190
Panama   205, 384, 425
paper   244
paper parks   352
Papua New Guinea   332
Para, Brazil   115
participatory approaches   92, 160–162, 197, 347,
    461, 467, 470–471
    see also engagement
partnerships   225–226, 462–463
PAs see protected areas
passive restoration   405
payments for ecosystem services (PES)
    community engagement   38–39, 463
    compliance   63
    mapping   87
    protected areas   375
    REDD   59, 476
    restoration   413, 416
    rewarding benefits   177–257
    subsidies   269, 292
    valuation   146
PBRs see People's Biodiversity Registers
peatlands   429
PEFC see Programme for the Endorsement of Forest
    Certification schemes
People's Biodiversity Registers (PBRs), India   63
permit trading schemes   328
Peru   142–143
PES see payments for ecosystem services
pharmaceutical industry   222, 227–228
phased performance payments   198
the Philippines   236, 422–423
phylogenetic indicators   81, 89
Pieters, J.   268
piggy backing services   196, 204–206
Pimampiro, Ecuador   416
PINC see Proactive Investment in Natural Capital
planning   162–163, 311, 370
political champions   62
political resistance   304, 327–328
political support   148, 187, 352, 367
pollination services   98
polluter pays principle (PPP)
    biodiversity loss   301, 304
    implementation   323
    liability rules   320
    monitoring   92–93
    PES   184–185
    sustainable action   463, 476, 478
pollution   24, 331–332, 466
population   19, 90
post-shrimp-farming mangroves   412

poverty
    biodiversity policies   60
    economic information   59
    ecosystem services   35–36, 457
    floodplain restoration   421–422
    GDP   82, 113–118
    illegal activity   332
    natural capital   475
    PES   193–194, 197
    protected areas   350
    vulnerability   160
    water subsidies   278
PoWPA see Programme of Work on Protected Areas
PPP see polluter pays principle
precautionary approaches   131, 163, 195, 268, 309,
    416, 427, 431–433
pricing
    accounting   107–108
    biodiversity losses   299–343
    biofuels   282
    complementary measures   460
    consumption, imports and exports   105
    ecosystem services   24–25, 132
    genetic resources   223
    GPP   244, 247
    hedonic   168, 170
    setting accurate   317–330, 476
    subsidies   267, 268, 278–280, 286
prior informed consent   227
private/public finance   377–379
private sector
    engagement   463
    environmental standards   305
    finance   213, 468
    gain above public loss   33
    greening supply chains   232
    monitoring   93
    offsets and biodiversity banking   317
    PES   191, 194
    protected areas   366, 377–378
    REDD+   204
Proactive Investment in Natural Capital (PINC)   212
proactive strategies   403, 430–433, 461
problem definition   56, 155
pro-conservation policies   33–35
procurement   242–247, 476
production
    efficiency   459
    genetic resources   222–223
    protected areas   366
    SNA   109
    stakeholders and interests   61
    subsidies   261, 267–273, 282, 291
    sustainable   465
production function approaches   142, 170
productivity   15, 20, 22, 27, 101, 356
product regulation   305
products and services, green   231–241
product traceability   107
Programme for the Endorsement of Forest
    Certification schemes (PEFC)   233
Programme of Work on Protected Areas (PoWPA),
    CBD   384–385
progressive water tariffs   286
property rights   49, 63–69, 132, 381

protected areas (PAs)
  community engagement   39
  entrance fees   329–330
  expansion   22, 477
  finance   454
  improvement   455
  PES   194
  REDD+   203
  sustainable action   466, 473
  tax revenues   217, 219–220
  value   2–3, 345–399
provisioning services   94–95, 101, 142–143, 209, 278
proxy indicators   89, 101
public goods
  biodiversity as   209–213
  biodiversity loss   25, 51
  ecosystem services value   132
  environmental standards   305–306
  GDP of the poor   113
  investment   403, 461
  liability   320
  neglect of   51, 108
  protected areas   367
  valuing nature   132
public level
  compensation   179, 219–221
  conservation funding   194
  debt   261
  environmental policy   52
  finance   216–219, 379–380
  levies   214–216
  loss from private sector gain   33
  organizations   112
  participation   161–162
  procurement   242–247, 476
  protected areas   379–380
  revenues and MBIs   326
  support for green markets   232
public–private partnerships   317, 416
pulpzyme   225

Q-methodology   172
qualitative approaches   94, 133–134
quantitative approaches   94, 133–134, 156, 158, 318–319
quick scan models   284

random utility models   170
Rausser, C.   223
reactive restoration   430
reallocation   407–408
recreation   314
REDD see Reducing Emissions from Deforestation and Forest Degradation
REDD+ see Reducing Emissions from Deforestation and Forest Degradation in developing countries
Red List, IUCN   19
Reducing Emissions from Deforestation and Forest Degradation (REDD)   59, 376, 386, 389
Reducing Emissions from Deforestation and Forest Degradation in developing countries (REDD+)
  bilateral cooperation   468
  climate change adaptation   427
  community engagement   38, 463
  PES   2, 179, 181, 199–214

  protected areas   219
  sustainable action   453, 464–465, 476
  valuation   146
reference levels   184–185, 203
reforestation   64, 98, 203, 208
reforming subsidies   2, 259–297, 303, 455, 465, 476
regional level
  accounting   110
  PES   199–200
  sustainable development scenarios   20
  valuation   149, 370
regional multi-country level   468
regulating services   28–29, 69, 94–96, 101, 143
regulation
  addressing biodiversity losses   299–343
  baselines   455, 476–477
  certification   240
  fisheries   275
  GPP   242
  PES   190, 194–195
  water   30, 306
  see also legal level
regulatory impact analysis (RIA)   151
rehabilitation   407–409, 417
relative decoupling   460
renewable and cultivated natural capital (RNC)   406
renewable energy subsidies   281–282
rent   223–224
replacement cost method   171
reporting   99, 293
resources see natural resources
responsibilities   462–464, 471
responsible citizens, responsible business   461
restoration   3, 140–141, 403–433 442–448, 461, 467
revealed preference methods   142, 168, 170
revenues   148–149, 261, 304, 320, 326, 381
  see also finance
rewards   2, 62, 177–257, 455, 461
  see also compensation
RIA see regulatory impact analysis
rice labelling   235
rights   64–65, 185, 366, 381, 388, 461
risk-based support   241
risks   163, 313–316, 353, 356, 432
rivers and river basins   64, 140–141, 414–415, 444, 468
RNC see renewable and cultivated natural capital
road infrastructure subsidies   277–278
roadmap for subsidy reform   285–286
road transport   268–269
robust accounting   108
robust indicators   99
rodent diversity   425
roundwood production   232, 234
rural communities   35–36, 113–114

Safari hunting   335
Sahel, Africa   21
salmon habitat restoration   136
Samadi Reef, Egyptian coast   381
Sami, Finland   221
satellite accounts   109
Saxony, Germany   219–220
SBSTTA see Subsidiary Body on Scientific, Technical and Technological Advice

Scheldt, Belgium–Netherlands 157–158
schistosomiasis 424
science 433, 458, 463–464, 467–468
Scotland 220, 246, 364
screening genetic materials 226
scrublands 142–143
SEA *see* strategic environmental assessment
sea turtle conservation 198
sector level
    GDP 117–118
    genetic resources 222
    indicators 84–85, 96–98
    innovation 461
    natural capital 27, 416
    regulations 306–307
    subsidies 264–265, 270–282
SEEA *see* System of Environmental and Economic Accounting
Segah watershed, Indonesia 58
self-regeneration 405
semi-natural grasslands 14
Sen, Amartya 461
Senegal 274, 424
Serengeti National Park, Tanzania 335
services 197, 278
    see also ecosystem services
sharing benefits 2, 179–180, 221–231, 461
sharing costs 367
short-term issues
    ecosystem services value 132
    Nagoya Protocol 230
    overcoming focus on 458
    protected areas 347, 365
    subsidy reform 292
    trade and environment 54
shrimp farming 32–33, 412
SIA *see* sustainability impact assessment
Sierra Leone 382
Simpson, R. D. 223
Sloping Land Conversion Programme, China 431
Small, A. A. 223
smart policy mixes 301–302, 336–337
SMART targets 93
SNA *see* System of National Accounts
social capital 26, 39, 104
social discount rates 157
social level
    equity and GDP 102
    investment 241
    property rights 68
    protected areas 371–372, 382–383
    restoration 413
    subsidies 266–267, 289–290
    water pricing 280
Social Stock Exchange 241
societal indicators 81, 102–107
socio-ecological systems 111
socio-economic issues 190–191, 420, 458
soil degradation 14–15, 431
South Africa 309, 413, 417, 420
South Korea 432
spatial level
    ecological fiscal transfers 217
    ecosystem services value 135–138

    mapping 206
    PES 182
    planning 52, 305
species diversity 18–19, 424–425
species extinction risk trends 91
species level headline indicators 92
Sperrgebiet, Namibia 162–163
spinner dolphins 381
spiritual resources 359
Sri Lanka 371
stakeholders 61, 159–162, 186, 195, 238–240, 287
standards 82, 90, 154, 235, 243–244, 301, 305–309
stated preference methods 142, 169, 171
Stern Review on the Economics of Climate Change 280, 362
stewardship 175–448
Stiglitz-Sen-Fitousi Commission on the Measurement of Economic Performance and Social Progress 81, 106
stimulus packages 292, 430–431
Stone, Richard 109
stormwater treatment 443
strategic destruction 229
strategic environmental assessment (SEA) 151–152, 155, 162–163
strategic impact assessments 266
Strategic Plan for Biodiversity, CBD 52–53, 283–284, 291, 453, 460, 462, 464–467
strict liability 319
sub-national level, baselines 203
Subsidiary Body on Scientific, Technical and Technological Advice (SBSTTA), CBD 93
subsidies
    economic assessment 59
    land conversion 32–33
    PES 184–185
    protected areas 389
    reforming 2, 259–297, 303, 455, 465, 476
substitution potential 9, 18, 36–38, 458
supply chains 231–232, 241–242, 244–455, 460, 476
supply side 112, 142–143, 180, 197, 460
support
    green markets 232
    national level 469
    PES 196–199
    political 148, 187, 352, 367
    protected areas 368–370, 383–388
supporting services 94, 143
sustainability impact assessment (SIA) 151
sustainable aspects
    action 453–454, 462–472
    agriculture 234–235, 429, 466
    fisheries 232–234, 459, 466
    indicators 101
    markets 477
    measurement tools 103–107
    protected areas 356, 365, 372–383
    public procurement 246
    smart policy mixes 336
    use of wildlife 335
sustainable development 462

Sweden 308
Switzerland 100
synergies 386–387
System of Environmental and Economic Accounting
    (SEEA), UN 82, 109, 468, 475
System of National Accounts (SNA) 83, 100, 105,
    108–109, 475

TAC *see* total allowable catch
Tanzania 335
taxes 148–149, 152, 179, 214–221, 267, 287, 289,
    337
see also market-based instruments
TDR *see* tradable development rights
tef 225
termite architecture 237
terrestrial biodiversity loss 16, 19
TEV *see* total economic value
TFP *see* total factor productivity
threshold effects 150
timber 106, 238, 243, 244
time scales for restoration 408–409
tipping points 21–22, 85, 477
Total Allowable Catch (TAC) 275, 319
total economic value (TEV) 34–35, 138–141
total factor productivity (TFP) 27
total system value (TSV) 135, 141
tourism 29, 235–236, 240, 358, 374–375, 381
tradable development rights (TDR) 325
tradable permit schemes 301, 317–319, 326,
    328–329
trade
    biodiversity banking 311
    deficits 103
    environment links 54
    illegal 335
    integrated policy assessment 164
    international 213
    liberalization 21, 54, 153
    wildlife 333, 335
trade-offs 31–35, 51–52, 54, 98, 157, 183, 368
traditional aspects
    finance 375–376
    knowledge 62–63, 159–160, 226–227, 241, 467
    wealth and well-being 102–103
transaction costs
    genetic resources 223, 228
    MBIs 328
    offsets and biodiversity banks 311
    PES 191, 195–196, 198
    protected areas 372
    REDD 207
    see also costs
transboundary issues 199–200, 331
transitional assistance 288–290
transition management 286
transparency
    accounting 108
    benefit-sharing 230
    future 461
    participation 160–161
    protected areas 368, 371, 386
    subsidies 261, 264, 287–288
    values 304

transport subsidies 265, 268–269, 277–278, 291
travel cost method 149, 168, 170
tropical coral reefs 16–17
trusts 215, 311, 382, 411
tsunami disaster 412, 430
TSV *see* total system value
Turner, W. R. 203
turtle conservation 198
tyranny of the average 113–114

Uganda 58
UK *see* United Kingdom
ultimatum game 229
UNCCD *see* United Nations Convention to Combat
    Desertification
uncertainty 51, 67, 163, 268, 314–316, 427
UNCLOS *see* United Nations Convention on the Law
    of the Sea
underlying drivers of biodiversity loss 24–26, 155
UNDP *see* United Nations Development Programme
UNEP *see* United Nations Environment Programme
UNFCCC *see* United Nations Framework Convention
    on Climate Change
unit benefits transfer 144
United Kingdom (UK) 243, 334
United Nations Convention on the Law of the Sea
    (UNCLOS) 275
United Nations Convention to Combat
    Desertification (UNCCD) 453, 462,
    465–467
United Nations Development Programme
    (UNDP) 87
United Nations Environment Programme
    (UNEP) 164, 206
United Nations Framework Convention on Climate
    Change (UNFCCC) 179, 199–214, 387, 427,
    453, 462, 464–467
United Nations subsidies 264
United States of America (US) 215, 316, 325, 411,
    421, 430
University of British Colombia 276
University of Queensland 353
urban areas 97, 216, 325
urgent ecological threats 472–474
US *see* United States of America
use rights 381
user pays principle 304, 323
see also polluter pays principle
use values 139

valuation
    asset 111
    costs and benefits 31–35
    decision support systems 58
    ecosystem services 55, 141–150,
        168–172, 414
    improvements 457
    indicators 101
    integrated 157–158
    keystone species 161
    MBIs 328–329
    natural capital 470
    protected areas 372–383, 388
    restoration 414, 417

SEEA 109
standard setting 309
watershed 152
see also monetary valuation
value
ecosystem services 9, 27–31, 55–59, 94, 129–173
genetic resources 221–228
illegal activities 334
nature 453, 455–462, 478
protected areas 2–3, 345–399
value function transfer 144
values 52, 304, 359, 366
VBWF *see* volume-based waste fees
vested interests 291
Vietnam 422
Vittel mineral water, France 191
volume-based waste fees (VBWF) 318
Vorarlberg, Austria 245
vulnerability 36, 114–116, 160, 333

waste 318, 331
water
climate adaptation 425–426
diseases 424
footprints 103
forests 97
GPP 244
investment 417–420
PES 181–182, 190–192, 194
pricing 286, 323–324
protected areas 356
regulation 30, 306
restoration 413, 421, 448
subsidies 265, 278–280, 286, 291
valuation 146
watersheds 138, 152, 187–190, 240, 411, 416
Waza floodplain, Cameroon 421–422

wealth 102–103
well-being 12, 35, 84–85, 102–103, 229, 364–365, 461, 475
wetlands
accounting 109–113
climate change adaptation 428
loss of 16
multiple values 55
restoration 417, 421, 426, 430, 443
WfW *see* Working for Water
white foot mouse 425
whole life costing (WLC) 244–245
wilderness areas 210, 211
wildlife crime 332–336
wildlife damage 219–221
wildlife–human conflict 360
wild pollinators 98
willingness to pay (WTP) 141–142, 152, 194, 223, 238, 329–330, 371
windows of opportunity 65, 288
WLC *see* whole life costing
Wolong Nature Reserve, China 68, 383
wood burning 281
Working for Water (WfW), South Africa 191, 413, 448
Working for Wetlands 417
World Bank 105, 112–113, 207, 431–433
World Summit on Sustainable Development 222, 283
World Trade Organization (WTO) 54, 264, 273, 276, 283, 291, 468
WTO *see* World Trade Organization
WTP *see* willingness to pay

Yangtze River, China 426, 431

Zimbabwe 237

Printed and bound by PG in the USA